STATE ARCHIVES OF ASSYRIA

VOLUME V

FRONTISPIECE. *Looting the temple of Haldi in Muṣaṣir.*
BOTTA AND FLANDIN, *Monument de Ninive* II, 141.

# STATE ARCHIVES OF ASSYRIA

Originally published by the Neo-Assyrian Text Corpus Project
of the Academy of Finland
in co-operation with
Deutsche Orient-Gesellschaft

Reprinted by Eisenbrauns

Editor in Chief
Simo Parpola

Managing Editor
Robert M. Whiting

Editorial Committee
Karlheinz Deller, Frederick Mario Fales, Simo Parpola,
Nicholas Postgate, Julian Reade

## VOLUME V

Giovanni B. Lanfranchi and Simo Parpola

## THE CORRESPONDENCE OF SARGON II, PART II

*Letters from the Northern and Northeastern Provinces*

Original publication of this volume was made possible in part by a grant
from the Research Council for the Humanities of
the Academy of Finland

Reprinted 2014, by permission of the Neo-Assyrian Text Corpus Project
Printed in the United States of America

www.eisenbrauns.com

ISBN 978-1-57506-326-3

Set in Times
Typography and layout by Teemu Lipasti
The Assyrian Royal Seal emblem drawn by Dominique Collon from original
Seventh Century B.C. impressions (BM 84672 and 84677) in the British Museum
Typographical encoding and Ventura Publisher format by Robert M. Whiting using Olivetti computers
with technical assistance from Timo Kiippa

The paper used in this publication meets the minimum requirements of the American National Standard
for Information Sciences—Permanence of Paper for Printed Library Materials, ANSI Z39.48–1984. ♾™

THE CORRESPONDENCE OF SARGON II
PART II

# LETTERS FROM THE NORTHERN AND NORTHEASTERN PROVINCES

*Edited by*
GIOVANNI B. LANFRANCHI
and
SIMO PARPOLA

*Illustrations*
*edited by*
JULIAN READE

Winona Lake, Indiana
EISENBRAUNS
2014

# FOREWORD

The basic manuscript of this volume was prepared by Giovanni B. Lanfranchi and Simo Parpola and provides the continuation of the publication of the correspondence of Sargon II begun in SAA I. The specific contributions of the individual authors are set forth in more detail in the Preface.

The production of this volume marks a significant departure from the previous volumes of the series in that it has been produced almost entirely by the staff of the State Archives of Assyria Project using Xerox Ventura Publisher and Olivetti computers. This procedure has made unnecessary a physical pasteup of the manuscript by writing the output of the Ventura Publisher directly to film. Redeveloping the processes used in producing earlier SAA volumes has cost time and effort, but it is hoped that it will be repaid by a saving in the production time and cost of future volumes.

We thank the Olivetti (Finland) Corporation for heavily subsidizing the acquisition of the hardware and software necessary to implement this new system as part of their ongoing sponsorship of the Project. I am particularly grateful to Timo Kiippa of the Helsinki University Press for advice and help in developing formats and fonts.

Our thanks are due to the Trustees of the British Museum and to the Musée du Louvre for permission to publish illustrative material in their keeping and again to the Finnish Ministry of Education for generous subsidies to help offset the costs of publication, and to the Academy of Finland for the primary financial support of the Project.

Helsinki, December 1990 — Robert M. Whiting

# PREFACE

The present volume has been prepared in close co-operation by the two editors, and they share the responsibility for the end product. Before embarking on the work, in August 1987, we agreed on a division of the work involved in manuscript preparation and on the general principles according to which the work was to be completed. Lanfranchi was to supply the introduction and the basic translation of the texts, while Parpola was to concentrate on the transliterations.

Virtually all the texts selected for the volume were collated by Parpola in March, 1988. The results were subsequently incorporated in the Project's database and a fresh printout of transliterations and indices was sent to Lanfranchi who in the course of 1989 prepared preliminary translations of all the texts on the basis of this material.

The translations made by Lanfranchi were scrutinized and edited by Parpola during the summer of 1990. This work was accompanied by a detailed orthographical and prosopographical analysis of the material, which made it possible to identify a great number of previously unknown writers, establish the final text order, and exclude from the volume a considerable number of irrelevant fragments. The critical apparatus and indices were compiled by Parpola in the fall, while Lanfranchi completed the introduction and scrutinized the revised translations in November. A final round of collations in the British Museum was completed by Parpola in December, 1990.

This book is the first volume in the SAA series produced using the Ventura desktop publishing setup acquired by the Project earlier this year, and marks a turning point in the Project's publishing activities. The credit for setting up the system and actually producing the electronic paste-up of the volume goes to the Managing Editor of the Project, Robert Whiting, assisted by Timo Kiippa of the Helsinki University Press.

The two previously unpublished tablet fragments in this volume are published by the kind permission of the Trustees of the British Museum. The staff of the Department of the Western Asiatic Antiquities of the Museum helped in every way in the study of the texts.

Galley proofs of the manuscript were read by Robert Whiting, Nicholas Postgate, F. M. Fales, and Julian Reade, who contributed many useful remarks. Results of collations and other corrections and modifications to the manuscript were entered by Laura Kataja.

December, 1990 G. B. Lanfranchi Simo Parpola

# CONTENTS


FOREWORD .......... VII

PREFACE .......... IX

INTRODUCTION .......... XIII

The Geographical and Historical Setting .......... XIII
The War with Urarṭu .......... XV
The Empire and Minor Independent States .......... XXI
Provincial Activity in Border Areas .......... XXVI
On the Present Edition .......... XXX
Notes .......... XXXIII
Abbreviations and Symbols .......... XXXV

TRANSLITERATIONS AND TRANSLATIONS

Letters from the Šubrian Frontier (1-83) .......... 1

1. Letters from Liphur-Bel, Governor of Amidi (1-20) .......... 3
2. Letters from Tušhan (21-43) .......... 17
   21-30 Ašipâ .......... 18
   31-43 Ša-Aššur-dubbu, Governor of Tušhan .......... 23
3. Letters from Vassal Kings and Bit-Zamani (44-51) .......... 37
   44-45 Hu-Tešub, King of Šubria .......... 38
   46 Unidentified Vassal King .......... 40
   47 Šarru-emuranni, Governor of Bit-Zamani .......... 41
   48-51 Aššur-patinu .......... 41
4. Letters from the Rab Šaqê Province (52-73) .......... 45
   52-61 Aššur-dur-paniya .......... 46
   62-73 Na'di-ilu, Chief Cupbearer .......... 54
5. Varia (74-83) .......... 61
   74-77 Mahdê .......... 62
   78-80 Aššur-belu-da''in, Governor of Halzi-atbar .......... 63
   81 Aššur-zeru-ibni to Nergal-eṭir .......... 65
   82 Šulmu-beli-lašme .......... 66
   83 Nabu-šarru-uṣur .......... 66

Letters from the Urarṭian Frontier (84-198) .......... 67

6. Letters from Kumme and Ukku (84-112) .......... 69
   84-103 Aššur-reṣuwa .......... 70
   104 Nabû-uṣalla, Governor .......... 81
   105-112 Varia and Unidentified .......... 82
7. Letters from Kurbail and Nearby Provinces (113-132) .......... 89
   113-125 Gabbu-ana-Aššur, Palace Herald .......... 90
   126-127 Aššur-belu-da'an .......... 98
   128-132 Varia and Unidentified .......... 99
8. Letters from Eastern Kurdistan (133-172) .......... 103
   133-144 Šulmu-beli, Deputy of the Palace Herald .......... 104
   145 Urda-Sin to the Palace Herald .......... 109
   146-147 Urzana, King of Muṣaṣir .......... 110

148-149 Unidentified High Official ... 112
150-151 Atanha-Šamaš ... 114
152-161 Aššur-alik-pani ... 115
162-163 Upaq-Šamaš ... 120
164-167 Bel-iddina, king of Allabria ... 123
168 Adâ to the Vizier ... 124
169 Issar-šumu-iqiša ... 125
170-171 Dinanu ... 125
172 Abat-šarri-uṣur ... 126
9. Fragmentary Letters Relating to Urarṭu and Zikirtu (173-198) ... 129

Letters from the Mannean Frontier (199-276) ... 141

10. Letters from Mazamua (199-226) ... 143
199-209 Šarru-emuranni, Governor of Mazamua ... 144
210-212 Nabû-hamatua, Deputy Governor ... 151
213-214 Kuškayu to Nabû-hamatua ... 152
215-225 Adad-issiya, Governor of Mazamua ... 153
226 Nabû-ahu-uṣur, Royal Bodyguard ... 160
11. Letters from Šamaš-belu-uṣur, Governor of Arzuhina (227-236) ... 163
12. Varia and Unassigned (237-276) ... 171
237-240 Mannu-ki-Adad ... 172
241 Adad-ibni ... 173
242 Aššur-balti-niše, Royal Bodyguard ... 173
243 Šarru-emuranni, City Lord of Qunbuna ... 175
244 Mušallim-Adad ... 175
245 Zabayu, Fort Commander of Appina ... 176
246 Bel-emuranni ... 176
247 Nanû ... 177

Letters from Assyria (Addenda to SAA I) ... 193

13. Letters from the King, the Crown Prince and the Treasurer (277-290) ... 195
277-281 Royal Letters ... 196
282 Crown Prince Sennacherib ... 199
283-290 Ṭab-šar-Aššur, Treasurer ... 200
14. Miscellaneous Letters (291-300) ... 205
291 Ṭab-ṣill-Ešarra ... 206
292 Šarru-emuranni ... 207
293 Nabû-ušabši and Iglî ... 207

GLOSSARY AND INDICES ... 215

Logograms and Their Readings ... 215
Glossary ... 217
Index of Names ... 243
Personal Names ... 243
Place Names ... 245
God and Star Names ... 249
Subject Index ... 250
List of Text Headings ... 258
Index of Texts ... 261
By Publication Number ... 261
By Museum Number ... 262
List of New Joins ... 264
List of Illustrations ... 264

COPIES AND COLLATIONS ... 265

PLATES I-II ... 273

# INTRODUCTION

In the first volume of this series, it was fittingly stressed that the existence of the Assyrian Empire of the eighth-seventh centuries B.C. was vitally dependent on a functional system of communications between the administrative centre and its periphery.[1] In this perspective, the Neo-Assyrian administrative letters which have come down to us represent an invaluable source for our knowledge of the organization and functioning of the vast empire created principally by the Sargonid kings. They give us a vivid picture of the "work in progress" in maintaining, developing and enlarging the political structure of the empire in its day-to-day evolution.

## The Geographical and Historical Setting

The letters published in this volume are of special interest because of the particular geographical area from which they originate. This area extends, in the shape of a broad crescent, roughly from the Euphrates to the Diyala river, surrounding and enclosing the Mesopotamian plain to the north and to the northeast. From the geographical point of view, the various territories which lie in this wide area all share a common feature: they represent the transition from the alluvial plain to the highlands of Anatolia and Iran. As such, the area of provenance of our letters may be described as comprising two basic elements: a territory of piedmont, slowly or swiftly rising to considerable altitudes; and a territory of high mountains in some places forming major systems, such as the eastern Taurus or the Zagros chain.

The special interest of this area stems from the fact that its geography affected the political entities at the time concerned. The piedmont was the seat of Assyrian provinces, of both ancient and recent establishment. In the mountainous territories, by contrast, a number of local communities or kingdoms still retained their independence, untouched by the expansion of the provincial system. Set apart from this constellation of small polities, to the north, another imperial structure, the kingdom of Urarṭu, long a major power in the Near East, still rivalled the Assyrian empire.

Generally speaking, the mountain territories as a whole represented the periphery of the Assyrian empire; but, at the same time, some of them (those placed on the northern borders) also represented the periphery of the Urarṭian empire. This means that we are dealing with areas on the fringes of established states which witnessed many kinds of interaction, both between the provinces and their small neighbours, and between the two imperial systems directly.

In this general framework, our letters are seen to deal with two kinds of information. The first is concerned with foreign relations, either with the major power of the Urarṭian empire, or with the minor independent territories. The information about Urarṭu, even if restricted to particular situations, offers exciting material for research, since it differs radically from the relatively few official sources (mostly royal inscriptions) which survive from the Urarṭian side. As for the independent territories, some of them were located precisely between the Urarṭian empire and Assyria, so that our texts also deals with their relations with Urarṭu — a fortunate situation which partly counterbalances the nearly total lack of such data on the Urarṭian side. Naturally, the correspondence also contains information on the internal situation of the independent territories, and in this way offers the reader a unique occasion to view historical and social developments in these otherwise forgotten lands.

The second type of information found in our letters is concerned with the internal situation of the Assyrian provinces, whether in their relations with foreign countries, or with the Assyrian central government, or among themselves. Similar data are available from other provinces, e.g. those situated on the western or southeastern borders of the empire, so that our letters provide an excellent opportunity for comparing the internal situation and social evolution of these lands.

The geographical provenance of our letters assumes a particular interest against the background of the historical developments which took place during the reign of Sargon II. The reign of this strong king represented the most impressive stage of the expansion of the Assyrian empire and of its consolidation as the dominant power in the Near East. The inscriptions of Sargon describe what appears as an irresistible succession of conquests in virtually all directions. To the west, all the independent states which separated Assyria from the Anatolian plateau were conquered and annexed to the provincial system; to the southeast, Assyrian influence was firmly established on the Iranian plateau; and to the south, a drastic solution was found for the Babylonian problem. Yet, on the northern and northeastern borders, Sargon's expansionist policies met with two major obstacles: the power of the Urarṭian kingdom, unchallenged in this area notwithstanding the successes of Tiglath-Pileser III, and the natural obstacles formed by the mountainous nature of the border territories. Our letters are an excellent source for the study of this conflict in detail, since they come from the very area which was affected by the military operations and diplomatic manœuvres of the conflicting powers.

# The War with Urarṭu

The rivalry between Assyria and Urarṭu, a contest for supremacy over large areas of the Near East, was difficult and prolonged. Even if open war between the two powers is attested only for the years 715 and 714,[2] there is reason to believe that the strife between the two kingdoms lasted from the beginning of Sargon's reign till its very end.[3] This long conflict affected the whole border area between Assyria and Urarṭu, from west to east.

## *The Western Sector*

Echoes of war permeate the correspondence of three western governors, Liphur-Bel of Amidi, Ašipâ and Ša-Aššur-dubbu of Tušhan. Even if Sargon's inscriptions do not mention a confrontation with Urarṭu in this area, the possibility of a large-scale conflict is described in letters 3 and 21. The former relates the state of readiness of the whole Urarṭian army, the latter tells of six Urarṭian governors assembled along the borders, while the Assyrian governor Ašipâ is keeping watch. No. 3 is interesting because it mentions the Urarṭian king Argišti, showing that the possibility of a conflict did not end with the death of Rusa I. A direct conflict is attested in no. 2, a letter of Liphur-Bel which tells of alleged Urarṭian attacks on Assyrian forts, and of the protest sent by the Assyrian governor to his Urarṭian counterpart. An Assyrian attack on a fort is described in no. 4.

The state of war also led to difficulties for the Assyrians in obtaining important materials such as timber, which was particularly abundant and valued in this area (see below): no. 3 tells of a fight to move an amount of delayed timber to Assyrian territory.

The situation in the area was complicated by the position of the independent state of Šubria, which lay north of these three provinces and south of Urarṭu. Its king, relying perhaps on the difficulty of his territory, conducted an ambiguous policy towards Assyria. Letter no. 35 shows him seizing and protecting Urarṭian deserters on their way to Assyria, while Assyrian deserters were held back and their extradition cunningly delayed with the excuse of illness.

Unfortunately, there are no means of assigning exact dates to these texts. No. 3 certainly dates from the reign of Argišti, but the accession year of this king still remains unknown. As for the others, the letters written by Ašipâ may precede those of Ša-Aššur-dubbu, since the former is known to have been active in the reign of Tiglath-Pileser III[4] and appears to have been followed in governorship of Tušhan by Ša-Aššur-dubbu.[5]

## *The Northern and Eastern Sectors*

The area most involved in the conflict with Urarṭu was, however, the northern and northeastern border of Assyria, as clearly stated in Sargon's inscriptions. The conflict was centred on supremacy over the wide territories of Mannea, which was subjected to the pressure of the two empires, either in the form of internal dissention between pro-Assyrian and pro-Urarṭian parties, or more directly through the direct conflict of the Assyrian and Urarṭian armies. The climax of the war was reached with the campaign conducted by Sargon in his eighth year (714) and described vividly in his famous letter to the god Aššur. This campaign led to a heavy defeat of the Urarṭians, which the Assyrian sources describe as having taken place on Mount Wauš, to the pillaging of a number of Urarṭian provinces, and finally to the sack of the city of Muṣaṣir with its temple of the Urarṭian national god Haldi, whose statue was abducted to Assyria.

A large group of letters, written by many different persons, pertains to these developments. The bulk of the correspondence comes from Aššur-reṣuwa, an Assyrian official residing in the city of Kumme; but reports are extant also from the Assyrian crown prince Sennacherib (who often acted as a substitute for his father during the latter's absence from Assyria), from vassal rulers, and from various officials. Unfortunately, once again there are only slim chances of ever firmly dating the letters in this group. As is well known, virtually no Neo-Assyrian letters contain a date; therefore, only internal analysis of content, with all the problems that are involved in this procedure, may give clues in this direction.

## *Datable Letters*

A firm dating may be obtained only for a small group of letters. No. 216 mentions, in a fragmentary context, Azâ, who is almost certainly to be identified with the ruler of Mannea who was dethroned and killed by his governors under Urarṭian influence in 716.[6] No. 218 mentions Aššur-le'i as receiving horses from Ullusunu, the Mannean king. Aššur-le'i is certainly the king of Karalla, and the episode has to be related to the alliance of these kings (together with Ittî of Allabria) instigated by Rusa against Sargon, which ended in Sargon's campaign to Mannea in 716 with the elimination of Aššur-le'i and Ittî, and the reinstatement of Ullusunu as pro-Assyrian king of Mannea.[7] No. 218 also mentions "the widow," a woman whose son is mentioned in no. 217 also. In the light of our dating, this widow could be identified with the wife of the Mannean king Azâ; and since no. 217 recounts a military confrontation between an Assyrian governor (Adad-issiya of Mazamua) and "the son of the widow," this man could be identified with Ullusunu.

No. 164, written by Bel-iddina, who was most probably the king of Allabria, is a report to Sargon about military preparations of the Urarṭian king after the latter had heard of Sargon's advance against the countries of Andia and Zikirtu. The wording of the letter ("The Urarṭian king ... ordered his magnates: 'Organize your troops, I shall array myself against the Assyrian king'") corresponds perfectly with what is described in Sargon's letter to Aššur, and places this letter at the crucial point of the 'Eighth Campaign' of 714, immediately before the battle on Mount Wauš. The same date may be assigned to a letter of Sennacherib which, referring to a message from Aššur-reṣuwa, informs Sargon that the Urarṭian king is marching towards Mannea: "He (Rusa) set out and entered the territory of the Manneans"[8] — a situation fitting that described in no. 164.

Another small group of letters may be attributed to the period immediately following the Eighth Campaign, although with no certain dating. The first (no. 88) is a letter from Aššur-reṣuwa reporting that two Urarṭian governors with their army are on the march towards Muṣaṣir. This letter cannot be separated from a famous letter of Urzana, king of Muṣaṣir, who relates the arrival of the same governors[9] and their celebration of rituals in the temple of his city (no. 147). Another fragmentary letter (no. 11) refers to the arrival of the governor of Waisi in Muṣaṣir. A fragmentary letter of Bel-iddina (no. 165) further reports on sacrifices performed by the Urarṭian king in a town whose name is regrettably broken.

The clue for dating these texts, which all seem to refer to the same occasion, is given by two details in the letter of Urzana: the facts that he addresses his letter to the Assyrian *nāgir ekalli*, quoting a prohibition issued by the latter against performing any ritual in the temple; and that he mentions a previous visit of Sargon to his city. The first detail points to the submission of Urzana to Assyrian dominion after the Eighth Campaign (when Muṣaṣir was administratively subordinate to the *nāgir ekalli*), the second is an evident reference to Sargon's "visit" to Muṣaṣir during the Eighth Campaign. Urzana says: "Could I hold him back? He did what he did," evidently a thinly veiled reference to the sack of his city. In the light of this, the group of letters may be dated *after* 714.

However, the most important dating criterion in these texts is the possibility of comparing them with the bilingual Assyro-Urarṭian inscriptions of Rusa I of Topzawa and Mergeh Kervan.[10] They describe Rusa's sacrifices in a border town, his arrival in Muṣaṣir, the military opposition of Urzana, who barred the temple door and tried to flee to Assyria; the recapture of Urzana, and his reinstatement as king of Muṣaṣir, after which he remained in that city, offering meals to the inhabitants of the country. In Urzana's letter to the *nāgir ekalli*, a question by the Assyrian official is quoted regarding the current whereabouts of the Urarṭian king and his likely intention to come to Muṣaṣir, to which Urzana answers that the king is coming, and will be followed by other governors. These indications seem to fit perfectly with the situation described in the Urarṭian bilinguals: frightened by the *nāgir ekalli*'s order, Urzana evidently tried to block Rusa, and fled towards Assyria. If these associations are correct, another historical problem, the much-debated dating of Rusa's bilinguals, would be solved by our letters.

## *Reports on Military Activities*

A large group of letters describes Urarṭian military movements, a type of information which was urgently and continuously needed in times of war. This information was obtained through scouts (*daiālu*), who were sent out to reconnoitre and spy, even as far as the Urarṭian capital, as one of the letters attests (see no. 85). The same activity was undertaken by the enemy, as is reported in a message about the capture of Urarṭian spies (no. 12). More generally, keeping the king constantly informed about what was going on in the Urarṭian kingdom was a service requested or required of many individuals, who wrote about the "news of the Urarṭians" (e.g., nos. 22, 113, 115, 144, 182), even from the western sector (no. 1). Particularly interesting is no. 113, written by the *nāgir ekalli* Gabbu-ana-Aššur, in which he confirms to the king that his messengers are in constant communication with three other governors (Nabû-le'i, Aššur-belu-da''in and Aššur-reṣuwa), two of whom are mentioned as informers of the crown prince Sennacherib in one of his letters (SAA I 31).

The kind of information obtained through this channel essentially concerned war preparations and operations which were being made behind the lines by the Urarṭians. So we hear of the departure of the Urarṭian army at the command of the king and his *turtānu* (no. 86); of the concentration of five Urarṭian governors with their troops in the city of Waisi (no. 87), or of the assembling of troops by the king and his entourage (no. 114); of military movements near the country of Andia (no. 177); or of the movements of the Urarṭian king and his commander-in-chief (no. 112).

Quite probably, information about the military activities of Assyria's allies was largely obtained through direct communication. Very interesting in this connection are two texts dealing with attacks of a Mannean king, in all probability Ullusunu, on Urarṭian territory. In no. 84, Aššur-reṣuwa forwards the information that "the Mannean (king) has attacked the Urarṭian cities in the district along the lake shore";[11] another fragmentary text refers to a Mannean attack against Urarṭian forts, which called for the swift intervention of the Urarṭian *turtānu* (no. 131).

These texts show clearly that the war between Assyria and Urarṭu deeply involved local rulers, who were able (and perhaps forced) to fight against imperial territories, in a turbulent scene of shifting alliances. This pattern is also evident in the letter of Bel-iddina to Sargon about the preparations of Rusa, mentioned above, in which we see the king of Hubuškia marching together with the Urarṭian king. The king of Hubuškia apparently was forced to change sides at least twice: he paid tribute to Sargon, who visited his city, in 715;[12] he then co-operated with Rusa before the battle on the Wauš, and finally went to pay tribute to Sargon at the end of that same campaign.[13]

Direct and certain information about battles between Assyrians and Urarṭians is unfortunately almost totally lacking. Perhaps the small fragment no.

273, which contains news about a storm and an attack of Assyrian soldiers coming out of fortresses, refers to such a battle. A surrender of Urarṭian soldiers is perhaps described in no. 184, where an Assyrian official proclaims: "You are subjects of the king, my lord; you are no longer subjects of the U[rarṭian]!"

## *Urarṭu's Internal and Dynastic Instability*

The effectiveness of imperial dominion was at times shaken by local rebellions, which led to military repression and severe punishment. On the Urarṭian side — the Assyrian one is well attested in royal inscriptions — such a situation is described in no. 166, which tells of the rebellion of a town against the Urarṭian king, and of military intervention by his commander-in-chief, the *turtānu*, in the context of a military campaign conducted by the king. No. 179 probably deals with the measures taken after a failed revolt in Urarṭian territory, and with the discharge of a governor and other officials in the wake of a general alarm in Urarṭu.

However, the most dangerous occurrence was internal strife caused by dynastic aspirations, which could materialize in open rebellion. A large group of letters informs Sargon on a revolt which took place within the Urarṭian empire, and led to military confrontations, trials and punishments. The main texts are nos. 91 and 93. The first mentions the arrest of 21 people in the Urarṭian capital and the killing of another 100 people, all involved in the revolt. The situation was truly dramatic, since the Urarṭian deputy commander-in-chief and another magnate, otherwise known as the governor of Muṣaṣir (no. 90), went to the capital, to be questioned by the king personally about the revolt, only to be set free later because they were found innocent. These two letters are quite probably linked to SAA I 8, a letter written by Sargon to Rusa of Urarṭu, mentioning the revolt against him and the defection of an Urarṭian governor (who was made commander-in-chief in Assyria). This same letter mentions hostile actions of Rusa against Mannea, and could refer to the wars of 715 (Urarṭian capture of Mannean forts)[14] and 714 (Urarṭian seizure of the Mannean province of Wišdiš).[15]

The Urarṭian commanders-in-chief were surely of royal lineage, as in no. 93 the "commander-in-chief of the right" is said to be "of the family of Sarduri," clearly the king who preceded Rusa on the Urarṭian throne. This same text seems to describe a crucial moment in Urarṭu: the murder of the sovereign, as the Assyrian informer tells that "his magnates surrounded him ... and killed him."

This important set of letters throws new light upon the feebleness of the Urarṭian dynasty, a matter perhaps hinted at in Sargon's "Letter to the God" with its cryptic references to the towns "of the father's house of Rusa" and "of Sarduri,"[16] and to the inscription on the statue of Rusa which was looted in Muṣaṣir, "with two horses and one charioteer of mine he (Rusa) took in his hands the kingship of Urarṭu," perhaps an indication of the illegitimacy of his ascent to the throne.[17]

## *The Cimmerian Problem*

The identity of the Urarṭian king murdered by his magnates is a problem linked with another long-debated issue, the interpretation of a large number of letters dealing with a crushing defeat suffered by the king of Urarṭu in or near Gamir, the territory inhabited by Cimmerians. The significance of this defeat is underlined both by the number of governors reported to have been killed (perhaps as many as 11) and by the very number of letters dealing with this matter (nos. 90, 92, 174 and probably no. 173).[18] A detailed description of the battle is lacking, but no. 90 tells us what happened immediately after: the Urarṭian king flees on a lone horse, while the rest of the army, ignoring his survival of the massacre, declares the crown prince Melarṭua (thus identified in no. 114) the new king. Letter 92 refers to the reorganization of the Urarṭian army in Guriania, a territory situated between Urarṭu and Gamir, and to the outbreak of a revolt in the city of Waisi. Two further letters report on an invasion of Cimmerian troops into Urarṭian territory (nos. 144 and 145) and on anxiety in Urarṭu, testified to by a call for help sent by the Urarṭian governor of Waisi to Urzana of Muṣaṣir.

The "Cimmerian defeat" has been amply discussed in various recent works, with respect to both its dating problems and its general interpretation. A direct succession of letters, pertaining to this event and to the Urarṭian revolt, has been proposed, linking together the texts about the defeat and the revolt in Urarṭu and suggesting for them a date preceding or contemporary with Sargon's Eighth Campaign.[19] The "Cimmerian defeat" has also been identified with Sargon's victory in his Eighth Campaign over Rūsa on Mount Wauš,[20] an identification which raises a large set of problems whose detailed exposition is beyond the scope of this Introduction. Suffice it to say that this hypothesis, if correct, would have important historical consequences. The Cimmerians would be the inhabitants of the district where that famous battle took place, the Mannean Wišdiš, and therefore a Mannean people (a thesis which was already expressed elsewhere);[21] they would become a people allied with the Assyrians, in whose name they would have fought against the Urarṭian king; and finally, the defeated king would be Rusa I, not his son Argišti, as assumed in earlier interpretations.[22]

As was anticipated above, this complex problem clearly involves the identity of the Urarṭian king killed by his magnates (no. 93). If the letter concerned describes the murder of Rusa, it would have to be dated after 714 since, as we have seen, Rusa was able to retake Muṣaṣir after the Eighth Campaign (which ended in late 714). However, the murdered king does not necessarily have to be Rusa; he could also be the prince Melarṭua who was raised to the throne after the "Cimmerian defeat" in total ignorance of Rusa's survival.[23]

However that may be, our letters show clearly that a whole page of Urarṭian history must be rewritten, particularly with regard to the stability of its throne and the cohesion of its structure.

# The Empire and Minor Independent States

The provinces where our letters originate were a pivotal place for relations with the independent communities and states bordering on the Assyrian empire. Many of these territories, due to their position between the two fighting empires, were directly, and in varying degrees, involved in the conflict. Owing to the selection dealt with in this volume, we have only very few examples of territories which were not directly involved in that war. From this point of view, the data provided by our texts on the relations between Assyria and independent states, which are essential for a full understanding of the relations between imperial and peripheral political structures, seem *ab origine* conditioned by an underlying specific political situation (the great war), which may condition in some way the nature of the documentation.

## *The Concept of Independent States or Communities*

A crucial problem which must be dealt with as a preliminary question in the matter of foreign relations, consists of establishing where the Assyrian imperial ideology considered the official border of the marginal provinces to end; that is to say, what countries and territories and communities were regarded as formally independent, and how relations with such entities were managed. This set of problems has obvious repercussions on the relations between kingdoms and on their different ranks, and on the relations between provincial government and foreign rulership; but also on the extension and the nature of Assyrian dominion in marginal lands.

The picture provided by our letters is not clear at all in this respect. While it seems roughly clear that some territories were considered fully independent because of the prerogatives which their rulers appear to have had in practice, this is not absolutely clear for many others. Hu-Tešub of Šubria was able to refuse the extradition of deserters to the Assyrian government (no. 35) or to bargain about this matter (no. 52), and to deny the consignment to Assyrian officials of timber cut in his own territories (no. 33). This points to his total autonomy from provincial government. Formally, also the sovereigns of Hubuškia and Muṣaṣir must be regarded as on the same level, as they were entitled to bring tribute to the Assyrian king (nos. 133 and 146).

On the other hand, the position of other territories is not well defined, nor is the institutional rank of their rulers clear. The case of Kumme, whose ruler might be identified with the often mentioned Ariye, may be paradigmatic in this regard. While Ariye is entitled to write directly to Assyrian crown prince

Sennacherib (SAA I 29), or to meet with the ruler of Ukku (SAA I 41), the status of the ruler of Kumme is said in no. 117 to be that of *bēl āli*, "city lord," a title normally referring to (recently subjugated) vassal rulers. Further, in no. 95 we hear that Kumme was totally in the hands of Assyria, and was subjected to a foreman of cavalry (obv. 12-15). On the other hand, in this same letter Argišti of Urarṭu complains about not having received any greetings from Kumme since his accession — a reference which would point towards a partial autonomy of that city (and its leader), at least in Urarṭian eyes. Historical developments which may have led to a change in the status of Kumme are otherwise unknown to us.

This problem involves even the status of some correspondents who bear clearly Assyrian names. It is the case of Aššur-reṣuwa, a man who wrote a large number of letters to Sargon (9 with his name preserved in the salutation, and 11 attributable to him on graphic and orthographic grounds), and who, just because of this plain fact, may be suspected to be a high official, even a provincial governor. Some of his letters deal with problems in Kumme (e.g., nos. 94, 97, 105), and this would lead one to consider him as a governor in charge of that area.[24] On the other hand, in letter no. 117, quoted above, Aššur-reṣuwa is listed, among others, as a "city lord." Further, in another letter (no. 106), Kummean citizens are described as no longer tolerating the Assyrian *qēpu*, while Aššur-reṣuwa asks for the elimination of high-ranking Kummeans, giving room for the suspicion that he is the *qēpu* in question. Since the *qēpu* is normally understood as an "official of the Assyrian king abroad,"[25] this would imply an independent status for Kumme, contradicting all that has been delineated above.

The matter clearly calls for further study, and this is connected with the long-lasting debate about the prosopography and *cursus honorum* of Assyrian officials; our correspondence is a valuable means to begin to face this problem.

## *Intensity of Communication*

A basic feature which emerges from our letters is a strong link in written communication between the empire and foreign communities. The volume of letters exchanged was obviously very high, judging from the number of references made to them. An extensive set of letters deals with direct relations between the imperial centre and provincial government, on one hand, and foreign rulers and communities on the other. These relations resulted in movements of people and information across the border and between administrative centres, even on the royal level.

Assyria was visited by foreign rulers or foreigners of royal blood bringing tribute (e.g., the Hubuškian king, no. 133 and 192; the crown prince of Andia, no. 171; the brother of Urzana of Muṣaṣir, no. 148), while emissaries and messengers of foreign countries formed an essential relay of communication (emissaries of Šubria, nos. 36 and 52; of Zikirtu, no. 169; of Labdudu, no. 194; messengers from Hubuškia, nos. 134, 162). Foreign visitors could move freely through the outer provinces towards the Assyrian capital, cf. nos. 138

and 203 (referring to seven rulers from the environs of Kumme, and city lords, probably Mannean, summoned by the king).

In the introduction to SAA I, it was stated that the letters from the reign of Sargon at our disposal may be regarded as a fairly representative sample of the whole of the original correspondence.[26] On this basis, the intensity of contact between foreign countries and Assyria revealed by our letters cannot be taken as accidental. It is clear that in Sargonid Assyria there was extensive political and cultural interchange between the imperial centre and periphery, in which different ideologies and cultural models met on a day to day basis. Assyria and Urarṭu being culturally and militarily by far the superior parties in this daily give-and-take, one may legitimately expect our letters to contain valuable information on the question of how marginal areas were gradually integrated into the imperial system.

## *Political and Social Relations*

Our correspondence reveals a number of instances of the political and social effects of imperial policies. As for the former, the whole "outside world" seems to have been totally conditioned by its relations with imperial politics. Imperial interference in the dynastic succession of an independent country, for instance, is attested by a very interesting fragmentary letter (no. 108), which is now basically understandable thanks to several recent joins. An unnamed individual has killed the legitimate queen of Habhu in order to raise an Urarṭian lady to the throne; faced with accusations of murder, he excuses himself by blaming the Urarṭian king for the assassination. The local populace, however, does not accept this fait accompli but mumbles: "An Urarṭian woman may not sit on the throne!" This situation has a parallel in the marriage of a daughter of Sargon to a ruler of Tabal,[27] which was meant to Assyrianize that Anatolian dynasty.

Another interesting case of imperial interference is provided by no. 31, where a king of Urarṭu pressures the ruler of Šubria by various means, among other things by demanding back "thc jewellery that my father and I have given to you," thus recalling the binding value of gifts exchanged between dynasts.

Imperial interference in local politics was exerted both overtly and covertly. On the one hand, we have Argišti's request for homage from Kumme (no. 95), mentioned above; on the other, the case of an Urarṭian informer secretly going to Ariye captured by the Assyrians, reported in no. 55. But perhaps the most devastating effect on local social compactness was caused by recruitment to imperial armies, a phenomenon which must have taken place as a matter of fact. On the Assyrian side, Kummean troops would serve under their local rulers, but they would be strategically directed by Assyrian commanders (no. 97), whereas vassal rulers were required to take part in Assyrian military expeditions (nos. 199 and 200). On the Urarṭian side, Urzana of Muṣaṣir was asked to provide military aid during the Cimmerian attack (no. 145), a situation exactly opposite to that presented in no. 139, where Muṣaṣirian troops were called by the Assyrian king.

On another level, imperial interference was caused by problems inherent in the imperial systems themselves. Deserters from imperial armies, political fugitives, as well as criminals constantly tried to take refuge in bordering lands which were formally autonomous. Many letters attest this important social phenomenon. Nos. 32, 34, 35, 52 and 54 deal with Assyrian (and Urarṭian, no. 35) deserters in Šubria, a land which evidently represented a kind of "sanctuary" until the time of Esarhaddon, who annexed Šubria in 673 and disposed of the Assyrian and Urarṭian deserters there.[28] Searches for criminals sometimes caused embarrassing moments in political relations, cf. no. 53, where a renegade officer flees to Šubria taking with him the seal of the Assyrian governor.

The subjection of formerly independent territories to Assyrian rule apparently resulted in friction between various elements of the local population. While the representatives of the Assyrian king may have been tolerated or welcomed by local rulers, other sectors of the populace were often less tolerant, resulting in unrest and demands for the removal of the local Assyrian delegates. A small group of letters reveals such a situation in Kumme, where the opposition to the Assyrian *qēpu* resulted in demands against Ariye, the ruler (no. 107), and led to a serious confrontation with Aššur-reṣuwa (no. 106). The story may have had a happy ending though (at least from the Assyrian point of view), for in one of the letters the Kummeans proclaim: "The king, our lord, is the lord of all; what can we say?" (no. 105).

Naturally, problems had occasionally to be solved by force: refusal to provide horses for the Assyrian king, for instance, was heavily punished (no. 202, probably in the Mannean area). Use of force, however, was not mandatory. The Assyrian approach to local problems may rather be perceived as generally cautious — a picture which decidedly contrasts with the stereotyped image of Assyrian cruelty and violence. In letter 203 an Assyrian governor fulfills the king's order to "speak kindly" to a local representative; another Assyrian official puts up a show of kindness in front of the men of Allabria (no. 202). Even long insubmissive mountain territories could be "appeased" by negotiations, which resulted in the acceptance of the "king's treaty," and with it, the re-imposition of labour and military duties (no. 78).

## *Economic Relations*

Economic relations, both in the form of formally established "unequal exchange" (tribute) and "parithetic exchange" of goods (trade), constituted a tight link between minor states and empires.

The mountain area northeast and east of Assyria was the prime breeding ground for horses, and tribute from that area was essentially composed of such animals. The crown prince of Andia could bring, probably as tribute, up to 51 equids (no. 171). Cattle and sheep were, however, not disregarded either. In no. 133, the king of Hubuškia brings to Assyria a tribute of this kind; in no. 136, Urzana of Muṣaṣir is reported to be on his way to Arbela with 56 horses and a good number of oxen and sheep.

The numbers of tribute animals mentioned in our letters are in general not particularly high, which makes it understandable that refusal to bring tribute was felt more as an ideological offence than as an economic loss. In no. 146, Urzana excuses himself for not being able to come with his tribute because of snow – probably on the very occasion which 'justified' Sargon's attack on Muṣaṣir: "Urzana of Muṣaṣir ... not submissive to my lordship ... did not embrace my feet with his heavy gift, and withheld his tribute and gift."[29]

Trade was the vital medium to acquire quality goods generally not obtainable through war (booty) or tribute and gifts. In the Assyrian empire, trade was carried on both by governmental authorities and licensed merchants, who enjoyed royal protection and were aided by local administrators. Rather surprisingly, trade of horses, probably considered a matter of nobility, appears to have been carried on even by foreign royalty: in no. 169, the king of Zikirtu is expected to sell horses to an Assyrian official, who deposits the money needed for the transaction in a stronghold.

Timber was probably also considered a commodity to be dealt with by royalty. According to no. 33, both Urarṭian and Šubrian kings objected to selling timber cut in their territories to the Assyrians. Evidently timber, like horses, was considered royal property, which would underscore the value of this material, particularly in view of its total lack in Mesopotamia. A royal timber monopoly thus seems not to be ruled out.

While merchants went around searching for horses in the east (nos. 208 and 224), unofficial trade was carried on locally. An interesting example of a routine infringement of custom duties is offered by no. 100, a letter which deals with smuggling of goods between Urarṭu and Assyria. Kummeans smugglers are reported to have bought precious merchandise in the Assyrian capitals, carried them to Kumme, and then sold it in Urarṭu, bringing back other precious goods to be sold in Assyria. Aššur-reṣuwa, the author of this letter, asks for their arrest and thorough examination. This text casts an unexpected ray of light on the constant ineffectiveness of borders vis-à-vis people's economic needs – a picture totally "blacked out" in the official records of Mesopotamia.[30]

## Imperial Activities in Border Provinces

Border provinces were essential cogs in the military and economic mechanism of the Assyrian empire. On one hand, they were the base for military control of bordering territories, which consisted of a constant surveillance of the situation in these territories and of military campaigns launched from time to time. On the other hand, they were an important target of economic exploitation, either as direct sources for materials needed in the heartland of the empire, or as regular conveyor belts of finished products extracted by means of taxation.

### *Provinces as Bases for Military Control*

Control of military activity in border provinces was a duty imposed upon governors, who acted as the king's representatives in providing and organizing the army, both as contingents locally installed and as groups centrally managed and sent to provinces for specific reasons.

Reporting briefly about the state of forts in the province was a widely attested procedure: many letters contain such a report immediately after the greeting formula (e.g., nos. 1-3, 6, 21-25). A number of letters deal with the problem of feeding the local troops (no. 60, 109, 126), a problem which, judging from the frequent communications to the king, must have been of constant difficulty for local administration and must have required particular attention on the part of the central authority. No. 109, in particular, shows the care given to reserve fields for the garrison's feeding requirements despite protests from the local populace. As for troops sent to outer territories, provincial governors had to report their movements, checking their accuracy (e.g., nos. 3, 72), and to provide for their sustenance (no. 68, referring to provisions for charioteers arriving from Que).

Border provinces were obviously the base for launching military campaigns abroad. Few examples of operations led by local authorities survive, and they seem to have been of limited extent: no. 3 refers to fighting to recover timber from a town, no. 5 probably refers to an attack on the same town, and no. 24 deals with deportation from a mountain town. A particularly interesting set of letters deals with the reviews of troops in preparation for a military campaign: the king asks precise details about the number and the composition of the available army, a request which is duly answered by governors or local authorities. No. 67 tells about an order from the king to review troops to be brought to him; no. 251 contains a short, detailed list of cavalrymen and charioteers, who were enlisted in groups of 200 (cavalrymen) and 100 (charioteers). The unnamed writer reports about present and missing individuals, and distinguishes between "king's men" and "chariot owners."

A most interesting and much debated text is no. 215, which contains a long and detailed list of military personnel described as "king's men" available in the province of Mazamua, including Assyrians, Itu'eans and Gurreans. This list has been used for determining the size and composition of the standard Assyrian chariotry unit,[31] however without taking into consideration the end of the letter which explicitly states that the figures listed pertain to the troops actually present at the review rather than the *whole* strength of the army.[32] Mazamua was the base for launching major campaigns into the Mannean and Median territories and the letter probably refers to one of them. Perhaps a similar occasion is recalled in no. 234, which refers to a military review and an order to send barley rations to Mazamua.

Letter no. 162 mentions the departure of Assyrian magnates and the visit of the otherwise unknown Zaba-iqiša to Rusa of Urarṭu. The mention of magnates recalls the expedition of year 713, which was led by them, while Sargon remained at home;[33] if the attribution is correct, this would be a welcome indication that the Urarṭian king was still alive the year after Sargon's Eighth Campaign.[34] Letters no. 199, 210, 226 and 250 deal with the preparation and activity of a campaign to the east. No. 250 is a detailed report about the arrival of the magnates in Kar-Aššur, about the quantities of day and month rations available for troops, and about a review of troops. The location of Kar-Aššur in eastern Babylonia[35] would favour a dating to the same year, 713, since the Eponym Chronicle lists Ellipi as an objective of the campaign of that year.[36]

The result of military campaigns was the distribution of booty and prisoners of war, both to the centre and to provincial administrations. No. 226, from Mazamua, mentions the sharing of booty of horses; if grouped with the other letters attributable to 713, this one could be placed in the autumn of that year.

Deportees and POWs appear to have been inspected at regular intervals and provided with food, drink and other necessities — a 'humanitarian' feature not included in the usual image of Assyrian war conduct. No. 156 is a report commenting on the miserable condition of a group of freshly arrived captives; no. 242 refers to rations of corn and salt given to deportees.

## *Economic Exploitation*

Provincial territory was a source of exploitation of fundamental importance to the central administration. It formed the primary basis for fixed state income, independent of the irregular and uneven quantities obtained as tribute from foreign kings or as booty from military campaigns. The *ilku*-duty ("forced" labour for the king), *iškāru*-duty (quotas on finished products and sheep), *nusāhē* (corn-tax) and other taxes[37] provided the centre with revenues and labour forces. Failure to punctually forward the *nusāhē* to the king was a serious fault, which earned a reprimand from the king personally (no. 82).

The pressure of the imperial centre upon the provincial system appears to have been sometimes excessive,[38] so that local authorities often complain of scarcity in their territories. See no. 117, where the sender attributes the lack of straw for pack animals in his province to forwarding all available supplies to Dur-Šarruken, the new capital under construction, and no. 120, referring to lack of reeds (though in this case a wish for increased supplies could be behind the request). Both letters were written by the *nāgir ekalli* Gabbu-ana-Aššur, who might be suspected of protesting, from his high position, against excessive pressure on his own province, and to be trying to reserve for himself a higher proportion of its income.

On the other hand, attention was duly paid to keeping local production on a regular standard: the communication of observations on rain quantity (nos. 274-276) to the king was certainly intended to relate to the state of crops.

In general, many economically precious raw materials were extracted from provinces and forwarded to the centre. The subjects of cutting and floating timber (e.g., nos. 4, 6, 7, 8, 127, 129)[39], as well as pulling up fruit tree saplings for the royal parks (nos. 27, 105; no. 268 deals with problems of transport) figure prominently in our corpus. The cutting and transport of bull colossi (nos. 17, 115, 117 and 118) or stone thresholds (no. 17) is also a frequent subject; long distance seems not to have posed a major problem, as one bull colossus is dealt with by Liphur-Bel, whose territory (Amidi) is far from central Assyria. Sheep were also forwarded to the centre (no. 263: 1,000 rams). Other letters deal with shipments of red wool to the king (no. 28, from Tušhan) and of hewn stone objects (no. 29, same provenance); a letter containing a fragmentary list of precious stones (no. 205, probably from Mazamua) and another mentioning carnelian from Kumme (no. 284) may possibly refer to the same matter.

Specialized manpower was also conveyed from the provinces to the central administration, possibly resulting in the impoverishment of local craftsmanship.[40] In no. 56, the author refuses to give junior master builders to the magnates, as senior ones had already been distributed to various points of the empire; in no. 71, an axe maker from Syrian Damascus is sent to the king by the chief cupbearer.

## *Economic Development*

While border provinces were exploited for the needs of the central administration, nonetheless the actions of the Assyrian king could also stimulate the local economy in various ways: the simple presence of Assyrian military and administrative personnel provided consumers who had to be maintained, at least to some extent, by trade with the local population — a matter often overlooked in historical research. Several letters show that extensive building activity was carried out in the provinces under the king's orders. No. 15 describes the building of a town and a fort in the province of Amidi, no. 210 the building of a fort in the province of Mazamua, and no. 211 the building of forts and houses in the bordering Allabria. Royal roads were built and repaired (no. 229, road to Mazamua), and were a medium for easy communication with the centre, thus facilitating commerce. Cf. especially no. 227, dealing with improving the mule express towards Mazamua.[41]

Installing troops and deportees to cultivate arable land in provinces (see, e.g., no. 14, concerned with Chaldean deportees in Bit-Zamani) could result in improvement of the local economy. Troops exempted from taxes evidently gave rise to a local economic circuit not burdened by contributions to the centre.[42] It was doubtless in the king's interest to increase the economic potential of the provinces, for the expansion of arable land was vital for creating a good basis for future exploitation (cf. no. 225, mentioning a royal order to three different governors to cultivate 1,000 homers of seed corn each).

Governors were naturally concerned with maintaining a high economic standard in their administrative sector. Materials needed by military installations were at times provided by the centre, cf. no. 48, listing equids, camels, sheep and carts, and no. 152, a request for new carts (notice, incidentally, the specification that these should be the "latest model," furnished "with linen above and with *tunimmu* leather below"). In order to keep up a good standards, local authorities were informed on how to deal correctly with corn distribution. In no. 289 the writer (probably the state treasurer Ṭab-šar-Aššur) explains the rationale behind providing garrison troops with rations taken from the corn tax:

"I give it, so they can cultivate their fields. If I did not allot it, they would take [the corn] they have harvested [prev]iously and eat it, and would not cultivate the fields but turn to me [with]out a superior, saying: 'Bread [*is being with*]*held from* us!'" (obv. 8ff).

## *Social Control and the Power of the Governors*

The capture of people fleeing from taxation, debt, or other obligations seems to have been the responsibility of an official called "mule stable attendant," *ša bēt kūdini* (nos. 48, 79). Quite large groups of people appear to have tried to escape from the "blessings" of the Assyrian government: no. 79 deals with the recapture and resettling of more than 380 Chaldean deportees. The picture of social disorders is enlarged by references to captured criminals or ones to be captured by a governor (nos. 227, 228, 231). However, this picture should not be exaggerated to suggest that Assyria in general was in a state of turmoil. The strongly expansionist policy carried out in the reign of Sargon, with its heavy strain on internal cohesion and effort, had evidently taken its toll in social disaffection.

On the other hand, Assyria's expansion brought affluence to its ruling class which surely affected the mutual relations between the provincial authorities. Allotting booty, prisoners of war and shares of taxes to incorporated territories must have created uneven or unfair situations in different provinces, and rivalry between governors. The very frequent letters denouncing the "foul" deeds of Assyrian authorities to the king (cf. nos. 81, 121, 149, 260; many more examples are known from outside the present corpus) are probably to be understood in this light. They provide evidence of continuous and large-scale variation in provincial competence, jealousy over the exploitation of annexed countries, and competition for territorial jurisdiction over mutually bordering areas.

## Letters from Assyria (Addenda to SAA I)

In this volume are published 24 fragmentary letters (nos. 277-300), which on epigraphical and other grounds belong to the correspondence edited in Volume I of this series. They deal mainly with building activities and related problems (nos. 281, 282, 291-296, 300, with river transport of timber (nos. 254-255) and bull colossi (nos. 290, 297-299). Very interesting is no. 282, dealing with palace reliefs of(?) the Old Palace depicting a Mannean campaign. This text may be added to the small roster of (roughly) datable letters, as the last campaign to Mannea was the one conducted in 714 (Sargon's Eighth). Interestingly, the text mentions that captions giving the names of Assyrian governors were to be fixed in the reliefs – a detail not paralleled by other textual evidence nor evident from the extant reliefs themselves.

No. 293 mentions the finishing of the winged 'claw' or 'hoof,' probably the leg of a piece of furniture, whose making is described in SAA I 51. Interestingly again, this same letter, in its fragmentary reverse side, seems to contain a slighting remark on the competence of the Babylonians engaged in the work: "Had it been at the disposal of the Assyrians, we would have retrieved it from them and quick[ly fin]ished it!" Such a remark, if correctly understood here, would strikingly illustrate the mental climate that fostered the war soon to break out between the two sister nations.

# On the Present Edition

The present volume continues the edition of the correspondence of Sargon begun in SAA I, and the general scope and objectives of this edition remain unchanged. The basic objective is to provide an up-to-date edition of the corpus that can be profitably used both by the specialist and the more general reader. While every effort has been expended to make it as complete and reliable as possible, no claim is laid to absolute "perfection." This can be achieved only after the texts have been subjected to a detailed and thorough analysis and their contents has been fully integrated with other contemporary evidence, which is beyond the scope of the present edition.

## *The Order of Texts in this Edition*

The order in which the texts are presented is, in principle, the same as in SAA I. The primary sorting criterion is prosopographical, so that all letters by the same sender, insofar as identifiable, appear together. The individual letter dossiers are arranged geographically, the general order being from west to east to south. Within each dossier, individual texts are arranged topically. Wherever possible within the limits of this arrangement, letters displaying similar orthographies, introductory formulae and other unifying features have been put together. No attempt at a chronological ordering of the material has been made. Senders whose identity or seat of office cannot be determined (or ones with only one extant letter) are to be found under "Varia and Unidentified" or "Miscellaneous Letters."

It goes without saying that a considerable number of fragmentary texts included in the volume would probably have been placed differently had they been completely preserved.

## *Texts Included and Excluded*

As indicated by its title, the volume is meant to contain all Assyrian letters published or identified to date that can with reasonable certainty be assigned to the correspondence of Sargon and that were written by persons stationed in the northern and and northeastern provinces of Assyria. The basic problems and methods involved in the selection process have been reviewed in ARINH

p. 118-134 and will not be further discussed here. It is necessary to point out once again, however, that some of the letters assigned to the Sargon correspondence may actually date from the beginning of the reign of Sennacherib (c. 705-702 BC), when the latter still resided in the North Palace, waiting for the completion of his SW Palace. There is generally no way of differentiating these letters from those written to or by Sargon, since the king is never identified by name.

Like SAA I, the present volume contains, in addition to letters from Nineveh, also a few Nimrud Letters. While as many as 17 letters found in Nimrud are related by subject matter and geographical provenience to texts edited in the present volume, only five of them have actually been included. The remaining 12 have been excluded since none of them can be *proved* to belong to the reign of Sargon, but some of them can *certainly* (NL 29, 49, 67, 100) and others with a great likelihood (NL 45, 75) be assigned to the reign of Tiglath-Pileser III. Since letters from the reign of Tiglath-Pileser seem to clearly outnumber those from the reign of Sargon in the Nimrud material, the likelihood for the unassignable letters to belong to Tiglath-Pileser's reign is considerable. Accordingly, we have considered it wisest to include only letters *certainly* assignable to Sargon's reign and leave the rest for a future volume on the correspondence of Tiglath-Pileser. The only deviation from this principle is NL 62 (no. 74), which may well date from the reign of Tiglath-Pileser (or Shalmaneser V) but has been included to supplement the otherwise very fragmentary dossier of Mahdê.

A large number of tiny fragments originally assigned to this volume were excluded as either not pertinent or not worth editing in their present condition. 24 fragments provisionally assigned to the volume or previously overlooked turned out, in the final analysis, to belong to the correspondence edited in SAA I. In order to make them available for study without further delay, it was decided to append them to the present volume.

## *Transliterations*

The transliterations, addressed to the specialist, render the text of the originals in roman characters according to standard Assyriological conventions and the principles outlined in the Editorial Manual. Every effort has been taken to make them as accurate as humanly possible. All the texts edited have been specifically collated for this volume with the exception of four Nimrud Letters in the collections of the Iraq Museum.

Results of collation are indicated with exclamation marks. Single exclamation marks indicate corrections to published copies, double exclamation marks, scribal errors. Question marks indicate uncertain or questionable readings. Broken portions of text and all restorations are enclosed within square brackets. Parentheses enclose items omitted by ancient scribes.

## *Translations*

The translations seek to render the meaning and tenor of the texts as accurately as possible in readable, contemporary English. In the interest of clarity, the line structure of the originals has not been retained in the translation but the text has been rearranged into logically coherent paragraphs.

Uncertain or conjectural translations are indicated by italics. Interpretative additions to the translation are enclosed within parentheses. All restorations are enclosed within square brackets. Untranslatable passages are indicated by dots.

Month names are rendered by their Hebrew equivalents, followed by a Roman numeral (in parentheses) indicating the place of the month within the lunar year. Personal, divine and geographical names are rendered by English or Biblical equivalents if a well-established equivalent exists (e.g., Esarhaddon, Nineveh); otherwise, they are given in transcription with length marks deleted. The rendering of professions is a compromise between the use of accurate but impractical Assyrian terms and inaccurate but practical modern or classical equivalents.

## *Critical Apparatus*

The primary purpose of the critical apparatus is to support the readings and translations established in the edition, and it consists largely of references to collations of questionable passages, scribal mistakes corrected in the transliteration, and alternative interpretations or restorations of ambiguous passages. Restorations based on easily verifiable evidence (e.g., parallel passages found in the text itself) are generally not explained in the apparatus; conjectural restorations only if their conjectural nature is not apparent from italics in the translation.

Collations given in copy at the end of the volume are referred to briefly as "see coll."

The critical apparatus does contain some additional information relevant to the interpretation of the texts, but it is not a commentary. Comments are kept to a minimum, and are mainly devoted to problems in the text, elucidation of names and lexical items, or Akkadian expressions necessarily left untranslated. The historical information contained in the texts is generally not commented upon.

## *Glossary and Indices*

The glossary and indices, electronically generated, follow the same pattern as the previous volumes. Please note, however, that the sorting program which previously treated short and long vowels as different letters has been modified, so that the order of short and long vowels now corresponds to that used in the major Assyriological lexicons.

## NOTES

[1] S. Parpola, SAA I p. xiii, quoting M. Liverani, "The Growth of the Assyrian Empire in the Habur/Middle Euphrates Area: a New Paradigm," *Les Annales Archéologiques Arabes Syriennes* 1984, p.110ff, now SAAB 2 (1988), p. 92.

[2] Generally, cf. Lie Sar. p. 18: 103-106 for year 715; pp. 22-28: 127-165, for 714. For the latter, see naturally also Sargon's letter to the god Aššur (TCL 3).

[3] Note the attempt to obtain Urarṭian support by the Kummuhian Mutallu (Winckler Sar. p. 116:112f), who was eliminated in 709 (thirteenth year of Sargon: Lie Sar. p. 79:467ff).

[4] Cf. S. Parpola, "Assyrian Royal Inscriptions and Neo-Assyrian Letters," ARINH (1981), pp. 132 and 138.

[5] Eponym (as governor of Tušhan) in 707: A. Ungnad, "Eponymen," RlA 2 (1938), p. 427, C$^{d}$ 13. It should be pointed out, however, that there is no evidence (except the introductory formula that he shares with Ša-Aššur-dubbu) that Ašipâ actually ever was a governor of Tušhan. It is equally possible that his seat of office was the neighboring city of Tidu.

[6] Lie Sar. p. 12:78-82.

[7] Lie Sar. p. 14:83-90.

[8] SAA I 29:31f. The letter became understandable in full thanks to two joins made by K. Deller; the attribution to 714 was advanced in Deller Zagros p. 104.

[9] The governors mentioned in the first letter are called "opposite me" and "opposite Ukku" by Aššur-reṣuwa (lines 6f and 12-r.1); Urzana speaks of the governor of Waisi and of the governor next to the Ukkean king (lines 9-10). On this equation, see G. B. Lanfranchi, "Some New texts about a revolt against the Urarṭian King Rusa I," OrAnt 22 (1983), pp. 128f.

[10] Recently edited by Salvini Zagros pp. 79-95.

[11] Salvini Zagros p. 21, was the first to show that the meaning of the verb *zaqāpu* in this text (ll. 4-7) means "to attack," and not "to revolt," as previously believed (cf. Deller Zagros p. 117).

[12] Lie Sar. p. 18:104.

[13] Lie Sar. p. 26:147f.

[14] Lie Sar. p. 16:101.

[15] TCL 3, 91.

[16] TCL 3, 404.

[17] On this matter, see my contribution quoted above, n. 9.

[18] See also SAA I 30-32, written by Sennacherib, and containing various reports on the defeat by different informers.

[19] See my contribution, n. 9 above.

[20] A.K.G. Kristensen, *Who Were the Cimmerians, and Where did they come from? Sargon II, the Cimmerians, and Rusa I*, Copenhagen 1988. For a study of this problem, and an analysis of the entire matter, see my *I Cimmeri. Emergenza delle élites militari iraniche nel Vicino Oriente (VIII-VII sec. a.C.)*, Padova 1990, and its English translation *The Cimmerians* (Padova 1991, in press).

[21] Salvini Zagros pp. 45f.

[22] See the pertinent bibliography in Salvini Zagros, p. 43, n. 186. A discussion of the chronology is found ibid., pp. 42-45.

[23] This thesis was put forward in my contribution in OrAnt 22 (above n. 9).

[24] In no. 104, a governor named Nabû-uṣalla appears to be in charge of a community of Kummeans. As pointed out in the critical apparatus, it is not at all certain, however, that he actually was in charge of the city of Kumme as well.

[25] CAD Q, p. 265 and 268, with bibliography.

[26] S. Parpola, SAA I p. xvii.

[27] Lie Sar. p. 32:197f.

[28] Borger Esarh. p. 106, Gbr. II, III 23-34.

[29] TCL 3, 309-312.

[30] For a similar example, or perhaps the very same situation, cf. SAA I 46.

[31] H.W.F. Saggs, "The Nimrud Letters, 1952 - Part VIII," Iraq 28 (1966), p.187; J.V. Kinnier Wilson, *The Nimrud Wine Lists*, London 1972, pp. 50-52.

[32] The crucial fragmentary sentence "[Perh]aps the [ki]ng, my lord, (now) says: 'Where are the rest of the troops?'" (r. 3-4) was correctly understood by the first editor (Saggs, ibid.) but not taken into account by later scholars.

[33] A. Ungnad, "Eponymen," RlA 2 (1938), p. 433, C$^{b}$ 3, 8. Cf. Lie Sar. pp. 28-32: 165-194.

[34] Contrary to the statement of his death after Sargon's sack of Muṣaṣir contained in Sargon's Annals (Lie Sar. p. 28:164f).

[35] Rost Tigl. p. 2:10; 42:7; 56:11.

[36] A. Ungnad, "Eponymen," RlA 2 (1938), p. 433, C$^{b}$ 3, 11. Sargon's annals do not contain any indication about Ellipi.

[37] On this matter, see Postgate, TCAE.

[38] No. 269, a request by the king to forward 7,000 homers of barley, may be perhaps understood in this way; cf. also SAA I 26 and 27.

[39] On this matter, see F.M. Fales, "Il taglio e il trasporto di legname nelle lettere a Sargon II," in O. Carruba - M. Liverani - C. Zaccagnini (eds.), *Studi orientalistici in ricordo di Franco Pintore*, Pavia 1983, pp. 49-92.

[40] M. Liverani, *Antico Oriente. Storia società economia*, Bari 1989, p. 826.

[41] See in detail for this text L. Levine, "K. 4765+ – The Zamua Itinerary," SAAB 3 (1989), pp. 75-92.

[42] Cf. no. 16, royal confirmation of Itu'eans' exemption from straw and barley tax; no. 263, gift of house, plough and field to an archer.

# Abbreviations and Symbols

## *Bibliographical Abbreviations*

| | |
|---|---|
| ABL | R. F. Harper, *Assyrian and Babylonian Letters* (London and Chicago 1892-1914) |
| ADD | C. H. W. Johns, *Assyrian Deeds and Documents* (Cambridge 1898-1923) |
| AO | tablets in the collections of the Musée du Louvre |
| AOAT | Alter Orient und Altes Testament |
| ARINH | F. M. Fales (ed.), *Assyrian Royal Inscriptions: New Horizons in Literary, Ideological and Historical Analysis* (Orientis Antiqui Collectio XVIII, Rome 1981) |
| BM | tablets in the collections of the British Museum |
| Borger Esarh. | R. Borger, *Die Inschriften Esarhaddons, Königs von Assyrien* (AfO Beiheft 9, Graz 1956) |
| Bu | tablets in the collections of the British Museum |
| CAD | Chicago Assyrian Dictionary |
| CT | Cuneiform Texts from Babylonian Tablets in the British Museum |
| Deller Zagros | K. Deller, *Ausgewählte neuassyrische Briefe betreffend Urarṭu zur Zeit Sargons II.*, in P.E. Pecorella - M. Salvini, *Tra lo Zagros e l'Urmia. Ricerche storiche ed archeologiche nell'Azerbaigian iraniano* (Rome 1984) |
| DT | tablets in the collections of the British Museum |
| GPA | J. N. Postgate, *The Governor's Palace Archive* (Cuneiform Texts from Nimrud 2, London 1973) |
| JRAS | Journal of the Royal Asiatic Society |
| K | tablets in the collections of the British Museum |
| LAS | S. Parpola, *Letters from Assyrian Scholars to the Kings Esarhaddon and Assurbanipal* I, II (Alter Orient und Altes Testament 5/1-2, Neukirchen-Vluyn 1970, 1983) |
| Lie Sar. | A. G. Lie, *The Inscriptions of Sargon II, King of Assyria* I (Paris 1929) |
| Menant, *Catalogue* | J. Ménant, *Catalogue des cylindres orientaux du Cabinet Royal des Médailles de la Haye* (La Haye 1878) |
| N. | tablets in the collections of the Musée du Louvre |
| ND | field numbers of tablets excavated at Nimrud |
| NL | H. W. F. Saggs, "The Nimrud Letters," *Iraq* 17 (1955), 21ff., etc. |
| OrAnt | Oriens Antiquus |
| Payne-Smith | J. Payne Smith (ed.), A Compendious Syriac Dictionary (Oxford 1903) |

| | |
|---|---|
| R | H. C. Rawlinson, *The Cuneiform Inscriptions of Western Asia* (London 1861-1884) |
| RCAE | L. Waterman, *Royal Correspondence of the Assyrian Empire*, I-IV (Ann Arbor 1930-1936) |
| RlA | Reallexikon der Assyriologie |
| Rm | tablets in the collections of the British Museum |
| Rost Tigl. | P. Rost, *Die Keilschrifttexte Tiglat-Pilesers III* (Leipzig 1893) |
| SAA | State Archives of Assyria |
| SAAB | State Archives of Assyria Bulletin |
| Salvini Zagros | M. Salvini, *La storia della regione in epoca urartea. I documenti*, in P.E. Pecorella - M. Salvini, *Tra lo Zagros e l'Urmia. Ricerche storiche ed archeologiche nell'Azerbaigian iraniano* (Rome 1984) |
| Sm | tablets in the collections of the British Museum |
| TCAE | J. N. Postgate, *Taxation and Conscription in the Assyrian Empire* (Studia Pohl, Series Maior 3, Rome 1974) |
| TCL | Textes cunéiformes du Louvre |
| TCL 3 | F. Thureau-Dangin, *Une relation de la huitième campagne de Sargon* (Musée du Louvre, Département des Antiquités Orientales. Textes Cunéiformes 3, Paris 1912) |
| Th | tablets in the collections of the British Museum |
| Winckler Sar. | H. Winckler, *Die Keilschrifttexte Sargons* (Leipzig 1889) |
| ZA | Zeitschrift für Assyriologie |

W and Y in the critical apparatus (followed by page number) refer to collations in RCAE and S. Ylvisaker, *Zur babylonischen und assyrischen Grammatik* (LSS 5/6, Leipzig 1912) respectively.

## *Other Abbreviations and Symbols*

| | |
|---|---|
| Aram. | Aramaic |
| Bab. | Babylonian |
| Hebr. | Hebrew |
| Syr. | Syriac |
| NA | Neo-Assyrian |
| NB | Neo-Babylonian |
| DN | divine name |
| GN | geographical name |
| RN | royal name |
| e. | edge |
| obv. | obverse |
| r., rev. | reverse |
| s. | (left) side |
| coll. | collated, collation |
| mng. | meaning |
| unpub. | unpublished |
| var. | variant |
| ! | collation |
| !! | emendation |
| ? | uncertain reading |
| : :. :: | cuneiform division marks |
| * | graphic variants (see LAS I p. XX) |
| 0 | uninscribed space or nonexistent sign |
| *x* | broken or undeciphered sign |
| ( ) | supplied word or sign |
| (( )) | sign erroneously added by scribe |
| [[ ]] | erasure |
| [...] | minor break (one or two missing words) |
| [......] | major break |
| ... | untranslatable word |
| ...... | untranslatable passage |
| → | see also |
| + | joined to |

# TRANSLITERATIONS AND TRANSLATIONS

## Letters from the Šubrian Frontier

# 1. Letters from Liphur-Bel, Governor of Amidi

COURTESY MOSUL MUSEUM

FIG. 1. *Assyrians beside a burning town, possibly in Hubuškian territory (reign of Assurnasirpal). Cf. nos. 11f.*
MOSUL MUSEUM.

## 1. No News is Good News

K 488

1 a-na LUGAL EN-ia
2 ARAD-ka $^{m}$NIGIN—EN
3 lu DI-mu a-na LUGAL EN-ia
4 DI-mu a-na KUR šá LUGAL
5 DI-mu a-na HAL.ṢU.MEŠ šá LUGAL
6 ŠÀ ša LUGAL EN-ia lu-⸢u?⸣ [DÙ]G!
7 i—su-[ri LUGAL be-lí]
8 i-qab-b[i ma]-⸢a⸣ m[i-i]-nu
9 ṭè-mu ša [KUR].⸢URI⸣-[a]-⸢a⸣
10 am!-ma!-⸢kam!⸣-[m]a
11 šu!-u ⸢ú!⸣-[di]-⸢ni!⸣
12 ⸢mi!-me!-ni!⸣
r.1 TA ŠÀ-bi
2 la i-li-ka
3 ṭè-en-šú-nu
4 la ni-šam-me
rest uninscribed

ABL 200

1 To the king, my lord: your servant Liphur-Bel. Good health to the king, my lord!

4 The land of the king is well; the forts of the king are well. The king, my lord, can be [gl]ad.

7 Perh[aps the king, my lord], will say: "Any news of the Urarṭian?" He is still over there; nobody has come from there, we haven't heard any news about them y[e]t.

## 2. Attacks on Forts

K 593

1 [a-na LU]GA[L! E]N!-[iá ARAD-ka $^{m}$NIGIN]—EN
2 ⸢lu⸣ DI-mu a-[na LUGAL EN]-iá
3 DI-mu a-na [KUR] ⸢ša!⸣ [LUG]AL
4 DI-mu a-na URU.HAL.[ṢU].MEŠ
5 ŠÀ-bu šá LUGAL EN-iá lu DÙG
6 ina UGU ṭè-me ša KUR.URI-a-a
7 LÚ*.A—KIN-⸢ia!⸣ [š]a! ina UGU!
8 LÚ*.EN.NAM [ša] pu!-u!-tú-u-a
9 áš-pur-ú-⸢ni!⸣ i[t!]-tal-ka
10 ki-i ša LUGAL be-lí iš-pur-an-ni
11 id-du-ba-áš-šú
12 ma a-ta-a a-ni-nu
13 sa-al-ma-ni at-tu-nu
14 at-tu-nu URU.HAL.ṢU.MEŠ-ni
15 tu-ṣa-ba-ta ma-a
r.1 ana-ku : mì-nu le-pu-uš
2 ma-a BE-ma ina ta-hu-me-ku-nu
3 ina URU.HAL.ṢU.MEŠ-ku-nu

ABL 548

1 [To the k]in[g, my lo]rd: [your servant Liphur]-Bel. Good health t[o the king], my [lord]!

3 [The land] of [the ki]ng is well; the for[t]s are well. The king, my lord, can be glad.

6 As to the news of the Urarṭians, the messenger of mine [wh]om I sent [to] the governor opposite me has come back; he spoke to him as the king, my lord, wrote me, saying: "Why do you capture our forts, while we are at peace?"

r.1 He said: "What should I do? If I have trespassed on your territory or your forts, call me to account."

**1** 6 See coll. 10ff See coll.

**2** → Deller Zagros p.120 with coll. by M. Salvini; recollated by S. Parpola, March 1988. 3 See coll. 11f The first quotation introduced by *ma* could theoretically represent the answer of the Urarṭian governor, but parallels indicate that words of the messenger are in question. Cf. *ina pitti dibbī ša š[arri issīšu ni]ddubub nuk* "[we] spoke [with him] in accordance with the king's words, saying: (...)" ABL 1003:12, similarly ABL 1070:16 and 1294 r.5;

4 *ah-ti-ṭí ina* ŠU.2-*ia*
5 *ba-i-a*[!] : LÚ*.*e-mu-qi-šú*
6 *i-si-šú pu-uh-ru*
7 *ina* URU.*har-da* EN.NUN
8 *i-na-ṣa-ar an-ni-i-u*
9 *ṭè-en-šú-nu*
rest uninscribed

5 His troops are assembled with him; he is keeping watch in Harda. This was the news about them.

## 3. Urarṭu gets Ready for War

Sm 760

1 *a-na* LUGAL EN-*iá* ARAD-*ka* $^{m}$NIGIN—EN
2 *lu-u* DI-*mu a-na* LUGAL EN-*ia*
3 DI-*mu a-na* KUR *ša* LUGAL
4 DI-*mu a-na* URU.HAL.ṢU.MEŠ
5 ŠÀ *ša* LUGAL EN-*ia lu-u* DÙG
6 *ina* UGU *ṭè-e-me ša* KUR.URI-*a-a*
7 LÚ*.*da-a-a-li a-sa-par*
8 *e-tam-ru ki-i an-ni-i-e*
9 *iq-ṭí-bi-ú-ni ma-a* LÚ*.EN.NAM
10 *ša pu-tú-un-ni* LÚ*.EN.NAM 2-*u*
11 *i-si-šú ina* URU.*ha-ar-da*
12 *pu-ut* LÚ*.SUKKAL EN.NUN *i-na-ṣur*
13 *ma-a* URU *a-na* URU : *a-di* URU.*ṭu-ru-uš-pa-a*
14 *ul-lu-a-te sa-ad-ra*
15 *ma-a* LÚ*.A—KIN *šá* $^{m}$*ar-gi-is-ta it-tal-ka*
16 *ma-a ina* UGU *dul*[!]*-li ša ṭè-mu*
17 *áš-kun-ka-a-ni ma-a* $dul_6$*-lu*
18 *ma-a la te-pa-áš ma-a* ANŠE.KUR.RA-*ka*
e.19 *šá-ki-il a-di* LÚ*.A—KIN
20 *a-šap-par-kan-ni*
r.1 GIŠ.ÙR.MEŠ *šá ina* URU.*e-zi-at*
2 *ik-lu-u-ni* LÚ*.*i-tú-a-a*
3 TA LÚ*.GAL—URU *a-sa-ap-ra*
4 *ina* ŠÀ *qa-ra-bi ú-se-te-qa*
5 LÚ*.2-*ú ša* LÚ*.GAL—URU.MEŠ-*šú-nu*
6 9 LÚ*.ERIM.MEŠ *i-si-šu ina* ŠÀ GIŠ.BAN
7 *ma-hu-ṣu* 2 *ina* ŠÀ-*šú-nu* ÚŠ
8 3 LÚ*.ERIM.MEŠ-*ni-šú-nu ut-ta-hi-ṣu*
9 *an-ni-i-ú ṭè-en-šú-nu*
10 LÚ*.*i-tú-a-a ša* É.GAL *šá ina* IGI-*iá*
11 TA UGU ÍD.*pu-rat-te i-suh-ru-ni*
12 TA LÚ*.SUKKAL *la*[!] *il-li-ku*
13 *a-sa-ap-ra-šú-nu* TA É 1-*en* É 2
14 TA ŠÀ URU *it-tu-ṣu-u-ni*
15 LUGAL *be-lí ina* UGU LÚ*.*na-sik*.MEŠ
16 *liš-pu-ra* LÚ*.ERIM—MAN *ki a-ha-iš*
17 *lu-še-ṣu-ú-ni* EN.NUN
18 *ina* URU.*la*[!]*-ru-ba i-si-ia*
19 *li-ṣu-ru a-di e-ṣa-du*
20 *nu-ka-na-šú-ú-ni*

ABL 424

1 To the king, my lord: your servant Liphur-Bel. Good health to the king, my lord!

4 The land of the king is well; the forts are well. The king, my lord, can be glad.

6 As to the news of the Urarṭians, the spies I sent to reconnoiter have informed me as follows:

9 "The governor opposite us is keeping watch with the deputy governor in the city Harda, opposite the Vizier; *levied* troops are positioned town by town in battle array as far as Ṭurušpâ.

15 "A messenger of Argisti has come by, saying: 'As to the work I ordered you to do, don't do it! Feed your horses until I send you a messenger.'"

r.1 I sent the Itu'eans with the village inspector for the logs which were held back in Eziat, and he got them moved through by fighting. The deputy of their village inspector and nine of his soldiers were struck down by a bow; two of them died. They wounded three of their soldiers. This was their report.

10 The Itu'eans of the Palace at my disposal have returned from the Euphrates; they did not go with the Vizier. I have sent for them, but (men) of one or two houses only have come out of the town. Let the king, my lord, write to the sheikhs; they should bring the king's men out jointly, to keep watch with me in Laruba, until we have collected the harvest.

contrast *issišunu addubub iqṭibûni mā* "we spoke with them and they said: (...)" ABL 1086:14. r.1 Logic implies that r.1ff, which theoretically could also belong to the speech of the messenger, represents the answer of the Urarṭian governor.

3 → Deller Zagros p.113f. 17 $dul_6$*-lu* sic (despite *dul-lu* in the preceding line). r.1 Or: "the Itu'ean" (scil. their prefect). r.18 See coll.

## 4. Floating Logs down the River

K 1924

beginning broken away
1′ x[x x x x x x x x]
2′ L[Ú.x x x x x x x]
3′ ⌈x⌉ [x x x x x x x]
4′ *a*[*r-x x x x x x x*]
5′ LÚ*.[x x x x x x x]
6′ *i-za-bil-*(*u*)*-ni* [x x x x]
7′ *ú-se-ṣi* [x x x x]
8′ ⌈URU⌉.HAL.ṢU.MEŠ *uh-t*[*ar-rid*]
9′ [*a-ta-m*]*ar-šú a-su*[*h-ra*]
10′ [x x x *t*]*a a* [x x x]
r.1 [*ina* U]GU $^{m}$*šá—aš-šur—du-b*[*u*]
2 *at-tal-ka ina pa-na-tú-u-*[*a*?]
3 UR[U?] *ṣa-bit* LÚ*.*ša*—HAL.ṢU.[MEŠ]
4 *ina* Š[À]-⌈*bi*⌉ *ú-se-ri-bu*
5 [LÚ*.*e-mu*]-⌈*qi*⌉ ŠÀ KUR-*šú-nu d*[*a*?-*ki-u*]
6 [*pu*]-⌈*uh*⌉-*ru a-na-ku* GIŠ.⌈ÙR⌉.[MEŠ]
7 ⌈*i-ba*⌉-*ši ina* ÍD *ak-t*[*ar-ra*]
8 *šá-pal* ⌈URU⌉.*e-zi-at šá* [GIŠ.ÙR.MEŠ]
9 *ú-še-taq-u-ni* LÚ*.*e-*[*mu-qi*]
10 *ina* ŠÀ-*bi* [x x x x x x]
rest broken away

CT 53 210

(Beginning destroyed)

6 carries [......]

7 brought out [......]

8 [*aler*]*ted* the forts.

9 [I sa]w him and retur[ned]

10 [......]

r.1 I went [t]o Ša-Aššur-dubb[u]; *the ci*[*ty*] was taken in [my] presence, and they brought garrison troop[s] into it.

5 [The tr]oops inside their country are *mo*[*bilized and* as]sembled.

6 As for me, I did throw the log[s] into the river. Downstream from Eziat, past [which] I float [the logs], there are tr[oops ...]

(Rest destroyed)

## 5. Bringing Soldiers into Eziat

K 13088

beginning broken away
1′ [x x x x] ⌈*né*⌉-*e-r*[*i-bi*]
2′ [x x x-*r*]*u-u-ni* : *e-t*[*a-rab*]
3′ [x x-*d*]*i ina* ŠÀ ANŠE.*ku-di*[*n*]
e.4′ [*ú-sa*]*r*?-*kib* 90 LÚ*.ERIM.MEŠ
5′ [URU!].⌈*i*⌉-*si-tú ina* ŠÀ-*bi*
6′ [*ina*] ŠÀ URU.*e-zi-at*
7′ *ú-se-ri-bi*
r.1 30 LÚ*.ERIM.MEŠ TA ŠÀ-*bi*
2 [*ú-s*]*e-ṣi pa-ni-u-t*⌈*i*⌉
3 [x x L]Ú.ERIM.MEŠ *ina* ŠÀ [x]
4 [x x x] ⌈*ú*⌉-*še-r*[*i-bu-ni*]
5 [x x x] ⌈x⌉ [x x x]
rest broken away

CT 53 478

(Beginning destroyed)

1 *I* entered [... through] the pa[ss of ...r]uni, [*mo*]*unting* [...] on mu[les].

4 *I* made 90 soldiers enter Eziat — there is a tower there — and brought 30 soldiers out of it. The *vanguard* [*who*] made the soldiers enter [......]

(Rest destroyed)

## 6. Transporting Logs

Rm 2,410

1 [*a-na* LU]GAL EN-*ia*
2 [ARAD]-⌈*ka*⌉ $^{m}$NIGIN—EN
3 [*lu* DI]-*mu a-na* LUGAL EN-*ia*

ABL 732

1 [To the ki]ng, my lord: your [servant] Liphur-Bel. [Good] health to the king, my lord!

**4** r.2 Or: "Before [my] coming, the city had been taken, and they were bringing ...."

FIG. 2. *Floating timber downstream (reign of Sennacherib).*
BM 124822.

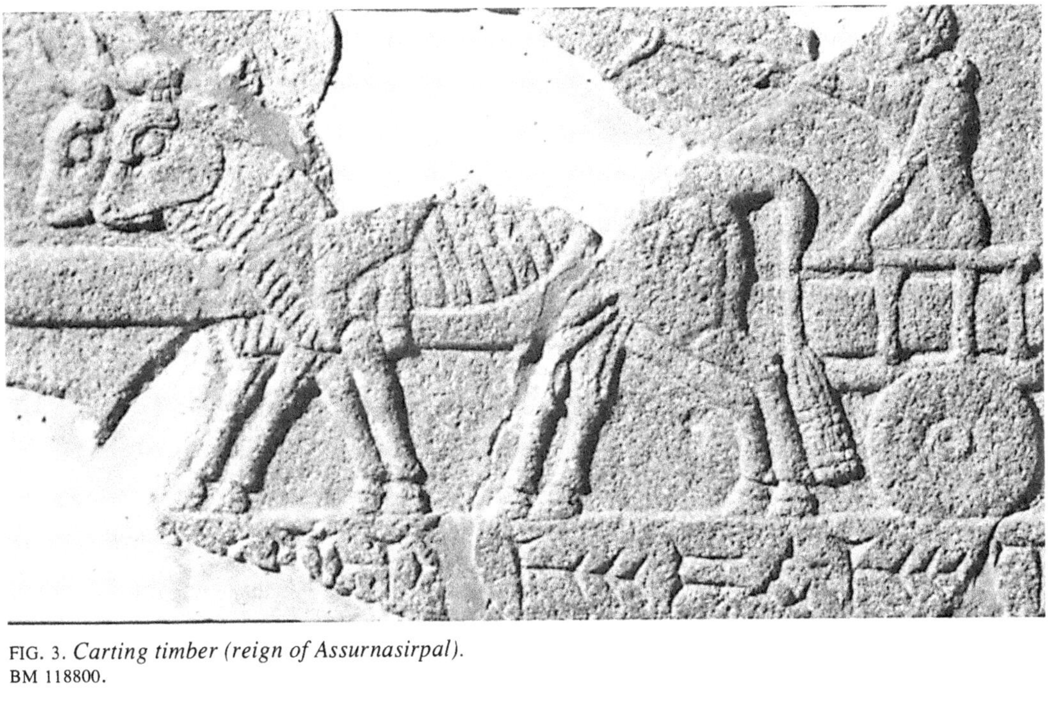



FIG. 3. *Carting timber (reign of Assurnasirpal).*
BM 118800.

4 [DI-*mu a*]-*na* KUR *šá* LUGAL
5 [DI-*mu a*]-*na* HAL.ṢU.MEŠ *ša* [LUGAL]
6 [ŠÀ *ša*] LUGAL EN-*ia lu* [DÙG]
7 [*x*]-*lim*-2-*me* GIŠ.[ŠÚ?.A?.MEŠ]
8 [*x*]-*lim*-2-*me* GIŠ.Ù[R!.MEŠ]
9 [*ina*] UGU ÍD *u*[*q*?-*ṭa-rib*]
10 [*x x*] LUGAL [*x x x*]
rest broken away
Rev. beginning broken away
1′ [*x x*]*x šu bu* [*x x x x*]
2′ [*x*].MEŠ *ina* Í[D? *x x x*]
3′ [*ki-ma*?] LÚ*.ERIM.MEŠ *ú-sa-an-*[*šil*]
4′ [*ina* UR]U!.HAL.ṢU.MEŠ *ú-se-r*[*ib*]
5′ [*l*]*a-ah-ru-ub ina* UGU Í[D]
6′ [*l*]*u-qa-rib ur-ki-ti*
7′ [*k*]*i-i šá* LUGAL *i-la-u-ni*
8′ [*l*]*e-pu-uš*
rest (4 lines) uninscribed

4 The land of the king [is well], the forts of the [king] a[re well]. The king, my lord, can [be glad].

7 I have b[rought *1*],200 [*door-beams*] and [*1*],200 roof-b[eams] to the river. [...] the king [...]

(Break)

r.2 [...] the [...]s in the *r*[*iver*].

3 [*As soon as*] I have bro[ught] *an equ*[*al number*] of troops [into the forts, I will promptly bring them to the ri[ver] bank; afterwards, the king, my lord, may do as pleases.

## 7. Log Driving

K 5555

beginning broken away
1′ 2-*lim* ⌜GIŠ⌝.[*x x x x x*]
2′ 5-*me* GIŠ.Ù[R.MEŠ *x x*]
3′ *pa-ni-um-*[*ma x x x x*]
4′ *ú-qa-ra-*[*bu-ni x x x*]
5′ *ki-ma* ⌜*a*⌝-[*x x x x x*]
6′ *i-t*[*al-x x x x x*]
rest broken away
Rev. beginning broken away
1′ [*x*] LUG[AL *x x x x*]
2′ *le-r*[*iš*! *x x x x x*]
3′ LUGAL *be*-⌜*lí*⌝ [*x x x x*]
4′ *ma-a* GIŠ.*x*[*x x x x*]
5′ *ar-hi-i*[*š x x x x*]
6′ A.MEŠ [*ina* ÍD *x x x*]
rest broken away

CT 53 280

(Beginning destroyed)
1 2,000 [*door*-beams ......]
2 500 roof-b[eams ......]
3 former [......]
4 bri[ng ......]
5 as soon as [......]
6 have co[me ......]
(Break)
r.1 [*of*] the ki[ng ......]
2 should req[uest ......]
3 The king, my lord, [*wrote to me*]:
4 "[...] the [logs]
5 quick[ly ...]" –
6 the water [in the river]
(Rest destroyed)

## 8. Fragment Referring to Messengers and Timber

K 15268

beginning broken away
1′ [*x x x x x x*] *a li* [*x x*]
2′ [*x x x x x*] ⌜*i*⌝-*pa-qí-d*[*u*]
3′ [*x x x x ú-s*]*a-hi-ru* $dul_6$-[*lu*]
4′ [*x x x x x š*]*a* ⌜*x x x*⌝ [*x*]

CT 53 631

(Beginning destroyed)
1 [......] ...
2 [......] they appoint
3 [... they have retu]rned [...] the wo[rk]
4 [......] of ...

**6** 8 See coll. r.1f See coll. r.3 Or: "have brought enough (*ú-sa-an-*[*ṣi*]) troops [into] the forts" (suggestion J. N. Postgate). r.4 See coll.
**7** r.2 See coll.
**8** Probably part of the same tablet as no. 9, with a gap of one line between K 1585:6′ and K 15268:1′; no physical join. Hand of Liphur-Bel.

5′ [x x x x x]-⸢i⸣ : *ki an-ni-[e]*
6′ [x x *ma-a*? LÚ*].⸢A⸣—KIN-*šú a-ni-[ni*?]
7′ [x x x x *i]—da-tuk-ka* [x]
8′ [x x x x x] *ina* IGI-*ia* [x x]
9′ [x x x x x x *s]a hi x*[x x]
rest broken away
Rev. beginning broken away
1′ [x x x x *š]a* GIŠ.ÙR.ME[Š]
2′ [x x x x x] *ni-it-te-et-[zi]*
3′ [x x x x GIŠ].ÙR.MEŠ *i-šá-du-[du]*
4′ [x x x x *a-n]a* EN.NUN [x]
5′ [x x x x *ú-še]-šib-ú-n[i]*
6′ [x x x x x] ⸢*ú*⸣ [x x x]
rest broken away

5 [... *spoke*] as follows:
6 "[*W*]*e are* his messengers
7 [......] after you [...]
8 [......] in my presence [...]
9 [......] ...[......]
(Break)
r.1 [...... o]f the logs
2 [......] we sto[od]
3 [......] will hau[l] the logs
4 [...... f]or the watch [...]
5 [...... se]ttled
(Rest destroyed)

## 9. ———

K 15085

beginning broken away
1′ [x x x x x] ⸢*paq-da*⸣-*šú-nu*
2′ [x x x x x] *ni iq-ṭí-bi*
3′ [x x x x *l]i*!-*is-hu-ru*
4′ [x x x x x]-*i-ú*
5′ [x x x x *š]a* ITI.ZÍ[Z]
6′ [x x x x ANŠE].*ku-din*!-[*ni*]
rest broken away
Rev. destroyed

CT 53 616

(Beginning destroyed)
1 [......] are entrusted to them
2 [......] said
3 [......] let them *return*
4 [......] ...
5 [...... On the ...th o]f She[bat] (XI)
6 [......] mul[es]
(Rest destroyed)

## 10. ———

K 15661

beginning broken away
1′ ⸢x⸣ [x x x x x x x]
2′ *an-na*-[x x x x x x]
3′ LÚ*.ERIM.M[EŠ x x x x x]
4′ URU.HAL.[ṢU x x x x x]
5′ *a-na* KUR—*a*[*š-šur* x x x x x]
6′ *ú-ma*-⸢*a*⸣ [x x x x x x]
7′ *ú*-[x x x x x x x x]
rest broken away
Rev. destroyed

CT 53 708

(Beginning destroyed)
2 he[re ......]
3 the troop[s ......]
4 the for[t ......]
5 to A[ssyria ......]
6 Now [......]
(Rest destroyed)

## 11. An Urarṭian Governor in Muṣaṣir

Rm 978

1 *a-na* LUGAL [EN-*ia*]
2 ARAD-*ka* $^{m}$[NIGIN—EN]
3 *lu-u* DI-*mu a*-[*na* LUGAL EN-*iá*]

ABL 1083

1 To the king, [my lord]: your servant [Liphur-Bel]. Good health t[o the king, my lord]!

**9** Probably part of the same tablet as no. 8 (with a one line gap between the two fragments).
**11** → no. 147; Deller Zagros p.108. The original of this text is thicker and coarser than usual in the letters of Liphur-Bel, and the scribal hand ("Liphur-Bel II") also makes a different ("hastier") impression. The orthography

4 DI-[mu] a-na KUR [ša LUGAL EN-iá]
5 [DI-mu] ⸢a-na⸣ [URU.HAL.ṢU.MEŠ]
rest (at least 20 lines) broken away
Rev. beginning (at least 20 lines) lost
1′ ⸢TA⸣ na!-x[x x x x x x x x x x]
2′ a-na ma-gu-ri! [x x x x x]
3′ KUR.hu-buš-ka-a-a i-s[a!-ap-ra-šú]
4′ ma-a la LÚ*.da-a-a-⸢URU⸣ [x x x]
5′ ma-a URU.nu-ra-a-a ša T[A x x]
6′ ih-li-qu-u-ni šú-n[u k]i-i LÚ*.EN.NAM [0]
7′ ša K[UR].ú-a-si a-na K[UR].mu-ṣa-ṣir ⸢e!⸣-[ru-bu-ni]
8e KUR.h[u]-buš-ka-a-⸢a⸣ [ina pa-ni-šú]
9e it-t[i]-it-su [ma-a BE-ma x x]
10e ta-šap-pa-r[a x x x x]
s.1 [x x x x x x x x x]x-šú ta-na-pa-ha
2 [x x x x x x x x x]x KUR.mu-ṣa-ṣir
3 [x x x x x x x x]x a-na nu-up-šá-te
4 [x x x x x x x x]x

4 The land [of the king] is we[ll, the forts] are [well. *The king, my lord, can be glad*].

(Break)

r.2 in order to make [...] agree [...],

3 the Hubuškian w[*rote to him*], saying: "[*They are*] no spies; they are Nuraeans who have run away fr[om ...]."

6 When the governor of Waisi en[tered] Muṣaṣir, the Hubuškians stood [in his presence, saying: "*If*] you send [......]

s.1 you light [...] his [......]
2 [......] Muṣaṣir
3 [......] for the lives [......]

## 12. Fragment Referring to Military Operations and Spies

Sm 96

Obv. broken away
Rev. beginning broken away
1′ [x KUR.hu-bu]š!-ka-a-a ⸢LÚ*.da!⸣-[a-a-li]
2′ [ša áš-pur-u]-ni TA* pa-ni-šú i!-s[uh?-ru-ni]
3′ [ma-a ina IGI?] URU šu-u : pu-u-tú x[x x x]
4′ [x x x ma]-a re-eh-ti ma-da[k!-ti x x x]
5′ [i-zu-q]u-pu ma-a ú-ma-a x[x x x]
6′ [ina UGU L]Ú.da-a-a-li KUR.U[RI-a-a]
7′ [ša LUGAL] be-lí iš-pur-an-ni [ma-a]
8′ [la LÚ*.GA]L!—HAL.ṢU ik-la!-[šú-nu-u]
9′ [x x KUR].hu-buš-ka-a-a [x x x]
10′ [x x m]a-a LÚ*.da-a-a-l[i am—mar]
11′ [ú-še]-zib-u-ni URU.MEŠ!-ni [e-tar-bu]
12′ [ina ma-ti-i]a i-šá-tu ni-[x x x]
13′ [x x x x] nu-uk la [x x x x]
14′ [x x x x x] a[l x x x x]
rest broken away

ABL 1043

(Beginning destroyed)

1 [*As to the ... of*] the [Hubu]škian, the sc[outs *whom I sent*] have *r*[*eturned*] from his presence, (reporting):

3 "He is [*in front of*] the city, opposite [...]. *They* [*have atta*]*cked* the rest of the [Urarṭian] cam[p]; now, [......]."

6 [As to] the Ur[arṭian] spies about whom the king], my lord, wrote me: "Has the [commanlder of the fort [not] held [them] back?" — [...] the Hubuškian [...] said:

10 "[Whichever] spie[s sa]ved themselves [have *entered*] the towns; we [*are sending*] fire (*signals*) [in m]y [country ...]."

13 I said: "*No* [......]

(Rest destroyed)

however (and, accordingly, the scribe) is the same as in the other Liphur-Bel letters. No. 12 is part of the same tablet but there is no physical join between the two fragments. No. 18 has the same ductus and tablet format but is not part of the same tablet. r.1, 3 See coll. r.2 W 295. r.3 Or: "s[ent ... to him]."

**12** Part of the same tablet as no. 11. r.1f, 4 See coll. r.3 Or "[in/at] the city." There is no room for restoring [KUR.URI-*a-a*] "the Urarṭian" at the beginning of the line. r.4 Or "he [has atta]cked/is atta]cking (*i-za-q*]*u-pu*) the rest of the/[his] cam[p]"; possibly also "the rest of [*his*] cam[p have atta]cked/[are atta]cking [...]."

**13** Previously unpublished; copy p. 265.

## 13. ———

K 19621

1′ [*x*]*x* ⸢*x x*⸣[*x x x x*]
2′ [*ṭ*]*è-mu ša* [*x x x x*]
3′ *ki-i ú-di-*[*ni* TA* É.GAL]
4′ *la-a i-ša*[*p-pa-ru-ni-ni*]
5′ A.[M]EŠ *ina* ÍD [*e-ṣu-ni*$^{?}$]
6′ LÚ*.*da-a-a-*[*li a-sa-par*]
7′ *ina re-eš* U[RU *it-tal-ku*$^{?}$]
8′ [*ma*]-*a x*[*x x x x x*]
rest broken away

K 19621

(Beginning destroyed)

2 news of [......]

3 Already before [they] wro[te to me *from the Palace*],

5 [(when) *there was little*] water in the river,

6 [I sent out] scou[ts];

7 [*they went*] to the 'head' of the ci[ty],

8 (reporting): "[......]

(Rest destroyed)

## 14. Chaldeans in Bit-Zamani

Rm 998

1 *a-na* [LUGAL EN-*ia*]
2 ARAD-*ka* [$^{m}$NIGIN—EN]
3 *lu-u* DI-*mu* [*a-na* LUGAL EN-*ia*]
4 DI-*mu a-n*[*a* KUR *šá* LUGAL]
5 DI-*mu a-na* URU.*b*[*i-rat ša* LUGAL]
6 ŠÀ-*bu ša* LUGAL E[N-*ia lu* DÙG]
7 *ki-i* LUGAL *be-lí* ⸢*a*⸣-[*na* KUR.*x x*]
8 *ú-na-miš-u-ni* LU[GAL *be-lí x x x*]
9 *iq-ṭí-ri-ib a-na-*[*ku x x x x*]
10 *a-na* KUR.É—*za-ma-n*[*i x x x*]
11 *ina* UGU LÚ*.ERIM—LU[GAL.MEŠ *a-sa-ap-ra*]
12 *nu-uk* 1-*me* LÚ*.ERIM.[MEŠ *x x x*]
13 *i-ṣal-ka b*[*i-la x x x x x*]
14 *le-pu-uš* [*x x x x x x x*]
15 [*x*] LÚ*!.3.⸢$U_5$⸣ [*x x x x x x x*]
rest broken away
Rev. beginning broken away
1′ [*ma*]-*a a-ta-a* [*x x x x x*]
2′ *ma-a* ANŠE.KUR.R[A.MEŠ *x x x x*]
3′ *ma-a a-ta-a x*[*x x x x*]
4′ *a-na* KUR.*kal-da-a-*[*a x x x*]
5′ *ma-a* ŠE.NUMUN.MEŠ *ina* Š[À-*bi le-ru-šú*]
6′ $^{m}$*hu-ma-ma-ti* $^{m}$[*x x x*]
7′ $^{m}$*hal-di*—AD—PAB ⸢PAB⸣ [*x x x*]
8′ $^{m}$*ka-nun-a-a* L[Ú.*x x*]
9′ $^{m}$*a-hu-tu-un* [*x x x x*]
10′ PAB 6 LÚ*.ERIM.MEŠ *ša* [*x x x*]
11′ *ra-qi-ú i-*[*x x x x*]
12′ *la-a i-ma-*[*gu-ru*]
13′ NUMUN.MEŠ-*šú-n*[*u la e-ru-šu a-na* LUGAL]

ABL 1193

1 To the [king, my lord]: your servant [Liphur-Bel]. Good health [to the king, my lord]!

4 [The land of the king] is well; the fo[rts of the king] are well. The king, [my] lo[rd, can be glad].

7 When the king, my lord, set out to [the country of ...], the ki[ng, my lord], arrived in [...], and I [wrote to ...] to Bit-Zaman[i ...] concerning the kin[g's] me[n]:

12 "Go and get 100 king's men, and come and b[ring them]; I should do [......]."

15 The 'third man' [......]

(Break)

r.1 "Why [...] the horses [...]?

3 "Why [......] to the Chaldeans? [They should cultivate] the arable fields [there]."

7 Humamati, [NN], Haldi-abu-uṣur brother [of NN], Kanunayu the [...], Ahutun and [NN], in all six men of [...] – they have been in hiding, [...], [and have] not agr[eed to cultivate] thei[r] arable fields.

**14** Hand of Liphur-Bel. → nos. 79 and 80. 7 Restore possibly ⸢*a*⸣-[*na* KUR.*mar-qa-si*]; the campaign to Gurgum in 711 was Sargon's only western campaign between 716 and 706. A date after 710 is implied by r. 4, which can only refer to Chaldeans deported and resettled in the north after the defeat of Merodach-Baladan. 13, 15 See coll.

**15** 17 See coll. r.12 Tablet *i-se-ši-ib*; scribal error.

14′ EN-*ia* [*a-sa-ap-ra* LUGAL *be-lí*]
15e *ki-i* [*šá i-la-u-ni le-pu-uš*]

14 [I have written to the king], my lord; [the king, my lord, may do] as [he deems best].

## 15. Building a Town, a Fort and a Palace

K 1966 + K 15607

1 [*a-na* LUGAL EN-*ia*]
2 [ARAD-*ka* $^{m}$NIG]IN—E[N]
3 [*lu*]-*u* ⸢DI⸣-[*mu*] *ana* MAN EN-*ia*
4 DI-*mu ana* KUR *ša* LUGAL
5 D[I-*m*]*u ana* HAL.ṢU.MEŠ
6 Š[À *š*]*a* MAN EN-*ia lu* DÙG
7 *in*[*a* UGU] A.ŠÀ.GA.MEŠ
8 *ša* ⸢É—AD⸣-*šú ša* $^{m}$*aš-šur—rém-a-ni*
9 ⸢*ša* LUGAL⸣ *be-lí iš-pur-an-ni*
10 LÚ*.*qur*-⸢*bu*⸣-*u-ti*
11 *up-ta-lìh-an-ni*
12 *ma-a* ⸢É?⸣ *gu-ub-bu*
13 ŠE.NU[MUN.MEŠ *r*]*a-am-me*
14 A.Š[À.MEŠ] LUGAL *be-lí*
15 ⸢*ú-da*⸣ [*x*] MU.AN.⸢NA⸣
16 ⸢URU⸣ [*ša*] *ina* A.Š[À 0]
e.17 ⸢LUGAL⸣ *á*[*r*!]-⸢*ṣip*!⸣-*u-ni* [0]
18 *ina* GIŠ.MI [LU]GAL ⸢EN⸣-[*ia*]
r.1 TA IGI [LÚ*.A]RAD.[MEŠ]
2 *ša* $^{m}$[*a*]-*ši-pa*-⸢*a*⸣
3 4-*me* A.[Š]À :. *a-si-qi*
4 *ina* UGU-*hi ur-ta-di*
5 URU.HAL.ṢU *ina* ŠÀ-*bi*
6 ⸢*ak*⸣-*ta-ra-ar*
7 [*x i*]*na* 1 KÙŠ : *kip-pu-tú*
8 ⸢*ša*⸣ URU :. É.GAL LUGAL
9 *ár-te-ṣip* ALAM LUGAL
10 *ina* ŠÀ-*bi e-te-ṣir*
11 2-*me* I.DIB LÚ*.ARAD LUGAL
12 *ina* ŠÀ-*bi ú*!!-*se-ši-ib*
13 ⸢*ú*⸣-[*ma*]-⸢*a*⸣ TA *ma-ṣi* LUGAL
14 [*be-lí* A.Š]À? *i-dan-u-ni*
15 [A.ŠÀ *š*]*a* É—AD-*šú*
16 [*x x x x x x*]*x*
last line broken away

CT 53 65

1 [To the king, my lord: your servant Liphu]r-Bel. [Go]od hea[lth] to the king, my lord!

4 The land of the king is well; the forts [are w]ell. The king, my lord, can be [gl]ad.

7 [As to] the fields of the patrimony of Aššur-remanni, about which the king, my lord, wrote me, the royal bodyguard shocked me when he said: "Give up the pro[perty], the well, and the arable land!"

14 (Regarding) the fields, the king, my lord, knows that [x] years ago I built a town in the king's field. Under the aegis of [the ki]ng, my lord, I have bought and added to it 400 (hectares of) field from [the sub]jects of [A]šipâ.

r.5 I have erected a fort there. The perimeter of the town is [...] cubits; I have built a royal palace and drawn the king's likeness inside it. I have placed 200 stone slabs there and settled the king's subjects there.

13 N[o]w, if the king, [my lord], really is giving (away) *the fi*[*eld*, the field o]f his patrimony [......].

## 16. Exempt Land Provides no Straw

K 690

1 *a-na* LUGAL [EN-*ia*]
2 ARAD-*ka* $^{m}$NIGIN—[EN]
3 *lu* DI-*mu ana* LUGAL EN-[*ia*]

ABL 201

1 To the king, [my lord]: your servant Liphur-[Bel]. Good health to the king, [my] lord!

**16** → TCAE p.263. 11 See coll. r.3 The last preserved sign looks like *ba*[*l*; see coll.
**17** Hand of Liphur-Bel II. 11 See coll.

FIG. 4. *Royal stela erected by an official (reign of Adad-nirari III).*
IRAQ MUSEUM, Baghdad.

4 LUGAL *be-li iq-ṭí-bi-*[*a*]
5 *ma-a* LÚ*.*i-tu-ʾa-a-a lu z*[*a*$^{!}$*-ku-u*]
6 A.ŠÀ GIŠ.BAN-*šu* ŠE.IN.N[U$^{!}$]
7 ŠE.PAD.MEŠ *za-ku-u* [0]
8 A.ŠÀ *ša aš-šur-a-a* [0]
9 *ša a-na a-ri-*⌈*šu*⌉*-*[*te* 0]
10 *nu-uk* [*x x x x*]
11 *la* ⌈*i*$^{!}$⌉*-*[*ma-gur x x x*]
rest broken away
Rev. beginning broken away
1′ ⌈*mi*⌉*-*[*x x x x x*]
2′ ŠE.IN.NU *la-bi-*[*ru* 0]
3′ *a-na* $dul_6$*-li a-ṣa-b*[*a-ta*]
4′ *ug-da-me-er ki-*⌈*i*⌉ [0]
5′ *ša* LUGAL *bé*$^{!}$*-li*$^{!}$ *i-la*$^{!}$*-*[*u-ni*]
6′ *le-pu-uš* [0]

4 The king, my lord, told [me] the Itu'ean (prefect) should be exempt, so his bow field is exempt from straw and barley (tax).

8 (As for) the field of the Assyrians, held in tenancy, I have told (them) [to ...], but they have not a[greed to ...]

(Break)

r.2 I have been using old straw for the work but have run out of it. May the king, my lord, do as he deems best.

## 17. Work on a Bull Colossus and Stone Thresholds

K 7509 + K 14673 (CT 53 579)

1 [*a-na* LUGAL EN-*ia*]
2 [ARAD-*ka* $^{m}$NIGIN—EN]
3 [*lu* DI-*mu a-na* LUGAL EN-*iá*]
4 [DI-*mu a-na* KUR *ša* LUGAL]
5 [DI-*mu a-na* URU.HAL.Ṣ]U.MEŠ
6 [ŠÀ *ša* LUGAL EN-*ia lu* DÙG]
7 [*x x x x x x*]*x*
8 [*x x* KUR.É]—*za-ma-na*
9 [*x x x a-n*]*a* EN.NUN
10 [*x x x x l*]*e-li-u*
11 [*x x x x l*]*u-ṣu-u-ni*
12 [*x x* NA$_4$.$^{d}$ALAD.$^{d}$]LAMA
e.13 [*x x x is-s*]*i-ia*
14 [*x x x liš*]*-du-du*
r.1 [*x x x x*]*x* UD.MEŠ *li-te-nu-ni*
2 [*x x x x*]*x* NA$_4$.$^{d}$ALAD.$^{d}$LAMA
3 [*x x x x* N]A$_4$.I.DIB.MEŠ
4 [*x x* $^{m}$*se-e*]—*gab-bar*
5 [*x x x* LUGAL] EN-*ia*
6 [*x x x x*] ⌈*ú*⌉*-qar-rab*
rest uninscribed

CT 53 386+

1 [To the king, my lord: your servant Liphur-Bel. Good health to the king, my lord]!

4 [The land of the king is well; the fo]rts [are well. The king, my lord, can be glad].

7 [......]
8 [... Bit]-Zamani.
9 [...] for the watch
10 [... should] come up
11 [... should] come out.
12 [... bull] colossus
13 [...] with me
14 [... they should] drag.
r.1 [... in x] days they should *alternate*.
2 [...] the bull colossus
3 [...] the stone thresholds
4 [... Se']-gabbar
5 [... the king], my lord
6 [...] I shall forward.

## 18. ———

K 7367

1 [*a-na* LUGAL EN-*iá*]
2 [ARAD-*ka* $^{m}$]⌈NIGIN⌉—E[N]
3 [*lu-u* DI-*mu*] *a-na* LUGAL EN-*iá*
4 [DI-*mu a-n*]*a* KUR *ša* LUGAL EN-*iá*
5 [DI-*mu a-na*] URU.HAL.ṢU.MEŠ
6 [ŠÀ-*bu ša*] LUGAL EN-*iá* [*lu* DÙG]

CT 53 335

1 [To the king, my lord: your servant] Liphur-B[el. Good health] to the king, my lord!

4 The land of the king, my lord, [is well]; the forts [are well]; the king, my lord, [can be glad].

**18** Hand of Liphur-Bel II.

7 [*x x x x*] ⸢*i*⸣-*ta-at-k*[*u x*]
8 [*x x x x* T]A KUR.[*x x*]
rest broken away
Rev. beginning broken away
1′ [*x x x x x*]*x* [*x x*]
2′ [*x x x ma*]-*a al-k*[*a*]
3′ [*x x a-na*] DI-*me*
4′ [*x x x x*]*x* LUGAL *be-lí*
5′ [*x x x x x*] TA* IGI-⸢*šú*⸣
6′ [*x x x x x-k*]*a*
rest (about 2 lines) broken away

7 [The ...] have left
8 [... fr]om the country [...]
(Break)
r.2 [......] "Come
3 [... *to*] *greet*
4 [...] the king, my lord,
5 [...] from his *presence*
(Rest destroyed)

## 19. Rendezvous

K 15154

1 *a-na* [LUGAL EN-*iá*]
2 ARAD-[*ka* $^{m}$NIGIN—EN]
3 *l*[*u* DI-*mu a-na* LUGAL EN-*iá*]
rest broken away
Rev. beginning broken away
1′ [*x x x x x*] ⸢*x*⸣ [*x x x*]
2′ [*x x x x x*] KASKAL [*x x x*]
3′ [*x x x x*] *ib x*[*x x x*]
4′ [*x x x x*] *ma-a* [*x x x*]
5′ [*x x x*] *ina* URU.*x*[*x x x*]
6′ [*ma-a a*]-*ni-nu ina x*[*x x*]
7′ *šu-nu it-ta-tak-k*[*u*]
8e *ma-a* 5 UD.MEŠ *ina* URU.[*x x*]
9e *ina pa-ni-ni rak-*[*x*]
s.1 [*x x x x x x x nu-uk mi-nu*] ⸢*ša*⸣ *ši-ti-ni am-ra*
2 [*qi-bi-a an-nu-rig ina pa-ni-šú*]-*nu a-da-gal*
3 [*ki-ma is-suh-ru-ni a-na* LUGAL EN-*i*]*a a-š*[*ap*]-*pa-ra*

CT 53 625

1 To [the king, my lord]: your [servant Liphur-Bel]. Go[od health to the king, my lord]!
(Break)

r.4 "We [shall be] in the city [... *by the ...th of* ...];
7 They left *on the f*[*irst*], saying: "[......] for 5 days in the city [...] before us."

s.1 [*I said*]: "Find out [what]ever it is [*and report it to me*]."
2 I am [now] waiting [for th]em, and sh[all] write [to the king, m]y [lord, as soon as they have returned].

## 20. ———

K 5507

1 [*a-na* LUGAL EN-*ia*]
2 [ARAD-*ka* $^{m}$NIGIN—EN]
3 [*lu* D]I-*mu a-n*[*a* LUGAL EN-*ia*]
4 [*dul-l*]*u ša* LUGAL [EN-*ia x x*]
5 ⸢*ina* U⸣GU GUD.M[EŠ *ša* $^{m}$*x x x*]
6 ⸢*a*⸣-[*n*]*a* LUGAL EN-[*ia iš-pur-an-ni*]
7 ⸢*ma-a*⸣ $^{m}$NIGIN—EN [*x x x x*]
8 [*x x x*] IGI LU[GAL *x x x*]
9 [*x*]*x hi* ⸢*x x*⸣ [*x x x x*]
10 [*x*] ⸢LUGAL⸣ *i*[*š*?-*x x x x*]
11 [*x x*] ⸢*a-na*⸣ [*x x x x*]
rest broken away
Rev. destroyed

CT 53 264

1 [To the king, my lord: your servant Liphur-Bel. Good he]alth t[o the king, my lord]!
3 [*We are doing*] the king's [wor]k.
4 As to the oxe[n concerning which NN wrote] to the king, my lord, saying: "Liphur-Bel [......]" —
8 [...] before the king [...]
(Rest too broken for translation)

# 2. Letters from Tušhan



FIG. 5. *Prisoners leaving a fort in mountain country (reign of Sennacherib).*
ORIGINAL DRAWING I, 70.

# 21. Tension on the Urarṭian Border

K 678

1 [*a-na* LUGAL] EN-*ia*
2 [ARAD-*ka* $^{m}$]*a-ši-pa-a*
3 [*l*]*u* DI-*mu a-na* LUGAL
4 EN-*ia a—dan-niš*
5 DI-*mu a-na* URU.*bi-rat*
6 *a-na* KUR *ša* LUGAL EN-*iá*
7 LÚ.3.$U_5$ *ša* LUGAL EN-*iá*
8 *ša il-li-kan-ni*
9 *ma-a* EN.NUN-*ka lu dan-na-at*
10 EN.NUN *dan-na-at a—dan-niš*
11 3 LÚ*.EN.NAM.MEŠ *ina* URU.*pu-lu-a*
12 ⸢3⸣ LÚ*.NAM.MEŠ *ina* URU.*da-ni-ba-ni*
13 *ina pu-tu-ni* TA ANŠE.*a-ṣap-pi*
14 *pu-uh-ru* : *a-ni-nu*
15 EN.NUN *ina pu-tu-šu-nu*
16 *ni-na-ṣar* : UN.MEŠ *gab!-bu*
17 *ina* É—BÀD.MEŠ-*ni* : *šu-nu*
18 GUD.MEŠ UDU.MEŠ *ina ba!-te*
19 *an-ni-te* [*š*]*a!* ÍD! *šu-*⸢*nu!*⸣
20 *a-ni-*[*nu ni*]*-za-*⸢*az*⸣
e.21 *ina* ⸢*x*⸣ *x*[*x x*]*x*
22 *ni-na-ṣar* [0]
r.1 *šu-uh* ŠE.IN.[NU]
2 *ša* LUGAL *be-lí* [*iš-pur-an-ni*]
3 *ina* ŠÀ ITI.ŠU A.[AN *la-a-šú*]
4 A.MEŠ *i-si-ṣu* LÚ*.2-*u*
5 LÚ*.GAL—URU.MEŠ *gab!-bu*
6 *i-tu-ur-du* : ŠE.IN.NU
7 *i-si-qi-u ša har-bi*
8 *am—mar i-ba-šu-u-ni*
9 *i-ta-an-nu* : *šu-uh*
10 LÚ*.*i-tu-ʾe-e ša* LUGAL
11 *be-lí iš-p*[*ur*]*-an-ni*
12 *a-na-ku* LÚ*.ERIM.MEŠ-*e*
13 *e-te-ri-iš ki-i*
14 *an-ni-e a-na* LUGAL EN-*iá*
15 *a-sa-bar* : *nu-ku* LÚ*.*i-tú-u*
16 *ša ina* KUR-*ia!* 5-*me* LÚ*.[ERIM].MEŠ
17 *ut-ru-te i-ba-ši*
18 *šu-nu i-si-ia*
19 [*l*]*u-u i-ṣu-ru* : *a-ta-a*
20 [*ina* U]RU.*gu-za-a-ni*

ABL 506

1 [To the king], my lord: [your servant] Ašipâ. The best of health to the king, my lord!

5 The forts and the land of the king, my lord, are well.

7 The 'third man' of the king, my lord, who came, told me: "Your guard should be strong!" The guard is very strong.

11 Three governors in Pulua and another three in Danibani are gathered with pack animals opposite us. We are keeping watch opposite them. All the people are inside fortified places; the oxen and sheep are on this side [o]f the river. We are standing by and keeping wa[tch] in [...].

r.1 As to the stra[w] concerning which the king, my lord, [wrote me, *there has been no*] *ra*[*in*] in Tammuz (IV) and water has become scarce, so the deputy and all the village managers have come down (from the mountains) to purchase straw. They have sold (them) whatever *harbu* (straw) there was.

9 As to the Itu'eans concerning whom the king, my lord, wr[ot]e me, did I ask for troops? I wrote to the king, my lord, as follows:

15 "Of the Itu'eans in my country, there is a surplus of 500 men who should have kept watch with me. Why [did they g]o [to] Guzana? Let them release the men to me."

**21** → 5 R 54,3. 16 Y 81, W 180. 19 See coll. 21 See coll.; line almost totally obliterated, no evidence of É—BÀD.MEŠ-*ni* shown in Harper's copy (ABL); cf. also 5 R 54,3. r.4 Copy 5 R 54,3 shows traces of A.⸢AN?⸣ [*la-a*]-⸢*šú*?⸣ at the end of the line; the signs in half brackets are no longer visible. r.5 Y 81, W 180. r.16 KUR-*ia* sic, not -*iá*; see coll.

FIG. 6. *Assyrian army archers, possibly Itu'eans (reign of Sennacherib).* BM 135198.

21 [*il-l*]*i-ku-u-ni*
22e [*nu-ku*] LÚ*.ERIM.MEŠ
23e [*lu-ra*]*-mu-u-ni*

## 22. News from the Urarṭian Border

K 14684

1 [*a-na* LUGAL EN-*ia*]
2 [ARAD-*ka* $^{m}$*a-ši-pa-a*]
3 [*lu* DI-*mu a-n*]*a* ⸢LUGAL⸣
4 [EN-*ia*] ⸢*a*⸣*—dan-niš*
5 [DI-*mu a-na* U]RU.*bi-rat*
6 [*a-na* KUR *ša*] LUGAL EN-*iá*
7 [*ina* UGU *ṭè-me*] *ša* KUR.URI-*a*-[*a*]
8 [*x x x x x*]*x* ⸢*ša*⸣ *pu-tú-u-*[*a*]
9 [*x x x x x x x*] ⸢*x*⸣ [*x*]
rest broken away
Rev. destroyed

CT 53 584

1 [To the king, my lord: your servant Ašipâ]. The bes[t of health t]o the king, [my lord]!

5 [The f]orts [and the land of] the king, my lord, [are well].

7 [*As to the news*] of the Urarṭians,

8 [......] opposite [me]

(Rest destroyed)

## 23. ———

DT 264

1 *a-na* LUGAL EN-[*ia*]
2 ARAD-*ka* $^{m}$*a-ši-pa-*[*a*]
3 [*l*]*u* DI-*mu a-na* LUG[AL]
4 [E]N-*ia a—dan-*⸢*niš*⸣
5 [DI]-⸢*mu*⸣ *a-na* URU.[*bi-rat*]
6 [*a-na*] KUR *ša* LUGAL [EN]-*ia*
7 [*x* L]Ú.NAM.M[EŠ *x x x*]
Rev. destroyed; last 3 lines uninscribed

ABL 508

1 To the king, [my] lord: your servant Ašipâ. The bes[t] of health to the ki[ng], my [lo]rd!

5 The [forts] and the land of the king, my [lord], are [we]ll.

7 [x] governors [......]

(Rest destroyed)

## 24. People from a Mountain Town

81-2-4,123

1 [*a-na*] LUGAL EN-*ia*
2 [AR]AD-*ka* $^{m}$*a-ši-pa-a*
3 [*l*]*u* DI-*mu a-na* LUGAL
4 [E]N-*ia a—dan-niš*
5 [D]I-*mu a-na* URU.*bi-rat*
6 ⸢*a*⸣*-na* KUR *ša* LUGAL [E]N-*ia*
7 UN.MEŠ *an-nu-te* ⸢URU⸣.*a-ba-a-a*
8 *ur-ki-ú-te* : *ša ú-ma-*⸢*a*⸣
9 *ú-še-ṣu-u-ni* : *a-na-ku* [0]
10 [*x* L]Ú.ERIM.MEŠ : *na-ši e*$^{!}$-[*x x*]
11 [*pa-a*]*n*$^{?}$ : MÍ.*ha-ri-ma-te* [0]
12 [*is-s*]*e-niš ur-ta-me* [0]

ABL 509

1 [To] the king, my lord: your ser[vant] Ašipâ. The bes[t] of health to the king, my lo[rd]!

5 The forts and the land of the king, my [lo]rd, are well.

7 (Regarding) these later people from Abâ whom *they are* now bringing out, I have, [*firs*]*tly*, left [x] men *carrying* ... [wi]th the prostitutes.

**22** Hand of Ašipâ.
**24** 9 Or: "*I am* bringing." 10 See coll.; possibly *na-ši e-*[*ni*] "with good looks" or *na-ši e-*[*qi*] "carrying the *ē*[*qu*] (symbol)." 15f See coll.

13 [*x* L]Ú.ERIM.MEŠ LÚ.*da-a-a-li* [0]
14 [*a-na*] *ma-ṣar-te ša né-ri-b*[*i*]
15 [URU.*a-ba*]*-a ša ina re-šu-šu-n*[*u*$^{!}$]
16 [*x x x x*] URU :$^{!}$ *ina* ⸢GÌR.2⸣ [*x x*]
17 [*x x x x*]*x*[*x x x x x*]
rest (2-3 lines and edge) broken away
Rev. beginning broken away; rest uninscribed

13 [I have assigned x] men as scouts to guard the pass of [*Ab*]*â above* them.

16 [...] the town at the foot [......]
(Rest destroyed)

## 25. Felling Trees in Šubria

K 1077

1 *a-na* ⸢LUGAL EN⸣*-ia*
2 ARAD*-ka* $^{m}$*a-*⸢*ši*⸣*-pa-*⸢*a*⸣
3 *lu* DI*-mu* ⸢*a-na*⸣ [LUGAL]
4 EN*-ia a—*⸢*dan-niš*⸣
5 DI*-mu a-na* URU.*bi-*⸢*rat*⸣
6 *a-na* KUR ⸢*ša*⸣ LUGAL E[N$^{!}$*-ia*]
7 KUR.*šu-ub-ri-a-a* [*ṭè-e-mu*]
8 *ina* URU.*ku-li-im-*⸢*me*$^{!}$⸣*-*[*ri*]
9 *i-ha-ra-aṣ* : *ina* [É.G]AL
10 *ki-i* ⸢*ha*⸣*-*[*an*]*-ni-ma* [*e-pu-šú*]
11 [*x x x ú-ṣ*]*a-bi-tú* [*x x x*]*x-ni*
12 [*x x x x*] *šu-u-tú* [*x x x*]
13 [*x x x x*] *i-sa-*[*x x*]
14 [*x x* GIŠ.ÙR].MEŠ GIŠ.ŠÚ.A.MEŠ
15 [*x x x x x x x*]*x*
rest broken away
Rev. beginning broken away
1′ [*x x x x x x*] ⸢*ka*$^{!}$⸣ [*x x x*]
2′ [GIŠ.ŠÚ.A.MEŠ$^{?}$ *ut*$^{?}$]*-ru-te* [*ina* Í]D$^{!}$
3′ [*a-kar-ra-ár a-z*]*a*$^{!}$*-bíl* : *a-*⸢*da*⸣*-an*
4′ ⸢LÚ*.ERIM$^{!}$⸣.[MEŠ] *gab-bu ina* KUR*-e*
5′ *ina* GIŠ.MURUB$_{4}$.MEŠ *bé-te* GIŠ.ŠÚ.A.MEŠ
6′ *bé-te* GIŠ.ÙR.MEŠ *i-ba-šú-ni*
7′ *i-na-ki-su*

ABL 507

1 To the king, my lord: your servant Ašipâ. The best of health to [the king], my lord!

5 The forts and the land of the king, [my] lo[rd], are well.

7 The Šubrian (king) makes a detailed [report] in Kulimme[ri], and [they *act*] *in* [*th*]*is way* in the Palace! They [have *s*]*eized* [......] and [...]

12 [...] he [...]

13 [...] ...

14 [... roof-be]ams and door-beams [...]
(Break)

r.2 [I shall th]row the [*rem*]*aining* [*door*-beams in the ri]ver, and transport and deliver them.

4 All (my) men are in the mountains, felling trees in groves where there are (trunks suitable for) door-beams and roof-beams.

## 26. No Water in the River

K 1931

beginning broken away
1′ [*x x*] ⸢*aš a*⸣ [*x x x*]
2′ ⸢*i-sa-ta*⸣*-pa*[*r x x x*]
3′ *t*[*a*]*-ta-al-*[*ka x x*]
4′ *a*[*m*] ⸢*x*⸣ *ra* [*x x x*]
5′ *x*[*x*].MEŠ [*x x x x*]
6′ *m*[*u x x x x x x*]
7′ *ud* [*x x x x x x*]
8′ *a* [*x x x x x x*]
e.9′ *la-a zi-*⸢*i*⸣*-*[*nu*]
10′ *la-a ku-up-p*[*u*]

CT 53 213

(Beginning destroyed)

2 has been sending [...]

3 *you* cam[e ...]
(Break)

9 [Because] it has neither rained nor snowed [...], the[re is] no water in the river.

**25** 11 See coll. r.2ff See coll.

11′ *i-zi-nu-nu-[ni]*
r.1 A.MEŠ *ina* ÍD *la-[áš-šú]*
2 TA É : TA [IGI LUGAL]
3 EN-*ia al-[lik-u-ni]*
4 *e-bi-ru-[u-ni* 0]
5 *né-ha-ku* ⸢*x*⸣ [*x x x*]
6 3-*lim* GIŠ.Š[Ú.A.MEŠ *x x*]
rest broken away

r.2 Ever since I ca[me] (back) from the [king], my lord, and cros[sed] (the river), I have been at ease [...].

6 3,000 door-bea[ms ......]

(Rest destroyed)

## 27. Pulling up Fruit Tree Saplings

81-7-27,35

1 [*a-na*] ⸢LUGAL⸣ [EN-*ia*]
2 [A]RAD-*ka* $^{m}$*a-ši-pa-[a]*
3 [*l*]*u* DI-*mu a-na* LU[GAL]
4 EN-*ia a—dan-[niš]*
5 DI-*mu a-na* URU.*bi-[rat]*
6 *a-na* KUR *ša* LUGAL E[N-*ia*]
7 *ina* UGU *zi-iq-p[i]*
8 *ša* LUGAL *be-lí* ⸢*iš*⸣-[*pur-an-ni*]
9 ⸢*ki*⸣-*i ṭè-e-m[u]*
10 *šá-ak-na-ku-u-ni* [0]
11 *qar-ba-te-šú šá-su-ma-[te*?]
12 *ša* GIŠ!.⸢*ha*!⸣-*ah-hi*
13 [GI]Š.*šá-*⸢*ah-šu*!-*ru*!⸣
14 ⸢*a*⸣-*ta-s[a]h*! *ú-[x x]*
15 [*x*]*x*[*x*] ⸢*x x*⸣ [*x x x*]
Edge destroyed
Rev. destroyed

ABL 510

1 [To] the king, [my lord]: your [se]rvant Ašipâ. [T]he [be]st of health to the ki[ng], my lord!

5 The fo[rts] and the land of the king, [my] lo[rd], are well.

7 As to the saplin[gs] concerning which the king, my lord, wr[ote me],

9 since the orde[r] was given to me, I have pulled up ...... of *plum* and *apple* trees [......]

(Rest destroyed)

## 28. Red Wool for the King

Sm 984

1 *a-na* LUGAL EN-*iá*
2 ARAD-*ka* $^{m}$*a-ši-pa-a*
3 *lu* DI-*mu a-na* LUGAL
4 EN-*ia a—dan-niš*
5 DI-*mu a-na* URU.*bi-rat*
6 *a-na* KUR *ša* LUGAL EN-*ia*
7 *ina šá-dàq-di-iš*
8 LUGAL *be-lí iq-ṭi-bi-a*
9 *ma-a* SÍG.*tab-ri-bu*
10 [*še*]*-bi-la an-nu-r[ig]*
11 [$^{m}$]*me-tu-[nu x x x]x*
12 [*x x x x x x*]
Edge broken away
r.1 [*x x x x x x*]
2 [*x x*]*x*[*x x*]*x*[*x x x*]
3 [0] *na-ṣu-[u-ni]*
rest (space of 10 lines) uninscribed

ABL 431

1 To the king, my lord: your servant Ašipâ. The best of health to the king, my lord!

5 The forts and the land of the king, my lord, are well.

7 Last year, the king, my lord, told me: "[S]end me red wool!"

10 Now then Metu[nu ......]

(Break)

r.3 have been brought [to me].

**27** 11 Obscure; see coll. Readings 4 KUŠ.*ma-[qar-rat]* or *šá su-pu[r*!*-gíl]* (suggestion J. N. Postgate) excluded.
12f See coll.
**28** 11 See coll.

## 29. Forwarding Hewn Stone Objects

K 847

1 *a-na* LUGAL [EN-*ia*]
2 ARAD-*ka* [ᵐ*a-ši-pa-a*]
3 *lu-u šu*[*l-mu*]
4 *a-na* LUGAL [EN-*iá a—dan-niš*]
5 DI-*mu a-na* [0]
6 URU.*bi-rat* [*a-na* KUR]
7 *ša* LUGAL EN-[*ia*]
8 *ina* UGU $NA_4$.[*x x*]
9 *ba-ti-iq-*[*ti*]
10 *ša* LUGAL *b*[*e*!-*lí*]
r.1 *ṭè-me* [0]
2 *iš-kun-a*!-*ni-*[*ni*!]
3 *an-nu-r*[*ig*]
4 4 *bi-*[*lat*]
5 $NA_4$.*ú-*[*x x*]
6 *ba-te-*[*iq-tú*]
7 *a-na* LU[GAL EN-*ia*]
8 *ú-se*!-[*bi-la*]

ABL 952

[1] To the king, [my lord]: your servant [Ašipâ]. The [best] of he[alth] to the king, [my lord]!

[5] The forts and the land of the king, my lord, are well.

[8] As to the hewn [...] stone about which the king, [my] lo[rd], gave [me] orders,

[r.3] I am no[w] se[nding] to the ki[ng, my lord], four tal[ents] of he[wn ...] stone.

## 30. ———

K 7352

1 [*a-na* LUGAL EN-*ia*]
2 [ARAD-*ka* ᵐ*a-ši-pa-a*?]
3 *lu* DI-*m*[*u a-na* LUGAL]
4 EN-*ia a—da*[*n-niš*]
5 DI-*mu* (*a-na*) URU.*bi-*[*rat a-na* KUR]
6 *ša* LUGAL E[N-*ia*]
7 *ta-hu-ma-t*[*e ša* KUR]
8 *gab-b*[*u x x x x*]
rest broken away
Rev. uninscribed

CT 53 328

[1] [To the king, my lord: your servant *Ašipâ*]. The be[st] of hea[lth to the king], my lord!

[5] The fo[rts and the land] of the king, [my] lo[rd], are well. Al[l] the borde[rs of the country ......]

(Rest destroyed)

## 31. Argisti Puts Pressure on Hu-Tešub of Šubria

K 1067 + K 1886 (CT 53 57)

1 *a-na* LUGAL ⸢EN⸣-*ia*
2 ARAD-*ka* ᵐ*ša—aš-šur—du-ub-bu*
3 *lu* DI-*mu a-na* LUGAL EN-*ia a—dan-niš*
4 DI-*mu a-na* URU.*bi-ra-a-ti*
5 *a-na* KUR *ša* LUGAL EN-*ia*
6 *ina* UGU *ṭè-e-me ša* LÚ.SANGA
7 *ša* URU.⸢*pe*⸣-*en-za-a ša* LUGAL *be-lí*
8 *iš-pur-an-ni ma-a mi-i-nu*
9 *ša* LUGAL KUR.URI-*a-a ina* UGU-*hi-šu*

ABL 139+

[1] To the king, my lord: your servant Ša-Aššur-dubbu. The best of health to the king, my lord!

[4] The forts and the land of the king, my lord, are well.

[6] As to the news of the priest of Penzâ about whom the king, my lord, wrote me: "What did the king of Urarṭu send and decree

**29** [9] Or "cheap, cut" (ore). "I cannot believe they weighed pieces of masonry, so you need a substance like alum which can be measured out into different weights" (J. N. Postgate). [10] Y 83. [r.2] See coll. [r.8] Y 83, W 267.

**31** → Deller Zagros p.112. [7] Y 76. [11f] See coll.; *pi-*⸢*qí*!⸣*-ti* certain, ⸢*ši-bu*⸣*-ti* (Deller, loc. cit.) excluded. It is uncertain whether the phrase in line 11 beginning with *ina* UGU belongs to the preceding or the following sentence. [r.3f] See coll.; *-ma*!*-nu* is certain, *-šu-nu* (Deller, loc.cit.) excluded. [r.8, 12] See coll. [r.17] *a-di-a-kan-ni* sic (for /addinakkanni/); cf. *adi akanni* ~ *adinakanni* "until now." [r.21] See coll.; on the basis of the context, *a-su-na-ka*

10 *iš-pur-an-ni ú-ki-nu-⸢šu!-u⸣-[ni]*
11 *ma-a ina* UGU LÚ.*pi!-[qí?]-ti ša* URU!.*[ta-s]i!*
12 *[x x x x x]x liš-ul x[x]-⸢si!⸣*
13 *[x x x x x x]* LUGAL EN-*ia*
14 *[x x x x x x* L]Ú.*qur-bu-ti*
15 *[x x x x* LÚ*].DUMU—*šip-ra-a-ni*
16 *[x x x x x] ša* URU.*pu-lu-u-a*
17 *[x x x x x]-u-ni ša* KUR.*al-zu-nu*
18 *[x x x x it-t]al-ku-u-ni [ina] bir-ti*
19 *[x x x ina bir]-ti* ŠEŠ.MEŠ-*šú*
20 *[uk-tin-nu? x x] za-ki-ti* LÚ*.SANGA *ina* UGU
21 *[x x x x x x x]* LÚ*.*qur-bu-ti*
22 *[x x x x x x] ⸢e!⸣-ta-rab!*
23 *[x x x x x x x x]-tú*
rest (3-4 lines) broken away
Rev. beginning (1-2 lines) broken away
1′ *[x x x x x] ⸢x x⸣ [x x x x x]*
2′ *[x x x x* URU].*ti!-di! [x x x x x]*
3′ *[ina ta-hu]-ú!-me! ša!* KUR!.*⸢šu!⸣-u[b!-ri-a]*
4′ *[x x]x-ma!-nu! :! ul-lu!-tú! : g[i-x x]*
5′ *[ša? na-g]i-e : ⸢a⸣-[nu]-su-nu [x x]*
6′ *[x x-r]u?-tu ina* URU.*pu-u-me i-za-⸢zu⸣*
7′ *[mx-x]-ra-a* LÚ.GAL—*da-a-⸢a-li!⸣*
8′ *[ša mhu—t]e!-šu-ub! :* LUGAL *be-lí ú-da*
9′ *[x x x š]a! mru-sa-a ú-sa-hi-ir*
10′ *[x x x x i]p-ti-qi-su ú-ma-a*
11′ *[x x x x] ina!* IGI! *⸢mhu⸣—te-šu-bu*
12′ *[x x x x x]-da! ⸢la!⸣ : me-me-ni*
13′ [LÚ*.DUMU—*šip-ri ina*] UGU!-*hi!-šú ina* URU.*pu-u-me*
14′ *[i-sa-bar ma]-a! šúm!-mu at-ta*
15′ *[x x x] kam-mu-sa-ka ma-a*
16′ *[x x x] :! du-ma-qi ša* AD-*u-a*
17′ *[š]a a-na-ku : a-di-a-kan-ni sa-[hi]-ra*
18′ [LÚ*].DUMU—*šip-ri ša il-li-kan-ni*
19′ *[ma]-a šul-mu a-na mhu—te-šub*
20′ *la-a ta-qa-bi ri-ik-su*
21′ *la ta-ma-har : a-su-na!-ka*
22′ ⸢LÚ*⸣.DUMU—*šip-ri mhu—te-šu-bu*
23′ *ina* UGU KUR.URI-*a-a* TA LÚ*.DUMU—*šip-ri-šú*
24′ *i-sa-bar : it-ta-lak ina meš!-⸢li!⸣*
25′ KASKAL : *ik-ta-la-šú : ma-a a-[di]*
26′ *al-la-ku-u-ni :* É—EN.MEŠ-*[ka?]*
27e *a-⸢qa!⸣-bu-u-ni : ma-a šú[m!-mu]*
28e *ú-[r]a-mu-ka tal-l[a!-ka]*
29e *la-šu ma [la?] ta-sa-hur*
s.1 *[x x x x x x x x]a x[x x x] ši an*
2 *[x x x x x x x] áš u [x x x]*.MEŠ ÚŠ!.MEŠ
3 *[x x x x x x a]k!-ṣur! [x x x m]a?-a*
4 *[x x x x x x]-ni li-din!*

for him *about* the official of [Ta]si? They should ask [...]" –

13 [......] the king, my lord,
14 [......] the royal bodyguard
15 [......] the messengers
16 [*of the governor*] of Pulua
17 [......] of Alzunu
18 [have co]me [... *and arbitrated* be]tween [... and] his brothers.
20 [*With*] clean [*hands*], the priest [...] to
21 [......] the royal bodyguard
22 [......] entered
(Break)

r.2 [...] Tidu [...]
3 [on the bor]der of Šub[ria]
4 [...] ... *levied* [...]
5 [*The ... of the dist*]*rict* [have ...ed] their equ[ip]ment
6 [...] are staying in Pumu.

7 The king, my lord, knows that [...]râ, the chief scout [of Hu-T]ešub, gave back [the ... o]f Rusa, and he [ap]pointed him [...]; now, there is no [......] in the presence of Hu-Tešub.

13 [The Urarṭian has sent] him [*a messenger*] to Pumu, saying: "If you stay [*in* ...], g[iv]e back the [... and] the jewelry [th]at my father and I gave you."

18 The messenger who came said: "Do not greet Hu-Tešub, and do not accept an agreement (*from him*), (*or*) *I shall punish* you!"

22 Hu-Tešub sent a messenger to the Urarṭian together with his messenger; he went, (but) in the middle of the journey he arrested him, saying:

26 "(You will be held) until I go and speak to [*your*] government; should they release you, you will g[o] and never return."
(Break)

s.2 [......] dead [...]s
(Rest too broken for translation)

(hapax legomenon) is tentatively taken as a present tense form of an otherwise unknown verb *swn* "to punish," cf. Syr. *šnw* "to punish, abuse, to inflict severe pain, punishment, torture" (Payne Smith, p. 587b). r.24, 27 See coll. *šú[m!-mu]* W 62. r.25f The laconic phrasing of the sentence makes it uncertain who the subject of *iktalašu* is. The sentence beginning with *adi* is logically connected with the preceding one, cf. NL 26 r.4ff: "They refuse to give their daughters (in marriage), saying: '(We won't give them) until they give us money.' Let them give them the money..." For other temporal *adi* clauses with a predicate in the present following the main clause, see nos. 4 r.19 and 32 r.17, ABL 306+ r.13, 433 r.15, 867:11, 1199 r.3, etc. r.29 Sic, see coll.; not *la-šu la* (Deller, loc.cit.). It is doubtful whether there is enough room for *[la]* in the break. s.1 Sic; probably a name.

# 32. Soldiers Captured by the Šubrians

K 469

1 *a-na* LUGAL EN-*ia*
2 ARAD-*ka* $^{m}$*šá—aš-šur—du-bu*
3 *lu* DI-*mu a-na* LUGAL
4 EN-*ia a—dan-niš*
5 DI-*mu a-na* URU.*bi-rat*
6 *a-na* KUR *ša* LUGAL EN-*ia*
7 2 LÚ*.SAG.MEŠ-*ia* 6 LÚ*.ERIM.MEŠ
8 *i-si-šú-nu* NA$_4$.KIŠIB *ina* ŠU.2-*šú-nu*
9 *ina* UGU ZÁH.MEŠ *ša ina* URU.*pe-en-za-a*
10 *a-sa-bar-šú-nu* 2 LÚ*.GAL—*ki-ṣir*.MEŠ
11 *i-si-šú-nu i-ta-at-ku*
12 LÚ*.ERIM.MEŠ *ú-se-ri-du-ni*

ABL 138

1 To the king, my lord: your servant Ša-Aššur-dubbu. The best of health to the king, my lord!

5 The forts and the land of the king, my lord, are well.

7 I sent two eunuchs of mine with six soldiers and a seal(ed order) for the deserters in Penzâ; they went off with two cohort commanders and had the men brought down.

**32** 11 Cf. W 62 correcting Y 76. 16 W 62. 20 See coll. r.13 W 62. r.16 See coll. r.20f W 62.

FIG. 7. *Eunuch officer with soldiers (reign of Sennacherib).*
BM 124789.

13 NINDA.MEŠ *ina* ŠÀ-*bi e-tak-lu*
14 ŠEŠ-*šú ša* KUR.*šub-ri-a-a*
15 *i-si-šú-nu-ma* [NINDA.ME]Š! ⸢*ina*⸣ ŠÀ-*bi*
16 *e-tak-la qa-*⸢*an*!⸣*-ni a-ha-iš*
17 *it-tu-ṣu-ú-ni*
18 *it-tal-ku-ú-ni*
e.19 KUR.*šub-ri-a-a*
20 *šu-ub-tú ina pa-na-*⸢*tú*⸣*-š*[*ú-nu*]
21 *ú-se-ši-bu*
r.1 2 LÚ*.SAG.MEŠ-*ia*
2 TA 6 LÚ*.ERIM.MEŠ *i-ta-ṣu*
3 LÚ*.GAL—*ki-ṣir*.MEŠ-*ia*
4 *ki-la-li ú-se-zi-bu*
5 *a-sa-bar-áš-šú nu-ku* LÚ*.ERIM.MEŠ
6 *ra-am-me ma-a a-šá-ʾa-al*
7 [*šú*]*m-mu ina* KUR-*ia* : *šu-nu a-da-an*
8 ⸢*a*⸣*-na-ku qa-ta-a-a ina kib-sa-ti*
9 [*a*]*t-ta-lak* : LÚ*.ERIM.MEŠ
10 *ina* URU.*bir-ti-šú ú-se-li-u*
11 LÚ*.*ta-zi-ru* LÚ*.*i-tú-ʾu-u*
12 *ša* LUGAL EN-*iá ša a-na-ka*
13 *ú-ka-lu*!*-ni* LÚ*.GAR-*nu*.MEŠ-*šú-nu*
14 LUGAL *be-lí liš-pu-ra*
15 *lil-*(*li*)*-ku-ni i-si-ia a-na*
16 *ma-ṣar-ti li-zi-zu*!
17 *a-di* GIŠ.ÙR.MEŠ *an-nu-te*
18 *ú-še-ṣu-u-ni* LUGAL *be-lí*
19e *ú-da* LÚ*.ERIM.MEŠ-*ia*
20e *in*[*a*!] URU.BÀD—$^{m}$MAN—GIN
21e ⸢*dul*!⸣*-lu e-pu-šú*
s.1 LÚ*.*šá—pet-hal-la-ti šu-nu ina* IGI-*ia*
2 *i-za-zu*

13 They had dinner there; the brother of the Šubrian (king) too dined with them there.

16 They set out together and were on their way home, when the Šubrians attacked them from an ambush and captured my two eunuchs and the six soldiers. Both of my cohort commanders escaped.

r.5 I wrote him: "Release the soldiers!" but he said: "I will inquire (into the matter); [i]f they are in my country, I shall give them back."

8 I [se]t out on their trail personally, but they had (already) taken the soldiers up to his fort.

11 The king, my lord, should send word that the prefects of the royal Taziru and Itu'u (troops) holding (fields) here should come and stand guard with me, until those beams are brought out.

18 The king, my lord, knows that my men are [wo]rking [in] Dur-Šarruken and I have only cavalrymen at my disposal.

## 33. Cutting Timber in Urarṭian Territory

82-5-22,109

1 *a-na* LUGAL EN-*ia*
2 ARAD-*ka* $^{m}$*ša—aš-šur—du-bu*
3 *lu* DI-*mu a-na* LUGAL [EN-*ia a—dan-niš*]
4 DI-*mu a-na* URU.*bi-ra-*[*a-ti*]
5 *a-na* KUR *ša* LUGAL E[N-*ia*]
6 *ša a-na* LUGAL EN-*iá áš-pu*[*r-an-ni*]
7 *nu-ku* KUR.*šu-u*[*b*]*-ri-a-a* [LÚ*.ERIM.MEŠ-*ia*]
8 *ú-ṣa-bit* ⸢LUGAL⸣ *be-lí* [*i-sap-ra*]
9 *ma-a* LÚ*.ERIM.MEŠ-*šú* : *pi-*[*it-ti*]
10 LÚ*.ERIM.MEŠ-*ka* : *ṣa-*[*bit a-di*]
11 ⸢*ú*⸣*-ra-mu-u-ni* : *x*[*x x x*]
12 [*x x*]*x* ⸢*a*!⸣*-ṣa*!*-bat* ⸢*a*!⸣*-*[*x x x*]
rest (about 10 lines)broken away
Rev. beginning (about 8 lines) broken away

ABL 705

1 To the king, my lord: your servant Ša-Aššur-dubbu. [The best] of health to the king, [my lord]!

4 The for[ts] and the land of the king, [my] lo[rd], are well.

6 When I wr[ote] to the king, my lord, that the king of Šu[b]ria had captured [my men], the king, my lord, [wrote me back]:

9 "Capt[ure] his men in eq[ual number] to your men, [until] he releases [them]."

12 [...] I took [......]

(Break)

**33** → ABL 138. 11f See coll. r.2 For restoration cf. no. 52:8, 84 r.1, 129:5. r.4 See coll. r.8 See coll.; cf. *am-mar* 5 *ú-*[*ba-ni*] LAS 54 r.1 and *am-mar* 2 *ú-ma-a-me* ABL 1285 r.27. r.9 See coll. r.19 See coll. s.1 Irony.

1′ ⌈*ša*!⌉ *a-na* LUGAL EN!-*iá*⌉ [*áš-pur-an-ni*]
2′ *nu-ku* 5-*me* GIŠ.ÙR.ME[Š *ina ta-hu-me*]
3′ *ša* KUR.URI-*a-a i-ta-*[*as-qu ú-ma-a*]
4′ LÚ*.3.$U_5$-*ia ša i*[*s-si-qu-u-ni*]
5′ *i-ti-ki-si* : *ina ši*[*d-di* ÍD]
6′ *ik-ta-ra-ra ki-*[*ma dul-lu*]
7′ *ug-da-mir* : *ú-n*[*am-ma-šá*]
8′ LÚ*.ERIM.MEŠ *ú-pa-har* ⌈*am*?⌉—*m*[*ar*?]
9′ 1-*me* LÚ*.ERIM.MEŠ *ú-za-ka* : *e-r*[*u*!-*bu*]
10′ GIŠ.ÙR.MEŠ *ina* ÍD *i-ka-ru-*[*ru*]
11′ *re-hu-ti* : *a-na* EN.NUN-*šú-n*[*u*]
12′ *ina* É *šu-ub-te-šú-nu ú-še-šá-*[*ab*]
13′ *i—su-ri* : *bar-tu* : *me-me-n*[*i*]
14′ EN.NUN *ú-da-ʾa-na*!
15′ ⌈TA⌉ IGI : *bar-ti* : *pal-ha-ku*
16e [LÚ*.E]N.NAM *ša* URU.*pu-lu-u-a*!
17e [*ša p*]*u*!-⌈*tú*!⌉-*u-a i-sa-bar*
18e [*ma*]-*a a-ta-a* :! LÚ*.A—*šip-ri*
19e *ša* PAB-*ia* :! *qàl-li*
s.1 [*la il-li-k*]*a* : *ma-a i-lu-u ina* IGI-*šu e-ra-b*[*a*]
2 [*x x x x x x x*]-*ú* : 3-*šú it-tal-ka*
3 [*x x x x x x x x*]-*ni* : *a-na a-ha-iš*
4 [*x x x x x x x x*] *iš-me*

r.1 As to what [I wrote] to the king, my lord: "They have *se*[*lected*] 500 roof-beams [in the territory] of the Urarṭian " —

4 [now] my 'third man' who *did the s*[*election*] has felled them and piled them up al[ong the river]. As so[on as] has has finished [the job], *he* will set [out] and assemble the troops.

9 I can free *up* [*to*] 100 men to en[ter] (the Urarṭian territory) and thro[w] the beams in the river; the rest I will ba[se] in the[ir] garrisons and ambush positions.

13 Some kind of an insurrection may occur; I am strengthening the guard — I am afraid of an insurrection.

r.16 [The gov]ernor of Pulua [o]pposite me has written me: "Why has the messenger of my little brother [*not com*]*e*? Is a god visiting him?"

s.2 [......] has come three times

3 [......] together

4 [...... *has not*] heard.

## 34. Problems with Cutting Timber in Šubria

K 7336 + K 7391 + K 13008

1 [*a-na* LU]GAL EN-[*ia*]
2 [ARAD-*ka*] m!*šá—aš-šur—du-bu*
3 [*lu* DI-*mu*] *a-na* LUGAL EN-*iá a—dan-niš*
4 [DI-*mu a-na*] URU.*bi-rat a-*⌈*na*⌉ [KUR *ša* LUGAL EN-*iá*]
5 [*ina* UGU *ṭè*]-⌈*e*⌉-*me ša* KUR.U[RI-*a-a ša* LUGAL *be-lí*]
6 [*iš-pur-an*]-*ni* [*ma-a*] *šá-ʾa-al* [*ṭè-e-mu har-ṣu*]
7 [*a-na*] ⌈LUGAL⌉ EN-⌈*ia*⌉ *a-sa-*⌈*bar*⌉ [*x x x x*]
8 [*x x ú-m*]*a*!-*a* ⌈*lu*!⌉-*šá-an-ni* [*la-áš-pu-ra*]
9 [KUR.*šub-ri*?]-*a-a* [T]A 2 LÚ*.[*x x x x*]
10 [*x x x x*]*x x*[*x*]*x* LÚ*.S[AG *x x x*]
lines 11-18 entirely gone
19 [*x x*]-*lak* ⌈*ú*?-*gam*?⌉-[*x x x x x*]
20 *a-na ka-a-*⌈*šu*⌉-*nu la* [*x x x x*]
21 *ni-ih-ti-liq ki-i an-*[*ni-e*]
22 *i-*[*s*]*i-šú-nu i-du-*⌈*bu-bu*⌉ *m*[*a-a x x x*]
23 *ina* É—EN.MEŠ-*ku-nu ma-a* ⌈*ni*⌉-[*x x x*]*x*
24 *it-tab-ši* ⌈*ma*⌉-*a ep-šá a-n*[*a x x x*]
25 [*m*]*a-a* LÚ*.EN.NAM *ú-di-*[*šú x x x x*]
26 [*e*]*p-šá* MU-*ku-nu da-mì-i*[*q*]-⌈*qa*⌉ [*x x x*]

CT 53 95

1 [To the ki]ng, [my] lord: [your servant] Ša-Aššur-dubbu. The best [of health] to the king, my lord!

4 The forts and [the land of the king, my lord, are well].

5 [As to the ne]ws of the Ur[arṭian(s) about which the king, my lord, wrote] me: "Inquire (about it)!" —

7 I have (already) sent [a detailed report to] the king, my lord, [......]! Let me [no]w [send it] for a second time.

9 [*A Šubri*]*an* with two [......]

10 [......] a eunuch [......]

(Break)

20 "[We did] not [...] you, so we deserted."

21 They spoke w[i]th them as follows: "[......] has occurred in the house of your lords [......]; do it, [...]!

25 "The governor *is* alo[ne]; do [...], and make yourself a go[od] name!"

**34** Script badly effaced; it impossible to read more than shown in the copy. 6 After *šá-ʾa-al* restore possibly [*ú-ṣi-ṣi*]. 8 See coll.

27 [*i*]-*si-šú-nu i-du-bu-bu* NINDA.MEŠ [*i-si-šú-nu*]
28 [*e*]-*tak-*⌈*lu*⌉ [*it*]-*tu-ur-du-u-*⌈*ni*⌉ [0]
29 [*x x x x*]*x-ti-e* KUR-*šú x*[*x x*]
30 [*x x x x x*]*x iq-ṭi-bi ma-*[*a*]
31 [*x x x x x x*] *ú-bal-*[*x x x*]
32 [*x x x x x x x*] *a a* [*x x x x*]
33 [*x x x x x x x x x x x x x*]
34 [*x x x x x x*]*x* LÚ*.[*x x x x*]
e.35 [*x x x x x it*]-*tal-ku* : ⌈*x*⌉[*x x x*]
36 [*x x x x x*] URU.[B]ÀD—$^{m}$[LUGAL—GIN]
37 [*x x x x x*] *a-na* ⌈LUGAL⌉
38 [*x x x x x*] ⌈ANŠE? *x x*⌉
r.1 [*x x x x x x*]-⌈*mi*?⌉-*i ma-a* ⌈*dul*$_6$⌉-[*lu*]
2 [TA LÚ*.ARAD].MEŠ *ša* LUGAL *gab-bu*
3 [*le-pu-uš*] ⌈*a*⌉-*na* LUGAL EN-*šú li-din*
4 [*ma-a la at-tú*]-*nu* LÚ*.ARAD.MEŠ-*e ša* LUGAL KUR—*aš-šu*[*r*]
5 [*š*]*a* GIŠ.ŠÚ.A GIŠ.A.AM GI.AMBAR *ina na-gi-*[*e*]
6 [*t*]*a-ki-sa-ni a-na* URU.⌈BÀD⌉—$^{m}$LUGAL—GIN
7 *ta-za-bi-la-ni ma-a* [TA IGI] KUR.*šub-ri-a-*[*a*]
8 *pal-ha-ku-u* LÚ*.DUMU—*šip-*[*ri-š*]*u*? *ša ina* [*x x*]
9 *ina* URU.⌈*il*?⌉-[*x x*]*x ina pi-*⌈*i*⌉ [*né-r*]*i-b*[*i*]
10 *ša* ⌈URU⌉.[*t*]*a-si ina* ⌈UGU⌉-*hi-ia it-*⌈*tal*⌉-[*ka*]
11 *ia-*⌈*ú ina*⌉ URU.*pe-en-za-a ina* UGU-*hi-šú* [0]
12 *a-sa-*⌈*pa-ar*?⌉ LÚ*.DUMU—*šip-ri-ia iq-*[*ṭi-ba-šú*]
13 ⌈*ma-a*⌉ [LÚ*].⌈EN⌉.NAM GIŠ.ÙR.MEŠ *e-r*[*i-ši*?]
14 [*ma-a x lim x*]-*me* GIŠ.ÙR.MEŠ *ina šid-di*
15 [KASKAL *ša a*]-*na* URU.*ta-si ina* UGU ⌈ÍD?⌉
16 [*kar-ru x x x x*]⌈*x x x*⌉[*x x x*]
17 [*x x x x x x x x x x x x x*]
18 [*x x x x x*]⌈*x*⌉ LÚ*.*šá*—⌈BAD-HAL⌉-*l*[*i*]
19 [*x x x x x*] ⌈*it*⌉-*ta-lak i-na-ki-si*
20 *mi-i-nu* ⌈*ša* LUGAL⌉ *be-lí i-qa-bu-u-ni*
21 KUR.URI-*a-a-e* GIŠ.ÙR.MEŠ *a-na* LUGAL EN-*iá*
22 *li-din* KUR.*šub-ri-a-a la-a* SUM-[*an*]
23 LÚ*.GAR-*nu*.MEŠ *ša* KUR.URI-*a-a ša* ⌈*pu*⌉-[*tú-u-a*]
24 *ia-mu-tú ina* KUR *it-tal-*⌈*ka*⌉ [*x*] *it-*[*x x*]
25 LÚ*.EN—*x*[*x x*]*x me ni* [*x x*] *ina dul*$_6$-⌈*lu*⌉
26 [*x x x x x*]*x*[*x*]*x a-na-k*[*u*]
27 [GIŠ.ŠÚ.A.MEŠ GIŠ.ÙR].MEŠ *ša ina na-gi-*[*e*]
28 [*x x x x x š*]*a a-na* LUGAL EN-*ia*
29 [*áš-pur-an-ni ma-a*] ⌈5⌉-*me šu-nu a-ta-*[*mar*]
30 [*x x x x a*]—⌈*dan*⌉-*niš* 1-*me* TA ŠÀ-*bi-šú-nu*
31 [*x x x x*]*x* 4-*me ša* ⌈*re*⌉-*hu-u-ni*
32 [*x x x x*] *ina* GIŠ.MURUB$_4$-*šú-*⌈*nu*⌉-*ma*
33e [*x x x x*]*x ṣa-hi-ti x*[*x*]

27 They spoke with them [*thus*, ha]d dinner [with them], and came down (from the mountain).

29 [...]... his country [...]

30 [......] said: "[......]

(Break)

35 [...... w]ent [...]

36 [...... D]ur-[Šarruken]

37 [......] to the king

38 [......] ...

r.1 [......]: "[He should do] wo[rk like] all [the subjects] of the king, and give it to the king, his lord.

3 "Are [yo]u [not] subjects of the king of Assy[ria, wh]o [have c]ut door-beams, *poplar* trees and reeds in the distri[ct] and are transporting them to Dur-Šarruken? Would I be afraid [of] the Šubrian?"

8 [H]is messen[ger] who [...] to the town [...], ca[me] to me at the mouth of the pass of [T]asi; I sent mine to him to Penzâ.

12 My messenger t[old him]: "[The g]overnor *as*[*ks for*] the beams. [x thousand x] hundred roof-beams [*are piled*] on the river bank along the [road t]o Tasi [......]"

(Break)

18 [......] has gone [to ... with] cavalry, and is cutting (the timber). What are the king my lord's orders? Would the king of Urarṭu give beams to the king, my lord, (when) the Šubrian does not?

23 Each of the prefects of the Urarṭian oppo[site me] has *gone* to (his) country [...]. The chief [......] at work [......].

26 (As to) [the *door-beams and roof-beam*]s in the district [..., about wh]ich [*I wrote*] to the king, my lord: "There are 500 of them," I have ins[pected] them; [*they are* v]ery [...].

30 100 of them [have been ...]; the remaining 400 [are ... and] they are (still) in their groves.

33 [...] desire [...]

34e [*šúm-ma*? LUGAL *be*]-⸢*lí*⸣ *i*-⸢*qa*⸣-[*bi x x*]
35e [*x x x ú*]-*še-ṣa-a* GIŠ.[*x x x*]
36e [*x x x x* L]Ú.GAL—É [*x x x*]
s.1 [*x x x x*] ⸢*ú-še-lu*⸣-*u-ni ina* ⸢*x*⸣[*x x x x x*] *da-an-qu š*[*a x x x x x*]
2 [*x x x x x x*] *ṣa ta* [*x x x x x*]*x* KUR.*šub-ri*-⸢*a-a*⸣ [*x x x x x x*]
3 [*x x x x x*] ⸢*áš*⸣ *ka*? [*x x x x x*] *sa* [*x x x x x x x*]
4 [*x x x x x*].MEŠ ⸢*x*⸣[*x x x x x x x x x x x x x*]

34 [*If the king*], *my* [*lo*]*rd, or*[*ders*],
35 [I shall br]ing out [the ...]
36 [...] the major-domo [...]
s.1 [*which* ......] *removed*, are good *for* [...].
2 [......] the Šubrian [...]
(rest too broken for translation)

## 35. The King of Šubria Refuses to Extradite Deserters

K 951

1 [*a-na* LUGAL EN-*ia*]
1 [*a-na* LUGAL EN-*ia*]
2 [ARAD-*ka* $^{m}$*ša—aš-šur—du-bu*]
3 [*lu* DI-*mu a-na* LUGAL EN-*ia a—dan-niš*]
4 [DI-*mu a-na* URU.*bi-ra-a-ti*]
5 [*a-na* KUR *ša* LUGAL EN-*ia*]
6 [ŠÀ *ša* LUGAL EN-*ia lu* DÙG].GA
7 [*x x x x x x x x x x*]*x-ru*
8 [*x x x x x x x* LÚ*].A—*šip-ri-ia*
9 [*x x x x x x* LÚ*.A]—*šip-ri-ia*
10 [*x x x x x x x x x*]-*me*
11 [*x x i*]*z-za-zu* [*x x x x x*]-*e-šu*
12 [*x x x*]*x* [*x x x x x x*]*x* UD-*me*
13 *x*[*x x x x x x x i*]-⸢*la*⸣-*ku-u-ni*
14 *a*-[*x x x x x x x x i*]-*du-al*
15 *ú-ma-a* LÚ*.A—*šip-ri-i*[*a*] ⸢*ú*⸣-*sat-bi-šu*
16 TA GIŠ.UL.MEŠ TA GI[Š.*x-x-t*]*i*
17 *i-na-ṣu-ru-šu a*-[*na* KUR.*šub-ri-a*]-*a a*-[*sa-a*]*l*
18 [*nu*]-*uk a-ta-a a-n*[*a*⸣] ⸢LÚ*.*ha-al-qu*⸣-[*t*]*e*
19 [*š*]*a* KUR.URI-*a-a* ⸢*ša*⸣ *ina* KUR—*aš-šur*.[KI] *ha-la-qu-ni-ni*
20 *tu-ṣa-bat* URU.[*x x x x x x x*]
21 *nu-uk a-ta-a* [*hal-q*]*u-te t*[*a-x x*]*x*
22 *la ta-da-na-na-a-ši ma-a* TA IG[I]
23 DINGIR.MEŠ *pal-ha-ku* LÚ*.GAL—*d*[*a-a-a-li*]
24 [*š*]*a* KUR.URI-*a-a a-na* ŠÀ [URU.*x x x*]*x*
25 50 ANŠE.GÌR.NUN.NA ⸢*i*⸣-*si-š*[*u e-tar-b*]*a*
26 ANŠE.GÌR.NUN.NA.MEŠ *i-ta-ah-ru-šu*
27 *a-na šá-a-šu* : *a-hi* GÌR.2.MEŠ
28 *si-pa-ri* AN.BAR *i-sa-ak-nu-šu*
29 *ú-sa-hi-ru a-na* [KUR.URI]-*a-a*
30 *i-ta-nu-šu a-sa-par-a*-[*šu nu-u*]*k a-ta-a*
31 *a-ba-ti mu-ru* ⸢*ša*⸣ KUR.⸢URI⸣-[*a-a*]
32 TA IGI DINGIR.MEŠ *la pal-ha*-[*k*]*a*

CT 53 160

1 [To the king, my lord: your servant Ša-Aššur-dubbu. The best of health to the king, my lord]!

4 [The forts and the land of the king, my lord, are well. The king, my lord, can be gl]ad.

7 [......]

8 [......] my messenger

9 [......] my [mes]senger

10 [......]

11 [... they s]tay [...] his [...]

12 [......] day(s)

13 [......] they come

14 [...... has been se]rving [...].

15 Now that my messenger wanted to make him leave, they protected him with *axes* and [...].

17 I a[sk]ed the [Šubria]n: "Why do you seize deserters [f]rom the Urarṭian (king) fleeing to Assyria, and [*settle them in*] the city? Why do you [*protect* dese]rters and not give them to us?" His reply: "I fear the gods."

23 A s[cout] commander of the Urarṭian [enter]ed [the town ...] with 50 mules. They took the mules from him, put iron shackles to his arms and feet and returned him to the [Urarṭi]an.

30 I wrote [him]: "Why are you not afraid of the gods, (you) *abati*, calf of the Urarṭ[ian]!"

**35** 31, r.11 The italicized words remain obscure; they are certainly not Assyrian but possibly (judging from the context) Šubrian. If so, the following Assyrian words might be explanatory translations, in which case *abati* would be the Šubrian word for "calf," etc. (for *ada* in r.11 cf. Urarṭian *ar*(*du*)- "to give," Melikišvili, *Die urartäische Sprache*, p.80).

e.33 LÚ*.*ṣi-ra-a-ni ša* KUR.[U]RI-*a-a*
34 *ina* UGU-*hi-šu i-lu-ku*
35 *i-la-ku-u-ni a-ki* [*ina* I]TI.AB
r.1 *ina* IGI LUGAL EN-*iá a-li-k*[*u*]-*u*-⸢*ni*⸣
2 10 LÚ*.ERIM.MEŠ *ša*—BAD-HAL-⸢*a*⸣-[*te š*]*u-nu*
3 *a-na* ŠÀ-*bi ih-tal-qu* [*x x*]*x*
4 40 LÚ*.ERIM.MEŠ TA ŠÀ UR[U?.*x*]*x-ri*
5 UN.MEŠ-*šú-nu ina* ŠU.2-*šú-nu i-ṣab-tú*
6 NA$_4$.*a-ru-a-ti-šú-nu i-ta-as-hu*
7 *a-na* ŠÀ-*bi i-tal-ku a-se-e-me*
8 *ma-a ma-ri-ṣi a—dan-niš ina* UGU
9 LÚ*.ERIM.MEŠ *an-nu-u-te a*-⸢*sa-al*⸣-*šu*
10 *e-gir-tú ina* UGU-*hi-ia i-sa-*[*pa*]*r*
11 *ma-a te-bal a-da ma-a* ERIM.⸢MEŠ⸣-*ku-*[*nu*]
12 *a-šá-par-a-ka ina* UGU LÚ*.ŠÁ[M]
13 ⸢*ša* LUGAL⸣ *be-lí iš-pur-a-ni* [0]
14 [*an-nu-rig*] *ina* É LÚ*.ARAD-*šú x*[*x x*]
15 *x*[*x x x x*]*x*.MEŠ *ina* IGI
16 ⸢LUGAL⸣ [EN-*iá*] ⸢*ú*⸣-*se-bi-la*

33 Emissaries of the [Ur]arṭian keep coming and going to him.

35 When I was visiting the king my lord [in] Kanun (X), 10 soldiers, (all) cavalrymen, deserted there; [*recently*], 40 soldiers from [...]ri took their people with them, pulled out their grinding slabs, and went there.

r.7 I heard that he had been very ill, so I asked him about those soldiers. He sent me a letter, saying: "*Tebal ada* – I shall send you yo[ur] men."

12 As to the bou[ght] slave concerning whom the king, my lord, wrote me, [*he has now turned up*] in the domain of his servant, and I am sending [the ...]s to the king, [my lord].

## 36. Joint Sacrifices

K 1137

beginning broken away
1′ [*x x x x x x*]*x* ⸢*mi-i*⸣-*nu* [*x x x*]
2′ [*x*] *ba iš* ⸢*x*⸣-*nu-ti ma-a*ʾ-*da*
3′ [UD]U.SISKUR.MEŠ *né-ta-pa-áš*
4′ [*šu-n*]*u a-na* KUR-*šú-nu i-ta*-⸢*ta*⸣-*ku*
5′ [*a-ni*]-*nu a-ni-šá* ⸢*x x x*⸣
6′ [*i-se*]-*niš* UN.MEŠ-⸢*šú-nu*⸣
7′ [*ša a-na*] KUR.URI *i*[*h-li-qu-ni*]
e.8′ [*i-su-u*]*h-ru-*[*ni x x*]
9′ [*x x x*]*x il*! *x*[*x x x*]
Rev. lines 1-5 destroyed
6 [*x x x x* LÚ*.*i-tu*]-ʾ*a-a-a*
7 [*x x x x x x x*]*x a*
8 [*x x x x x x x x*] ⸢*ku*⸣
rest broken away

CT 53 163

(Beginning destroyed)

1 [......] what [...]

2 ... We made many sacrifices. [The]y went away to their country, (while) [w]e [...ed] hither.

6 Their people, [who] had f[led to] Urarṭu, have [like]wise [retu]rned [...]

(Break)

r.6 [...... the It]u'eans [...]

(Rest destroyed)

## 37. Defense Against Accusations

K 7458

1 [*a-na* LUGAL EN-*ia*]
2 [ARAD-*ka* m*šá—aš-šur—du-bu*]
3 [*lu* DI-*mu a-na* LUGAL EN-*iá a—dan-niš*]
4 [DI-*mu a-na* URU.*bi-rat a-na* KUR *ša* LUGAL EN-*iá*]

CT 53 101

1 [To the king, my lord: your servant Ša-Aššur-dubbu. The best of health to the king, my lord]!

4 [The forts and the land of the king, my lord, are well].

r.14 "In the domain of his servant": i.e., in my domain.
**36** 2, 8f See coll.

5 ⸢ša i ri⸣ [x x x x x x x x]
6 LUGAL be-lí ⸢lu⸣ [la-a x x x x]
7 l[a] LÚ*.ta-zi-r[u x x x x x]
8 ú-pa-za-ar : [x x x x x x]

9 LUGAL be-lí lu ⸢la⸣-a ⸢i⸣-[x]-⸢x⸣[x x]
10 šúm-mu a-na-⸢ku⸣ LÚ*.⸢ṣi⸣-x[x x x x]
11 la mu-qa-⸢a⸣-a la a-[x x] ⸢la a⸣-[x x]
12 UDU.MEŠ ina IGI UN.MEŠ LÚ*.[x]x [x] du [x x]
13 a-na-ku an-⸢na⸣-[ka] ⸢x⸣ [x l]ak a ⸢sa⸣ [x x]
14 ⸢ú?⸣-še-ṣa [x] a [x x]-ni-ia ina UGU [x x]
15 ⸢e x⸣ [x x x i]-sa-(a)ʾ-lu ma-⸢a⸣ [x x]

16 [x GUD].MEŠ ⸢6?⸣ UDU.MEŠ a-ta-mar LÚ*.⸢ta⸣-[zi-ru]
17 [x x]x a ⸢GUD⸣ šu-u-tú a-di re-eh-⸢tu⸣
18 [iš]-ʾa-lu-ni i—su-ri LUGAL be-lí
19 [i]-qa-bi ma a-ta-a LÚ*.qur-bu-ti ú-ki-iš
20 [L]UGAL be-lí i-sa-bar ma-a 4 GUD.MEŠ ša ṣa-hi-ti
21 [t]a-ti-[š]i ⸢GUD⸣.MEŠ ⸢ša⸣ si-[ni?-t]i ina ŠÀ
22 GUD.MEŠ a-[si-qi] ⸢x⸣ [x]⸢x⸣ an-nu-rig

23 ina ŠÀ URU.MEŠ ša KUR—aš-šur ⸢e⸣-[ku?]-lu ki-ma
24 ina IGI LUGAL EN-ia at-tal-k[a a-na L]UGAL EN-iá
25 ú-kal-lam : a-na-ku GUD.MEŠ [ina ŠU].⸢2⸣ man-ni
26 ú-ba-ʾa-a la-⸢a x x⸣ [x x x x] a
27 [ina UG]U ⸢UN⸣.MEŠ ša LUGAL be-lí iš-⸢pur⸣-[an]-ni
28 [ša x x]x NINDA.MEŠ i-gi-⸢ru-ú-ni⸣ a-na-⸢ku⸣
29 [x x x] a-sa-bar nu-ku LÚ*.ARAD.MEŠ ša LUGAL
30 [at-t]u-nu ⸢x x LUGAL⸣ be-lí ⸢x⸣ [x] ṣa
31 [x x]x ma-a ⸢x x⸣ lu ⸢x⸣ nu
32 [x x x] ⸢x x⸣ [x x] LÚ*.ARAD.MEŠ [š]a LUGAL
33 [x x x x x x] da-⸢la⸣-hu
e.34 [x x x x x] ⸢e⸣-ṣi-i
35 [x x x x x ap?-t]a-làh
36 [x x x x x ú]-se-li
37 [x x x x x x] ⸢x x⸣-ni
r.1 [x x x x x x] it-ta-lak
2 [x x x x x x] DINGIR.MEŠ-šu
3 [x x x x x]x-$^{d}$AG i-se-niš
4 [x x x x x]x.MEŠ-ši-na
5 [x x a-na LUGAL] EN-iá a-sa-bar
6 [nu-ku LÚ*.EN—pi-q]i-ta-ti la-ak-la
7 [x x x x x]-ik ma-a ki-la-šú-nu

5 (......) who [......] — the king, my lord, should [*not believe him*]!

7 No Tazir[u ......]

8 *I* do [*not*] conceal [...].

9 Let the king, my lord, not [...]!

10 If I [......], I will not be able to [...] and to [...].

12 The sheep are at the disposal of the people; [......].

13 I [...] here; I have [......],

14 and will bring out [...]. My [*servant*]s have [...ed] to [...] and questioned (him). He said:

16 "I have seen [... ox]en and *six* sheep." The Taziru is the [...] of the ox, until they have inquired about the rest.

18 Perhaps the king, my lord, will [s]ay: "Why was the royal bodyguard delayed?"

20 [The k]ing, my lord, wrote: "You have appropriated four oxen of *value*" — but I have [*taken*] oxen from among *br*[*an*]*ded* oxen (only)! They *are actually ea*[*ti*]*ng* them in the cities of Assyria!

23 As soon as I com[e] to the presence of the king, my lord, I shall show [the k]ing, my lord, whom I hold accountable for the oxen. No [......].

27 [As] to the people about whom the king, my lord, wrot[e to m]e, [the ones who] quarreled [...] bread, I have written [*to them*]: "[Yo]u are subjects of the king; [...] the king, my lord, [...]."

31 They (said): "[......]

32 [......] the subjects of the king

33 [......] *disturb*

34 [......] *Is it little*?

35 [...... *I*] got afraid

36 [...... *I mo*]*ved up* [......] ...

r.1 [......] he went

2 [......] his gods

3 [......]-Nabû together

4 [......] their [...]s

5 [...] I wrote [to the king], my lord: "Let me detain [and ... the offi]cials," and he said: "Detain them!"

**37** 5 Possibly one line missing before this line. 10 Possibly LÚ*.⸢ta!⸣-[zi-ru. r.10 Text BI-*bu*. r.12 Text *up-ta-zi-ni*; scribal error. r.18 At end read possibly *la-a mu-qa-*[*a-a*].

8 [*x x x am—mar*$^{?}$ NU]MUN—LUGAL TA URU.MEŠ
9 [*x x x* A.ŠÀ.MEŠ] GIŠ.SAR.MEŠ *mi-i-nu*
10 [*x x x x x*]*x gab*$^{!!}$*-bu šu-nu ú-du-u*
11 [*a-na-ku-u x x* T]A ŠÀ-*bi a-ti-ši*
12 [*x x x x*] ⸢A⸣.ŠÀ.MEŠ GIŠ.SAR.MEŠ *up-ta-zi-ir*$^{!!}$
13 [*x x x x-b*]*i-u* URU.MEŠ ⸢*ša*⸣ *a-na* NUMUN—LUGAL
14 [*x x x ta-ad*]*-nu-ni* : ⸢*ša x* GUD⸣.MEŠ UDU.MEŠ
15 [*x x x x*]*-a-ti x*[*x x*] ⸢*x*⸣ *ú-di-ni*
16 [*x x x* L]Ú.ERIM.MEŠ ⸢*x x*⸣ [*x*] *bi*
17 [*x x x x*]*-šú-nu* : *šúm-m*[*u*] ⸢*da-an-qu*⸣
18 [*x x x x*] *la a-mu-*[*x*] ⸢*x*⸣ [*x x*]
19 [*x x x x*]*x ta* ⸢*x x x*⸣ [*x x x*]
20 [*x x x x*] LÚ*.ARAD.MEŠ *š*[*a x x x*]
21 [*x x x x*] *ina* IGI-*ia* ⸢*šu-nu*⸣ [*x x*]
22 [*x x x x*] ⸢*x x x*⸣ [*x x x*]
rest (about 10 lines) broken away

8 They know [*the property* which] the king's [off]spring [have *taken*] from the cities, [the *fields*] and orchards, what[ever ...], every [...];

11 [*could*] I (really) have taken [... fr]om it, and concealed [...] the fields and the gardens?

13 [...] The towns which [have be]en given [...] to the king's offspring, which [...] oxen and sheep [...]

15 [... not] yet [...]

16 [...] the men [...]

17 their [...]; if they are good

18 [...] I *do* not [...]

19 [...] ... [...]

20 [...] the subjects of [...]

21 [...] are in my presence [...]

(Rest destroyed)

## 38. A Visit by Duri-Adad and a Royal Delegate

K 8989

1 [*a-na* LUGAL *b*]*e*$^{!}$*-lí-*[*ia*]
2 [ARAD-*ka* $^{m}$*š*]*a—aš-šur—d*[*u-bu*]
3 [*lu* DI-*m*]*u a-na* LUG[AL *be-lí-ia*]
4 [*an-nu-r*]*i* $^{m}$BÀD—$^{d}$I[M LÚ*.*x x*]
5 [$^{m}$*x-x*]*x-tú-šú* LÚ*.*qe-e-pu* [*i-si-šu*]
6 [*it-ta*]*l-ka mi-nu ša di-b*[*i-šú-ni*]
7 [*ša ṭ*]*è-en-šú-u-ni ina* ŠU.2 $^{m}$ARAD—[*x a-šap-pa-ra*]
8 [*ú*]-⸢*ma*⸣*-a an-nu-ri* $^{m}$BÀD—$^{d}$IM *x*[*x x x*]
9 [*il*]*-lak* LÚ*.*qe-pu i-si-šu il-l*[*ak-ma*]
10 [*i*]*l-lu-ku* ŠÀ-*bu* [*ša* LUGAL EN-*iá lu* DÙG.GA]
11 [*x x pa*]-⸢*né*$^{!}$⸣*-e-a* [*x x x x*]
rest broken away
Rev. traces of several lines but nothing legible

ABL 703

1 [To the king, my l]ord: [your servant Š]a-Aššur-d[ubbu. Good h]ealth to the kin[g, my lord]!

4 Duri-A[dad the ...] has just come [*with* ...]*tušu*, the (royal) delegate; [I *shall write*] through Urda-[...] whatever he had to te[ll] and [rep]ort.

8 Right now, Duri-Adad [...] is leaving, and the delegate is lea[ving] with him; they are on their way. [The king, my lord, can] be glad.

11 [...] my presence [......]

(Rest destroyed)

## 39. Fragment Concerning Tree Trunks

K 16047

rest broken away
1′ [*x x x š*]*a ina* UR[U.*x x x*]
2′ [*x x x*]*x šu-u* [*x x x x*]

CT 53 726

(Beginning destroyed)

1 [... wh]ich are in the cit[y ...]

2 [...] he [...]

**38** 5 See coll.; possibly [*pa-n*]*a-tú-šú* LÚ*.*qe-e-pu* [*ša* URU.*x x*] "[bef]ore him the legate [of ...] (had come)."
8.11 See coll.
**39** Hand of Ša-Aššur-dubbu.

3′ [*x x x*] *ina* ÍD [*x x x x*]
4′ [*x x x*] *tu x*[*x x x x*]
5′ [*x* GIŠ].⌜Ù⌝R.MEŠ [*x x x x*]
6′ [*x x*] *i*⌜*d*⌝*—da-a-*[*te x x x*]
7′ [*x x š*]*a nu-*[*x x x x x*]
8′ [*x x x*] *a-na* [*x x x x x*]
rest broken away
Rev. destroyed

3 [...] in the river [...]
4 [...] ... [...]
5 [...] the beams [...]
6 [...] afterwards [...]
7 [... wh]ich we [...]
8 [...] to [...]
(Rest destroyed)

## 40. A Šubrian Emissary on his Way to the King

K 536

1 [*a-na* LUGAL EN]-*ia*
2 [ARAD-*ka* $^{md}$*x—x*]*x*—GIN-*in*
3 [*lu* DI-*mu a-na* LUGAL] ⌜EN-*ia*⌝
4 [DI-*mu a-na* URU.*bi-ra-a*]-⌜*ti*!⌝
5 [*a-na* KUR *ša* LUGAL E]N-⌜*ia*?⌝ [0]
6 [*x x x x x x x*] ⌜*x*⌝ [*x*] ⌜*x*⌝
7 [*x x x x x x x*] ⌜*x*⌝ [*x x x*]
8 [*x x x x x x*] ⌜LUGAL⌝ [*x x x*]
9 [*x x x x x*] ⌜*x im x*⌝ [*x*]
10 [*x x x x la*?] *nu-ú-da ša* ⌜*x*⌝ [*x* (*x*)]
11 [*x x x x x i*]*q-ṭí-bu-u-ni ma-a ut-t*[*a-mi-iš*]
12 [*x x x x x x m*]*a-a la ú-na*[*m-mi-iš*]
13 [*x x x x x x x*] *ma-a ina* [*x x*]
14 [*x x x x x x x x*] *nu* [*x x*]
illegible traces
illegible traces
illegible traces
18 *nu-pa-*[*x x x x x x x x x*]
19 *ma-a* [*x*] *lik* [*x x x x x*] ⌜*x x*⌝
20 ⌜*x*⌝[*x x x x x x x x x*]*x tú*
21 *ma-*[*a* EN.NUN]-*šú-nu i-na-*⌜*ṣu*⌝-*ru*
e.22 *a-sa-par* ⌜*it*⌝-*tal-ku i-šá-*ʾ*u-u-l*[*u*]
23 *ṭè-e-mu har-ṣu il-la-ku-u-ni*
r.1 *i-qab-bu-u-ni a-na* LUGAL EN-*ia*
2 *a-šap-pa-ra an-nu-rig* LÚ*.MAH
3 KUR.*šub-ri-a-a ina* IGI LUGAL EN-*ia il-la-ka*
4 *mi-nu ša di-ib-bi-šú-nu-ni* [*ina*] IGI LUGAL EN-*ia*
5 [*x x x x*]-*ni i—*⌜*su*⌝-*ur-ri* [*x x*]
lines 6-10 destroyed
11 *la-a x*[*x x x x x x x*]
rest uninscribed

CT 53 4

1 [To the king], my [lord: your servant ...]-ka''in. [Good health to the king], my lord!

4 [The for]ts [and the land of the king, m]y lo[rd, are well].

(Break)

10 [......] we [*don't*] know [...]
11 [......] told me: "He has se[t out]
12 [......] "He has not s[et out]
13 [......] "In [...]
(Break)

21 "They are keeping [an eye] on them."

22 I have sent (scouts) to go and inquire; (when) they come back with a detailed report, I shall write to the king, my lord.

r.2 A Šubrian emissary is just coming to the king, my lord. [*Let them* ...] in the presence of the king, my lord, whatever they have to say. Perhaps [......]

(Rest destroyed)

**40** 2 *x*]*x*—GIN-*in* sic; reading [$^{m}$*ša—aš-š*]*ur—du-bu*! excluded.

## 41. ———

K 15640

beginning broken away
1′ [*x x x*]⸢*x*⸣-*a* ⸢LÚ*.EN⸣.N[AM]
2′ [*ša pu*]-*tú-u-a an-na-ka* [0]
3′ [*x x x*] *šu-ú* GIŠ.KIN.GE[ŠTIN.MEŠ]
4′ [(*x*)*x x*]-⸢*ú*⸣ LÚ*.ERIM.MEŠ [0]
5′ [*x x x x*] É 10 *x*[*x x x*]
rest broken away
Rev. destroyed

CT 53 697

(Beginning destroyed)

1 [...]a, the gov[ernor oppo]site me is here.

3 He is [...]; the gra[pes]

4 [...] the men

5 [...] *where* 10 [...]

(Rest destroyed)

## 42. ———

K 11315

beginning broken away
1′ [*x x x x*]-*šú-nu i*-[*x x*]
2′ [*x x x*]*x-ṣu-ú*-[*ni*]
3′ [*x x-l*]*i*?-*te-šú-nu ina* [*x x*]
4′ [*x x x*]-*bu-u da*-[*x x*]
5′ [*x x-l*]*ak-áš*-⸢*šu*⸣ [*x x*]
6′ [*x x x*] *ṣu ni* [*x x*]
7′ [*x x x d*]*u-ub-bu* [*x x*]
e.8′ [*x x x*] GIŠ.SAR [*x x*]
9′ [ŠÀ]-*bi* LUGAL E[N-*ia*]
r.1 [*lu* DÙG.GA] *ù re-e*[*h-ti*]
2 ⸢ŠEŠ⸣.MEŠ-*šú-nu ú-še-ṣ*[*u-ni*]
3 *i-ba-ši* URU.*la-bir-a-a*
4 [*i-b*]*a-ši* URU.*sak-ku-a-na-a-a*
5 [*an-n*]*u-rig ú-ma-a an-nu-te* DU-*u*-⸢*ni*⸣
6 [*ma*]-⸢*a*⸣ : Á.2-*ni ina* ŠÀ KUR—*aš-šur*.KI
7 [*ni-t*]*u-bíl ma-a ú-za-*ʾ*u-u-na-ši*
8 [*ma-a ina*] É.⸢GAL *ṭè*⸣-*e-mu*
9 [*x x x x x x x*]*x an* [*x*]
rest broken away

CT 53 424

(Beginning destroyed or too broken for translation)

7 [... s]peak [...]

8 [...] garden [...]

9 The king, [my] lo[rd, can be glad].

r.1 Also, they are bring[ing out] the re[st] of their brothers, including people from Labir and Sakkuana. [No]w then, these have come and said:

6 "[Should we l]ay hands on Assyrian territory, we would be ...ed; re[port to] the Palace [......]"

(Rest destroyed)

**41** Orthography and sign forms favour assignation to either Liphur-Bel or Ša-Aššur-dubbu.
**42** Hand resembles that of Ša-Aššur-dubbu.

# 43. Fetching Beams

K 5568

1 [*a-na* LUGAL *be-lí-ia*]
2 [ARAD-*ka* [m]*x x x x x*]
3 [*lu* DI-*mu a-na* LUGAL] ⸢EN⸣-*ia*
4 [*ina* UGU *x x x x*]-*a-a*
5 [*ša a-na* É.GAL[?]] *a-hu-ru-u-ni*
6 [*nu-uk* GIŠ.ŠÚ.A].MEŠ *li-in-tú-hu*
7 [[md]*x—bal*]-*liṭ* LÚ*.*qur-bu-tú*
8 [[m]*x x x*] *i-si-šú-nu*
9 [*id-du-ub-b*]*u ma-a* GIŠ.ŠÚ.A.MEŠ
10 [*x x x*]*x-ni mì-i-nu*
11 [*x x x*] *i-du-ba-ka-nu-ni*
12 [*x x x x*] LÚ*.GAL—50.MEŠ-[*k*]*u-nu*
13 [*x x x x x*] LÚ*.EN—[*x x*]
rest broken away
Rev. beginning broken away
1′ [*x x x x x x*]*x*
3′ [*x x x x*]*x x*[*x*].MEŠ
4′ [*x x x x*]-*du-šú*
5′ [*x x x x x*]*x*
6′ [*x x x x*] ⸢*x x*⸣

CT 53 283

1 [To the king, my lord: your servant NN. Good health to the king], my lord!

4 As to the [...]ans [concerning whom] I appealed [to the *Palace*, saying]: "Let them fetch [the door-beam]s" — [...]-balliṭ the royal bodyguard [and NN have spok]en with them (as follows):

9 "[...] the beams [*and do*] whatever [...] said to you;

12 [... y]our commanders-of-fifty [......]

(Rest too broken for translation)

# 3. Letters from Vassal Kings and Bit-Zamani



FIG. 8. *Oxen, sheep and captives (reign of Assurbanipal).*
ORIGINAL DRAWING V, 31.

# 44. Troops in Hubuškia

K 1871

1 *a-n[a* LUGAL EN-*iá a—dan-niš*] ⸢*a*⸣*—dan-niš*
2 *lu-[u* DI-*mu* ARAD-*ka* $^{m}$*hu]—te-šub*
3 *na*!-[*gi-u x x x x x x*]*x* ⸢*i*⸣*-qab-bu-niš-šú*
4 [*x x x x x x x x x*]*x*
5 [*x x x x x x x x x b*]*i*
6 [*x x x x x x x x x*]-*šu*
7 [*x x x x x x x* LÚ*.NA]M.MEŠ
8 [*x x x x x x x x x*]*x*
9 [*x x x x x x x x x*]-*a*
rest broken away
Rev. beginning broken away
1′ [LÚ*.*šá*]—⸢*pet*!⸣-*hal* LUG[AL? *x x x x x*]
2′ [*ina*!] UGU LÚ*.NIGIR—É.GAL *x*[*x x x x*]
3′ *ina* UGU *e-mu-qi ša ina* KUR.*hu-ub-uš-ki-a*
4′ *ina qa-an-ni šu-nu-ni ina* UGU-*hi e-gir-ti*
5′ *an-ni-tú a-na* ⸢*ku*?⸣*-in*!-⸢*ti*!⸣ *a-sa-par*
rest uninscribed

CT 53 54

1 The very [best of health] t[o the king, my lord! Your servant Hu]-Tešub.

3 A di[strict of *Urarṭu*] called [...]

(Break)

7 [...... gove]rnors

(Break)

r.1 [The *cava*]*lry of the ki*[*ng of* ...]

2 [*have ...ed ag*]*ainst* the palace herald.

3 *On account of* the troops which are in Hubuškia, outside (the border), I am sending this letter of mine to ....

# 45. Urarṭian Offensive against Mannea and Zikirtu

K 1037

1 *a-na* LUGAL EN-*iá a—dan-niš a—dan-niš*
2 *lu-u* DI-*mu* ARAD-*ka* $^{m}$*hu—te-šub*
3 *ina* UGU *ṭè-e-me ša* KUR.URI-*a-a*
4 [*š*]*a* LUGAL EN *iš-pur-an-ni ma-a*
5 [*mi*]-*i-nu ša taš-mu-u-ni ár-hiš*
6 [*šup-ra*] *ki-i* ⸢*x*⸣ *sur-rat áš-mu-u-ni*
7 [*a-na* LUGA]L! ⸢EN!-*iá*!⸣ *a*?-*sa*!-*par ú-ma-a*
8 [*x x x x x x x* IT]I.APIN
9 [*x x x x x x x* LÚ*.GA]L.MEŠ
rest (at least 10 lines) broken away
Rev. beginning broken away
1′ [*x x x x x x* U]RU?.*a-x*[*x x x*]
2′ [*x x x x x*.ME]Š? *ša* URU.HAL!.⸢ṢU!⸣
3′ [*x x x x*]-⸢*ú*⸣ *ma-a šúm-ma* 0!
4′ [*in-ta-ra-ṣa*]-*áš-šú ina* KUR.*man-na-a-a iz-za-a*[*z*]
5′ [*ma-a šú*]*m*!-*mu i-ta-at-ra-ṣa-áš-šú*
6′ *ina* U[GU] KUR.*zi-kir-ta-a-a*

ABL 215

1 The very best of health to the king, my lord! Your servant Hu-Tešub.

3 As to the news of the Urarṭians concerning which the king, my lord, wrote me: "[Write me] quickly whatever you have heard" —

6 (even) when I heard *false* ..., I wrote [to the kin]g, my lord! Now [...... *on the ...th of*] Marchesvan (VIII)

9 [...... *the magn*]*ates*

(Break)

r.1 [......*the to*]*wn* A[...]

2 [...... have ...]ed the [...]s of the fort.

3 "If [things have gone badly] for him, he will be sta[ying] in Mannea; [i]f things have

**44** → Deller Zagros p.107. r.1ff See coll. r.2ff The fragmentary context makes it impossible to determine the meanings of *ina muhhi* in these lines with certainty, and various alternative renderings are within the possibilities. r.5 See coll.; *ás-sa*-⸢*ṭar*?⸣ (Deller loc.cit.) excluded.
**45** → Deller Zagros p.107. 6f See coll. r.1f, 5 See coll.

FIG. 9. *Assyrian attack on Pazaši, a border fortress between Mannea and Zikirtu.*
BOTTA AND FLANDIN, *Monument de Ninive* II, 145.

7′ *iz-zu-qu-pu*
8′ *ki-i an-ni-e a-se-me*

gone well for him, he *will have attacked* the Zikirteans."

8 This is what I have heard.

## 46. A Wronged Vassal

Sm 1809

beginning destroyed
1′ ⌜*ma-a la i*⌝-[*x x x x x x x*]
2′ *ina* ZAG-*ka* [*x x x x x x x*]
3′ *ma-a man-nu mi*-[*x x x x x x x*]
4′ *ú-ma-a* LUGAL EN [*x x x x x x*]
5′ *gi is li x*[*x x x x x x*]
6′ URU.MEŠ-*ni-ia i*-[*kaš-šu-du* ARAD.MEŠ-*ni-iá*]
7′ *ša a-na na-gúr-te* [*x x il-li-ku-ni*]
8′ *ú-ṣab-bu-tú* LÚ.GAL—[*x x x x x*]
9′ *šu-tú ina* UGU *man-ni in*[*a x x x x*]
10′ TA IGI $^{m}$*a-ši-pa-a ú-x*[*x x x x*]
11′ URU.MEŠ-*ni i-kaš-šad* ARAD.MEŠ-*ni-iá ú-k*[*aš-ša-da*]
12′ *a-šab-bar muk a-le-e mì-li*[*k-ka* 0]
13′ *ṭè-mu-ma la i-šak-kan* LÚ*.*kal*-[*la-bu*]
14′ *ša ina* IGI-*ia* LUGAL *ip-q*[*i-du*]-*ni* [0]
15′ 3-*šú* 4-*šú* TA LÚ*.A—KIN-*iá* [*a-sa-bar*]
16′ *ba-ši-i*ʾ *ṭè-mu-ma la* [*iš-kun*]
17′ *a-na* LÚ*.A—KIN-*iá ú-ti*-[*ra*]
e.18′ *ma a-ṣa-bat ina* ŠÀ *si*-⌜*bar*⌝-[*ri*]
19′ *e-si-ip-ka*
blank space

r.1 LÚ*.2-*i-šú ina* IGI-*šú i-za-za*
2 *a-a-ši a-di* KUR-*ia i-na-zi-ra-a-ni*
3 LUGAL EN *di-ib-bi an-nu-te a-na* $^{m}$SUHUŠ—$^{d}$IGI.D[U$^{?}$]
4 *liš-al a-ta-a e*-⌜*hu-la*$^{?}$ *x x*⌝ [*x*]*x-ni*
5 *ki-i ša* ZAG *ù* K[AB *x x x x*]-*ni*
6 *mi-nu i-qab-bi-ú ina* ⌜IGI⌝ LUG[AL E]N-*iá*
7 ⌜*d*⌝*e-ek-tú a*-[*a-š*]*i lib*$^{!}$-*bi i*-[*k*]*aš-šad*
8 [*dib*]-*bi* ⌜*ma*⌝-*a-d*[*u-u-t*]*e*$^{!}$ *i*-⌜*na*⌝-[*zi*]-*ru-šú*
9 [*ú-m*]*a-a* LUGAL EN ⌜*lu*$^{!}$ *la*⌝ [*x x x x x x*]
10 [LUGA]L *at-tah*-[*ra x x x x x x x*]
11 [*ú*]-*ma-a la* [*x x x x x x x*]
12 [*x*] *ki-i š*[*a* LUGAL *be-lí i-la-u-ni*]
13 [*le-p*]*u-uš l*[*a x x x x x x x*]
14 [*ina*] UGU-*iá tu*-[*x x x x x*]
15 [*x* T]A ⌜*x x x x*⌝ [*x x x x x*]
rest broken away

CT 53 132

(Beginning destroyed)

1 "he does/they do not [......]
2 "at your right [......]
3 "Who [......]?"
4 Now, the king, [my] lord [......]
5 ...[......]

6 [They conquer] my towns [and] seize [*my subjects*] who [*have gone* to ...] for *hired employment*. He is chief [...]; on behalf of whom does he [...] from the presence of Ašipâ [...], conquer (my) towns and per[secute] my subjects?

12 I keep writing: "Where is [your] sense?" but he does not give any *reason*. [I have] many times over [sent] the *kal*[*lāpu*] whom the king ap[poin]ted in my service with my messenger, but *to no avail*. [He has not given] any *explanation* but has retur[ned] my messenger, (saying): "I will seize you and wrap you up in iron chains!"

r.1 His deputy stands in his presence and curses me and my country.

r.3 The king, my lord, should ask Ubru-Pali[l] about these matters! Why does he [...] me? When people [*slander*] me right and left, what will they say in the presence of the ki[ng], my [lo]rd? [I sh]all be slain; he will reach my very heart.

r.8 But ma[ny thi]ngs will c[ur]se him!

9 [N]ow the king my lord should not [...]! I have appealed to [the kin]g; [n]ow [let him] not [......].

12 [The king, my lord, may a]ct as [he deems best. ......]

13 [ag]ainst me [......]

(Rest destroyed)

**46** 13, 16 The meaning "reason, explanation" assigned to *ṭēmu* is based on the context; if, as seems likely, the writer complaining about an Assyrian governor is a vassal king, subject to the Assyrian king only, the normal meaning of *ṭēmu* ("order") would seem to be excluded. r.3 See coll.

# 47. Having Mares Serviced

Sm 548 + Sm 887

1 *a-na* LUGAL EN-*iá*
2 ARAD-*ka* $^{m}$LUGAL—IGI.LAL-*a-ni*
3 *lu-u* DI-*mu a-na* LUGAL EN-*iá*
4 DI-*mu a-na a-ṣa-pi*.ME[Š!]
5 *ša* LUGAL EN-*iá*
6 DI-*mu a-na* LÚ*.ARAD.MEŠ
7 *ša* LUGAL EN-*iá*
8 DI-*m*[*u*] ⸢*a*⸣-*na* KUR.É—*za-ma-ni*
9 *a-du* I[TI!.Š]U! MÍ!.AN[ŠE!.KU]R!.RA!
10 *ú-šar-kab*
11 Ú.*pu-e*
12 *a-na-kis*
13 *a-na bir-te ra-da*!-*bi*
14 *ša bu-li*
15 *a-na* MÍ.ANŠE.KUR.RA
r.1 *a-na* 15 *ša* ITI.ŠU
2 *la-al-li-ka*
3 IGI.MEŠ! *ša* LUGAL EN-*iá*
4 *la*-⸢*mur*?⸣ KIN-*i*
5 *i—su-ri*
6 *bir-ti me-eh-ri*-⸢*iá*!⸣
7 *a-ma-ra-kù*!
8 *dul-li*
9 *in*[*a*! UR]U.BÀD—LUGAL—*i*!-⸢*ku*?⸣
10 [*l*]*a-mur*

ABL 757

1 To the king, my lord: your servant Šarru-emuranni. Good health to the king, my lord!

4 The pack animals of the king, my lord, are well; the subjects of the king, my lord, are well; the land of Bit-Zamani is well.

9 I will have the m[ar]es serviced until [Tam]muz (IV); in between the urging of the herds to the mares, I am cutting hay.

r.1 On the 15th of Tammuz I would like to come and *see* the face of the king, my lord, (*about*) *my work* —

5 Perhaps I am lagging behind my colleagues; I should inspect my work i[n] Dur-Šarruken.

# 48. Receiving a Shipment of Animals and Wagons

K 1889 (ABL 921) + K 5572 + K 7327 + K 15383

1 ⸢*a*⸣-*na* LUGAL E[N-*ia*]
2 ARAD-*ka* $^{m}$*aš-šur—pa-*[*ti-nu*]
3 *lu-u šul-mu a-n*[*a* LUGAL] EN-*ia*
4 $^{m}$DINGIR—DU-*k*[*a* L]Ú.*šá*—É—*ku-din*
5 [*š*]*a*! [*x x x aš*]-*šur*! *na-ṣa-an-ni*
6 [*it-tal-ka* (*x*)] 15 ANŠE.*ku-din*.MEŠ
7 ⸢5⸣2 AN[ŠE *x* ANŠ]E.A.AB.BA
8 43 GUD 2 G[I]Š.GAG.LIŠ.LAL.MEŠ
9 4 GIŠ.*tal-lak*.MEŠ *a-ta-šar*
10 *at-ta-har k*[*i*]-⸢*i*⸣ *an-ni-e*
11 *iq-ṭi-bi-a ma-a* LÚ*.ARAD.MEŠ-*ia*
12 [*ur*]-*ta-mu-*[*u*]-*ni ih-tal-qu*
13 *an*!-*nu-ri*[*g i*]*a-mu-tú* MU.MEŠ-*šú*
14 *a*-⸢*du*!⸣ URU.MEŠ *b*[*é-e*]*t šú*-⸢*nu-ni*⸣
15 [*a-s*]*a-ṭar ina* UGU LUGAL EN-*ia*
16 [*ú*]-*se-bi-la*
r.1 [*x x x x*] *ina* ŠU *x*[*x*]
2 [*x x x x x*] *tú* LÚ*.SA[G]

CT 53 58

1 To the king, [my] lo[rd]: your servant Aššur-pa[tinu]. Good health t[o the king], my lord!

4 Ilu-illik[a, the] *mule stable attendant* [w]ho brings me [...], [has come], and I have checked and received from him 15 mules, 52 don[keys], [x] camels, 43 sheep, 2 carts, and 4 wagons.

10 He told me this: "My servants have left me and run away!"

13 [I have] now [wr]itten down the names of each of them, including the towns w[he]re they come from, and am herewith sending (this information) to the king, my lord.

r.1 [...] in the hand [of ...]

2 [...] the eunu[ch]

**47** 11, 20ff, r.10f, 14 See coll. r.4 See coll. and cf. no. 126:6f *la-al-lik-ka* IGI.2.MEŠ *ša* MAN EN-*ia la-mur*; also 294 r.11f, *lal*!-*li-ka pa-ni ša* LUGAL [EN-*ia l*]*a-mur*. The signs after ⸢*mur*⸣ are perfectly clear but their interpretation remains obscure. KIN perhaps here logogram for *dullu*?
**48** 5, 7 See coll.

3 [*x x x x x*] ⌜*x-da-te*⌝
4 [*x x x x x*] ⌜*x ih*⌝*-tal-qu*
5 *x*[*x x x x x*] *ina* KUR.⌜É⌝—*za-ma-na*
6 *x*[*x x x x x*] ⌜*na*⌝ *kal* ⌜*zu*?⌝ *tú*
7 *x*[*x x x x x*] *ina* URU.⌜*gu*?*-za*?⌝*-na*
8 [*x x*]⌜*x*⌝[*x x x*] ⌜URU?.*ta*⌝-[*x x*]
9 [*x x x x x x x x x*]*-te*
10 [*x x x x x x x x*]*x-tú*
11 2 [*x x x x* LÚ*].ARAD.M[EŠ]*-ia*
12 *x*[*x x x x* LU.GAL—*da*]*-ni-bat*
13 ⌜*x x*⌝[*x x x x x*] *a-na-ku*
14 *x*[*x x x x x x x*]*x-da*
15 *id-x*[*x x x x*] ⌜LÚ*.ARAD?⌝.M[EŠ]
16 *la-a* ⌜*x*⌝[*x x*]⌜*x x x*⌝
17 LÚ*.*e*-[*x x x x x x x x x*]
one line destroyed

3 [...] ...
4 [...] have run away
5 [......] in Bit-Zamani
6 [......] ...
7 [......] in *Guza*na
8 [...... *in*] Ta[...]
(Break)
11 two [......] my servants
12 [...... *the chief vic*]*tualler*
13 [......] myself
14 [......] ...
15 [...] servants
16 do not [......]
17 the [...] official [......]
(Rest destroyed)

FIG. 10. *Consignment of stock including camels (reign of Shalmaneser III).* BM 124652.

## 49. ———

82-5-22,140

1 *a-na* LUGAL EN-*ia*
2 ARAD-*ka* $^{m}$*aš-šur—pa-ti*$^{!}$-⸢*nu*⸣
3 *lu-u šul-mu*
4 *a-na* LUGAL EN-*ia*
5 GIŠ.*bat-x*[*x*]*x* [GÍD$^{?}$].DA.MEŠ
6 $^{md}$*x*[*x x x x x*]*x*
7 L[Ú$^{!}$.*x x x x x*]-*ni*
8 *x*[*x x x x x x x x*]
rest broken away
Rev. uninscribed

ABL 922

1 To the king, my lord: your servant Aššur-patinu. Good health to the king, my lord!

(Rest destroyed or too fragmentary for translation)

## 50. ———

K 14665

1 [*a-na* LUGAL EN-*ia*]
2 [A]RAD-*ka* $^{m}$*aš-šur—*[*pa-ti-nu*]
3 [*l*]*u šul-mu a-n*[*a* LUGAL EN-*ia*]
4 ⸢*e*⸣-*gír-tú ša* [*x x x x*]
5 [*š*]*a* LUGAL EN-*ia* [*x x x x*]
6 [ARA]D.MEŠ-*ni ša* [*x x x x x*]
7 [*ina*] UGU GÌR.2 [*x x x x x*]
8 ⸢*ú*⸣-*sa-zi-*[*zu x x x x x*]
9 [*x x x*]*x x*[*x x x x x x*]
rest broken away
Rev. destroyed

CT 53 573

1 [To the king, my lord]: your [se]rvant Aššur-[*patinu*. Go]od health t[o the king, my lord]!

4 A letter from [NN, *a servant* o]f the king, my lord, [*has come to me*].

6 [The serv]ants of [......]

7 have made [them] stand *on* the feet [......]

(Rest destroyed)

## 51. Fragment Referring to a Messenger

K 15321

beginning broken away
1′ [*x*]*x x*[*x x x*]
2′ ⸢*ma*⸣-*a* ⸢*ú*$^{?}$⸣-[*ma-a*]
3′ LÚ*.A—K[IN]
4′ *ša* $^{m}$*aš-šur—p*⸢*a*⸣-[*ti-nu*]
5′ *il-la-*[*ka*]
Edge uninscribed
r.1 *ina* UGU [*x x x*]
rest broken away

CT 53 641

(Beginning destroyed)

2 "The messen[ger] of Aššur-pa[tinu] is n[ow] com[ing]."

r.1 As to [...]

(Rest destroyed)

**49** 2, 5, 7 See coll.

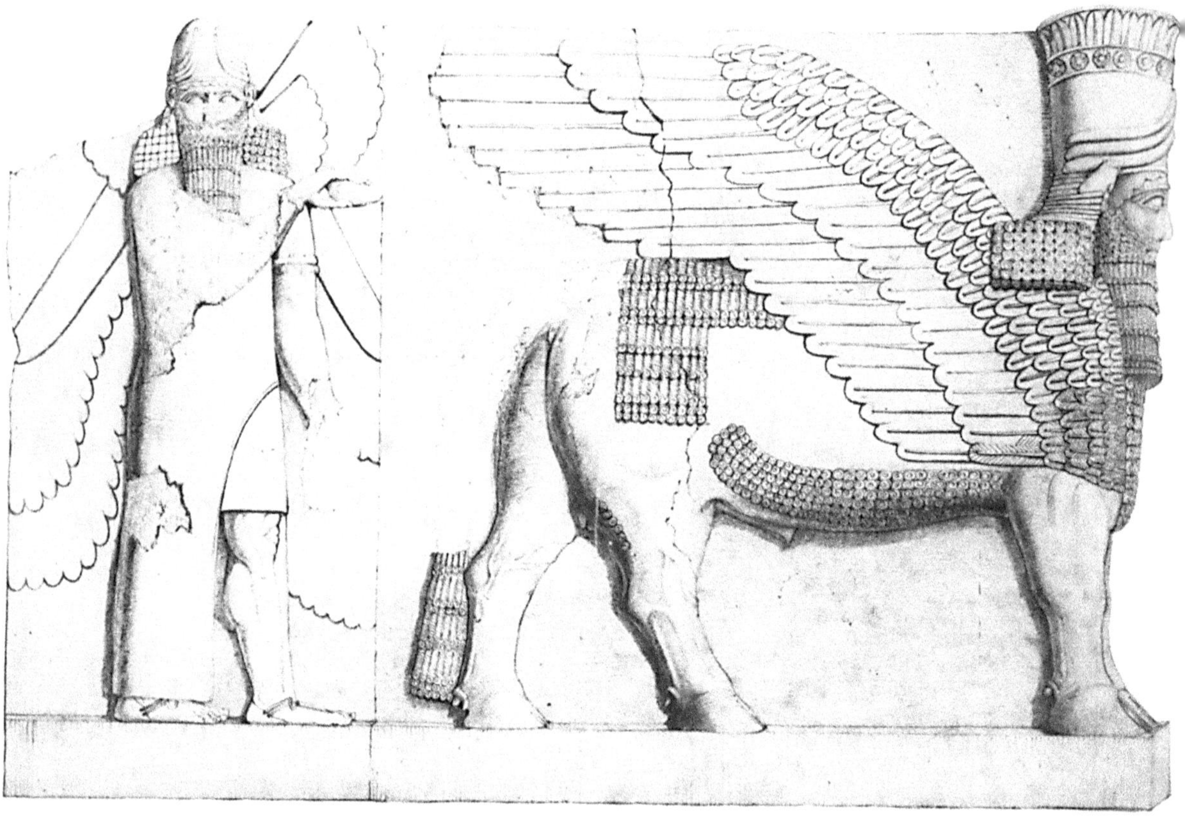

# 4. Letters from the Rab Šaqê Province



FIG. 11. *Human-headed bull colossus (reign of Sennacherib).*
ORIGINAL DRAWING I, 32.

## 52. Šubrian Emissaries on their Way to the King

K 525

1 *a-na* LUGAL *be-lí-ia*

2 ARAD-*ka* $^{m}$*aš-šur*—BÀD—IGI-*ia*

3 *lu šul-mu a-na* LUGAL *be-lí-ia*

4 UD-23-KÁM *ša* ITI.ŠE LÚ.MAH.MEŠ

5 KUR.*šu-bur-a-a ina* URU.*šá-bi-ri-šú*

6 *it-tal-ku-u-ni is—su-ur-ri* LUGAL *be-lí-i*$^{!}$

7 *i-qab-bi ma-a man-nu šú-nu* $^{m}$*ia-ta-a*ʾ

8 LÚ.GAL—URU.MEŠ-*šú ša qa-ni ta-hu-me*

9 *ša* KUR.URI-*a-a* ⌈$^{m!}$*a*$^{!}$⌉*-bi—ia-qa-a* UN.MEŠ KUR *šú-u-tú*

10 *i-si-šú it-tal-[k]u-u-ni i—su-ur-ri*

11 LUGAL *be-lí i-qab-bi ma-a a-ta-a* ŠEŠ-*šú*

12 ⌈TA*⌉ LÚ.2-*i-šú* ⌈*ša*⌉ *ina ma-šar-ti*

13 *iq-bu-u-ni ma-[a] il-lak-u-ni la il-lik-u-ni*

14 *ma-a* $^{m}$*hu—te-šub ma-ri-ṣi ma-a an-nu-te*

15 *a-na te-gír-te it-tal-ku-u-ni*

16 LÚ.ERIM.MEŠ—LUGAL LÚ.UN.MEŠ KUR

17 *ša šad-daq-diš ina šal-še-ni ina ra-bu-še-ni*

18 TA* *pa-an il-ki* TA* IGI ERIM.MEŠ—MAN-*te*

19 *ih-li-qu-u-ni ina* ŠÀ-*bi*

20 *e-ra-bu-u-ni a-na šú-na-šú-nu*

21 *ina* ŠÀ-*bi e-gír-*⌈*te*⌉.MEŠ

e.22 *i-sa-ṭa-ru*

23 *a-na te-gír-te-šú-nu*

24 *i-sa-ak-nu*

r.1 *na-ṣu-u-ni a-na* LUGAL *be-lí-ia*

2 *ú-šá-áš-mu-u-ni ù* LÚ.ERIM.MEŠ *pa-ni-(u)-te*

3 *ša ú-ma-a* TA* *pa-an dul*$_{6}$*-li* LUGAL

4 *ih-hal-li-qu-u-ni ina* ŠÀ-*bi i-lak-u-ni*

5 A.ŠÀ.MEŠ GIŠ.SAR.MEŠ É.MEŠ *id-da-na-šú-nu*

6 *ina* ŠÀ KUR-*šú ú-ša-aṣ-bat-su-nu*

7 *ina* ŠÀ-*bi kam-mu-su an-nu-te* LÚ.MAH.MEŠ-*ni*

8 *ša il-lik-u-ni-ni a-na te-gír-te šú-u-tú*

9 $^{m}$*hu—te-šub ma-ri-ṣi ma-a ni-il-lik*

10 *né-mur an-nu-rig il-lak-u-ni*

11 *la ke-e-tu ši-i-te e-gír-tú an-ni-tú*

12 *a-na* LUGAL EN-*ia ú-šá-áš-mu-u-ni* 8$^{!}$ ERIM.MEŠ

13 1 ANŠE.*ku-du-nu* 3 ANŠE.MEŠ *ša* TA* LÚ*.MAH.MEŠ

ABL 252

1 To the king, my lord: your servant Aššur-dur-paniya. Good health to the king, my lord!

4 The Šubrian emissaries came to Šabirešu on the 23rd of Adar (XII).

6 Perhaps the king, my lord, will say: "Who are they?" (They are) Yata', his man in charge of the towns near the Urarṭian border, and with him Abi-yaqâ, a local inhabitant.

10 Perhaps the king, my lord, will say: "Why did his brother and his deputy, who at the review said they would come, not come?" They say: "Hu-Tešub is ill; these (people) have come *to bargain*."

16 They have written down on clay tablets the king's men and the people of the country who last year, the year before and three years ago ran away from labour duty and military service, ending up there, and have set them *as their bargain*; they are going to bring (the tablets) and read them to the king, my lord.

r.2 Yet the *prime* men who now escape the king's work and go there – he gives them fields, gardens and houses, settles them in his country, and there they stay.

7 These emissaries who came to *bargain*, Hu-Tešub being ill, said: "We will go and see"; they are now coming, but (when) they read the said tablet to the king, my lord, it is not the whole truth.

12 Eight men, one mule and three donkeys have come with the emissaries.

**52** → TCAE p.271f. 6 See coll. 9 W 98. 12 See coll. r.2 Or "previous, former, senior men." The suggested translation presumes that *pānîu* here has the connotation "first(-ranking)" well attested for its Bab. equivalent *mahrû*. r.12 Y 78, W 98.

14 *il-lik-u-ni-ni* LUGAL *be-lí iq-ṭí-bi-a*
15 *ma-a ki-ma* LÚ.MAH.MEŠ-*ni il-lak-u-ni*
16 *ma-a* ${}^{m}$*aš-šur—bi-su-nu i-si-šú-nu*
17 *lil-li-ka šum-ma* LUGAL *be-lí i-qab-bi*
18 *i-si-šú-nu lil-li-ka*
19 *lid-di-bu-bu mi-i-nu ša a-bat-u-ni*
20 LUGAL *be-lí liš-pu-ra*

14 The king, my lord, told me: "When the emissaries come, Aššur-bessunu should come with them" – if the king, my lord, so orders, he may go and speak with them. Let the king, my lord, write me what his orders are.

## 53. A Murderer Flees to Šubria

K 506

1 *a-na* LUGAL *be-lí-ia*
2 ARAD-*ka* ${}^{m}$*aš-šur*—BÀD—IGI-*ia*
3 *lu-ú šul-mu a-na* LUGAL *be-lí-ia*
4 LÚ.GAL—50-*ia šú-u ša* LÚ.*gur-ra-a-a* URU.*mu-dur-na-a-a*
5 *a-na* LÚ.*ha-za-ni ša* URU.*mu-dur-na i-du-ka*
6 TA* *mar* KASKAL *il-li-kan-a-ni la il-li-ka*
7 *dul*$_6$*-lu* TA* ŠEŠ.MEŠ-*šú la e-pu-uš*
8 TA* *pa-an ip-ta-làh* 15 LÚ.*gur-ra-a-a*
9 *ina qa-a-ti-šú i-ṣab-bat a-na* KUR.URI-*a i-la-ka*
10 *it-tal-ku-u-ni iq-ṭí-bu-u-ni ana-ku* ${}^{m}$DINGIR—*da-la-a*
11 *a-na* KUR.*šu-bur-a a-sa-pa-ra mu-ku a-lik*

ABL 251

1 To the king, my lord: your servant Aššur-dur-paniya. Good health to the king, my lord!

4 A commander-of-fifty of mine, of the Gurrean (troops) from *Meturna*, killed the mayor of *Meturna*. From the moment the expedition came, he did not show up to do work with his fellows but, afraid of his deed, took with him 15 Gurreans and went away to Urarṭu.

10 (When) they came and reported it to me, I sent Il-dalâ to Šubria, saying: "Go and bring

FIG. 12. *Assyrian army spearmen with crested helmets, possibly Gurreans (reign of Sennacherib).* ORIGINAL DRAWING VI, 33.

12 LÚ.ARAD.MEŠ-*ni-ka še-ri-da it-tal-ka*
13 LÚ.ARAD.MEŠ-*ni-šú ú-se-ri-da-a ana*[!]*-ku*[!] *ú-sa-hi-ir*
14 LÚ.A—*šip-ri-ia ina* GABA ᵐDINGIR—*da-la-a a-sa-pa-ra*
15 *mu-ku* LÚ.GAL—50 *ha-ni-u* TA* L⸢Ú⸣.ERIM.MEŠ-*šú*
16 *mu-ku* KUR-*ú ù né-rab-a-ni gab-bu*
17 *ina* UGU-*hi-šú ú-*[*ta*]*-hi-iṣ-ṣi*
18 *mu-ku at-ta ri-di-pi* ⸢*i*[!]—*da*[!]⸣*-tú-šú a-lik*
19 *ir-ti-di-bi a-na* KUR.*šu-bur-a it-*(*ta*)*-la-ka*
20 LÚ.GAL—50 TA* LÚ.ERIM.MEŠ-*šú*
21 *ina* URU.*mar-hu-ha* URU.[*bi*]*r*[!]*-te*
22 *ša* KUR.*šu-bur-a-a e-ta*[*r*]*-bu*
23 ᵐDINGIR—*da-la-a e-ta-am-m*[*a*]*r-šú*
24 [*t*]*a*[!]*-mit-tú i-si-šú i-sa-a*[*k*[!]*-na*]
e.25 *ma-a a-lik* $NA_4$.KIŠIB *ša* L[Ú.EN.NAM]
26 [*i*]*ṣ*[!]*-ṣa al-la-ka lu re-*[*qa-ka*]

27 LÚ.GAL—50-*ia* TA* 1-*me* L[Ú.ERIM.MEŠ]
r.1 *ša* GIŠ.*a-ri-te* URU.*mar-hu-ha-a-a*
2 *i—da-at* ᵐDINGIR—*da-la-a it-tal-ku-u-ni*
3 *ina* KASKAL *i-zu-ku-pu* LÚ.ARAD.MEŠ-*ni ša* LUGAL EN-*a*
4 *et-ku la-áš-šú mi-mi-ni ina* ŠÀ-*bi-šú-nu*
5 *la i-du-ku* LÚ.GAL—50 *ú-ta-hi-iṣ-ṣu*
6 *is-su-hur ina* URU.*mar-hu-ha e-tar-bu*

7 *an-ni-nu ša ú-ma-a ri-id-pu a—*⸢*da*[!]⸣*-at* LÚ.GAL—50
8 *ni-iš-ku-*(*nu*)*-u-ni la* (*i*)*-ṣi-bu-tú la i-di-nu*
9 LÚ *ip-tu-gu tu-ra* LÚ.ARAD.MEŠ-*ni ša* LUGAL EN-*a*
10 *la-bi-ru-ú-te ša ina* ŠÀ-*bi kam-ma-su-u-ni*
11 *ú-še-ṣu-u-ni* [[*x*]] *i-du-nu*

down your servants." He went, but did he bring down his servants?

13 I sent my messenger back to Il-dalâ, telling him: "This commander-of-fifty and his men! I have *hurt* the whole mountain (area) and all the passes because of him! Go in pursuit after him!"

19 Pursuing him, he went to Šubria. The commander-of-fifty and his soldiers ente[r]ed Marhuha, a [fo]rt of the Šubrian (king). Il-dalâ saw him and ma[de a sw]orn agreement with him: "Come and [b]ring me the seal of the go[vernor] and [you] shall be fr[ee]."

27 My commander-of-fifty and 100 Marhuhaean [ho]plites went after Il-dalâ and attacked him on the road. The servants of the king, my lord, were on their guard; none of them got killed, and they wounded the commander-of-fifty. They turned back and entered Marhuha.

r.7 We, who organized the present pursuit of the commander-of-fifty — they did not arrest him and hand him over but took the man away! Once again, they are (only) bringing forth and handing over old subjects of the king, my lord, who have been living there.

## 54. A Sanctuary for Fugitives

Rm 68

beginning broken away
1′ [*x x x x x x x* LU]GAL *be-lí*
2′ [*x x x x ša* LUGAL *be*]*-lí iš-pur-an-ni*
3′ [*ma-a a-a-ka š*]*u-tú iq-ṭí-bu-u-ni*
4′ [*ma-a* TA *mar šá*]*-ga-lu-u-ni*
5′ [*x x x x ih-ti*]*-liq a-na* KUR.*šub-ri-a*
6′ [*it-ta-lak i—su-r*]*i* LUGAL *be-lí i-qab-bi*
7′ [*ma-a i-s*]*uh*[!]*-ra* TA* KUR.*šub-ri-a*
8′ [*it-ta-la-ka a-sa-ʾa-a*]*l ú-ta-ṣi-ṣi*
9′ [*ma-a* TA É *ih-l*]*i-qu-u-ni a-na* KUR.*šub-ri-a*
10′ [*il-li-ku-u-ni a*]*h—hur a-na* KUR
11′ [*la is-hu-r*]*a la il-li-ka*

ABL 1176

(Beginning destroyed)

1 [The ki]ng my lord [*should know this*].

2 [As to what the king], my [lo]rd, wrote me: "[Where] is he?" — They told me: "[After he had] been deported [..., he fl]ed [and went] to Šubria."

6 [Perha]ps the king, my lord, will say: "[Has he retu]rned [and come back] from Šubria?" [I have aske]d and investigated; [they say that since he fl]ed [and went] to Šubria, [...; he has not] yet [retur]ned and come back to the country.

**53** 13,17,24f See coll.
**54** The orthographic and linguistic features of this letter do not favour assignation to Aššur-dur-paniya, Ašipâ, Ša-Aššur-dubbu, or any other sender in the present volume; the scribe (and hence the sender) remains unidentified.
7, 12, 17, 21f See coll.

12′ [*x x x x x*]-*us ina* UGU 1!
13′ [*x x x x x x*] *nu-uk at-ta*
14′ [*x x x x x x*]-*ar nu-uk ú-ma-a*
15′ [*x x x x x x*] *ina* IGI-*ka kam-mu-su*
16′ [*x x x x x x*].MEŠ-*ia la im-qu-ut*
17′ [*x x x x x x ṭ*]*è-e-mu-ma*!
18′ [*la áš-me x x x a*]*h* LÚ *an-ni-u*
19′ [*x x x x x x x*] *ina* KI.TA ŠU.2
e.20′ [*x x x x x x x*] KUR.*šub-ri-*[*a*]
21′ [*x x x x x x-n*]*i*! LUGAL *be-lí*
22′ [*x x x x x x x*] URU.*bir-te*!
23′ [*x x x x x x x x*] *hal-qu*
r.1 [*x x x x x x*]*x ina pi-i* DÙG.GA
2 [*x x x x ina* UGU *x*]*x*.MEŠ *ša* LUGAL
3 [*be-lí iš-pur-an-n*]*i ma-a ana-ku*
4 [*x x x x x š*]*um*!-*mu lib-ba-šú-nu*
5 [*x x x x x x*]*x lib-ba-šú-nu*
6 [*x x x x x x*] É.KUR *šu-tú*
7 [*x x x x la i*]-*ṣab-bat la* SUM-*an*
8 [*x x x x x x*] 1-*en* :. URU DUG$_4$.GA
9 [*x x x x x x-m*]*u*! *ma-ṣar*!-*tú-šú*
10 [*x x x x x x*] ⌈É!⌉.KUR [*b*]*ir-ti*
11 [*x x x x nu-u*]*k* ARAD.MEŠ ⌈*ša*⌉ LUGAL
12 [*x x x x x x*]-*ah* ARAD.MEŠ [*š*]*a* LUGAL
13 [*x x x x x* LUGAL *be*]-*lí i-qab-bi*
14 [*x x x x*] LUGAL *ú-ra-mu-ni*
15 [*x x x x x ina*] UGU LÚ*.*da-a-a-li*
16 [*x x x x x x*]*x-šú a-na šá-šú*
17 [*x x x x x x*]-*ṣab-ba-tú-ni*
18 [*x x x x x x x*] *i—su-ri*
19 [*x x x x x x x-t*]*i am-mu-te*
20 [*x x x x x x x x x x x x*]*x*
rest broken away

12 [I sent ...]... to [...], saying: "You [......]; now, [......] is staying in your court!"

16 [*He replied*: "He] has not fallen into my [hand]s, [*nor* ... have I heard] any report [*about him*]."

18 [......] this man

19 [......] secretly

20 [......] Šubri[a]

21 [......] the king, my lord

22 [......] the fort

23 [......] have fled

r.1 [...] with kind words [...].

2 [As to the ...]s about whom the king, [my lord, wrote m]e: "I [......]; if they want [......]" —

5 they want [......]

6 [......] he is [*in*] the temple

7 [......] He does not seize and give [him]

8 [......] a town *is said*

9 [......] his guard

10 [......] the temple [be]tween

11 [... I said]: "[*You are*] the king's subjects [...]." [......] the king's subjects.

13 [Perhaps the king], my [lo]rd, will say: "[...]" — [... who] leave the king's [......].

15 [A]s to the scout to whom his [......]

17 [...] will take

18 [......] perhaps [......] those

(Rest destroyed)

## 55. A Captured Informer

Sm 807

1 [*a-na* LUG]AL *be-lí-*[*ia*]
2 [ARAD-*ka*] $^{m}$*aš-šur—*BÀD—IGI-⌈*ia*⌉
3 [*lu-u š*]*ul-mu a-na* LUGAL *be-lí-*[*ia*]
4 [LÚ.*da-a*]-*a-li-ia ša ina* ŠÀ K[UR-*i*]
5 [*šu-n*]*u-u-ni* LÚ.EME *šu-*[*ú ša*]
6 [TA* URU.*i*]*r*!-*gi-is-ti-a-ni a-n*[*a x x*]
7 [$^{m}$*a-r*]*i-e a-na* KUR-*i i*[*l-lik-u-ni*]
8 [LÚ.*d*]*a-a-a-li-ia iṣ-ṣab-*[*tu-ni-šú*]
9 [*a-s*]*a-al-šú mu-ku mi-*[*i-nu*]
10 [*ṭè-e*]-*mu ša* KUR.U[RI!-*a-a*]
11 [*ma-a* KUR.*x*]*x-ti-na-a-a x*[*x x x x*]
12 [*x i*]*l* [[*x*]] *is*!-*x*[*x x x*]
13 [*x x l*]*a-a ú-ṣa x*[*x x x*]
rest broken away
Rev. destroyed

ABL 741

1 [To the ki]ng, [my] lord, [your servant] Aššur-dur-paniya. [Good] health to the king, [my] lord!

4 My [sco]uts in the m[ountain] have captured an informer [who] was g[oing from A]rgistiani t[o Ar]iye, over the mountain.

9 [I as]ked him about [the ne]ws of the Ura[rṭian], and he informed me:

11 "The [...]tinaean(s) [...]

12 ......

13 [has n]ot [*yet*] come out [...]

(Rest destroyed)

12 The upright wedge following UGU is probably accidental; the signs are clearly legible and the reading *šá* assumed in Harper's copy is excluded.

**55** 5 See coll. 11 The broken sign before *ti* is not *e*; see coll.

# 56. Master Builders and Apprentices

K 1175 (ABL 253) + K 1179 + K 1207

1 *a-na* LUGAL *be-lí-ia*
2 ARAD-*ka* $^{m}$*aš-šur*—BÀD—IGI-*ia*
3 *lu-ú šul-mu a-na* LUGAL *be-lí-ia*
4 *ina* UGU LÚ.TIN.MEŠ *ša* LUGAL *be-lí*
5 *iš-pur-an-ni ma-a a-na* LÚ.GAL.MEŠ QÀL.MEŠ
6 *di-i-ni ma-a p*[*i*]*l-ku-šú-nu ina* ŠÀ-*bi*
7 *le-pu-uš* 16 LÚ.TIN.MEŠ-*ni-ia*
8 3 *ina pa*-⸢*an*⸣ LÚ.600—É.GAL
9 3 *ina* MURUB$_4$ [URU] *dul*$_6$*-lu e-pu-uš*
10 10 *ša pil-ki* [0] *ina* BÀD
11 *i-ra-ṣip-u-ni* P[AB] 16 LÚ.TIN.MEŠ
12 *ša dul*$_6$*-lu e-*[*p*]*a-áš-šú-u-ni*
13 *ù* DUMU.MEŠ-*šú-nu* QÀL.MEŠ
14 LÚ.*tal-mi-da-*[*ni šu-nu*]
15 *dul*$_6$*-lu mi-mi-*[*ni la e-pu-šú*]
16 *ina* ŠÀ-*bi-šú*$^!$-[*nu*]
17 *la ha-ki-*[*im*]
r.1 *ú*$^!$*-ni-na-a-te ina i*$^!$—*d*[*a*$^!$*-tu-šú-nu*]
2 *i-za-bi-lu mu-ku dul*$_6$-[*lu ša*]

CT 53 33

1 To the king, my lord: your servant Aššur-dur-paniya. Good health to the king, my lord!

4 As to the master builders concerning whom the king, my lord, wrote me: "Give junior ones to the magnates, so they can perform their work assignment with their help";

8 (out of) my 16 master builders three are with the palace herald, three are working in the centre [of the city], and ten are engaged in bricking my work allocation of the city wall. (This makes) a total of 16 master builders engaged in work.

13 As for their junior sons, [they are] apprenti[ces], incapable of doing any (serious) work; it is not within their understanding. They just carry chests af[ter them].

r.2 I said: "The master builders have

FIG. 13. *Hauling a winged bull (reign of Sennacherib). Cf. nos 57f and 297.*
ORIGINAL DRAWING II, 65.

3 LÚ.TIN.MEŠ *i-ba-áš-ši* [*mi-mi-ni*]
4 *la a-dan-na* LÚ.TIN.[MEŠ 6]
5 *ina* UGU *pil-ki ša* [$MURUB_4$ URU]
6 *ša* LÚ.600—É.GAL [*a*]-*na*[!]-*ku*[!]
7 *a-ti-din ù d*[*$ul_6$-lu*] *ia-u*
8 *ina* UGU-*hi-ia* KALAG-[*an*] *a—dan-niš*
9 10 LÚ.TIN.MEŠ-*ni* [*an*]-*nu-ti*
10 *ša ina pa-ni-ia* [*la*] *ú-ṣu-u*
11 $SIG_4$-⌜*ma*⌝[!] [*x x*]*x* [*i*]-*ha-pi-u*

wo[rk] to do, I cannot give away [any of them]." I have (already) given [six] master builder[s] to the work assignment of the [centre of the city] and the palace herald, and my own w[ork] is a great burden on me.

9 [The]se ten master builders at my disposal can[not] go out; they will [*not*] even break a brick [...].

# 57. Raising Bull Colossi in Adia

K 7398

1 [*a-na* LUGAL EN-*ia*]
2 [ARAD-*ka* $^{m}$*aš-šur*—BÀD—IGI]-*ia*
3 [*lu* DI-*mu a-na* LUGAL] EN-*ia*
4 [*ina* UGU $NA_4$.$^{d}$ALA]D.$^{d}$LAMA *ša* URU.*a-d*[*i*]-⌜*a*⌝
5 [*ša* LUGAL *be-lí*] *iš-pur-an-ni*
6 [*x x x ú-š*]*at-ba-šú-nu-u-ni*

CT 53 346

1 [To the king, my lord: your servant Aššur-dur-pani]ya. [Good health to the king], my lord!

4 [As to the bull] colossi of Ad[i]a [about which the king, my lord], wrote me, [*the ... by which*] I am going to raise them

**56** 16, r.1, 6, 11 See coll.

7 [*x x x ú*$^{?}$]*-ni-na-a-ti*
8 [*x x x x*] *it-tan-nu-ni*
9 [*x x x x*] ⌜*a*⌝*-na* GAR*-nu-u-ti*
10 [*x x x x ú*]*-pa-ha-šú-nu*
rest broken away
Rev. uninscribed

7 [... *c*]*hests*
8 [...] they have given me
9 [...] to the *prefects*
10 [... *will*] *modify* them
(Rest destroyed)

## 58. Raising Bull Colossi in Adia

79-7-8,273

beginning broken away
1′ [*x x x x x*] *šú-u-tú*
2′ [*x x x x x*] *šú-u*
3′ [*x x x ub*]*-bal-u-ni-šú*
4′ [*x x x*]⌜*x*⌝[*x*]*-at*
5′ [*x x x is*]*—su-ur-ri*
6′ [LUGAL *be-lí*] *i-qab-bi*
7′ [*ma-a a-ke-e d*]*ul*$_{6}^{!}$*-lu te-pa-áš*
8′ [*x x x*] ⌜*a*⌝*-na ga-ma-ri-šú*$^{!}$
9′ [*x x x*] *ú-šá-da-ba*
10′ [*x x x* UR]U$^{!}$.*a-di-a*
11′ [*x x* NA$_{4}$].⌜$^{d}$⌝ALAD.$^{d}$LAMA.MEŠ
12′ [*x x x a-šá-d*]*a-da*
rest broken away
Rev. uninscribed

ABL 1419

(Beginning destroyed)
1 [......] he is [...]
2 he [......]
3 [th]ey are bringing to him [......]
4 [......]
5 [Pe]rhaps [the king, my lord], will say:
7 "[*How*] are you doing [the w]ork?"
8 [...] to finish it
9 [...] I am raising
10 [...] Adia
11 [...] bull colossi
12 [I] shall h[aul ......]
(Rest destroyed)

## 59. A Chaldean Bodyguard

Rm 2,462

1 [*a-na* LUGAL EN*-a*]
2 ARAD*-ka* $^{m}$*aš-šur—*BÀD*—pa-ni-*[*ia*]
3 *lu-u* DI*-mu a-na* LUGAL EN*-a*
4 TA* UGU $^{m}$AD*—ul—i-di*
5 LÚ*.*qur-bu-te* KUR.*kal-dà-a-a*
6 *ša* LUGAL EN *iš-pur-an-ni*
7 *ma-*[*a x*]*x su* [*x x*]*x*
8 ⌜*a*$^{!}$⌝ [*x x x*] ⌜*x*⌝ [*x x x x*]
9 [*x x x x*]*x*[*x x x x*]
rest broken away
Rev. uninscribed

ABL 742

1 [To the king, my lord]: your servant Aššur-dur-pani[ia]. Good health to the king, my lord!

4 As to Abi-ul-idi, the Chaldean bodyguard about whom the king, my lord, wrote to me: "[...]... [...]

(Rest destroyed)

**57** Hand of Aššur-dur-paniya; does not join no. 58.
**58** New copy p. 265. Hand of Aššur-dur-paniya; does not join no. 57.
**59** 7f See coll.

# 60. Providing for Troops

K 7528

beginning broken away
1′ [*x x x x x x x x x*] *gab-bi-*[*x*]
2′ [*x x x x x x*] A.ŠÀ.MEŠ-*šú-nu* [0]
3′ [*x x x x x*]*x ad-ra-te-šú-nu* [0]
4′ [*x x x x-l*]*i ù* 20 ANŠE ŠE.NUM[UN.MEŠ]
5′ [*x x x* URU].*bir-te ina* ŠÀ-*bi i-si-*[*te*]
6′ [*x x x*]*-ma ù* ERIM.MEŠ *an-n*[*i-šá*]
7′ [*x x x x k*]*i-i* $^{m}$*aš-šur—re-ṣu-*[*u-a*]
8′ [*x x x x x*]*x a-a-ka-m*[*e*$^{?}$*-ni x*]
rest broken away
Rev. destroyed

CT 53 389

(Beginning destroyed)
1 [......] all
2 [......] their fields
3 [......] their threshing floors
4 [...]; moreover, 20 homers of se[ed] corn
5 [... of] the fort in the tow[er]
6 [...] and the troops hith[er]
7 [......] when Aššur-reṣ[uwa]
8 [......] anyw[here]
(Rest destroyed)

# 61. ———

K 5609

beginning broken away
1′ ⸢*x*⸣ [*x x x x x x x x x*]
2′ LÚ.[*x x x x x x x x x*]
3′ *a-sa-*[*par x x x x x x*]
4′ *ṭ*[*è-e-mu x x x x x x*]
5′ *ma-*⸢*a*⸣ [*x x x x x x x*]
6′ *ma-*⸢*a*⸣ [*x x x x x x x*]
7′ *ma-*⸢*a*⸣ [*x x x x x x x*]
8′ *it-*[*x x x x x x x x x x*]
rest broken away
Rev. beginning broken away
1′ [*x x x*] ⸢*x*⸣ [*x x x x x*]
2′ ⸢*x*⸣ *gam šá* [*x x x x x*]
3′ *mi-mi-n*[*i x x x x x x*]
4′ ⸢*it*⸣*-x*[*x x x x x x x x x*]
5′ Í⸢D⸣ [*x x p*]*a-an* [*x x x x*]
6′ $^{m}$*qa-*[*x x x*] *ri r*⸢*i*⸣ [*x x x x*]
7′ *i—da-at am-m*[*u*$^{?}$*-ti x x x x*]
8′ $^{m}$⸢*x x*⸣ *ul* ⸢*la*⸣ *a x*[*x x x x*]
9′ ⸢*x x*⸣ *ib šú-u* [*x x x x x*]
10′ *giš-ri ih-*[*x x x x x x*]
11′ ⸢*it*⸣*-ta-lak* [*x x x x x x*]
12′ [*x*]*x ik x*[*x x x x x x x*]
rest broken away

CT 53 296

(Too broken for translation)

**60** Orthography points to Aššur-dur-paniya, but cf. no. 109.
**61** Hand of Aššur-dur-paniya.

## 62. Meeting the King on the Way

Sm 521

1 *a-na* LUGAL *be-lí-ia*
2 ARAD-*ka* $^{m}$I—DINGIR
3 *lu šul-mu a-na* LUGAL *be-lí-ia*
4 *an-nu-rig* LUGAL *be-lí* [[*ut*$^{!}$-*ta*$^{!}$-*mì*$^{!}$-*ši*$^{!}$]]
5 *il-la-ka a-na-ku lal-lik-ka*
6 *a-du* URU.*šá-bi-ri-šú*
7 *ina*$^{!}$ GABA LUGAL *be-lí-ia*-⸢*a*$^{!}$⸣
8 *mi-i-nu ša* LUGAL [*be-lí i-qab-bu-ni*]
9 LUGAL *be-lí liš-p*[*u-ra i—su-ri*]
10 LUGAL *be-lí i-*[*qab-bi*]
11 [*m*]*a-a* ANŠE.KUR.RA.[MEŠ *x x*]
12 [*x x*]*x* ⸢*x*⸣ *x*[*x x x x*]
rest (about 5 lines) broken away
Rev. beginning (about 5 lines) lost
1′ [*x x*]⸢*x x*⸣[*x x x*]
2′ ⸢*ha*⸣-[*nu*$^{?}$-*t*]*e* ŠE.IN.[NU.MEŠ]
3′ *liš-pu-*[*r*]*u*$^{?}$ [*x x x*]
rest uninscribed

ABL 729

1 To the king, my lord: your servant Na'di-ilu. Good health to the king, my lord!

4 Now that the king, my lord, has set out and is coming, should I come as far as Šabirešu to meet the king, my lord? May the king, my lord, wr[ite me] what the king my lo[rd's orders are].

9 [Perhaps] the king, my lord, will s[ay]: "The horses [...]

(Break)

r.2 ... should se[n]d straw [......]

(Rest destroyed)

## 63. Subjugating Bit-Amukani

K 665

1 [*a-na* LUGAL] *be-lí-ia*
2 [ARAD-*ka* $^{m}$]I—DINGIR
3 [*lu šul-mu*] *a-na* LUGAL EN-*ia*
4 [*ina* UGU] $^{m}$⸢*na*⸣-*ṣib*—DINGIR
5 [*ša*] ⸢LUGAL⸣ *be-lí*$^{!}$ ⸢*iš-pur*⸣-*an-ni*
6 [*ma-a i*]*na ša* [*x x x x*]*x*
7 [*x x*] *tu* [*x x x x*]*x*
8 [*x*]*x me x*[*x x x x*]*x*
9 *ina* ⸢*da*$^{!}$⸣-*t*[*i*$^{!}$ EN.NUN-*šú-nu l*]*i-ṣur*
10 *la-áš-šú* [*la i-šá-man*]-*ni*
11 *la* ⸢*ú*⸣-[*pa-har-šú-n*]*u*
12 *ina* É [*ina* IGI LUGAL *be*]-*lí-ia*
13 *la a*[*l-lik-u-ni šu-t*]*ú*$^{?}$
14 *e-rab* [*ina* IGI-*i*]*a*$^{?}$
15 ZAG *u* KAB *a*-⸢*sa-na*⸣-*par-šú*
16 [*ina*] IGI-*ia i-za-az*
17 [*k*]*i-i an-ni-e*
r.1 [LU]GAL *be-lí liš-pur-áš-šu*
2 *ma-a* É—$^{m}$*ú-kan-a-a*
3 *gab-bu pa-hi-ir*
4 *ma-a ina* IGI LÚ*.GAL—KAŠ.LUL
5 *it-zi ma-a mi-nu*
6 *ša i-qa-ba-kan*$^{!}$-*ni e-pu-uš*
7 LUGAL *be-lí e-gír-tú*
8 *ina* UGU $^{m}$MAN—IGI.LAL-*ni*
9 *liš-pu-ra* É—$^{m}$*ú-kan-a-a*
10 *gab-bu lu-pa-hi-ra*
11 *ki-i an-ni-e*

ABL 194

1 [To the king], my lord: [your servant] Na'di-ilu. [Good health] to the king, my lord!

4 [As to] Naṣib-Il [about whom] the king, my lord, wrote me: "In [......]

(Break)

9 "Afterwa[rds, he should k]eep [watch over them]."

10 He does not [obey] me at all and is not [*assembling* th]em.

11 Before I visi[ted the king], my [lo]rd, he used to enter my [court]; I sent him on various errands, and he stayed [in] my presence. Let the king, my lord, write him [as] follows: "Assemble the whole Bit-Amukani, stay with the chief cupbearer, and do whatever he commands you!"

r.7 Let the king, my lord, (also) send a letter to Šarru-emuranni; he should assemble the whole Bit-Amukani and say to them as

**62** Same scribe as in letters of Aššur-dur-paniya! 4,7,12 See coll. r.1ff See coll.

FIG. 14. *The king on the road (reign of Assurnasirpal).*
BM 124557.

12 [*l*]*i-qi-ba-áš-šú-nu*
13 [*ma*] *a*$^{!}$*-ta-a a-na*
14 [$^{m}$*n*]*a*$^{!}$*-ṣib*—DINGIR *ina* UGU *dul-li*
15 [LU]GAL$^{!}$ *la ta-šá-me-a*
16 [*šu*]*-tú iq-ṭi-bi-a*
17 [*ma*]-⌜*a*$^{!}$⌝ LÚ*$^{!}$.ERIM$^{!}$.MEŠ
18 [*la*] *i-šá-mu-u-ni*

follows: "Why do you not obey [N]aṣib-Il regarding the [ki]ng's work?"

16 [H]e told me that the men [do not] obey him.

**63** 4, 9, r.12, 14 See coll.

## 64. Horses from the East

K 146

1 ⸢*a-na* LUGAL⸣ [EN]-⸢*ia*⸣
2 ⸢ARAD-*ka* $^{m}$I—DINGIR⸣
3 ⸢*lu-u* DI-*mu a-na* LUGAL⸣ EN-*ia*
4 UD-2⸢7-KÁM⸣
5 1-*me*-⸢20 ANŠE.KUR⸣.RA *pa-ni-iu-te*
6 *ša* ⸢$^{md}$PA—*rém-a-ni*⸣
7 *ina* URU.*ur-zu-hi-na*
8 *iq-ṭa-ra-bu-u-ni*
9 UD-28-KÁM *ina* ŠÀ-*bi-ma šú-nu*
10 UD-29-KÁM *ú-na-mu-šú*
11 *al-lak ina* URU.*sa-re-e*
12 *ú-še-bir-šú-nu*
13 UD-30$^{!!}$-KÁM
14 *ina* URU.*sa-re-e-ma*
15 *ak-la-šú-nu*
16 *a-di* É
r.1 EGIR.MEŠ
2 *i-qar-bu-u-ni-ni*
3 *i-se-niš* ANŠE.KUR.RA.ME
4 *ga-mu-zu*$^{!}$
5 *lip-šu-hu*
6 *bur-ba-a-ni*

ABL 192

1 To the king, my [lord]: your servant Na'di-ilu. Good health to the king, my lord!

4 The first 120 horses of Nabû-remanni arrived in Arzuhina on the 27th. They will be there for the 28th and set out (again) on the 29th.

11 I shall go and bring them across (the river) to Sarê and keep them in Sarê for the 30th, until the later (horses) reach me.

r.3 *All the same*, the horses have been *heavily pressed*; the *foal*s should rest out.

## 65. An Arrival Report

BM 123359 (1932-12-10,302)

1 *a-na* LUGAL EN-*ia*
2 ARAD-*ka* $^{m}$I—DINGIR
3 *lu-u* DI-*mu*
4 *a-na* LUGAL EN-*ia*
5 UD-11-KÁM
6 *ina* URU.*ha-da-at*$^{!}$-*ti*
7 *a-na-ku*
8 ARAD.MEŠ-*ni ša* LUGAL
9 *ša ina* IGI-*ia*
10 DI-*mu*
Rev. uninscribed

Iraq 7 99

1 To the king, my lord: your servant Na'di-ilu. Good health to the king, my lord!

5 I am in Hadattu on the 11th day; the king's subjects in my command are well.

## 66. Fragment of a Military Report

K 7493

1 [*a-na*] LUGAL [EN-*ia*]
2 [ARAD-*ka*] $^{m}$I—⸢DINGIR⸣
3 [*lu* DI]-*mu a-na* LUGAL [EN-*ia*]

ABL 195

1 [To] the king, [my lord: your servant] Na'di-ilu. [Good] health to the king, [my lord]!

**64** 13 Tablet UD-20-KÁM (scribal error); see coll. r.4, 6 Sic; see coll. Both *ga-mu-zu* and *bur-ba-a-ni* seem to be Aramaic loanwords; cf. Syr. *gmz* "to mangle clothes, press heavily" (Payne Smith, pp. 71f) and *bar bānā* "calf, bullock that has not yet been yoked" (ibid. 53b).
**65** 6 See coll.

4 [*ša* LUGAL] *be-lí iš-*[*pur-an-ni*]
5 [*ma-a* LÚ*.*e*]-⸢*mu*⸣-*qi* ⸢*ša*⸣ L[Ú.*x*]
6 [*x*]*x-šú*$^{?}$ URU.[*x x x*]
rest broken away
Rev. uninscribed

4 [As to what the king], my lord, wr[ote me: "The tr]oops of the [......]
(Rest destroyed)

## 67. Assembling Troops

K 5503 + K 14663

beginning broken away
1′ [*m*]*a-a* [*e-mu-qi-ka*]
2′ [*l*]*u-u pu-*[*uh-ru ár-hiš*]
3′ [[*ina pa-ni-ia al-ka*]]
4′ [LU]GAL *be-lí ú-da*
5′ ⸢*e*⸣*-mu-qi-ia gab-b*[*u*]
6′ [*b*]*a-ta-ba-ti ša* U[RU]
7′ *šu-nu ina* ŠÀ-*bi* 3 [UD.MEŠ]
8′ *i-pa-hu-ru* [*x x*]
9′ *ap-ti-*⸢*qi*⸣*-di* [*x x*]
10′ LÚ*.GAL—É-*i*[*a*]
11′ *e-mu-qi ú-p*[*a-har*]
12′ [*ana*]-*ku* 1 UD-*me mar-*[*di-tú*]
13′ [T]A ŠÀ URU.[*x x x*]
e.14′ [*la*]*l-li-*[*ka x x*]
15′ [*x x x x x*]
r.1 [L]UGAL *be-lí* [*ṭè-e-mu*]
2 [*l*]*iš-kun* [*x x x x*]
3 [*dul*$^{?}$]-*lu ina* UG[U *x x x*]
4 [*x x*] *ra* [*x x x x*]
5 [*x x x*]*x x*[*x x x x*]
rest broken away

CT 53 85

(Beginning destroyed)

1 [As to what the king, my lord, wrote me]: "[Your troops] should be as[sembled; *come to me, quickly*]" –

4 [the ki]ng, my lord, knows that all my troops are around the ci[ty]; they can be assembled within three [days].

9 I have appointed [...]; m[y] major-domo [will] ass[emble] the troops, and I [shall] *co*[*ver*] in one day the *st*[*retch* f]rom the city [... to ...].

r.1 [The k]ing, my lord, should give [orders that ...]

2 [wo]rk on [......]

(Rest destroyed)

## 68. Chariot Troops from Que

K 1213 (ABL 624) + K 14622

1 *a-na* [LUGAL] EN-⸢*ia*⸣
2 ARAD-*ka* $^{m}$[I]—DINGIR
3 *lu-u* DI-*mu a-na* LUGAL EN-*ia*
4 *ina* UGU LÚ*.EN—GIŠ.GIGIR.MEŠ
5 KUR.*qu-ú-a-a ša* LUGAL *be-lí*
6 *iš-pur-an-ni ma-a šá-*⸢ʾ*a*⸣*-al*
7 *ú-ṣi-ṣi šúm-ma* NINDA.[MEŠ-*šú*]-⸢*nu*⸣
8 ŠE.NUMUN.MEŠ-*šú-nu* [*l*]*a-*[*áš-šú*]
9 *ma-a šup-ra* UN.ME[Š *x x x*]
10 *ša i-si-šú-nu* [*x x x x*]
rest broken away
Rev. uninscribed

CT 53 40

1 To [the king], my lord: your servant [Na'di]-ilu. Good health to the king, my lord!

4 As to the chariot troops from Que about whom the king, my lord, wrote to me: "Enquire and investigate, and if they [have no] food and seed, write me" –

9 the people [...] who are with them [......]

(Rest destroyed)

**66** 5f See coll.
**68** 7 See coll.

## 69. On an Army Unit

Sm 333

1 *a-na* LUG[AL EN-*ia*]
2 ARAD-*ka* $^{m}$I—⸢DINGIR⸣
3 *lu-u* DI-*mu a-na* LUGAL EN$^{!}$-*ia*
4 *ina* UGU *ki-iṣ-ri-ia ša be-lí*
5 *iš-pur-an-ni ma-a* ⸢*ki*$^{!}$-*ṣar*$^{!}$⸣-*ka*
6 *ina re-eš ša x*.MEŠ-⸢*ka*⸣
7 *lu-u šá-ki-ni* ⸢*ú*$^{!}$-*ma*$^{!}$⸣-[*a*]
8 DINGIR.MEŠ-*ni ša* [LUG]AL *e*-⸢*tap*⸣-*šú*
9 *a-ki* LUGAL *be*-[*lí*] ⸢*ip*$^{?}$-*qi*$^{?}$⸣-[*da*]-*ni-ni*
10 *a-na e-ta*-[*qi x x x x x*]
11 *ú-la-a a*-[*x x x x x*]
12 *ina* UGU ⸢$^{m!}$⸣*ki-ṣ*[*ir*$^{?}$—*aš-šur x x x*]
13 *ina* UGU *dul-l*[*i x x x x x*]
14 *ša* LUGAL *i*[*š-pur-an-ni x x*]
15 *la-a-šú* LU[GAL$^{!}$ *x x x x x*]
16 ŠÀ-*bi* LU[GAL$^{!}$ EN-*ia lu-u* DÙG.GA]
rest broken away
Rev. beginning broken away
lines 1-2 unreadable
3′ PAB [*x x x x x x*]*x*
4′ [*x x*] ⸢*a*⸣-*a* ⸢*x*⸣ *nu ti*
5′ *ù* LÚ*.⸢GAL⸣.MEŠ *mar ša*
6′ *i-la-ku-ni-ni*
7′ GUD.MEŠ *a-na ma-za-si*
8′ *ina pa-na-tú-šú-nu*
9′ *ú-šá-za-zu*
rest uninscribed

CT 53 125

1 To the kin[g, my lord]: your servant Na'di-ilu. Good health to the king, my lord!

4 As to my army unit about which my lord wrote me: "Your unit should be placed at the head of your ...!" —

7 now the gods of the [kin]g have taken action: when the king, [my] lo[rd *appoin*]*ted* me, [......] to mo[ve on].

11 Otherwise, [......] to Kiṣ[ir-Aššur].

13 As to the wor[k ...] about which the king w[rote me], there is no [...]; the ki[ng ......]. The king, [my lord, can be] gl[ad].

(Break)

r.5 Further, they will make the oxen *stand in position* before all the magnates who are coming.

## 70. Fragment Referring to Oxen

K 4701

1 *a-na* LUGAL EN-[*ia*]
2 ARAD-*ka* $^{m}$I—[DINGIR]
3 *lu-u* DI-*mu a-n*[*a* LUGAL EN-*ia*]
4 *ina* UGU GUD.MEŠ
5 *pi-qi-tú ša ina* IGI-*i*[*a*]
6 *ša* LUGAL *be-lí* [0]
7 [*ṭ*]*e-e*-⸢*mu*⸣ [*iš-kun-an-ni*]
8 [*x x*]*x*[*x x x x x*]
rest broken away
Rev. destroyed

ABL 1018

1 To the king, [my] lord: your servant Na'di-[ilu]. Good health t[o the king, my lord]!

4 As to the oxen entrusted in m[y] charge about which the king, my lord, [gave me or]ders [......]

(Rest destroyed)

## 71. An Axe Maker from Damascus

K 542

1 *a-na* LUGAL EN-[*ia*]
2 ARAD-*ka* $^{m}$I—DINGIR
3 *lu-u* DI-*mu a-na* LUGAL
4 EN-*ia*

ABL 193

1 To the king, [my] lord: your servant Na'di-ilu. Good health to the king, my lord!

**69** 5ff, 9, 12, 16 See coll.

5 *ina* ⸢UGU⸣ $^{m}$*ši-im-ka-ia*
6 LÚ*.[NA]GAR!—*pa-*⸢*a*⸣*-ši*
7 URU.⸢*di*⸣*-maš-qa-a-a*
8 *ša* [LUGAL] *be-lí*
9 ⸢*iš-pur-an*⸣*-ni*
10 ⸢*an-nu-rig*⸣
11 *ina* ŠU.2 LÚ*.A—KIN-*ia*
12 [*ina*] *pa-an* LUGAL
13e [E]N-*ia*
r.1 ⸢*ú*⸣*-se-bi-la-šú*

5 As to Šimkaya, the axe [m]aker from Damascus whom [the king], my lord, wrote me about, I am herewith sending him to the king, my [lo]rd, in the charge of my messenger.

## 72. Returning from the River

Sm 1821

1 [*a-na* LUG]AL *be-l*[*í-ia*]
2 [ARAD-*ka*] $^{m}$⸢I?⸣—[DINGIR]
3 [*lu šul*]-*mu a-n*[*a* LUGAL EN-*ia*]
4 [*ina* UGU] LÚ*.*i-*[*tu-ʾa-a-a*]
5 [*ša* TA U]GU Í[D.*pu-rat-ti*?]
6 [*is-hu-r*]*u-u-ni* [*x x x*]
7 [*x x x*]*x-ni* ⸢*ma*⸣-[*a x x x*]
rest broken away
Rev. destroyed

CT 53 852

1 [To the kin]g, [my] lo[rd: your servant] Na'di-[ilu. Good hea]lth t[o the king, my lord]!

4 [As to] the I[tu'eans who return]ed [fr]om the ri[ver *Euphrates* ......]

(Rest destroyed)

## 73. ———

K 16050

1 [*a-na* LUGAL *be-lí-ia*]
2 [ARAD-*ka* $^{m}$*x x x x x*]
3 [*lu* DI-*mu a-na* LUGAL *be*]-⸢*lí-i*⸣*a*
4 [*x x x x x x x*] *a*
5 [*x x x x x x*] *še*
6 [*x x x x x ú*]-*ba-la-ni*
7 [*x x x x* UD-*x*]-KÁM
8 [*x x x x x x*] URU.*šá-bi-r*[*i-š*]*ú*
9 [*x x x x x x*]-*z*[*u*]
rest broken away
Rev. uninscribed

CT 53 729

1 [To the king, my lord: your servant NN. Good health to the king], my [lo]rd!

4f [......]

6 [......] is bringing
7 [...... on the ...th] day
8 [......] Šabirešu
9 [... ente]red
(Rest destroyed)

**71** 6 See coll.

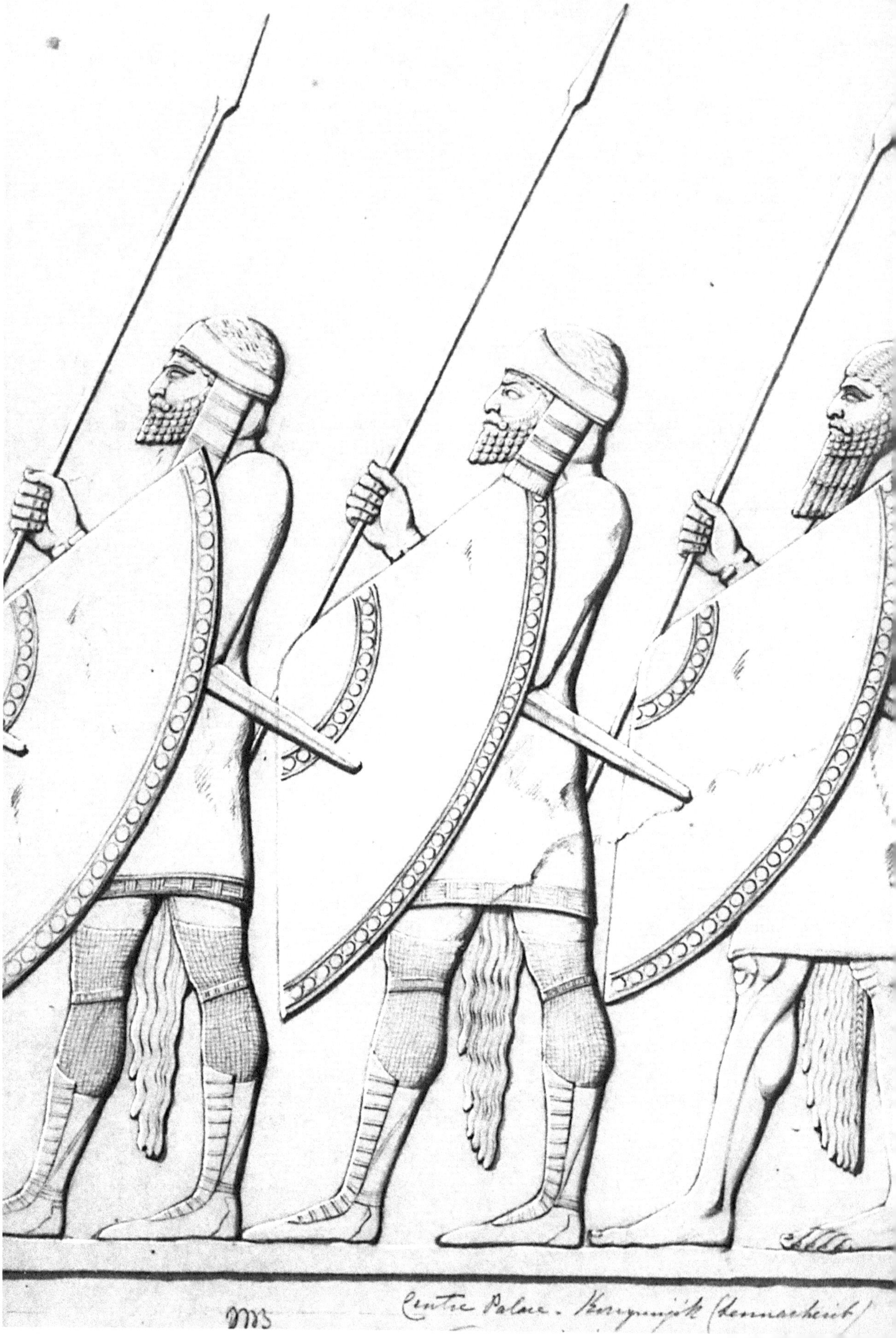
Centre Palace. Kouyunjik (Sennacherib)

# 5. Varia



FIG. 15. *Troops from different provinces in the Assyrian king's bodyguard (reign of Sennacherib).* ORIGINAL DRAWING VI, 34.

## 74. Mule Express not Available

ND 2367

1 *a-na* LUGAL *be-lí-ia*
2 ARAD-*ka* $^{m}$*mah-de-e*
3 *lu-u* DI-*mu a-na* MAN EN-*ia*

---

4 *kal-li-ú ša ni-*[*d*]*a-nu-ni*
5 LÚ*.*q*[*u*]*r-*[*b*]*u-ti ša il-lak-*[*an-n*]*i*
6 *ma-a* [*a*]*-bat* MAN *ši-i-ti*
7 *ma-a a-di* URU.*šá-bi-ri-šú*
8 *lil-lik* A[NŠ]E$^{?}$ *ša ina* (IGI)-*ia*
9 *u*[*g-d*]*a-me-*[*r*]*a* LUGAL *be-lí*
10 *ú-da a-di* URU.*šá-bi-ri-šú*
11 *ú-ru-u la ú-k*[*al-la*]
12 *ša il-l*[*ak*]*-ú-n*[*i*]
13 *la i-sa-hur-ú-ni*
e.14 ANŠE.*ú-ra-te-ia*
15 [*g*]*am-mu-ra*
r.1 LUGAL *be-lí lu ú-da*
2 [*š*]*a* URU.*kal-ha* ⸢*ú-rat*⸣.MEŠ
3 *nu-še-taq* GIŠ.GIG[IR]
4 *ú-ra-a-a* LÚ*.*mu-*[*kil*—KUŠ.P]A.M[EŠ-*ia*]
5 $^{md}$PA-*u-a* [LÚ*.*q*]*ur-bu-ti*
6 *a-di* U[RU.*šá*]*-bi-ri-šú*
7 *i-tal-*[*ku š*]*a* U[R]U.*š*[*á*]*-bi-ri-šú*
8 *ú-s*[*e-ti-q*]*u* LUGAL *be-lí*
9 *li*[*š-ʾa-a*]*l liš-pu-ra*
10 *m*[*a-a*] *al-*[*k*]*a ina* GÌR.2.ME-*ia*
11 *al-la-ka la-a* GIŠ.GIGIR
12 *la ú-ra-a-a*
13 *la-a* LÚ*.*mu-kil*—KUŠ.PA.MEŠ-*ia*

NL 62

1 To the king, my lord: your servant Mahdê. Good health to the king, my lord!

---

4 (As to) the mule express that we provide and the royal bodyguard who com[es] citing a royal order that he should go as far as Šabirešu — he has used up the [...] in my possession!

6 The king, my lord, knows that I do not main[tain] a team (to go) as far as Šabirešu; the ones that go do not return. My teams are used up; the king, my lord, should know (this).

r.2 We let the teams from Calah go by; my chariot, my team and [my] [dri]ver went (with) Nabû'a the bodyguard as far as Šabirešu, and those of Šabirešu le[t them go] by.

6 Let the king, my lord, inve[stigate]; let him send word that I come, and I shall come on foot! I have no chariot, no team, no driver!

## 75. News from Šubria

K 1211

1 *a-na* LUGAL *be-lí-*⸢*ia*⸣
2 ARAD-*ka* $^{m}$*mah-de-e*
3 *lu* DI-*mu a-na* LUGAL EN-*ia*
4 *ina* UGU [LÚ*.MA]H$^{?}$ KUR.*šub-ri-a-a*
5 *ša* [LUGAL *be-lí iš-p*]*ur-an-ni*
6 *m*[*a*$^{!}$*-a x x x x x x x x x*] *x*
rest destroyed
Rev. uninscribed

ABL 987

1 To the king, my lord: your servant Mahdê. Good health to the king, my lord!

4 As to the Šubrian [*emiss*]*ary* about which [the king, my lord, wro]te me: "[......]"

(Rest destroyed)

**74** → no. 227. Mahdê may be writing here as governor of Nineveh, an office he is known to have held in the reign of Shalmaneser V (year 725).

**75** 4 See coll.

## 76. ———

K 14672

1 [*a-na* LUGAL *be*]-*lí-ia*
2 [ARAD-*ka* $^{m}$*ma*]*h-de-e*
3 [*lu* DI-*mu*] ⸢*a*⸣-[*n*]*a* LUGAL EN-⸢*ia*⸣
4 [*x x x x x x x x*]*x* [*x*]
rest broken away
Rev. destroyed

CT 53 578

1 [To the king], my [lo]rd: [your servant Ma]hdê. [Good health] to the king, my lord!
(Rest destroyed)

## 77. ———

Sm 1675

Obv. destroyed
Rev. beginning broken away
1′ ⸢2⸣ UTÚL 3 [*x x*]
2′ *ma-a ina* KUR.*šub-r*[*i-a-a*]
3′ *at-ti-di-*[*ni*]

---

rest uninscribed

CT 53 847

(Beginning destroyed)
1 "I have giv[en] two pots and three [...s] to the Šubr[ian]."

---

## 78. Imposing the King's Treaty

K 669

1 *a-na* LUGAL EN-*ia*
2 ARAD-*ka* $^{m}$*aš-šur*—EN—KALAG-*in*
3 *lu-u* DI-*mu a-na* LUGAL EN-*iá*
4 URU.LÚ*.*uš-ha-a-a*
5 URU.LÚ*.*qu-da-a-a*
6 *ša* LUGAL EN-*lí ina* UGU-*hi-šú-nu*
7 *iš-pur-an-ni*
8 *ina* UGU *pe-e ša* LUGAL EN-*iá*
9 *ih-ta-an-šú*
10 URU.MEŠ-*ni ša* UD.MEŠ
11 *ša* $^{md}$UTU—DINGIR-*a-a*
12 *la ha-an-šu-ni*
13 *ú-ma-a an-nu-rig*
14 LÚ*.*qur-bu-te up-ta-hi-i*[*r*]
15 *ina* UGU-*hi-ia na-ṣa*!!
16 *ú-sa-li-im-šú-nu*
e.17 *ša il-ka-šú-ni*
r.1 *il-ku-šu i-ti-*[*din*]
2 *ša* LÚ*.ERIM.MEŠ—MAN-*šu-*[*ni*]
3 LÚ*.ERIM.MEŠ—MAN *i-ti-*[*din*]
4 KUR-*ú gab-bu* ⸢*a*⸣-[*de-e*]
5 LUGAL *i-ta-ṣar* [0]
6 ŠÀ-*bu* LUGAL EN-*iá l*[*u* DÙG.GA]
7 LÚ*.*e-mu-qi* [*šu-n*]*u*
8 *ša ina* IGI-*ia lu-ra-*[*mi-š*]*ú-nu*
9 *ú-la-a ma-*⸢*ṣar*⸣-*tú* [0]
10 *li-ṣu-ur* [0!]

ABL 246

1 To the king, my lord: your servant Aššur-belu-da''in. Good health to the king, my lord!

4 The Ušhaeans and Qudaeans about whom the king, my lord, wrote me, have submitted to the king my lord's command; (these) towns which were not submissive in the days of Šamaš-ila'i, the royal bodyguard has now assembl[ed] and brought over to me.

16 I have made peace with them. Those obliged to provide labour have provided it, and those obliged to provide king's men have provided them.

r.4 The whole mountain (area) has observed the king's tr[eaty]; the king, my lord, ca[n be glad].

7 Shall I relea[se] the troops at my disposal, or should they (continue to) keep the watch?

**76** This fragment does not join no. 105.
**78** → TCAE p. 270. r.10 See coll.

11 URU.*mu-ma-a-a* [0]
12 *i-ba-ši la ha-an-šú-ti*
13 *la-li-ki ina* UGU *pe-e* LUGAL
14 *is-si-šú-nu la-da-bu-ub*
15 *ú-la-a mi-nu ša* LUGAL
16e *i-qab-bu-u-ni*
17e *liq-bi*

11 The Mumaeans are unsubmissive; shall I go and negotiate with them about the king's command? If not, let the king, my lord, tell me what his orders are.

## 79. Capturing Runaways

K 513

1 *a-na* LUGAL EN-*ia*
2 ARAD-*ka* $^{m}$*aš-šur*—EN—KALAG-*in*
3 *lu-u* DI-*mu a-na* LUGAL EN-*ia*
4 LÚ*.*ša*—É—*ku-din*
5 *ša ina* UGU UN.MEŠ KUR *hal-qu-te*
6 *ú-še-ṣa-an-ni*
7 LÚ*.ERIM.MEŠ TA* *ba-ta-ba-ti-ia*
8 *ú-se-ṣi-a i-ta-an-na*
9 KUR.*hal-zi*—AD.BAR-*a-a*
10 *gab-bi-šú-nu ma-aʾ-da*
11 *hal-qu ina* ŠÀ-*bi* KUR.MEŠ
12 *gab-bu šu-nu*
13 LÚ*.*ša*—É—*ku-din*
14 *da-li-ih ma-a* KASKAL
15 *ka-ri-im an-nu-rig*
16 $^{md}$PA-*ú-a*
r.1 LÚ*.*ša*—É—*ku-din*
2 *ša ina* IGI LÚ*.*kal-da-a-a*
3 *pa-qi-du-ú-ni*
4 3-*me*-80 ZI.MEŠ *na-aṣ-ṣa*
5 TA* ŠÀ-*bi-šú-nu ina* ŠÀ KUR.*ia-su*$^{!}$-*me*
6 *ina* ŠÀ KUR.É—*za-ma-ni*
7 *re-e-hu e-gír-tú*
8 *ina* UGU-*hi-šú liš-pur-ú-ni*
9 *ki-i ša* KUR.*kal-da-*[*a-a*]
10 *ú-še-ṣa-an-ni ú-ga-m*[*ar*$^{!}$-*u-n*]*i*
11 *ki-i ša* UN.MEŠ KUR *hal-qu-te*
12 *ú-pa-har-an-ni*
13 *ú-bal-an-ni*

ABL 245

1 To the king, my lord: your servant Aššur-belu-da''in. Good health to the king, my lord!

4 The *mule stable attendant* whom I brought forth in search of the runaway people of the country has brought forth men from my neighbourhood and given them to me. All Halziatbareans have run away in great numbers and are (scattered) all over the *countries*. The *mule stable attendant* is desperate, saying: "*It is an impasse.*"

15 Now Nabû'a, the *mule stable attendant* who was appointed in charge of the Chaldeans, has brought me 380 persons; a number of them remain in Yasumu and in Bit-Zamani.

r.7 Let them send him a letter (telling him) how he is to bring forth the Chaldea[ns] compl[etely], and how he is to assemble the runaway people of the country and bring them to me.

## 80. Building a Fort and Houses for Deportees

K 1027

1 *a-na* LUGAL EN-*ia*
2 ARAD-*ka* $^{m}$*aš-šur*—EN—KALAG-*in*
3 *lu-u* DI-*mu a-na* LUGAL EN-*ia*
4 *a-na* URU.*bi-ra-a-te*
5 *a-na* [*m*]*a-ṣar*$^{!}$-*te*
6 *ša* LUGAL EN-*ia* DI-*mu*
7 ˹*dul*˺-*lu ša* URU.HAL.ṢU
8 [*ša ina* Š]À$^{!}$ MURUB$_{4}$ URU
9 [*x x x*] 2 LÚ

ABL 247

1 To the king, my lord: your servant Aššur-belu-da''in. Good health to the king, my lord!

4 The forts and the [ga]rrison of the king, my lord, are well.

7 The work on the fort [i]n the centre of the town [...]. Two men [......]

(Break)

**79** 11 Or "all over the mountains." 14f Or "the campaign is delayed" (J. N. Postgate). r.5 W 96.
**80** 8 See coll.

FIG. 16. *Chaldean prisoners (reign of Assurbanipal).*
BM 124945.

rest broken away
Rev. beginning broken away
1′ [*x x x x x*] ⸢LUGAL⸣
2′ [EN.NUN *i-na-ṣ*]*u-ru*
3′ LÚ*.*kal-da-a-a*
4′ É.MEŠ-*šú-nu i-ra-ṣi-pu*
5′ UD-20-KÁM *ša* ITI.KIN
6′ *ina* UGU $SIG_4$.MEŠ
7′ *ú-ta-me-di*

r.1 [...... the ... *of*] the king [ke]ep [the watch]. The Chaldeans are building their houses.

5 On the 20th of Elul (VI) I started working on the bricks.

## 81. A Case Against the Governor

AO 4506

1 IM $^{m}$*aš-šur*—NUMUN—DÙ
2 *a-na* $^{m}$U.GUR—KAR-*ir* PAB-*u-a*
3 DI-*mu a-a-ši*
4 *lu-u* DI-*mu a-na* PAB-*u-a*
5 *ú-ma-a an-nu-*[*rí*]*g*
6 LÚ*.A—KIN-*ia i-la-ka*
7 *ina* UGU-*hi* LÚ*.GAL—SAG
8 *it-tal-ka ina* UGU-*hi*
9 *de-ni ša* LÚ*.EN.NAM
10 *ša* KUR.*hal-zi*—AD.BAR
11 *ina* UGU-*hi* URU.*e-hi-man-a-a*
12 *ma-a* LÚ*.ARAD.MEŠ-*ia*
13 *at-tu-ú-ni*
14 *ú-ma-a* LÚ*.A—KIN
15 [*ina*] ⸢UGU⸣-*hi* LÚ*.GAL—[SAG]
16 ⸢*il-lak*⸣-*a*
17 *it-*[*x x*]-*si-i*
r.1 [*a*]*t-ta* [*x*] *mu u ku mi*
2 *a-na ma-ni-ma šup-ra*

TCL 9 68

1 A tablet of Aššur-zeru-iddina to Nergal-eṭir. I am well; may my brother be well.

5 My messenger is n[ow] on his way to the chief eunuch. He has left on account of the claim of the governor of Halziatbar concerning the Ehi*man*eans: "You are my servants!"

14 Now that the messenger is going to the chief [eunuch, ...];

r.1 You [...]; write to anybody!

**81** 11 Cf. SAAB 2 (1988) 16 r.1 and 3 (1989) 66 r.13; the name may also be read Ehiniš, cf. URU.*Ši-ib-hi-niš/ni-iš* (AOAT 6 s.v. Šibṭiniš).

3 *la-a* ŠEŠ-*a-a* ⸢*at*⸣-*ta-a*
4 *mi-nu šá ṭè-mu-u-ni*
5 PAB-*u-a li-iš-pur*

3 Are you not my brother? Let my brother write (me) whatever the news (may be).

## 82. Paying the Corn Tax

K 4306

1 *a-na* LUGAL EN-*ia*
2 ARAD-*ka* $^{m}$DI-*mu*—EN—*la-áš-me*
3 *lu* DI-*mu a-na* LUGAL EN-*ia*
4 *ina* UGU *ša* LUGAL *b*[*e-lí*]
5 *iš-pur-a-ni* [*ma-a si-mìn*]
6 ŠE.NUMUN.MEŠ [*a-ra-ši*]
7 *e-te-te-q*[*i ma-a*]
8 *te-lit ad-r*[*a-te a-le-e*$^{?}$]
9 53 LÚ*.[*x x x x x*]
10 *ú-šá*-[*x x x x x*]
11 [*x*]*x*[*x x x x x x*]
rest broken away
Rev. beginning broken away
1′ [*ma*]-*a a-na* [*x x x x x*]
2′ *ú-ma-a* [*x x x x x x*]
3′ LÚ*.*mu-šar*-[*kis x x x x*]
4′ *e-ta-x*[*x x x x x x*]
5′ *la-a*$^{!}$ ŠE.*tab*-[*ku x x x x x*]
6′ 30 ANŠE.KUR.RA.MEŠ [*x x x*]
7′ ⸢*ša*$^{!}$⸣ LUGAL EN-*i*[*a x x x*]
8′ [LÚ*.*qu*]*r*$^{!}$-*bu-te* ⸢*i*$^{!}$⸣-[*x x x*]
9′ [*an-n*]*u-rig* $^{m}$*man-nu*—GIM—PAB.MEŠ$^{!}$
10′ [LÚ*.*qu*]*r-bu-te ša* ŠE.*nu-sa-hi*
11′ [*is-s*]*u-hu-u-ni* LUGAL EN-*i*$^{!}$
12e [*liš*]-*al-šu šúm-mu* (ŠE).PAD.MEŠ
13e *i-ba-šú-u-ni*

ABL 1012

1 To the king, my lord: your servant Šulmu-beli-lašme. Good health to the king, my lord!

4 As to what the king, [my] l[ord], wrote to me: "[The time for cultivating] the fields has elaps[ed; *where is*] the yield of the thresh[ing-floor]?" —

9 53 [......]

(Break)

r.1 "to [......]." Now [NN],

2 the recruitment offi[cer ...]

3 ha[s ......]

4 neither stored [grain *nor* ...]

6 30 horses [...]

7 of the king, m[y] lord, [...]

8 [the royal] bodyguard [...].

9 [N]ow, the king, my lord, [should a]sk Mannu-ki-ahhe, the [roy]al bodyguard who [extra]cted the corn-tax, whether there is any barley (here).

## 83. Fragment of a Military Report

K 1042

1 *a-na* LU[GAL *be*]-⸢*lí*⸣-*ia*
2 ARAD-*ka* $^{md}$PA—MAN—PAB
3 *lu* DI-*mu a-na* LUGAL *be-lí-ia*
4 LÚ*.*da-a-a-li-ia*
5 [T]A É-*a-ni it-tu-ṣu-u-ni*
6 [*ki-i an*]-⸢*ni-e*⸣ *iq-ṭí-bu-u-ni*
rest broken away
Rev. beginning broken away
1′ [*x x x x x x x x*]*x*
2′ *ša a-na* LUGAL *be-lí-iá áš-pur-a-ni*
3′ *nu-uk* LÚ*.EN.NAM *an-ni-u*
4′ *a-na* KUR.*ki-ir-me-si* KUR-*e*
5e *i-tal-ka la-áš-šú*
6e *la il-li-ka*
7e *am*$^{!}$-*ma-kam-ma šu-u*

ABL 769

1 To the ki[ng], my [lo]rd: your servant Nabû-šarru-uṣur. Good health to the king, my lord!

4 My scouts have come out [fr]om the Interior and reported to me [as foll]ows: "[......]"

(Break)

r.2 As to what I wrote the king, my lord: "This governor has come to Mount Kirmesi" — it is not so, he has not come but is still there.

**82** → TCAE p.293f. 6, r.4, r.9 See coll. r.11 EN-*i*$^{!}$ sic, see coll.
**83** r.7 Tablet QAR-*ma-kam-ma*; scribal error.

# Letters from the Urarṭian Frontier

# 6. Letters from Kumme and Ukku



FIG. 17. *Assyrian soldiers in hill country (reign of Sennacherib).*
ORIGINAL DRAWING VI, 13.

## 84. The Mannean King Raids Urarṭian Cities

81-2-4,55

1 *a-na* LUGAL EN-*ia*
2 ARAD-*ka* $^{m}$*aš-šur—re-ṣu-u-a*
3 *lu-u šul-mu a-na* LUGAL EN-*iá*
4 KUR.*man-a-a i-na* ŠÀ URU.MEŠ-*ni*
5 *ša* KUR.URI-*a-a*
6 *i—na-gi-e ša šid-di*
7 *ti-amat i-zu-qu-pu*
8 *i-ti-ši e-te-li*
9 $^{m}$*a-ba*$^{!}$*-lu-qu-nu* LÚ*.EN.NAM
10 *ša* URU.*mu-ṣa-ṣi-ri*
11 $^{m}$*ṭu-un-ba*$^{!}$*-un* LÚ*.EN.NAM
12 *ša* ⸢URU⸣.*kar-si-par-*[*ri*]
r.1 *i-na* UGU *ta-hu-m*[*e*]
2 *ša* KUR.*man-a-a i-tal-ku*
3 *a-na ma-ṣar-te*
4 KUR.URI-*a-a*
5 *i-na* URU.*ṭu-ru-uš-pa-a šu-u*
6 UDU.SISKUR.MEŠ-*šú e-pa-áš*
7 LÚ*.EN.NAM.MEŠ *gab-bu*
8 *i—pa-ni-šú šu-nu*

ABL 381

1 To the king, my lord: your servant Aššur-reṣuwa. Good health to the king, my lord!

4 The Mannean has attacked the Urarṭian cities in the district along the lake shore but has left and gone up (the mountains).

9 Abaluqunu, the governor of Muṣaṣir, and Ṭunbaun, the governor of Kar-sipar[ri], have gone to the Mannean border, to guard (it).

r.4 The Urarṭian is in Ṭurušpâ, making his sacrifices. All the governors are with him.

## 85. Spying on the Urarṭian Capital

K 1907

1 *a-na* LUGAL *be-lí-iá* ARAD-*ka* $^{m}$*aš-šur—re-ṣu-u-a*
2 ⸢*lu* DI-*mu*⸣ *a-na* LUGAL *be-lí-iá*
3 ⸢*ša* LUGAL⸣ *be-lí iš-pur-an-ni ma-a* LÚ*.*da-a-a-li-ka*
4 ⸢*a*⸣-[*n*]*a qa-an*$^{!}$*-ni* URU.*ṭu-ur-uš-pa-a šu-pu-ur*
5 *ma-*⸢*a ṭè-e*⸣*-mu har-ṣu liš-ul-lu*
6 *x*[*x x x x*]*x*[*x*]*x*[*x x x*]
rest broken away
Rev. beginning broken away
1′ ⸢4$^{!}$ LÚ*⸣.NAM.MEŠ *ina* ŠÀ URU.[*ṭu-ur-uš-pa-a*]
2′ *ú-ra-du-ni dul-lu* ⸢*e*$^{!}$⸣-[*pu-šu*]
rest uninscribed

ABL 148

1 To the king, my lord: your servant Aššur-reṣuwa. Good health to the king, my lord!

3 As to what the king, my lord, wrote me: "Send your spies to the environs of Ṭurušpâ to find out a detailed report!"

(Break)

r.1 [Fo]ur governors are coming down to [*Ṭurušpâ*] *to do service* (in the temple).

**84** → Deller Zagros p.117. → no. 131. With regard to its orthography and scribal hand, this tablet differs considerably from the other letters of Aššur-reṣuwa. 9,11 See coll. 12 Break with room for *-ri* at end of line.
**85** 4, r.1 Y 77, W 66. r.2 See coll. For the translation cf. nos. 84 r.5ff and 147:11f; "to perform work" is also possible.

## 86. The Army of Urarṭu on the March

81-2-4,60

1 [*a-na* LU]GAL *be-lí-*⸢*ia*⸣
2 [ARAD-*ka*] $^{m}$*aš-šur—re-ṣu-u-a*
3 [*lu* D]I-*mu a-na* LUGAL *be-lí-ia*
4 [*ina* S]AG.DU ITI *ša* ITI.BARAG
5 [LUG]AL KUR.URI-*a-a* TA* URU.*ṭu-ur-uš-pa-*[*a*]
6 *it-tu-ṣi a-na* URU.*el-iz-za-da*
7 ⸢*i*⸣*-tal-lak* $^{m}$SAG.DU-*a-nu*
8 LÚ.*tur-ta-nu-šu ina* ŠÀ
9 URU.*ú-e-si i-tal-lak*
10 ⸢L⸣Ú.*e-muq-qi ša* KUR.URI
11 *gab-bu de-et* LUGAL
12 [*a*]*-na* URU.*el-iz-za-du*
13 [*i*]*-ra-di-a i—su-ri*
14 LUGAL *be-lí i-qab-bi*
r.1 [*ma-a a*]*-ke-e*
2 [*šak-na ú-d*]*i-na*
3 [*ṭè-e-mu l*]*a áš-me*
4 [*x x x*]-⸢*ni*⸣
rest uninscribed

ABL 492

1 [To the ki]ng, my lord: [your servant] Aššur-reṣuwa. [Good hea]lth to the king, my lord!

4 [The ki]ng of Urarṭu has left Ṭurušpâ [on the fir]st of Nisan (I) and gone to Elizzada. Kaqqadanu, his commander-in-chief, has gone to Waisi. The whole Urarṭian army is marching [t]o Elizzada, following the king.

13 Perhaps the king, my lord, will say: "[H]ow [*are they positioned*]?" —

r.3 I have [n]ot heard [any report ... y]et.

## 87. The Urarṭian Troops Concentrate in Waisi

K 645

1 [*a-na* LUGAL EN-*ia*]
2 [ARAD-*ka* $^{m}$*aš-šur—re-ṣu-u-a*]
3 [*lu* D]I-⸢*mu*⸣ *a-na* LUGAL E[N-*ia*]
4 [5] LÚ*.EN.NAM.MEŠ *ša* KUR.URI-[*a-a*]
5 *ina* ŠÀ URU.*ú-e-si e-ta*[*r-bu*]
6 $^{m}$*se-ti-nu* LÚ*.EN.NAM *ša p*[*u*!-*t*]*u*!-⸢*ni*⸣
7 $^{m}$*kaq-qa-da-nu ša pu-tu* [0]
8 KUR.*ú-ka-a-a* $^{m}$*sa-ku-a-ta-a*
9 *ša* KUR.*qa-ni-un* $^{m}$*si-ip-li-a*
10 *ša* KUR.*al-zi* $^{m}$*ṭu-ki*!
11 *ša* KUR.*ár-mir-a-li-u*
12 *an-nu-te* MU.MEŠ-*šú-nu*
13 TA* ⸢3!⸣ LÚ*.EN—*pir-ri*
14 *ina* ŠÀ-*bi* URU.*ú-e-si*
15 *e-tar-bu ú-ma-a*
16 *i—da-tu-šu-nu*
17 *ul-lu-a-te* KUR *ú-tu-li-u*
18 LÚ*.*e-mu-qi i-kal-*⸢*lu*?-*u*?⸣
19 LUGAL TA* ŠÀ URU.*ṭu-ur-*⸢*uš*⸣-[*pa*]-*a*
20 *i-tu-ṣi*
r.1 *ina* ŠÀ URU.⸢*ha*?⸣-*za*!-*un*
2 *i-tal-lak*
3 *ša* LUGAL *be-lí iš-pur-an-ni*
4 *ma-a* LÚ*.*da-a-a-li šu-pur*

ABL 444

1 [To the king, my lord: your servant Aššur-reṣuwa. Good] health to the king, [my] lo[rd]!

4 [Five] governors of the Urarṭ[ian] have ent[ered] Waisi: Setinu, the governor o[p-po]site us; Kaqqadanu, the one opposite the Ukkeans; Sakuatâ of Qaniun; Siplia of Alzi; Ṭuki of Armiraliu: these are their names.

13 They have entered Waisi with three *unit* commanders. Now, after their (arrival), they have raised the *levies* of the country, and are keeping the army *in readiness*.

19 The king has moved out of Ṭuruš[p]â and gone to *Wazaun*.

r.3 As to what the king, my lord, wrote me: "Send out scouts!" — I have sent them twice:

**86** → Deller Zagros p.103. r.3 The preterite rarely occurs after *udīna/i* in lieu of the present tense, but is also attested in no. 112:7, SAA I 225:6 and 255 r.3. r.4 See coll.
**87** → Deller Zagros p.103. Hand of Aššur-reṣuwa. 6, 10, 13, r.1 See coll.

5 *a-na* 2-*šú a-sa-par*
6 *i-se-nu-te i-tal-ku-ni*
7 *di-ib-bi an-nu-te iq-ṭí-bu-ni*
8 *i-se-nu-te-ma ú-di-na*
9 *la ú-ṣu-ni*

the first have come back and told me these things; the others have not yet come out.

## 88. The Urarṭian Troops Set out to Muṣaṣir

Rm 2,3

1 *a-na* LUGAL ⸢*be*⸣-[*lí-iá*]
2 ARAD-*ka* $^{m}$*aš-šur—re-ṣu-u-a*
3 *lu* DI-*mu a-na* LUGAL *be-lí-iá*
4 3-*lim* LÚ*.ERIM.MEŠ GÌR.2.MEŠ
5 LÚ*.GAR-*nu-te* LÚ*.GAL—*kal-lab*.MEŠ
6 *ša* $^{m}$*se-e-ti-ni* LÚ*.EN.NAM
7 *ša pu-tu-u-a*! *a-na* URU.*mu-ṣa-ṣir*
8 *ú-ta-me-šu* ÍD.MI
9 *e-tab-ru* ANŠE.*a-ṣap-pu-šú*
10 ⸢*n*⸣*am*!*—ma-la ša* $^{m}$*se-e-ti-ni*
11 *ina*! *pa-ni-šu šu-ú*
12 *ša* $^{m}$*su-na-a*
13 LÚ*.EN.NAM
r.1 *ša pu-ut* KUR.*ú-ka-a-a*

ABL 380

[1] To the king, [my] lo[rd]: your servant Aššur-reṣuwa. Good health to the king, my lord!

[4] 3,000 *foot soldiers*, their prefects, and the commanders of the *kallāpu* troops of Setini, the governor opposite me, have set out towards Muṣaṣir and crossed the Black River. All the pack animals of Setini are with him.

**88** → Deller Zagros p.107. [7] W 144. [8] Black River: probably Gadar Chai.

FIG. 18. *Urarṭian troops (reign of Shalmaneser III).*
BM 124652.

2 LÚ*.ERIM.MEŠ-*šu*
3 *ú-ta-mi-šu-ma*
4 *a-na* URU.*mu-ṣa-ṣir*
5 *a-se-me ma-a* LUGAL
6 *ina* ŠÀ URU.*ú-e-si*
7 *il-lak ú-di-na*
8 *la ú-nam-maš*

12 The troops of Sunâ, the governor opposite Ukku, have also set out towards Muṣaṣir.

r.5 I have heard that the king is in Waisi; he will be going but has not yet departed.

## 89. The King of Muṣaṣir Taken to Urarṭu

80-7-19,30

1 *a-na* [LUG]AL [EN-*ia*]
2 ARAD-*ka* [ᵐ*aš-šur—re-ṣu-u-a*]
3 *lu* DI-*mu a-*[*na* LUGAL EN-*ia*]
4 URU.HAL.ṢU [*ina* URU.*x x*]
5 TA* *pa-an* ᵐ*kaq*!*-q*[*a*!*-da-ni*]
6 LÚ*.EN.NAM *ep-p*[*u-šu*]
7 ⸢*a*⸣-[*n*]*a*! ᵐ*ur-za-a-ni* [LUGAL]
8 ⸢*ša*!⸣ KUR.*mu-ṣa-ṣi*[*r iṣ-ṣa-bat*]
9 [L]Ú.UN.MEŠ-*šú i*[*k-ti-rik*]
10 ⸢*ina*⸣ ŠÀ *ú-e-si* [*ú-se-rib*]
11 ᵐ*a-ri-ṣa-a ina* UG[U *x x x*]
12 ⸢*i*!⸣*-lak* ᵐ*a-r*[*i*!*-e x x*]
13 [*x x*]*x* ⸢*x*⸣ *x*[*x x x x*]
rest broken away
Rev. uninscribed

ABL 1196

1 To [the ki]ng, [my lord]: your servant [Aššur-reṣuwa]. Good health t[o the king, my lord]!

4 They are building a fort [*in* ...] because of Kaqq[adanu], the governor.

7 [*He has seized*] Urzana, [*the king*] of Muṣaṣi[r], *ga*[*thered*] his people, [and *taken them*] to Waisi.

11 Ariṣâ is on his way to [NN]. *Ar*[*iye* ...]
(Rest destroyed)

## 90. The Urarṭian King Flees and his Son is Made King

79-7-8,292

beginning broken away
1′ [*x x x x x*] *i-r*[*u-x x x*]
2′ [*x x x x* KUR.U]RI-*a-a* [*x x*]
3′ [*x x x x x*] *ip-la-*[*hu-ni*]
4′ [*x x x x*]-⸢*a*⸣ *a-na a-*⸢*hi*⸣*-t*[*i-šú x x*]
5′ [9 LÚ*.EN].⸢NAM⸣.MEŠ-*šú d*⸢*e*⸣*-e-k*[*u*!]
6′ [LÚ*.EN.N]AM *ša pu-ut* LÚ*.GAL KAŠ.LU[L]
7′ [LÚ*.EN].NAM *ša pu-tú-ni*
8′ [LÚ*].EN.NAM *ša pu-ut* ᵐ*ša—aš-šur—du-bu*
9′ LÚ*.EN.NAM *ša pu-ut* URU.*mu-ṣa-ṣi-ri*
10′ LÚ*.EN.NAM *ša* KUR.*ú-a-za-e*!
11′ LÚ*.EN.NAM *ša* KUR.*ši-ib-*⸢*ṭu*?⸣-[*r*]*u*?
12′ 2 LÚ*.EN.NAM.MEŠ *ša pu-ut* [KUR].*kar-*UD.KA.BAR
13′ LÚ*.EN.NAM *ša* KUR.*šá-*⸢*at*⸣*-te-ra*
14′ PAB 9 LÚ*.EN.NAM.MEŠ-*šú*
15e *de-e-ku*
r.1 *ù* LUGAL-*šú-nu ina a-hi-te-šú*
2 *ina* ŠÀ *e-da-ni-e e-te-*⸢*li*!⸣
3 KUR-*ú i-ṣa-bat* [0]

ABL 646

(Beginning destroyed)

2 [... the U]rarṭian(s) [...]

3 [...... who] got afr[aid]

4 [...] *secre*[*tly* ...]

5 [Nine] of his [gov]ernors were kil[led: the gover]nor opposite the chief cupbe[arer, the gove]rnor opposite us, the governor opposite Ša-Aššur-dubbu, the governor opposite Muṣaṣir, the governor of Wazae, the governor of Šib*ṭu*[*r*]*u*, two governors opposite Kar-siparri, the governor of Šattera — in all nine governors of his were killed.

r.1 Their king, however, escaped *secretly* on a lone (horse) and took to the mountains.

**89** → Deller Zagros p.108. 4 Cf. SAA I 29:8ff. 5, 7f, 12 See coll.
**90** → Deller Zagros p.99. 10ff, r.8 See coll.

4 *zi-ba-te* : *ša ma-dàk-t*[*i*]
5 [LU]GAL-*šú-nu la-a e-mu-ru* [0]
6 [*la*] *ú-du-u a-ki ú-š*[*e*$^{!}$*-zib-u-ni*]
7 [*it-ta*]*-ṣu* $^{m}$*me-la-ar-*[*ṭu-a*]
8 [*ina* U]Š$^{!}$ KASKAL *a-na* LUGAL-*u-t*[*e* 0]
9 [*is-sak*]*-nu-uš* :.$^{!}$ $^{m}$*me-la-a*[*r-ṭu-a*]
10 [LUGAL]*-ú-tú* :$^{!}$ ⸢*ú*⸣-[*x x x*]
rest broken away

The rear parts of the camp did not see their [ki]ng and did [not] realize that he had sa[ved himself].

7 [So they lif]ted up Melar[ṭua] and [ma]de him king [alo]ng the road; Mela[rṭua ...]ed [the king]ship [......]

(Rest destroyed)

## 91. Revolt against the King of Urarṭu

K 194

1 *a-na* LUGAL *be-lí-iá* ARAD-*ka* $^{m}$*aš-šur—re-ṣu-u-a*
2 *lu* DI-*mu a-na* LUGAL *be-lí-iá*
3 *ina* UGU $^{m}$*na-ra-ge-e* LÚ*.GAL—*ka*$^{!}$*-ṣir*
4 *ša a-na* LUGAL *be-lí-iá áš-pur-an-ni*
5 *nu-uk* 20 LÚ*.SAG.MEŠ *i-si-šu*
6 *ša ina* UGU LUGAL *id-di-bu-ub-u-ni*
7 *ṣa-ab-bu-tú ú-ma-a* LUGAL KUR.URI-*a-a*
8 *ina* URU.*ṭu-ur-uš-pa-a e-ta-rab*
9 *ú-sa-ni-iq-šú-nu* ERIM.MEŠ *re-hu-te*
10 *ša i-si-šú-nu i-sa-du-ú-ni*
11 *a-di* LÚ*.SAG.MEŠ *a-di* LÚ*.*ša*—$SU_6$.MEŠ
12 1-*me šu-nu* ERIM.MEŠ *de*$^{!!}$*-e-ku*
13 $^{m}$*ur-ṣe-né-e* LÚ*.*tur-ta-nu* 2-*u*
14 ŠEŠ-*šú ša* $^{m}$*ab-li-uq-nu*
15 *ina* ŠÀ URU.*ṭu-ur-uš-pa-a ṣa-bi-ti*
16 $^{m}$*ab-li-uq-nu ina* URU.*ṭu-ur-uš-pa-a*
17 *i-tal-ka a-na šá-a-šú a-na* ŠEŠ-*šú*
18 *an-ni-e i-sa-al-šú-nu* GÍR$^{!}$ *me-me-ni*
19 *la-a qur-bu i-ti-ši*
20 *ur-ta-mi-ú-šú-nu*
21 *ina* UGU $^{m}$*i-ṣi-ie-e*
22 *ša* LUGAL *be-lí iš-pur-an-ni*
e.23 *me-me-ni la*$^{!}$ *ú-da*
24 É *šu-ú-tu-u-*⸢*ni*⸣
r.1 *a-sa-na-al me-me-ni*
2 *la i-qab-bi-a šúm-mu*
3 *mé-e-te šúm-mu ba-al-ṭa*
4 LÚ*.A—KIN *ša ina* ŠÀ KUR.⸢*ú*⸣*-ki* [[*x*]]
5 *a-šap-par-u-ni la-áš-*⸢*šú*⸣$^{!}$ *la e-mar-šú*
6 *i-sa-na-al me-me-ni*
7 *la i-qab-ba-áš-šú*
8 *ú-ma-a a-šap-par i-ša*$^{!}$*-ú-lu*
9 *ú-ṣu-uṣ a-na* LUGAL
10 *a-šap-par*

ABL 144

1 To the king, my lord: your servant Aššur-reṣuwa. Good health to the king, my lord!

3 As regards Naragê, the chief tailor about whom I wrote to the king, my lord: "He and 20 of his fellow eunuchs who conspired against the king have been arrested" —

7 the king of Urarṭu has now entered Ṭurušpâ and questioned them. They have dragged forth and killed the rest of the people involved in the plot — 100 men, including the eunuchs and the bearded courtiers.

13 Urṣenê, the deputy commander-in-chief, brother of Abliuqnu, was likewise arrested in Ṭurušpâ. When Abliuqnu came to Ṭurušpâ, he (i.e. the king) questioned him and this brother of his. No sword was *drawn*; they let them go.

21 As to Iṣiye about whom the king, my lord, wrote me, nobody knows where he is; I keep inquiring, but nobody can tell me whether he is alive or dead.

r.4 The messenger whom I send to Ukku never sees any trace of him; he keeps inquiring, but nobody tells him anything. I am now sending (spies) to inquire and investigate, and shall write (again) to the king, my lord.

**91** → Deller Zagros p.116f. 12 Tablet KI-*e-ku*; scribal error. 18 Lit., "no sword was present/involved." The translation "they were not involved in anything" suggested by Deller, loc.cit., is attractive but seems excluded, as the tablet almost certainly has GÍR not *ina*$^{!}$ ŠÀ$^{!}$. See coll. and cf. ŠÀ in r.4. r.4 See coll. The fragmentary sign at the end of the line could be [*i*]*s* or just an erasure.

# 92. The Urarṭian King Gathers his Troops after Defeat

K 1080 + K 12992 (RCAE III 65)

1 *a-na* LUGAL *be-lí-ia* ARAD-*ka* $^{m}$*aš-šur—re-ṣu-u-a*
2 *lu* DI-*mu a-na* LUGAL *be-lí-ia* DI-*mu*
3 ⸢*a*!⸣-[*n*]*a* KUR *ša* LUGAL DI-*mu a-na* URU.HAL.ṢU
4 *lu* DI-*mu a-na* LUGAL *be-lí-iá*
5 KUR.*gu-ri-a-ni-a* KUR.*na-gi-ú*
6 *bir-te* KUR.URI *bir-te* KUR.*ga-mir-ra*
7 *šu-ú ma-da-at-tú a-na* KUR.URI-*a-a*
8 *i-da-an a-ki-i* KUR.URI-*a-a*
9 *ina* UGU KUR.*ga-mir-ra il-lik-u-ni*
10 *a-ki-i a-bi-ik-tú ina* ŠÀ KUR.URI-*a-a*
11 *ta-áš-šá-ki-nu-ni* LÚ*.ERIM.MEŠ *a—mar* TA* *ma-ka*
12 [*i*]*n*!-*na*-⸢*su*?-*x-ni*!⸣ [*ina*? KUR.*g*]*u*!-*ri*!-⸢*a*!⸣-*ni*-⸢*a*⸣ 0
13 *an-ni-ú am-mu-t*[*e x x x x*]
14 *am-mu-te i-ṣa-bat x*[*x x x x x x*]
15 *i-šak-kan ki-i* [LUGAL KUR.URI-*a-a*]
16 TA*! ŠÀ LÚ*.KÚR!-*š*[*u x x x x x x*]
17 *ina pa-an* KASKAL-*šu* [*x x x x x*]
18 *an-nu-te* ⸢*ú*!⸣-[*x x x x x x x x*]
19 ⸢*x x x*⸣ [*x x x x x x x x x*]
rest (1-2 lines and edge) broken away

Rev. beginning (2-3 lines only) broken away
1′ *k*[*i*!-*x x x x x x x x x x x*]
2′ *ša i*[*l*!-*x x x x x x x x x x*]
3′ 8-*lim* L[Ú.ERIM.MEŠ *x x x x x*]
4′ *ku-pu n*[*i*!] *ki*! [*x x x* LÚ*.NAM.MEŠ?]
5′ KUR.URI-*a-a ša ina* Š[À *x x x x*]

6′ *ina* UGU LUGAL KUR.URI-[*a-a it-tal-ku*?]
7′ LÚ*.NAM.MEŠ *an*!-*nu*!-*te*! [*x x x x x x*]
8′ *ina* ŠÀ IGI.2.MEŠ [*ša*] LUG[AL! *x x x x*]
9′ URU.HAL.ṢU.MEŠ [*x x x x x x x x*]
10′ LUGAL *be-lí i-q*[*ab*?-*bi x x x x x*]
11′ *i-tal-lak an*-⸢*nu*!⸣-*x*[*x x x x x x x x*]
12′ LÚ*.A—KIN.MEŠ ⸢*il*?-*lu*?-*ku*⸣ [*x x x*]
13′ *ina*! UGU-*hi-šú-nu r*[*a*?-*x*]*x x*[*x x*]
14′ *a-du zi-bu*-[*tú*? *x x x*]-*u-ni*
15′ *ina* UGU-*hi-šú-nu ṭè*-[*e-mu ša*] ⸢LUGAL⸣
16′ [*ina*!] URU.*ṭu-ur-uš-pa-a* ⸢*šu*⸣-*ú*

ABL 146+

1 To the king, my lord: your servant Aššur-reṣuwa. Good health to the king, my lord!

3 The land of the king is well; the fort is well; may the king my lord be well!

5 Guriania is a district between Urarṭu and Cimmeria; it pays tribute to the Urarṭian king.

8 When the Urarṭians went against Cimmeria and the Urarṭians suffered defeat, whatever troops [...]ed from there [*to* G]uriania, this [...] some of them and took others as captives, putting [...].

15 When [the king of Urarṭu *escaped*] from his enemy,

17 before his trip [......]

18 these [......]

(Break)

r.3 8,000 s[oldiers ...]

4 snow ... [......].

5 The Urarṭian [*governors*] who were i[n ...]

6 [*marched*] against the [king of] Urarṭu.

7 These governors [......]

8 in the eyes [of] the kin[g ......]

9 the forts [......]

10 the king, my lord, *sa*[*ys* ......]

11 went ... [......].

12 messengers are going [......]

13 to them [......]

14 until *the rea*[*r part* ...] to them.

15 Ne[ws of] the king: he is [in] Ṭurušpâ.

**92** → Deller Zagros p.98. 3 See coll. 12 See coll. The first sign is too long for *i*; the third sign looks like ⸢*su*⸣ or ⸢*zu*⸣; there is room for the preposition *ina* in the break between *-ni* and KUR; after *-a-ni-a*, the end of the line is uninscribed. 13 The referent of *anniu* "this" remains unclear. r.2, 4, 10 See coll. In r.4, reading ⸢*qar*!-*hi*!⸣ "ice" (Deller, loc. cit.) is excluded. r.11 Coll. Deller ibid.; possibly *annur*[*ig*] "now." r.12f See coll. r.14 Cf. no. 90 r.4; less likely *zi-bu* "vulture(s)."

# 93. A Coup d'État in Urarṭu

K 7466 + K 13024 (CT 53 462)

beginning broken away
1′ [*ina*] ⌜URU⌝.[*x x x*]
2′ [*ša q*]*a-ni* URU.*ú*-⌜*e*⌝-[*si*]
3′ [L]Ú.GAL.MEŠ-*šú*
4′ [*i*]*l-ti-bi-ú-šu*
5′ *i-du-ku-šu*
6′ LÚ*.*tur-ta-nu*
7′ [*š*]*a* ZAG *ša qi-i-ni*
8′ [$^{m}$]⌜$^{d}$⌝[15]—⌜BÀD⌝
e.9′ [*x x x*]*x x*[*x*] ⌜*x*⌝ [(*x*) *b*]*i*
r.1 [*x x x*] Š[À *x*] ⌜*x*⌝ [*x x*]*x*
2 [*ú*]-*di-na ina* URU.*ṭu-u*[*r-uš-p*]*a-a*
3 [*la*] *e-rab-ba* [0]
4 [*i—s*]*u-ri* LUGAL *be-lí* [0]
5 [*i-qab*]-*bi ma-a* [*x*] KUR.[*x x*]
6 [*x x* UR]U.HAL.ṢU *a*-[*x x x*]
7 [*x x x*] *la ú-d*[*u-u x x*]
8 [*x x š*]*a* URU.HAL.Ṣ[U *x x*]
9 [*x x x*] ⌜*x* URU.*ú*⌝-[*e-si x*]
rest broken away

CT 53 365+

(Beginning destroyed)

1 His magnates [sur]rounded him in [..., at the ou]tskirts of Wai[si], and killed him.

6 The right-hand commander-in-chief, of the family [of Sar]duri, [......] but has [not y]et entered Ṭu[rušp]â.

r.4 [Per]haps the king, my lord, [will s]ay: "[...]

6 [...] *the fort* [...]

7 [...] they do not kn[ow ...]

8 [... o]f *the for*[*t* ...]

9 [...] W[aisi]

(Rest destroyed)

# 94. Houses in the Environs of Kumme

Sm 677

1 [*a*]-⌜*na*⌝ LUGAL *be-lí-iá*
2 ⌜ARAD⌝-*ka* $^{m}$*aš-šur—re-ṣu-u-a*
3 [*lu*] DI-*mu a-na* LUGAL *be*-[*lí-iá*]
4 [*ina* UG]U É.MEŠ *ša* URU.*x*[*x x x*]
5 [*x x*]*x ša qa-an-ni* URU.*ku*-[*um-me*]
6 [*x*] LÚ*.ZI.ME *šu-nu* [*x x*]
7 [*x x š*]*a* URU.*ṭ*[*u*!-*ur-uš-pa-a*]
8 [*x x x*]*x x*[*x x x*]
rest broken away
Rev. uninscribed

ABL 491

1 [T]o the king, my lord: your servant Aššur-reṣuwa. [Good] health to the king, [my] lo[rd]!

4 [As t]o the houses of the town [...] in the environs of Ku[mme],

6 they are [...] persons [...]

7 [... o]f *Ṭ*[*urušpâ*]

(Rest destroyed)

# 95. Argisti's Message to the Kummeans

K 1258 + Sm 1934 (CT 53 858)

1 [*x x x x x x x x x*] ⌜*x x x*⌝
2 [*x x x x x i*]-*si-šú-nu i-tal-lak*
3 [*x x x*] ⌜*x*⌝ [*x* T]A *bé-et ina* GIŠ.GU.ZA
4 ⌜*ka*⌝-*mu-sa*-[*ka-ni š*]*a a-na* DI-*me-ia*
5 *taš-pur-ni ma-a la*-⌜*áš*!-*šú*⌝ [*ina* Š]À *aš-šur* DINGIR.MEŠ-*ku-nu*
6 *ina* UGU-*hi-ia il-lak ù*! *ma-a a-se-me*
7 *ma-a ig-da-na-ru*-[*ru m*]*a-a a-ta-a*

CT 53 172+

(Beginning destroyed)

2 "[......] went [w]ith them [...]

3 "[... 'Ever s]ince [I ha]ve been on the throne, there has not really been (anybody) you have sent to greet me; (everybody) comes to me [in the na]me of Aššur and your gods.'

6 "He further said: 'I have heard that you are scar[ed]; why are you scar[ed]? Even

**93** Hand of Aššur-reṣuwa. r.6, 8 Or: "the city of Birate."
**95** → Deller Zagros p.109f. 5 See coll.

8 *ta-ag-da-⸢na-ra⸣-[ra ma]-a $^{m}$ur-sa-a-ma*
9 *ina* UGU *ha-pe-e ša* [KUR-*ku-nu*]
10 *la id-di-bu-ub* [*a-na-ku-ma*]
11 *la ad-da-bu-ub šu-nu ki-⸢i⸣* [*an-ni-e*]
12 *ú-sa-pi-lu ma-a ki-i* ARAD.MEŠ [KUR—*aš-šur*.KI]
13 *a-ni-nu-ni ša pa-an* ⸢ANŠE⸣.BAD-HAL-*lu* [*ina*] UGU-[*hi-ni*]
14 *i-lak ma-a* ⸢É⸣.[ME]Š URU.⸢*ku*⸣-*um-me*
15 *ina* UGU-*hi-ni kar-*[*ra ma-a x x*]
e.16 *ina* UGU-*hi* ⸢*x x x*⸣
17 *ma-a la mu-qa-ni* GÌR.2.MEŠ-*ni*
18 *a-a-ka-me-ni la ni-šak-kan*
r.1 *an-nu-te di-ib-bi*
2 *ša* LÚ*.A—KIN *an-ni-ú i-di-bu-u*[*b-u-ni*]
3 *a-na š*[*a*]-*ni-e* UD-*me* $^{m}$*a-ri-e*
4 *ina pa-a*[*n* $^{m}$*a*]-⸢*ri*⸣-*ṣa-a ina pa-an* LÚ*.SAG
5 *an-ni-*[*e š*]*a ina* ŠÀ ⸢URU⸣.*ku-um-me*
6 *i-d*[*u-bu*]-*ub* ⸢*ma*⸣-*a* LÚ*.A—KIN [*x*]
7 TA* *meš-li* ⸢ANŠE.KUR.RA *ip*⸣-*t*[*aq-du*]
8 *ma-a* ANŠE.KUR.RA [*ša*] *a-*⸢*šá*⸣-*ru-*[*u-ni*]
9 *la-*⸢*áš*⸣-*šú ma-a e-*[*x x*]*x* ERIM.ME[Š *x*]
10 [*x x x x x x x x ina* U]GU-*ka*
11 [*x x x x x x x x x x x-n*]*i*$^{?}$
12 [*x x x x x x x x x x x-n*]*i*$^{?}$
13 [*x x x x x x x x x x x-d*]*u*$^{?}$
14 [*x x x x x x x x x x x-n*]*i*$^{?}$
rest broken away

Rusa did not speak about destroying [your country; nor have I] spoken about it.'

[11] "They responded like th[is]: 'Since we are subjects [of Assyria], a foreman of cavalry is [our su]perior. (Only) the houses of Kumme are left to us; [*we have authority*] *over them* (*only*), we cannot put our feet anywhere.'" These were the words spo[ken] by this messenger.

[r.3] The following day, Ariye s[po]ke with [A]riṣâ and this eunu[ch w]ho is in Kumme:

[6] "They have com[missioned] half of the horses to *the* messenger; there are no horse[s] (left) for me to review. [...] troops [...... t]o you [......]

(Rest destroyed)

# 96. An Ukkean Messenger and his Dispatch

K 910

1 *a-na* LÚ*.IGI.DUB *be-lí-iá*
2 ARAD-*ka* $^{m}$*aš-šur—re-ṣu-u-a*
3 *lu* DI-*mu a-na be-lí-iá*
4 LÚ*.A—KIN *ša* KUR.*ú-ka-a-a*
5 *ša a-na* KUR.URI *e-lu-u-ni*
6 *a-na* KUR—*aš-šur*.KI *i-tu-ri-di*
7 TA* ŠÀ KUR—*aš-šur*.KI *ina* KUR LÚ*.⸢SIPA$^{?}$⸣ GAL
8 [*e*]-⸢*te*⸣-*ti-iq ina* URU.*mu-ṣa-ṣir*
rest broken away
Rev. beginning broken away
1′ *x*[*x*]*x*[*x x x x*]
2′ *a-bi-te an-ni-te*
3′ *be-lí lu ú-da*$^{!}$
4′ *mi-i-nu ša ši-ti-ni*
5′ *ša* ŠÀ *e-gír-te*
6′ *an-ni-te ina* É.GAL
7′ *la-áš-pur*
8e *di-ib-bi an-nu-te*
9e *ku-un-nu-te*
10e ⸢*šu*⸣-*nu* UGU *be-lí-iá*
11e *a-sap-ra*

ABL 145

[1] To the treasurer, my lord: your servant Aššur-reṣuwa. Good health to my lord!

[4] The messenger of the Ukkean who went to Urarṭu has come down to Assyria, and proceeded from Assyria to the land of the *Great Shepherd*. In Muṣaṣir [......]

(Break)

[r.2] My lord should know the [*heart*] of this matter. I will write to the palace everything that was written in this letter; I am writing to my lord only these ascertained facts.

**96** → Deller Zagros p.119f. [7] See coll.; W 64. LÚ.NIGÍR—É.GAL excluded.

# 97. Troop Movements in Kumme

K 1170

1 [*a-na* LÚ*].I[GI.DUB *be-lí-iá*]
2 [ARAD-*ka* $^{m}$]*aš-šur—r*[*e-ṣu-u-a*]
3 [*lu* D]I-⸢*mu*⸣ *a-na* [*be-lí-iá*]
4 ⸢*ina* UGU⸣ ERIM.MEŠ *ša ina* UR[U.*ku-um-me*]
5 ⸢*ša be*⸣*-lí iš-pur-an-ni* [*am-mu-te*]
6 *ú-se-li am-mu-*[*te*]
7 *ú-di-na la ú-ša*!*-la*[*k*]
8 $^{m}$*a-ri*!*-e* $^{m}$*a-ri-ṣa-a* [0]
9 *a-nu-su-nu tar-ṣa-at ú-*[*di-na*]
10 *la ú-na-maš-ú-ni* [0!]
11 *ki-ma ú-na-maš-ú-ni* [0]
12 LÚ*.A—KIN-*iá ina pa-na-at-*(*u*)*-šú-*[*nu*]
13 *i-lak ina* UGU-*hi-ia* [*i-sa-hu-ra*]
14 *be-lí ú-da* UD.MEŠ [*x x x*]
15 [*x x x*] *da* [*x x x x*]
rest (about 3 lines) broken away
Rev. beginning (about 3 lines) broken away
1′ ⸢*i-di-in*⸣ [*x x x x x x*]
2′ GURUN.BURU$_{14}$ *e-t*[*a-ṣi-di*]
3′ *šúm-mu be-lí ú-m*[*a*?*-x x*]
4′ *pa-ṭi-ra-a-te ú-*[*x x x*]
5′ *be-lí liš-pur* LÚ*.*i-tu-*[*ʾa-a-a*]
6′ *ša* URU.BÀD—$^{d}$UTU [0]
7′ *ša* URU.*bar-za-ni-iš-*[*ta*]
8′ *le-lu-ni* ERIM.MEŠ *an-nu-*[*te*]
9′ *li-ip-ṭu-ur-u-ni ša* [*be-lí*]
10′ *iš-pur-an-ni ma-a* 50 LÚ*.*i-*⸢*tu*⸣*-*[*ʾa-a-a*]
11′ *ina*! URU!.15—BÀD-*a-ni* ⸢*lu*!⸣*-*[*x x*]
12′ [*x x*]*-ṣi*! LÚ*.⸢*ú*?⸣*-*[*x x x x*]
rest broken away
s.1 [*x x*]*x ina* IGI $^{m}$DI—EN—*la-áš-me be-lí lu-x*[*x x x*]

ABL 147

1 [To the] tr[easurer, my lord, your servant] Aššur-r[eṣuwa. Good h]ealth to [my lord]!

4 As to the troops in [Kumme] about whom my lord wrote me, I have moved up [some of them], but have not yet got the others under way.

8 The equipment of Ariye and Ariṣâ is in order, but they have not y[et] departed; when they do set out, my messenger will go ahead of [them], and [then *return*] to me.

14 My lord knows that the days [......]
(Break)

r.1 [...] *was strong* [......]

2 I have r[eaped] the harvest. If my lord *o*[*rders*], I shall [...] *reed altars*. My lord should send word that the It[u'eans] of Dur-Šamaš and Barzaniš[ta] come up here to relieve the[se] troops.

9 As to what [my lord] wrote me: "Let 50 It[u'eans ...] *to* Sarduriani [...]
(Break)

s.1 My lord should [......] in the presence of Šulmu-beli-lašme.

# 98. Where Did All That Wine Go?

K 1501 + K 7393 + K 9783 + K 13082

1 *a-na* LUGAL EN-*ia*
2 ARAD-*ka* $^{m}$[*aš-šur*]—*re-*[*ṣu-u-a*]
3 *lu* DI-*mu* ⸢*a-na*⸣ LUGA[L EN-*i*]*a*
4 $^{md}$IM—A—AŠ LÚ*.*q*[*ur-b*]*u-ti*
5 *ša un-qu* ⸢*ina* UGU⸣-[*hi-i*]*a na-ṣa-ni*
6 *ina* UGU ⸢DUMU⸣ $^{m}$⸢*x*⸣-[*x*]*-ur-da-a*
7 *ša* KUR.⸢*hal*⸣*-z*[*i*—AD.BAR *a*]*-na-ku*
8 *ù* L[Ú.*qur-bu-t*]*i ni-tab-ba*
9 *ina* URU.*ku-u*[*m-me ni*]*-tal-ka*
10 $^{m}$*a-ri-e* ⸢*x*⸣-[*x*]-⸢*x*⸣*-na-ši*

CT 53 42

1 To the king, my lord: your servant [Aššur]-re[ṣuwa]. Good health to the kin[g, m]y [lord]!

4 Adad-aplu-iddina, the ro[yal body]guard who brought me the sealed order concerning the son of [...]urdâ of Halz[iatbar] —

7 the bodyguard and I got up and [w]ent to Ku[mme]. Ariye [*received*] us, but did [not]

**97** 8 W 65. 12 See coll. r.4 *pa-ṭi-ra-a-te* possibly with J. N. Postgate "relief units(?)" (cf. r.9) rather than "reed altars," but the suggested meaning is not otherwise attested. r.11 See coll.; at end, reading ⸢*i*!⸣-[ (W 66) excluded. r.12 See coll.
**98** The form of *ša* in this letter is distinctively Aššur-reṣuwa's. r.4ff The implication of the passage seems to

11 *ṭè-e-mu-⸢ma⸣*[!] [*la*] ⸢*iš*⸣*-kun-*⸢*na*⸣*-na-ši*
12 *i-tab-ba* [*ina* É].GAL *i-tal-ka*
13 LUGAL *be-lí* [*lil-l*]*i*[?]*-ka i-si-šú*
14 *lid-bu-ub* ⸢LÚ*⸣.[*x-x*].⸢MEŠ⸣
15 *bi* ⸢*x*⸣ [*x x x x*]*x* ⸢*ša*⸣ LUGAL *be-lí-ia*
16 *x*[*x x x x x x x*] ⸢*ri*⸣
17 [*x x x x x x x x g*]*ab-bi*
rest broken away
Rev. beginning broken away
1′ *ma-*⸢*a*⸣ [*x x x x x x*]
2′ LUGAL *be-lí lu* [*x x x x*]
3′ *ki-i an-ni-e l*[*i-i*]*q-ba-š*[*u*]
4′ *ma-a a-na man-ni-ma*
5′ 6 ANŠE ŠE.PAD.ME[Š] 4 ANŠE GEŠTIN.MEŠ
6′ 20 UDU.HI.A.MEŠ *ta-din*
7′ *ú-ma-a* LÚ*.*qur-b*[*u*]
8′ *an-ni-iu-ma šu-u-tu*
9′ *a-du bé-et* ⸢*un*⸣*-qu*
10′ *ina* UGU*-hi-ia tal-lak-an-ni*
rest uninscribed

give us any orders; he left and went [to the Pala]ce.

13 The king, my lord, should [*g*]*o* and speak with him. The [...] officials

15 [...] of the king, my lord

16 [......]

17 [......] all

(Break)

r.2 Let the king, my lord, [...] and say to h[im] as follows: "To whomever did you give 6 homers of barley, 4 homers of wine and 20 sheep?"

7 Now, this one will be the *closest relat*[*ive*] until a (further) sealed order reaches me.

## 99. ———

K 15389

beginning broken away
1′ ⸢*a-du*⸣ [*x x x x x x x x*]
2′ LUGAL EN-[*ia x x x x x x*]
3′ *a-na* KUR.*me-*[*ṣa*[?]*-a-a x x x x x*]
4′ *ú-ma-a*[*l*[!]*-x x x x x x*]
5′ *tu-sa-lim* [*x x x x x x x*]
6′ *a-du*[!] *x*[*x x x x x x x*]
7′ *gab-bi* [*x x x x x x x*]
8′ *a-*⸢*na*⸣ KUR—*aš-šu*[*r x x x x x x*]
9′ *ṭè-ma-ni* [*x x x x x x*]
10′ EN.NUN [*x x x x x x*]
11′ TA* [*x x x x x x*]
e.12′ *a-na* KUR—*aš-š*[*ur x x x x x x*]
13′ *la-al-li*[*k x x x x x x*]
Rev. lines 1-6 destroyed
7 *e-*⸢*x x*⸣ [*x x x x x x*]
8 *a-na* ⸢URU⸣.[*x x x x x x*]
9 ⸢LUGAL⸣ *b*[*e-lí x x x x x x*]
10 *x*[*x x x x x x x x x*]
rest broken away

CT 53 656

1 *until* [......]
2 the king, [my] lord, [......]
3 to Me[......]
4 *fil*[*led* ......]
5 *you have pacified* [......]
6 as far as [......]
7 all [......]
8 to Assyr[ia ......]
9 the *news* [......]
10 the watch [......]
11 *from* [......]
12 to Assyr[ia ......]
13 I will g[o ......]
(Break)
r.8 to the city [......]
9 the king, [my] lo[rd ......]
(Rest destroyed)

## 100. Smugglers on the Assyrian Border

N. III 3158

1 [*a-na* LU]GAL *be-lí-ia*
2 [ARAD-*k*]*a* ^m^*aš-šur—re-ṣu-u-a*
3 [*lu*] DI-*mu a-na* LUGAL *be-lí-ia*

TCL 9 67

1 [To the ki]ng, my lord: [yo]ur [servant] Aššur-reṣuwa. [Good] health to the king, my lord!

be that the items mentioned had been paid as tribute to the king of Urarṭu. r.7 The noun *qurbu* is otherwise known from NA legal documents only, where it seems to have the meaning "close relative." Reading LÚ.*qur-b*[*u-ti*] "bodyguard" is excluded after collation.

4 $^{m}$*bu-ri-e* $^{m}$*e-zi-ie-e*
5 $^{m}$*ga-ma-lu* $^{m}$*e-hi-ie-e*
6 PAB$^{!}$ 4 *ša* ŠU.2 $^{m}$*a-ri-a-ṣa-a*
7 $^{m}$*ku-ma-a-a* $^{m}$*bi-ri-a-un*
8 P[AB] 2 *ša* ŠU.2 $^{m}$*a-ri-e*
9 6 $^{m}$*ku-*⸢*ma*⸣*-a-a* ⸢*an*⸣*-nu-ti*
10 *il-lu-ku ina* ŠÀ URU.*bu-su-si*
11 *ša* É LÚ*.GAL—KAŠ.LUL *ú-šu-bu*$^{!}$
12 URU.*bu-su-sa-a-a ṣa-hi-ta-a-*⸢*te*⸣
13 *ša* KUR—*aš-šur*.KI TA* URU.*kal-hi*
14 TA* URU.*ni-nu-a i-laq-qi-u*
15 *a-na* $^{m}$*ku-ma-a-a an-nu-te*
16 *i-du-nu* $^{m}$*ku-ma-a-a an-nu-te*
17 ⸢*ina* ŠÀ⸣ URU.*a-i-ra*
18 É $^{m}$SAG.DU-*a-ni*
19 *ša*$^{!}$ ŠU.2 $^{m}$*sa-ni-ie-*⸢*e*⸣
20 EN—URU LÚ*.AR[AD$^{!}$]
r.1 ⸢*ša*⸣ LÚ*.EN.NAM *ša* URU.*kal-hi*
2 *ina* ŠÀ-*bi e-ru-bu* TA* ŠÀ-*bi*
3 *ina* ŠÀ-*bi* KUR$^{!}$.URI$^{!}$ *ú-bu-lu*
4 TA* *ma-ak-ka ṣa-hi-ta-a-te*
5 *a-na ni*$^{!}$*-šá*$^{!}$ ⸢*ú*$^{!}$⸣*-ba-al*$^{!}$*-u-ni*
6 LUGAL *be-lí ina* UGU $^{m}$[*sa-ni*]*-ie-e*
7 EN—URU *liš*$^{!}$*-*⸢*pur*⸣ $^{m}$*ku-ma-a-a an-nu-te*
8 *lu-ṣa-bi-it ina* UGU LUGAL *be-lí-iá*
9 *lu-še-bi-la* LUGAL *be-lí liš-al-šú-nu*
10 *ṣa-hi-ta-a-te an-na-te* TA* *a-a-ka*
11 *i-na-šu-ni a-na a-a-šá i-da*$^{!}$*-nu-ni*$^{!}$
12 *man-nu* TA* ŠU.2-*šú-nu i-ma-har-u-ni*
13 *man-nu ú-še-bar-ru-šu-nu-u-ni*
14 $^{m}$*ku-ma-a-a an-nu-te*
15 *hal-qu-u-te šu-nu*
16 ⸢TA*$^{!}$⸣ URU.*ku-um-me*
17 *hal-qu*

4 Burê, Eziye, Gamalu and Ehiye, in all four (men) under Ariaṣâ; Kumayu and Biriaun, in all two (men) under Ariye — these six Kummeans go and stay in Busustu, a town in the domain of the chief cupbearer.

12 The inhabitants of Busustu purchase Assyrian luxury items in Calah and Nineveh and sell them to these Kummeans. These Kummeans enter the town Aira of the house of Kaqqadanu, ruled by Saniye, a city lord subject to the governor of Calah, and bring (the merchandise) from there to Urarṭu. From over there they import luxury items here.

r.6 The king, my lord, should write to [Sani]ye, the city lord, that he should arrest these Kummeans and send them to the king, my lord.

9 The king, my lord, should ask them where they buy these valuables, where they sell them, who receives them from their hands, and who lets them pass (the border).

14 These Kummeans are runaways; they have run away from Kumme.

# 101. Fragment of a List of Valuables

K 17736

beginning broken away
1′ [*x x x* URU.*k*]*u-um-m*[*e*]
2′ [*x x x-z*]*u*$^{?}$ *i—su-r*[*i*]
3′ [LUGAL *be-l*]*í i-qab-bi*
4′ [*ma-a m*]*i-i-nu ši-i-na*
5′ [*ṣa-hi-ta*]*-a-te*
e.6′ [*x x x x x*]*-te*
r.1 [*x x x x x*] URUDU.MEŠ
2 [*x x x x*]*-ha* URUDU.MEŠ
3 [*x x x x*]*x-tú* KUŠ.MEŠ
4 [*x x x x*]*-me iš-pat* ⸢URUDU⸣
5 [*x x x x*] ⸢*x x x x*⸣
rest broken away

K 17736

(Beginning destroyed)
1 [... K]umm[e]
2 Perhaps [the king], my [lord], will say: "[W]hat are the [...*val*]*uables*?
r.1 [......] of bronze
2 [......] of bronze
3 [......]... of leather
4 [...] *hundred* bronze quivers
(Rest destroyed)

**100** → photo pl. I-II. r.5 *a-na ni*$^{!}$*-šá* (collated from photo) is a back formation from *annēša* "hither" by analogy to *ana hur/ah–hur*, etc.
**101** Previously unpublished; copy p. 265.

## 102. ———

K 13140

beginning broken away
1′ [*x x x*] ⸢*a*⸣ [*x x x x*]
2′ [URU.Š]À$^{?}$—URU-*a*-⸢*a*⸣ [*x x x*]
3′ [*x*] *za-ab-lu ú* [*x x*]
4′ [*x x*]*x* URU.*ku-mu x*[*x x x*]
5′ [*šu*]-*ú* ⸢*ú*⸣-[*x x x*]
6′ [KUR].⸢*ú*⸣-*ka*-[*a-a x x*]
7′ [*x x*]*x* ⸢*x*⸣ [*x x x x*]
rest broken away
Rev. beginning broken away
1′ [*x*]*x x*[*x x x x x x x*]
2′ [*x*] $^{md}$UTU—HAL-⸢*ni*⸣ *šu-x*[*x x*]
3′ [*x x*]-*ba ina* UGU-*h*[*i x*]
4′ [*x x* $^{m}$]*a-ri-e* [*x x x*]
rest broken away

CT 53 492

(Beginning destroyed)
1 [......]
2 *from the* [*In*]*ner City* [...]
3 [...] transported [...]
4 [...] Kumme [...]
5 [*H*]*e* [...]
6 the Ukk[ean(s) ......]
(Break)

r.2 [...] Šamaš-išmanni [...]
3 [...] *to* [...]
4 Ariye [......]
(Rest destroyed)

## 103. Manhunt

K 1111

beginning (about 10 lines) broken away
1′ [*ma*]-⸢*a ina* URU⸣.[*x x x x*]
2′ [L]Ú.ERIM.MEŠ *i*-[*ba-áš-ši-i*]
3′ *ina* ŠÀ-*bi ina*$^{!}$ [ŠU.2-*šú-nu*]
4′ *la in*$^{!}$-*q*[*u*$^{!}$-*tu*]
5′ $^{m}$*sa-ni-ie* LÚ.⸢EN—URU⸣
6′ TA* $^{m}$*kaq-qa-da-a-ni*
7′ *a-sa-par na-ṣu-ú-ni*
8′ *a-sa-ʾa-al-šú-nu mu-uk* LÚ.ERIM.MEŠ
9′ *a-le-e ma-a* LÚ*.ERIM.MEŠ *ig-du-ru*
e.10′ *a-ki an-ni-e iq-ṭi-bu-u-ni*
11′ *ma-a* LÚ*.ERIM.MEŠ *ina* ŠÀ-*bi*
r.1 *šu-nu* : *ma-a ši-du*
2 *lu-ri-ku-na-ši a-du* É
3 LÚ*.ERIM.MEŠ *ina qa-ti-ni*
4 *i-ma-qa-tu ni-ni*
5 *šúm-ma* LUGAL *b*[*e-lí*] *i-qa-bi*
6 $^{m}$*sa-ni-ie* [*x x x n*]*i*$^{!}$
7 ⸢*ina*$^{?}$⸣ IGI [*x x x x x x*]
rest broken away

ABL 590

(Beginning destroyed)
1 "Have the men re[ally] not fallen into [their hands] in the city [...]?"

5 I sent Saniye, the city lord, and Kaqqadanu to bring (them), and asked them where the men are.

9 They said: "The men have got scared," and informed me as follows: "The men are in there; let them extend the ... for us until they fall into our hands."

r.5 If the king, [my] lo[rd], orders, Saniye [*and Kaqqadan*]*u* [...] before [......]
(Rest destroyed)

## 104. For his Royal Ears Only

K 539

1 *a-na* LUGAL *be-lí-ia*
2 ARAD-*ka* $^{md}$PA—*ú-ṣal-l*[*a*]
3 *lu* DI-*mu a-na* LUGAL *be-lí-ia*

ABL 206

1 To the king, my lord: your servant Nabû-uṣall[a]. Good health to the king, my lord!

**102** r.3 At the beginning of the line restore either [*e-tar*]-*ba* "[ente]red" or [*iq-ṭar*]-*ba* "arrived."
**103** 1ff, r.5ff See coll.
**104** → no. 105. The sender may be identical with the Nabû-uṣalla of CT 53 72 (SAA I 237, a letter from the governor of Naṣibina), and hence the present letter may refer to Kummeans deported from the province of Guzana (cf. SAA I 233). 9, 17 See coll. r.4 See coll.

4 3 LÚ*.ERIM.MEŠ *dan-nu-ti šú-nu*
5 *ša* LÚ*.*ku-um-ma-a-a*
6 *i-tal-ku-ni ina pa-ni-ia*
7 *ina pa-an* $^{m}$DUMU—$^{d}$15 LÚ*.*qur-bu-ti*
8 *i-ti-ti-su*
9 *ki an-ni-e iq-ṭí-bu-ú-n[i]*
10 *ma-a* UN.MEŠ-*ni* É LUGAL
11 *iq-bu-ú-ni lil-li-ku*
12 *ma a-na na-ši* LÚ*.A—KIN-*ka*
13 *ina* É.GAL *lu-bi-la-na-ši*
14 *ma a-bu-tú ši-i*
15 [*ša*] KUR *šá-ni-ti*
16 [*ina pa-a*]*n* LUGAL *ni-qa-bi*
17 [*ma x x*]*x-ka ša* GÌR!.2
18 [*la-a n*]*i*!*-qa-ba-ka*
r.1 [*ma*] *a-na* ⸢LÚ*.*qur*⸣*-bu-ti-ma*
2 [*l*]*a-a ni-qa-bi*
3 [*m*]*a-a ú-la-a ina* É.GAL
4 ⸢*la*!⸣ *tú-bi-la-na-a-ši*
5 *ma-a ina ši-a-ri*
6 *ina li-di-iš*
7 *ina pa-an* LUGAL *ni-qa-bi*
8 *ma-a pa-an* LÚ*.EN.NAM
9 *pa-an* LÚ*.*qur-bu-ti*
10 *ni-iq-ṭí-bi ma-a la im-ma-gúr*
11 *ina* É.GAL *la-a ú-ba-lu-na-ši*
12 *mi-i-nu ša* LUGAL *be-li*
13 *i-qa-bu-ni*

4 Three powerful men of the Kummeans have come and had an audience with me and Mar-Issar, the royal bodyguard. Here is what they said to me:

10 "Our people may go where the king said, but your messenger should take us to the Palace. There is a matter [concerning] another country we (wish to) discuss [in] the king's [pres]ence. [...] ...; we [will] not tell it to you, [n]or will we tell it to the royal bodyguard.

r.3 "Else if you do not take us to the Palace, sooner or later we shall say to the king:

8 "'We spoke with the governor and the royal bodyguard, but they did not agree to bring us to the Palace.'"

12 What are the king my lord's orders?

## 105. The Kummean Leaders Comply with the King

K 464

1 *a-na* LUGAL [*be-lí-iá*]
2 ARAD-*ka* [$^{m}$*x x x x*]
3 *lu-u* DI-*mu a-n*[*a* LUGAL EN]-*ia*
4 *ša* LUGAL *be-lí ina* ŠÀ-*bi un-qi*
5 *ú-še-bal-a-ni a-na-ku*
6 $^{m}$15—BÀD LÚ*.*qur-bu-tú*
7 [*d*]*i-ib-bi am—mar il—li-bi-ni*
8 [*ni*]*-du-ba-áš-šú-nu un-qu*
9 [*ša*] *ina* UGU-*hi-šú-nu tal-li-kan-ni*
10 [*nu*]*-sa*!*-šá-me-šú-nu i-da-bu-bu*
11 [*ma*]-⸢*a*!⸣ LUGAL *be-lí-i-ni be-*⸢*lí*!⸣ *š*[*a*!] *gab-bi*
12 [*šu*]*-ú ma-a a-ni-nu mi-nu ni-*⸢*qa*!⸣*-bi*
13 *ma-a* LÚ*.*ku-ma-a-a-e am—mar ina* KUR.KUR.MEŠ
14 É.MEŠ *ú-kal-lu-u-ni*
15 LUGAL BE-*ni* É *ṭa-bu-u-ni*
16 *lu-bi-li ù* LÚ*.*ku-ma-a-a-e*
17 LÚ*.*da-ia-a-li ša* TA* URU.*ku-me*
18 *a-na na-gúr-tú il-li-ku-u-ni*
19 *ú-di-ni la il-la-ku-*[*u-ni*]

ABL 544

1 To the king, [my lord]: your servant [NN]. Good health t[o the king], my [lord]!

4 As to what the king, my lord, wrote me in the sealed order, I and Issar-duri, the royal bodyguard, told them every word that was in it and let them hear the sealed order [which] came concerning them. They say:

11 "The king, our lord, is the lord of all; what can we say? The king, our lord, may take all the Kummeans who hold houses in (other) countries to wherever it is appropriate."

16 But the Kummean scouts who went from Kumme for *hire* have not yet returned but are still there! The king, [my] lo[rd],

**105** Not hand of Aššur-reṣuwa. → no. 104. 10ff See coll. 22 See coll.; W 191 excluded. r.2 Signs clear; reading *hal-qu-ni* excluded. r.10 See coll.

20 *am-ma-ka-ma šú-nu* LUGAL *be-*[*lí*]
21 *liš-al lu-ṣi-ṣi i—s*[*u-ri*]
22 ⌜*qa*!*-ni*!⌝ *am-mu-te*
23 *ú-šá-ga-lu-šú-nu*
24 LUGAL *be-lí ina* URU.*ku-me*
25 *lu-sa-hi-ir-šú-nu*
r.1 LUGAL *be-lí ú-da a-ki* [0]
2 TA* ŠÀ KUR.URI *bat-qu-ni* [0]
3 *ina* KUR—*aš-šur a-na na-gúr-te šú-nu-ni*
4 *ina* UGU GIŠ.*ziq-pi ša* LUGAL *be-lí*
5 *iš-pu-ra-ni ku-up-pu*
6 *qar-hu* KALAG-*an ú-di-ni*
7 *le-ma-tú-hu* SAG.DU DINGIR GIBIL
8 *ša* ITI.ŠE *ina* URU.BÀD—$^{m}$LUGAL—GI.NA
9 ⌜*i*⌝*-ma-tú-hu ú-bu-lu*
10 [*a*]*l*!*-la-ka ṭè-me ú-ta-ra*

should inquire and investigate: may[be] they are getting deported with those (other Kummeans).

24 The king, my lord, should return them to Kumme. The king, my lord, knows that they are needed in Urarṭu, and that they are in Assyria for *hire* (only).

r.4 As to the saplings about which the king, my lord, wrote me, there is much snow and ice, so they cannot be picked up yet; they will pick them up and bring them to Dur-Šarruken at the beginning of the new moon of Adar (XII). I shall (then) come and give my report.

## 106. The Kummeans versus the Royal Delegate

79-7-8,260+316

CT 53 138

beginning broken away
1′ ⌜*ir*⌝*-t*[*a-x x x x x x x x x x*]
2′ *in-tu-a-*[*ta x x x x x x x x x*]
3′ [DI]NGIR.MEŠ-*ni ša* [LUGAL EN-*ia lu ú-du-u šúm-mu*]
4′ [*d*]*ul*$_6$*-lu an-n*[*i-ú la x x x x x x*]
5′ [*šú*]*m-mu ni-si-*[*aṭ x x x x x x x x*]

(Beginning destroyed or too broken for translation)

2 died [......]

3 [I swear by the g]ods of [the king, my lord,] that th[is w]ork [...]; if we have been negli[gent, may ......]!

**106** Same scribe as in nos. 107 and 108.

FIG. 19. *Representing Assyrian power (reign of Assurbanipal).*
BM 124802.

6′ [L]UGAL *be-lí i-*[*x x x x x x x x x*]
7′ ⸢*e-ta*⸣-*pa-áš* [*x x x x x x x x x*]
8′ ⸢*ù*⸣ ARAD *ša* L[UGAL EN-*ia x x x x*]
9′ [*a*]-*na-ku ki-i x*[*x x x x x x x x x*]
10′ [*k*]*i-i* DINGIR.MEŠ *e-*[*pa-šu-u-ni a-na-ku*]
11′ [*ina p*]*i-ti le-p*[*u-uš x x x x x*]
12′ [L]Ú.*ku-ma-a-a š*[*a ina pa-ni-ti a-na*] ⸢LUGAL⸣ [EN-*ia*]
13′ [*i*]*h-hu-ru-ni* [*is*]-*su-uh-ru-ni ina* UG[U-*hi-ia*]
14′ [*i*]*t-tal-ku-ni ma-a* URU.*ku-um-mu gab-bi-šú*
15′ [L]Ú.*qe-e-pu la i-na-ši-ú ma-a a-ni-*[*nu-ma*]
16′ [*ni-n*]*a-ši ma-a pu-tu-hu na-ṣa-ni* [0]
17′ [ᵐ*aš-šur*]—⸢*re*⸣-*ṣu-u-a iq-ṭí-bi ma-a* 4 ERIM.MEŠ [*šu-nu*]
18′ [*lu-š*]*e-li-ú* UD.MEŠ *ša an-na-ka a-n*[*a-ku-ni*]
19′ [*pa-n*]*a-tu-u-a lu la il-lu-ku* KUR *i-da-*[*ki-u*]
20′ [*i-ba*]-*ši iq-ṭí-bi-a ma-a ina* IGI-*ka lu š*[*u-nu*]
21′ [NINDA.MEŠ *le*]-*kul* A.MEŠ *li-is-si-u ki-i si-*[*mìn*]
22′ [*x x x*] *le-li-u ú-ma-a šúm-mu la* [*x x*]
23′ [*x x x*] *ma-a lu ka-la-ʾu di-ib-b*[*i* DÙG.GA.MEŠ]
24′ [*is-si-šú-nu li*]*d-bu-bu* LÚ*.*qe-e-pu x*[*x x x*]
25′ [LÚ*.ERIM.MEŠ *lu l*]*a i-kal-li-*⸢*ú*⸣ [*x x x x*]
e.26′ [*x x x il-l*]*ik-u-ni x*[*x x x x x*]
Rev. destroyed

[6] [The k]ing, my lord [......]
[7] *has* done [......]
[8] I am a servant of the k[ing, my lord ...];
[9] when [......]
[10] and when the gods ta[ke action, I] wi[ll do accor]dingly [...].
[12] The Kummeans w[ho previously] appealed [to] the king, [my lord, h]ave returned and [c]ome t[o me], saying: "The city of Kummu in its entirety can't stand the royal delegate; [but] we can, and will bear the responsibility."

[17] [Aššur]-reṣuwa has said: "[There are] four men [who should be] removed; they must not walk (free) in my presence while I [am] here; they are inci[ting] the country."
[20] [In f]act, he told me: "T[hey] should stay with you and be provided with [foo]d and drink; when the ti[me *is right*] let them disappear."
[22] Now, if it is not [..., and the ... *insists*]: "Let them be detained," [he sho]uld speak k[indly with them]; the royal delegate [and the ... should n]ot detain [the men].
[26] [... who w]ent [......]
(Rest destroyed)

## 107. Kill the Assyrian Delegate!

K 7402

beginning broken away
1′ [LÚ*.KÚR.MEŠ *ša* UR]U.⸢*ku*⸣-*um-me* TA* ŠÀ-*bi-*⸢*ku*⸣-[*nu*]
2′ [*še-ṣi-a ú*]-*ma-a an-nu-rig* URU.*ku-um-m*[*u*]
3′ [*gab-bi-šu ina*] UGU ᵐ*a-ri-e i-sa-ak-nu*
4′ [*x x x x*]*x ina* UGU *du-a-ki*
5′ [*ša* LÚ*.*qe-pi*] ⸢*i*⸣-*da-bu-bu*
e.6′ [*ina* ŠÀ UD-*me š*]*a* ⸢*e*⸣-*gír-tú*
7′ [*ša* ᵐ*aš-šur—re-ṣ*]*u-u-a* TA* LÚ*.A—KIN
r.1 [*ša x x x ina* UGU-*hi-ia i*]*l-lik-u-ni-ni*
2 [*x x x x x x x x x*]-*ka*
13 [*x x x x x x x x x*]*x-ib-šú-nu*
rest broken away

CT 53 98

(Beginning destroyed)
[1] "'[*Drive the enemies* of] Kumme from yo[ur] midst!'
[2] "Now then [the whole] city of Kumm[u] has turned [ag]ainst Ariye; they [...] speak of killing [*the royal delegate*]."
[6] [The day th]at the letter [of Aššur-reṣ]uwa came [to me] with the messenger [of ...]
(Rest destroyed)

**107** Same scribe as in nos. 106 and 108f.

# 108. An Urarṭian Woman on the Throne of Habhu

K 1186 + K 7303 + K 7477 (CT 53 370) + K 13037 + K 15610 (CT 53 679)

1 a-na LUGAL E[N-ia ARAD-ka $^{m}$x x x x]
2 lu DI-mu a-[na LUGAL be-lí-ia]
3 LÚ*.A—KIN-ia ⸢ša⸣ [IGI LÚ*.IGI.DUB k]a-a-a-m[a-nu]
4 DI-mu iq-ṭí-ba-[ni ma-a at]-ta ṭè-e-[mu]
5 ta-sa-kan-an-ni ma-[a a-na] LÚ*.IGI.DUB qi-[bi]
6 ma-a IGI LÚ*.A—KIN-ia [du-g]ul ma-a a-mur ⸢a⸣-[na-ku]
7 ina UGU LÚ*.IGI.DUB a-šap-par ma-a UD-mu ⸢ka⸣-[x x]
8 ina URU.kip-šú-na a-na-ku ma-a IGI LÚ*.⸢A⸣—[KIN-ka]
9 LÚ*.IGI.DUB i-da-gal ma at-ta [la taš-pur]
10 la LÚ*.A—KIN-ka i[l$^{!}$-l]i-ka [x x x x]
11 ⸢ú-ma⸣-[a an-nu-rig] UN.M[EŠ KUR x x x]
12 [x x x x x x x]x u[r x x x x]
13 [a]-⸢na⸣-ši [x x x x x] x[x x x x]
14 [qi]-bi-a la-áš-šú-m[a x x x x x x x x]
15 [dul$_6$]-la-šú-nu le-pu-[šú x x x x x x x]
16 [a]-na ša-ši-ma iq-[ṭí-bi ma-a dul-lu la te-pa-šá]
17 [m]a-a ra-me-a a-di UD-[me x x x x x x]
18 ú-pa-har-šú-nu ma-lu-⸢ú⸣ [x x x x x x]
19 i-ta-bu-ku a-na-ku [x x x x x x]
20 Ì.MEŠ ina SAG.DU.MEŠ-šú-nu [a-tab-ba-ak]
21 an-nu-te šú-nu di-bi-šú [ša ina pa-ni-ia]
22 id-bu-bu-ni a-na-ku a[s-sa-ʾa-al-šú]
23 nu-uk pi-i-ka la ta-[ap-te-e nu-uk is-si-šú]
24 la ta-da-bu-bu ki-i [an-ni-e x x x]
25 iq-ṭí-bi ma-a SU$_6$.MEŠ [x x x x x x]
26 ma-a KUR gab-bi-šá gal-l[u$^{?}$-bu x x x x]
27 ŠEŠ-šú TA* $^{m}$i-ṣi-[ie-e x x x x x]
28 ina UGU di-ib-bi am-[mu-te x x x x]
29 ša ina É.GAL áš-pur-[an-ni x x x x]
e.30 TA* LÚ*.tur-gu-ma-[ni x x x x x]
31 ma-a dul$_6$-lu [x x x x x x x x]
32 a-bat LUGAL [x x x x x x x x x]

r.1 ú-sa-p[i-il x x x x x x x x]
2 ša-pal GÌR.[2 x x x x x x x x]
3 ma-a ú-ma-a ⸢x x⸣[x x x x x x x]
4 li-is-hu-ra li[l-li-ka x x x x x x]
5 liq-ba-šú ma-a al-k[a x x x x x x x]
6 la-áš-šú-ma É r[i x x x x x x x]
7 ha-nu-me-šú la iš-me [x x x x x x x]
8 a-na LÚ*.A—KIN ša LÚ*.[IGI.DUB si-par-ri AN.BAR]

CT 53 37+

1 To the king, [my] lo[rd: your servant NN]. Good health t[o the king, my lord!]

2 My messenger permane[ntly (appointed) in the presence of the treasurer] has greeted m[e, saying]:

4 "You ordered me to sa[y to] the treasurer: '[Wa]it for my messenger; see, I am going to write to the treasurer.' I was in Kipšuna for [x] days, and the treasurer kept waiting for [your] mess[enger], but you [did not send word], nor did your messenger come [...].

11 "Now [then] the peop[le of the country ......]

12 [......]

13 '[I] bear [......]

14 [te]ll me; *if* not [......],

15 should they do their work [......]?'

16 He told her: '[Do not do the work]; leave it until the day [......]. I am going to gather them. *Filling* [......] they pour [...]; I [am going to ...] and [pour] oil upon their heads.'"

21 These were the words [that] he spoke [in my presence]. I [asked him]: "Did you not [open] your mouth and speak [with him]?" He said [...] as [follows]:

25 "The beards [of ... and] the whole country have been trim[med. NN] and his brother [have ......] with Iṣi[ye]

28 concerning th[ose] matters [...]

29 about which I wrote to the Palace [...]

30 with an interpreter [...]:

31 'Work [......]

32 the king's word [......].'

r.1 He *answ*[*ered*: '......]

2 under the feet [......]

3 'Now [......]

4 should return, c[ome ......]

5 and tell him: Come [......]!

6 If not, and (if) ...[......]

7 does not listen to ...[......],

8 I am going to put the messenger of the [*treasurer* in irons].

**108** Same scribe as in nos. 106, 107 and 109.

9 *a-šak-kan-šú* LÚ*.A—KIN [*x x x x x x x*]
10 [L]Ú.A—KIN-*ia ki-i x*[*x x x x x x x*]
11 [*ki*]-⌈*i*⌉ LÚ*.A—KIN *ša* [*x x x x x x x*]
12 [*a*?-*q*]*a-ba-šú-ni ma*-⌈*a*⌉ [*x x x x x x x*]
13 GÌR.2-*šú a-a-ka-me-ni* [*x x x x x x x*]
14 *ma-a pu-tu-hu ša* [*x x x x x x x*]
15 *ù a-na ana—mi-ni* [*x x x x x x x*]
16 *ki-i ša pa-ni-tú* [*x x x x x x x x*]
17 *a-di-nu-ni ú-ma-a* [*ki-i*] ⌈*an-ni*⌉-*ma* [*x x x x*]
18 *ù di-ib-bi ša* U⌈N⌉.MEŠ KUR *ina* ŠÀ U[D-*me x x*]
19 *i-du-bu i-si-šú ma-a a-ta-a ki-i* [*an-ni-e*]
20 *te-pu-uš* MÍ.NIN—ŠEŠ-*ka* DUMU—ŠE[Š-*ka*]
21 *ta-du-uk ma-a* TA* *ma-ṣi te-pu-š*[*ú-u-ni*]
22 *ma-a nu-ú-da ma-ṣi ki-*[[*i*]] *at-ta x*[*x x x*]
23 *ta-du-ku-ni* MÍ KUR.*hab-hi ù ur-k*[*i-tú*]
24 ⌈Ì.MEŠ⌉ *ina* UGU *t*[*a-t*]*a-ba-ak ma-a* KUR.[URI-*a-a*]
25 *i-du-ak-*[*ši*] MÍ.KUR.URI-*tú ina* GIŠ.[GU.ZA]
26 *la tu-šab* [*ù šá*]-⌈*a*⌉-*ru iq-ṭí-bu-*[*ni-šú*]
27 *ma-a* LUGAL [*x x x x x x x x x x*]
28 *a-ni-nu* [*x x x x x x x x x x x*]
29 [*x x x x x x x x x x x x x x x*]
s.1 *ina* É.GAL *a-sa-par ki-*[*i x x x*]-*a-ni mi-nu ša* LUGAL *be-lí ṭè-e-mu*
2 *i-šak-ka-nu-ni a-n*[*a* ARAD-*šú liš-pu-r*]*a*

9 The messenger [......]

10 my messenger *like* [......].'

11 When the messenger of [......]

12 [*I*] had told him: '[......],'

13 [he did not set] foot anywhere at all [but said]:

14 '[I will bear] the responsibility for [......].

15 And why [......]?

16 Just as I previously gave [......], so [I will] now [give ...].'"

18 And the things that the people of the country speak with him [these] days! "Why did you do th[is] — kill the sister of your brother and the son of [your] brot[her]? From what you have done, we know well enough that you killed [*her*], a woman of Habhu; and afterwards you 'pour oil' upon it, saying: 'The [Urarṭia]n killed [her].' An Urarṭian woman may not sit upon the throne!"

26 They told [him an *unsubs*]*tantiated rumor*: "The king [......]

28 We [......]

29 [......].

s.1 I have [now] sent [*my messenger*] to the Palace. When [..., *may*] the king, my lord, [*write*] to [his servant] whatever he orders.

## 109. Allocating Fields for Garrison Troops

K 7551

beginning broken away
1′ [*x x x x x x*]*x-šu-nu ma-*[*a x x x*]
2′ [*x x x x a*]*t-tú-nu nu-uk* LUG[AL *x*]
3′ [*x x x x*]-⌈*ú*⌉-*bu ki-i ša* LUGAL [*be-lí*]
4′ [*ṭè-e-m*]*u iš-ku-na-ni a-na x*[*x x x*]
5′ [*ú*]-*še-ra-da-šú-nu mi-nu ša* LUG[AL *be-lí*]
6′ [*i*]-*qa-bu-ni ú-la-a ia-mut-*[*tu*]
7′ [*ina*] ŠÀ A.ŠÀ-*šú* GIŠ.SAR-*šú lu kam-mu-*[*su*]
8′ [*a*]-*na* DUMU—LUGAL *lip-lu-hu* [0]
9′ [*a*]-*ta-a* URU *gab-bi-šú* A.ŠÀ.M[EŠ]
10′ [*ša* URU.*b*]*ir-tú i-na-ši-*⌈*ú*⌉ [0]
11′ [*x x* LÚ*.*qur*]-*bu-te*! *ša x*[*x x x x*]
12′ [*x x x x x*]*x* [*x x x x x*]
rest broken away
Rev. destroyed

CT 53 394

(Beginning destroyed)

1 [...] them. He said: "[...]."

2 [I said]: "You are [...]; the ki[ng ...]."

3 I am bringing them down to [...] as the king, [my lord], ordered me. What are the king my [lord's] orders?

6 Alternatively, each (of them) should st[ay in] his (own) field or garden, and fear the Crown Prince. [W]hy should the whole town take away field[s of the f]ort?

11 [NN the royal body]guard who [......]

(Rest destroyed)

**109** Same scribe as in no. 108 etc. 8 See coll.

## 110. A Letter to the Treasurer

Sm 1162

1 *a-na* L[Ú.IGI.DUB EN-*ni*]
2 ARAD-*ka* $^{m}$*a-*[*ri-e*]
3 $^{m}$*a-ri-ṣa-a* [*lu* DI-*mu*]
4 *a-na* LÚ*.IGI.D[UB EN-*ni*]
5 *ša* LÚ*.IGI.D[UB *be-lí*]
6 [*i*]*š-pur-ni ina* U[GU *x x x*]
7 *i—ti-ma-l*[*i x x x x*]
8 ⸢*x x*⸣ [*x x x x x*]
rest broken away
Rev. uninscribed

CT 53 127

1 To the [Treasurer, our lord]: your servant A[riye] and Ariṣâ. [Good health] to the Trea[surer, our lord]!

5 As to what the trea[surer, my lord, w]rote me abo[ut ...], yesterday [......]

(Rest destroyed)

## 111. Report on Timber Transport

K 746

1 4-*me*-70 GIŠ.ÙR.MEŠ
2 UD-3-KÁM *ina* UGU ÍD *qur-bu*
3 1-*me* LÚ.ERIM.MEŠ *ša* KUR.*ú-ka-a-a*
4 30 *ša* $^{m}$*a-ri-e*
5 30 *ša* $^{m}$*ú-ri-ṣa-a*
e.6 PAB 60 ERIM.MEŠ *ša* URU.*ku-ma-a-a*
r.1 PAB 1-*me*-60 ERIM.MEŠ
2 TA* $^{m}$*aš-šur—re-ṣu-u-a*
3 *ina* ŠÀ URU.*ú-ra*
4 ⸢GIŠ.ÙR⸣.[MEŠ] *i-za-bi-lu*

ABL 490

1 On the third day, 470 beams were available on the river bank.

3 100 men of the Ukkeans, 30 men of Ariye, 30 men of Ariṣâ, in all 60 men of the Kummeans, all together 160 men are transporting the beam[s] to Ura with Aššur-reṣuwa.

## 112. Urarṭian Movements in Waisi

K 13147

beginning broken away
1′ [*x x x* $^{m}$*kaq*]*-qa-*[*da-nu*]
2′ [*x ina pa*]*-na-tu-u-*[*šu*]
3′ [*ina* IT]I.⸢DUL⸣ *ina* ŠÀ URU.*ú-e-*[*si*]
4′ [*e*]*-tar-ba* LUGAL
5′ [*i*]*—da-tú-u-šu e-tar-ba*
6′ [*ú-d*]*i-na ina* UGU ERIM.MEŠ
e.7′ [*am-mu*]*-te la-*⸢*a*⸣ *áš-me*
8′ [*mi-nu*] *ša ši-ti-ni*
r.1 [*šúm-m*]*u i-du-ku-šu-nu*
2 [*šúm-mu*] *ú-šá-gal-u-šú-nu*
3 [LÚ*.A—*š*]*ip-ri ša* $^{m}$*ur-za-na-a*
4 [LUGAL KUR.*mu*]*-ṣa-ṣi-ri*
5 [LÚ*.A—*šip-ri ša*] $^{m}$*ú-ri-ṣa-a*
6 [*ina* UGU-*hi-ia it*]*-tal-ku-n*[*i*]
7 [*x x x x x x*] ⸢*x*⸣ [*x*]
rest broken away

CT 53 114

(Beginning destroyed)

1 [B]efore [him, Kaq]qa[danu had en]tered Wai[si] in Tishri (VII); the king entered the city [af]ter him.

6 I have [not y]et heard what happened to [tho]se men, [wheth]er they [have] been killed [or] deported.

r.3 [A mess]enger of Urzana, [king of Mu]ṣaṣir, [*and a messenger of*] Ariṣâ have [c]ome [*to me*]

(Rest destroyed)

**110** → Deller Zagros p.116. 2 A written over a horizontal wedge; see coll.

# 7. Letters from Kurbail and Nearby Provinces



FIG. 20. *Troops in mountain country (reign of Sennacherib).*
ORIGINAL DRAWING VI, 20

## 113. All Quiet on the Northern Front

K 574

1 *a-na* LUGAL EN-*ia*
2 ARAD-*ka* $^{\mathrm{m}}$*gab-bu—ana—aš-šur*
3 *ina* UGU *ṭè-e-me*
4 *ša* LUGAL EN *iš-ku-na-ni-ni*
5 *ina* UGU *ma-ṣar-ti*
6 *ša* KUR.*ú-ra-ar-ṭa-a-a*
7 TA* É *ina* URU.*kur-ba-ìl*
8 *e-ru-bu-u-ni*
9 LÚ*.DUMU—*šip-ra-ni-ia*
10 *ina* UGU $^{\mathrm{md}}$PA—ZU
11 *ina* UGU $^{\mathrm{m}}$*aš-šur*—EN—KALAG-*an*
12 *ina* UGU $^{\mathrm{m}}$*aš-šur—re-ṣu-*⸢*u-a*⸣
13 *il-lu-ku il-la-ku-u-ni*
14 *ši-*⸢*ir*!!⸣*—šu-me-e*
15 *ša* L[Ú!] *ša*! *m*[*e*!]*-me-ni*
16 *la né-*[*ṣi-in i*]*a-mu-ut-tum*
17 *dul-lu-š*[*u*! *ep*]*-pa-áš*
18 *gír-ru-tú me-me-ni la-a-šú*
r.1 *a-ki an-ni-e*
2 *ni-sa-*[*n*]*am-me*
3 *ma-a* KUR.*ú-ra-ar-ṭa-a-a*
4 TA ŠÀ URU.*ṭu-ru-uš-pi-a*
5 *la ú-ṣi-a*
6 *ù* [*a-n*]*i-nu ma-ṣar-tú*
7 *ša* L[UGAL EN] *ṭè-e-mu*
8 *iš-*[*ku-na*]*-ni-ni*
9 *ni-na-*[*ṣar*] *la ni-ši-aṭ*
10 UD-⸢16⸣-[KAM *š*]*a* ITI.ŠU
11 *ina* URU.*kur-*⸢*ba-ìl*⸣ *aq-ṭí-rib*
12 UD-20-KAM *ša* ITI.NE
13 *e-gír-tú ina* UGU LUGAL EN-*ia*
14 *a-sap-ra*

ABL 123

1 To the king, my lord: your servant Gabbu-ana-Aššur.

3 As to the orders that the king, my lord, gave me concerning the watch of the Urarṭian, ever since I entered Kurbail my messengers have been going back and forth to Nabû-le'i, Aššur-belu-da'an and Aššur-reṣuwa.

14 We have not [gotten] a whiff of anybody or anything. Everybody is doing h[is] work, there is no hostility at all.

r.1 We keep hearing as follows: "The Urarṭian has not come out of Ṭurušpâ." Nevertheless, [w]e are ke[eping] the watch about which the k[ing, my lord,] ga[ve] me orders — we are not negligent.

10 I arrived in Kurbail on the 16th day of Tammuz (IV), and am sending (this) letter to the king, my lord, on the 20th of Ab (V).

## 114. The King of Urarṭu Gathers his Army

K 635

1 *a-na* LUGA[L EN-*ia*]
2 ARAD-*ka* $^{\mathrm{m}}$*gab*!!-[*bu—ana—aš-šur*]

CT 53 7

1 To the kin[g, my lord]: your servant Gab[bu-ana-Aššur].

**113** 14f See coll. The reading *ši-*⸢*ir*!!⸣ is virtually certain; *ši-*⸢*ṭir*⸣ (W 157) is excluded. *šīr šumê* properly means "roasted meat"; in the present context, an idiomatic colloquial meaning like "smell, scent, sniff," or "whiff" must be involved. 17 W 157.

**114** → Deller Zagros p.103f. 2 See coll. The first sign of the name is badly effaced but does look like I; both the orthography and the introductory formula imply, however, that the sender is Gabbu-ana-Aššur. There is room for the required signs in the break at the end of the line. 9 Sic (see coll.); *ša* [*pu-t*]*u-ni*! or [*pu-t*]*u-*⸢*ú*!!⸣-[*a*] excluded.

3 KUR.⸢*ú-ra-ar-ṭa*⸣*-a-*[*a*]
4 *e-mu-*⸢*qe*⸣*-šú ina* KUR.*ú-a-za-na*!
5 *up-tah-*⸢*hi-ir*⸣ [0]
6 *bé-et pa-*[*ni*]-⸢*šú-ni*⸣ [*l*]*a áš-me*
7 $^{m}$*me-la-ar-*⸢*ṭu-a*⸣
8 LÚ*.A-*šú* ⸢$^{m}$*a-ba*⸣-[*l*]*i-*⸢*ú*⸣*-qu-nu*
9 LÚ*.EN.NAM ⸢*ša*⸣ [KUR.*x x*]*x-pa*
10 *a-di e-m*[*u-qe-šú-nu*]
11 [*x*] *x*[*x x x x x*]
rest broken away
Rev. beginning broken away
1′ ⸢*x x x*⸣ [*x*] KUR.⸢MEŠ⸣
2′ *i-*⸢*za-qu*⸣*-pu*
3′ ⸢LUGAL⸣ *be-lí lu-u ú-da*
4′ LUGAL EN *lu-u la*
5′ *i-qab-bi ma-a* [*k*]*i-i*
6′ *taš-m*[*u*]*-u-ni ma-a a-ta-a*
7′ *la* ⸢*taš*⸣*-pu-ra*

3 The king of Urarṭu has assembled his army in Wazana; I have [n]ot heard where he intends to go.

7 His son Melarṭua, and Aba[l]iuqunu, the governor [of ...], together with [their] tro[ops ......]

(Break)

r.1 [...] they will attack [...]... The king, my lord, should know this; the king, my lord, should not say: "Why did you not write even though you heard?"

## 115. Retrieving Captured Soldiers

K 1043

1 [*a-na* LUGAL EN-*ia*]
2 ⸢ARAD⸣-[*ka*] $^{m}$[*gab-bu—ana—aš-šur*]
3 UGU *ṭè-me ša* KUR.U[RI-*a-a*]
4 *a-sa-par nu-uk mì-i-*[*nu*]
5 *ṭè-en-šú-nu ma-a* 6 LÚ*.ERIM.[MEŠ-*ni*]
6 *ša* ZÍD.*e-ṣi-di-a-te*
7 *a-na* URU.HAL.ṢU.MEŠ
8 *ú-še-lu-u-ni ú-ṣab-bi-tú*
9 *a-na* LÚ*.GAL—É *a-sa-par*
10 *nu-uk* Á.2-*ka*
11 *ina* ŠÀ-*šú-nu la tu-bal*
12 *nu-uk šu-up-ru*
13 UGU $^{m}$*a-bi-le-e*
r.1 [*m*]*a a-ta-a* LÚ*.ERIM.MEŠ-*ni*
2 *tu-ṣa-bi-ta nu-uk*
3 *mi-nu ša e-pal-ka-ni*
4 *ár-hiš šup-ra*
5 UD-17-KAM NA$_4$.$^{d}$ALAD.$^{d}$LAMA
6 [U]GU ÍD *uq-ṭa-ri-ib*
rest uninscribed

ABL 579

1 [To the king, my lord: your] servant [Gabbu-ana-Aššur].

3 As to the news of Ura[rṭians], I wrote: "Wha[t] is the news of them?" They were reported to have captured six [*of our*] soldier[s] who were moving provisions up to the forts.

9 I wrote to the major-domo: "Don't try to take them by force. (Instead) write to Abilê: 'Why have you seized our men?' and quickly write me what he replies."

r.5 I moved the bull colossus to the river bank on the 17th.

## 116. Arrests in Kumme

K 1224

beginning broken away
1′ $^{m}$⸢*e*⸣-[*x x x x*]
2′ *ša* ŠU $^{m}$⸢*a*⸣-[*ri-e*]
3′ $^{m}$*ba-bi-*⸢*su*?⸣-[*x*]
4′ *ša* ŠU $^{m}$*a-ri-a-*⸢*ṣa*⸣-[*a*]
5′ *la-a ina* KUR-*e* [0]
6′ ⸢*i*⸣*-ṣa-ba-s*[*u-nu*]
rest broken away

CT 53 170

(Beginning destroyed)

1 E[...], a subordinate of A[riye], and Babisu[...], a subordinate of Ariaṣ[â]; he did not capture th[em] in the mountain [......]

(Break)

Rev. beginning broken away

1′ [*x*] ⸢*ta bi*⸣ [*x x x*]
2′ *i-ṣa-ab-t*[*u-šú-nu*]
3′ *a-na* UGU LUGAL [EN-*ia*]
4′ *ú-se-bi-la-*[*šú-nu*]
rest uninscribed

r.1 [They] have been arrested ... [...], and I am herewith sending [them] to the king, [my lord].

## 117. Delays in Timber Delivery

K 1182 (ABL 619) + K 1543 + K 1917

1 *a-na* LUGAL [EN-*ia*]
2 ARAD-*ka* m[*gab-bu—ana—aš-šur*]
3 UGU *ši-bir-te* [*ša ta-li-ka-ni*]
4 *ma-a a-ta-a* [GIŠ.ÙR.MEŠ *na-mar-ku-u*]
5 *a-di a-ki man-n*[*i x x x x*]
6 m*aš-šur—re-ṣu-u-*[*a* KUR.*x x-a-a*]
7 KUR.*ku-ma-a-a* K[UR.*x x x-a-a*]
8 KUR.*ba-bu-ta-*[*a-a* KUR.*x x-a-a*]
9 KUR.*ú-ka-a-a* KUR.*i*[*l-x-a-a*]
10 KUR.*ú-li-a-a* KUR.*me-ṣa-*[*a-a*]
11 PAB 10 EN—URU.URU.MEŠ 2 *mar-di-*⸢*a*⸣*-*[*te*]
12 *e-tab-ku-u-ni a-di* UGU-*hi-ia*
13 *a-na-ku a-na ú-di-ia*
14 3 *mar-di-tú a-tab-ka*
15 DINGIR.ME-*ni ša* LUGAL EN-*ia*
16 ⸢*lu*⸣*-u-di-ú šúm-ma ina* ŠÀ UD-*m*[*e*]
17 *ša* GIŠ.ÙR.MEŠ *ina* UGU-*hi-ia*
18 DU-*u-ni-ni* LÚ*.E[N?—*x x*]
19 *ú-še-ra-ni-ni* GIŠ.[ÙR.MEŠ]
20 ⸢*šúm*⸣*-ma la-a ina ki-b*[*ir*?] ÍD]
e.21 [*n*]*a*!*-ta-na*!*-a-a x*[*x x x*]
22 A.MEŠ *ina* ÍD *la* [*e-ṣu-ni*]
23 *mar-ṣa-te* ⸢*ša*⸣ [ÍD *x x x*]
r.1 GIŠ.ÙR.[MEŠ *x x x x x*]
2 30 *áš-*⸢*la*?!⸣*-ni*! *x*[*x x x x x*]
3 4-*me*-60 GIŠ.Ù[R.MEŠ *x x x*]
4 TA KUR.*ni-x*[*x x x x*]
5 *ša* KUR.*qu-*⸢*ru*⸣*-b*[*a x x*]
6 *a-*⸢*na*⸣ LUG[AL *x x x x x*]
7 *nu-uk a-*[*lik*? *x x x x*]
8 *ma-a a-nu-t*[*e x x*] ⸢*x*⸣ [*x x*]
9 *a-ta-har* UD-2⸢5⸣-⸢KÁM⸣ [*x x-t*]*e*
10 [*ina*] *né-ri-bi* ⸢*ša*⸣ URU.DI-EN-*ia*
11 [*ú-s*]*e-li* UD-26-KÁM GIŠ.ÙR.MEŠ
12 [*re-hu*]*-te a-ka-ra-ár*
13 [*x x x*]*-a ú-še-la x*[*x*]
14 [*x*]*x*[*x x*]*x* ⸢*ni*?!⸣ *nu* [*x x x*]
15 ⸢*x*⸣[*x x x x x x x*]
16 *a-na* [*x x x x x x*]
rest (4 lines) uninscribed

CT 53 35

1 To the king, [my lord]: your servant [Gabbu-ana-Aššur].

3 As to the message [*which I got*]: "Why [*are the beams late*]?" –

5 *up to now* [...], Aššur-reṣuw[a, the ...ean], the Kummean, [the ...ean], the Babutean, [the ...ean], the Ukkean, the I[l...ean], the Uliean, the Meṣa[ean], in all 10 city lords have hauled (the beams) to me (over a distance of) two stag[es], while I had to haul them for the third stage alone!

15 By the gods of the king, my lord, the day that the beams came to me, the [...] (official) did not *leave* me; (I swear) the [beams] are on the [*river*] *ba*[*nk*] ..., but the water in the river is [low], and the difficult spots of [the river *are many*].

r.1 [I have ...ed] the beams and [...] 30 ropes;
3 460 be[ams ...]
4 from *the pa*[*ss* ...]
5 of Qurub[a ...]
6 to the ki[ng ...]
7 I told (him): "*G*[*o* ......]!"
8 He said: "I have received *my equipment* [......]."

r.9 I [mov]ed [the ...]s up [to] the pass of *Denya* on the 25th day and shall pile up [the re]st [of] the beams on the 26th; [...] I shall move up [......]

(Rest destroyed)

**117** → Deller Zagros p.117ff. 21, r.2 See coll. r.5, 14 See coll.

FIG. 21. *Under arrest (reign of Assurbanipal).*
BM 124793.

# 118. Complaint on Disobedience

K 503

1 *a-na* LUGAL EN-*ia*
2 ARAD-*ka* $^{m}$*gab-bu—ana—aš-šur*
3 NA$_4$.I.DIB.MEŠ
4 NA$_4$.$^{d}$ALAD.$^{d}$LAMA
5 *ina* UGU-*hi-ia*
6 [*k*]*a*$^{!}$-*ár-ri*
7 UN.MEŠ KUR
8 *mi-mi-e-ni*
9 *la im-ma-gúr*$^{!}$
10 *a-na dul*$_6$$^{!}$-*l*[*i*$^{!}$-*i*]*a*
11 *la ú-*[*ṣu-u-ni*]
e.12 *ma-a* ERIM.ME[Š-*ka*]
13 ⸢*a*⸣-*ni-*⸢*ni*$^{!}$⸣-[*e*]
r.1 ⸢*la*$^{!}$ *i*$^{!}$-*šam-*[*u-ni*]
2 *a-na-ku*$^{!}$-*u* [*x x*]
3 *an-nu-*⸢*te*⸣ *m*[*i*$^{!}$]-⸢*i*⸣-*nu*
4 *ša i-ba-šu-u-ni*
5 *ša la-šu-u-ni*
6 *ki-i a-he-iš*
7 ⸢*la*$^{!}$⸣-*šú la* ⸢*i*$^{!}$⸣-*šam-u-ni*

ABL 125

[1] To the king, my lord: your servant Gabbu-ana-Aššur.

[3] Stone thresholds and bull colossi are imposed upon me, but the people of the country totally refuse to g[o forth] to my wor[k], saying: "Are we [your] men?"

[r.1] They do not lis[ten to me] — am I [...]?

[3] These (people) unanimously and categorically disobey me in every possible way.

# 119. Complaint on Lack of Straw

K 491

1 ⸢*a*⸣-*na* ⸢LUGAL⸣ EN-*ia*
2 ARAD-*ka* $^{m}$*gab-bu—ana—aš-šur*
3 ŠE.IN.NU.MEŠ *gab-bu*
4 *ina* KUR-*ia a-na* URU.BÀD—$^{m}$MAN—GIN.NA
5 *ša-a*[*k*$^{!}$]-⸢*lu*⸣ *an-nu-rig*
6 LÚ*.*mu-šár-kis*.MEŠ-*ni*
7 *i—d*[*a*]-*tú-u-a i-du-lu*
8 ŠE.IN.NU.MEŠ *a-na a-ṣap*.MEŠ
9 *la-áš-šú ú-ma-a*
10 *mi-nu ša* LUGAL *be-lí*
11 *i-qa-bu-u-ni*
Rev. uninscribed

ABL 122

[1] To the king, my lord: your servant Gabbu-ana-Aššur.

[3] All the straw in my country is reserved for Dur-Šarruken, and my recruitment officers are now running after me (because) there is no straw for the pack animals.

[9] Now, what are the king my lord's instructions?

# 120. Leave me Some Booty, Please

K 903

1 [*a-na* LUGAL E]N-⸢*ia*$^{!}$⸣
2 [ARA]D-⸢*ka*⸣ $^{m}$*gab-bu—a-na—aš-šur*

ABL 124

[1] [To the king], my [lo]rd: your [serva]nt Gabbu-ana-Aššur.

**118** r.1f See coll.
**119** → TCAE p.255. [5] See coll. [7] I.e., "begging or pestering me" (for straw). The idiom refers to dogs running around or after their master, wagging their tails and begging for morsels, as often in contemporary petitions.

3 GI.AMBAR.MEŠ
4 *mar i-ba-šú-ni*
5 *a-na ma-te-ni*
6 LÚ*.*qur-bu-te*
7 *a-na pa-ni pa*!*-qi-ni*
8 *hu-ub-tú*
9 ⸢*i*⸣*-si-te*
r.1 [*lu*]*-ra-mu-ni*
2 GI.AMBAR.MEŠ
3 *a-na* É—*i-si-te-ia*
4 *la-áš-šu*

3 Whatever reed there is in our country, the royal bodyguard is ...ing over it.

8 [Let] them leave me the *booty* of the (depot) tower. There are no reeds for my tower.

## 121. Protest against False Accusations

K 468 + K 1154 (CT 53 164)

1 *a-na* LUGAL EN-*ia*
2 ARAD-*ka* $^{m}$*gab-bu—ana—aš-šur*
3 UGU UN.MEŠ *ša* $^{m}$*ar-za-a-a*
4 *ša* LUGAL EN *iš-pur-a-ni*
5 *ma-a* UN.MEŠ *ša ina* GIŠ.*le-*ʾ*i*
6 *šak-nu-u-ni ma-a ki-ṣir*
7 *ša ak-ṣur-u-ni a-di-na-kan-ni*
8 *ma-a ha-nu-u-te lu ina pa-ni-ka*
9 *ù ma-a* UN.MEŠ
10 *ut-ru-u-ti*
11 [*š*]*a ina* GIŠ.*le-*ʾ*i*
12 [*l*]*a áš-ṭa-ru-u-ni*
13 [*ma*]-⸢*a*⸣ *a-na* $^{m}$*ar-za-*⸢*a*⸣-[*a*]
14 *di-ni* [0]

ABL 121+

1 To the king, my lord: your servant Gabbu-ana-Aššur.

3 As to the people of Arzâ about whom the king, my lord, wrote me: "I have given you the people entered on the writing-board, the cohort which I formed; these are at your disposal. However, give Arzâ the rest of the people whose (names) I [did n]ot write in the writing-board" —

**120** 7ff See coll.; signs absolutely clear.

FIG. 22. *Writing down the details (reign of Sennacherib).*
ORIGINAL DRAWING VI, 5.

15 UN.MEŠ-*ma ša la-a* [0]
16 GIŠ.*le-ʾi* [0]
17 [*l*]*a-áš-šu ina pa-ni-i*⸢*a*⸣
18 [*k*]*e-e-tú* TA* ŠÀ-*bi*
e.19 [UN.ME]Š *ša* GIŠ.*le-ʾ*[*i*]
20 [*ša* L]UGAL EN [0]
r.1 [*i-d*]*i-na-an-ni* [0]
2 [*x x*] *ina pa-ni-*⸢*šú*⸣ [0]
3 *a-ki* LÚ*.A—*šip-ri* [0]
4 *ša* LUGAL *i-si-i*⸢*a*⸣
5 *a-na* ⸢URU.*kur-ba*⸣-[*il*]
6 *i-*[*li-ku-ni*]
7 [*x x x x x*]
8 [*x x x x x*]
9 *m*[*a x x*]*x* ⸢*x*⸣[*x x*]
10 ⸢*de*!*-et*?!⸣ *ha-ni-*⸢*e*?!⸣ [0]
11 *ú-hur* TA* *a-a-k*[*i*!]
12 *ih-tal-qu-u-ni* [0]
13 *i-na* UGU-*hi-ia i-tal-*⸢*ku-ni*⸣
14 *a-na mi-ni di-ib-bi*
15 *la-áš-la-mu*!*-te* LUGAL EN
16 *i-sa-na-me* UN.MEŠ
17 *a—mar ša* LUGAL EN
18 *ik-ṣur-u-ni i-di-na-ni*
19 *ha-nu-te ina pa-ni-ia*
20e [[UN.MEŠ *ša la* GIŠ.*le-ʾi*!]]
21e [[*la-áš-šú*!]]

[15] There are no people not on the writing-board at my disposal! In fact, from [the peo-p]le in the writing-[board whom] the king, my lord, gave me, [x] are at his disposal!

[r.3] When the king's messenger c[ame] with me to Kurba[il]

(Break)

[10] After this, (*others*) disappeared from the temple and came to me.

[r.14] Why does the king, my lord, pay attention to groundless allegations? Only those people whom the king, my lord, organized and gave me are in my service. [[There are no people not on the writing-board (in my service).]]

## 122. Anticipating Criticism

79-7-8,154

1 *a-na* [LUGAL *be-lí-ia*]
2 ARAD-[*ka* $^{m}$*x x x x x*]
3 ⸢*lu*⸣ [*šul-mu a-na* LUGAL EN-*ia*]
4 *x*[*x*].⸢MEŠ⸣ *a-x*[*x x x x x*]
5 *x*[*x*]*x da* [*x x x x x*]
6 ⸢*i*⸣*-si-ia* [*x x x x x*]
7 GUD.MEŠ UDU.MEŠ [*x x x x*]*-ni*
8 *it-tan-na* [*x x x x x*] *aš*
9 *la-a* GIŠ.GEŠTIN [*x x x x x*]
10 TA* ŠÀ *x*[*x x x x x x*]
11 *ša* ⸢*e*?⸣*-x*[*x x x x x x x*]
12 GUD.MEŠ [*x x x x x x x*]
13 *x*[*x x x x x x x x x*]
14 [*x x x x x x x x x*]
15 [*x x x x x x x x x*]
e.16 *a-n*[*a x x x x x*]
17 *be-*⸢*lí*⸣ [*x x x x x*]
r.1 LUGAL EN LÚ.*x*[*x x x x*]
2 *a-na ka-li-e x*[*x x x*]
3 *ina* ŠÀ *mi-i-ni lu-šal-*[*x x*]
4 ANŠE.SAL.HÚB.MEŠ DUMU MU.A[N.NA]
5 *ša ina pa-ni-ia ú-x*[*x x x*]

CT 53 137

[1] To [the king, my lord: your] servant [NN]. Go[od health to the king, my lord]!

(Break)

[6] with me [......]
[7] gave me the oxen and sheep [......]
[9] neither wine [nor ......]
[10] from [......]
[11] which [......]
[12] oxen [......]

(Break)

[16] t[o ......]
[17] my lord [......].

[r.1] The king, my lord, sh[ould] posthaste [send] a [......]; by what means can I [...]? The one-ye[ar-old] mares that I have [......].

**121** r.10ff See coll. r.15 Sic (over erasure); W 57. Cf. *di-ib-bi la šal-mu-ti*, NL 59 s.3. r.20f See coll.

6 *an-nu-rig* LÚ.EN—*p*[*i-qit-ti-ia*]
7 LÚ.A.BA *i-si-šú il-la*[*k*]
8 *ina pa-an* LUGAL EN-*ia le-ru-bu*
9 LUGAL EN *liš-al-šú-nu mi-i-nu*
10 *ina* URU.*bir-te ú-ra-mu-u-ni*
11 LUGAL EN *lu-u la i-qab-bi*
12 *ma-a ap-ti-qi-su la e-pu-uš*
rest uninscribed

6 Now, an offi[cial of mine] is leaving with a scribe; let them enter into the presence of the king, my lord, and let the king, my lord, ask them what I/he/they left in the fort.

11 May the king, my lord, not say: "I appointed him, and he did not achieve (anything)!"

## 123. ———

Sm 2071

destroyed beginning broken away
r.1′ [*x x x x*]*x-u* ⸢*a-ta*?⸣-[*x x x x*]
2′ [*x x-b*]*il ma-a šúm-ma* UD-1-⸢KÁM *e*?⸣-[*x x*]
3′ [*ma-a k*]*i-i a-he-iš ni-qar-ri-ib*
4′ [*ni*]-*mat-ta-ah ú-ma-a*
5′ *mi-i-nu ša* LUGAL *be-lí i-qab-bu-u-*[*ni*]

CT 53 859

(Beginning destroyed)

2 "If the 1st day [is ...], we shall get there and fetch it together."

5 Now, what are the king my lord's instructions?

## 124. A Matter of Loyalty

K 12959

beginning broken away
1′ [*x x x x x*] ⸢*x x x*⸣ [*x*]
2′ [*x x x x* LU]GAL EN *ú-da*
3′ [*x x x x x* U]RU.HAL.ṢU.MEŠ
4′ [*x x x x* LUG]AL EN-*ia ad-di*⸢*n*⸣
5′ [LUGAL *be-lí lu la*] *i-qab-bi*
6′ [*ma-a* LÚ.*par-ri*]-*ṣu šú-ú*
7′ [*x x x x* L]Ú.ARAD.MEŠ *ša* LUGAL
8′ [*am—mar ina pa-ni-i*]*a-a-ni*
9′ [*x x x x x x x*] ⸢*i*⸣
rest broken away
Rev. destroyed

CT 53 440

(Beginning destroyed)

2 [... the kin]g, my lord, knows

3 [......] the forts

4 [......] I gave [to the ki]ng, my lord.

5 [May the king, my lord, not] say: "He is [a trait]or!"

7 [... all] the king's subjects [who are in] my [service]

(Rest destroyed)

## 125. ———

79-7-8,52

1 *a-na* LUGAL [EN-*ia*]
2 ARAD-*ka* $^{m}$*g*[*ab*?-*bu—ana—aš-šur*]
3 *ša* LUGAL EN [*iš-pur-an-ni*]
4 *ma-a i-ba-á*[*š-ši-i*]
5 *ina* URU.NINA *ina* [*x x x*]
6 $^{m}$*tu-ʾa-ia* [*x x x*]
7 [*x x*]⸢*x x x*⸣[*x x x x*]
rest broken away
Rev. beginning broken away
1′ [*x x*]⸢*x x x*⸣[*x x x x*]

ABL 1414

1 To the king, [my lord]: your servant G[*abbu-ana-Aššur*].

3 As to what the king, my lord, [wrote to me]: "Is the[re] in Nineveh, in [...], Tu'ayu [......]?"

(Break)

**125** 2 See coll.; topmost horizontal might be accidental. 4 See coll.; *-na-* (W 363) excluded. 6 Note $^{m}$*tu-ú-a-a* L[Ú*.*x x x* no. 281:12 (from Sennacherib).

2′ *ma-a* LÚ *ka-*[*x x x*]
3′ *ma-a* LÚ *ah-*[*x x x*]
4′ *ma-a* É LÚ.[*x x x*]
5′ *ba-ʾu-ú* [*x x x x*]
6′ *ú-ma-a x*[*x x x x*]
7′ URU.*tú-ur-*[*x x x x*]
8′ *a-lik-u-n*[*i x x x x*]
9e *a-ta-ma*[*r a-na* LUGAL]
10e EN-*ia* [*as-sap-ra*]

r.2 "the [...], the [...], and the house of the [......] have been searched [...]."

r.6 Now, [when] I went [...to] *Tur*[...], I sa[w ...], and (subsequently) [wrote to the king], my lord.

## 126. Feeding the Troops

K 567

1 *a-na* LUGAL EN-*ia*
2 ARAD-*ka* $^{m}$*aš-šur*—EN—KALAG-*an*
3 *lu-u* DI-*mu a-na* MAN EN-*ia*
4 $^{d}$AG *u* $^{d}$AMAR.UTU *a-na* MAN EN-*ia*
5 *lik-ru-bu ina* UD-22-KAM
6 *ana-ku nu-uk la-al-lik-ka*
7 IGI.2.MEŠ *ša* MAN EN-*ia la-mur*
8 $^{m}$*ka-ku-la-nu* LÚ*.*qur-bu-te*
9 *a-na ir-ti-ia* TA *lib-bi* URU.[*x*]-⸢*li*$^{!}$-*te*$^{!}$⸣
10 *ú-sa-hi-ra-a-ni ma-a a-l*[*ik*$^{?}$]
11 LÚ*.ERIM.MEŠ-*ka pa-ṭi-ir* :$^{!}$ *šú*[*m-mu*]
12 *la il-li-ku ma-a* LÚ*.ERIM.[MEŠ-*ka*]
13 *ina bu-bu-te i-mut-tú* [*x x x*]
14 *ša* 5 ITI.MEŠ ŠE.*tab-ku a-t*[*an*$^{!}$-*na-šú-nu*]
15 ⸢1$^{!}$⸣ *qa-a-a* Ì.MEŠ 1 *qa-a-*⸢*a*⸣ [NINDA.MEŠ]
16 [1 *q*]*a-a-a* Ú.ZAG.HI.⸢LI⸣.[SAR *x x*]
17 [*i-se*]-⸢*niš*⸣ *a-tan-na-šú-nu* [*x x x*]
18 [*ha-ra*]-*me-ma ana-ku at-*[*tu-ṣi*$^{?}$]
19 [*x x* UG]U LÚ*.ERIM.[MEŠ *x x*]
e.20 [*x x x-t*]*ar*$^{!}$-*bu*$^{!}$ [*x x x*]
21 [*x x x-t*]*i*$^{!}$ *x*[*x x x*]
r.1 [*x x x-n*]*i*$^{!}$-*tu*$^{!}$ [*x x*]
2 [*x x x*] *ku-um šú-nu* [*x x*]
3 [*ina bat*]-*ti*—*bat-ti* ⸢*ša*$^{!}$⸣ UR[U$^{!}$.*x x*]
4 [*kam*]-*mu-su*$^{!}$ TA IGI *ku-*[*pe-e*]
5 *la i-lak-ka šú-nu l*[*a x x x*]
6 *ú-ma-a an-nu-*⸢*rig*⸣ [*x x* (*x*)]
7 TA $^{m}$*ka-ku-la-a-ni a-*[*na* URU$^{?}$]
8 *i-tal-lu-ku i-ru-bu* [0$^{?}$]
9 *ša* MAN *be-lí iš-pur-an-ni* [0]
10 *ma-a a-ta-a* LÚ*.GAL—É-*k*[*a*$^{!}$]
11 *ina lib-bi la-šu* 10 LÚ*.E[N$^{?}$—*x*]
12 *ša a-na* MAN EN-*ia a-qa-b*[*u*$^{!}$]-*u*$^{!}$-[*ni*]
13 *ša-mu-ru a*—*dan-niš*
14 *ši-a-*⸢*h*⸣*u*$^{!}$ *šu-ú*
15 *a-*⸢*na*⸣ MAN EN-*ia a-sa-*⸢*par*⸣-*ra*

ABL 243

1 To the king, my lord: your servant Aššur-belu-da'an. Good health to the king, my lord! May Nabû and Marduk bless the king, my lord!

5 On the 22nd day, I said: "I'll go and see the eyes of the king, my lord," (when) I met Kakkullanu the royal bodyguard, (who) turned me back from the town [*A*]lite, saying: "G[o] and release your troops: i[f] they do not go, [the] men will die of hunger!"

13 [...], I g[ave them] 5 months worth of stored grain; I also gave them 1 litre of oil, 1 litre of [*bread*, and 1 li]tre of cress [...].

18 [La]ter on, I *de*[*parted* ...... *t*]*o* the troop[s];

20 they [en]tered [......]

(Break)

r.2 lest they [*starve*]. They are [st]aying [in the en]virons of the city [...]; they cannot [depart] because of sn[ow].

6 Now then they are going about and entering [the city] with Kakkullanu.

9 As to what the king, my lord, wrote me: "Why is yo[ur] major-domo not there?" – the ten [*city*] *lords* about whom I spoke with the king, my lord, are extremely *fierce*; I did write to the king, my lord, *in full earnest*.

**126** 9 There is only room for a narrow sign such as A or ZA in the break. 11, 14f, 20f See coll. r.1, 4, 10f See coll. r.14 See coll. and critical note on no. 243:20; ⸢LÚ*$^{!}$⸣.A—⸢KIN$^{!}$⸣ (W 95) excluded.

## 127. Log Towing

K 1932 (ABL 244) + K 12957

1 *a-na* LUGAL *be-lí-ia*
2 ARAD-*ka* $^{m}$*aš-šur*—EN—KALAG-*an*
3 ⌈*lu*⌉-*u* DI-*mu a-na* LUGAL *be-lí-ia*
4 $^{d}$PA *u* $^{d}$ŠÚ *a-na* LUGAL *be-lí-ia*
5 *lik-ru-bu* : DI-*mu a-na ma*-⌈*a*⌉-*te*
6 *ša* LUGAL BURU$_{14}^{!}$ ⌈*x x*⌉ [*x x x x*]
7 [*ib-ta*]*l-ṭa*$^{!}$ : ŠÀ-*bu š*[*a* LUGAL EN-*ia*]
8 *lu* D[ÙG.GA] GIŠ.⌈ÙR$^{!}$⌉.M[EŠ *ša* LUGAL *b*]*e*-[*lí*]
9 *iq-bu*-[*u-n*]*i*$^{!}$ : 50$^{!}$ [*x x x x x x*]
10 *a-sa-da*-[*ad x x x x x x x x*]
11 *a-na-ku* ⌈EN.NUN⌉ [*x x x x x*]
12 *a-na*-⌈*ṣar*$^{!}$⌉ EN.NUN *x*[*x x x x x*]
13 *ša* $^{m}$*aš-šur—rém-a*-⌈*ni*⌉ [*x x x x*]
14 ⌈*a*$^{?}$⌉-*na-ṣar*$^{!}$ ⌈*a*⌉-*x*[*x x x x x*]
rest broken away
Rev. uninscribed

CT 53 63

1 To the king, my lord: your servant Aššur-belu-da'an. Good health to the king, my lord! May Nabû and Marduk bless the king, my lord!

5 The land of the king is well; the harvest [...; ... has recov]ered; [the king, my lord], can be gl[ad].

8 (As for) the log[s about which the king, my lo]rd, sp[oke], I have tow[ed] 50 [......].

11 I am keeping watch [......]. I am keeping watch [......] of Aššur-remanni [......]

(Rest destroyed)

## 128. Fragment of a Report on Urarṭu

K 1940

1 [*a-n*]*a* LUGAL [*be-lí-ia*]
2 [ARAD]-*ka* $^{md}$P[A—ZU$^{?}$]
3 [*l*]*u* DI-*mu a-na* LUGAL *b*[*e-lí-ia*]
4 [D]I-*mu a-na* URU.*bi-ra-t*[*i*]
5 DI-*mu a-na* KUR *ša* LUGAL *be-lí*-[*ia*]
6 *ša* LUGAL *be-lí ṭè-e-mu iš-k*[*un-an-ni*]
7 *ma-a* LÚ*.A—KIN-*ka a-na* URU.*bi*-[*ra-ti*]
8 [*šu*]*p*-⌈*ru*⌉ *ma-a* ⌈*ṭè-e*⌉-*m*[*u ša*] KUR.[URI-*a-a*]
9 [*hu*]-*ur-ṣu šup*-[*ra x x x x*]
10 [*x*] ⌈*a*⌉-*na* KUR.[*x x x x x x*]
rest broken away
Rev. destroyed

CT 53 215

1 [T]o the king, [my lord]: your [servant] Na[bû-*le'i*]. Good health to the king, [my] l[ord]!

4 The *forts are* well; the land of the king, [my] lord, is well.

6 As to the order which the king, my lord, ga[ve me]: "Send your messenger to Bi[rate] and send me a detailed repo[rt on] the [Urarṭian]" –

10 [...] to the country [......]

(Rest destroyed)

## 129. Where are the King's Logs?

Rm 2,460

beginning broken away
1′ ⌈*nu-uk* 1-*me*-20 GIŠ.ÙR⌉.MEŠ
2′ *ša* LUGAL *a-le-e*
3′ *šu-ú i-su-hur iq-ṭi-bi-a*
4′ *ma-a* GIŠ.ÙR.MEŠ *šal-ši-u-te*
5′ *ú-se-ri-ba ina ta-hu-me*
6′ *ša* KUR.*qu-ru-ba u*[*r-t*]*a-me*

CT 53 872

(Beginning destroyed)

1 I (wrote him): "Where are the king's 120 logs?" He returned and told me: "I have brought in the third (installment of) logs, and l[ef]t it on the border of Quruba."

**127** 6ff, 14 See coll.
**128** Same scribe as in no. 129, 130 and 131. Could be part of the same tablet as no. 130 and 131. 2 The suggested restoration of the sender's name is conjectural. 4 Or: "The city of Birate is well."
**129** Same scribe as in no. 128. r.6 See coll.

7′ KUR.⸢*ú*⸣-[*x x x x x x*]
rest broken away
Rev. beginning broken away
1′ *x*[*x x x x x x x x x*]
2′ *i-s*[*u-x x*] *x*[*x x x x x*]
3′ *a-na* KUR.*ú-ka-a-a iq-ṭí-b*[*i*]
4′ *ma-a e-mu-qi ša* LUGAL *a-na mì-ni*
5′ *ina* UGU-*hi-ia tú-ba-*⸢*la*⸣
6′ *a-na-ku-ma a-ba*$^{!}$*-ak*
7′ *ki-i e-mu-qi ú-na-me-šá-ni*
8′ KUR.*ú-ka-a-a* [*iq-ṭi-b*]*i-a*
9′ [*ma-a x x x x x x*]-⸢*x*⸣-[*k*]*a*
rest broken away
s.1 *x x x*]*x* GIŠ.ÙR.MEŠ KUR.*né-ru-bu x*[*x x x x*
2 *x x x*] *a-na* LÚ*.A—KIN *ša ma-da-*[*a*] [*x x x x*
3 *x x x*] ⸢KUR⸣ URU.*pa-ie-e* LÚ*.ERIM.M[EŠ *x x x x*
4 *x x x*] UR[U.*x x x x*

7 The U[kkean ......]
(Break)

r.2 He re[turned ...] and said to the Ukkean: "Why do you bring the king's troops to me? I will have them removed." When the troops departed, the Ukkean [said to m]e:
9 "[... yo]ur [......]
(Break)

s.1 [......] the logs (at) the pass [......]
2 [......] to the messenger of Adâ [......]
3 [......] of the town Paye the men [......]
4 [......] the ci[ty ......]
(Rest destroyed)

## 130. Urzana has Left the Town

81-7-27,46

beginning broken away
1′ ⸢*la ni-ip*⸣*-t*[*i x x x x x x*]
2′ *ša* KUR *gab-b*[*u x x x x x x*]
3′ *ú-bal ma* [*x x x x x x x*]
4′ *ma* GÌR.2.MEŠ *ša* L[UGAL *x x x x*]
5′ *ma ú-la-a a-n*[*a x x x x x*]
6′ *ma* LÚ*.ERIM.MEŠ 2-*me x*[*x x x x x*]
7′ UGU LUGAL *be-lí-*[*ia x x x x*]
8′ *ma at-ta x*[*x x x x x x*]
9′ *ša i-qa-ba-na-*[*ši-ni x x x x*]
10′ UD-2-⸢KÁM⸣ [T]A *pa-ni-i*[*a x x x x*]
11′ [*x x x x*]*x ra* [*x x x x x*]
rest broken away
Rev. beginning broken away
1′ [*it-t*]*a-ta-*[*ku x x x x x*]
2′ *iš-ku-*[*x x x*]
erased
4′ *a-na* $^{m}$*sa-ni-ie* [*a-sa-par nu-uk*$^{?}$]
5′ *mì-nu ṭè-mu i*[*š-x x x x*]
6′ UGU LUGAL *be-lí-i*[*a x x x x*]
7′ *ma-a* $^{m}$*ur-za-ni* UR[U.*x x x x x*]
8′ *ma šúm-ma* LÚ*.NIGÍR—⸢É⸣.[GAL *x x x*]
9′ [*x x* LÚ*].⸢A⸣—*šip-ri* [*x x x x x*]
rest broken away
s.1 [*ú-ma-a an-nu*]*-rig* LÚ*.A—KIN-*ia ša* [*x x x*]
2 [*x x ina* U]GU LUGAL *be-lí-ia a-sa-par-šú* LUGA[L *be-lí*]
3 [*liš*]*-al-šú*

CT 53 918

(Beginning destroyed)
1 We did not disclo[se ......].
2 He is bringing all the [...] of the country [......], saying: "[*Let us grasp*] the feet of the k[ing of ...]; otherwise, [*we should* ...] t[o ......] 200 soldiers."
7 [He has ...] to the king, [my] lord, [...]: "You [......]."
9 What(ever) he tells us [...].
10 On the 2nd day [... fr]om m[y] presence [......]
(Break)
r.1 [they w]ent [away ...]
2 *pla*[*ced* ...]
4 [I *wrote to*] Saniye: "What order *did he g*[*ive him? I must write*] to the king, m[y] lord."
7 He (responded): "Urzana [*has left*] the to[wn ...]; if the pal[ace] herald, [*my lord, orders*], a messenger [......]
(Break)
s.1 [Now th]en I am sending [t]o the king, my lord, the messenger of mine who [......]; the kin[g, my lord, may a]sk him.

**130** Possibly part of the same tablet as no. 128 and 131. r.4ff The suggested restorations are all conjectural.

## 131. An Attack on Urarṭian Border Forts

K 13004

beginning broken away
1′ [*x x x* UR]U.*bi-ra-ti ša* KUR.UR[I-*a-a*]
2′ [*ša ina* UGU] *ta-hu-mi-šú i-zu-q*[*u-pu*]
3′ [ERIM.MEŠ-*šú ina* U]RU.*bi-ra-ti ú-se-l*[*i*]
4′ [LÚ*.*tur-t*]*a-nu ša* KUR.URI-*a-a a-di* [*e-mu-qi-šú*]
5′ [*a-na a*]-⌜*a*⌝-*li it-ta-lak* [*x x x*]
6′ [*x x x x x*] *ina na-gi-*⌜*e ša*⌝ [*x x x*]
rest broken away
Rev. destroyed

CT 53 454

(Beginning destroyed)

1 [The Mannean] has atta[cked] the forts of the [king of] Urarṭu [which are situated on] his border, and let [*his troops*] occupy the forts.

4 [The] Urarṭian [commander]-in-chief has gone [to he]lp with [his troops ...]

6 [...] in the district of [......]

(Rest destroyed)

## 132. Letter of Accompaniment

K 1028

1 *a-na* L[UGAL *be-lí*]-*ia*
2 ARAD-⌜*ka* $^{m}$⌝[$^{d}$*aš-šur*$^{?}$]—*rém-an-ni*
3 *lu* DI-*mu a-na* LUGAL *be-lí-ia*
4 DI-*mu a-na* KUR
5 *ša* LUGAL *be-lí-ia*
6 *lib-bi* KUR
7 *a—dan-niš ṭa-a-ba*
8 *ina* UGU UN.MEŠ
9 *ša* LUGAL [*be-lí*]
rest broken away
Rev. beginning broken away
1′ [*u*]*s-s*[*e-bi-la*]

ABL 978

1 To the ki[ng], my [lord], your servant [*Aššur*]-remanni. Good health to the king, my lord!

4 The land of the king, my lord, is well; the mood the land is very good.

8 As to the people about whom the king, [my lord, *wrote me* ......]

(Break)

r.1 I am herewith sen[ding them *to the king, my lord*].

**131** → no. 84. Possibly part of the same tablet as no. 128 and 130.

# 8. Letters from Eastern Kurdistan



FIG. 23. *Horses from the north-east (reign of Shalmaneser III).*
BM 124652.

## 133. King of Hubuškia Arrives with Tribute

K 676

1 [*a*]-*na* LUGAL EN-*ia*
2 ARAD-*ka* ᵐDI-*mu*—EN
3 *lu-u* DI-*mu a-na* LUGAL EN-*iá*
4 TA* URU.BÀD—LUGAL—GI
5 DU-*ak* LÚ*.A—KIN-*ia*
6 TA* ŠÀ-*bi* URU.*a-ni-su*
7 *ina* URU.EN-*an ina* [GA]BA!-*ia*
8 *i-tal-ka ma*-[*a*]
9 ᵐ*ia*!-*an-zu*-⸢*ú*!⸣ [0]
10 KUR.*hu*!-*buš*!-*a-a* [0]
11 *ma-a* UD-24-KÁM [0]
12 *i-na* URU.⸢*ú*!⸣-*a*!-[*si*]
13 *e-ta*-⸢*rab*!⸣ [0]
r.1 *i-na* URU.*har-ra*-[*ni-a*]
2 *i-tu*-*ṣ*[*i*!]
3 *ma-a šúm-ma i-na* ŠÀ-*bi*
4 URU.*har-ra-ni-a la e*-*l*[*i*!]
5 UD-26-KÁM *ina* URU.PÚ-*te*
6 *ú-la-a ina* URU.*har-ra-ni-a*
7 *e-te-li* UD-27-KÁM
8 *ina* URU.PÚ-*te* ANŠE.KUR.MEŠ
9 GUD.NITÁ.MEŠ-*šú*! ⸢UDU!⸣.MEŠ!-*šú*
10 1-⸢*en*!⸣ UD-*mu i—pa-na-tú-šú*
11 [*i-na*] *pu-ut*! URU.*a-ni-su*
12 [*i*]-*tal-ku-ni*
13 [*x* A]NŠE.KUR.MEŠ
14 [*x* GU]D!.MEŠ
15 [*x x* UDU.NIT]A?.MEŠ
16e [*x x* (*x*)]-*šú-nu*
17e [*x x i*]-⸢*si*!⸣-*šú*
18e [*x x x*] ⸢*x x*⸣ [*x x*]
s.1 [*šúm-m*]*a* LUGAL *be-lí i-qa-bi la-li*!-[*ki*]
2 [*i-s*]*i-šú*! *la-da-bu-ub*

ABL 890

1 [T]o the king, [my lord]: your servant Šulmu-beli. Good health to the king, my lord!

4 (When) I was coming back from Dur-Šarruken, my messenger, coming from Anisu, met me in Adi*an* and said:

9 "Ianzû, (king) of Hubuškia, has entered Wa[isi] on the 24th, and is going to Harra[nia]. If he does not go up to Harrania, he will be in *Bur*te on the 26th; else if he does go up to Harrania, he will be in *Bur*te on the 27th."

r.9 The horses and his oxen and sheep came in one day ahead of him opposite Anisu. [He has wi]th him [x] horses, [x ox]en and [x shee]p [plus] their [......].

s.1 [I]f the king, my lord, so orders, I sha[ll go] and speak [wi]th him.

## 134. A Message from Hubuškia

K 7370

1 [*a-na* LUGAL EN]-*ia*
2 [ARAD-*ka* ᵐD]I-*mu*—EN
3 [*lu-u* DI]-*mu a-na* LUGAL EN-*ia*

ABL 931

1 [To the king], my [lord: your servant Š]ulmu-beli. [Good] health to the king, my lord!

**133** 7, 9f, 12ff, r.2, 17 See coll. r.19 W 255. s.1 See coll.
**134** 5 See coll.

4 [*ša a-n*]*a* LUGAL EN-*ia*
5 [*áš-pur*]-*a-ni nu-uk* KUR.*hu-bu*[*š*$^{!}$-*ka-a-a*]
6 [*is-s*]*ap-ra ma-a* LÚ*.A—KIN-[*ia*$^{?}$]
7 [*ina* IGI-*k*]*a li-li-ka*
8 [*ú-ma*]-*a an-nu-rig* [0]
rest broken away
Rev. destroyed

[4] [As to what I wr]ote [t]o the king, my lord: "The Hubu[škian has wri]tten to me: 'Let [*my*] messenger come [to yo]u'" —
[8] [n]ow then [......]
(Rest destroyed)

## 135. Information about the King of Hubuškia

K 14571

1 *a-na* [LUGAL EN-*ia*]
2 ARAD-*ka* [$^{m}$DI-*mu*—EN]
3 *lu* DI-*mu a-n*[*a* LUGAL EN-*ia*]
4 UD-30-KÁM *ša* ITI.ŠE [*ina* URU.*x x*]
5 *e-tar-ba* UD-1-[KÁM *ša* ITI.BARAG]
6 KUR.*hu-buš-ka-a-a* [*x x x x*]
7 *ina* KUR.*hu-buš-ki-*⸢*a*⸣ [*x x x x*]
8 [*x x x*]*x* ⸢*x x*⸣ [*x x x x*]
rest broken away
Rev. beginning broken away
1′ [*x x*] *la* [*x x x x x*]
2′ ⸢*al*$^{!}$-*l*[*i*$^{!}$-*x x x x x*]
3′ *ma-a* [*x x x x x x*]
4′ $^{m}$*sal*-[*x x x x x x*]
5′ *i-n*[*a x x x x x x*]
6′ *i-šá*-[*x x x x x x*]
7′ *i-š*[*i*$^{!}$-*x x x x x x*]
8′ ŠÀ [*x x x x x x x*]
9′ É [*x x x x x x*]
10e *m*[*a*$^{!}$-*a x x x x x*]
11e *ina* Š[À$^{!}$ *x x x x x*]
12e [*x*] *x*[*x x x x x x*]
s.1 [*x x x x x x x*]-*bi-lu-ni*

ABL 1466

[1] To the [king, my lord]: your servant [Šulmu-beli]. Good health t[o the king, my lord]!
[4] I entered [...] on the 30th of Adar (XII); on the 1[st of Nisan (I)] the Hubuškian [......]
[7] in Hubuškia [......]
(Reverse too broken for translation)

## 136. Urzana on his Way to Assyria

K 1079

1 *a-na* LUGAL EN-*ia*
2 ARAD-⸢*ka*⸣ $^{m}$DI-*mu*—EN
3 *lu*-⸢*u* DI⸣-*mu a-na* LUGAL EN-[*ia*]
4 $^{m}$⸢*ur-za*⸣-*na* UD-10-KÁM
5 *ina* URU.*a*-⸢*la*$^{!}$⸣-*mu iz-za-az*
6 ⸢UD$^{!}$⸣-[11-KÁM] *ina* URU.*hi-ip-tú*$^{!}$-*ni*
7 [UD-12-KÁM] *ina* URU.*mu-ši*
8 [UD-13-KÁM *ina* U]RU.1-*te*
9 [UD-14-KÁM *ina* URU.*arb*]*a*$^{!}$-*il*$^{!}$
rest (about 6 lines) broken away
Rev. beginning broken away
1′ [*x x*]*x*[*x*]*x*[*x x x*]

ABL 891

[1] To the king, my lord: your servant Šulmu-beli. Good health to the king, [my] lord!
[4] Urzana is staying in Alamu on the 10th ; on the [*11*th] he will be in Hiptuna, [on the *12*th] in Muši, [on the *13*th] in *Isse*te, [on the *14*th in Arbe]la.
(Break)

**135** r.2,4,7ff See coll.
**136** → Deller Zagros p.120f. Coll. I.L. Finkel, 1981 and S. Parpola, 1988. Does not join no. 137. r.2 See coll.

2′ ⸢5⸣6$^{!}$ KUR.MEŠ [*x x*]*x*.⸢MEŠ$^{!}$⸣
3′ 2-*lim* ⸢UDU⸣.[NITÁ.MEŠ *x x*]
4′ *ni-sa-a*[*p-ra x x*]
5′ 1-*me* GIŠ.[*x x x x*]
6′ *na-mu*[*r-tú x x x x*]
7′ *mi-nu* [*ša ṭè-mu-ni*]
8′ LUGAL *b*[*e-lí lip-ru-us*]
9′ [*li*]*š*$^{!}$-⸢*pu*$^{!}$⸣-[*ra*]

r.2 We have se[nt ...] 56 horses, [x oxe]n, and 2,000 sh[eep]; 100 [...], the audience gift, [...].

r.7 Let the king, [my] lo[rd, decide] what his [orders are] and write [me].

## 137. Arrival of Tributaries

K 10875

beginning destroyed
1′ [*x x*] *x*[*x x x x x x*]
2′ [$^{m}$*na*]-*nu-u* ⸢LÚ*⸣.S[AG *x x*]
3′ [*i*]-*si-šú-nu* 2 ANŠE.KUR.[MEŠ]
4′ [*x*] GUD.NITÁ.MEŠ *ina* ŠU.2-*šú-nu*
5′ [UD-1]2-KÁM *ina* URU.*hi-ip-tú-ni*
6′ [*i*]*t-ta-bal-kàt-u-ni*
7′ [*ra*$^{?}$-*d*]*i-a-te-šú*-⸢*nu*⸣
8′ [*x x d*]*i* ⸢*x*⸣ [*x x x*]
e.9′ [*il-l*]*a-ku-ni* [0]
blank space
r.1 [*ša* LU]GAL EN
2 [*iš-p*]*ur-an-ni ma-a*
3 [*šúm-m*]*a il-la-ku-u-*[*ni*]
4 [*me-m*]*e-ni i-si-šú-n*[*u*]
5 [*lu*] *la i-da-bu-*[*ub*]
6 [LÚ*].*rak-su*.MEŠ [0]
7 [*i-s*]*i-šú-nu up-t*[*a-qid*]
8 [*ú-ma*]-⸢*a mi*⸣-*nu š*[*a* LUGAL]
rest broken away

CT 53 414

(Beginning destroyed)

2 [... to]gether with [Na]nû, the e[unuch ...] came across (the mountain) to Hiptuna on the 12th bringing 2 horses and [x] oxen with them.

7 Their [*gu*]*ides* [......], but they [are co]ming.

r.1 [As to what the ki]ng, my lord, [wro]te to me: "[I]f they come, [nob]ody should speak with th[em]" —

6 I have appo[inted] *recruits* [wi]th them. [No]w, what are t[he king my lord's orders]?

(Rest destroyed)

## 138. Forwarding Local Rulers to the King

K 1613

beginning broken away
1′ [*ša*] ⸢LUGAL⸣ *be-lí i*[*š-pur-an-ni*]
2′ [$^{m}$*a-d*]*a-a* TA* KUR.*ni-*[*x-x-a-a*]
3′ [UR]U.*ul-ú-a-a* URU.*x*[*x x x x*]
4′ [KUR].*me-ṣa-a-a* TA* $^{m}$*da-*[*x x x x*]
5′ [PAB] ⸢7⸣ ARAD.MEŠ-*ni ša* LUG[AL EN-*ia*]
6′ [TA*] $^{m}$*lu-ul-lu-pa-*[*a-a x x x*]
7′ [*ina* U]GU LUGAL EN-*iá* [*ú-se-bi-la*]
8′ [*x x x*]-*ši* $^{m}$*da-a-*[*x x x x*]
9′ [*x x x*] $^{m}$*am—ra*-⸢*i*⸣ [*x x x x*]
10′ [*x x x x*]*x i-tal-k*[*a x x x*]
11′ [*x x x x x*]-*u ki-i* [*x x x x*]
rest broken away
Rev. destroyed

CT 53 192

(Beginning destroyed)

1 [As to *the city lords* about whom] the king, my lord, w[rote to me, I am herewith sending t]o the king, my lord:

2 [Ad]â, along with the Ni[...ean, the ...ean], the Uluean, [the ...ean], and the Meṣaean, along with Da[...],

5 [in all] 7 subjects of the kin[g, my lord, together with] Lullupa[yu ...].

8 [...] Da[...]

9 [...] Am-ra'i [...]

10 [...] cam[e ...]

11 [...] as [...]

(Rest destroyed)

**137** Hand of Šulmu-beli. 2 → no.247:2; there is no room in the break for any other name ending in *-nû* (Asinû, Hirinû, I(a)mannû) attested in the NA corpus.

## 139. Troops from Muṣaṣir Summoned by the King

K 826

1 *ina* UGU LÚ*.ERIM.MEŠ
2 KUR.*mu-ṣa-ṣir-a-a*
3 *ša* LUGAL SAG-*su-nu*
4 *i-šu-u-ni*
5 *ina* URU.*si-ha-na*
6 *ša mad-bar šu-nu*
7 *ni-iš-pu-u-ru*
8 *lu-bi-lu-ni-šu-nu-u*
9 *ú-la-a ina mad-bar-ma*
10 *lu*$^{!}$ *šu-nu*
Rev. uninscribed

ABL 448

1 As to the men from Muṣaṣir whom the king summoned, they are in Sihana, on the plain. Shall we send word and have them brought here, or should they stay in the plain?

## 140. Fragment of a Military Report

K 14096

1 *a-na* LUGAL EN-*ia*
2 ARAD-*ka* $^{m}$DI-*mu*—[EN]
3 *lu-u* DI-*mu a-na* [LUGAL EN-*ia*]
4 ⸢*ina* UGU *ṭè-e*⸣-[*me x x x x*]
rest broken away
Rev. uninscribed

CT 53 509

1 To the king, my lord: your servant Šulmu-[beli]. Good health [to the king, my lord]!

4 As to the ne[ws of ......]

(Rest destroyed)

## 141. Summoning a Chariot-Man

Sm 1189

1 *a-na* LUGAL EN-*iá*
2 ARAD-*ka* $^{m}$D[I-*mu*—E]N
3 *lu-u* D[I-*mu a-na* LUGAL E]N-*iá*
4 UGU $^{m}$[*x x x x*]
5 LÚ*.3.[$U_5$ *x x x*]
6 *ša* [$^{m}$*x x x x*]
7 DUMU [*x x x x*]
8 *ša* L[UGAL *be-lí*]
9 *iš-pu*[*r-an ni ma-a*]
10 *re-s*[*u i-ši*]
11 *ma-a x*[*x x x x*]
12 ⸢T⸣A *x*[*x x x x*]
13 ⸢*i*⸣-*x*[*x x x x*]
r.1 [*iq-ṭí-bu-n*]*i ma-a* EN—GIŠ.⸢GIGIR⸣
2 [*ša i*]-*si-šú*
3 [*i-l*]*u*-⸢*ku*⸣-*u-ni*
4 [*x*] ⸢*x*⸣ *i-na-ši*
5 [*ma*] *ina* URU.⸢*arba*$^{!}$-*ìl*$^{!}$⸣
6 ⸢*i-ta*⸣-*lak*
rest uninscribed

CT 53 131

1 To the king, my lord: your servant Š[ulmu-be]li. [Good] heal[th to the king], my [lo]rd!

4 As regards [NN], the 'third [man' ...] of [NN] son of [NN], about whom the k[ing, my lord], wro[te me]: "Sum[mon him; ...] with [...]"

(Break)

r.1 [They told m]e: "The chariot owner [who go]es [wi]th him will summ[on him]; he has gone to Arbela."

**139** Hand and orthography of Šulmu-beli.
**141** r.5 See coll.

## 142. Having an Official Whipped

Sm 1293

beginning broken away
1′ [*x*]*x* [*x x x x x x x x*]
2′ [*i*]*na* UR[U.*x x x x x x x*]
3′ 2-*šú* 3-*šú* ⸢*x*⸣[*x x x x x*]
4′ *nu-uk pa-an* ⸢LÚ⸣.[*x x x*]
5′ *a-na* URU.*ba-qar x*[*x x x x*]
6′ *ku-pu-u še-ri-*⸢*da*⸣ [*x x x*]
7′ *la i-ša-ma-a-ni* [*ki-i* LUGAL]
8′ *be-lí a-na* URU.*k*[*al-hi šu-tú-ni*]
9′ *pa-an* LUGAL EN-*ia* [*ṭè-mu*]
10′ *ú-te-re nu-u*[*k x x*]
e.11′ [*ina* É].⸢GAL *ap*⸣-[*x x x*]
12′ [*x x x x x x x x x*]
r.1 [*x x x x x x x x x x*]
2 [*x*]⸢*x*⸣ [*x x x x x x x x*]
3 [*l*]*a ip-ti nu-u*[*k x x x x*]
4 [*ṭ*]*è-mu la iš-k*[*un x x*]
5 LUGAL *be-lí i-sa-a*[*p-ra*]
6 *a-na* URU.*kal-hi na-ṣ*[*u-ni-šu*]
7 LUGAL *be-lí iq-ṭí-b*[*i*]
8 *ma-a* ŠÀ KUŠ.*mar-šá-n*[*i x x*]
9 *li-ṭu-šú ana-ku pa-an* [*x x x*]
10 *aq-ṭí-bi nu-*[*uk x x x x*]
rest broken away

CT 53 840

(Beginning destroyed)

2 [......] in the city [...].

3 I have several times [told him to go] to Baqar to the [...] and bring down ice, but he does not obey me.

7 [When the king], my lord, [was] in C[alah], I gave to the king, my lord, the following [report]: "I have *ap*[*pointed* ... in the Pa]lace [...]

(Break)

r.3 "He has not opened [...], nor giv[en or]ders [to ......]."

5 The king, my lord, (then) se[nt] word; [he] was brou[ght] to Calah, and the king, my lord, order[ed] him to be whipped with [...] leather straps.

9 I (however) said to [the king, my lord]: "[......]

(Rest destroyed)

## 143. Merchants Killed and Detained

Rm 2,539

1 [*a-na* LUGAL EN-*ia*]
2 [ARAD-*ka* $^{m}$DI-*mu*—EN]
3 [*lu* DI-*m*]*u a-*[*na* LUGAL EN-*ia*]
4 [LÚ.A]—*šip-ri* [*ša x x x*]
5 [*ina m*]*a-a-ti-*⸢*ni*⸣ [*x x x x x*]
6 [*šu*]*l-mu* [*x x x x x*]
7 [*i-n*]*a* UGU L[Ú.DAM.QAR.MEŠ]
8 [*š*]*a* LUGAL *be-lí i*[*š-pur-an-ni*]
9 2 LÚ.DAM.QAR.MEŠ [*x x x x x*]
10 *ša i-*[*d*]*u-ku-ni a-ki* [*x x x x x*]
11 1-*e*[*n x x š*]*a* LUGAL E[N-*ia x x*]
12 *x*[*x x x x x x x x x x x x x*]
13 *x*[*x x x x x x x x x x x x x*]
rest broken away
Rev. beginning broken away
1′ *ša ina* [*x*]⸢*x*⸣ [*x x x x x x x x*]
2′ *i-na* [U]GU KUR.KUR.[MEŠ *x x x x x*]
3′ *a-na šul-me a-*⸢*x x*⸣ LU[GAL *x x x*]
4′ LÚ*.DAM.QAR.MEŠ-*ia ik-ta-*[*la x x x*]
5′ *a-na-ku* LÚ*.DAM.QAR.MEŠ-*šu la* [*x x x*]
6′ *mì-i-nu ša* LUGAL *be-lí* ⸢*i*⸣-[*qab-bu-u-ni*]

CT 53 874

1 [To the king, my lord: your servant Šulmu-beli. Good heal]th t[o the king, my lord]!

4 [A mes]senger [of ... *has arrived* in] our [co]untry; [he *sends the king his* re]gards.

6 [A]s to the [merchants ... about wh]om the king, my lord, w[rote me, ...]

9 2 merchants [......]

10 who were killed, when [......],

11 a [... o]f the king, [my] lo[rd ......]

(Break)

r.1 who in [......]

2 upon all the countri[es ......]

3 to greet the king, [my] lo[rd ...].

4 He has deta[ined] my merchants [and ...ed them], while I [have] not [detained] his merchants; what are the king my lord's instructions?

7′ AD-*ia* AD—AD-*ia* [*x x x x x*]
8′ LÚ*.GAL—*da-ni-bat* ŠE.[*x x x x x*]
9′ ⌜*i*⌝—[*su-r*]*i* LUGAL [*be-lí i-qab-bi*]
rest broken away

(7) (In the days) of my father and my grandfather, [...] the chief victualler [...ed] the corn [...]. Pe[rha]ps the king, [my lord], will say: "[......]"

(Rest destroyed)

## 144. Cimmerians and the Urarṭian King

ND 1107

1 [*a-na* LUGAL *be-lí-ia*]
2 [ARAD-*ka* $^{m}$*x x x x x*]
3 ⌜*lu*⌝ [*šul-mu a-na* LUGAL EN-*ia*]
4 *šul-mu a-n*[*a* KUR *ša* LUGAL]
5 *šul-mu a-na* U[RU.HAL.ṢU.MEŠ]
6 *ina* UGU *ṭè-e-me š*[*a*!] KUR.URI-*a-a*]
7 *ša* LUGAL *be-lí i*[*š-pur-an-ni*]
8 *ma-a ṭè-mu har-ṣ*[*u šup-ra*]
9 KUR.*g*[*i*]-⌜*mir*⌝-[*a-a x x x*]
10 ⌜*ma*?⌝-[*a x x x x x x x x*]
rest broken away
Rev. beginning broken away
1′ [*x x x x*]*x-ú* L[Ú.*x x x*]
2′ [*x x x x*] *ša* $^{m}$*a-r*[*a-x x x*]
3′ [*x x m*]*ah-ru x*[*x x x x*]
4′ [*n*]*i*?-*ma-ag*?-*gu-ru né-er-r*[*ab*? *x x*]
5′ KUR.*gi-mir-a-a ina* UGU-*hi* ⌜*i*⌝-[*x x*]
6′ *ina* ŠÀ KUR.*ú-ṣu-na-li* [*ma-dak-tú*]
7′ ⌜*i*⌝-*sa-kan ṭè-e-mu* [*la ah-ru-uṣ*]
8′ TA* KUR.*hu-ub-buš-a-*[*a x x*]
9′ UGU $^{m}$*ur-za-na a-*[*sap-ra*]
10′ *nu-uk ṭè-*⌜*e*⌝-[*mu ša x x*]
11′ *hur-ṣa* [*x x x x x x x x*]
rest (a few lines) broken away
s.1′ [*x x x x x x d*]*i la-a a-šá-me* [*mì-i-nu*]
2′ [*ša* LUGAL *be-lí i-qa-bu-ni l*]*i-iš-pa-ru-u-ni* [0]

GPA 243

1 [To the king, my lord: your servant NN]. Go[od health to the king, my lord]!

4 [The land of the king, my lord] is well; the f[orts of the king, my lord], are well.

7 As to the news o[f the Urarṭian] about which the king, my lord, wr[ote me]: "[Send me] a deta[iled] report!" —

9 the Cimme[rian(s) ......]

(Break)

r.2 [...] of Ar[a ...]

3 [...] were *received* [...]

4 ....... [...]

5 The Cimmerian (king) has [...ed] on *it* and pitched [*his camp*] in Uṣunali; [*I do not have a full*] report (yet). [...] with the Hubušk[ian].

10 I have written to Urzana: "Send a detailed repo[rt on ...]"

(Break)

s.1 I have not [yet] heard [......].

2 Let them write me [what the king my lord's orders are].

## 145. Cimmerian Invasion of Urarṭu

K 485

1 *a-na* LÚ.NIGÍR—É.GAL
2 EN-*ia*
3 ⌜ARAD⌝-*ka* $^{m}$ARAD—$^{d}$30
4 [LÚ].⌜*ga*⌝-*me-ra-a-a*
5 ⌜*x an*?⌝-*ni*!-*ú*
6 ⌜*it*!-*tu*!⌝-*ṣi* TA* ŠÀ-*bi*
7 ⌜KUR!.*ma*!-*na*!⌝-*a-a*

ABL 112

1 To the Palace Herald, my lord: your servant Urda-Sin.

4 The Cimmerian (king) has departed from Mannea this [...] and entered Urarṭu. He is ... [in] Hu'diadae; Sarduri is [...] in Ṭur[u]špâ.

**144** → Deller Zagros p.104. r.4 Possibly "we agree to ent[er ...]." We have not been able to collate the original and the readings indicated by question marks are thus entirely conjectural.

**145** → Deller Zagros p.102 (with new copy by M. Salvini); Pinches, JRAS 1913, 609ff. Coll. S. Parpola, March, 1988. 5f, 8ff, s.1f See coll.

8 ⸢*ina*! ŠÀ!-*bi*!⸣ KUR.URI
9 ⸢*e*!⸣-*tar-ba*
10 [*ina* UR]U!.⸢*hu*?⸣-*u*ʾ-*di-a-da-e*
11 [*x x*]*x* ⸢*x x*⸣ $^{md}$15—BÀD
12 [*ina* UR]U!.⸢*ṭu*!-*ru*!⸣-[*u*]*š*!-⸢*pa*!⸣-*a*
13 [*x*] ⸢ŠÀ?⸣ [*x*] *šá*!-*ki-ni*
14 ⸢LÚ!.DUMU⸣—*šip-ri*
15 *šá* LÚ.EN.NAM
e.16 URU.*ú-e-s*[*i*!]
17 UGU $^{m}$*ur-*[*za*]-*ni*
18 *it-*⸢*tal*!⸣-[*ka*]
r.1 *ina* UGU [*kit*?-*ri*?]
2 *ma-a* ⸢*e*!-*mu*⸣-*qi-k*[*a*]
3 *lil-li-ku-ni*
4 *ina* UGU URU.*pu-li-a-a*
5 *ina* UGU URU.*su-ri-a-na-a-a*
6 KUR.URI *gab-bi-šú*
7 *ip-ta-làh*
8 *a—da-niš*
9 *e-mu-qi ú-pa-hu-ru*
10 *ma-a i—su-ri*
11 *ki-ma ku-pu-u*
12 *i-di-i-ni*
13 *ma-a ni-za-qu-pu*
14 *ina* UGU-*hi-šu*
15 *ina* UGU *hu-ub-ti*
16 *an-ni-e*
17e *ša iq-bu-ni*
18e *ma-a hu-ub-tú*
19e [*i*]*h-ta-bat*
s.1 *i-ba-ši i-qab-bi-u ma-a šá na-gi-e*
2 *šá* URU.⸢*ar*!⸣-*hi*! ⸢*x x*⸣-*ši*! *ma-a a-*[*d*]*i*? ZI *kar n*[*i*?]

[14] The messenger of the governor of Wais[i] has gone to Ur[za]na *for* [*help*], saying: "Let yo[ur] troops come *to* (*aid*) the people of Pulia and Suriana."

[r.6] All of Urarṭu is extremely frightened. They are assembling troops, saying: "Perhaps we can attack him, once there is more snow."

[r.15] As to this booty which they said he has taken, they do say that of the district of Arhi, [...]......

## 146. A Letter of Excuse

Sm 1056

1 [*a*]-*na* LUGAL EN-*ia*
2 ARAD-*ka* $^{m}$*ur-za-na-a*
3 *lu-u* DI-*mu a-na* LUGAL BE!-*ia*
4 LUGAL BE-*i* : *ú-d*[*a*]
5 *a—bé-e-ti* GUD.NITÁ.M[EŠ]
6 *ù* UDU.NITÁ.MEŠ *ia-a-k*[*a*?]
7 *ku-pu-ú* : KASKAL.MEŠ
8 *ú-ṣa-bi-it* : ⸢*ka*⸣-*a-ni*
9 *a-da-ga-la* : *la il-la-k*[*a*]
10 [*r*]*a-qu-te-ia* : *ina* IGI LU[GAL]
11 ⸢*la*!⸣ *al-la-ak* : *ú*!-[*la-a*]
12 *a-ta-al-ka* : T[A *x x*]

ABL 768

[1] [T]o the king, my lord: your servant Urzana. Good health to the king, my lord!

[4] The king, my lord, knows *my affair*. Whe[re] are the oxen and the rams?

[7] Snow has blocked the roads. (As) I am looking out now, it is impossible: I cannot go empty-handed to the presence of the ki[ng].

[11] Or (suppose) I went and had to return from [...: *I might ... and die* in] the enemy country.

r.4f *palāhu* "to be afraid of" is construed with *issu pān*, not *ina muhhi*; hence r.4f must be connected with the verb *alāku* in line 3. Cf. r.13f.

**146** → Deller Zagros p.115f. [3] See coll. [5] *a—bé-e-ti* sic (collated); obscure. Possibly standing for *abitī* (/abat+i:/) "my matter," with an irregular shift of stress to the penultimate syllable, or for *ab-bēti* (/an+be:ti/) "to/in the house, at home," or simply for *bēt*(*e*) "where, what." All these interpretations involve various difficulties. [6] The last sign is not ⸢*nu*⸣ (Deller); see coll. [15] See coll.

13 *a-su-uh-ru* : *x*[*x x x*]
14 [*ina*] KUR.*na-ki-ri* [*a-mu-at*]
15 *ia-ú* : ⸢ŠÀ⸣!⸣-*b*[*i x x x x*]
16 *ú-še-er* : *ši*[*x x x x x*]
17 *ka-ši-du* [*x x x x x x*]
18 ⸢*ša*⸣ LUGAL BE-[*i iš-pur-an-ni*]
19 *ma-a* : ⸢2⸣ [*x x x x x x x*]
20 4-*me x*[*x x x x x x x*]
21 ⸢*a*⸣-*ma*-[*x x x x x x x*]
e.22 *a-n*[*a x x x x x x*]
23 LUGAL *x*[*x x x x x x*]
r.1 *ši*-[*x x x x x x x*]
2 *ša ak-x*[*x x x x x*]
3 *nu-ru* ⸢*ú*⸣-[*x x x x x*]
4 *a—bé-e-t*[*i x x x x*]
5 *il-li-k*[*a x x x*]
6 $^{d}$*aš-šur* $^{d}$E[N $^{d}$PA]
7 $^{d}$*iš-tar be-lit* [MURUB$_4$ *u* MÈ]
8 KÚR.MEŠ-*ka a-a-b*[*i*!-*ka*]
9 *li-ik-šu-du* [*x x*]
10 *ina šap*!-*la* [G]ÌR!.2.[MEŠ-*ka*]
11 *liš-ku-nu* : ⸢GIŠ⸣.P[A?-*ka*]
12 UGU KUR.KUR.MEŠ *ga*[*b-bu*]
13 *lu-ṭa-i*-[*bu*]

15 My heart [is ...], humble [...], *reaching* [...].

18 As to what the king, [my] lord, [wrote me]:

19 "2[......]
20 400 [......]
21 [......]
22 t[o ......]
23 the king [......]
r.1 [......]
2 which I [......]
3 [*bring*]s light [......]
4 *wher*[*e* ......]
5 came [......]

6 May Aššur, B[el, Nabû], and Ištar, the Lady [of Battle and Fight], vanquish your enemies and fo[es], put [your ...] under [your f]eet, and make [your] ru[le] bene[ficial] for a[ll] the countries.

## 147. Urarṭian Governors in Muṣaṣir

Rm 2,2

1 [I]M $^{m}$*ur-za-na*-[*a*!]
2 *a-na* LÚ*.NIGIR—É.[GAL]
3 *lu* DI-*mu a-na ka*-[*šá*!]
4 [*š*]*a taš-pur-an-ni*
5 *ma-a* LUGAL KUR.URI-*a-a*
6 *a-di* LÚ*.*e-muq-qi-šú*
7 *kar-ka-te-e* : *i-lak*
8 *ma-a a-a-ka ú-šab*

ABL 409

1 A [tab]let of Urzana to the pa[lace] herald. Good health to y[ou]!

4 As to [wh]at you wrote me: "Is the king of Urarṭu on his way (there) with assembled troops? Where is he staying?" –

**147** → Deller Zagros p.114f; new copy by M. Salvini ibid. p.115. Cf. also 5 R 53,1.

FIG. 24. *Seal of Urzana, king of Muṣaṣir.*
MENANT, *Catalogue* pl. VII.

9 LÚ*.EN.NAM *šá* URU.*u-a-si*
10 LÚ*.EN.NAM *ša qa-ni* KUR.*u-ka-a-a*
11 *i-tal-ku-u-ni : dul-lu*
12 *ina* É—DINGIR : *e-pu-šú*
13 *i-da-bu-ub : ma-a* LUGAL
14 *i-lak ina* URU.*u-a-si ú-šab*
15 *ma-a* LÚ*.NAM.MEŠ *ah—hu-ru*
e.16 *i-la-ku-u-ni*
r.1 *ina* URU.*mu-ṣa-ṣir*
2 *dul-lu e-pu-šú*
3 *šá taš-pur-an-ni*
4 *ma-a : ša* ⌜*l*⌝*a pi-i*
5 *ša* LUGAL *me-me-ni*
6 Á-*šú ina dul-li*
7 *lu la ú-ba-la*
8 *ki-i* LUGAL KUR—*aš-šur*.KI
9 *i-lik-an-ni : ak-tal-šú-u*
10 *šá e-pu-šú-ni : e-tap-šá*
11 *ú an-ni-u : a-ke-e*
12 *lak-la-šú*

9 the governor of Waisi and the governor next to the Ukkean have come and are doing service in the temple. They say:

13 "The king is on his way; he is staying in Waisi, and further governors are coming to Muṣaṣir to do the service."

r.3 As to what you wrote me: "Nobody may take part in the service without the king's permission" —

8 when the king of Assyria came here, could I hold him back? He did what he did. So how could I hold back this one!

## 148. A Visit by Urzana's Brother

Sm 358

1 [*a-na* LUGAL EN-*ia*]
2 [ARAD-*ka* $^{m}$*x x x x x*]
3 *lu* DI-*mu* [*a-na* LUGAL EN-*ia*]
4 *aš-šur* EN ⌜$^{d}$⌝[PA UD.MEŠ GÍD.DA.MEŠ]
5 *li-di-n*[*u-nik-ka x x x x*]
6 *ina* KUR.*mu-uṣ*-[*ṣa-ṣir šu-u x x x*]
7 LÚ.EN.NAM.MEŠ [*x x x x x*]
8 UGU *ṭè-e-me ša* KUR.URI-[*a-a*!]
9 ŠEŠ-*šú ša* $^{m}$*ur-za-n*[*a-a*]
10 [*ina* IG]I! $^{m}$DI-*mu*—EN ⌜*i*⌝-[*tal-ka*]
11 [*ma-a*] ⌜*i*⌝-*su-hu*-[*ru x x x*]
12 [*x x p*]*a-ni x*[*x x x x*]
Edge broken away
Rev. beginning (4 lines) broken away
1′ [*x x*] ⌜*i*? *na*⌝ *x*[*x x x*]
2′ ⌜*ša*!⌝ É—GIŠ.*mu-x*[*x x x x*]
3′ *a-za-qa-ap ina* URU.*x*[*x x x*]
4′ *a-na-ku dul*$_6$-*lu ša x*[*x x x*]
5′ *e-pa-áš lib-bu ša* L[UGAL EN-*ia*]
6′ *lu* DÙG.GA [0]

ABL 1048

1 [To the king, my lord: your servant NN]. Good health [to the king, my lord]! May Aššur, Bel, and [Nabû] giv[e you length of days]!

5 [... is] in Muṣ[aṣir]; [*the rest of*] the governors [......].

8 As to the news of the Urarṭ[ian], the brother of Urzan[a] has c[ome t]o Šulmu-beli, [saying]: "He has returned [...]"

(Break)

r.2 I shall set it up [in the ...] of the [...] palace.

3 I am in the city of [...], working on the [...]. The ki[ng, my lord], can be glad.

## 149. The Foul Dealings of the Deputy

K 463

1 *a-na* LUGAL EN-*ia* ARAD-*ka* $^{m}$[*x x x x*]
2 *lu* DI-*mu a-na* LUGAL [EN-*ia*]

ABL 1273

1 To the king, my lord: your servant [NN]. Good health to the king, [my lord]!

**148** → Deller Zagros p.121f. 10, 12, r.1ff See coll. r.3 Possibly URU.*k*[*u-um-me*]; see coll.
**149** 4f DINGIR *ša* sic; see coll. For the construction cf. *am—mar š*[*a ina*] UGU $^{m}$*e-ṭè-ru am-ru-ú-n*[*i*] ABL 1093:15.

3 LUGAL *be-lí ú-da ki-i* [*x x x*]
4 DINGIR! *ša*! [*x*]*x-ni i-na* U[GU KUR.*har-ga-a*]-⸢*a*?⸣
5 ⸢*am*!⸣-*ra-š*[*u*!-*nu*?-*n*]*i šu-nu š*[*a* LUGAL] EN-*ia*
6 *šu-nu* [*x x x x x x*] EN *il-ki*
7 *šu-nu* [*x x x x i*]*h*!-*ta-an-šu*
8 *ha-pu*-⸢*su*!⸣-[*nu x x x u*]*h*!-⸢*ta*⸣-*pi-ú*
9 *i-t*[*a-x x x x*]-*u-šú-nu*
10 *ina š*[*a*? *x x x x*] ⸢*pa*?⸣ [*x*] *ku* [*x x*]
11 [*x*]*x x*[*x x x x x x x x*]
12 [*ma-a*]ʾ!-⸢*da*! LUGAL *be*!⸣-*lí x*[*x x x*]
13 [*x x x*] ⸢KUR!.*har*!-*gu*! 3?⸣ *a-x*[*x x x*]
14 *hab*!-*bu-ul* [*x* M]A!.NA KUG!.UD! L[Ú!].2!-*ú*!
15 *ša* LÚ.600—⸢É⸣.[G]AL [*ina*] *qab*-⸢*si*! URU!.*arba*!-*ìl*!⸣
16 *i-ta-har-šu ú-ma-a tu-*[*u-r*]*a*!
17 *ma-a* 3-*lim*-6-[*me* ZI?.M]EŠ! *ma*!-*a* ÚŠ.ME[Š *x*]
18 *ša* UN.MEŠ ⸢É!⸣.[MEŠ *ga*]*b*!-*bi i-la-*[*qi*]
19 UN.MEŠ *an-*[*nu*]-⸢*ti*!⸣ [*la-a*] UN.MEŠ-*šú*
20 *ša* [LÚ*.2]-⸢*ú*! *ša*! LÚ!.600!⸣—KUR *šu-nu*
21 *x*[*x x x x x*] T[A?] ᵐ*ku*!-*ia-ka-a*
22 [*x x x x x x x*]*x šu-nu*
23 [*x x x x i-d*]*u*!-*ak*!-*šú-nu*
24 [LÚ.2-*ú ša* LÚ.600]—É.GAL
r.1 *i-tal-ka ma-a* UN.MEŠ-*ia šu-nu*
2 *ina* UGU KUR.*har-gi pu-a-gi*
3 *i-da-bu-ub* KUR.*har-ga-a-a*
4 *i-tal-ka a-na* ⸢*pa*⸣-*ni-ia i-te-et-zi*
5 *ma-a* ⸢*la*!⸣-*a* ⸢*qa*!-*la*!⸣-[*ka*!] *ú-pa-ṣu-ni*
6 *an-nu-rig* [KUR.*h*]*ar-ga-a-a*
7 *i-na p*[*a*!-*an* LUGAL EN-*ia ú-se-bi-la*]
8 LUGAL *be-lí* [*liš-al-šú mi-nu ša* LÚ.2-*ú*]
9 LÚ.[600—É.GAL TA *pa-ni-šú iš*]-⸢*šú*!-*ú*⸣-[*ni*]
10 ⸢*di*?-*in*?⸣-*šú* [0] *li-ip-ru-s*[*u*]
11 *a-ta-a i-na tuk-ka-ni ma-a-t*[*i*!]
12 *i-ga-mar bir-ti* IGI.2.MEŠ-*šú* [0]
13 *lu-ma-di-du* TA* *ša* ŠU.⸢2⸣-[*ia*]
14 ⸢*lu*!⸣ *la*! *i-da-bu*-⸢*ub*⸣ [0]
15 [*x x x x x x x x x*]
16 [*x x x x x x x x x*]
17 [*x x x x x x x x x*]
18 LÚ!.E[N?]—⸢*x x*⸣ [*x x x x x x x*]
19 *ina* UGU-*hi-*[*ia i-tal-ku-ú-ni*]
20 *a-sa-ʾa-al-šú*-⸢*nu*!⸣ *m*[*a*!-*a x x x x*]
21 *a-ni-nu ina kas-pi* ⸢*ta*!-*da*!-*an*!-*ni*!⸣
22 *ma-a* LÚ.DAM.QAR-*ni-ni nu-ú-da*
23 *an-nu-rig ina* ŠU.2 LÚ.DUMU—*šip-ri-ia*
24 ⸢*ú-se-bi*!-*la*!⸣ LUGAL *be-lí* [0]
25 *liš*!-[*ʾa*]-⸢*al*!⸣-*šú-nu* [0]

3 The king, my lord, knows that [...], the god of *our* [...] *is ... upon* [*the Hargean*]*s*. They are [the king] my lord's (people).

6 [They ......], they perform the labour duty, they [have] submitted [to ...]. Their [...] have been utterly destroyed, their [......]
(Break)

12 The king, my lord, [... mu]ch;
13 [...] of Hargu is indebted [...].
14 The deputy of the palace herald has (already) received from him [x mi]nas of silver [in] the middle of Arbela. Now, ag[ai]n, they say: "3,6[00 person]s *are dying* [...]; he is buying up [a]ll the ho[uses] of the people."

19 Th[e]se people [are not] people of [the deputy] of the palace herald!
21 [...] *fr*[*om*] Kuyakâ
22 [...] they are
23 [... he is ki]lling them.
24 The [deputy] of the palace [herald] has come [...] and said: "They are my people!" He is plotting to take over the land of Hargu.
r.4 The Hargean (ruler) has come and had an audience with me, saying: "Be not silent (while) I am being crushed!" [I am] now [sending] the [H]argean t[o the king, my lord]; let the king, my lord, [ask him what] the [deputy of the palace herald] has ta[ken from] him, and decide his case.
11 Why is he destroying [my] country by oppression? Let it be impressed upon him that he may not lay claims to people under [my] jurisdiction.
(Break)
18 The [...s of ... have come] to [me]; I asked them [...], and they said: "[...]; we are to be sold – we know our merchants!"

23 I am now sending (them) with a messenger of mine; let the king, my lord, que[st]ion them.

7f, 11ff, 18, 20ff See coll. 16 Or: *i-ta-har šu-ú ma-a*. 17 Or "have died." r.4f, 10, 13f, 18, 20f, 24f See coll.

# 150. Curbing a Slave Trader

K 1897

1 [*a-na* LUGAL] EN-*ia*
2 [ARAD-*ka* $^{m}$*a-t*]*an-ha*—$^{d}$UTU
3 [*lu šul-mu a-n*]*a* LUGAL EN-*ia*
4 [$^{m}$*a-tar—ha-a*]*m* LÚ*.DAM.QAR É$^{!}$ *lik*$^{!}$*-la-šú*
5 [*ina* KUR.*hab-r*]*u-ri šu-ú* UD-*mu*
6 [*ša ina pa-n*]*a-tú-u-a ha-ri-ip ina* URU.*har-gi*
7 [*il-l*]*ak kas-pu-šú ina* ŠÀ-*bi*
8 [*x x x*]*x ú-šá-da-an*
9 [*x x ina* ŠÀ]-*bi* ⌈*e-tap*⌉*-šu a-ṣa-ba-su*
10 [*mu-uk la*] DUMU—LUGAL EN-*ni*
11 [*ki-i a*]*n-ni-i ma-a me-me-ni*
12 [LÚ*.ŠÁM].MEŠ *a-na ka-a-ri lu-u la ú-ši-la*
13 [*a-t*]*a-a at-ta* LÚ*.ŠÁM.MEŠ
14 [*ina* M]A.NA$^{!}$*-a-a tú-še-li*
15 [*šá-da*]*q*$^{!}$*-di-iš bé-et* LUGAL EN
16 [*la*]*-a ú-ši-bu-u-ni*
17 [LÚ*.Š]ÁM *a-na* URU.*ka-a-ri*
18 [*ú-se-li*] LUGAL EN *ina qa-*⌈*ti*$^{!}$⌉*-*[*šú*]
19 [*lu-ba-ʾi x*]*x* ⌈*a*$^{!}$⌉ *x*[*x x x x*]
rest (about 5 lines) broken away

Rev. beginning broken away
1′ [$^{m}$*x x x ša*] ŠU.2 $^{m}$*za-m*[*i-x x x*]
2′ [$^{m}$*x-x-x*]*x-aʾ* ARAD *ša* $^{m}$*x*[*x x*]
3′ [$^{m}$*x-x-x*]*-am ša* ŠU.2 $^{m}$*har-mi-*[*x*]
4′ [3 LÚ .DA]M.QAR.MEŠ *an-nu-tú šu-nu*
5′ [LÚ*.IGI].MEŠ-*ia*$^{!}$ *ina* ŠÀ *la qur*$^{!}$*-bu*$^{!}$*-ni*
6′ [*ki-i*] $^{m}$*a-tar—ha-am* LÚ*.DAM.QAR
7′ [*x x x*]*x*.MEŠ *e-lu-u-ni*
8′ [$^{m}$*hab*$^{?}$]*-si šu-u* UGU $^{m}$DI-*mu*—EN
9′ [LÚ*.2-*u* L]Ú.600—É.GAL *a-sap-ra*
10′ [*x x x*]*x ki-ma* ⌈*né*⌉*-ru-bu*
11′ [*i-tú-ṣ*]*i*$^{?}$*-a* $^{m}$⌈*lu*⌉*-qu*
12′ [$^{m}$*x-x*]*-am i-sa-he-iš*
13′ [*ina* IGI LU]GAL EN-*ia ú-bal*
14′ [LUGAL E]N *liš-ʾa-al-šú-nu*
15′ [*ki-i*] *an-ni-e a-se-me*
16′ [*ma-a*] $^{m}$*hab-si* $^{md}$AMAR.UTU—*rém-ni*
17′ [*ina* UR]U.*arba-ìl šu-nu*

CT 53 59

1 [To the king], my lord, [your servant At]anha-Šamaš. [Good health t]o the king, my lord!

4 The Palace should detain the merchant [Atarha]m (who) is [in Habr]uri.

6 Earlier, before my time, he used to go to Hargu and collect his money [...] there. (When) they made [... *the*]*re*, I arrested him, saying:

10 "[Did not] the crown prince, our lord, rule [lik]e this: 'Nobody shall put [bought] men up for sale in a *trade colony*?' [W]hy then have you put bought men up for sale [at one m]ina each?"

15 [Last ye]ar, when the king my lord was not yet enthroned, [he had already put a bo]ught man up for sale in a *trade colony*. The king, my lord, [should call him] to account [......]

(Break)

r.1 [NN], a subordinate of Zam[i...; ...]a', a servant of [NN], and [...]am, a subordinate of Harmi[...] — these [three mer]chants are my [*witnesses*]; they are not involved.

6 [When] Atarham the merchant went up to [...], I sent a certain [Hab]si to Šulmu-beli, [the deputy of] the palace herald. As soon as he gets back through the pass, he will bring both Luqu and [...]am [to the ki]ng, my lord; [the king, my lo]rd, should question them.

15 I have been informed [as] follows: "Habsi and Marduk-remanni are [in] Arbela."

# 151. ———

K 15291

1 [*a-na* LUGAL EN-*ia*]
2 [ARAD-*ka* $^{m}$*a-ta*]*n-ha*—$^{d}$[UTU]
3 [*lu šul-mu a-n*]*a* LUGAL EN-[*ia*]

CT 53 637

1 [To the king, my lord: your servant Ata]nha-[Šamaš. Good health t]o the king, [my] lord!

**150** 4 See coll. 12 The determinative URU prefixed to *kāru* in line 17 as well as the general context (business carried on outside the Assyrian heartland) suggest that *kāru* here means "trade colony" rather than plain "market." 14, 18, r.5 See coll. r.12 In view of r. 3 it is questionable whether Atarham is to be restored here.

4 [*ina* UGU *x x x*]*x-na-a-*⸢*a*⸣
5 [*ša* TA É.GAL *ina*] UGU-*hi-ia*
6 [*iš-pur-u-ni-ni*] *ma-a ina* URU.*arba-ìl*
7 [*x x x x*] ⸢É⸣.GAL
8 [*x x x x* T]ÙR É.GAL
9 [*x x x x x*] *i-ṣab-ta-ni*
10 [*x x x x x x*] *šap ku-ṣ*⸢*i*?⸣
11 [*x x x x x x x*] ⸢*x*⸣ [*x*]
rest broken away
Rev. destroyed

4 [As to the ...]nean(s) [about whom they wrote] me [from the Palace]: "In Arbela [...] the palace
8 [... the cou]rtyard of the palace
9 [...] seized me
(Rest destroyed)

## 152. Request for New Carts

K 1031 + K 1251

1 *a-na* LUGAL EN-*ia*
2 ARAD-*ka* $^{m}$*aš-šur—a-lik—pa-ni*
3 *lu* DI-*mu a-na* LUGAL EN-*ia*
4 *di-ib-bi an-nu-ú-te ša* LUGAL *be-lí*
5 *ina* UGU $^{m}$*pi-ha-me* LÚ*.2-*e*
6 UGU EN.NUN.MEŠ UGU *ṭè-ma-a-ni*
7 *ina* UGU *ha-ar-du-ut-te ša dul-la-ni*
8 *iš-pur-an-ni* LUGAL *be-lí a-na* ARAD-*šú*
9 [*i*]-*sa*!-*ra-aṣ a—dan-niš*
10 [*x x*]*x* LÚ*.GAL—É *ša* LUGAL [*be-lí*]
11 [*x x*]*x* ⸢*x x x x*⸣ *ma* [*x x*]
12 [*x x x x x x x* ]-*a-a*
13 *x*[*x x x x x x-a*]*n-ni*
14 *a-*⸢*na*!⸣ [*x x x x*] EN.NUN.MEŠ
15 *a-*⸢*na*⸣ [*x x x*] LÚ*.GAL—URU.MEŠ
16 *a-n*[*a x x x š*]*a*! URU.MEŠ-*ni*
17 *a-*[*na x* URU.*bi-ra*]-*a-te ú-pa-qa-da-šú-nu*
18 *ina* ⸢UGU!⸣ [URU.*bi-ra*]-*a-te*! ARAD.MEŠ-*ni*
19 *ša* ⸢LUGAL⸣ [EN-*i*]*a* ⸢*ša*⸣ *an-na-ka*
20 ⸢ŠÀ!⸣-*b*[*u*! *ša* LUGAL] EN-*ia a—dan-niš lu* DÙG.GA
21 ⸢*ú*!-*ma*⸣-*a* ⸢*an*?-*nu*?-*ra*!⸣ LUGAL *be-lí i-sa-ap-ra*
22 [LÚ*].ERIM!.MEŠ—LUGAL-*ia* GIŠ.GIGIR.MEŠ BAD-HAL!-*lum*
23 [*ki-i*] ⸢*ša*⸣ LUGAL *iš-pur-an-ni ú-sa-ak*
24 [*e-d*]*a-nu ša* LUGAL *be-li iš-kun-an-ni*
e.25 [*a-n*]*a*!-*ku a-du* ERIM.MEŠ—MAN-*ia*
26 [*a*]-*du e-mu-qi-ia ina* IGI-*at*
27 [LU]GAL *be-lí-ia ina* ⸢URU⸣.*arba-ìl a-na-ku*
r.1 [GIŠ.*l*]*e*!-[ʾ]*u-*⸢*ú*!⸣ *ša*! *dul*!-*la*!⸣-*a-ni*!
2 [*ša*] LUGAL *iš-pur-an-ni* ⸢*ma*!⸣-[*a bi-la*]
3 [*is-s*]*i-ia ú-ba-la* ⸢*a-na*⸣ [LUGAL]
4 EN-*ia ú-ša-áš-ma*
5 *an-ni-tú* LUGAL *be-lí a-na* ARAD-*šú le-pu-uš*
6 GIŠ.*qir-si-ia pa-ni-ú-te i-ba-áš-ši*
7 *la* ⸢*dam*!⸣-*qu šá-ni-ú-te eš-šu-u-te*

ABL 784

1 To the king, my lord: your servant Aššur-alik-pani. Good health to the king, my lord!

4 These words that the king, my lord, wrote me about Pihame, the deputy (governor), about the garrisons, about the reports, and about prompting the works — the king, my lord, did greatly ... his servant!

10 [...] the major-domo whom the king, [my lord]

11 [......]

12 [*As to* the *Itu'*]eans [about *whom the king, my lord, wrote*] me, I shall appoint them to [...] the garrisons, to [the ... of] the village inspectors, t[o the ... o]f the towns, and t[o the *fort*]*s*.

18 [The king], my lord, can be glad indeed about the [for]ts and the servants of the king, [m]y [lord], who are here.

21 Now that the king, my lord, has written to me, I shall assign my king's men, chariotry and cavalry as the king wrote me, and I shall be in the [ki]ng my lord's presence in Arbela with my king's men and army by the [dea]dline set by the king, my lord.

r.1 I shall bring [wit]h me [the wr]iting-[bo]ard on the works (in progress) [which] the king wrote [I should bring], and I shall have it read to [the king], my lord.

5 May the king, my lord, do this (favour) to his servant! My previous carts were not good and I have ...ed new ones, but they are

**151** 10 See coll.
**152** 9, 11 See coll. r.7 W 235. r.8 *ú*-TAR-*si* sic; see coll. r.11, 20f See coll.

8 *ú*-TAR-*si la ga-am-mu-ru*
9 *ina* UGU mdIM—*ib-ni* LUGAL *be-lí* ⸢*li*⸣-*iš-pu-ra*
10 GIŠ.*qir-si* SIG5.MEŠ *ša* NIM.[MA] ⸢TÚG?⸣.GADA
11 *ša* KI.TA KUŠ.⸢*tu*?⸣-*nim-me* ⸢*is*⸣-*se-niš*
12 *l*[*i*!-*iš-pur*]-⸢*ú*⸣-[*ni*] *an-ni*-⸢*ú*⸣ *šu*!-*u*
13 [*x x x x*]*x ša ma*!-*ṭi-a*-⸢*ku*!-*ú*!⸣-*ni*
14 [*x x x*] *gab-bu* [*x x x x*]
15 [*x x x x x x x x x x*]
16 [*x x x*] *x*[*x x x x* ] *x*[*x*]
17 [*x x x*] *ina* UGU m*tar*!-*d*[*i*!]-⸢*tú*!⸣—*aš-šur*
18 [ARAD *ša* LUGAL] ⸢*be*⸣-*lí-ia i—su-ri*
19 [LUGAL *be-lí i-qab*]-*bi ma-a a-ta-a*
20 [*x x x x x*]*x* ⸢*ša*! KASKAL⸣-*šú*
21 [*x x x x x x x*]*x* ⸢*ma*!-*la*!⸣
last two lines rubbed off

not ready. May the king, my lord, write to Adad-ibni, that they should [*send* me] good carts, (furnished) with linen abo[ve] and with *tunimmu* leather below.

12 This is [*the only thing*] that I am lacking.

14 [...] all [......]

(Break)

17 As to Tard[i]tu-Aššur, [the king] my lord's [servant], perhaps [the king, my lord, will sa]y: "Why [...] of his expedition [......]?"

21 [......] once

(Rest destroyed)

## 153. ———

K 14109

1 [*a-na*] LUGAL E[N-*ia*]
2 [ARAD-*ka*] m*aš-šur—a-lik—*[*pa-ni*]
3 [*lu* DI]-*mu a-na* LUGAL [EN-*ia*]
rest broken away
Rev. beginning broken away
1e [*x x*] ⸢*x x x x*⸣ [*x x*]
2e [*x-t*]*a-lak* [*x x*]

ABL 786

1 [To] the king, [my] lo[rd: your servant] Aššur-alik-[pani. Good] health to the king, [my lord]!

(Rest destroyed or too broken for translation)

## 154. Fragment on Allegations

Rm 55

1 *a-na* LUGAL EN-*ia*
2 ARAD-*ka* m*aš-šur—a-lik—pa-an*
3 *lu* DI-*mu a-na* LUGAL EN-*ia*
4 *ina* UGU *ša* mEN—SUM-*na ina pa-an* LUGAL EN-*ia*
5 *iq-bu-u-ni ma-a* [*x x x*]*x*.MEŠ
6 *a-na* LÚ*.⸢2?⸣-[*e x x x x x*]
7 *šu-u-tú in*[*a x x x x x x*]
8 [*a*]-⸢*na*?-*ku*?⸣ [*x x x x x x*]
rest broken away
Rev. beginning broken away
1′ *x*[*x x x x x x x x x x*]
2′ *šúm-ma* L[Ú.*x x x*] ⸢*x x*⸣
3′ *a-na* É—EN.MEŠ-[*šú-nu i-pal-l*]*àh-u-ni*
4′ *e-mar-u-ni a* ⸢*hu da*?⸣ *ni*
5′ *lal-li-ka ina pa-an* LUGAL
6′ EN-*ia* TA* LÚ *ha-ni-u*
7′ *la-ad-bu-ub*

ABL 787

1 To the king, my lord: your servant Aššur-alik-pani. Good health to the king, my lord!

4 As to what Bel-iddina said in the presence of the king, my lord: "The [...]s [...] to the *depu*[*ty* ...],"

7 he [......]

8 I [......]

(Break)

r.2 whether the [...s res]pect [their] government and *are devoted* to it ...

5 Let me come and speak with this man in the king my lord's presence.

**153** r.1f See coll.
**154** 6, r.4 See coll.; W 235.

## 155. Fragment Concerning a Royal Order

Bu 89-4-26,1

1 *a-na* LUGAL EN-*i*[*a*]
2 ARAD-*ka* $^{m}$*aš-šur—a-lik—pa-n*[*i*]
3 *lu* DI-*mu a-na* LUGAL ⸢EN⸣-[*ia*]
4 *ina* UD-5-KÁM $^{m}$⸢*aš-šur*!—EN!?⸣-*x*[*x ina* IGI-*ia*]
5 *it-tal-ka* ⸢*ṭè-e*⸣-[*mu*]
6 *ša* LUGAL *be*!-[*lí*]
7 *iš-ku-nu-šú*!-[*u-ni*]
8 *iq-ṭí*!-*ba-a*[*n-na-ši*]
9 *ina* U[GU *x x*]*x a* [*x x x*]
10 *ma-*[*a x x x x x x x x*]
rest broken away
Rev. beginning lost
1′ ⸢*x x x x*⸣ [*x x x*]
rest (space of 8 lines) uninscribed

ABL 788

1 To the king, m[y] lord: your servant Aššur-alik-pan[i]. Good health to the king, [my] lord!

4 On the 5th day Aššur-bel-[...] came [to my presence] and communicated [us] the or[der] which the king, [my] lo[rd], gav[e] him about [...]:

10 "[......]

(Rest destroyed)

## 156. Inspecting Deportees

K 1231 + K 14575 (CT 53 522) + K 16578 (CT 53 808)

1 [*a-na* LUGAL *b*]*e*-⸢*lí*⸣-[*ni*]
2 [ARAD.MEŠ-*n*]*i-k*[*a*]
3 [$^{m}$*aš-šur—a*]-*lik—pa-ni*
4 [$^{md}$U.GU]R—MAN-*a-ni*
5 ⸢*lu šul*⸣-[*m*]*u a-na* L[UGAL EN-*ni*]
6 *ina* UGU *ša* LUGAL [EN-*ni*]
7 *iš-pur-an-na-ši*-[*ni*]
8 *ma-a ki-ma* LÚ*.EN.[NAM?]
9 *iq-ṭar-ba ma-*[*a*]
10 TA* LÚ*.*hu-ub-*[*te*]
11 ⸢*an*⸣-[*na-k*]*a*!-*a*!-⸢*ma*?⸣ *x*[*x x*]
12 UD-6-KÁM ⸢$^{m}$⸣[*x x x x x*]
13 *ina* URU.*šu-*[*x x x*]
14 *iq-ṭar-ba* [*an-nu-rig*]
15 LÚ*.*hu-ub-*[*tú* 0]
16 *né-e-ta-*[*mar*]
e.17 *a-na* LUGAL [EN-*ni*]
18 *ni-sa-ap-*[*ra*]
r.1 UN.MEŠ *e-ta-*[*an-šú*]
2 *a—dan-*[*niš*]
3 ⸢*šá*?⸣-*ár*!-*bu la*[*m*?-*šú-nu*]
4 *e-ta-kal* KUR.⸢MEŠ⸣-[*ni*]
5 [*i*]*m*!-*tar-qu-šú-nu*
6 *qu-ba-te-šú-nu*
7 *il-la-ku-u-ni*
8 [L]UGAL EN-*ni lu ú-da*
rest uninscribed

ABL 988+

1 [To the king, our l]ord: [yo]ur [servan]ts [Aššur-a]lik-pani and [Nerg]al-šarrani. Good health to the k[ing, our lord]!

6 As to what the king, [our lord], wrote to us: "When the gov[ernor] arrives, [...] th[e]re with the capti[ves]" –

12 [NN] arrived in Šu[...] on the 6th; we have [now] inspec[ted] the captiv[es] and are herewith writing to the king, [our lord].

r.1 The people are ve[ry] we[ak]; *weather* has eaten up [their] *loo*[*ks*] and the mountains have crushed them. They are coming *ague-stricken*.

8 [The ki]ng, our lord, should know (this).

**155** 4, 6ff See coll.
**156** 10f, r.3ff See coll. r.3 The sign LAM appears to have here the phonetic value /lan/. r.6 *qubbatu* may be an Aramaic loanword, cf. Syr. *qūbābā* "ague, shivering fit."

COURTESY TRUSTEES OF THE BRITISH MUSEUM

FIG. 25. *Deportees (reign of Assurbanipal).*
BM 134386.

# 157. ———

K 13048

1 [*a*]-*na* [LUGAL *be-lí-ni*]
2 [ARAD].MEŠ-*n*[*i-ka* $^{m}$*aš-šur—a-lik—pa-ni*]
3 [$^{m}$]$^{⌈d⌉}$U.GUR—M[AN—*a-ni*]
4 [*l*]*u šul*-[*mu a-na* LUGAL EN-*ni*]
5 *ša* LUGAL *i*[*š-pur-an-na-ši-ni*]
6 *a-na ṭu-bi* [*u su-lum-me-e*$^{?}$]
7 *a-na* KUR.É—*a*[*b-da-da-a-ni*]
8 2 UD.MEŠ *ina* [*x x kam-mu-sa-ni*]
9 *me-me-ni is-si*-[*ni la x x x*]
10 [*x*].*x ba* [*x x x x x x x*]
rest broken away
Rev. uninscribed

CT 53 470

[T]o [the king, our lord: your serv]ants [Aššur-alik-pani and] Nergal-ša[rrani]. Good [health to the king, our lord]!

5 The king having s[ent us] for good relations [*and peace*] to Bit-A[bdadani],

8 [we stayed] two days in [... *but* no]body [...ed] with [us]

(Rest destroyed)

# 158. Fragment of a Military Report

DT 218

1 *a-na* LUGAL *b*[*e-lí-ni*]
2 ARAD.MEŠ-*ka* $^{m}$[*aš-šur—a-lik—pa-ni*]
3 $^{md}$U.GUR—M[AN-*a-ni*]
4 *lu šul-mu a*-[*na* LUGAL EN-*ni*]
5 *ina* UGU LÚ*.*e*-[*mu-qi* 0$^{?}$]
6 [*š*]*a* LUGAL EN-[*ni iš-pur-an-na-ši-ni*]
7 [*ṭè*]-*en-šú-nu x*[*x x x x*]
rest broken away
Rev. destroyed

ABL 1359

1 To the king, [our] lo[rd]: your servants [Aššur-alik-pani] and Nergal-ša[rrani]. Good health t[o the king, our lord]!

5 As to the tr[oops] about [wh]om the king, [our] lord, [wrote us, *no*] news of them [......]

(Rest destroyed)

# 159. Fragment Concerning a Royal Utterance

K 13142

1 [*a-na*] LUGAL *be*-[*lí-ia*]
2 [ARAD-*ka*] $^{m}$*aš-šur—a-lik*—[*pa-ni*]
3 [*lu* DI]-*mu a-na* LUGAL [EN-*ia*]
4 [*ki-i*] LUGAL *be-lí*
5 [*a-na*] ⌈É⌉ LÚ*.600—É.GA[L]
6 [*iš-pu*]-*ra*$^{!}$-*ni-ni*
7 [LUGAL *be*]-*lí iq-ṭí-bi*-[*a*]
rest broken away
Rev. completely broken away

ABL 785

1 [To] the king, [my] lo[rd: your servant] Aššur-alik-[pani. Good] health to the king, [my lord]!

4 [When] the king, my lord, [se]nt me [to the ho]use of the palace her[ald, the king], my [lo]rd, said [to me]:

(Rest destroyed)

**157** 6 Though *sulummû* "peace" is otherwise not attested in NA letters, the suggested restoration is considered possible in view of the occurrence of the phrase *ṭūbu u sulummû* as a sterotyped political *terminus technicus* in other contemporary documents. 7 The restoration is virtually certain since no other NA eastern toponym beginning with KUR.É– fits the traces following É.

**159** 5ff See coll.

# 160. Guarding the Camp

81-2-4,438

beginning broken away
1′ [*x x x x x x x x*] ⸢*x*⸣ [*x x x x*]
2′ [*x x x x x x*]-*u-ni* TA* *pa-ni* [*x x x*]
3′ [*x x x x x x*] *ha-ram-me-ma d*[*ul-lu*]
4′ [*x x x x x š*]*a* URU.HAL.ṢU.MEŠ *x*[*x x*]
5′ [*x x x ina šá*]-*li-in-ti né-t*[*a-rab*]
6′ [*x x x x x*] *šak-na-ni* EN.NUN [*dan-nat*]
7′ [*mì-i-nu ša* LUGAL *be*]-*lí i-šap-pa-*[*ra-an-ni*]
8′ [*x x x x x*] BÀD *ma-dak-te x*[*x x x*]
9′ [*x x x x*] ⸢*ú*⸣-*da ki-i* LUGAL *b*[*e-lí x x*]
10′ [*x x x x*] *a-na ṣe-er maš-ki* [*x x x*]
11′ [*x x x x*]*x* LÚ*.600—É.GAL *si-*[*x x x*]
12′ [*x x x* LÚ*].600—É.GAL *a-ni-nu x*[*x x x*]
13′ [*x x x x ga-a*]*m*-⸢*ri*⸣ LÚ*.[*x x x x*]
14′ [*x x x x x x*]*x i-qab-*[*x x x x*]
15′ [*x x x x* E]N.NUN *ša m*[*a-dak-te*]
16′ [*dan-na-at* ŠÀ]-*bu ša* LUGAL [EN-*ia lu* DÙG.GA]
17′ [*x x x x*] LUGAL *be-lí* [*x x x x x*]
18′ [*x x x*] *šu-nu ta tab ab* [*x x x x*]
19′ [KUR.*hu-buš-k*]*a-a-a* TA* *pa-an* [*x x x x*]
20′ [*x x x* L]Ú.ARAD *ša* [*x x x x x*]
21′ [*x x x*] LUGAL *be-*[*lí x x x x x*]
rest broken away
Rev. destroyed

CT 53 914

(Beginning destroyed)
2 [......] from [...]
3 [......] Later, the w[ork]
4 [...... o]f the forts [...].
5 We en[tered sa]fely, and are [encam]ped [...]. The guard [is strong].
7 [*What orders*] does [the king my l]ord, sen[d me]?
8 [...] the wall of the camp [...].
9 [...*I*] know that the king, [my] l[ord ...]
10 [...] on leather [...]
11 [...] the palace herald [...]
12 [...] the palace herald *and* we [...],
13 [... fi]nished [...]
14 [...] sa[y ...]
15 [The gu]ard of the c[amp is strong];
16 the king, [my lord, can be glad].
17 [...] the king, my lord, [...]
18 [...] they ... [...]
19 [the Hubušk]ian from [...]
20 [...] servant of [...]
21 the king, [my] lo[rd ......]
(Rest destroyed)

# 161. ———

K 1029

1 *a-na* LUGAL EN-*ia*
2 ARAD-*ka* $^{m}$*aš-šur—a-lik—pa-ni*
3 *lu-u* DI-*mu a-*⸢*na*⸣ LUGAL EN-*i*[*a*]
4 *ina* UGU ⸢*š*⸣*a* LUGAL *be*$^{!}$-[*lí*]
5 *iš-*[*pur*]-*an-ni*
6 ⸢*ma-a*⸣ [*x x*]-⸢*a*⸣-*a* ⸢*ša*⸣ [*x x x*]
rest broken away
Rev. beginning lost
1′ ⸢*x x*⸣*x*[*x x x x x*]
rest uninscribed

ABL 783

1 To the king, my lord: your servant Aššur-alik-pani. Good health to the king, m[y] lord!

4 As to what the king, [my] lo[rd], wr[ote] me: "The [...]ean who [......]
(Rest destroyed)

# 162. Zaba-iqiša Joins the Camp of Rusa

K 534

1 [*a-n*]*a* LUGAL E[N-*ia*]
2 [AR]AD-*ka* $^{m}$*ú-pa-*[*qa—*$^{d}$UTU]
3 *lu* DI-*mu a-na* LUG[AL EN-*ia*]

ABL 441

1 [T]o the king, [my] l[ord]: your [ser]vant Upa[q-Šamaš]. Good health to the ki[ng, my lord]!

**161** 4, r.1 See coll.
**162** → Deller Zagros p.108f.

4 UD-20-KÁM *ša* ITI.[Š]U
5 [L]Ú.GAL.MEŠ TA* ŠÀ URU.*ie-e-ri*
6 *ú-ta-mi-šu a-na*
7 URU.*bir-te ša* $^{m}$10—*rém-a-ni*
8 *i-tal-ku* $^{md}$É.A—MAN—DÙ
9 *i-si-šu-nu i-ta-lak*
10 [*a-n*]*a-ku ina* ŠÀ URU.*ie-e-ri*
11 [*a-na-k*]*u* : *a-ki* LUGAL *be-lí*
12 [*iq-bu-u*]*-ni* : EN.NUN
13 [*ša* $^{mí}$Í]D.*za-ba*—BA-*šá*

4 The magnates departed from Yeri on the 20th of [Tam]muz (IV) and went to Fort Adad-remanni; Ea-Šarru-ibni went with them. I am in Yeri, [keepin]g watch over Zaba-iqiša, *as* the king, my lord, [told] me.

4ff → ADD 1096; Levine, SAAB 3 (1989) 88f. 11 *a-ki* is taken as a scribal error for *a-ki ša*, cf. no. 163 r.7.

FIG. 26. *Assyrian camp (reign of Assurbanipal).*
ORIGINAL DRAWING V, 26.

14 *[a-na-ṣa]r* UGU *ṭè-me*
15 *[ša* $^{m}$Í]D.*za-ba*—BA-*šá*
e.16 [LÚ*.DU]MU—*šip-ri*
17 *[ša* U]RU.*hu-bu-us-ka-a-a*!
18 *[ina* U]GU LÚ*.*sar-tin-ni*
r.1 *⸢i⸣-tal-ka iq-ṭí-bi*
2 *[ma]-⸢a⸣ ú-ta-mi-šu-šu*
3 *[ina* UG]U $^{m}$*ur-sa-a i-tal-lak*
4 *[a-bu-tú k]u-un-tú ši-i-ti*
5 *[ṭè]-mu*! *⸢a!⸣-ni-ú* 2-*šu*
6 [3-*š*]*u*! : *⸢a⸣-ki a-ni-e*
7 *[a-se]-me* [0] *a!-na!-ku an-nu-rig*
8 EN.⸢NUN⸣-[*šu*] *a-na-⸢ṣar⸣*

14 As to the news [of] Zaba-iqiša, [a mes]senger [of] the Hubuškian has come and told the *sartinnu*: "He has been made to depart, and he is on his way [t]o Rusa."

r.4 It is a substantiated rumor; [I have he]ard it [reported] like this ma[ny] times. I am keeping an eye on [him] now.

## 163. Settling a Complaint by the Augurs

Rm 2,4

1 *a-na* LUGAL EN-*ia*
2 ARAD-*ka* $^{m}$*ú-paq*—$^{d}$*šá-maš*
3 *lu-u* DI-*mu*
4 *a-na* LUGAL EN-*ia*
5 *ina* UGU LÚ*.*šá*—EN.NUN
6 *ša* TA* LÚ*.*da-gíl*—MUŠEN.MEŠ
7 *ša* LUGAL *be-lí*
8 *iš-pur-an-ni*
9 *ma-a ina* IGI-*ka*
10 *lu-uk-ta-ti-ni*
11 *ma-a mì-i-nu*
12 *ša* TA* IGI LÚ*.*da-gíl*—MUŠEN.MEŠ
13 *i-šu-u-ni*
e.14 *[l]u-u-sa-hi-ri*
15 *[l]id-din*
r.1 *a-sa-a'-la*
2 *ú-ta-ṣi-ṣi*
3 *me-me-ni* [[TA* *pa!-ni!-šú!*]]
4 TA* *pa-ni-šú-nu*
5 *la i-ši*!
6 [[*ina* UGU-*hi-šú i!-du!-bu-bu!*]]
7 *ú-ma-a* : *a-ki ša* LUGAL
8 EN : *iq-bu-u-ni*
9 LÚ*.*šá*—EN.NUN *ur-ki-iu-u*
10 *ina* IGI-*šú-nu*
11 *ak-ta-la*
12 *am-mì-iu-u*
13 *a-na* EN.NUN-*šú*
14 *i-ta-ta-ka*

ABL 410

1 To the king, my lord: your servant Upaq-Šamaš. Good health to the king, my lord!

5 As to the guard with the augurs, about whom the king, my lord, wrote me: "He should be tried in your presence, and he must give back whatever he took from the augurs" —

r.1 I have carried out a thorough investigation; he has taken nothing from them, [[though they complained about him]].

7 Now, I have kept the *reserve* guard in their service, as the king, my lord, commanded; the other one has gone back to his garrison.

17 See coll.
**163** r.3, 5 See coll. r.4f written over erasures. r.9 Or "later/second/junior guard."

## 164. King of Urarṭu Facing Battle with Sargon

K 621

1 [*a-na*] LUGAL EN-*ia*
2 ⸢ARAD⸣-*ka* $^{m}$EN—AŠ
3 *ina* UGU *ṭè-me*
4 *ša* KUR.URI-*a-a*
5 LÚ.KIN.A *ša* KUR.*an-di-a-a*
6 LÚ.KIN.A *ša* KUR.*zi-ki-ra-a-a*
7 *ina* ŠÀ-*bi* URU.*ú-a-si*
8 *i-tal-ku-u-ni*
9 *i-qi-ṭí-bu-ni-šú*
10 *ma-a* LUGAL KUR—*aš-šur*
11 *ina* UGU-*hi-ni*
12 UD-*mu ša* LÚ*.KIN.A.MEŠ
13 *e-mu-ru-ni*
14 *ú-ta-mì-ši*
15 *ina* KUR.*zi-ki-ti-a*
Edge uninscribed
r.1 *šu-tú a-di*
2 *e-mu-qi-šu*
3 *ù* KUR.*hu-ub*!-*ka-a-a*
4 5 *ma*!-*di-tú*
5 *i-si*!-*šú*! *i-tal*!-*ka*
6 *i-su-*⸢*hu*⸣-*ra*
7 *ina* LÚ.GAL.MEŠ-*šú i-iq-ṭí-bi*
8 LÚ.*e-mu-qi-ku-*(*nu*) *ka-ṣa-ra*
9 *ma-a* $in_6$—*ni-ri-te* LUGAL KUR—*aš-šur*
10 ⸢*a*!⸣-*sa-di-ri*
11 [*b*]*a*!-*ti-qí*!-*tú ši-i*
12 [*ina*] UGU *sa-di-ri*
13 *ba*!-*ti-qí-tú ši-i*

ABL 515

1 [To] the king, my lord: your servant Bel-iddina.

3 As to the news of the Urarṭian, a messenger of the Andian and a messenger of the Zikirtean have gone to Waisi and told him: "The king of Assyria is upon us."

12 The day he saw the messengers he set out to Zikirtu, he himself with his troops.

r.3 The Hubuškian too went with him, for five stages. (Then) he turned back and ordered his magnates: "Organize your troops, I shall array myself against the Assyrian king."

11 This is from [in]formers; (the part) concerning the arraying is from informers.

## 165. King of Urarṭu Sacrificing on a Campaign

K 4695 + K 16529 (CT 53 793)

1 *a-na* LUGAL [EN]-⸢*i*⸣*a*
2 ARAD-*ka* $^{m}$E[N]—AŠ
3 *lu* DI-*mu a-na* LUGAL EN-*ia*
4 *ina* UGU *ṭè-me*
5 *ša* KUR.URI-*a-a* :! U[D *x*]*x* ⸢*x*⸣
6 *ú-ta-me-š*[*i x x x*]
7 *ina* ŠÀ-*bi* URU.*a-*[*x x x*]
8 UDU.*ni-qi a-d*[*i*! LÚ*.GAL.MEŠ-*šú*]
9 *e-pa-ša ši-*[*pir-tu ša*]
10 KUR.*hu-ub*!-*ka-a-*[*a ta-tal-ka*]
11 [*ina*] *pa-ni-šú ma-a* [*x x*]
12 [*x*] ⸢*a*⸣-*ba*!-*ta-*[*x x*]
rest broken away
Rev. completely obliterated or uninscribed

ABL 1298+

1 To the king, my [lord]: your servant B[el]-iddina. Good health to the king, my lord!

4 As to the news of the Urarṭian, he set out [*on the* ... *d*]*ay* and was making sacrifices in the city of A[... *on the* ...*th*] wi[th his magnates], (when) a *me*[*ssage* from] the Hubuškian [came] to him:

11 "[...]...[......]

(Rest destroyed)

**164** → Deller Zagros p.108. r.3, 5 See coll. r.7 *i-iq-ṭí-bi* sic. r.10 W 182.
**165** 5 See coll.; reading U[D]-⸢*x*-KAM/KÁM⸣ excluded. 8, 10, 23 See coll.

## 166. Revolt in Urarṭu

K 5462

beginning lost
1′ [*x*]*x*[*x x*]*x*[*x x*]
2′ *i—ha-ri* URU.*š*[*u*-(*x x*)]
3′ *i-ṣa-ba-ta* LÚ*!.*hu*-[*ub-tú*!]
4′ *ša* TA* *na-ka*
5′ TA* *na-ka*
6′ *ina* ŠÀ-*bi ú-še-ra-ba*
r.1 *ù* URU.*kar*-URUDU.MEŠ
2 *i-si-šú i-ti-ki-ri*
3 LÚ.*tur-ta-nu-šu*
4 *ina* Š[À-*bi qa-r*]*a-bu ú-pa-ša*
5 [*x x x x x*] *a*?
rest broken away

ABL 1325

(Beginning destroyed)

1 [...] has captured [...] in the *moat* of the town Š[u...], and is bringing cap[tives] from *various places* into it.

r.1 Furthermore, the city Kar-siparri has revolted against him, and his commander-in-chief is engaged in [bat]tle [the]re.

(Rest destroyed)

## 167. Military Movements in Urarṭu

K 15081

beginning broken away
1′ [*x x x x* KUR].⸢URI⸣-*a-a it*-[*x x*]
2′ [*x x x x x*] *ip-tu-uh*-[*ru*]
3′ [*x x x* URU].⸢*ú*⸣-*a-si du*-[*x x*]
4′ [*x x x x*] *i—pa-an* LUGAL EN-[*ia*]
5′ [*x x x x* U]RU.*ú-a-s*[*i x x x*]
6′ [*x x x x x*]-*ab-bi* [*x x x x*]
rest broken away
Rev. destroyed

CT 53 615

(Beginning destroyed)

1 [......] the Urarṭian has *go*[*ne*]

2 [......] have assem[bled]

3 [...... *in*] Waisi [...]

4 [......] in the presence of the king, [my] lord,

5 [......] Wais[i ...]

(Rest destroyed)

## 168. Report on the Urarṭian Camp

Rm 557

1 *a-na* LÚ*.SUKKAL
2 BE-*iá* ARAD-*ka*
3 m*a-da-a lu* DI-*mu*
4 *a-na* LÚ*.SUKKAL BE-*iá*
5 [*i*]*na* ⸢UGU⸣ *ṭè-me*
6 [KUR.URI?]-⸢*a*⸣-*a ša be-li*
7 [*iš-pur-an-n*]*i ina* ŠÀ-*bi*
8 [*x x x x x x*]*x*
rest (at least 8 lines) broken away
Rev. beginning broken away
1 [*x x x x x x*]*x*
2 [*x x x x x x*]-⸢*ri*!⸣
3 *i*!-⸢*na* MI?⸣ [*x x x*.M]EŠ
4 *ina* ŠÀ-*bi-š*[*u i-sa*]-*kan*
5 *ina* ŠÀ-*bi i*!-⸢*x x*⸣-*a-a*
6 *ina* ŠÀ-*bi* KUR.*ú-lu-a-za*!

ABL 1081

1 To the vizier, my lord: your servant Adâ. Good health to the Vizier, my lord!

5 As regards the news [of *the Urarṭi*]an about which my lord [wrote m]e, in [......]

(Break)

r.4 *On the night of* [... he pla]ced [...]s within it; he is encamped in ..., within Ulua-

**166** Hand of Bel-iddina. 1ff See coll. 4f By analogy to *issēn* ... *issēn* "one ... the other," *ša ūme ša ūme* "day by day," and like expressions, *issu naka issu naka* is assumed to have a distributive meaning here.
**168** r.2ff See coll.

7 *šá-ki-ni* É *pa-ni-šú-ni*
8e *a-na* LÚ*.SUKKAL BE-*iá*
9e *a-sap-ra*
s.1 [*x x x x x-n*]*i a-sap-*(*ra*$^{?}$)
2 [*x x x x x*] ⌜*a*⌝*-sap-ra*

za; I have written to the vizier, my lord, where he intends to go.

s.1 I have written [all that I have heard ...]

2 I have written [......].

# 169. King of Zikirtu as Horse Trader

K 537

1 *a-na* LUGAL EN-*iá*
2 ARAD-*ka* $^{md}$15—MU—BA-*šá*
3 *an-nu-rig* LÚ.MAH.MEŠ
4 LÚ*.*zi-gír-ta-a-a* DU-*u-ni*
5 LÚ*.DUMU—*šip-ra*$^{!}$*-ni* : *ša* KUR.URI-*a-a*
6 *ša ina* UGU LÚ*.[*zi*]*-gír-ta-a-a*
7 DU-*u-ni* : *ṣa-bu-tú* : *i-si-šú-nu*
8 DU-*u-ni* : *ina* UGU : KA
9 *ša* LÚ*.*zi-gír-ta-a-a kas-pu*
10 *ú-se-li* : *ina* URU.*dan*$^{!}$*-ni-te*
11 *a-sa-kan* : *ma-a* : *ana* : KUR.*pa-áš-šá-te*
12 ANŠE.KUR.RA.MEŠ SUM-*ka*
13 *ú-ma-a* : *bir-ti* IGI.2.MEŠ
14 *ša* LÚ*.MAH.MEŠ
15 *lu-u-ma-di-du*
r.1 *ma-a*ʾ*-da* : LÚ*.MAH.MEŠ
2 KA-*šú-nu* : *ú-šá-bal-ku-tú*
3 *ma-a* TA* UGU : *ša* : LÚ*.EN-*ni*$^{!}$
4 *la ni-iš-me* : *a-na* LÚ*.MAH
5 2-*e* : LUGAL : *liš-al* : *šu-u-tú*
6 DU ZU : *a-ki a-na* LÚ*.*tur-tan*
7 *ṭè-e-mu* : *iš-kun-u-ni*
rest uninscribed

ABL 205

1 To the king, my lord: your servant Issar-šumu-iqiša.

3 The emissaries of the Zikirtean (king) are now coming; the messengers of the Urarṭian who had gone to the [Zi]kirtean are coming with them as captives.

8 I have had money brought up and deposited in the stronghold, (relying) on the word of the Zikirtean, who said: "I shall sell you the horses in Paššate."

13 Now let it be impressed upon the emissaries, as the emissaries are trying hard to back out of their word, claiming: "We have not heard about (such a promise) by our lord."

r.4 The king should ask the second emissary; he knows that he gave the order to the commander-in-chief.

# 170. Appointing an Attendant to a Eunuch

K 1892

1 [*a-na* LUGAL EN-*ia*]
2 [ARAD-*k*]*a* $^{m}$*di-*[*na nu*]
3 [*lu-u* DI]*-mu a-na* L[UGAL EN-*ia*]
4 [*ša* LUG]AL *be-lí iš—šad-*[*dag-diš*]
5 [*iš-p*]*ur-ni-ni* LÚ*.SA[G]
6 [*ša*] LUGAL *be-lí iq-bu-*[*u-ni*]
7 [*m*]*a-a i—pa-ni-šú* [*x x x*]
8 [$^{m}$]*iš-me*—DINGIR *ina* ⌜*pa-ni*⌝-[*x x*]
9 [*k*]*i-i* [*x x x x x x*]
rest broken away
Rev. beginning broken away
1′ [*x x x k*]*as r*[*u x x x*]
2′ [*x x x*]*-ṭu-ru* G[Ú *x x*]
3′ [*x x x*]*-tar-ra ri* [*x x*]
4′ [*x x s*]*u-sa-a-a x*[*x x x*]

CT 53 204

1 [To the king, my lord: y]our [servant] Di[nanu. Good] health to the k[ing, my lord]!

4 [As to what the ki]ng, my lord, [wro]te me last y[ear], the eunu[ch about whom] the king, my lord, said: "[Appoint ...] to his service!" — Išme-ilu [is now] in [his] service.

9 When [......]

(Break)

r.4 [the *Bu*]susean(s) [...]

**169** → copy 5 R 53,4. r.3, 6 See coll.
**170** → SAA I 258; no. 171.

5′ [*x x x š*]*a* KUR.*bi*[*r-a-te*]
6′ [*x x x*] ⌜*e-ru-bu*⌝ [*x x*]
7′ [*x x x x x x x x*]

5 [... o]f Bi[rate]
6 [...] enter [...]
(Rest destroyed)

## 171. Arrival of Foreign Princes with Horse Tribute

Sm 51

1 $^{m}$*ia-la-*[*x x*]
2 DUMU—LUGAL KUR.*an-d*[*i-a-a*]
3 *i-la-ka a-*[*na x x*]
4 $^{md}$MAŠ.MAŠ—EN—PAB LÚ*.M[AH]
5 *i-si-šu* [0]

6 16 ANŠE.KUR.RA.MEŠ ⌜SA$_5$⌝.MEŠ
7 13 KUR.MEŠ *ir-gi-ni*
8 14 KUR.MEŠ GI$_6$.MEŠ
9 1 KUR *har-šá-a-a*
10 1 KUR *tu-a-nu*
11 6 KUR MÍ.HÚB.MEŠ
r.1 5 ANŠE.GÌR.NUN.NA.MEŠ-*šú*
2 PAB 51 KUR.MEŠ *ša* DUMU—LUGAL
3 KUR.*an-di-a-a*

4 $^{m}$*a-bat*—LUGAL—PAB LÚ*.MAH
5 KUR.*man-na-a-a* : *i-si-šú-nu*
6 *i-la-ka*
7 *a-sa-al-šú*
8 *ma-a na-mur-tú* [0]
9 *i-ba-ši*
10 ŠU.2-*ti-ku-n*[*u-u*]
11 *ma-a* ⌜*pa*!*-x x*⌝ [*x*]
12 *a*!*-na x*[*x x x x*]
13e *ma-a m*[*i-i-nu*]
14e *šá ú-*[*x x x*]
15e *ú-q*[*a-x x x*]

ABL 466

1 Yala[...], the crown prince of And[ia], is coming t[o ...], accompanied by the em[issary] Nergal-belu-uṣur.

6 16 red horses; 13 *irginu* horses; 14 black horses; 1 Haršean horse; 1 *tuanu* horse; 6 mares; 5 mules; in all 51 horses from the crown prince of Andia.

r.4 Abat-šarri-uṣur, the Mannean emissary, is coming with them. I asked him: "Is the audience gift with you?"

11 He said: "[......] to [......];

13 "what[ever ...] ...[...]."

## 172. Nabû-ereš under Surveillance

Rm 2,5

1 *a-na* LUGAL EN-*a*
2 ARAD-*ka* $^{m}$*a-bat*—MAN—PAB
3 *lu* DI-*mu a-na* LUGAL EN-*a*
4 *ina* UGU $^{md}$PA—KAM-*eš*
5 LÚ*.*kal-da-a-a*
6 *ša* LUGAL *be-lí iš-pur-an-ni*
7 *ma-a šap-li qa-ti*
8 *ma-ṣar-tú-šú li-ṣu-ru*
9 TA* *mar* LUGAL *be-lí*
10 *iš-pur-an-ni*
11 *a-sa-par ma-ṣar-tú-šú*
12 *šap-la qa-ti*
e.13 *it-ta-aṣ-ru*

ABL 411

1 To the king, my lord: your servant Abat-šarri-uṣur. Good health to the king, my lord!

4 As to the Chaldean Nabû-ereš about whom the king, my lord, wrote me: "He should be watched secretly" —

9 the very moment the king, my lord, wrote me, I sent (word), and they have been watching him secretly.

**171** Hand of Dinanu. → TCAE p.279. 3f, r.11f See coll.

r.1 *ú-ma-a*
2 *an-nu-ri*
3 *ú-tam-me-šá*
4 *il-la-ka*
5 *ma-a a-na šul-me*
6 *ina* É.GAL *al-lak*

r.1 Now then he has set out and is on his way, going to the Palace to greet (the king), as he says.

# 9. Fragmentary Letters relating to Urarṭu and Zikirtu



FIG. 27. *A rider, possibly Urarṭian, pursued (reign of Tiglath-Pileser III). Cf nos. 90 and 173f.*
BM 118905.

## 173. Report on an Urarṭian Defeat

K 7420

beginning broken away
1′ [*ša b*]*e-lí i-*[*x x x x*]
2′ [*ki*]-⌜*i*⌝ *an-ni-e* [*iq-ṭi-bu-ni*]
3′ [*ma*]*-a* LUGAL-*šú-nu* ⌜LÚ*⌝.[GAL.MEŠ-*šú*]
4′ [*ina*] KASKAL *bé-et i*[*l-lik-u-ni*]
5′ [*m*]*a-a de-ek-tu-šú-*[*nu ma-a*ʾ*-da*]
6′ ⌜*i*⌝*-du-ku ma-a* LÚ*.GA[L.MEŠ-*šú x*]
7′ [*d*]*e-e-ku ba-ti-i*[*q-tú*]
8′ [*l*]*a-a ah-ru-ṣa ki-*[*i*]
9′ [*š*]*a e-pa-šu-u-ni a-*[*na*]
10′ [E]N-*ia la-a áš-p*[*u-ra*]
11′ ⌜*ú*⌝*-ma-a* TA ŠÀ [KUR.*x x*]
12′ [*ina* Š]À KUR-*ia e-*[*tar-bu-ni*]
13′ [URU.*b*]*i-ra-t*[*e*! *x x x x*]
e.14′ [*x x x*]*x a* [*x x x x*]
Rev. destroyed

CT 53 99

(Beginning destroyed)

1 [about which] my [lo]rd [*inquired*, they previously informed me] as follows:

3 "Their king [and *his magnates*] have been [utterly] defeated on (their) expedition; [x] of his magna[tes] have been killed."

7 I did [no]t have more detailed information, and (thus) did not wr[ite] t[o] my [lo]rd how it happened.

11 Now they have e[ntered] my country from [...] and [*are ...ing*] *the forts* [...]

(Rest destroyed)

## 174. The Defeat of the King of Urarṭu

K 14683

beginning broken away
1′ [*x x x x*]*x ša* [*x x x*]
2′ [*x x x* K]UR.URI-*a-a* [*ina* KUR.*gi-mir*]
3′ [*bé-et i*]*l-li-ku-u-*[*ni x x x x*]
4′ [*x x x ga*]*b-bu de-e-*[*ku* 1-*en*]
5′ [TA ŠÀ-*bi l*]*a is-hu-r*[*a x x x*]
6′ erased
7′ blank
rest broken away
Rev. destroyed

CT 53 583

(Beginning destroyed)

1 [...] of [...]

2 [When] the (king) of Urarṭu [w]ent [against the Cimmerians, a]ll [his governors and his troops] were kil[led; n]ot [one] has returned [from there].

(Rest destroyed)

## 175. ———

K 15114

beginning broken away
1′ ⌜*i*⌝*-x*[*x x x x x x*]
2′ *i-tú-*[*x x x x x x*]
3′ *i-du-k*[*u x x x x x*]
4′ *i-qa-bi* [*x x x x x*]

CT 53 621

(Beginning destroyed)

3 kill[ed ......]

4 says [......]

**173** → Deller Zagros p.100. 6 Possibly "[three] of his magnates"; cf. ABL 197 r.12 (SAA I 31). 13 Or "the city of Birate". See coll.
**174** → Deller Zagros p.100.

5′ *i-na me-*[*x x x x x*]
6′ *ša pu-ut* [*x x x x x*]
7′ ⸢*a*⸣*-di* [*x x x x x*]
rest broken away
Rev. destroyed

5 in the [......]
6 opposite [......]
7 as far as [......]
(Rest destroyed)

# 176. Military Movements in the Northeast

Sm 1961

beginning broken away
1′ *x*[*x x x x x x x x x*]
2′ *nu-*[*x x x x x x x x x*]
3′ KUR—*aš-š*[*ur x x x x x x x x*]
4′ 1-*en x*[*x x x x x x x x*]
5′ *a-na* KUR.*an-d*[*i-a x x x x x x*]
6′ *a-na* KUR—*aš-šur*.K[I *x x x x x x*]
7′ *ug-da-dam-*[*mar x x x x x x*]
8′ *har-ra-nu ša* [*x x x x x x*]
9′ *al-la-ka bi-i*[*s x x x x x*]
10′ *man-nu ša* Á.2-*š*[*ú x x x x x*]
11′ *a-bat-taq is-se-niš* [*x x x x x*]
12′ LUGAL KUR—*aš-šur*.KI *ina* U[GU *x x x x*]
13′ *né-rab* KUR.*su-a* [*x x x x*]
14′ *ša* LÚ*.SIPA *ina* UG[U *x x x x*]
15′ [*a*]*n-nu-ti taq-x*[*x x x x*]
rest broken away
Rev. beginning broken away
1′ *x*[*x x x x x x x x x x*]
2′ *a-n*[*a x x x x x x x x x*]
3′ *ša x*[*x x x x x x x x x x*]
4′ *an-ni-*[*x x x x x x x x x*]
5′ *a-x*[*x x x x x x x x x x*]
6′ *x*[*x x x x x x x x x x*]
7′ *ša x*[*x x x x x x x x x x*]
8′ *a-na* [*x x x x x x x x x*]
9′ *a-x*[*x x x x x x x x x x*]
rest broken away
s.1′ [*x x x*] *al-li-kan-ni* LÚ*.LUL.MEŠ *sa*!-⸢*r*⸣*a-nu ša* LÚ*.*x*[*x x*]
2′ [TA ŠÀ *né*]*-ri-bi it-ta-ṣu-šú-nu ke-et-tu a-x*[*x x*]
3′ [*x x ina*] ŠÀ KUR.URI *la ah-ṭi*

CT 53 133

(Beginning destroyed)

3 *Ass*[*yria* ......]
4 one [......]
5 to And[ia ......]
6 to Assyria [......]
7 [will be] completed [......]
8 the road to [......]
9 I shall go [......]
10 Whoever [*lays*] hands [on ......]
11 I shall cut [...]; *at the same time* [...]
12 the king of Assyria aga[inst ......]
13 the pass of Sua [......]
14 *which* the Shepherd [......]
15 [t]hese [......]
(Break)
(Reverse too broken for translation)

s.1 [*When*] I came [to ...], they brought the criminals and thieves of [...] away [from the p]ass. Truly, [...]; I did not trespass [up]on Urarṭian territory.

# 177. Military Movements in the Urarṭian Camp

K 14686

beginning broken away
1′ [*x x a-se*]*-me ma-a ina b*[*a-x x x*]
2′ [*x x it*]*-ta-lak ina* UG[U *x x x*]
3′ [*x x x*] KUR.*an-di-a-a* ⸢*x*⸣ [*x x x*]
4′ [*x x š*]*a* KUR.URI-*a-a* [*x*] PAB [*x x x*]

CT 53 122

(Beginning destroyed)
1 [... I have hea]rd that he has gone to [...].
2 As to [......] the Andian [...],
4 [the ... o]f the Urarṭian [...]

**176** Possibly fragment of a royal letter to the king of Urarṭu; → SAA I 8. s.1 See coll.

5′ [*x x*] ⸢*i-tu*⸣*-rid* [URU].MEŠ-*ni* [*x x x*]
6′ [*x x x x x*] ⸢*x*⸣ [*x x x x x x*]
other side broken away

5 has descended [to ... and ...ed] the [*citi*]*es* [...]
(Rest destroyed)

## 178. Fragment of a Report on Urarṭu

K 15015

beginning broken away
1′ [*x x x x x x x*] *nu-uk* 1-*me*
2′ [*x x x x x x x*]*-u-ni*
3′ [*x x x x x x x*]*-sa-kan*
4′ [*x x x x x x x*] ⸢UD⸣*-me*
5′ [*x x x x x x* GIŠ.Ù]R.MEŠ
6′ [*x x x x x x* LÚ].⸢A⸣—KIN-*šú*
7′ [*x x x x x x x*] *x* [*x*]
e.8′ [*x x x x x x x x x*]
9′ [*x x x x x x*] ⸢*mu*⸣ *na* ⸢*an*⸣
10′ [*x x x x x x*] *ana-ku*
11′ [*x x x x* DING]IR.MEŠ-*ni ša* LUGA[L]
12′ [*be-lí-ia l*]*u-u-du-u*
r.1 [*šum-ma x x x*] 1-*lim* LÚ.*i-tú-*ʾ*u*
2 [*x x x x* URU.*ṭ*]*u-ru-uš-pa-a*
3 [*x x x x ú*]*-ba-*ʾ*u-u-ni*
4 [*x x x x x*] ⸢*a*!⸣*-sap-ra*
5 [*x x il-l*]*ik-u-ni ú-sa-hi-ir*
6 [*x x x ma*]-⸢*a*⸣ LUGAL KUR.URI-*a-a*
7 [*x x x x*]-⸢*te*⸣ *i-sap-ra*
8 [*ma-a x x*]-⸢*ku*⸣*-nu*! *lil-*⸢*li-ku*⸣
9 [*x x x x*] KUR.URI-*a*-[*a x x*]
10 [*x x x x x š*]*a* [*x x x*]
rest broken away

CT 53 124

(Beginning destroyed)
1 [...... I said]: "100
2 [......]ed
3 [......] placed
4 [......] day
5 [...... be]ams
6 [......] his messenger
(Break)
10 [...] I [...].
11 [By the go]ds of the kin[g, my lord],
r.1 [......] 1,000 Itu'eans
2 [...... Ṭ]uruspâ
3 [*will*] *call* [... *to account*].
4 I have sent [*my messenger* to ...];
5 [having g]one [...], he [sent] back [...], saying:
6 "The king of Urarṭu has written [to] *his* [governors]:
7 "Your [troops] should go and [...]."
9 The Urarṭian [......]
(Rest destroyed)

## 179. Purge in an Urarṭian Province

K 4677

Obv. destroyed
Rev. beginning broken away
1′ *x*[*x x x t*]*e*! ⸢*ru*!⸣ [*x x*]
2′ *il-li-kan-ni* : *ma-a-tu* [0]
3′ *e-ta-ka* : LÚ.EN.NAM [0]
4′ *i-si-šu* : *ina* URU.*ṭu-ur-uš*-[*pa-a*]
5′ *i-ti-ši* : *pa-a-tu* [0]
6′ LÚ.2-*u* LÚ.GAL—URU.MEŠ-[*ma*]
7′ ⸢*pa*!⸣*-tu-ú* : KALAG.MEŠ *ša* KUR [0]
8′ [*ina*] ŠÀ-*bi-šú-nu* : *ir-tu-*ʾ*u-b*[*u*]
9′ [*x x*]*x-tú*! :! *ma-a* : *a-ta-a*
10′ [*ki*]-⸢*i*⸣ *at-tu-nu* : *tu*-[*x x*]
11′ [*x x x*] LÚ.*šá*—UGU—[*x x*]
rest broken away

ABL 1295

(Beginning destroyed)

r.1 [*Ever since the king of Urarṭu*] came [...], the country *has been in a state of alarm*. He has taken the governor with him to Ṭuruš[pâ]; he has been discharged.

5 The deputy and the village manager have been discharged [as well]. The mighty of the land have been raging among themselves [...], saying:

9 "Why, [wh]en you [...],

10 [...] the overseer of [......]"

(Rest destroyed)

**179** r.5, 7ff See coll.

## 180. Troubles in Urarṭu

K 16551

beginning broken away
1′ [*x x x x* K]UR$^{?}$-*e* [*x x*]
2′ [*x x x*] LÚ*.EN.NA[M.MEŠ]
3′ [*x x x*] *ina da-at* [LUGAL]
4′ [*x x x i*]*l-la-ku-*[*ni*]
5′ [*x x x x x i*]*š is* [*x x*]
rest broken away
Rev. destroyed

CT 53 799

(Beginning destroyed)
1 [...... the *mount*]*ain* [...]
2 [......] the gov[ernors]
3 [......] after [the king]
4 [... ar]e co[ming]
(Rest destroyed)

## 181. News of Urarṭu

K 14687

1 [*a-na* LUGAL EN-*ia*]
2 [ARAD-*ka* $^{m}$*x x x x*]
3 [*lu* DI-*mu a-na* LUGAL E]N-*ia*
4 [*ina* UGU *ṭè-me ša* KU]R.[U]RI-*a-a*
5 [*ša* LUGAL *be-lí iš*]-*pur-an-ni*
6 [*x x x x x* L]Ú.S[A]G
7 [*x x x x x*] *áš-pur-an-ni*
8 [*x x x x x*]-*bi*
rest broken away
Rev. uninscribed

CT 53 586

1 [To the king, my lord: your servant NN. Good health to the king], my [lo]rd!

4 [As to the news of] the [Ur]arṭian [about which the king, my lord, wr]ote me,
6 [NN], the e[un]uch [whom] I sent [to ......]
(Rest destroyed)

## 182. Fragment of a Military Report

79-7-8,267

1 [*a-na* LUGAL *be-lí-ia*]
2 [ARAD-*ka* $^{m}$*x x x x x*]
3 [*lu* DI-*mu a-na* LUGAL] ⸢EN⸣-[*ia*]
4 [*ina* UGU KUR.URI$^{?}$]-*a*-⸢*a*⸣
5 [*ša* LUGAL *be-lí*] *iš-pur-an-*[*ni*]
6 *m*[*a-a mi-i-nu*]-*u*[*m-ma*]
7 *ṭ*⸢*è*⸣-[*en-šú*]-⸢*nu*⸣ *i-x*[*x x x*]
8 *ša iš*$^{!}$-*ʾa*-⸢*al*⸣$^{!}$-[*x x x*]
9 LÚ*.SAG *šu-tú x*[*x x x*]
10 *ša ina pa-ni-šú-nu* [*x x x*]
11 [*x x x*] *ina* ⸢*x*⸣ [*x x x x*]
rest broken away
Rev. beginning broken away
1′ *ha-*[*x*]-⸢*x*⸣-*šú-nu* [*x x x*]
2′ *e-te-nu-na-š*[*i x x*]
3′ *bat-qi-ni* TA* ŠÀ-*bi* [*ni-ti-ši*]
4′ *ú-ma-a i-na-ṣ*[*u-ru-šú*]
5′ *a-ni-nu a-ke-e* [*né-pu-uš*]
6′ *ki-iṣ-r*[*u š*]*a* LUGAL *be-*[*lí*]
7′ *ik-ṣur-u-ni šu-u-*[*tu*]
8′ [*š*]*um-mu ina pa-an* LUGAL [EN-*ia*]
9′ [*t*]*a-ri-iṣ ki-*⸢*i*⸣ [*x x*]

CT 53 891

1 [To the king, my lord: your servant NN. Good health to the king, my] lord!

4 [As to the *Urarṭ*]*ians* [about whom the king, my lord], wrote me: "[*Whatev*]*er* is the ne[ws about th]em?" –
8 [...] who asked [......].
9 He is a eunuch [...]
10 who in their presence [......]
(Break)

r.1 their [...] *changed* [...] for us, [*and we took*] our replacement from it. [They are] guar[ding him/them] now.

5 How [should] we [proceed]? It is a cohort formed by the king, [my] lo[rd]; if it suits the king, [my lord], [let them ...] *like* [...];

**182** 8 See coll.

10′ [*lu-u*]*m*?-*mi*-[*du x x x*]
11e [*ú*]-*la-a* [*x x x x*]
12e [*x x*] *e* [*x x x x x*]

11 [oth]erwise [……]
(Rest destroyed)

## 183. Sending People to Palace

K 14291

beginning broken away
1′ [*x x x x-r*]*u ina* UG[U]
2′ [*x x x-b*]*u-ti*
3′ [*x x x* L]Ú.SAG
4′ [*x x x x*] KUR.URI
5′ [*x x x x*] ⌜É⌝ LUGAL
6′ [*x x x x x*]-*si-hu*
Edge uninscribed
r.1 [*x x x x-š*]*ú-nu*
2 [*x x an-nu*]-*rig*
3 [*a-na* É].GAL
4 [*ú-se-bi-l*]*a-šú-nu*
rest uninscribed

CT 53 519

(Beginning destroyed)
1 […] *upon* (*it*)
2 [… *royal body*]*guard*
3 […] eunuch
4 […] Urarṭu
5 […] the royal house
6 […]…
r.1 [… t]heir […].
2 [I am herew]ith [sen]ding them [to the Pa]lace.

## 184. Urarṭian Subjects Submit to Assyria

K 12970

beginning broken away
1′ [*x x*] ⌜*x x x*⌝ [*x x x x x x*]
2′ *ur*-⌜*ke*!-*te*!⌝ *i-ta-la*-⌜*ak*?⌝ L[Ú.ERIM.MEŠ *up-tah-hir*]
3′ 50 ⌜*ina* ŠÀ⌝-*bi-šú-nu* GAZ.ME[Š *x x x*]
4′ *ma-a* LÚ*.ARAD.MEŠ-*ni ša* LUGAL EN-*iá at-t*[*ú-nu*]
5′ *ma-a la* LÚ*.ARAD.MEŠ-*ni ša* KUR.*u*[*r-ar-ṭa-a-a*]
6′ [*a*]*t-tú-nu ih-ta-an-šú* [*x x x x*]
r.1 [*x x x x*] KALAG.ME[Š *x x x x*]
2 [*x x x x*]-*te x*[*x x x x x*]
3 [*x x x*] 2-*lim x*[*x x x x x*]
rest broken away

CT 53 445

(Beginning destroyed)
2 Later he went and [*assembled*] the m[en]; 50 of them we[re] killed. [He *proclaimed*]:
4 "Y[ou] are subjects of the king, my lord; [y]ou are no longer subjects of the U[rarṭian]!"
6 They submitted [……]
r.1 […] stro[ng ……]
2 [……]
3 […] 2,000 [……]
(Rest destroyed)

## 185. Fragment of a Report on Urarṭu

K 16522

beginning broken away
1′ [*x x x x x x x*]*x a*
2′ [*x x x x x x*] *ina* UGU-*hi*
3′ [*x x x x* KUR.U]RI-*a-a*
4′ [*x x x x x*] ⌜URU?⌝.*uš-ti*
5′ [*x x x x*]-*šú* ŠE.PAD.M[EŠ]
rest broken away
Rev. destroyed

CT 53 789

(Beginning destroyed)
2 […] as regards
3 […… the Ura]rṭian
4 [……] *the town Ušti*
5 […] barley rations
(Rest destroyed)

## 186. Exchanging Messengers

K 9971

beginning broken away
1′ [*x x x x x*]*x* [*x x*]
2′ [$^{md}$*x*—API]N-*eš* ⸢LÚ*.A⸣—[SIG$^{?}$]
3′ [*x x x*]-*a-a ša* ŠU.2 [$^{m}$*x x*]
4′ [*it-tal*$^{?}$-*k*]*u*$^{?}$-*u-ni* LUGAL ⸢*ú*⸣-[*da*]
5′ [*x x x p*]*a-ti-ú-te* [*šu-nu*]
6′ [LÚ*.A—KIN-*i*]*a ina* UGU-*hi*-[*šú*]
7′ [*a-sa-par*] *ki-ma-a*
8′ [*ina* UG]U-*ia i-suh-ra*
e.9′ [*ár-hiš ina*] UGU LUGAL
10′ [EN-*ia a-ša*]*p-pa-ra*
Rev. destroyed

CT 53 407

(Beginning destroyed)

2 [...-er]eš, a [...], [*and* ...]*ayu*, a subordinate of [NN, have *co*]*me to me*. The king kn[ows that *they are*] *distant* [...].

6 [I have now sent] m[y messenger] to [*him*]; as soon as he returns [t]o me, [I shall immediately w]rite to the king, [my lord].

(Rest destroyed)

## 187. Military Operations in Muṣaṣir

K 11801

beginning broken away
1′ [*x x x* $^{m}$*ur*]-*za*-⸢*ni*⸣ [*x x x x x*]
2′ [*x x x* UR]U.HAL.ṢU.M[EŠ *x x x*]
3′ [*x x x n*]*u-ṣa-bat ina* ŠÀ UR[U.*x x*]
4′ [*x x x ina*] UGU ÍD *ú*-[*x x x*]
5′ [*x x x*] *ina pu-tu-uš-š*[*ú x x*]
6′ [*x x* $^{m}$*ur-sa*]-*a-ma ina* UGU-*hi* [*x x x*]
7′ [*x x x i*]-*sak-nu-uš* [*x x x*]
8′ [*x x x x x*] *šu-nu-ni* [*x x x*]
9′ [*x x x x x*] *ša* EN [*x x x*]
10′ [*x x x x x*] ⸢*la*⸣ [*x x x x*]
rest broken away
Rev. destroyed

CT 53 427

(Beginning destroyed)
1 [... Ur]zana [...]
2 [...] the fort[s ...]
3 [... w]e capture; in the ci[ty ...]
4 [... t]o the river [...]
5 [...] opposite hi[m ...]
6 even [Rus]a *against* [...]
7 [... they pl]aced him [...]
8 [...] they are [...]
(Rest destroyed or too broken for translation)

## 188. Fragment referring to Zikirtu

K 5533

beginning broken away
1′ [*x x x x x x*] ⸢*x*⸣ [*x x*]
2′ [*x x x x x x*] *li x*[*x x*]
3′ [*x x x x x* A].ŠÀ *e*-[*te-riš*]
4′ [*x x x la i-d*]*i-na-áš-šu*
5′ [*x x x x* U]GU KUR.*zi-g*[*ír-te*]
6′ [*x x i-ta-n*]*a-áš-šu i-sa-pa-*[*ra-šu*]
7′ [*x x x x*] LÚ*.A—KIN-*i*[*a x x*]
8′ [*ina* UGU KUR.URI]-*a-a a-sa-al-š*[*ú*]
9′ [*ki-i an-ni-e*$^{?}$ *i*]*q-ṭí-bi-a ma-a x*[*x x*]
rest broken away
Rev. destroyed

CT 53 272

(Beginning destroyed)
3 [...] *re*[*quested a fi*]*eld* [...]
4 [He did not g]ive him [...]
5 [... *ab*]*out* Zik[irtu],
6 [gav]e him [...] and sen[t him *to me*].
7 [...] m[y] messenger [...]
8 I asked h[im about the *Urarṭ*]*ian*, and he informed me [as follows]:
(Rest destroyed)

**186** 2f Or "[...-er]eš, a [...]ean *chariot* [*fighter*] ..."

## 189. ———

Sm 1742

beginning broken away
1′ *[a]-⸢na⸣ ú-[ṣe-e x x x]*
2′ *[ina* K]A-*ia x[x x x x x]*
3′ *[ú]-⸢ma-a⸣* MAN KUR.*z[i?-kir-te x x]*
4′ *[x x x] ú-rat [x x x x]*
5′ *[x x x x]-u* LÚ.*[x x x]*
6′ *[x x x x x] ⸢x⸣[x x x x]*
rest broken away
Rev. destroyed

CT 53 912

(Beginning destroyed)
1 *[t]o g[o out ......]*
2 *[in]* my [mou]th [......]
3 *[N]ow, the king of Z[ikirtu]*
4 [...] a team *[of horses]*
(Rest destroyed)

## 190. Arrested by the Governor

K 1862

Obv. surface rubbed off
r.1 *[ša ina* U]GU *ta-hu-u-me*
2 *[ša]* É—⸢AD⸣-*šú-u-ni*
3 [TA] $^{m}$*aš-šur*—MAN-*a-ni*
4 *[a?]-sa-pa-[[]]ar-šú*
5 [LÚ*].EN.NAM *i-ṣa-bat-s[u]*
6 *[ú]-ma-a* $^{m}$*a-da-a*
7 *[a-na]* ⸢$^{m}$⸣*ba-zi-ia* ⸢A?⸣-*[šú]*
8 *[ša* K]UR!.*uk-ka-[a-a]*
rest broken away

CT 53 194

(Beginning destroyed)

r.1 [I] sent him [with] Aššur-šarrani [to the ...] on the border [of] his father's household; the governor arrested [him].

6 [N]ow Adâ [has ...ed] Baziya, the *s[on* of] the Ukk[ean]
(Rest destroyed)

## 191. ———

ND 1112

beginning broken away
1′ *⸢x x⸣ [x x x x x x x x]*
2′ *i-la-k[a? x x x x x x x]*
3′ *ina* ŠÀ KUR.*[x x x x x x]*
4′ KUR-*e i-[x x x x x x]*
5′ SAG.DU GIB[IL *x x x x x x]*
6′ *ina* KUR.*mu-ṣa-[ṣi-ri x x x x]*
7′ *⸢e⸣-[x x x x x x x x]*
rest broken away
Rev. uninscribed

GPA 244

(Beginning destroyed)

2 *is coming* [......]
3 in the country [......]
4 the mountains [......]
5 at the beginning of the mo[nth ......]
6 in Muṣa[ṣir ......]
(Rest destroyed)

## 192. The Hubuškian has Arrived

K 10895

Obv. broken away
Rev. beginning broken away
1′ *[ma]-⸢a* URU⸣.*[x-x-a-a]*
2′ *i-sa-a[p-ra]*
3′ *ma-a* KUR.*hu-[buš-ka-a-a]*
4′ *a-na* URU.*x[x x x x]*
5′ *iq-ṭa-[ra-bu-u-ni]*

CT 53 415

(Beginning destroyed)

1 "The (ruler) of [...] has writ[ten to me]: 'The Hu[buškian] has arr[ived] in [...].'"

6′ UD-14-KÁM ᵐ[*x x x*]
7′ LÚ*.2-*ú* ⌜*a*⌝-[*na x x x*]
8′ [*a*]-*sa-a*[*p-ra* 0]
rest uninscribed

6 On the 14th day, [I] se[nt *Šulmu-beli*], (my) deputy, t[o ...].
(Rest uninscribed)

# 193. Fragment Mentionning Šulmu-beli

K 5518

beginning broken away
1′ *x x x x*]⌜*x*⌝ [*x x x x x*
2′ *x x x*]*x-šú ša* ⌜*e*⌝-[*x x x*
3′ *x x* ᵐ]⌜D⌝I-*mu*—EN *x*[*x x x*
4′ *x x x x*] *qi* [*x x x x*
rest broken away
Rev. destroyed

CT 53 261

(Beginning destroyed)
2 [...] *his* [...] *who* [......]
3 [......] Šulmu-beli [......]
(Rest destroyed)

# 194. Emissaries from Labdudu

K 13006

1 [*a-na* LUGAL E]N-*ia*
2 [ARAD-*ka* ᵐ*man-nu*—*k*]*i*—URU.*arba-ìl*
3 [*lu* DI-*mu a-na* LU]GAL EN-*ia*
4 [*x x x x x* KU]R!.*hu-buš-ki-a*
5 [*x x x x x*] *nu-ta-me-ši*
rest broken away
Rev. beginning broken away
1′ [*x x*] ⌜*x x*⌝ [*x x x x*]
2′ [*x x*]*x-na-áš-ta*-[*x x x*]
3′ [*i*]—*su-ri* UGU *x*[*x x x*]
4′ [*i-š*]*á*!-*mu-na-ši* LÚ*.*lab*!-[*d*]*u*!-[*da*!]-[*a-a*]
5′ [*e-l*]*u-ni*! *i-la-ku-u-ni*
6′ [*a-na*?] *a*!.*a-e* KASKAL *ni-li-ka*
7′ [*ina* GABA] LÚ*.MAH.MEŠ *ú-ma-a*
8′ [*x x*] *le*!-⌜*lu*!⌝-*u-ni ú-la-a*
9e [*x x x-n*]*i mi-nu ša ṭè-e-mu-ni*
10e [LÚ*.A—KIN LUGAL] *ina*! GABA-*ni*
11e [*liš-pu-ra lil*]-*li-ka*
12e [*x x x x*]

ABL 936

1 [To the king], my [lo]rd: [your servant Mannu-k]i-Arbail. [Good health to the k]ing, my lord!
4 [......] Hubuškia
5 [......] we have departed
(Break)
r.2 ... [......]; perhaps they [will o]bey us as regards [...].
4 The Lab[d]ud[eans are coming] up and getting here; which way should we take to [meet] the emissaries? Now, should they come up [to ...], or [...]?
9 [*Let the king send a messenger*] to come and [tell] us what the orders are.

# 195. Messenger from Hubuškia

K 14675

beginning broken away
1′ [*i*]—⌜*su*⌝-*ri* L[Ú.*x x x*]
2′ [*ša*] URU.*hu-bu-u*[*š-ki-a*]
3′ [*i-s*]*i-ia i-l*[*a-ku-u-ni*]
4′ [*x x x*] TA* *x*[*x x x x*]
rest broken away
Rev. destroyed

CT 53 581

(Beginning destroyed)
1 [Pe]rhaps the [*emissaries*] of Hubu[škia] will co[me wi]th me
4 [...] from/with [......]
(Rest destroyed)

**194** 4, r.2ff, 8ff See coll.

# 196. A Letter from Hubuškia

K 10363

lines 1-3 destroyed
4 [x x x x x] ⸢a⸣ [x x x]
5 [x] ša É $^{m}$⸢tu!-ú⸣-x[x x x]
6 [ki]-i DUMU-šu in-[na-bit-u-ni]
7 [x $^{m}$u]r-ma-ak-in-n[u x x x]
8 [la-a i]l-li-ka x[x x x x]
9 [x x x] $^{m}$ia-ú—ʾ[a-x x x x]
10 [an-nu-r]ig šu-u [x x x x x]
11 [$^{m}$a-t]a-a—id-ri [ina pa-ni-ia]
12 [i-t]i-ti-is-s[u x x x x]
13 [x x K]UR-e TA* KUR.hu-b[u-uš-ki-a]
14 [x x x]x KUR.hu-bu-⸢uš⸣-[ki-a x x]
15 [x x x x] ina UGU [x x x x]
rest broken away
Rev. beginning broken away
1′ [x] ⸢x x x⸣ [x x x x x x x]
2′ [m]a-a 1-en šu-u x[x x x x x]
3′ [š]u-u $^{m}$EN-ŠU-u-a L⸢Ú⸣.[x x x x]
4′ ⸢ú⸣-ma-a ma-ʾa-a[d x x x x]
5′ [p]u-tu!-uš-šu-nu u [x x x x]
6′ [x T]A ŠU.2 LUGAL x[x x x x x]
7′ [ša a-n]a LUGAL be-l[i-ia aq-bu-u-ni]
8′ [mu]-uk TA* ma-ṣ[i LUGAL be-li]
9′ [a-n]a KUR.hu-bu-uš-[ki-a iš-pur-an-ni-ni]
10′ [a]-na ia-a-ši ina x[x x x x]
11′ [x x x]-lu-u-ni ù [x x x]
12′ [x x K]UR.hu-b[u]-uš-[ki-a x x]
13′ [x x x] ⸢x⸣ [x x x x x x]
two lines broken away

CT 53 409

(Beginning destroyed)

5 [...] of the house of Tu[...],
6 [wh]en his son *f[led]*,
7 [... *U*]*rmakinn*[*u* ...]
8 [did not] come [...]
9 [...] Iau-'a[...]
10 [No]w he and [...]
11 [At]â-idri [had an au]dience [with me]
13 [... the mo]untain from Hub[uškia]
14 [...] Hubuš[kia ...]
15 [...] on [...]
(Break)

r.2 "*There is one* [...];
3 *he is* Bel-qatua [...]."
4 Now, muc[h ...]
5 opposite them [...]
6 [...] the hands of the king [...].
7 [As to what I said t]o the king, [my] lo[rd]: "Ever sinc[e the king, my lord, sent me t]o Hubuš[kia], they have [...]ed me in [...] and [...]
12 [...] Hub[u]š[kia ...]
(Rest destroyed)

# 197. ———

K 13096

beginning destroyed
1′ [x]x ⸢x⸣ [x x x x x x x]
2′ a-n[a x x x x x x x x x x]
3′ [x x x x x x x x x x x x]
4′ [x x x x x x x x x x x x]
5′ [x x x x x x x x x x x x]
6′ [x x]x ⸢$^{m}$⸣$^{d}$AMAR.UTU—x[x x x x x]
7′ [TA] ŠÀ-bi ik-[x x x x x]
8′ [x] ⸢$^{md}$MAŠ⸣—ku-x[x x x x x]
9′ [u]k-tal-li-[x x x x x]
e.10′ [x x x x] ša [x x x x x]
11′ LÚ*.kal-lap—ši-pir-[te x x x]
r.1 iš-ka-šú i-[x x x x x]
2 LÚ*.kal-lap—ši-pir-t[ú x x x x]
3 liš-ʾa-al šúm-ma ina [x x x x x]
4 a-na URU.har-ma-s[a-a-a x x x]

CT 53 485

(Beginning destroyed)

6 [...] Marduk-[......]
7 [from] there [......]
8 Inurta-ku[......]
9 show[ed ......]
10 [......]
11 The *kallāpu* messenger [......]
r.1 [...]ed his work quota [...]
2 Let [*the king, my lord,*] ask the *kallāpu* messenger [...] whether in [...]
4 to Harmas[aeans ......]

**196** r.5 See coll.

5 URU.*ha*[*r-g*]*a-a-a* : *a-n*[*a x x x x*]
6 É *tu-um-ta-l*[*ik-x x x x x x*]
7 GAZ-*šú ma-a bi-*[*x x x x x*]
8 *a-na* DUMU-*ia* [*x x x x x x*]
9 É *ma-a at-*[*x x x x x x x*]
10 *šu-ú* MÍ [*x x x x x x x x*]
11 *tu-se-x*[*x x x x x x x x x*]
12 [T]A *x*[*x x x x x x x x x*]
13 ⌜*x*⌝ [*x x x x x x x x x x*]
rest broken away

5 Ha[rg]aeans to [......]
6 When you have taken coun[sel ......]
7 *kill* him [......]
8 to my son [......]
9 *my* house [......]
(Rest destroyed or too broken for translation)

## 198. On the Road Again

K 14588

Obv. destroyed
Rev. beginning broken away
1′ [*x x x x*] *x*[*x x*]
2′ [TA* ŠÀ URU].BÀD—$^{d}$U[TU]
3′ [*bé-et*] LUGAL *be-lí*
4′ [*i*]*š-pur-ra-ni-ni*
5′ ⌜*ú*⌝*-ta-me-š*[*i*]

CT 53 533

(Beginning destroyed)

r.2 I have [*now*] set out [from] Dur-Ša[maš to where] the king, my lord, sent me.

# Letters from the Mannean Frontier

# 10. Letters from Mazamua



FIG. 28. *Assyrian chariots and horses (reign of Assurbanipal).*
AO 19909.

## 199. Time to Set Out for a Campaign

K 630

1 *a-na* LUGAL *be-lí-ia*
2 ARAD-*ka* $^{m}$LUGAL—*e-mur-an-ni*
3 *lu* DI-*mu a-na* LUGAL EN-*ia*
4 *ša* LUGAL EN *iš-pur-an-ni*
5 *ma-a a-ta-a ta-ha-ru-pu*
6 *tu-na-me-še ma-a ina* IGI LÚ*.EN.NAM
7 *ša* URU.*arrap-ha la ta-ad-gul*
8 *a-na* LÚ*.EN.NAM *ša* URU.*arrap-ha*
9 KASKAL *am-mì-ú kar-ma-šu a—dan-niš*
10 TA* URU.*za-ban ú-na-ma-áš*
11 *a-na šá-al-še ina* ŠÀ-*bi šu-u*
12 *an-ni-ú* KASKAL *a-na* KUR.*par-su-a*
13 *al-lak a-la-bi-ia ba-si ha-ni-e*
14 *šu-ú ah-tú-ru-pu a-na* URU.*bir-te*
15 *e-te-li ina šad-dàq*$^{!}$-⸢*diš*$^{!}$-*ma*$^{!}$⸣
16 *a-na-ku šu-ú pu-u*[*t*$^{?}$ *ha-ni-e*]
17 [*x x x*] ⸢*x*⸣ *i x*[*x x x x*]
rest (about 5 lines and edge) broken away
Rev. beginning (3-4 lines) broken away
1′ [*x x x* ANŠ]E.⸢KUR⸣.RA.M[EŠ *x x x*]
2′ [*ina* URU.HAL].⸢ṢU$^{!}$⸣ *la ú-ra-ma* [*x x x*]
3′ LÚ*.*za-ku-ú ina* ŠU.2-*ia a*-[*ṣa-bat*]
4′ *a-na* KUR—*za-mu-u-a ú-ra*-[*da*]
5′ *e-ṣa-du e-ṣi-di ina* IGI LÚ*.A—⸢KIN⸣
6′ *ša* LUGAL EN-*ia a-da-gal*
7′ *mì-nu ša* LUGAL EN *i-qa-bu-ni*
8′ *ki ma-ṣi-en* LUGAL EN *i-qi-bu-ni*
9′ *ma-a* DUMU $^{m}$EN—SUM-*na i-si-ka*
10′ *lil-li-ki šu-u* TA* ERIM.MEŠ-⸢*ni*⸣
11′ *lil-li-ki* $^{md}$PA—*ha-mat-u-a*
12′ *a-na-ka li-mar-ku dul-lu*
13′ *ša* LUGAL EN-*ia le-pu-šu*
14′ *bat-qu ša* URU.HAL.ṢU.MEŠ *ša* LUGAL EN-*iá*
15′ *lik-ṣu-ru*
2 lines uninscribed

ABL 311

[1] To the king, my lord: your servant Šarru-emuranni. Good health to the king, my lord!

[4] As to what the king, my lord, wrote to me: "Why did you set out early without waiting for the governor of Arrapha?" –

[8] for the governor of Arrapha, the road in question is very slow. He sets out from Zabban, and it takes him three days to get there, while I can make a round-trip to Parsua going this way.

[13] For this very reason I went up to the fort first. Last year, too, I and he [...] accordingly [...]

(Break)

[r.1] [...] Shall I not leave [the h]orses [*and free men*] in [the fo]rt, but ta[ke] the [*horses*] and free men with me, go d[own] to Mazamua, and reap the harvest? I am waiting for the king my lord's messenger; what are the king my lord's orders?

[r.8] Since the king, my lord, said: "The son of Bel-iddina should go with you," let him go with the troops, and let Nabû-hamatua stay here to do the work of the king, my lord, and *repair* the forts of the king, my lord.

## 200. Sending Boys to War

K 689

1 *a-na* LUGAL EN-[*ia*]
2 ARAD-*ka* $^{m}$LUGAL—IGI.LAL-[*an-ni*]
3 *lu* DI-*mu a-na* LUGAL [EN-*ia*]

ABL 312

[1] To the king, [my] lord: your servant Šarru-emuranni. Good health to the king, [my lord]!

**199** → TCAE p.274f. [13] I.e., the fort of Adad-remanni? → no. 162. [15ff. r.2] See coll.
**200** Same scribe as in no. 199.

4 *ša* LUGAL EN *iš-pu[r-an-ni]*
5 *ma-a e-mu-qi-ka ku-ṣ[u*!*-ru]*
6 *lu et-ka-ka ma-a šúm-mu [ta-ri-iṣ]*
7 KASKAL *ša a-na* URU.*hi-ri-te ša* ⸢*ú*⸣-[*x x*]
8 *a-lik la-áš-šu la ta-ri-ṣi*
9 *kaq-qu-ru ma-ri-ṣi bir-te* KUR.MEŠ-*ni*
10 *šu-ú* A.MEŠ *kar-ku* ÍD *da-ʾa-na*
11 *la a-na* KUŠ.*maš-ki-ri ka-ra-ri*
12 *i-la-ka la a-na* KUŠ.*ka-la-ki*
13 LUGAL EN *ú-da* ERIM.MEŠ A.MEŠ
14 *la i-la-ʾu-ú e-mu-qi*
15 *pu-uh-ra al-lak e-l*[*i*]
16 ⸢*a*⸣*-na* KUR.*su-um-bi a-na* UR⸢U⸣.[*x x*]
17 [*a-l*]*a*!*-bi-a ina* KUR.É—⸢*ha*⸣*-ban* [*x x*]
18 [*x x*]*x* ⸢*x*⸣ [*x x x*] ⸢*x*⸣ [*x x*]
rest broken away
Rev. beginning broken away
1′ [*x x x x*] ⸢*x*⸣ [*x x x x x*]
2′ [*ah-tú-r*]*u-up x*[*x x x x*]
3′ *ina pa-ni-šú a-da-*[*gal šu-tu-ma*]
4′ *ih-tú-ur-pa-ni i*[*na*] ⸢*pa-ni*⸣*-ia*
5′ *i-da-gal* DUMU $^{m}$EN—SUM-*na ina šad*!*-dàq-diš*
6′ *i-si-ia a-na* KASKAL *la i-li-ki*
7′ ERIM.MEŠ SIG$_5$.MEŠ *ik-ta-la* LÚ*.TUR.MEŠ
8′ *qa-lu-te i-si-ia ú-se-ṣi*
9′ *ú-ma-a* LÚ*.*šá*—É—*ku-din* LUGAL EN
10′ *liš-pu-ra lu-še-ṣi-šú i-si-ia*
11′ *lil-li-ki ú-la-a i-bal-ka-ta*
12′ *i-ma-qu-ut ina* UGU *mur-ṣi e-*⸢*te*⸣*-ka*
13′ *la-áš-šu i-si-ia* ⸢*la*!⸣ [*i-la-ka*]
14′ LÚ*.TUR.MEŠ-*ni-ma q*[*a*!*-lu-te*]
15′ *i-si-ia ú-še-ṣa* [ERIM.MEŠ SIG$_5$.MEŠ]
16′ *i-ka-al-la* [0]

4 As to what the king, my lord, wro[te me]: "Orga[nize] your army and be on the alert! If [feasible], take the road to Hirite by [...]" —

8 it is not at all feasible! The terrain is difficult; it lies between the mountains, the waters are constricted and the current is strong, not fit for using either wineskins or keleks. The king, lord, knows that the men cannot *swim*.

14 The troops are assembled, and I am going up to Sumbi, making a detour to [...], [*then descending*] to Bit-Hamban [......]

(Break)

r.2 [I could have gone f]irst [...] and wai[ted] for him, [but he] left before me and is waiting f[or] me.

r.5 Last year the son of Bel-iddina did not go with me to the expedition but kept the best men at home and sent with me young boys only. Now let the king, my lord, send me a *mule stable attendant* to make him come forth and go with me.

11 Otherwise, he will (again) back off, fall away, *keep alert grudgingly*, and certainly not [go] with me, but will only send y[oung] boys with me, keeping [the best men] at home.

4f, 7 See coll. r.2ff Or: "waited f[or] me."

FIG. 29. *Raft (kelek) supported on skins, and boat, on Tigris (reign of Assurbanipal?).* ORIGINAL DRAWING IV, 78.

## 201. ———

K 14093

1 [a-n]a LUGAL EN-i[a]
2 [ARAD]-ka $^{m}$LUGAL—e-mur-[an-ni]
3 [lu DI]-mu a-na LUGAL EN-[ia]
4 [LÚ*.EN.N]AM$^{!}$ ša URU.ár-z[u$^{?}$-hi-na]
5 [x x x x]x b[i x x]
rest broken away
Rev. destroyed

ABL 321

1 [To] the king, m[y] lord: your [servant] Šarru-emuranni. [Good he]alth to the king, [my] lord!

4 [The govern]or of *Arz[uhina* ......]
(Rest destroyed)

## 202. Horses for the King

K 610

1 a-na LUGAL be-lí-ia
2 ARAD-ka $^{m}$LUGAL—IGI.LAL-ni
3 lu DI-mu a-na LUGAL be-lí-ia
4 ša LUGAL be-lí iš-pur-an-ni
5 ma-a šúm-ma ANŠE.KUR.RA.MEŠ
6 a-mu-te ša pi-i-te na-me-di
7 ina ŠU.2-ka i-tuq-tu-u-ni
8 ⸢ma⸣-a i-ṣa še-bi-la-áš-šú-nu
9 LÚ.DAM.QAR.MEŠ KUR.ku-me-sa-a-a
10 i-ta-⸢áš$^{?}$-ru⸣$^{!}$ ina$^{!}$ ⸢UGU$^{!}$⸣ a-he$^{!}$⸣-iš
rest (about 3 lines) broken away
Rev. beginning (2-3 lines) broken away
1′ be$^{!}$-⸢lí$^{?}$⸣ x[x x x x x]
2′ a-da-gal ina ⸢pa⸣-n[i-šú-nu]
3′ ki ma-ṣi-in ina UGU-hi-i[a]
4′ la-a i-lik-u-ni-ni
5′ a-sa-par LÚ*.ARAD.MEŠ-ni
6′ ša LUGAL be-lí-ia
7′ URU.ki-ba-at-ki
8′ ig-ta-al-du
9′ UN.MEŠ pi-i GÍR AN.BAR
10′ i-sa-ak-nu
11′ ki-i URU.ki-ba-at-ki
12′ ig-la$^{!}$-du-u-ni
13′ ip-ta-al-hu
14e i-sa-pa-ru-u-ni
15e ina UGU-hi-ia$^{!}$ e-da-nu
16e a-sa-kan-šú-nu
17e ⸢šúm⸣-ma i-⸢tal⸣-ku-⸢ni⸣
s.1 [x x na-ṣ]u-u-ni ina UGU LUGAL ú-še-bal-šú-nu
2 [x x x]x-ki ⸢ša⸣ LUGAL a-ta-ṣa

ABL 310

1 To the king, my lord: your servant Šarru-emuranni. Good health to the king, my lord!

4 As to what the king, my lord, wrote me: "If horses of *such size* fall into your hands, get them and send them to me!" —

9 Kumesaean merchants have reviewed (their stock and) together [...]
(Break)

r.1 my lord [......].

2 I waited f[or them], but since they did not come to m[e], I sent the servants of the king, my lord, to terrorize Kibatki, and they put people to the sword. After this act of terror on Kibatki, they got afraid and wrote to me, and I imposed a deadline upon them.

17 If they come and bring [*the horses*] I shall send them to the king.

s.2 I have fetched the king's [...].

**201** 4 The last sign actually looks like *n[u*; see coll.
**202** 10, r.1, 7, s.2 See coll.

## 203. When the King Established the Debt Remission

Sm 1045

1 *a-na* LUGAL *be-lí-ia*
2 ARAD-*ka* ᵐLUGAL—IGI.LAL-*ni*
3 *lu* DI-*mu a-na* LUGAL EN-*ia*
4 *ina* UGU GEŠTIN.MEŠ *ša* LUGAL
5 *be-lí iš-pur-an-ni*
6 *ma-a* 2-*me* ANŠE GEŠTIN.MEŠ
7 *a-na ma-ṣar-te ú-li*
8 *a—mar ša* LUGAL *be-lí*
9 *iš-pur-an-ni ú-ta-li*
10 *ina* UGU ᵐ*kù*!-KÁ—*sa-tar*
11 *ša* LUGAL *be-lí iš-pur-an-ni*
12 [*ma*]-*a ina pi-i* DÙG.GA
13 [*i*]-*si-šú du-ub-bu*
14 [*pi*]-⸢*i*⸣-*ia*!-*a-ma la pa*!-*te*!
15 [*ki-i ša* LUG]AL *be-lí*
16 [*iš-pu*]*r-an-ni*
17 [*ina pi-i* DÙG.G]A-⸢*ma*!⸣
rest (1-2 lines and edge) broken away
Rev. beginning broken away
1′ [*x x x*]*x* [*x x x*]
2′ [*x x x*] *pa-an* [*x x x*]
3′ [*ina pa-n*]*i*-⸢*ia*⸣ *i-za*!-[*x x x*]
4′ *ú-ma-a a-sa-*[*par* 0]
5′ LÚ*.*tar-gu*!-*ma-nu i*[*na x x*]
6′ *a-mar a-na* LUGAL *be-lí-ia*
7′ *a-na-ši-a*! *ú-še-bal*
8′ *ina* UGU LÚ*.EN—URU!-*a-ni*
9′ *ša* LUGAL *be-lí iš-pur-an-ni*
10′ *ma-a šum-ma i-tal-ku-u-ni*
11′ *ina pa-ni-ka ma-a* ⸢*i*!⸣-*ṣa*
12′ *ina* UGU-*hi-ia še-bi-la*
13′ DINGIR!.MEŠ-*ni* ⸢*ša*⸣ LUGAL *le*-⸢*pu*⸣-*šú*
14′ DUMU—KÁ.⸢DINGIR⸣.RA.KI
15′ *ina* UGU LUGAL *be-lí-ia*
16′ *i-tal-ku-u-ni a-na ma-hi-ir-te*
17′ *ki-i du*!-*ra-ru*
18′ LUGAL *be-lí iš-kun-u-ni*
19′ UN.MEŠ TA* *pa-ni-šú-nu*
20e *ma-a-a'-du*
21e *ú-se-ṣi-a*
22e LUGAL *be-lí* ⸢*a*⸣-*bu-t*[*ú*!]
s.1 [*x x x l*]*i-qi-bu-ni-šú-nu* TA IGI *ga-li-te* [*x x x x*]*x li-gi-ru-ru*

ABL 387

1 To the king, my lord: your servant Šarru-emuranni. Good health to the king, my lord!

4 As to the wine about which the king, my lord, wrote me: "Set aside 200 homers for the garrison!" — I have set aside as much of it as the king, my lord, wrote.

10 As to Kubaba-satar about whom the king, my lord, wrote me: "Speak nicely with him!" —

14 my [mo]uth is closed. [As the ki]ng, my lord, [wr]ote me, [I shall speak nic]ely [with him ......]

(Break)

r.3 [He] *will st*[*ay* in] my [pre]sence.

4 I have now se[nt] (word), and I shall find an interpreter in [...], acquire him for the king, my lord, and send him.

8 As to the city lords about whom the king, my lord, wrote me: "If they come to you, get them and send them to me!" — may the gods of the king make (that happen)!

14 Citizens of Babylon have come to (visit) the king, my lord. *Previously*, when the king, my lord, established the debt-remission, he released many people from their possession. The king, my lord, should [...] the matter and let them be informed so they become scared of [...] deportation.

## 204. Sending a Message to Mannea

K 1875

1 [*a-na* LUGAL *be-lí-ia*]
2 [ARAD-*ka* ᵐLUGAL—IGI.LAL-*ni*]
3 [*lu* DI-*mu a-na* LUGAL EN-*ia*]

CT 53 56

1 [To the king, my lord: your servant Šarru-emuranni. Good health to the king, my lord]!

**203** Same hand as in no. 202. 10, 14ff, r.3 See coll. r.5 Y 79, W 145. r.11, 13, 17, s.2 See coll.
**204** 1ff Number of missing lines ascertainable from the reverse.

4 [DI-*mu a-na* URU.HAL.ṢU.MEŠ]
5 [*a-na* KUR *ša* LUGAL EN-*ia*]
6 *di-*⸢*ib-bi*⸣ [*am-mu-u-te*]
7 *ša ina* ŠU.2 [$^{md}$PA—PAB—PAB]
8 LÚ*.*qur-bu-*[*tú*] ⸢LUGAL *be-lí*⸣
9 *ina* UGU-*hi-ni iš-pur-a*[*n-ni*]
10 *ma-a ki-i ha-an-ni-*⸢*i*⸣
11 *ina* UGU DUMU $^{m}$*in-ṣab-ri*
12 *šup-ra* ⸢*ki*⸣*-i* $^{md}$PA—PAB—⸢PAB⸣
13 *iq-rib-an-ni*
14 *ina* ⸢ŠÀ⸣-*bi* UD-*mì-*[*im*]*-ma*
15 [$^{md}$]⸢UTU⸣—GIN-[*i*]*n*
16 [LÚ] *tak-lu ú-mu-ru*
17 [*š*]*a* ⸢*dib*⸣-[*b*]*i i-la-u-ni*
18 *ša* LÚ*.GAL—*bir-te*
r.1 *dib!-bi ki-i ša* LU[GAL]
2 *be-lí iš-pur-an-*⸢*ni*⸣
3 *ina pi-i* LÚ*.A—KIN
4 *ša* LÚ*.GAL—*bir-te ni-sa-kan*
5 UD-4-KÁM *it-tu-uṣ-ṣi*
6 *a-na* URU.*i-zir-te it-ta-l*[*ak*]
7 GIM *is-suh-ra mì-nu*
8 *ša i-qab-ba-na-ši-ni*
9 [*ina*] UGU LUGAL EN-*ia*
10 [*a*]*-šap-pa-r*[*a*]
rest uninscribed

4 [The forts and the land of the king, my lord, are well].

6 [As to those] words which the king, my lord, sent [us] through [Nabû-ahu-uṣur], the royal bodygu[ard]: "Send in this way to the son of Inṣabri" –

12 when Nabû-ahu-uṣur arrived, on that very same d[a]y Šamaš-ukin, a trustworthy and chosen [man] of the fort commander, able in words –

r.1 we implanted the very words that the king, my lord, sent us, in the mouth of (this) messenger of the fort commander; he left on the 4th day and went to Izirtu.

7 As soon as he returns, [I] shall write [t]o the king, my lord, everything that he tells us.

## 205. Precious Stones

Sm 754

1 *a-na* LUGAL *b*[*e-lí-ia*]
2 ARAD-*ka* $^{m}$MAN—IGI.[LAL-*ni*]
3 *lu* DI-*mu a-n*[*a* LUGAL EN-*ia*]
4 *a-du* É *a-x*[*x x x*]
5 NA$_4$.*mil-hu x*[*x x x*]
6 NA$_4$.*nu-*KUR-*x*[*x x x*]
7 *ina pa-na-tú-*⸢*u!*⸣-[*a*]
8 *ina* UGU *ṣa-p*[*i-ú-ti*]
9 *uq-ṭa-r*[*i-bi x x x*]
10 [LUGAL] EN ⸢*a ki*⸣ [*x x*]
11 [*x x*].MEŠ *tar-x*[*x x x*]
12 [LÚ*.K]AB.SAR ⸢*ki*⸣-[*x x*]
13 [*x x*]*x ni* [*x x x*]
rest broken away
Rev. beginning broken away
1′ [*x x x*]*x*[*x x x*]
2′ [*ša ina* U]RU!.*kal!-*[*ha a-na* LUGAL]
3′ [E]N-*ia aq-b*[*u-u-ni*]
4′ [*nu*]*-uk la-x*[*x x x*]
5′ *ina* ŠÀ-*bi nu-x*[*x x x*]
6′ *šúm-ma* SIG$_5$-*a*[*t x x x*]
7′ *ina* ŠÀ-*bi-šá n*[*u!-x x x*]
rest (3 lines) uninscribed

ABL 758

1 To the king, [my] lo[rd]: your servant Šarru-em[uranni]. Good health t[o the king, my lord]!

4 While I [*was in* ...],
5 *milhu* stone [...]
6 *nukur*[...] stone [...]
7 at [my] disposal [...]
8 to the *dy*[*ers*]
9 I provi[ded ...]
10 The king, my lord, [...]
11 ...[...]
12 [en]graver [...]
(Break)

r.1 [As to what] I sa[id to the king], my [lo]rd, [in] Cal[ah]: "I will [...] and we will [...] *with* it" –

6 if that is all right, we shall [......] *with* it.

**205** New copy p. 265.

## 206. Opening the Treasury

K 1987 (CT 53 225) + K 7384 (ABL 319)

1 *a-na* LUGAL *be-lí-ia*
2 ARAD-*ka* $^{m}$LUGAL—*e-mur-an-ni*
3 *lu-u šul-mu a-na* LUGAL *be-lí-iá*
4 UD-27-KAM TA* *sa-an-ti*
5 É *na-kam-ti ša hu-še-e*
6 *ša ina né-ri-bi ša* É *ina* É.GAL
7 *ša ina* UGU *tam-le-e ni-ip-te*$^{!}$*-te*
8 4-*me*-20 GÚ.UN URUDU *hu-še-e*
9 [*n*]*i-ih-ti-aṭ ina* É—ŠU.2
10 [*ša* L]Ú$^{!}$.KAŠ.LUL *ni*$^{!}$*-is*$^{!}$*-sa-k*[*an*]
11 [*x* GÚ.U]N *ú-de-e* URUDU$^{!}$
12 [*x x x x n*]*i-ih-*[*ti-a*]*ṭ*
13 [*x x x x x*] ⸢*ud*⸣ [*x x*]
rest broken away
Rev. beginning broken away
1′ [*x x x-a*]*n* URU$^{!}$
2′ [*x x* É.GAL—*m*]*a-šar-ti*
3′ [*x x x x*] ⸢*ú*⸣*-la-a*
4′ UD-29-KAM ⸢*ša*⸣ É$^{!}$.GAL$^{!}$—*ma-šar-ti*
5′ *né-ep-pa-áš ina re-eh-ti*
6′ UD-*me-ni a-na* URU.BÀD—MAN—GIN
7′ *ni-il-lak* TÚG.GADA.MEŠ
8′ *am-ma-ti ni-kan-na-ak*

ABL 319+

1 To the king, my lord: your servant Šarru-emuranni. Good health to the king, my lord!

4 On the 27th day, at dawn, we opened the treasury of metal scraps at the entrance to the house in the palace upon the terrace.

8 [We] weighed 420 talents of bronze scraps and plac[ed] it in the storehouse [of] the cupbearer.

11 We also weighed [x talen]ts of bronze objects [...]

(Break)

r.1 [......] city,
2 [...... *of* the R]eview [Palace].
3 Alternatively, we can do the (*inventory*) of the Review Palace on the 29th and go in the remaining days to Dur-Šarruken, to seal those tunics.

## 207. ———

Rm 2,474

1 [*a*]*-na* LUGAL *be-lí-ia*
2 [ARAD]-*ka* $^{m}$LUGAL—IGI.LAL-*ni*
3 [*lu* DI-*mu*] *a-na* LUGAL EN-*ia*
4 [$^{md}$*x*]—PAB-*ir* LÚ*.*qur-bu-te*
5 [URU.*x*]-⸢*š*⸣*i-ma-a-a*
6 [*x x x*] *ina* URU.*kar*—$^{d}$MAŠ$^{!}$.MAŠ$^{!}$
7 [*it-tu-bi-l*]*a-an-ni*
8 [*x x x x x*]*x-te*
rest broken away
Rev. uninscribed

ABL 761

1 [T]o the king, my lord: your [servant] Šarru-emuranni. [Good health] to the king, my lord!

4 The royal bodyguard [...]-naṣir [*has brou*]*ght* [... *Ba*]*šimeans* to Kar-Nergal [......]

(Rest destroyed)

## 208. ———

K 14578

beginning broken away
1′ UGU ⸢LÚ*⸣.*x*[*x x x x x*]
2′ *til-li a-*[*na x x x x*]
3′ LÚ*.*qur-bu-*[*te x x x x*]
4′ TA* LÚ*.2-[*e x x x x*]
5′ *i-tal-k*[*u-ni x x x x*]
6′ *iš-šú-u-ni* [*x x x x x*]
7′ *ša i-*[*x x x x x x*]

CT 53 527

(Beginning destroyed)
1 As to the [......]
2 equipment t[o ......],
3 the royal bodyguar[d ......]
4 with the depu[ty ......]
5 cam[e ......]

**207** Same hand as in no. 202 etc. 6ff See coll.

8′ ANŠE.KUR.[RA *x x x x x*]
9′ ⌜*an*⌝ [*x x x x x x x*]
rest broken away
Rev. beginning broken away
1′ *i*-[*x x x x x x x*]
2′ *la* [*x x x x x x x*]
3′ *a*-*k*[*i x x x x x x*]
4′ *a*[*k x x x x x x x*]
5′ *x*[*x x x x x x x x*]
rest broken away

6 took [......]
7 which [......]
8 hors[e(s) ......]
(Reverse too broken for translation)

FIG. 30. *Royal bodyguards (reign of Assurnasirpal).*
BM 124558.

## 209. ———

K 16500

1 *a-na* LUGAL [*be-lí-ia*]
2 ARAD-*ka* $^{m}$MAN—[IGI.LAL-*ni*]
rest broken away
Rev. uninscribed

CT 53 779

[1] To the king, [my lord]: your servant *Šarru-*[*emuranni*].
(Rest destroyed)

## 210. Taking over the Forts of Allabria

K 617

1 *a-na* LUGAL EN-*ia*
2 ARAD-*ka* $^{md}$PA—*ha-mat-u-*[*a*]
3 *lu-u šul-mu a-na* LUGAL
4 EN-*ia šul-mu a-na*
5 URU.HAL.ṢU.MEŠ *ša* LUGAL
6 EN-*ia e-gír-ti*
7 TA* IGI LÚ*.EN.NAM
8 LÚ*.KUR.*ma-da-a-a ú-se-ṣi-ia-a*
9 *ma-a* LÚ*.A—KIN$^{!}$-*ka ina* É.GAL
10 *lu-bíl* UN.MEŠ KUR
11 *ša* DUMU $^{md+}$EN—SUM-*na*
12 *dib-bi* DÙG.GA.MEŠ *i-si-šú-nu*
13 *ad-du-bu-ub*
14 ŠÀ-*bi ú-sa-áš-kin-šú-nu*
15 LÚ*.DUMU $^{md+}$EN—SUM-*na*
16 EN *hi-i-ṭu šu-ú*
17 [L]Ú.*par-ri-ṣu šu-ú*
r.1 [*a-bat* LUGAL] *la i-šá-am-me*
2 [*muk at-t*]*u*$^{!}$-*nu ia-a-mut-tu*
3 [*ina* É-*šú*] *ina* ŠÀ A.ŠÀ-*šú*
4 ⸢*dul*⸣-*la-ku-nu ep-šá*
5 ŠÀ-*ba-ku-nu lu-u* DÙG.GA-*ku-nu*
6 *muk*$^{!}$ LÚ*$^{!}$.ARAD.MEŠ *ša* LUGAL
7 *at-tu-nu né-e-hu*
8 *dul-la-šú-nu ep-pu-šú*
9 TA* ŠÀ 6 URU.HAL.ṢU.MEŠ
10 *ú-se-ṣi-šú-nu*
11 *muk*$^{!}$ *a-lik al-ka*
12 *ia-a-mut-tu ana* UGU A.ŠÀ
13 *li-ir-ṣip lu-ši-ib*
14 LÚ*.ARAD.MEŠ *ša* LUGAL EN-*ia*
15 *ina* ŠÀ-*bi e-tar-bu*
16 EN.NUN *dan-na-at*
17 *a-di* LÚ*.EN.NAM
18 *il-la-kan-ni*
19e *mì-ni ša* LUGAL E[N]
20e *ṭè-e-me*
21e *iš-ku-nu-šu-u-*[*ni*$^{!}$]
22e *ep-pa-á*[*š*]

ABL 208

[1] To the king, my lord: your servant Nabû-hamatu[a]. Good health to the king, my lord!
[4] The forts of the king, my lord, are well.

[6] A Mede forwarded me the (attached) letter from the governor, saying: "Let your messenger bring it to the Palace."

[10] I have spoken kindly with the countrymen of the son of Bel-iddina and encouraged them. The son of Bel-iddina (himself) is a criminal and a traitor; he does not obey [the king's orders].

[r.2] [I said]: "Do your work, each in [his house and] field, and be glad; you are now subjects of the king."

[7] They are peaceful and do their work. I have brought them out from six forts, saying: "Go! Each one of you should build (a house) in the field and stay there!"

[14] The king my lord's subjects have entered (the forts); the guard will be strong until the governor comes. I am doing everything the king, [my] l[ord], ordered him (to do).

**209** [2] Or: Man[nu-ki-...].
**210** [9] W 85. [r.6] See coll.; W 85. [r.11] Y 77.

## 211. Building Forts

Sm 1933

1 *a-na* LUGAL [EN-*ia*]
2 ARAD-*ka* $^{md}$P[A—*ha-mat-u-a*]
3 *lu-u* DI-*mu a-na* [LUGAL EN-*ia*]
4 DI-*mu a-na* URU.HAL$^{!}$.Ṣ[U$^{!}$.MEŠ]
5 *ša* LUGAL EN-[*ia x x x x*]
6 LÚ*.GAL—⸢*ú*⸣-*r*[*a-te x x x*]
7 TA* LÚ*.⸢EN⸣.NA[M *x x x x*]
8 ⸢*uq*⸣-*ṭ*[*ar-ri-ba*]
9 *ma-a* ⸢*pa*$^{!?}$⸣-*x*[*x x x x x*]
10 $^{m}$⸢*aš-šur*⸣—*x*[*x x x x x*]
11 [*x x x x x x x*]
e.12 [*x x x x x*]
r.1 LUGAL EN *lu-u ú-*[*di*]
2 LUGAL EN *lu-u la-*[*a*]
3 *i-qab-bi ma-a* LÚ*.ARAD [0]
4 *še-e-ṭu šú-ú ma-a*
5 *dul-lu la-a e-pa-áš*
6 LÚ*.ARAD.MEŠ *ša* LUGAL EN-*iá*
7 MI *ù kal* ⸢UD⸣-[*mu* 0]
8 *a-ra-di e-b*[*ir-tú*]
9 *ina kal* UD-*mu* DI$^{!}$-⸢*x x*⸣
10 *i-šá-hu$^{!}$-ṭu$^{!}$ ina* Š[À *x x*]
11 *ú-qa$^{!}$-ru$^{!}$-b*[*u$^{!}$* 0]
rest uninscribed

ABL 1068

1 To the king, [my lord]: your servant Na[bû-hamatua]. Good health to [the king, my lord]!

4 The for[ts] of the king, [my] lord, are well.

5 [NN], a te[am] commander, br[ought me a *letter*] from the govern[or ...], saying: "[......] Aššur-[......]

(Break)

r.1 The king, my lord, should k[now] (this).

2 The king, my lord, should not say: "He is a negligent servant; he does not do (his) work."

7 I drive the servants of the king, my lord, day and night; they are glazing kiln-[fired bricks] all day long [...] and bringing them into [...].

## 212. Fragment Mentioning an Interpreter

K 12010

beginning destroyed
1′ [*x x x x x a-k*]*e-e* ⸢*la*⸣ [*x x x*]
2′ [*x x x x*]-⸢*a*⸣ *ma-a* LÚ*.UN.M[EŠ *x x*]
3′ [*x x x x*]-*šá ma a-ke-e* [*x x x*]
4′ [*x x x*]-⸢*ú*⸣-*ni ma-a* LÚ*.*tar-*[*gu-ma-nu*]
5′ [*x x x x*]-*a ma-a na-mur-*[*tú x x x*]
6′ [*x x x x*]*x*-⸢*la*⸣ *ma-a* LÚ*.*t*[*ar*$^{?}$-*x x x*]
7′ [*x x x x x x x x*] ⸢*a*⸣ [*x x x x*]
rest broken away
Rev. destroyed

CT 53 432

(Beginning destroyed)
1 [... *h*]*ow* not [...]
2 [......] "the peopl[e ...]
3 [...]; "how [...]
4 [...] "an inter[preter]
5 [...] "the audience gi[ft ...]
6 [...] "the in[terpreter]
(Rest destroyed)

## 213. A Case Concerning a Town

Th 1905-4-9,281

1 IM $^{md}$PA—*ha-am-mat-u-a*
2 ARAD-*ka* $^{m}$*ku-uš-ka-a-a*
3 *lu* DI-*mu a-na* EN-*iá*

ABL 1407

1 A letter (to) Nabû-hamatua: your servant Kuškayu. Good health to my lord!

**211** 4, r.9ff See coll.
**212** 3 Or: *ma-a ke-e-*[*tu* "honestly."

4 *de-e-ni*
5 *ša* URU ŠU.2-*a-a*
6 *ša a-qa-ba-kan-ni*
7 *ina pa-ni* $^{m}$*aš-šur*—MAN—PAB
8 *qi*!-*bi*
9 *e-gír-ti liš-pu-ru*
e.10 ⸢*ki*!⸣ [*á*]*r*?-*hi*[*š*!]
r.1 *a-na* LÚ*.*šá*—UGU—URU
2 *šúm*!-*mu a-na*
3 LÚ*.*šak-nu*
4 *liš-pu-ru*
5 *ma-a* LÚ
6 TA* ŠÀ-*bi*
7 GIŠ.SAR *lu-še-li*
8 [*l*]*a-ah-ri-di*
9 *ina* ŠÀ-*bi-šú*

4 Please present before Aššur-šarru-uṣur the case of the town in my hands which I told you about.

9 Let him *qu*[*ick*]*ly* send a letter to the city overseer or to the prefect, telling him to remove everybody from the orchard.

r.8 I will *keep vigil* there.

## 214. Envelope of the Previous Letter

Th 1905-4-9,281A

1 IM $^{md}$PA—*ha-am-mat-u-a*
cylinder seal impression
2 ARAD-*ka* $^{m}$*ku-uš-ka-a-a*
e.3 *lu* DI-*mu a-na* EN-*ia*
4 *a—dan-niš*

ABL 1407A

1 A letter (to) Nabû-hamatua:
2 your servant Kuškayu.
3 The best of health to my lord!

## 215. The Troops of Mazamua

ND 2631

1 [*a-na* LUG]AL EN-*ia*
2 [ARAD-*ka*] $^{md}$IM—KI-*ia*
3 [*lu* D]I-*mu a-na* LUGAL EN-*ia*
4 [*š*]*a* LUGAL EN *ṭè-e-mu iš-ku-na-ni-ni*
5 *ma-a e-mu-qi ša* KUR—*za-mu-u-a*
6 *a-šur*! ⸢*šup*⸣-*ra* 10 GIŠ.GIGIR.MEŠ
7 20!! GIŠ.*ut*-⸢*tar*⸣-*a-te* 10 *ša* ANŠE.KUR.RA.MEŠ
8 10 *ša* ANŠE.*ku-di-ni* 30 ANŠE.*ú-ra-te*
9 97 ANŠE.BAD-HAL-*lu* 11 LÚ*.*mu-kil*—KUŠ.PA.MEŠ
10 12 LÚ*.3.U$_5$.MEŠ [3]0 LÚ*.A.SIG$_5$
11 53 LÚ*.GIŠ.GIGIR.MEŠ [ANŠ]E.*ú-ra-te*
12 PAB 1-*me*-6 ERIM.ME[Š 30] GIŠ.GIGIR.MEŠ
13 1-*me*-61 LÚ*.*šá*—*pet-hal*-[*a-t*]*e* 1-*me*-30!! LÚ*.GIŠ.GIGIR.MEŠ
14 52 LÚ*.*zu-un-zu-ra-hi* PAB 3-*me*-43
15 LÚ*.GIŠ.GIGIR.MEŠ [8] LÚ*.*šá*—É—2-*e*
16 12 LÚ*.KA.KÉŠ 20 LÚ*.KAŠ.LUL
17 12 LÚ*.*kar*-⸢*ka*⸣-*di-ni* 7 LÚ*.NINDA.MEŠ
18 10 LÚ*.MU PAB 69 UN.MEŠ É

NL 89

1 [To the ki]ng, my lord: [your servant] Adad-issiya. [Good] health to the king, my lord!

4 [As t]o the order that the king, my lord, gave me: "Review the troops of Mazamua and write me!" — (here are the facts):

6 10 chariots; 20 large-wheeled chariots, 10 (of them) horse-drawn, 10 mule-drawn; 30 teams; 97 riding horses; 11 chariot drivers; 12 'third men'; [3]0 chariot fighters; 53 grooms of the [t]eams, in all 106 men and [30] chariots.

13 161 cavalrymen, 130 grooms, 52 ...: in all 343 grooms.

15 [8] *lackeys*, 12 tailors, 20 cupbearers, 12 confectioners, 7 bakers, 10 cooks: in all 69 domestics.

**213** 10 See coll.; *šúm-mu* excluded. r.2 See coll.
**215** 6 Copy *a-šá*; not collated. 7 Copy 2 GIŠ.*ut-tar-a-te*. 13 Copy 1-*me*-30 (not collated). r.6 Copy ⸢*ú-ba-lu*⸣.

19 8 LÚ*.*um-ma-ni* 23 LÚ*.UŠ—ANŠE.MEŠ
20 1 LÚ*.*mu-tir—ṭè-me* 80 LÚ*.*kal-ba-*⌈*te*⌉
21 PAB 6-*me*-30 KUR.*aš-šur-a-a*
22 3-*me*-60 LÚ*.*gur-*⌈*ru*⌉ 4-*me*-40 KUR.*i-*⌈*tú*⌉
e.23 PAB-*ma* 1-*lim*-4-*me*-30 ERIM.MEŠ—MAN
r.1 *a-di pa-ni-ú-te ša a-na-ka-[ni]*
2 *a-di ša* LÚ*.*qur-bu-te na-ṣa-ni*
3 *[i—s]u-ri* [LU]GAL EN *i-qa-bi*
4 *[ma]-*⌈*a*⌉ *re-[e]h-*⌈*te*⌉ *e-mu-q[i] a-*⌈*le*⌉*-e*
5 LÚ*.GAL—É-*i[a n]a-*⌈*mar*⌉*-ku re-eh-te*
6 *e-mu-qi* ⌈*ú-ba-la*!⌉

19 8 scholars, 23 donkey drivers, 1 information officer, 80 *dispatch-riders*.

21 In all 630 Assyrians.

22 360 Gurreans, 440 Itu'eans.

23 All together 1,430 king's men, including the previous ones which have been here, plus the ones whom the royal bodyguard brought.

r.3 [Perh]aps the [ki]ng, my lord, (now) says: "Where are the rest of the troops?" M[y] major-domo is delayed but will [la]ter bring the rest of the troops.

## 216. Fragment Mentioning Azâ, King of Mannea

79-7-8,264

1 *a-na* LUGA[L EN-*ia*]
2 LÚ*.ARAD-*ka* $^{m}$[$^{d}$IM—KI-*ia*]
3 *lu-u* DI ⌈*a*⌉-*n[a* LUGAL EN-*ia*]
4 UD-*mu ša* LÚ*.[*e-mu-qi*? *x x*]
5 *ša* KUR.URI-*a-[a x x x x x]*
6 $^{m}$*a-za-a [x x x x x x x]*
7 *e-ta-x[x x x x x x x]*
8 *a-na* L[Ú.*x x x x x x x*]
9 *ni-[x x x x x x x x x]*
rest (about 7 lines) broken away
Rev. beginning broken away
1′ *i-ta[l-x x x x x x x]*
2′ *i-tu-x[x x x x x x x]*
3′ *i-ta-lak [x x x x x x]*
4′ *[ma]-a a-ta-a [x x x x x]*
5′ NINDA.MEŠ *la-a [x x x x x]*
6′ LÚ*.600—É.GAL *x[x x x x x]*
7′ *ma-a* ⌈KUR.URI⌉*-a-a [x x x x x]*
8′ TA* [*x x*] *x[x x x x x x]*
9′ L[Ú.*x x x*] 7 [*x x x x x*]
10e *re-ha-ti x[x x x x x x]*
11e *ma-a ša [x x x x x x]*
s.1 [*x x x x x* L]Ú.*sar-tin-ni* ⌈*ma*⌉*-a i-ši*
2 [*x x x x x x*]*x kur-ru*

CT 53 885

1 To the kin[g, my lord]: your servant [NN]. Good health t[o the king, my lord]!

4 The day that the [*army and the* ...] of the Urarṭian [......],

6 Azâ [......]

7 ...[......]

8 to the [......]

9 *we* [......]

(Break)

r.1 *ca[me]*

2 [......]

3 came [......],

4 saying: "Why [......]

5 no bread [......]?"

6 The palace herald [......]

7 "The Urarṭian [......]

8 from/with [......]

9 [...] 7 [...]

10 the rest [......]

11 "*Of* [......]

s.1 [......] the *sartinnu*; take [...]

2 and put [......].

## 217. Preparing for War in Mannea

79-7-8,234

1 *a-na* LUGAL EN-*ia*
2 ARAD-*ka* $^{md}$IM—KI-*ia*
3 *lu* DI-*mu a-na* LUGAL EN-*ia*

ABL 342

1 To the king, my lord: your servant Adad-issiya. Good health to the king, my lord!

**216** Hand of Adad-issiya.

4 2 LÚ*.GAL—*ki-ṣir*.MEŠ
5 *ša* BAD-HAL-*li ina* URU.*sa-an-ha*
6 *ina* URU.*ú-lu-ši-a*
7 *ina* UGU LÚ*.ARAD.MEŠ *ša* LUGAL
8 *ša ina* ŠÀ-*bi a-sap-*[*r*]*a*
9 *i-ta-at-ku e-tam-ru-šú-nu*
10 *til-li ša ina* ŠÀ-*bi* ŠE.PA[D].MEŠ
11 *ša ṭup-pi-šú-nu i-ba-ši ina* ŠÀ-*bi*
12 *ú-hu-ta-ri-du-šú-nu*
13 *ma-ṣar-ta-šú-nu dan-na-at*
14 *a—dan-niš* ŠÀ-*bu ša* LUGAL
15 EN-*ia lu* DÙG.⌜GA⌝
16 md*kù*!-KÁ—DINGIR-*a*-⌜*a*⌝
17 LUGAL EN *ú-da*
18 EN *li-šá-ni šú-u*
r.1 *ina* URU.*ti-ik-ri-iš*
2 *a-sap-ár-šu šu-ú*
3 *ṭè-mu an-ni-ú ih-tar-ṣa*
4 *iq-ṭi-ba-a-na-a-ši*
5 *ina* UGU LUGAL EN-*ia ni-sap-ra*
6 *am—mar* UD-*mu*.MEŠ *ša ina ta-hu-me*
7 *ša* KUR.*man-na-a-a ma-dàk-tú*
8 *šá-ak-na-ku-u-ni* DUMU MÍ.*al-mat*!*-te*
9 *i—pu-tú-u-a-a ma-dàk-tú*
10 *ina* UGU *ta-hu-me-šu šá-ki-in*
11 *ina* ŠÀ UD-*mu ša* mdMAŠ.MAŠ—EN—PAB
12 DU-*a-ni ú-na-me-šá-a-ni-ni*
13 *ina* KUR.*man-na-a-a e-ru-bu-u-ni*
14 LÚ*.3.$U_5$-*ia ina* UGU-*šú*
15 *a-sap-ra muk*! *na-me-šá*
16 *ma-a mar-ṣa-ak* : mu*muk*!
17e DUMU-*ka li-li-ka*
18e *ma-a ma-ri-ṣi-ma*
s.1 *ma-a* ŠEŠ-*u-a* TA* ERIM.MEŠ-*ia áš-par* LÚ*.3.$U_5$
2 *a-sap-ra ú-di-ni ina* IGI-*ia la i-qa-rib-u-ni*
3 *re-eh-ti* LÚ*.*e-mu-qi ša* LÚ*.EN—URU.MEŠ
4 *ina* IGI-*ia šú-nu*

4 I se[n]t two cavalry cohort commanders to Sanha and Ulušia to the king's subjects who are there. They went and saw them: the equipment (they had received) there and the barley rations specified in their tablet were there.

12 They warned them, and their guard is very strong. The king, my lord, can be glad.

16 The king, my lord, knows that Kubaba-ila'i masters the language. I sent him to Tikriš, and he gave us this detailed report. We are herewith sending it to the king, my lord.

r.6 All the time I have been encamped on the Mannean border, the son of the widow has been encamped opposite me on his side of the border.

11 The very day that Nergal-belu-uṣur came here ordering me to depart and I entered the Mannean territory, I sent my 'third man' to him, saying: "Set out!" He said he was sick. I said: "Let your son come!" He said: "He is sick too; I shall send my brother with my troops."

s.1 I sent the 'third man,' but he (i.e., this brother) has not yet showed up. The rest of the troops of the city lords are with me.

## 218. Ullusunu Bribes Aššur-le'i of Karalla

Sm 935

beginning (about 10 lines) broken away
1′ ⌜*ma*⌝*-a ina* [*x x x x x x x*]
2′ É MÍ.*a*[*l*!*-mat*?*-te*? *x x x x*]
3′ *ma-a* m*aš-šur*—Z[U *x x x x x*]
4′ *i-ta-la-k*[*a x x x x*]
5′ *šal-mu šu-u i*-⌜*sa*⌝-[*x x x*]
6′ mdPA—*ha-mat-u-a ina* UG[U-*hi-ia*]
7′ *i-sap-ra ma-a* m*aš-šur*—Z[U 0]
8′ *ina* UGU m*ú-li-su-ni* ⌜*il*⌝*-lak*
9′ *ma-a* 5 KUR.RA.MEŠ m*ú-li-su-nu*

ABL 1058

(Beginning destroyed)

1 "in [......]

2 "*the house of* the wi[dow ......]

3 "Aššur-le'[i ...]

4 came [...]

5 he is safe and has [...].

6 Nabû-hamatua wrote m[e] that Aššur-le['i] is going to Ullusunu, and that Ullusunu

**217** 10, 16, r.15 See coll.
**218** Same scribe as in no. 221. 2, r.13f See coll.

10′ *a-na* $^{m}$*aš-šur—*ZU *i-ti-din* KUR.RA.MEŠ
11′ *ša i-di-na-šú-u-ni* $^{md}$PA*—ha-mat-u-a*
12′ *ina* ŠÀ*-bi e-gir-te a-na* UZU.MEŠ*-ni*
13′ *i-sa-ṭar ú-se-bi-la*
14′ *e-gir-a-te ša* $^{md}$PA*—ha-mat-u-a*
15′ *ina* URU.NINA *pa-an* LUGAL EN*-iá*
e.16′ *ú-se-ri-ba*
r.1 *i-si-si-i-u* TA* UGU
2 LÚ*.SAG *ša* $^{m}$*aš-šur—*ZU *ša pa-an*
3 $^{md}$PA*—ha-mat-u-a ša* LUGAL EN
4 *iš-pur-an-ni* 3*-su* MU.AN.NA
5 TA* É *pa-an* $^{md}$PA*—ha-mat-u-a*
6 *ih-li-qa-an-ni la i-lak*
7 *a-na še-ru-di a-ki-i*
8 *qa-ab-si* KUR*-šú lu-u-še-ti-qu-u-ni-šú*
9 TA* UGU $^{m}$EN—PAB.MEŠ LÚ*.DAM.QAR
10 *ša* LUGAL EN *iš-pur-an-ni*
11 *šá-pal* ŠU.2 *a-šap-pa-r*[*a*]
12 *ú-bal-u-ni-šú ina* U[GU LUGAL EN*-iá*]
13 *ú-še-bal-a-šú* DI!-[*mu a—dan-niš*]
14 [*a*]-⌜*na*!⌝ URU!?.HAL!.ṢU! *x*[*x x x x*]
rest broken away

has given five horses to Aššur-le'i. Nabû-hamatua has itemized the horses he gave him by colour in a clay tablet (which) he (also) sent me. I have forwarded the letters of Nabû-hamatua to Nineveh, and they will have read them to the king (by now).

r.1 As to the eunuch of Aššur-le'i who is with Nabû-hamatua, about whom the king my lord wrote me, it is the third year already since he fled to Nabû-hamatua, so it is not possible to get him down from there. Let them bring him over to me when he is inside his country.

9 As to Bel-ahhe, the merchant about whom the king, my lord, wrote, I shall secretly send word that they bring him to me, and I shall (then) send him t[o the king, my lord].

r.13 [Everything is fi]ne [wi]th the fort [...]
(Rest destroyed)

# 219. Fragment of a Report on Mannea

K 5528

beginning broken away
1′ [*x x x šar*]*-ru-tú ša* [*x x*]
2′ [*x x x š*]*a* BANŠU[R *x x*]
3′ [*x x x x*]*x* $^{m}$*aš-šur*—MAN—[*x x*]
4′ [*x x x x*] $^{m}$*aš-šur*—Z[U *x x*]
5′ [*x x x i*]*—da-a-te-šú-*[*nu*?]
rest broken away
Rev. destroyed

CT 53 271

(Beginning destroyed)
1 [... ki]ngship of [...]
2 [... o]f the table [...]
3 [......] Aššur-šarru-[...]
4 [......] Aššur-le['i ...]
5 [......] after th[em]
(Rest destroyed)

# 220. Military Operations in Mannea

K 5481

beginning broken away
1′ [*x x x*] ⌜EN*-ni*⌝ [*x x x x x*]
2′ [*x x x*] *i-ṣa-ab-*[*tu x x x x*]
3′ [LÚ**.e-mu-q*]*i-šú ina* ŠÀ*-bi* ⌜URU⌝.[*x x x*]
4′ [*x x x*] *ma-a* $^{m}$*ul-su-*⌜*un*⌝*-n*[*u*]
5′ [*x x x-b*]*u ma-a* LÚ**.e-mu-*⌜*qe-e*⌝*-*[*šú*]
6′ [*ša*? *il-l*]*i-ku-ni-ni ma-a ina* Š[À *x x*]
7′ [*e-tar-bu is*]*—su-ri šu-*[*u x x x x*]
8′ [*x x x*] ARAD.MEŠ*-ia* [*x x x x*]
9′ [*x x la*] *ú-ṣi ina n*[*é-ri-bi*? *x x*]
10′ [*x x x x*] *la-a* [*x x x x*]
rest broken away
Rev. destroyed

CT 53 250

(Beginning destroyed)
1 [...] our lord [...]
2 [...] have seiz[ed ...].
3 His [*troops are*] in [...].
4 [...] "Ullusun[u]
5 [...] "[His] army, [which] had come [..., *has*] *en*[*tered* ...].
7 [Pe]rhaps h[e ......]
8 [...] my servants [...]
9 [... has not] emerged [...] in the *p*[*ass* ...]
10 [...] not [......]
(Rest destroyed)

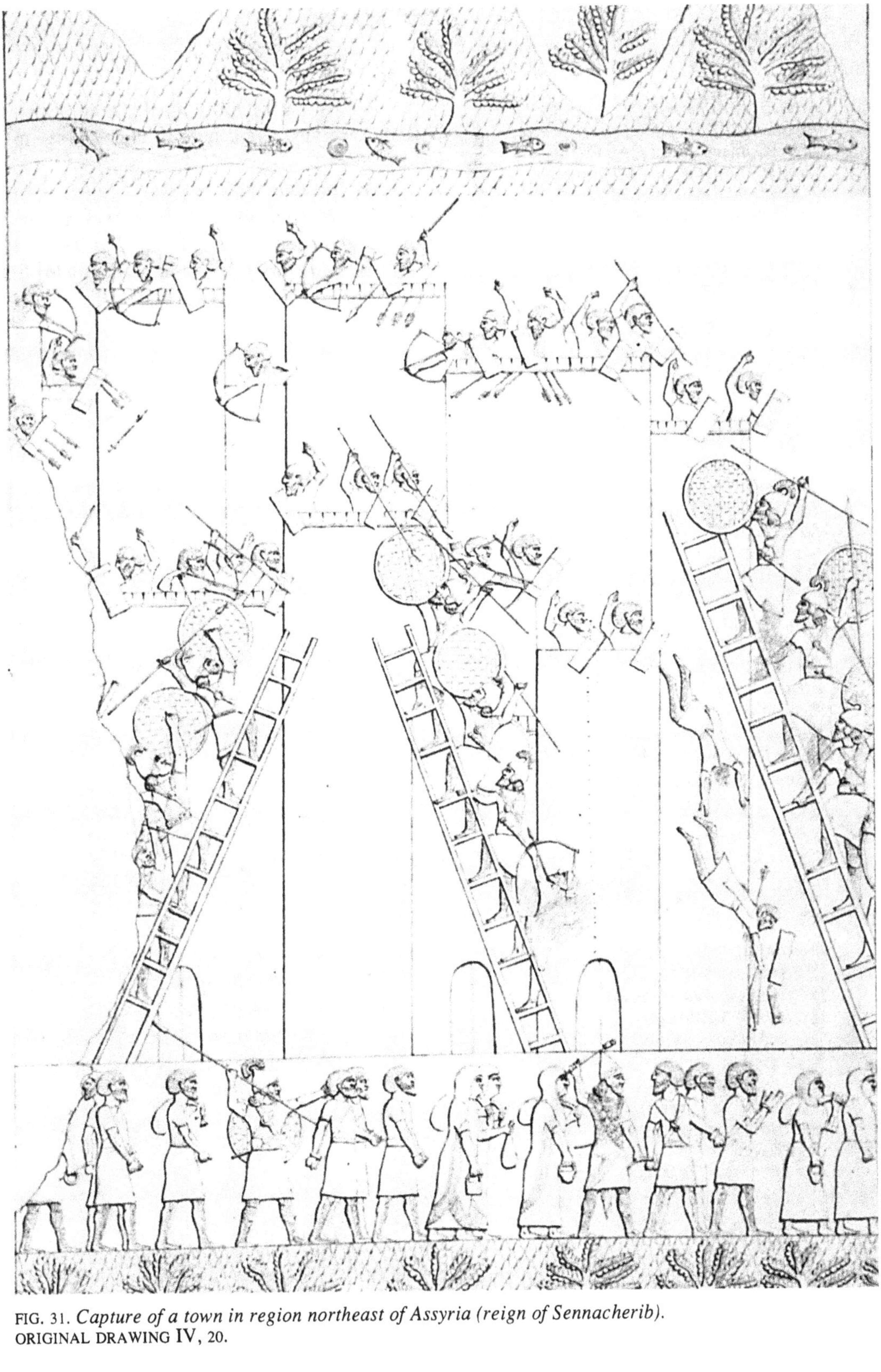

COURTESY TRUSTEES OF THE BRITISH MUSEUM

FIG. 31. *Capture of a town in region northeast of Assyria (reign of Sennacherib).*
ORIGINAL DRAWING IV, 20.

# 221. News from Mannea

79-7-8,160

1 *a-na* [LUGAL EN-*ia*]
2 ARAD-*ka* $^{m}$[$^{d}$IM—KI-*ia*]
3 *lu-u* DI-*m*[*u a-na* LUGAL EN-*ia*]
4 *ša* LUGAL E[N *iš-pur-an-ni ma-a*]
5 *a-ta-a mì-*⸢*i*⸣*-n*[*u ši-ti-ni*]
6 *ša* KUR.*man-na-a-a* ⸢*taš*⸣*-*[*me*? *la taš-pu-ra*]
7 *ina ta-hu-mì-i-ni* [*it-tal-ka*]
8 UDU.SISKUR.MEŠ-*šú*! [*e-tap-šá*]
9 *i-su-hu-ru x*[*x x x x*]
10 *ina* UGU-*hi-šú a-na* DI-[*me it-tal-ku*]
11 LÚ*.A—*šip-ri*.MEŠ *š*[*a*? *x x x*]
12 TA* URU.MAŠ-*d*[*a*?*-x x x x x*]
13 DI-*mu ša* [*x x x x x x*]
rest (about 4 lines) broken away
Rev. beginning broken away
1′ ⸢*x x x*⸣ [*x x x x x x*]
2′ É *i-ba-áš-*[*šu*]*-u-ni* [*x x x*]
3′ TA* UGU $^{md}$[*x x x x*]
4′ *ša* LUGAL E[N *iš-pur-an-ni*]
5′ *ma-a a-ta-*[*a x x x x*]
6′ *ina* ⸢*pa*⸣*-ni-i*[*a x x x x*]
7′ *la* ⸢*i-ma*⸣*-*[*x x x x x x*]
8′ *la* ⸢*i*⸣*-ma-*[*x x x x x x*]
9′ *ša* LÚ*.[*x x x x x x*]
10′ *iq-*⸢*qi*⸣*-*[*x x x x x x*]
11′ *i-t*[*a*!*-x x x x x x*]
12′ $^{m}$DI!*-m*[*u*!—EN *x x x x x x*]
13′ *i*—KASKAL-*šú-nu* [*x x x x x*]
14′ *ina* UGU [*x x x x x x*]
15e *i-*[*x x x x x x x x*]

ABL 1416

1 To [the king, my lord]: your servant [Adad-issiya]. Good he[alth to the king, my lord]!

4 As to what the king, [my] lo[rd, wrote me]: "Why have you [not sent me] a[ny *news*] of the Mannean that you have *h*[*eard*]?" —

7 [he *has come*] to our border, [made] his sacrifices, and returned (home); [the ... *have* gone] to greet him.

11 The messengers o[f ... *have come*] from *Bar*[..., and presented him] the greetings of [...].

(Break)

r.2 [......] where they are [...].

3 As to [NN] about whom the king, [my] lo[rd, wrote me]: "Wh[y does he *not* ...] to m[y] presen[ce]?"

7 He does not [...]

8 he does not [...]

9 of the [......]

10 ...[......]

11 ...[......]

12 Šulm[u-beli ......]

13 in their expedition [......]

14 *to* [......]

(Rest destroyed)

# 222. Military Movements in Mannea

K 14685

beginning broken away
1′ [*x x x x x x*] ⸢*a u*⸣
2′ [*x x x x* KUR.*man*]*-na-a-a*
3′ [*x x x x* KUR.U]RI*-a-a*
4′ [*x x x x* ŠÀ]*-bi-i-ni*
5′ [*x x x x*]*x* DUMU URU.*ša-*⸢*x*⸣
6′ [*x x x x*]*x* KUR.UR[I]*-a-*[*a*]
7′ [*x x x x x*] *du* [*x x x*]
rest broken away
Rev. destroyed

CT 53 585

(Beginning destroyed)

2 [...... the Man]nean(s)

3 [...... the Ura]rṭian(s)

4 [......] our [*hear*]*t*

5 [...... NN] from the city of [...]

6 [......] the Urar[ṭ]ia[n]

(Rest destroyed)

**221** Hand of Adad-issiya. 8, 11f, r.12 See coll.

## 223. Preparing for Battle with Urarṭian Troops

K 1120

beginning broken away
1′ *ina* [*x x x x x*]
2′ *mar* [*x x x x*]
3′ *re-he ú-*⸢*sa*?⸣*-x*[*x x*]
4′ *ma-a* LÚ**.e-mu-*⸢*qi*⸣
5′ *ša* KUR.URI *ina* UGU
6′ *ta-hu-me*
r.1 *i-tal-ku-u-ni*
2 *ma-a i—ni-ir-ti-šú-nu*
3 *i-tú-*⸢*ṣi i*⸣*-ta-lak*
4 *a-na* [*x x x*]
5 *ša*! [*x x x x*]
rest broken away

ABL 596

(Beginning destroyed)

1 as many as [...] remain in [......]...

4 "The Urarṭian troops advanced to the border; he went out to meet them in [...] of [......]"

(Rest destroyed)

## 224. Buying Horses in the East

K 1252A

1 *a-na* LUGAL EN*-ia*
2 ARAD*-ka* mdIM—KI*-ia*
3 *lu-u* DI*-mu a-na* LUGAL EN*-ia*
4 *ina* UGU LÚ*.DAM.QAR.MEŠ
5 *ša* LUGAL EN *ṭé-mu*
6 *iš-kun-an-ni-ni*
7 m*šá-ri-i* URU*.kan-nu-u*ʾ*-a-a*
8 *ina* URU*.ur-zu-hi-na*
9 $in_6$*—ni-ir-ti-iá*
10 70 KUR.RA.MEŠ *ina* ŠU.2*-šú* [0]
11 *a-sa-*ʾ*a-al-šú*
12 mu*muk re-eh-ti* [0]
13 KUR.RA.MEŠ*-ka a-li-i* [0]
14 *ma-a* 2*-me* KUR.RA!.[MEŠ]
15 [*ma*]*-a a-ma*?*-k*[*a*]
r.1 [*a-s*]*i-qi*! *ma-a*! *u*[*b*!*-ba-la*]
2 [*x*] *i x*[*x x x x*]
3 $in_6$*—ni-i*[*r-ti-iá*]
4 TA* UGU [KUR.RA.MEŠ]
5 *a-sa-*ʾ*a-*[*al-šú*]
6 *ma-a gab-bi-*[*šú-nu*]
7 *ni-si-qi ma-a x*[*x x*]
8 $in_6$*—ni-ir-ti-i-k*[*a*]
9 *i-lak-u-ni*
10 21 KUR.RA.MEŠ
11 2 ANŠE.NUN.NA
12 *ša* mdPA—SU
13 URU*.kal-ha-a-a*
14 *ša* ŠU.2 m*sa-ni-i*
15 *ina* URU*.ur-zu-*⸢*hi-na*⸣
16 $in_6$*—ni-ir-ti-iá*

ABL 529

1 To the king, my lord: your servant Adad-issiya. Good health to the king, my lord!

4 As to the merchants about whom the king my lord gave me orders, I met Šarî of Kannu' in Arzuhina. He had 70 horses.

11 I asked him where the rest of his horses were, and he said: "[I have bou]ght 200 horses over there and will b[ring them] (later)."

r.2 [I also met NN] and ask[ed him] about [the horses]; he said: "We have bought [all of them]; they are on their way towards yo[u ...]."

10 I encountered 21 horses and 2 mules of Nabû-eriba of Calah, a subordinate of Sanî, in Arzuhina.

**223** → Deller Zagros p.120. Hand of Adad-issiya. 3ff, r.5 See coll.
**224** 14ff See coll. r.1 W 187. r.7 See coll.

## 225. Not All Reap What They Sow

K 5435B + K 7304 + K 7360

1 [*a-na* LUGAL EN-*ia*]
2 [ARAD-*ka* $^{md}$IM—KI—*ia*]
3 [*lu* DI-*mu a-na*] LUGAL E[N-*ia*]
4 [*ina* UGU] ŠE.NUMUN [*š*]*a* LUGAL EN *iš-p*[*ur-an-ni*]
5 [*ma-a* $^{md}$]AG—⸢*x*⸣ 1-*lim* ŠE.NU[MUN]
6 [*l*]*e-ru-*⸢*uš*?⸣ *ma-a* $^{m}$*man-nu—ki*—⸢$^{d?}$IM?⸣
7 [1?-*li*]*m le-ru-uš ma-a* ⸢*at-ta*⸣
8 [1?-*li*]*m-ma* ⸢*a*⸣-*ru-uš*
9 [*i*]*a*?-*a-ka l*[*a m*]*u-qa-a-a pu-ut*
10 [*x x*]*x*.MEŠ-*te* ⸢*dan*⸣-*na-te a-na-ku*
11 [*e*]-*ra-áš šu-nu* ŠE.NUMUN
12 [*e*]-*ta-ár-šú* TA* ŠÀ-*bi* ⸢*i-ku*⸣-*ul*
13 [TA*] ŠÀ-*bi* KUR.RA.MEŠ-[*šú-nu*]
14 ⸢*ú*⸣-*šá-ku-ul* TA* [ŠÀ-*bi*]
15 [ŠE].NUMUN *i-ru-*[*šu*]
16 [*x*] ⸢*x x*⸣ T[A] KUR.*ma-d*[*a-a-a*]
17 [*ú*]-*ṣa-bi-tu* TA* ⸢*ur*⸣ [*x x x*]
18 [*x x*] ⸢*x x x*⸣ [*x x x x x*]
rest broken away
Rev. obliterated

CT 53 79

[1] [To the king, my lord: your servant Adad-issiya. Good health to] the king, [my] lo[rd]!

[4] [As to] the seed corn [about wh]ich the king, my lord, wr[ote me]: "Nabû-[...] must cultivate 1,000 (homers of) seed, Mannu-ki-*Adad* must cultivate [*1*],*000*, and you too must cultivate [*1*],*000* (homers of) seed corn" – [*wh*]*ere?* I cannot do it!

[10] [I] cultivate corn in the face of harsh [...]. They, by contrast, having planted their seed, [e]at from it, feed [their] horses [fr]om it, and (even) cultiva[te s]eed fro[m it].

[16] [They] have seized [...] from the Med[es ......]
(Rest destroyed)

## 226. Orders to Magnates

K 510

1 *a-na* LUGAL EN-⸢*ia*!⸣
2 ARAD-*ka* $^{md}$PA—PAB—PAB
3 *lu-u* DI-*mu a-na* LUGAL EN-*iá*
4 *ina* É LUGAL *be-lí*
5 *ina* UGU LÚ.GAL.MEŠ
6 *iš-pur-an-ni-ni*
7 *am—mar* LUGAL *be-lí*
8 *ṭè-e-mu iš-kun-an-ni-ni*
9 *gab-bu a-du-ba-šú-nu*
10 *ina* UGU URU É *š*[*a*]*k*!-*nu-u-ni*
11 URU.*ir-*⸢*šu*?⸣-*mu*
12 *ina* ŠU.2-*šú-nu*
13 *ár-hiš ina* UGU
14 LUGAL *be-lí-ia*
15 *il-la-ku-u-ni*
16 *ina* U[GU] $^{m}$⸢MAN⸣—IGI-*ni ša* LUGAL
17 *be-*[*lí ṭ*]*è-e-mu iš-kun-an-ni-ni*
e.18 *nu-uk* ANŠE.KUR.RA.MEŠ
r.1 LÚ*.ERIM.MEŠ-*ka*
2 1-*en lu*! *la i-ma-ṭi*
3 *nu-uk bi*!-*is*! *la ina pa-a*[*n*]
4 LUGAL [[0]] *e-ti-q*[*u*]
5 *ina* UGU $^{md}$PA—*ha-mat-u-a*
6 *ša* LUGAL *be-lí iq-bu-u-ni*

ABL 884

[1] To the king, my lord: your servant Nabû-ahu-uṣur. Good health to the king, my lord!

[4] The king, my lord, sent me to the magnates; I have (now) communicated them all the orders that the king, my lord, gave me.

[10] As to the town where they are encamped, Ir[š]umu is in their hands; they are soon to leave for the king, my lord.

[16] As [to] Šarru-emuranni, about whom the king, [my] lo[rd], gave me [or]ders, (I told him): "Not one of your horses and men may be missing *if* they are to pass before the king."

[r.5] As to Nabû-hamatua, about whom the king, my lord, told me: "Let him come and receive the booty from them!" –

**225** 6 See coll.

7 *ma-a šu-u* DU-⌈*ka*⌉ *hu*!*-ub*!*-tú*
8 ⌈*li*⌉*-hur*!*-šú-nu ki-i an-ni-e*
9 LÚ*.GAL.MEŠ *iq-ṭi-bu-ni*
10 *ma-a la*! *ú-šam-ṣa la i-la-ka*!
11 *ma-a a-na* LÚ*.2-*e ša*! KUR.*ha-ban*
12 *ni-da-an ina* UGU LÚ*.GAL.MEŠ
13 *ša* LUGAL *be-lí iq-bu-u-ni*
14 *ma-a* 50-*a-a* BAD-HAL *ina pa-ni-šú-nu*
15 *lik-li-u ma-a re-eh-te*
16 ANŠE.KUR.RA.MEŠ-*šú-nu ina* UGU-*hi-iá*
17 DU-*u-ni aq-ṭi-ba-šú-nu*
18 *la i-ma-gu-ru ma-a il-lu-ku*
19 *ina*! *šid*!*-di* KASKAL! *i-mut-tú*
20e *ma-a i-si-ni*
21e *i-la-ku-u-ni*

8 the magnates said to me as follows: "He cannot come; we shall give it to the deputy (governor) of (Bit)-Hamban."

r.12 As to the magnates about whom the king, my lord, told me: "They may each keep 50 riding horses at their disposal, the rest of their horses should come to me!" —

17 I told them (this), but they disagreed, saying: "(If) they go, they will die along the way; they will come with us."

# 11. Letters from Šamaš-belu-uṣur, Governor of Arzuhina



FIG. 32. *Ferry-boats on the Tigris (reign of Assurbanipal).*
ORIGINAL DRAWING IV, 77.

# 227. Post Stations and Criminals

Rm 2,1

1 *a-na* LUGAL EN-*ia*
2 ARAD-*ka* $^{md}$UTU—EN—PAB
3 *lu* DI-*mu a-na* LUGAL EN-*iá*
4 *ina* UGU *ka-li-ie ša* LUGAL *be-lí*
5 ŠU.2 $^{m}$URU.*arba-ìl-a-a iš-pur-an-ni*
6 *ma a-ta-a ka-li-iu-u la-šú*
7 *ki-i* TA* $^{m}$SUHUŠ—KASKAL LÚ*.*qur-bu-te*
8 *i-li-kan-a-ni a-na-ku ina* URU.*ur-zu-hi-na*
9 *i—pa-na-tú-šú-nu* 2 ANŠE.*ku-din*
10 *ina* KI.TA $^{m}$SUHUŠ—KASKAL *ar-ta-kas*
11 *ina* URU.*arrap-ha i-ṣa-bat* 2 ANŠE.*ku-din*
12 *ina* KI.TA $^{m}$URU.*arba-ìl-a-a ir-ta-kas*
13 *a-na* KUR.*ma-za-mu i-ta-lak*
14 LUGAL *be-lí liš-a*[*l*! *šú*]*m-ma la*
15 *ú-ru-u ša* AN[ŠE.*ku-din*] *ina* URU.BÀD—*ta-li-ti*
16 *ú-ru-u ša* ANŠE.⌜*ku-din*⌝ *ina* URU.*ta-ga-la-gi*
17 *ú-šá-zi-zu-ú-ni*
18 TA* URU.*ur-zu-hi-na i-tú-ṣi*
19 2 ANŠE.*ku-din ina* KI.TA-*šú ka-li-iu-u*
20 *a-na ka-li-e a-di* URU.*a-ra-ak-di*
21 *ki-i ú-ma-a i-li-kan-a-ni*
22 É LUGAL *be-lí iš-pur-šu-u-ni*
23 *a-na-ku ina* URU.*ur-zu-hi-na*
24 2 ANŠE.*ku-din ina* KI.T[A-*šú*]
e.25 *ar-ta-kas* [0]
r.1 ⌜*a*⌝-*di* URU.BÀD—*ta-li-*⌜*ti*⌝
2 [[*hu x x nu x ši*]]
3 [[*hu ma x x x x*]]
4 LUGAL *be-lí ú-da*
5 *ki-i* URU.*ar-zu-hi-na*
6 *ina* ŠÀ *is-pi-lu-ur-te*
7 *ka-ri-ru-u-ni mar-di-tú*
8 TA* URU.*ur-zu-hi-na a-di*
9 URU.*a-ra-ak-di a-na ú-ma-me*
10 *ta-da-in* LUGAL *be-lí*
11 *a—ṭè-mu liš*!-*kun*
12 *ka-*[[*šá*! *ka*!]]-*li-iu-ú*
13 *ina* URU.BÀD—MÍ.ANŠE.MEŠ-*te*
14 *lu-šá-zi-zu a-he-ii-ši*
15 *nu-ti-in ina* UGU LÚ*.LUL.MEŠ
16 *ša* LUGAL *be-lí iš-pur-an-ni*
17 *ma-a ina* UGU LÚ*.TUR.MEŠ-*ni*

ABL 408

1 To the king, my lord: your servant Šamaš-belu-uṣur. Good health to the king, my lord!

4 As to the express service about which the king, my lord, wrote me through Arbailayu: "Why isn't there any express service?" –

7 When he came to me with the royal bodyguard Ubru-Harran, I harnessed before their coming two mules in Arzuhina for the use of Ubru-Harran. He took them to Arrapha, harnessed two mules for the use of Arbailayu, and went on to Mazamua.

14 Let the king, my lord, a[sk whet]her I did not station a team of [mules] in Dur-Taliti and another one in Tagalagi! When he departed from Arzuhina, there were two mules for his use from one express-station to another, as far as Arrakdi.

21 As he now came, (going) to where the king, my lord, had sent him, I harnessed two mules in Arzuhina for [his] use as far as Dur-Taliti (...).

r.4 The king, my lord, knows that Arzuhina is situated at a crossroads; the stage from Arzuhina to Arrakdi is a strain for the animals. The king, my lord, should give orders that a mule-express be stationed in Dur-Atanate, so we can strengthen each other.

15 As to the criminals about whom the king, my lord, wrote me: "They have fallen upon the menservants of the chief confec-

**227** 14 See coll. 16 URU.*ta-ga-la-gi* sic; signs clear. r.2f See coll. r.11f Y 80, W 152; see coll.; both lines written over erasures. The initial *a*, not erased, is likely to have belonged to the erased sentence.

18 *ša* LÚ*.GAL—SUM.NINDA *ina* KUR.*ba-bi-ti*
19 *i-tú-uq-tu a-sa-al*
20 *ú-ta-ṣi-ṣi me-me-(ni) la-šú*
21 *ù la ni-iš-me* LUGAL *be-lí*
22 *i-sap-ra ma-a šúm-ma* LÚ*.LUL.MEŠ
23 *la tu-ṣa-bit ma-a lu tu-da*
24 *ki-i at-ta tu-šal-lum-ni*
25 LÚ*.*pa-ri-ṣu-u-te*
26e *ša* URU.*arrap-ha*
27e *ša* É LÚ*.ŠÚ.NIGÍR—É.GAL
s.1 *up-ta-at-hu-ru ina* ŠÀ *i-za-qu-pu ú-ma-[a* LÚ*.ERIM.MEŠ]
2 *ú-se-li i-na-ṣur šúm-ma ú-ṣa-bit-u-ni ina* IG[I LUGAL EN-*ia*]
3 *ú-bal-u-ni-šú-nu a-nu-rig* LÚ*.LUL.MEŠ-*te ša* É LÚ*.[*sar-tin-ni*$^{?}$]
4 *ša qa-an-ni* URU.*ur-zu-hi-na in-qut-u-ni ina* IGI LUGAL EN-[*iá ú-se-bi-la*]

tioner in Babiti" – I have asked and enquired, but there is nothing, and we have not heard anything.

21 The king, my lord, wrote me: "If you do not catch the criminals, be sure you will have to pay" –

25 the criminals of Arrapha (and) of the domain of the palace herald have banded together and are *making raids* there. I have now moved [troops] up to keep watch; if they catch them, they will bring them t[o the king, my lord].

s.2 For now [I am sending] to the king, [my] lord, the criminals of the house of the [*sartinnu*] who fell (into my hands) near Arzuhina.

## 228. Criminals Again

K 1124

beginning destroyed
1′ [*x x x*]*x* [*x x*]
2′ *ú-se-bíl* [$^{m}$*x x x*]
3′ ⌜ARAD-*šú*⌝ *ša* LÚ*.E[N$^{!}$.NAM]
4′ [*x x x*]*x šu-ú* [*ù*]
5′ ⌜É$^{?}$⌝-*su ina ba-t*[*i am-mì-ti*]
6′ [*kam*]-*mu-su* : *mì*-⌜*i*$^{!}$⌝-[*nu*]
7′ *ša* LUGAL *be-lí* [[*x x*]]
8′ *i-q*[*a*$^{!}$]-*bu-u-ni i-se-niš*
9′ LÚ*.LUL.MEŠ *šú-nu*
10′ [$^{m}$]*ni-mar-ka-a-a*
11′ [ARA]D-*šú ša* DUMU—LUGAL
12′ ⌜*ú*⌝-*ṣa-bi-ti*
13′ [*in*]*a*$^{!}$ É.GAL *na-aṣ-ṣa*
14′ ⌜$^{m!}$⌝AD—*ra-me*
r.1 $^{m}$*da-la*—DINGIR PAB 2
2 URU.*ur-zu-hi-na-a-a*
3 2 URU.*arrap-ha-a-a i-si-šú-nu*
4 *ina* É.GAL *ú-sa-ni-qu-šú-nu*
5 LÚ*.LUL.MEŠ *ša i-si-šú-nu*
6 [*an-nu-ri*]*g*$^{?}$ *ú-s*[*e*$^{!}$-*bi-l*]*a*
rest broken away

ABL 599

(Beginning destroyed)

2 I have sent [......].

3 [NN], a servant of the go[vernor of ...] and his family are [st]aying on the [other] side (of the river). Wha[t ar]e the king my lord's orders?

8 Likewise, there are some criminals (whom) Nimarkayu, a [serv]ant of the Crown Prince, seized and brought to the Palace:

14 Abi-ram and Dala-Il, in all two Arzuhinaeans, and with them two Arraphaeans; they have questioned them in the Palace.

r.5 I am [*no*]*w* s[ending over] the criminals who were their accomplices.

(Rest destroyed)

## 229. Clearing up the Royal Road to Mazamua

K 1516

beginning (about 10 lines) broken away
1′ *x*[*x x x x x x x*]
2′ *ina* ŠÀ-*bi* [*x x x x*]

ABL 635

(Beginning destroyed)

2 there [......].

**228** Same hand as in no. 229. 3, 5f, 8, 13f See coll.

3′ *a-ki ha-*[*an-ni-im-ma*]
4′ *ṭè-e-*[*mu a-sa-kan-šú*]
5′ *nu-*⸢*uk*⸣ [*x x x x x*]*x*
6′ *i-šá-*[*x x x x x*]*-*⸢*ú*⸣*-ni*
7′ KASKAL.GÍ[D *x x x x*]
8′ *nu-u*[*k x x x x*]*x*
9′ *ma-a* [*x x x x x*]
e.10′ ⸢É⸣ [*x x x x x x*]*x*
11′ *ma-a ma-a*ʾ*-*⸢*da a*⸣*-na* Z[AG]
12′ *a-na* 150 : *i-šap-pu-r*[*u*]
r.1 TA* ŠÀ*-bi* URU.*sa-re-*⸢*e*⸣
2 *a-di* URU.BÀD—*a-ta-na-t*[*e*]
3 *ana-ku ú-pa-sa-ak*
4 TA* URU.BÀD—*a-ta-na-t*[*e*]
5 *a-di* URU.BÀD—*ta-li-ti*
6 URU.*arrap*!*-ha-a-a ú-pa-su-ku*
7 TA* URU.BÀD—*ta-li-ti*
8 *a-di* ŠÀ*-bi* URU.*a-za-ri*
9 [*ana-ku-m*]*a*! *ú-pa-sa-ak*
traces of one more line; rest broken away

3 [I gave him] the follo[wing] ord[er]: "[......]
(Break)

9 [He said]: "[......]; where [......], they are sending [...] to the ri[ght] and left on various errands.

r.1 I remove [...] from Sarê to Dur-Atanate, the Arraphaeans remove [...] from Dur-Atanate to Dur-Taliti, [I] remove [the ...] again from Dur-Taliti to Azari
(Rest destroyed)

## 230. A Military Review

K 5392

beginning broken away
1′ [*x x x x x*]*x ina* [*x x*]
2′ [*x x x x*] *pa-su-k*[*u x*]
3′ [*ša* LUGAL] *be-lí iš-pur-an-*[*ni*]
4′ [*ki-i* T]A *ma-šar-ti al-*[*lik-an-ni*]
5′ [*x x*]*-ti-ia* LÚ*.3.[U$_5$*-ia*]
6′ [LÚ*.DIB]—⸢*a-pa*⸣.MEŠ *ina* ⸢*x*⸣ [*x x x*]
7′ [*x x x*] *ab* ⸢*ba*⸣ [*x x x x*]
8′ [*x x x*] KASKAL [*x x x x x*]
rest broken away
Rev. destroyed

CT 53 240

(Beginning destroyed)
2 [......] remov[ed ...].
3 [As to what the king], my lord, wrote [me, *when*] I c[ame fr]om the review, my [..., my] 'third [man' and the chariot d]river
(Rest too broken for translation)

## 231. Fragment Concerning Criminals

K 14635

beginning broken away
1′ [*x x x x*] ⸢*li-ir*⸣*-di-ia*
2′ [*x x x*] LÚ*.LUL.MEŠ
3′ [*x x x x x*] *li-li-i*[*k*]
rest broken away
Rev. destroyed

CT 53 553

(Beginning destroyed)
1 [......] should lead
2 [......] the criminals
3 [......] he should go
(Rest destroyed)

**229** Same hand as in no. 228. r.9 See coll.
**230** Same hand as in no. 228; could be part of the same tablet as no. 231
**231** Same hand as in no. 228; part of the same tablet as no. 230?

## 232. The Governor of Dur-Šarruken Wants More Fields

Rm 993

1 [*a-na* LUGAL EN-*ia*]
2 [ARAD-*ka* $^{md}$UTU—EN—PAB]
3 ⌜*lu*$^{!}$⌝ D[I-*mu a*]-*na*$^{!}$ [LUGAL EN-*ia*]
4 ⌜*ina*⌝ [UGU] ⌜URU$^{?}$⌝.[MEŠ *ša*] ⌜KUR⌝.*ha-a-ú*
5 ⌜*ša*$^{!}$⌝ $^{m!}$*ki-ṣir*—[*aš-š*]*ur*$^{!}$ *ina*$^{!}$ IGI$^{!}$ LUGAL EN-[*ia*]
6 [*i*]*q*$^{!}$-[*b*]*u*$^{!}$-*u*$^{!}$-*ni*$^{!}$ [*ma*]-*a* 2-*me* A.ŠÀ ⌜*ša*$^{!}$⌝
7 [*ina qa*]-⌜*ni*$^{!}$⌝ : ⌜*li*⌝-*di-nu-u*-⌜*ni*⌝ [0]
8 [*x* URU].⌜MEŠ$^{!}$⌝-*ni ša* KUR.*si-ru-ra*
9 5$^{!}$ [UR]U$^{!}$.MEŠ-[*ni*] *ša* É LÚ*.SANGA
10 [$^{d}$]⌜EN$^{?}$⌝ [*x x x š*]*a* ŠU.2 LÚ*.GAL—[SAG$^{?}$]
11 [*x x x x x*]-*ú ina*$^{!}$ IGI$^{!}$ $^{m}$*k*[*i*$^{!}$-*ṣir—aš-šur*]
12 [*x x x x x x*] URU.MEŠ [*x x*]
rest (about 10 lines) broken away
Rev. beginning broken away
1′ [*x x x x x*] ⌜*ú*$^{!}$⌝-*ma-a* $^{m!}$*ki*-⌜*ṣir*⌝—[*aš-šur*]
2′ [*i-qa-bi*] *ma-a qa-ni* URU.*ur-zu-hi-na*
3′ ⌜*ù*⌝ *ina* ⌜URU$^{!}$⌝.BÀD—*ta-li-ti*
4′ *la a-na-ši ma-a* URU.MEŠ-*ni-ma*
5′ *ša ina* IGI LUGAL *a-qa-bu-u-ni*
6′ ⌜*lu*$^{!}$⌝ *šú-nu* [*i*$^{!}$]-*na-ši-ú an-nu*-⌜*rig*⌝
7′ [*i*]*l*$^{!}$-*ku ša* KUR.*ha-a-ú*
8′ [0 *i*]*na* UGU URU.MEŠ-*ni an-nu-te*
9′ ⌜*i*$^{!}$⌝-*la-ku-u-ni* : *a-sa-ṭar ina* UGU [LUGAL E]N$^{!}$-[*ia*]
10′ [*ú*]-*se*$^{!}$-*bi-la mì-i-nu šá*$^{!}$ LU[GAL$^{!}$ *be-l*]*í*$^{!}$
11e [*i-q*]*a*$^{!}$-*bu-u-ni* [0]

ABL 1192

[1] [To the king, my lord: your servant Šamaš-belu-uṣur]. Good [health t]o [the king, my lord]!

[4] A[s to] *the t*[*owns* of] the country Hau, about which Kiṣir-[Ašš]ur [s]aid to the king, [my] lord: "Let them give me 200 (hectares) of field in their environs" –

[x town]s of Sirura and 5 [tow]ns of the house of the priest [of] *Bel* [...], under the jurisdiction of the chief [*eunuch*], are [...] at the disposal of K[iṣir-Aššur].

[12] [...] the towns [...]

(Break)

[r.1] Now, Kiṣir-[Aššur claims]: "I do not *extract* (*labour duty*) in the environs of Arzuhina or in Dur-Taliti. It is the towns I mentioned to the king that *extract it*."

[6] I have now written down the [lab]our duty which Hau carries for these towns, and [I am] herewith sending it to [the king, my lo]rd. What are the k[ing] my [lord]'s [or]ders?

## 233. The King Gets an Old Boat

81-7-27,39

1 *a-na* LUGAL EN-*ia*
2 ARAD-*ka* $^{md}$UTU—EN—PAB
3 *lu-u* DI-*mu a-na* LUGAL EN-*ia*
4 LUGAL *be-lí ú*$^{!}$-*da*$^{!}$
5 ŠE.*ki-su-tú* TA* *na-ak*
6 *a-na* KUR.*am*$^{!!}$-*pi-ha-a-bi ni-za-bi-lu-ni*
7 GIŠ.MÁ *ši-i la-bir-tú*
8 *ša ti-ib-nu* ŠE.*ki-su-tú*$^{!!}$
9 *mì-i-nu ša i-ba-šu-u-ni*
10 *ina* ŠÀ-*bi nu-še-ba-lu-u-ni*
11 *i-x*[*x x x x x x*]
rest destroyed
Rev. beginning broken away
1′ *šúm-m*[*a ta-ri-iṣ*]
2′ TA* LUGAL EN-*i*[*a* 0]
3′ *lu-u ta-li-ki*
rest uninscribed

ABL 802

[1] To the king, my lord: your servant Šamaš-belu-uṣur. Good health to the king, my lord!

[4] The king, my lord, knows that we transport fodder from here to Ampihabi. There is an old boat we use for shipping straw, fodder and all sorts of things [......]

(Break)

[r.1] If [it is all right], she may go with the king, m[y] lord.

**232** Hand of Šamaš-belu-uṣur. [4, 11, r.6, 9] See coll.
**233** [4] Y 83, W 239. [6] Y 83; see coll. [8] Tablet ŠE.*ki-su-nu*; scribal error. Y 83; see coll.

# 234. Barley to Mazamua

K 1093

beginning destroyed
1′ *nu-*[*x x*]*-*⸢*ki*!*-da*!⸣
2′ *ša nam-*⸢*mu*⸣*-ši*
3′ *a-na ma-šar-te*
4′ $^{m}$*iš-me*—DINGIR LÚ*.GAL—*ki-ṣir*
5′ *un-qu* KUG.GI
6′ *na-aṣ ina* UGU*-hi-ni*
7′ *ik-ta-na-la-a-na-ši*
8′ *ma-a* ŠE.PAD.MEŠ
9′ *zi-ib-la*
r.1 *a-na* KUR—*za-mu-u*
2 *mì-nu ša* LUGAL *be-lí*
3 ⸢*i*⸣-[*q*]*ab-bu-u-ni*
4 [*x x x*] ANŠE.KUR.MEŠ
5 [*x x x x*]-⸢*ú*⸣*-te*
6 [*x x x x x*]*x*
7 [*x x x x x*] ⸢EN?-*iá*!⸣
8 [*x x x x x*] ⸢*x*⸣
9 [*x x x x x*]-⸢*ni*⸣
rest broken away

ABL 582

(Beginning destroyed)

1 We [*are ready*] to set out for the review, but Išme-ilu, the cohort commander, brings us the (king's) golden stamp seal and holds us up continually, saying: "Bring barley rations to Mazamua!"

r.2 What does the king, my lord, say?

4 [...] horses

(Rest destroyed)

# 235. ———

K 16496

beginning broken away
1′ *x*[*x x x x x x x x*]
2′ *li-x*[*x x x x x x*]
3′ *ú-d*[*a x x x x x*]
4′ *ina* UGU [*x x x x x*]
5′ *ša* L[UGAL *x x x x x*]
6′ *lu* [*x x x x x x x*]
7′ *a-*[*x x x x x x x x*]
rest broken away
Rev. destroyed

CT 53 777

(Beginning destroyed)

3 kno[ws ......]

4 As to [......]

5 about which the k[ing, my lord, *wrote me*]

(Rest destroyed)

# 236. ———

DT 68

beginning broken away
1′ [$^{m}$]*a-ri-*[*e x x x x x*]
2′ MÚD.MEŠ *ša* [*x x x x x*]
3′ ⸢*ša*⸣ LÚ*.ARAD ⸢*x*⸣ [*x x x x*]
4′ *ina* KUR.*man-na-a-a* [*x x x x*]
5′ *ina* ŠÀ*-bi* DINGIR.MEŠ [*ša* LUGAL EN*-ia*]
6′ ⸢1*-me*⸣-90 *ma x*[*x x x x x x*]
rest broken away
Rev. destroyed

CT 53 135

(Beginning destroyed)

1 Ari[ye ......]

2 the blood which [......]

3 of the servant [......]

4 In Mannea [......]

5 with the help of the gods [of the king, my lord],

6 190 [......]

(Rest destroyed)

**234** 1ff, r.7f See coll.
**235** Script as in no. 229.

# 12. Varia and Unassigned



FIG. 33. *Prisoners from the northeast (reign of Sennacherib).*
AO 19913.

## 237. Appointing a City Lord

K 1046

1 *a-na* LUGAL EN-*ia*
2 ⸢ARAD-*ka*⸣ $^{m}$*man-nu—ki—*$^{d}$IM
3 [*lu*] DI-*mu a-na* LUGAL EN-*ia*
4 [DUMU] $^{m}$*ba-bu-ú* EN—URU
5 [*ina* UG]U-*hi-ia i-tu-ur-*[*d*]*a*
6 [ŠÀ-*b*]*u*! *a-sa-kan-šú*
7 [*x x x*]*x ap*!*-ta*!*-aq-da-šú*
8 [*x x x x* LU]GAL EN-*ia*
rest broken away
Rev. uninscribed

ABL 902

1 To the king, my lord: your servant Mannu-ki-Adad. [Good] health to the king, my lord!

4 [The son of] Babû the city lord has come down [t]o me (from the mountain). I have [en]couraged him and appointed him [.... The ki]ng, my lord, [*can be glad*].

(Rest destroyed)

## 238. Buying Ungelded Bulls

K 1071

1 [*a-na*] LUGAL EN-*ia*
2 [ARAD]-*ka* $^{m}$*man-nu—ki—*10
3 ⸢*lu*⸣ DI-*mu a-na* LUGAL
4 ⸢EN⸣-*ia ina* UGU GUD.MEŠ
5 [*šak-l*]*a*!*-lu-tu*
6 [*ša*] LUGAL BE.LUM
7 [*iš-pur-a*]*n-ni*
8 [*x x x*]*x*[*x x x*]
rest broken away
Rev. beginning broken away
1′ [*x x x x*]⸢*x x x*⸣
2′ [TA*] *pa-an* LÚ*.*i-tú-ʾa-a-*[*a*]
3′ *ina* ŠÀ KUG.UD *li-qi-a*
4′ *ni-la-qi* [[*x*]]
5′ [[*x*]]

ABL 903

1 [To] the king, my lord: your [servant] Mannu-ki-Adad. Good health to the king, my lord!

4 As to the [unge]lded oxen [about which] the king, my lord, [wrot]e me

(Break)

r.1 [As to what the king, my lord wrote me]: "Buy [... fr]om the Itu'eans with silver!" — we are buying (them).

## 239. ———

K 13027

1 [*a-na* LUGA]L EN-*ia*
2 [ARAD-*ka* $^{m}$*ma*]*n-nu—ki—*$^{d}$IM
3 [*lu* DI-*mu a-na* L]UGAL EN-*i*⸢*a*⸣
4 [*ina* UGU $^{m}$*x x*]*x—*$^{d}$UTU [0?]
5 [*x x x x x p*]*íl*!-[*x*]
rest broken away
Rev. completely broken away

ABL 904

1 [To the kin]g, my lord: [your servant Ma]nnu-ki-Adad. [Good health to the k]ing, my lord!

4 [As to ...]-Šamaš [......]

(Rest destroyed)

**237** 6 See coll.
**238** 5 See coll.
**239** 5 See coll.

## 240. ———

K 13120

1 [*a-na* LUGAL] EN-*ia*
2 [ARAD-*ka* $^{m}$*man-n*]*u—ki—*$^{d}$IM
3 [*lu* DI-*mu a-na*] LUGAL EN-*ia*
4 [LÚ*.*e-mu-qi*]-⌈*ia*⌉ *ú*-⌈*ta*⌉-*me-šá*
rest broken away
Rev. destroyed

ABL 905

1 [To the king], my lord: [your servant Mann]u-ki-Adad. [Good health to] the king, my lord!

4 My [troops] have set out [......]
(Rest destroyed)

## 241. A Babylonian Asks for Audience

K 498

1 *a-na* LUGAL *be-lí-ia*
2 ARAD-*ka* $^{md}$IM—DÙ
3 *lu šul-mu a-na* LUGAL
4 *be-lí-ia*
5 DUMU—KÁ.DINGIR.RA.KI
6 *šu-u ina* UGU-*hi-ia*
7 *it-tal-ka ma-a di-bi*
8 *ina* KA-*ia ma-a ina* É.GAL
9 *lu-bi-lu-u-ni*
10 *ú-ma-a an-nu-rig*
11 *ina pa-an* LUGAL *be-lí-ia*
12 *ú-se-bi-la-šu*
13 LUGAL *be-lí liš-al-šu*
14 *mì-nu ša di-bi-šú-u-ni*
r.1 UD-28-KAM TA* ŠÀ
2 URU.*za-ad-di*
3 *ina pa-an* LUGAL *be-lí-ia*
4 *ú-se-bi-la-šu*

ABL 522

1 To the king, my lord: your servant Adad-ibni. Good health to the king, my lord!

5 A Babylonian has come to me, saying: "I have things to say; let them take me to the Palace" –

10 now then I am sending him to the king, my lord; let the king, my lord, ask him what he has to say.

r.1 I sent him to the king, my lord, on the 28th from Zaddi.

## 242. Resettling Captives

K 541

1 *a-na* LUGAL EN-*ia*
2 ARAD-*ka* $^{m}$*aš-šur*—TÉŠ—UN.MEŠ
3 *lu* DI-*mu a-na* LUGAL
4 *be-lí-ia*
5 TA* (UGU) LÚ*.*hu-ub-te*
6 *ša* LUGAL *be-lí*
7 *iš-pur-an-ni*
8 *at-tu*$^{!}$*-bíl*$^{!}$ *ana-ku*
9 LÚ*.2-*ú* TA* URU.*tah*-URU
10 *a-du* URU.*kar*—$^{d}$UTU
11 ⌈*nu*$^{!}$⌉-*se*$^{!}$*-rib nu-up-ta-qid*
12 [ŠE.PAD.MEŠ] *ša* ITI UD$^{!}$.MEŠ
Edge uninscribed
r.1 [0] *ina ša* 8 *qa* 1/2 *qa-at*
2 MUN ŠE.*ku-dim-me*
3 *at-ti-din* DI-*mu*
4 *a—dan-niš*

ABL 207

1 To the king, my lord: your servant Aššur-balti-niši. Good health to the king, my lord!

5 As to the captives about whom the king, my lord, wrote me, I have brought them (there).

8 I and the deputy (governor) have entered them from Tahal as far as Kar-Šamaš, and appointed (them).

12 I have given out [provisions] for a whole month, [by the sea]h of 8 litres, and half a cup of salt and *cress*. Everything is fine.

**242** 8f, 11f See coll.; UD (l. 12) over erased MEŠ. r.1f See coll.

FIG. 34. *Prisoners under guard (reign of Assurbanipal).*
ORIGINAL DRAWING VI, 15.

FIG. 35. *Prisoners under escort (reign of Assurbanipal).*
ORIGINAL DRAWING V, 31.

## 243. Portrait of a Vassal

K 5291

1 *a-na* LUGAL E[N-*ia*]
2 ARAD-*ka* $^{m}$LUGAL—IGI.LAL-[*an-ni*]
3 *lu-u* DI-*mu a-na* LUGAL [EN-*ia*]
4 *la-a* DUMU LÚ*.EN—URU ⸢*ša*⸣ U[RU.*x x*]
5 *a-na-ku* LÚ*.*un-za-ar-h*[*u*]
6 LÚ*.ARAD *ša* LUGAL EN-*ia a-na-ku*
7 LUGAL *be-li ina* URU.*qu-un-bu-na*
8 *ip-taq-da-ni mi-i-nu*
9 *ša a-ma-ru-ni ša a-šam-mu-ni*
10 *ina pa-an* LUGAL EN-*ia a-qab-bi*
11 *me-me-ni* TA IGI LUGAL *la*! *ú*-⸢*ba*!-*zar*!?⸣
12 *ina* UGU LÚ*.ARAD.MEŠ-*ni* ⸢*ša* LUGAL⸣ [EN-*ia*]
13 *ša* TA URU.*gar-ga-mis ina* URU.*ar*-[*zi-zi*]
14 *il-li-ku-ni-ni*
15 *ša ina* É.GAL *ina* UGU-*hi-šú*-⸢*nu*!?⸣
16 *áš-pu-ra-ni ú-ma-a an-nu-rig*
17 *ú-sa-aṣ-bit a-na* LUGAL EN-*ia*
e.18 *a-ti-din ina* ŠÀ-*bi an-ni-e*
19 *ina* É.⸢GAL⸣ *li-ih*!-⸢*hi*!?⸣-[*kim*]
20 *ki-i ši-a-hu*
r.1 TA LUGAL *a-da-bu-bu-ni*
2 *ú-ma-a* $^{m}$*da-da-a*
3 LÚ*.*ar-zi-za-a-a*
4 *ma*-⸢*a a-ta-a kar*!?⸣-*ṣi-ia*
5 *ina* É.GAL *ta*!-*kul*! $^{m}$*da-da-a*
6 *la-a* EN *de-ni-i*[*a*] ⸢*šu-ú*⸣
7 *me*-⸢*me*⸣-*ni-šú ina pa*-⸢*ni*⸣-[*ia la-áš*]-*šú*
8 *ú-ma-a ina* É.GAL ⸢*a-na*⸣ [*da-ba-bi*]
9 *ina* UGU-*hi-ia* ⸢*i*?⸣-[*ta-lak*]
10 LUGAL *be-li liš-*ʾ*a-a*[*l* 0]
11 ⸢*šum*!?⸣-*ma me-me-ni-šú ina* ⸢*pa-ni*⸣-[*ia*]
12 *i-ba-ši* LÚ*.A—KIN.MEŠ-⸢*šú*⸣
13 *ka-a-a-ma-nu ina* URU.*x*[*x x*]*x*
14 *ina ka-la-ma-ri i*[*l-lu-ku*]
15 *il-la-ku-ni* ⸢UD?⸣ *x*[*x x x x*]
16 *ša* UN.MEŠ KUR-*ia x*[*x x x x*]
17 UN.MEŠ KUR-*ia* [*x x x x x*]

ABL 317

1 To the king, [my] lo[rd]: your servant Šarru-emur[anni]. Good health to the king, [my lord]!

4 I am not the son of the city lord of [*Qunbuna*]; I am a house-born slav[e], a servant of the king, my lord! The king, my lord, appointed me in Qunbuna; I tell everything that I see and hear to the king, my lord, I do not conceal anything from the king.

12 As to the king [my lord]'s subjects who came to Ar[zizi] from Carchemish, about whom I wrote to the Palace, I have now had them arrested and am herewith handing them over to the king, my lord. From this act, it should be understood in the Palace that I speak *earnestly* with the king.

r.2 Now, Dadâ the Arzizean (has said to me): "Why have you slandered me in the Palace?"

5 Dadâ does not have a lawsuit against me; [there is noth]ing belonging to him in [my] possession. [He has] now [gone] to the Palace in order to [*litigate*] against me; let the king, my lord, investigate whether there is anything belonging to him in [my] possession.

12 His messengers constantly g[o back] and forth to the city [...] early in the morning;

16 [......] of the people of my country [......]

17 the people of my country [......].

## 244. The Forts are Fine

83-1-18,103

1 *a-na* LUGAL EN-*ia*
2 ARAD-*ka* $^{m}$*mu-šal-lim*—$^{d}$IM
3 *lu-u* DI-*mu a-na* LUGAL EN-*ia*

ABL 946

1 To the king, my lord: your servant Mušallim-Adad. Good health to the king, my lord!

**243** Scribal hand resembles closely that of nos. 199-200. The sender may accordingly be identical with the governor of Mazamua who authored nos. 199ff. 11 See coll. 15 W 123. 19 See coll. 20 Sic (see coll.); all signs absolutely clear. W 123 ⸢-*ri*!⸣ excluded. Cf. no. 126 r.14 and Hebr. *śiaḥ* "business, concern" (L. Koehler and W. Baumgartner, *Lexicon in Veteris Testamenti Libros*, p.919b), Syr. *sāḥā* "earnest desire, eagerness" (Payne-Smith, p. 364a). r.9, 13ff See coll.

4 DI-*mu a-na* URU.HAL.⸢ṢU.MEŠ⸣
5 *ša* LUGAL EN-[*ia* 0]
6 TA* URU.HAL.ṢU.MEŠ *š*[*a*! *x x*]
7 *a-du* URU.HAL.ṢU.[MEŠ *x x x*]
8 DI-*mu* É LUGAL [*be-li x x*]
9 [LÚ*].⸢*ši*!⸣-*kin*—[*ṭè-mi*]
rest (about 10 lines) broken away
Rev. beginning lost
1′ [*x x x x*]⸢*x x*⸣[*x*]
2′ [*x x x x*]-*ra-a-ni*
3′ *x*[*x x x*] LUGAL EN-*ia*
4′ *a*-⸢*sa-pa-ra*!⸣ É! LUGAL *be-li*
5′ *i-qa-bu-u-ni kar-ru*
6′ *ṭè*!-*ru*!-*bu*!
7′ LUGAL *be-li a-na* ARAD-*šú*
8′ *l*⸢*i-iš*⸣-*pur-ra*
9′ *ku-um a-mu-tu-ni*

4 The forts of the king, [my] lord, are well; (everything) is fine from the forts o[f ...] as far as the fort[s of ...].

8 *When* the king, [my lord, ...] *the com*[*mandant* ......]
(Break)

r.3 I have sent [...... to] the king, my lord; they will be placed where the king, my lord, orders. May the king, my lord, send ... to his servant, lest I die.

## 245. Flooded by Refugees

83-1-18,18

1 *a-na* LUGAL EN-*ia*
2 ARAD-*ka* $^{m}$*za-ba-a-a*
3 LÚ*.GAL—URU.HAL.ṢU
4 *ša* URU.*ap-pi-na*
5 *lu* DI-*mu a-na* LUGAL EN-*iá*
6 DI-*mu a-na* URU.HAL.ṢU
7 DI-*mu a-na* LÚ*.ARAD.MEŠ
8 *ša* LUGAL EN-*ia*
9 LÚ*.SAG LÚ*.*šá*—UGU—É
10 [*š*]*a*? $^{m}$*su-it-ka-a*
11 [LÚ*.EN?—U]RU *ih-tal-qa*
12 [*a-na* U]RU.*ap-pi-na*
13 [*it-tal-k*]*a* LÚ*.*ma-aq-tu-tú*
rest (about 5 lines) broken away
Rev. beginning (about 5 lines) lost
1′ [*ina* SAG] ⸢ITI?⸣ *ša* ⸢ITI.APIN⸣
2′ [*a-na* É.G]AL! *a-sa-par*
3′ [LÚ*].*ma-aq-tú ina* ŠU.2-*šú*
4′ [LÚ*].A—*šip-ri*.MEŠ
5′ *ša i-si-šú it-tal-ku-nu*
6′ *šu-ú a-da-kan-ni*
7′ *la il-li-ka*
5 lines uninscribed

ABL 343

1 To the king, my lord: your servant Zabayu, the commander of the fort Appina. Good health to the king, my lord!

6 The fort and the servants of the king, my lord, are well.

9 The eunuch who is overseer of the household o[f] Suitkâ [the ci]ty [*lord*], has fled and [com]e [to] Appina. Deserters [......]
(Break)

r.1 I sent [... to the Pala]ce [on the 1]st of Marchesvan (VIII); a deserter is (coming) with him. The messengers accompanying him have come, but up to now he himself has not come.

## 246. Waiting for Scouts to Come back

K 1021

1 *a-na* ⸢LUGAL⸣ *be-lí-iá*
2 ARAD-*ka* $^{m}$EN—IGI.LAL-*ni*
3 *lu* DI-*mu a-na* LUGAL EN-*iá*

ABL 309

1 To the king, my lord: your servant Bel-emuranni. Good health to the king, my lord!

**244** 6, 9, r.4 See coll. r.6 Sic; see coll.; obscure. W 265.
**245** 10, r.1f See coll.

4 *ina* UGU *li-šá-ni ša* LUGAL
5 *be-lí iš-pu-ra-an-ni*
6 *a-sap-ra* LÚ*.*da-a-a-li*
7 *ú-di-ni la il-la-ku-u-ni*
8 *ina pa-an-šú-nu a-da-gal*
9 *a-ka-an-ni ṭè-e-mu*
10 *a-na* LU[GAL EN-*iá ú-ta-ra*]
11 ⌜*a*?-*pa*?⌝-[*x x x x x*]
rest (about 6 lines) broken away
Rev. beginning (about 5 lines) broken away
1′ ⌜*x x x x*⌝ [*x x x x x*]
2′ *lid-di-nu lu-b*[*i-lu-ni*]
3′ *ú-la-a la-a ša du-l*[*u*?-*x*]
4′ *ši-i* LÚ *ut-ru i-ba-š*[*i*!]
5′ *is-si-šú i-za-za*
6′ *lid-di-nu-niš-šú lu-bi-la*
7 *ša*—LÚ*.BAD-HAL *li-zi-zi*
8′ EN.NUN-*šú li-ṣur*
rest uninscribed

4 As to the rumour about which the king, my lord, wrote me, I have sent out scouts but they have not yet come back.

8 While waiting for them, [I am submitting] the ki[ng, my lord], this report.

(Break)

r.2 They should give it and b[ring it to me].

3 Or if it is not to be ... and there happens to be a man in his company he can dispense with, let them give it to him, and let him bring it.

7 A cavalryman should be there to guard him.

## 247. A Sealed Royal Order

K 14113 + K 14643 (CT 53 560)

1 [*a-n*]*a* LUGAL EN-*ia*
2 [ARAD]-*ka* ^m*na-nu-u*
3 [*lu* D]I-*mu a-na* LUGAL EN-*ia*
4 [*ina* UG]U ^m*me-ṣa-te*—[*i*]*b*!-*ni*
5 [^m*x-x*]*x-na-a ša* LUGAL *be-lí*
6 [*iš-pur-a*]*n-ni pi-ti*! *un-qi* LUGAL
7 [*x x x*] ⌜*x x*⌝ [*x x k*]*a*
rest broken away
Rev. destroyed

CT 53 513+

1 [To] the king, my lord: your [servant] Nanû. [Good] health to the king, my lord!

4 [As t]o Meṣate-[i]bni and [...]nâ about whom the king, my lord, [wrote] me, in accordance with the king's sealed order [......]

(Rest destroyed)

## 248. ———

K 16055 + K 16074

beginning destroyed
1′ ⌜*ša*⌝ *ina x*[*x x x x x*]
2′ *ina* UGU-*hi x*[*x x x x*]
3′ *a-sap-r*[*a x x x x*]
4′ *ša* UN.[MEŠ *x x x x*]
5′ *a-ki ša* [*x x x x*]
6′ *ta-qí-pu-*[*ni x x x*]
7′ *la-ak-l*[*a x x x x x*]
8′ LÚ*.EN—*pi-*[*qit-te x x*]
9′ *ap-ti-*[*qid x x x x*]
10′ *a*[*p x x x x x x*]
rest broken away
Rev. beginning broken away
1′ *ša ma-*[*x x x x x*]

CT 53 730

(Beginning destroyed)

1 which in [...]

2 *on account of it* [...]

3 I wro[te ...]

4 of the people [...]

5 Just as you trust [in ...],

6 I shall hold ba[ck ...]

8 I app[ointed] an offi[cial ...]

(Break)

r.1 of ...[...]

**246** 11, r.3 See coll.
**247** Probably part of the same tablet as no. 248, with a one-line gap between the two fragments. See copy p. 265.
**248** Part of the same tablet as no. 247. r.2 Or *še-b*[*i-la* "send".

2′ ŠE.*tab-k*[*i x x x x x*]
3′ *ina* UG[U *x x x x x*]
4′ ⸢*ú*⸣-[*x x x x x x*]
5′ ⸢*ša*⸣ [*x x x x x x*]
6′ ⸢*x*⸣ [*x x x x x x x*]
7′ *a*-[*x x x x x x x*]
8′ *a*[*s-x x x x x x*]
9′ *i*-[*x x x x x x* ]
rest uninscribed

r.2 stored grain [......]
(Rest too broken for translation)

## 249. Stormy Night

K 1876

beginning broken away
1′ *ina* [*x x x x x x x x*]
2′ URU.MAN—⸢*iq-bi*⸣ *x*[*x x x x*]
3′ *ša* A.MEŠ *ina* ŠÀ-*bi* ⸢*a*⸣-[*x x x*]
4′ *ku-tu-li-šu-nu ša in*[*a x x*]
5′ *ina* ŠÀ-*bi ni-ik-te-ti*-[*ir*]
6′ *ina* MI *ša* UD-4-KAM *šá-a-r*[*u*]
7′ *dan-nu ša a—dan-niš i-z*[*i-qa*]
8′ TÚG.*maš-kan*.MEŠ *gab-bu mi*-[*hu-u*]
9′ *i-ba-áš-ši ú-ta-s*[*i-hi*]
10′ UN.MEŠ *ip-tal-hu a—dan-n*[*iš*]
11′ ANŠE.KUR.MEŠ *ina* ŠÀ-*bi a-ha*-[*iš*]
12′ *it-ta-ad-bu-ku ina* U[GU]
13′ MUL.*kip-pi-te ú-s*[*ar-ri*]
14′ *ina* UGU MUL.*taš-ka*-[*a-ti*]
15′ [*i*]*t-tu-ú-ah* [*x x*]
16′ [ŠÀ-*bu*] *ša* LUGAL EN-[*ia lu* DÙG]
rest broken away
Rev. beginning broken away
1′ ⸢*uk*⸣-*t*[*a-x x x x x x*]
2′ *ina* ŠÀ-*bi* [*x x x x x*]
3′ ⸢*gab-bu*⸣ [*x x x x x*]
4′ ⸢*am-x-u-ni*⸣ [*x x x x x*]
5′ *a-na-ku* [*x x x x x x*]
6′ *ša* DUMU [m]E[N—SUM-*na*? *x x x*]
7′ *ina* UD-4-KAM *ina x*[*x x x x*]
8′ EN.NUN *i-si-šú* [*x x x x*]
9′ *il-lak-u-ni* [*x x x x*]
10′ *iq*-⸢*ṭar-bu*⸣-*u-ni* [*x x x x*]
11′ *i*-[*x x x*]*x x*[*x x x x*]
rest broken away

CT 53 197

(Beginning destroyed)
1 in [......]
2 Šarru-iqbi [......]
3 where there is water [...]
4 their *rear side* [...]
5 We waited there.

6 On the night of the 4th day an extremely strong wind was bl[owing]. The sto[rm] was so (strong) it tor[e off] all the tents; people got panicked, horses piled together making a heap.

12 It started at (the culmination of) the Circle star (Corona) and subsided at (the culmination of) the Triplet star (α Herculis). [*All is well*]; the king, my lord, [*can be at ease.*]

(Break)
r.2 there [......]
3 all [......]
4 ... [......]
5 I [......]
6 of the son of *B*[*el-iddina* ......]
7 on the 4th day in [......]
8 watch with him [......]
9 going [......]
10 arrived [......]
(Rest destroyed)

## 250. Assembling Troops for War and Counting Rations

K 1424 (CT 53 47) + K 4282 (ABL 1290)

1 ⸢*a-na*⸣ L[UGAL *be-lí-ia*]
2 ARAD-*ka* [m*x x x x x*]

CT 53 47+

1 To the k[ing, my lord]: your servant [NN]. Good heal[th to the king, m]y [lord]!

**249** The scribe who wrote this tablet is not identifiable by orthographic and epigraphic analysis. 4 Or "reserves." 14f I.e., about 3.5 hours later, see Schaumberger, ZA 50 (1952) p.228.

**250** The scribe who wrote this tablet is not identifiable by orthographic and epigraphic analysis; cf. r. 24!

3 *lu-u šul-m*[*u a-na* LUGAL *be-lí-i*]*a*
4 UD-2-KAM *ina* U[RU.*kar—*$^{d}$*aš-šur ni-i*]*q*$^{!}$*-ṭi-rib*
5 LÚ.*tur-ta-nu* [*x x x* LÚ.GA]L—KAŠ$^{!}$.LUL$^{!}$
6 $^{m}$*tak-lak—a-na—*E[N $^{m}$HAL-*n*]*i*$^{!}$*—aš-šur*
7 *ù* LÚ.EN.NAM.[MEŠ *ša* URU.*si-ʾi-me*]*-e*
8 URU.*til-e* URU.*gu-za-n*[*a* URU.*i-sa*]*-na*
9 *an-nu-ti šú-nu* LÚ.GAL.MEŠ *š*[*a i-s*]*i*$^{!}$*-ni*$^{!}$
10 *ina* URU.*kar—*$^{d}$*aš-šur iq-ri-bu-u-ni*
11 *ù li-bit* LUGAL *gab-bu*
12 [*x*]*x-li-ih-ti* LÚ.GAL.MEŠ *me-me-ni*
13 [*la iq*]-⸢*ri-ba ki-ṣir* $^{m}$U⸣.[GUR—K]AR$^{!}$-⸢*ir*⸣
14 *pa-*⸢*ni-u*⸣ *ša i-qar-rib-an-ni re-šu*$^{!}$
15 *ni-na-áš-ši šúm-mu* LUGAL *be-lí i-qab-bi*
16 *ma-a sa-*[*d*]*ir-tú si-id-ra* ⸢*ma*$^{!}$*-a*⸣ *ina* UGU
17 ⸢*e*⸣*-mu-qi e-ti-iq an-nu-rig*
18 [LÚ*].GAL—*ki-ṣir-ia ša ina pa-an* LUGAL
19 [*be-lí-i*]*á áš-pu-ra-an-ni*
20 [*x x x x*] ⸢*x*⸣ [AN]ŠE.KUR.RA.MEŠ
21 [*x x x x x x*] *pa-na-tu-uš-šú*
22 [*x x x x x x x x x*]⸢*x*⸣
rest (1-2 lines and edge) broken away
Rev. beginning (1-2 lines) broken away
1′ [*x x x x x x x x*]*x*[*x x x*]
2′ [*x x x*]⸢*x*⸣[*x x x x* L]UGAL *né-p*[*a*$^{!}$*-áš*]
3′ ⸢*ù*⸣ *ina* UGU Š[E$^{!}$.*tab-ki ša* LU]GAL *be-lí*
4′ *iš-pu-ra-an-ni* [*ma-a* ŠE].*tab-ku*
5′ *ša* ITI UD.MEŠ-*te* [*ša* U]RU-*ka še-bi-la-a-ni*
6′ *an-nu-rig* ŠE.*ki-su-tú ša a-ṣap-pi*
7′ *ù* ŠE.*tab-ku ša* UD.MEŠ *ina bat-ta-ta-a-a*
8′ *ni-sa-ṭar ina* UGU LUGAL *be-lí-iá nu-se-bi-la*
9′ 4$^{!}$-*me*-70 ANŠE ŠE.*ki-su-tú* 5-*me*-49$^{!}$ ANŠE 4BÁN
10′ [ŠE.*ta*]*b-ku ša* ERIM$^{!}$.MEŠ PAB 1-*lim*-19 ANŠE 4BÁN *ša* 1 UD-*me*
11′ [*x x x x*]*x* L[Ú] 1-⸢*me*⸣-8$^{!}$ ANŠE ŠE.*ki-su-tú*
12′ ⸢1-*me*-55$^{!}$⸣ AN[ŠE ŠE.*tab*]-*ku ša* ERIM$^{!}$.MEŠ PAB 2-*me*-63 ANŠE 6BÁN
13′ *ša* 1 UD-*me ša* [*x x x*] *ša* URU.MEŠ-*šú-nu*
14′ *ina* ⸢NAM$^{!}$⸣ URU.*la-h*[*i-ri x x x x*]
15′ [PAB 5-*me*-7]8 ANŠE ŠE.[*ki-su-tú ša* 1 UD-*me*]
16′ [17-*lim*-3-*me*]-40 ANŠE ŠE.PAD.MEŠ ⸢*ša* ITI⸣
17′ [PAB 7-*me*-5 ANŠE] ŠE.*tab-ku ša* ERIM.MEŠ *ša* 1 UD-*me*
18′ [21-*lim*-1-*me*-50 A]NŠE ŠE.PAD.MEŠ *ša* ITI
19′ [PAB 38-*lim*-4-*m*]*e*-90 ANŠE ŠE.*ki-su-tú* ŠE$^{!}$.*tab*$^{!}$-⸢*ku*⸣
20′ [*ša* ITI ERIM.MEŠ—L]UGAL$^{!}$ *a-du*$^{!}$ *ša* LÚ.GAL.MEŠ
21′ [*x x x x*]-⸢*su*$^{!}$⸣ *ù ina* UGU *sa*$^{!}$*-dir-te*
22′ [*ša a-na*] LUGAL *be-lí-iá áš-pu-ra-an*$^{!}$*-ni*
23′ [*um-ma* LUGAL] *be-lí i-*[*qab-b*]*i*$^{!}$
24e [*ni-is-dir* L]Ú$^{!}$.A.BA *ša né-m*[*ur*$^{!}$*-u-ni*]
25e [*x x an-n*]*i-tú* ⸢*i-sa*$^{!}$*-ṭar*$^{!}$⸣ [*x x x*]
26e [*x x x*]*x me* [*x x x x x x*]

4 [We ar]rived in [Kar-Aššur] on the 2nd day. The commander-in-chief, [the ..., the chie]f cupbearer, Taklak-ana-Be[l, Išmann]i-Aššur, and the governor[s of Si'imm]ê, Tillê, Guzan[a and Isa]na: these are the magnates w[ho] arrived [with u]s in Kar-Aššur.

11 As for the whole royal entourage and the ... of the magnates, none have arrived. We are readying the first contingent of Ne[rgal-e]ṭir which is arriving, just in case the king, my lord, should say: "Draw up the battle array and proceed *against* the army!"

17 Right now the cohort commander of mine whom I sent to the king, [m]y [lord, ...] horses [...] in front of him [......]

(Break)

r.2 We are d[oing the k]ing['s work].

3 And as to the sto[red grain concerning which the ki]ng, my lord, wrote me: ["Send me (data on) the sto]red grain (consumed) by your [*ci*]*ty* in a calendar month!" — we have now itemized the daily (consumption) of pack-animal fodder and stored grain, and are herewith sending (this information) to the king, my lord:

9 470 homers of fodder, 549 homers 4 seahs of [sto]red grain for soldiers, in all 1,019 homers 4 seahs daily, [......].

11 108 homers of fodder, 155 ho[mers 6 seahs of sto]red grain for soldiers, in all 263 homers 6 seahs daily, which [...] and their cities [...] in the province of Lah[iru].

15 [In all, 57]8 homers of [fodder daily], making [17,3]40 homers of grain rations per month; [in all 705 homers] of stored grain for soldiers daily, (making) [21,150 ho]mers of grain rations per month; [all told, 38,4]90 homers of fodder and stored grain [per month for the k]ing's [men], plus what the magnates [...].

21 And as regards the battle array [of which] I wrote [to] the king, my lord, [if the king], my lord, so or[der]s, [we shall draw it up].

24 A scribe se[lected] by us wro[te th]is [*letter*].

(Rest destroyed)

4ff, 9, 13f, 16, r.2f, 9f, 13f, 20ff, 25 See coll.

# 251. Reviewing Cavalry and Chariot Troops

K 946 + K 15639 (CT 53 797)

1 *a-n*[*a* LUGAL *be-lí-ia*]
2 ARAD-[*ka* $^{m}$*x x x x*]
3 *lu* [DI-*mu a-na* LUGAL EN-*ia*]
4 [*ina* UGU LÚ.*ša*—BAD-HAL.MEŠ]
5 [*ša* LUGAL *be-lí*]
6 [*ṭè-e-mu*]
7 *iš-ku-na-*[*an-ni*]
8 *a-ta-š*[*ar-šú-nu*]
9 1-*me*-6 LÚ*.*š*[*a*!—BAD-HAL.MEŠ]
10 *am-ru-te* ⸢9⸣[4! LAL-*e*]
11 *ša* ŠU.2 $^{md}$[*x x x*]
12 LÚ*.*šak-ni in*[*a* UGU]
13 LÚ*.EN—GIŠ.GIGIR.MEŠ LU[GAL] *be-lí*
14 *ṭè-e-mu la iš-*[*k*]*u-na-an-ni*
15 TA LÚ*.*ša*—BAD-[HAL.ME]Š-*ma*
16 *a-ta-šar-šú-nu*
r.1 10 LÚ*.EN—GIŠ.GIGIR.MEŠ
2 21 LÚ*.ERIM—MAN-*šú-nu*
3 PAB 31 LÚ*.EN—GIŠ.GIGIR.MEŠ
4 *am-ru-te* 6⸢9⸣ [LA]L-*e*
5 *ša* ŠU.2 $^{m}$*tu-t*[*i-i* LÚ*.*mu*]-*šár-kis*
6 1-*me*-50 ANŠE.KU[R.RA.MEŠ]
7 *ú-tu-si-i*[*k x x x*]
8 *an-nu-rig* [*x x x*]
rest uninscribed

ABL 567+

1 To [the king, my lord: your] servant [NN]. Good [health to the king, my lord]!

4 [As to the cavalrymen about whom the king, my lord], gave [me orders], I have revie[wed them]: 106 [cavalry]men seen, 9[4 missing], under the command of the prefect [NN].

13 The ki[ng], my lord, gave me no orders re[garding] the chariot owners, but I have reviewed them too along with the ca[valry]: 10 chariot owners, 21 of their king's men, in all 31 chariot owners seen, 69 [miss]ing, under the command of the [recru]itment officer Tut[î].

r.7 I have assigned 150 hor[ses ...];
8 now [...].

FIG. 36. *Cavalry in action (reign of Sennacherib).*
ORIGINAL DRAWING I, 70.

## 252. ⸺

K 10913

    beginning broken away
1'  [x x x x x x x]x a [x x]
2'  [x x x x x x-ta]l-ka [x]
3'  [x x x x x x x] nam [x x]
4'  [x x x x x x x] ⌈x⌉ [x x]
5'  [x x x x x x x x x x]
6'  [x x x x x x x x x x]
7'  [x x x x x x x x x] x[x]
8'  [x x x x x x LÚ*].⌈A⌉—šip-ri-i[a]
9'  [x x x x x x t]a-hu-ma-[ni]
10'  [x x x x x x x] LUGAL [be-lí]
11'  [x x x x x x x]x x[x x]
    rest broken away
Rev.  beginning broken away
1'  [x x x x x x UR]U.arrap-ha
2'  [x x x x lu?-š]á-aṣ-bi-t[u]
3'  [x x x x x x]x
4'  [x x x x x GI]Š.nar-kab-tu
5'  [x x x x x x]-⌈tan⌉-na
6'  [x x x x x x x]-lam
7'  [x x x x x] ⌈a⌉-tan-na
    rest uninscribed

CT 53 420

(Beginning destroyed)

8  [......] my messenger
9  [...... the b]order[s]
10  [......] the king, [my lord]
(Break)
r.1  [......] Arrapha
2  [......] they [should] provide
3  [......]
4  [......] the chariot
5  [...... g]ave
6  [......]
7  [...] I have given [...]

## 253. Beams from the Zagros

K 7389

beginning broken away
1′ [*x x*] *x*[*x x x x x x x x*]
2′ [*ina*] ⸢U⸣GU LÚ.[*x x x x x x x*]
3′ GIŠ.*mi-ih-r*[*i x x x x x x*]
4′ URU.*arrap-ha-a-*[*a x x x x x*]
5′ GIŠ.ÙR.MEŠ *ša* ⸢*a-na*⸣ [*x x x x x*]
6′ GIŠ.*ṣar-bu-tú x*[*x x x x x*]
7′ 2-*me* GIŠ.ÙR.MEŠ [*x x x x x*]
8′ [*a*]*t-ta-at-ha* [*x x x x x x*]
9′ [*x x*] ⸢*a*⸣-*ta-*[*x x x x x x x*]
rest broken away
Rev. beginning broken away
1′ ⸢TA*⸣ ŠÀ-*bi-šú-nu* [*x x x x x*]
2′ *li-di-nu-ni* [*x x x x x x x*]
3′ *ina har-*⸢*pu*⸣*-ti* [*x x x x x x*]
4′ ⸢*x*⸣ [*x x x x x x x x*]
rest broken away

CT 53 343

(Beginning destroyed)

2 [As] to the [......]
3 *mihru* tree [......]
4 Arraphaeans [......]
5 the beams which to [......]
6 poplar tree [......]
7 I have fetched 200 beams [......]
(Break)

r.1 from their midst [......]
2 let them give me [......]
3 in early [......]
(Rest destroyed)

## 254. Logdriving in Isana

Sm 339

beginning broken away
1′ [*x x x x*] ⸢*at*⸣ [*x x*]
2′ [*x x x x*] *i-za-z*[*u-ni*]
3′ [*aq-ṭi-ba-á*]*š-šú* :. :. *nu-u*[*k*]
4′ [TA*] ⸢ŠÀ⸣ LÚ*.ARAD.MEŠ-*ka*
5′ ⸢*še*⸣*-bi-la* :. *ina* IGI-*ia*
6′ *li-zi-zi* :. *la i-ma-gúr*
7′ *la ú-še-ba-la*
8′ *ina* UGU KUR.*ra-ṣa-pa-a-a*
9′ EN—*pi-qi-ti* : *ša* LUGAL EN
10′ *iš-pur-an-ni* : *ma pu-ṭu-ur-šú*
11′ *i-si-ka* : *li-du-lu*
12′ ⸢*a*⸣*-sa-ap-ra* :. *ina* UGU
13′ [L]Ú.*šá*—UGU—É *ša* L[Ú.EN.NAM]
14′ [*š*]*a* URU.*kal-ha* : *la* [*i-ma-gúr*]
15′ [*l*]*a i-ba-ṭar-*[*šú x x*]
16′ [*a-n*]*a*! *ša-šú* :. *la* [*x x x*]
e.17′ [*x x*] ⸢*i*⸣ *x*[*x x x x x*]
18′ [*x x x x x x x x x*]
Rev. lines 1-2 destroyed
3 [*ina* U]GU ⸢*x*⸣ [*x x x x x*]
4 ⸢2⸣5 GIŠ.Ù[R.MEŠ *x x x*]
5 [*ina* UG]U ÍD :. ⸢*ú*⸣-[*x x x*]
6 [GIŠ.Ù]R.MEŠ [*x x x*]
7 [*x x x*]*x-tú mu-x*[*x x x*]
8 [*x x x*]*x gi-il-*⸢*te*?⸣
9 [*x* URU].⸢*i*⸣*-sa-na-a-a*
10 [*x x x*] *ina pu-tú-u-a*
11 [*x x x i*]*-ma-tú-hu*

CT 53 126

(Beginning destroyed)

2 [......] standing [in ......]

3 [I told] him: "Send me one [of] your subjects, to stay in my presence," but he has not agreed to send me one.

8 As to Raṣappayu, the official concerning whom the king, my lord, wrote to me: "Release him, and let him serve with you!" I have written to the household overseer of the [governor o]f Calah, but he has not [agreed] to release [him, *so I have*] not [*hired*] him.

(Break)

r.3 [As t]o [......], I *am b*[*ringing*] 25 log[s ... t]o the river. [The l]ogs [......]

(Break)

9 [...] Isanaeans [......] opposite me will pick up [*the logs*].

**254** r.16 See coll.

12 [*x x x*] ⸢*i*⸣-*qab-bi*
13 [*ma-a* GIŠ].ÙR.MEŠ *ina* ŠÀ
14 [URU.*i-sa*]-*na*! : *kar-ru*
15 [md*x*—*x*.M]EŠ!—AŠ *ina* UGU-*hi*
16 [*a-s*]*a*!-*ap*-⸢*ra*!⸣
17 [*x x x x x x*] *x*[*x x*]
rest broken away

12 [*Should the king*] say: "[There are l]ogs piled up in [Isa]na," [I have se]nt [...]-iddina for [them ......]
(Rest destroyed)

# 255. Transport of Beams

K 14655

beginning broken away
1′ [*x x x x*] *hi* [*x x x*]
2′ [*x x x x*] GIŠ.MEŠ ⸢*šá*⸣ *ina* IGI-[*x*]
3′ [*x x x x*] ⸢Í⸣D-*ma*
4′ [*x x uq-ṭ*]*a-ri-bu*
5′ [*x x x* KUR].*ta-ba-li*
6′ [*x x x x*] *it-bu-uk*
7′ [*x x x x*]*x-ba-a-ti*
8′ [*x x x x x x x*]-*ti*
rest broken away
Rev. destroyed

CT 53 569

(Beginning destroyed)

2 [...] the trees which are at [my/his] disposal [...]
3 [...] the river
4 [they b]rought
5 [...] Tabal
6 [...] he has piled up [...]
(Rest destroyed)

# 256. Problems with Sheep

K 4277

beginning broken away
1′ [*lu-u* DI]-*mu a*-[*na* LUGAL EN-*ia*]
2′ [*ina* UG]U! UDU.MEŠ *š*[*a x x ša* LUGAL]
3′ [*be-lí*] *iš-pur-a*-[*ni*]
4′ [*ma-a*] ⸢*a*⸣-*ta-a* ⸢UDU⸣.MEŠ TA* Š[À *x x*]
5′ [*t*]*a-ka-la*-⸢*ši*⸣ LUGAL *be*-[*lí*]
6′ [U]DU.MEŠ *a-na* DINGIR.MEŠ-*ni-šu ik*-[*ta-la*]
7′ [*š*]*úm-ma ina* UGU-*hi la ú-ra*-⸢*da*⸣
8′ *re-ʾi-šu-nu-u a-kal-la*
9′ mdPA—NUMUN—AŠ *ina pa-ni-ia*
10′ ⸢*i*⸣-*ti-it-zi ma-a* m*ša*—DINGIR!—*du-bu*
11′ [U]DU.MEŠ *uk-ta-ši-di*
12′ [*ma*]-*a* 1-*lim*-3-*me* UDU.MEŠ *ṣu-ʾu-bat*
13′ [*x x*]*x an-nu-ti* ⸢*x x x*⸣[*x*]*x*
rest broken away
Rev. beginning broken away
1′ [*x x x*]-⸢*da*!⸣-*a*ʾ *iq-ṭi*-[*ba-šú-nu*]
2′ [*ma-a al*]-*ka-ni ra*!-*ʾi*-[*a* (*x*)]
3′ [*x x x*]*x ni i*⸢*s*⸣ *ṭè-e*-[*mu*]
4′ [*liš-ku-nu*]-*šu-nu* [*šú*]*m-ma* ŠÀ MAN! [0]
5′ [*ina* KUR.*m*]*u*!-*da-bar*! É UDU.MEŠ-*i*⸢*a*⸣
6′ [*i-ra*]-*ʾu-u-ni* UDU.MEŠ
7′ [*x x*].MEŠ *pa*-⸢*na*⸣-*tu-šú-nu li-ri-ʾu*

ABL 1288

[To the king, my lord: your servant NN. Good heal]th t[o the king, my lord]!

2 [As] to the sheep of [... about which the king, my lord], wrote [me]: "Why do [yo]u withhold the sheep fr[om ...]?" —

5 it is the king, [my] lo[rd], who has wi[thheld] the [sh]eep for his gods! If he does not add to them, (how) can I hold back their shepherds?

9 Nabû-zeru-iddina had an audience with me, saying: "Ša-ili-dubbu has driven away [she]ep; 1,300 *ṣuʾbu* sheep

13 [...] these [......]

(Break)

r.1 [...-ya]da' sa[id to *them*]: "[Co]me and graze!"

3 [Let ... give] them or[ders; i]f it pleases the king, let them graze the sheep and [*goats*] at their disposal [in the s]teppe, where my sheep [are being g]razed.

**256** 2, 5, 10, r.1f, 4f See coll. Reading Ša-*Aššur*-dubbu in line 10 excluded.

8′ [*ša* LUGAL *be*]-*lí ina* UGU $^{md}$PA—NUMUN—AŠ
9′ [*iq-bu-ni ma*]-⌜*a*⌝ *ki-i ina pa-an* ARAD.[MEŠ-*x*]
10′ [*x x x*]*x-ni ma-a i-x*[*x x x*]
11′ [*x x x*]*x iq-ṭi-ba*-[*šú-nu ma-a*]
12′ [*x x x x*].MEŠ *ša* [*x x x x*]
rest broken away

8 [As to what the king], my [lo]rd, [said] about Nabû-zeru-iddina: "When he [...] before [...] servant[s ...], he said [to them ...]
(Rest destroyed)

## 257. Sheep from Dur-Yakin

81-2-4,94

beginning broken away
1′ [*x x x x x x x x x x*]*x*
2′ *a-x*[*x x*] *ša-ku-lu a*-⌜*sa*⌝-[*par*? *ina*] UGU-*hi*
3′ UDU.MEŠ *an-nu-te ša* LÚ*.*um-ma-ni*
4′ *ša* TA* URU.BÀD—*ia-ki-ni*
5′ *ú-ṣu-ni-ni šú-nu a-na* LÚ*.GAL—10.MEŠ-*te*
6′ *ša* URU.BÀD—*ia-ki-na-a-a*
7′ *ina* UGU-*hi-šú-nu e-rab-u-ni*
8′ *ip-taq-du ma-a* 2-*a-a* ERIM.MEŠ
9′ *ina* ŠÀ-*bi-šú-nu pi-iq-da*
10′ *li-ir-ʾu-ú-šú-nu*
11′ *a-di* PAB.MEŠ-*ku-nu*
e.12′ *il-lak-u-ni-ni*
r.1 *i-da-nu-ni-šú-nu*
2 *ú-ma-a* LUGAL *iq-ṭí-bi*
3 TA* IGI *gab-bi-šú-nu*
4 *ni-mah-har ina* UGU LÚ*.UŠ—IGI.DUB
5 *ša* LUGAL *be-lí iq-bu-ni*
6 *ma-a lil-li-ka* URUDU.MEŠ
7 *ša* ARAD.MEŠ *ša* LÚ*-GAL.MEŠ *i-ma-su-ni*
8 GIŠ.*qab-li-tú ina pa-ni-šú*
9 *a-na-ku ina* URU.*ni-nu-a a-na-ku*
10 [*a-k*]*an-ni at-ta-har-šú-ma*
11 [*ina* IGI] LUGAL EN-*ia ú-se-bi-la-šú*

ABL 867

(Beginning destroyed)
2 [...] *are being fed*. I have *wr*[*itten* ab]out these sheep of the scholars, which came forth from Dur-Yakin; they have entrusted them to the commanders-of-ten to whom the Dur-Yakinites are entering, saying:
8 "Appoint two men each from among them to graze them, until your brothers come and give them out."

r.2 Now that the king gave the command, we shall receive them from all of them.
4 As to the *attendant* of the treasurer about whom the king, my lord, said: "He should come" —
6 the copper which is being refined by the servants of the magnates, (as well as) the ... are at his disposal, and I have been in Nineveh.
10 I have now received him and sent him [to] the king, my lord.

## 258. Supplying Oxen and Sheep

K 1426 + K 16478 (CT 53 766)

beginning broken away
1′ [LÚ*.EN].NA[M *ša* KUR.*x x*]
2′ 1-⌜*me* GUD⌝.MEŠ *e*-⌜*ri*⌝-[*iš*]
3′ LÚ*.EN.NAM *ša* KUR.*si*-[*ʾi-me-e*]
4′ 2-*me* GUD.MEŠ 2-*lim* UDU.M[EŠ]
5′ *e-ri-ša-an-ni*
6′ *ú-ma-a š*[*úm-ma*] LUGAL *be*-[*lí*]
7′ *i-qa*-[*bi x x x*]
rest broken away
Rev. destroyed

CT 53 517+

(Beginning destroyed)
1 [The gov]ern[or of ...] has as[ked *me*] for 100 oxen; the governor of Si['immê] has asked me for 200 oxen and 2,000 sheep. Now, i[f] the king, [my] lo[rd] ord[ers, ......]
(Rest destroyed)

FIG. 37. *Supplies of oxen and sheep (reign of Sennacherib).*
ORIGINAL DRAWING VI, 5.

## 259. Distributing Provisions

K 13085

1′ ⸢É⸣ [*x* ANŠE A.ŠÀ *x x*]
2′ *ab-t*[*a-taq x x x x*]
3′ *a-ta-na-*⸢*áš*⸣*-*[*ši-na x x x*]
4′ ŠE.NUMUN.MEŠ-*ši-n*[*a me-me-ni*?]
5′ *ina* ŠÀ-*bi la-a-*[*šu x x*]
6′ 1-*me* ŠE.PAD.MEŠ [*x x x*]
7′ ⸢*ku*⸣-*um* ŠE.NUMUN.MEŠ-[*ši-na*]
8′ ⸢*i*⸣-*ti-ši-*[*a* 0]
r.1 [*x x*]*x ina* URU.*za-ba*[*n x x x*]
2 [*ina*] *qa-an-n*[*i x x x x x*]
3 DUMU.MÍ *ina* [*x x x x x*]
4 *a-ta-n*[*a-x x x x x*]
5 [*x*]*x x*[*x x x x x x*]
rest broken away

CT 53 480

(Beginning destroyed)

1 I *pa*[*rceled out*] a plot [*of x hectares of field in* ...] and gave (it) [to them ...].

4 They had no seed corn [*whatever*] there, (so) they took 100 (homers) of barley [*from* ...] instead of [*their*] seed corn.

r.1 [The ...] in Zabba[n ...]
2 outside [...]
3 *my* daughter in [...]
4 I *ga*[*ve* ......]
(Rest destroyed)

## 260. Insults and Accusations

K 1438

1′ [*x x*]⸢*x x*⸣[*x x x x x x x*]
2′ *ša* LUGAL EN-⸢*i*⸣[*a*!] ⸢*lu*?⸣-*x*[*x x x*]
3′ LÚ*.DUMU—*šip-ri-ia a-sa-pa-*[*ra*]
4′ LÚ*.DUMU—*šip-ri-ia ih-t*[*i-si*]
5′ *ma-a a-ta-a* UGU LÚ*.ARAD.MEŠ-*ni*
6′ *ša* LUGAL *ta-da-bu-bu*
7′ *ma-a na-ka-ra-ka i-si-ku-nu*
8′ *ma-a i-na* KUR.*ma-ti-ia*
9′ *i-na na-gi-ia-a la tú-ra-da*
10′ *ma-a re-hu-ti la ú-ra-*⸢*ma*⸣-*ka*
11′ A.ŠÀ.MEŠ É.MEŠ *ina* ⸢UGU!⸣ *x*[*x x x*]
12′ *in-ta-a*ʾ-*da* [*x x x x*]
13′ [*š*]*a*? LUGAL *x*[*x x x x x*]
rest broken away

Rev. beginning broken away
1′ ⸢TA*! *pa-an*⸣ LUGAL EN-*ia a-*[*x x x*]
2′ *ma-a hi-bi-la-te-ka mar ih-b*[*il-u-ka-ni*]
3′ [*l*]*i*!-*di-na-ka a-bat* LUGAL
4′ *la-a iš-me hi-bi-la-te-ia*
5′ [*l*]*a*!-*a i-di-na* TA* É LUGAL
6′ *be-lí a-hu-ru-u-ni* LÚ*.ARAD.MEŠ-*ni*
7′ *ša* LUGAL *be-lí-ia* É *i-ma-ru-ni*
8′ *i-du-ka i-ha-bat* KASKAL.MEŠ LUGAL.MEŠ-*ni*
9′ *ú-sa-ha-ri*!-*ri a-na-ku*
10′ TA* É *la ú-ṣa* UGU *du-a-ki-ia*
11′ *i-da-bu-bu* : *ú-ma-a*
12′ *pa-an* LUGAL E[N!-*ia x x x*]
rest broken away

ABL 463

(Beginning destroyed)

2 [......] of the king, my lord.

3 I sen[t] my messenger, but he insu[lted] my messenger, saying: "Why do you plot against the king's subjects? I am at war with you, do not come down to my country and my district! I will not release the rest to you!"

11 The [...] have amassed fields and houses [...]

12 [o]f the king [......]

(Break)

r.1 I [*was notified*] by the king my lord's court: "He should repay you the debts that he ow[es you]." He has not obeyed the king's order though, and has [n]ot paid his debt to me; from the moment I appealed to the king, my lord, he has been killing and robbing the king my lord's servants wherever he sees them, laying waste the king's roads.

9 I cannot leave my house; he is plotting to kill me. [*I am*] now [*on my way*] to the king, [my] lo[rd ......]

(Rest destroyed)

## 261. Dividing the Booty

K 7797

beginning destroyed
1′ [*x x x x*] ⸢*x*⸣ [*x x x*]
2′ ⸢3⸣-*lim*-3-*me*-50 L[Ú.ZI.MEŠ]
3′ ⸢TA*⸣ URU.⸢DU6!⸣—*da*-[*x x*]
4′ *a*-⸢*di*⸣ URU.*sa*-⸢*za*⸣-*n*[*a-a*]
5′ ⸢*ni-ib*⸣-*ti-ar* ⸢m!⸣EN—[*x x*]
6′ [m*x x x*]-*ni* m*gab-bu—ana—aš-šur* [0]
7′ [m*x x x x*]*x* mI—DINGIR
balance destroyed

Rev. beginning destroyed
1′ [*x x x*] LUGAL [*x x x*]
2′ ⸢m!⸣*mu-sa*-⸢*ni*⸣ [*x*]
3′ LÚ*.*qe-pu ša* URU.*x*[*x x*]
4′ *ina* É-*šú* N[Á]
5′ ⸢*a-na*⸣-*ku* 9BÁN 7 [*qa x x*]
balance destroyed

CT 53 398

(Beginning destroyed)

2 We have selected 3,350 p[eople]

3 from Til-da[...]

4 as far as Sazan[â].

5 *Bel*-[...],

6 [NN], Gabbu-ana-Aššur,

7 [NN], Na'di-ilu

(Break)

r.1 [...] the king [...]

2 Musan[i],

3 the legate of [...]

4 sleeps in his house.

5 I [...] 9 seahs 7 [litres ...]

(Rest destroyed)

**260** 2, 11, r.1, 9 See coll.
**261** 2, r.2 See coll.

## 262. ———

K 15606

beginning broken away
1′ [*x x x x*] *a*[*l x x x*]
2′ [*ina* UG]U $^{md}$PA—*x*[*x x x*]
3′ [*x x*] ⸢LÚ*⸣.A—*šip-ri-šú* [*x x x*]
4′ [*ma*] *a*-⸢*a*⸣-*ʾu* [*x x x x x*]
5′ [T]A *x*[*x x x x x x x*]
6′ [*l*]*a ir-x*[*x x x x x x*]
7′ LÚ*.*qur*-⸢*bu*⸣-[*tú*] ⸢*x*⸣ *x*[*x x x*]
8′ [*m*]*a-a ina* ŠÀ-*bi* UR[U.*x x x x*]
9′ [*x*]*x qa te* [*x x x x x*]
rest broken away
Rev. destroyed

CT 53 676

(Beginning destroyed)

2 [*As t*]*o* Nabû-[......]
3 [...] his messenger [..., saying]:
4 "*What* [......]
(Break)
7 The royal bodygu[ard ......]
8 "In the ci[ty ......]
9 ... [......]
(Rest destroyed)

## 263. Arrival of Rams

81-2-4,100

beginning broken away
1′ [*x x x*]⸢*x x x*⸣[*x x*]
2′ [*š*]*a* LUGAL *be-lí iš-pur-*[*an-ni*]
3′ *ina* ŠÀ-*bi* UD-*mi ša e-gír-t*[*ú*]
4′ *pa-ni-tú ta-li-kan-ni*
5′ *a-sa-par ú-ba-lu-ni-šú*
6′ *ina* UGU UDU.NITÁ.MEŠ *li-mi*
7′ *ša* LUGAL *be-lí iš-pur-an-ni*
8′ *an-nu-rig ina* ŠU.2
9′ LÚ*.DUMU—*šip-ri-ia ú-se-bi-la*
10′ *ina* UGU $^{m}$*qur-di*—$^{d}$1[5]
11′ [L]Ú.*ma-hi-ṣi ša* LUGAL [*be-lí*]
12′ [*i*]*š-pur-an-ni ma-a* ŠÀ [*šá-áš-kin-šú*]
13′ [É] GIŠ.APIN A.ŠÀ *a*-[*x x*]
14′ [*x x x*]⸢*x x x*⸣[*x x*]
rest broken away
Rev. destroyed

ABL 1206

(Beginning destroyed)

2 [As to NN about wh]om the king, my lord, wrote [me], I had sent word on the very day that the previous lette[r] arrived: they are bringing him.

6 As to the 1,000 rams about which the king, my lord, wrote me, I am herewith sending them over with my messenger.

10 As to Qurdi-Iss[ar], the *archer* about whom the king, [my lord, wr]ote me: "*Encou*[*rage him, and give him a house*], a plough, and a field [......]"

(Rest destroyed)

**263** [1] See coll.

FIG. 38. *Rams and sheep (reign of Sennacherib).* ORIGINAL DRAWING VI, 7.

## 264. ———

Sm 1872

beginning broken away
1′ [*x x x x x x x x*] ⸢*iq-ṭi-bi*⸣
2′ [*x* LÚ*.*i-t*]*u-ʾa-a-a ša* LÚ*.2-*e*
3′ [*x x x x*] LÚ.SIPA *sa-kul-la-te*
4′ [*x x x* LÚ*].*da-a-a-li* TA* ŠÀ-*bi*
5′ [*x x x pa-n*]*i-u-te a-na* EN.NUN-*šú-nu*
6′ [*x x x x* U]N.MEŠ SUM-*ka-nu-ni*
7′ [*x x x x x*] *ša* É $^{m}$*ba-bu-*[*u*]
8′ [*x x x x x x*]*x bir* KUR [*x x x*]
rest broken away
Rev. destroyed, except for right edge:
1′ [*x x x x x x x x x x x x x*]-*a*
2′ [*x x x x x x x x x x x x x*]*x*
3′ [*x x x x x x x x x x x x-d*]*a-ni-šu*

CT 53 856

(Beginning destroyed)
1 [...] said:
2 ["... the I]tu'eans of the deputy
3 [......] herdsman
4 [...] scouts from [the pre]vious
5 [... *have gone*] to their *garrison*
6 [...... who] give/gave people to you
7 [...] of the house of Babû
8 [......] ... the country [......]
(Reverse too broken for translation)

## 265. Cherchez la Femme

79-7-8,262

1 *a-na* L[UGAL *be-lí-ia*]
2 ARAD-*ka* $^{m}$[*x x x x x*]
3 *a-na* UGU $^{m}$*x*[*x x x x*]
4 *ša* LUGAL *be-l*[*í iš-pur-an-ni*]
5 *ma-a šá-a-la* [*ú-ṣi-ṣi*]
6 *ma-a man-nu* MÍ.M[EŠ *x x x*]
7 *ša a-na* ŠÀ-*b*[*i x x x*]
8 ⸢*a-ta*⸣-*a a-*[*x x x x*]
9 [*x x x x x x x x x*]
10 *ir-*[*x x x x x x x x*]
11 *i-*⸢*x*⸣[*x x x x x x*]
rest broken away
Rev. beginning broken away
1′ *ú-*[*x x x x x x x*]
rest uninscribed

CT 53 882

1 To the ki[ng, my lord]: your servant [NN].

3 As to [NN] about whom the king, [my] lord, [wrote to me]:

5 "Ask [and investigate] who [...] the [...] women who [...] t[o ...]! Why [......]?"

(Rest too broken for translation)

## 266. Fragment Referring to Public Works

K 15380

1 *a-na* LUG[AL *be-lí-ia*]
2 ARAD-*ka* [$^{m}$*x x x x x*]
3 $dul_6$-*lu š*[*a x x x x*]
4 $dul_6$-*lu* [*x x x x x*]
5 ⸢*ša*⸣ [*x x x x x x*]
rest broken away
Rev. beginning broken away
1′ ⸢$dul_6$?⸣-[*lu x x x x x*]
2′ $dul_6$-*l*[*u x x x x x*]
3′ *ina* ŠÀ-*b*[*i x x x x*]
4′ (upside down) [*x x x x x x*] *hu*? *e*

CT 53 651

1 To the ki[ng, my lord]: your servant [NN].

3 The work o[n ...] and the work [...], which [......]

(Break)

r.1 the wo[rk ...],
2 the wor[k ...],
3 *in* [......]
(Rest destroyed)

**265** 3ff The fragment CT 53 819 may refer to the same royal order, cf. ibid. obv.2′ff: *ša* LUGAL *be-*[*lí ṭè-e-mu*] *iš-ku-n*[*a-an-ni-ni*] *ma-a* ⸢*ša*⸣-*a*[*l ú-ṣi-ṣi*] *ma-a man-nu* [MÍ.MEŠ? *x x*].

## 267. Fragment Concerning Public Works

K 15090

1 [*a-na* LUGAL EN-*ia*]
2 ARAD-*k*[*a* $^{m}$*x x x x x*]
3 *lu* DI-*mu a*-[*na* LUGAL EN-*ia*]
4 *ina* UD-11-KAM *ša* I[TI.*x x x*]
5 [*d*]*ul*$_6$-*lu gab-bu š*[*a x x x x x*]
6 [*x a-d*]*u*$^{?}$ UD$^{!}$-20-[KAM *x x x x x*]
rest broken away
Rev. destroyed
s.1 [*x x x x x x x x x x*]*x x*[*x x x*]
2 [*x x x x x x x x x x*]*x e-ta*[*m-ru*]
3 [*mi-nu ša* LUGAL *be-lí i-qa-bu-u-ni liš*]-*pa-ru*-[*ni*]

CT 53 617

1 [To the king, my lord]: yo[ur] servant [NN]. Good health t[o the king, my lord]!

4 On the 11th of [...]
5 the whole [w]ork o[n ...]
6 [... un]til the 20[th ...]
(Break)

s.2 [......] they s[aw ...].
3 [*Let them wr*]*ite* [*me what the king my lord's orders are*].

## 268. Refusal to Transport Saplings

Sm 1231

1 [*a-na* LUGAL$^{?}$]
2 *be*-⌜*lí*⌝-[*iá*]
3 ARAD-*ka* [$^{m}$*x x x x*]
4 *ina* UGU *x*[*x x x x x*]
5 *ša* TA* [É.GAL$^{?}$ *x x x*]
6 *iš-pur*-[*u-ni-ni x x*]
7 GIŠ.*zi*[*q-pi x x x*]
8 *qur*-[*bu x x x x*]
9 URU.ME[Š *x x x x x*]
10 *gab-bu* [*x x x x x*]
11 *ú-dan*-[*x x x x x*]
12 *la-áš*-[*šú x x x x*]
13 *la i-ma*-[*gur*$^{?}$ *x x x*]
14 LÚ*.[*x x x x x x*]
e.15 *la i*-[*x x x x x*]
16 GIŠ.*ziq*-[*pi x x x x*]
r.1 *ma-a e*-[*x x x x x*]
2 *ina pa*-[*x x x x x*]
3 *ma-a k*[*a-x x x x x*]
4 *la ni*-[*x x x x x*]
5 *ma za-ku*-⌜*a*⌝-[*ni x x x*]
6 LÚ*.GAR-*nu* [*x x x x*]
7 *ha-na-k*[*a x x x x*]
8 *ṭè-mu x*[*x x x x x*]
9 *ku-mu za-k*[*u-ti*$^{?}$ *x x x*]
10 LÚ*.GAR-*nu* [*x x x x x*]
11 *liš-pur* [*x x x x x*]
12 ⌜*x x*⌝ [*x x x x x*]
last line destroyed

CT 53 836

1 [To *the king*, my] lord: your servant [NN].

4 As to [the *saplings*] about which they wr[ote to me] from [the Palace ..., ...] sapl[ings of ...] are [now] avail[able ...].

9 The towns [......]
10 all [......]
11 ...[......]
12 [They] absolutely [...] refu[se to obey me]; they do not [...] the [... *and do not transport*] the sapl[ings], saying: "[......]
(Break)

r.4 "We shall not [......, w]e are exempt [......]."
6 The prefect [......]
7 her[e ......]
8 an order [......].
9 Instead of exe[mpted men ...], the prefect should send [......].

**267** 6 See coll.
**268** r.2 Restore *ina pa*-[*ni*- or *pa*-[*na-tu*-.

## 269. Delivery of Barley

K 7334

1 [*a-na* LUGAL *be-lí-ia*]
2 [ARAD-*k*]*a* [$^{m}$*x x x x x*]
3 [*lu* D]I-*mu* [*a-na* LUGAL EN-*ia*]
4 [*ša*] LUGAL *be-lí* [*iš-pur-an-ni*]
5 [*ma*]-*a* ŠE.PAD.MEŠ *ša* [*x x x*]
6 [*š*]*a ina pa-ni-*[*ka*]
7 [*ma*]-⸢*a*⸣ *a-na* $^{m}$*ki-ṣi*[*r—aš-šur*]
8 [*di*]-*ni* 7-*lim* ŠE.P[AD.MEŠ]
9 [*ina* GI]Š.BÁN *ša* 6 *qa ina* [*pa-ni-ia*]
10 [$^{m}$*man*]-*nu—ki—arba-ìl* L[Ú$^{?}$.*x x*]
11 [*ù*] LÚ*.A.BA.MEŠ [*x x ša*]
12 [*i-l*]*i-ku-ni-ni si-*[*x x x*]
13 [*x x*]*x it-tah-ṣ*[*u x x x*]
14 [*x* LUG]AL EN [*x x x x*]
rest broken away
Rev. destroyed

CT 53 324

1 [To the king, my lord: y]our [servant NN. Go]od health [to the king, my lord]!

4 [As to what] the king, my lord, [wrote me]: "[Gi]ve Ki[ṣir-Aššur] the barley of [... wh]ich is at [your] disposal!" –

8 there are 7,000 (homers) of ba[rley, (measured) by a s]eah of 6 litres, at [my disposal].

10 [Man]nu-ki-Arbail, the [...] official, [and] the [...] scribes [who ca]me here *hit* the [......]

14 [the ki]ng, [my] lord [......]

(Rest destroyed)

## 270. ———

Sm 770

1 [*a-na* LUGAL EN$^{!}$-*ia*]
2 [ARAD-*ka* $^{m}$*x x x x*]
3 [*lu* DI-*mu*] *a-*[*na* LUGAL EN-*ia*]
4 [DI-*mu*] *a-n*[*a x x x*]
lines 5-8 destroyed
9 ⸢*x*⸣ [*x x x x x x x*]
10 ANŠ[E$^{?}$.*x x x x x x x*]
11 LUGA[L *x x x x x x x*]
12 *la-a* [*x x x x x x x*]
13 LÚ*.*i-t*[*u-ʾu-u x x x*]
14 *i-si-ia* [*x x x x x*]
15 *i-sa-par* [*x x x x x*]
16 [*i*]-*si-k*[*a x x x x x*]
17 [*x*] ⸢*i*⸣-*da-*[*x x x x x*]
18 [*x*] *ana-ku x*[*x x x x x*]
19 [*x x*] *la* [*x x x x x*]
e.20 [*x*] *i-*[*x x x x x x*]
Rev. beginning broken away
8 *x*[*x x x x x x x x*]
9 *ši-*[*x x x x x x x x*]
10 *m*[*a x x x x x x x x*]
rest (about 10 lines) broken away
s.1 [*x x x x x-r*]*a-an-ni* [*x x x x x*]
2 [*x x x x x*] ⸢*a*⸣-*sa-par ina* UG[U *x x x x*]
3 [*x*] *man-nu i-da-na ma-a ina* [*x x x x*]
4 [*x x x x x*] *šu-nu* [*x x x x*]

CT 53 827

1 [To the king, my lord: your servant NN. Good health] t[o the king, my lord]!

4 [*The forts* of the king, my lord], are [well].

(Break)

11 the king [......]
12 not [......]
13 the It[u'eans ......]
14 with me [......]
15 sent, [saying: "...]
16 with you [......]
17 [...] *aft*[*er* ......]
18 [...] I [......]

(Break)

s.2 [......] I sent to [......]
3 Who will give [...]?" He said: "[......]
4 [...] they [......]

## 271. ———

K 1884

1 [*a-na* LUGAL *be-lí-ia*]

2 ⌈ARAD⌉-[*ka* $^{m}$*x x x x x*]

3 *lu* [DI-*mu a-na* LUGAL EN-*ia*]

4 *a*-[*ki x x x x x x*]

5 *i*-[*x x x x x x x*]

6 *ina* [*x x x x x x x*]

rest broken away

Rev. beginning broken away

1′ [*x* M]A.N[A *x x x x*]

2′ [K]I.LAL-*šu* [*x x x x*]

3′ *ni-da-da-x*[*x x x*]

4′ *nu-še*-[*x* (*x*)]

rest uninscribed

CT 53 200

1 [To the king, my lord: your] servant [NN]. Good [health to the king, my lord]!

4 Wh[en ......]

(Break)

r.1 its [we]ight is [x] minas [...].

3 We shall [...] and *b*[*ring it in*].

## 272. Rain and Travel Problems

K 4756

lines 1-10 broken away

1′ [*x x x x x x x*]-*ti*

2′ [*x x x x x x x*]

3′ [*x x x x x x x*]-*te*

4′ [*x x x x x x x x*]

5′ [*x x x x x x x x*]

6′ [*x x x x x x x x*]*x*

r.1 [A.AN.M]EŠ *ina* UGU-*hi-šú*

2 ⌈*i*⌉-*za-nun* : *šúm-mu qar-hu*

3 *ina* UGU-*hi-šú* : *la iq-ru-hu*

4 *ina meš-la-a-ti ša* ITI.ZÍZ

5 *nu!-ra-ma*

rest (space of 15 lines) uninscribed

ABL 1305

(Beginning destroyed)

r.1 It is [now] raining on it. If ice does not form on it, we can leave it in mid-Shebat (XI).

## 273. An (Urarṭian?) Defeat

K 16534

beginning broken away

1′ [*x x x z*]*i!*-⌈*i!-nu!?*⌉ *ina* UG[U *x x*]

2′ [*ma-a*ʾ-*da*] ⌈*i*⌉-*zu-nu-u*[*n* 0]

3′ [*x x i?*]-*si-a-aṭ* KUR—*aš*-⌈*šur*⌉.K[I-*a-a*]

4′ [*x x x*] TA* ŠÀ URU.HAL.ṢU.MEŠ

5′ [*i-tu*]-*ṣu-u-ni de*-⌈*ek*⌉-[*tú*]

6′ [*ina* ŠÀ-*bi-šú*]-⌈*nu*⌉ *i-du-u*[*k-ku*]

7′ [*x x x x*] ⌈*i*⌉-*du-k*[*u x x*]

rest broken away

Rev. destroyed

CT 53 795

(Beginning destroyed)

1 [...] it was raining [*heavily*] on [...].

3 [... was ca]reless; the Assyria[ns ... c]ame out of the forts and *infl*[*icted*] a defe[at on th]em.

7 [Th]ey killed [...]

(Rest destroyed)

# 274. Heavy Rain

Sm 163

beginning broken away
1′ [*zi*]-⌜*i*⌝-[*nu*]
2′ [*m*]*a*$^{!}$-*a*ʾ-*d*[*a*$^{!}$]
3′ ⌜*a*⌝—*dan-niš i*$^{!}$-*z*[*u*$^{!}$-*nun*]
4′ [G]IŠ$^{!}$.*pi-sa-nu*
5′ 1-*me* ANŠE A$^{!}$.MEŠ
6′ *ú-se-*⌜*li*$^{!}$⌝
Edge uninscribed
Rev. illegible

ABL 1265

(Beginning destroyed)
1 It rai[ned] extremely heavily.

4 The water trough raised 100 homers (20,000 litres) of water.
(Rest destroyed)

# 275. Steady Rain

K 15638

beginning broken away
1′ *ina* U[GU *x x x x*]
2′ UD-20-[KAM *zi-i-nu*]
3′ *ú-*⌜*sa*⌝-[*ri-ia*]
4′ 2 UD.MEŠ [*ma-a*ʾ-*da*]
5′ *i-zu-*[*nu-un*]
6′ GIŠ.*pi-s*[*a*$^{!}$-*nu*]
7′ [*x*] *x*[*x x x*]
rest broken away
other side destroyed

CT 53 695

(Beginning destroyed)

2 It star[ted to rain] on the 20th day, and it rai[ned heavily] for two days.

6 The water [trough *raised x homers of water*].
(Rest destroyed)

# 276. Fragment Reporting on Rainfall

K 14641

beginning broken away
1′ U[D$^{?}$ *x x x x x*]
2′ *ina* UR[U.*x x x x*]
e.3′ [*m*]*a-a*ʾ-*d*[*a a—dan-niš*]
r.1 ⌜*i*⌝-*zu-*[*nu-un*]
2 ŠÀ-*bu ša* LU[GAL EN-*ia*]
3 ⌜*lu*⌝-[*u* DÙG.GA 0]
rest broken away

CT 53 558

(Beginning destroyed)
1 [*On the ...th*] *da*[*y* ...] it rai[ned] extremely heav[ily] in the ci[ty ...].

r.2 The k[ing, my lord], can [be glad].
(Rest destroyed)

# Letters from Assyria

# (Addenda to SAA I)

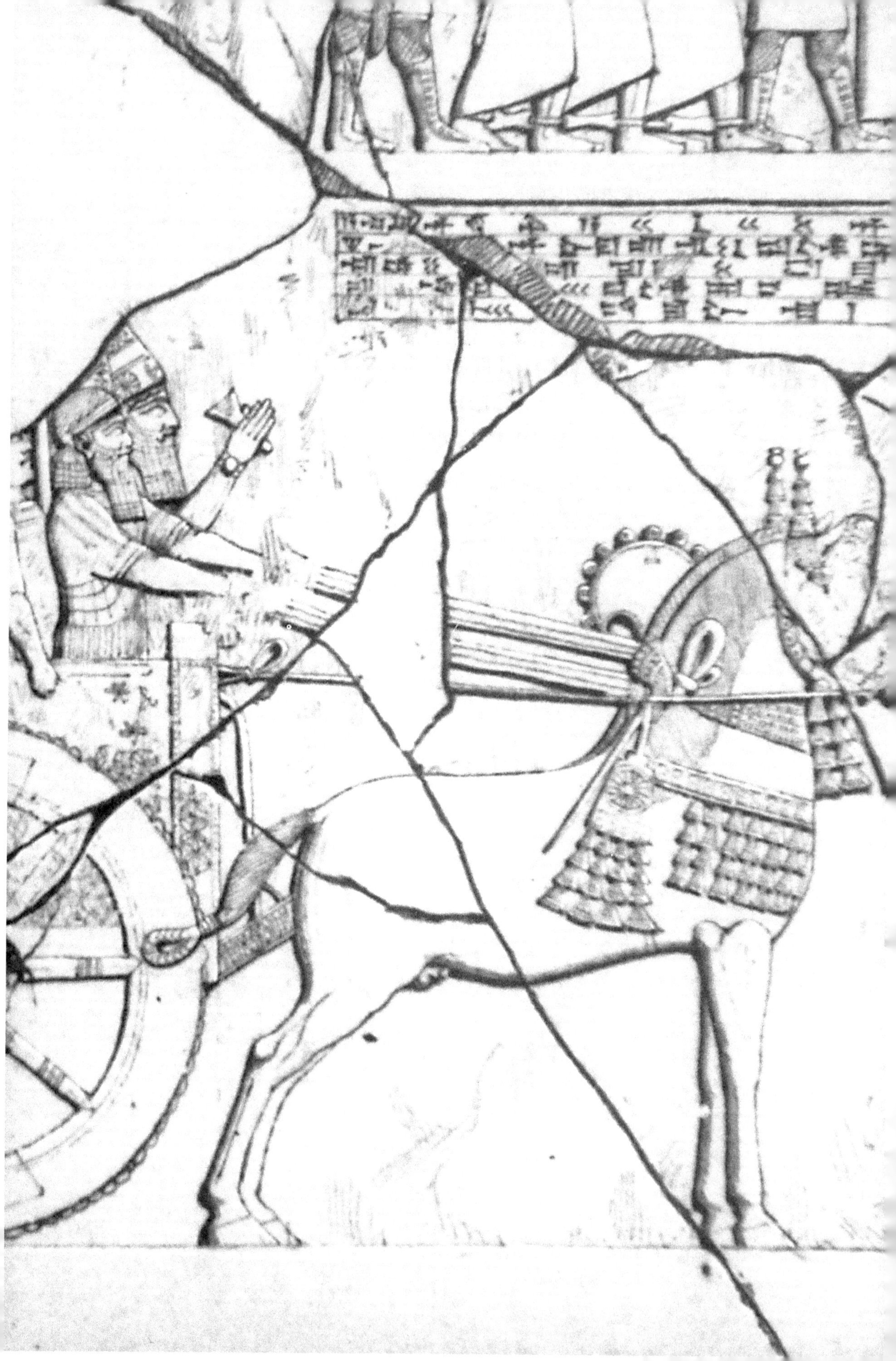

# 13. Letters from the King, the Crown Prince and the Treasurer



FIG. 39. *King in his chariot, with caption.*
ORIGINAL DRAWING V, 31.

# 277. Assembling Troops

K 7301

beginning broken away
1′ [*ina* URU$^{?}$].⸢*ur*⸣-*z*[*u*$^{?}$-*hi-na x x x x*]
2′ [*an-nu*]-*rig a-s*[*a-ap-rak-ku-nu ki-ma x x*]
3′ [*ú-s*]*e-bi-la* TA* [$^{m}$*x x x du-ub-ba*]
4′ [*šu*]-*tú ina* É.GAL *ina* U[GU *x x x x*]
5′ [*ma*]-⸢*a*⸣ *a-ta-a dul*$_6$-*l*[*u x x x x x*]
6′ [*ma*]-*a ina* UGU *man-nu ta*-[*x x x x x*]
7′ [EN—U]RU$^{?}$-*u-te-e ú-s*[*e-x x x x x*]
8′ [*š*]*u-u at-tu-nu a-d*[*i e-mu-qi-ku-nu*]
9′ [*a*]-*di* ERIM.MEŠ *ša* GIŠ.GI[GIR$^{?}$ *x x x x*]
10′ [LÚ*].*gur-ru* LÚ*.*i-tu*-[ʾ*u x x x x x*]
11′ [LÚ*].*zu*$^{?}$-*ku* LÚ*.*ka*⸢*l*$^{?}$⸣-[*la-pu x x x*]
12′ [*pu*]-*uh*-⸢*ra*⸣ [*x x x x x x x*]
13′ [*x*] *ta ṣa* [*x x x x x x x*]
14′ [*x x*] *a x*[*x x x x x x x*]
Edge broken away
r.1 [*x x x x x x x x x x x*]
2 [*mu-u*]*k* ⸢*la*⸣ [*x x x x x x x x x*]
3 [*na*]-*mar-ku* ⸢*lu*⸣ [*x x x x x x x x*]
4 [*x* D]UMU—LUGAL $^{m}$*x*[*x x x x x x*]
5 [*l*]*a ú-bal l*[*a x x x x x x*]
6 [$^{m}$*m*]*a-nu—ki-i*—$^{d}$[IM$^{?}$ *x x x x*]
7 [*m*]*a-a ki-i x*[*x x x x x x*]
rest broken away

CT 53 305

(Beginning destroyed)

1 [in] Arz[uhina ......].

2 I am w[riting to you righ]t now: [*after I have*] sent [..., *speak*] with [NN *wh*]*o* [*has written*] to the Palace ab[out ...]:

5 "Why [*is*] the wor[k *delayed*]? To whom did you [......]? *Have they p*[*romoted* NN] as city [lord]?"

8 He is [...]; as for you, [*be ready*] wi[th your army and wi]th your ch[ariot] troops, assemble the Gurreans, the It[u'eans, the ...], the *exempt infantry*, the *kal*[*lāpu* troops and ...]

(Break)

r.2 [*I said*:] "No [......]
3 [de]layed [......]
4 [... the cr]own prince [......]
5 does [n]ot bring [......]
6 Mannu-ki-[*Adad* ......]
7 "As [......]
(Rest destroyed)

# 278. ———

K 15608

beginning broken away
1′ [*x x x x x-i*]*a šu-ú x*[*x x*]
2′ [*x x x x x*]-⸢*a*⸣-*a* URU.*a-ra-za*-⸢*a*$^{!}$⸣.[*a*]
3′ [*x x x x š*]*u-ú* ⸢*šu*⸣-*pur-šu* [0]
4′ [*x x x x*] ⸢*e*⸣-*mu-qi ša* [*x x*]
5′ [*x x x* T]A ŠÀ-*bi it*-[*tu-ṣi*]
6′ [SIG$_5$-*iq a—da*]*n-niš am—mar* [*x x*]
7′ [*x x x x*] *ku-tal-l*[*i x x*]
8′ [*x x x x x*]*x du x*[*x x x*]
9′ [*x x x x x*] ŠE.PAD.[MEŠ *x x*]
10′ [*x x x x x x x*] ⸢*x*⸣ [*x x x*]
rest broken away
Rev. beginning destroyed
1′ [*x x x x x x x x*] ⸢*x x*⸣ [*x*]
2′ [*x x x x x x x x*]*x tú* [*x*]
3′ [*x x x x x x x x*] *ta* [*x*]
4′ [*x x x x x x x p*]*a l*[*u x*]
rest broken away

CT 53 677

(Beginning destroyed)

1 [...] he is my [...]
2 [...]ean(s) and Arazean(s)
3 [...] he is [...]. Send him
4 [...] the army of [...]
5 [...] has de[parted fr]om there.
6 (The situation) [is ve]ry [good]. Whatever [...]
7 [...] the re[ar ......]
8 [......] barley [...]
(Rest destroyed)

# 279. Military Matters

K 9526

beginning broken away
1′ [*x x x x x x*] ⸢*x x*⸣ [*x x x x*]
2′ [*x x x x x x*] É.GAL [*x x x*]
3′ [*x x x x x x*]*x du ul* [*x x x*]
4′ [*x x x x* $^{m}$*gab*$^{?}$*-bu*$^{?}$]—⸢*a*⸣*-mur ša x*[*x x*]
5′ [*x x x at-ta tu*]*-ú-da ki-*⸢*i*⸣ [*x x*]
6′ [*x x x x x*]*x-ru-u-ni il-*[*x x x*]
7′ [*x x x-b*]*u-u-ni an-nu-rig* [*x x x*]
8′ [*x e-mu-q*]*i-ia kar-ka-ti* LÚ**.x*[*x x x*]
9′ [*x x x x x*]*x-li a-du* AN[ŠE.*x x x*]
10′ [*x x x x x x* L]Ú.GAL—SAG *i-*[*x x x*]
11′ [*x x x x x x*]*x a-na* [*x x*]
12′ [*x x x x x ma*]*-*⸢*a*⸣ LUGAL *be-*[*lí x x*]
13′ [*x x x x x x x*] ⸢*x x*⸣ [*x x x x*]
rest broken away
Rev. beginning broken away
1′ [*x x x x x x*] ⸢*sa*⸣ *x*[*x x x*]
2′ [*x x x x x*] LÚ*.*qur-bu-ti ša* [*x x*]
3′ [*x x x x-n*]*i ša* É.GAL 1*-en* [*x x*]
4′ [*x x x it-tal*]*-ku-u-ni* : *ma-a* [*x x*]
5′ [*x x x x x š*]*ap-ra-a-ni la* [*x x*]
6′ [*x x at-ta tu*]*-ú-da ki-i* [*x x x*]
7′ [*x x x x x i*]*l-lak-ni x*[*x x x*]
8′ [*x x x x x x*]*x-ú* LÚ*.*qur-b*[*u-ti*]
9′ [*x x x x x i*]*na pa-ni* URU.*ku-*[*x x*]
10′ [*x x x x x-t*]*a a-na* LÚ*.[*x x x*]
11′ [*x x x x x ina*] UGU *ṭè-*⸢*e*⸣*-*[*me x x*]
12′ [*x x x x x x*]*-nu it-t*[*a-x x x x*]
13′ [*x x x x x x*]*x hu* [*x x x x*]
14′ [*x x x x x x x*] ⸢*x*⸣ [*x x x x*]
rest broken away

CT 53 403

(Beginning destroyed)
2 [......] palace [...]
3 [......] ... [...]
4 [...... *Gabbu*]-amur who [...]
5 [...... *You*] know that [the ...]
6 [who ...]... *g*[*o and*]
7 [...]. Now, [...]
8 [*with*] my assembled [tr]oops [...]
9 [...] *together with the h*[*orses* ...]
10 [...] the chief eunuch [...]
11 [...] to [...]
12 [...... say]ing: "The king, [my] lor[d, ...]
(Break)
r.2 [...] the royal bodyguard who [...]
3 [...] one [...] of the palace [...]
4 [... *have co*]*me*, saying: "We have been sent [to ...]" —
5 [*that is*] not [*true*]!
6 [*You*] know that [the ...]
7 [who] goes [...]
8 [......] the royal bo[dyguard]
9 [......] *before* the city *Ku*[...]
10 [......] to the [...]
11 [A]s to the ne[ws of ...]
(Rest destroyed or too broken for translation)

# 280. Oxen and Wagons

K 12964

1′ [*x x x*] ⸢*a*⸣ [*x x x x x*]
2′ [*x x x*] ⸢*x*⸣ [*x x x x x*]
3′ [*x x x x x x x x x x*]
4′ [*x x x x x x x x x x*]
5′ [*x x x*]*x* [*x x x x x*]
6′ [*x x x*] *a-na* [*x x x x x*]
7′ [*a*]*-na* ANŠE.*ú-*[*rat x x x x*]
8′ *a-na* LÚ*.A—KI[N *x x x x x*]
9′ *at-ta-ṣ*[*a x x x x x x*]
10′ *šu-*[*x x x x x x x x x*]
11′ [*x x x x x x x x x x*]

CT 53 442

(Beginning destroyed)
6 [...] to [......]
7 [t]o the te[ams ......]
8 to the messen[ger ...]
9 I bro[ught ......]
(Break)

**279** Taken as a royal letter partly on epigraphic grounds (e.g., the unusual form of the sign *ra* which also occurs in SAA I 9, 10, 13, 18 and 28), partly on the basis of the content (note, e.g., obv. 8). 5, r.6 For the restoration cf. SAA I 18 r.11.

e.12′ ⸢$^{m}$*sa*⸣-[*x*]*x*-⸢*x*⸣-[*x x x x*]
13′ *ṭè-e-mu a-s*[*a-kan-šu*]
14′ *nu-uk ki-ma x*[*x x x*]
r.1 GUD.MEŠ TA* GIŠ.*tal*-[*lak-a-te*]
2 *ta-at-ta-ṣa a-na* $^{m}$[*x x x di-ni*]
3 *nu-uk ha-ram-ma-*[*ma x x x*]
4 *mi-i-nu ah—hur x*[*x x x x*]
5 *an-na-a-te še-ṣi-*[*a x x x*]
6 ⸢*la tu*⸣-*šar-ba-*[*x x x x*]
7 [*x x*] *ù* GIŠ [*x x x x*]
8 [*x x*]*x a-na* [*x x x x x*]
9 [*x x*]*x a-na x*[*x x x x*]
10 [*x x x*]*x-šu i*[*š-x x x x*]
11 [*uq*]-*ṭar-rib* [*x x x x*]
12 [*x*] ⸢*ú*⸣-*bi-x*[*x x x x x*]
13 [*x x x*] ⸢*x*⸣ [*x x x x*]
rest broken away
s.1 [*š*]*a ep-pa-lu-ka-a-n*[*i x x x x x x*]

12 I g[ave him] these orders: "As soon as you have brought [...] the oxen and the wa[gons, give them] to [NN]; later on, [......]."

r.4 What else? Let these [...]s go out too, don't let [...] grow [...]
(Break)

11 [... ap]proached [...]
(Break)

s.1 [wh]ich I answered you [...]

## 281. Trees for the Royal Orchards

K 1183

1 *a-n*[*a* LUGAL EN-*ia*]
2 ARAD-*ka* $^{m}$30—[PAB—MEŠ—SU]
3 *lu šul-mu a-na* L[UGAL EN-*ia*]
4 *šul-mu a-na* [KUR—*aš-šur*.KI]
5 *šul-mu a-na* ⸢É⸣.[KUR.MEŠ-*te*]
6 *šul-mu a-na* URU.*b*[*i-rat ša* LUGAL *gab-bu*]
7 ŠÀ-*bu ša* LUGAL E[N-*ia a—dan-niš lu* DÙG.GA]
8 2 GIŠ.UB.MEŠ KALAG.[MEŠ *x x x x x x*]
9 UD-5-KAM *ša* IT[I.*x x x x x x x*]
10 *a-na* URU.*šu-u-r*[*i*? *x x x x x*]
11 UD-7-KAM *ša* IT[I.*x x x x x x*]
12 $^{m}$*tu-ú-a-a* ⸢LÚ*!⸣.[*x x x ina pa-ni-ia*]
13 *it-tal-ka ku-*[*x x x x x*]
14 *ina* ŠÀ GIŠ.KIB *x*[*x x x x x x*]
15 *ša* GIŠ.SAR [*x x x x x x*]
rest broken away
Rev. beginning broken away
1′ GIŠ.[*x x x x x x x x x x*]
2′ GIŠ.ŠUR.M[AN *x x x x x x x x*]
3′ *gab-bu šu-*[*x x x x x x x*]
4′ *ina* ŠÀ-*bi* ⸢*šu*?⸣ [*x x x x x x x*]
5′ GIŠ.KIN.GEŠTI[N *x x x x x x x*]
6′ *it-ta-ha-*[*ar x x x x x x*]
7′ *ṭè-e-mu a-sa-*[*kan x x x x*]
8′ *dul-lu ša* ITI.BARA[G *x x x*]
rest uninscribed

CT 53 36

1 To [the king, my lord]: your servant Sin-[ahhe-riba]. Good health to the k[ing, my lord]!

4 [Assyria] is well, the tem[ples] are well, [all the king's] fo[rts] are well. The king, [my] lo[rd], can be [glad indeed].

8 Two big ... trees [......]
9 on the 5th day of [......]
10 to the city Šur[u ......]
11 On the 7th of [......]
12 Tu'ayu [......]
13 came [*to me* ......]
14 among the medlar(s) [......]
15 of the orchard [......]
(Break)
r.1 [...] tree [......]
2 cypres[ses ......]
3 all [......]
4 there [......]
5 grape[s ......]
6 recei[ved ......]
7 I gave orders [......]
8 the rites of Nisan (I) [......]

**280** r.6 Or: ⸢*la tu*⸣-*šar-ba-*[*ṣa* "do not let [them] lie (idle)" (suggestion J. N. Postgate).

# 282. Palace Reliefs

K 7517

1 [*a-na* LUGAL EN-*ia*]
2 [ARA]D-*ka* ⸢m⸣[DÙG—IM—*aš-šur*]
3 *lu* DI-*mu a-n*[*a* LUGAL EN-*ia*]
4 *ša* LUGAL *be-lí iš-*[*pur-an-ni ma-a*]
5 MU.MEŠ *ša* LÚ*.EN.N[AM.MEŠ *ina x x x*]
6 *a-ta-a la za-qu-*[*pa* LUGAL *be-lí*]
7 *ú-da hu-li-ni* [*pa-ni-ú*]
8 *ša a-na* KUR.*man-na-*⸢*a*⸣-[*a x x x*]
9 ⸢*ni*⸣-*il-lik-u-ni in*[*a* É.SIG$_4$.MEŠ$^?$]
10 [*ša*] É.GAL *la-bir-*[*te x x x x*]
11 [*x x*] *né-e-ta-x*[*x x x x*]
rest broken away

Rev. beginning broken away
1′ [*x x*]*x* ⸢*lu* LÚ.UŠ⸣-*x*[*x x x x*]
2′ [M]U.MEŠ LUGAL.MEŠ LÚ.*x*[*x x x x*]
3′ [*p*]*i-tu-a-te ina* I[GI *x x x x*]
4′ [M]U.MEŠ-*šú-nu x*[*x x x x x*]
5′ [*x x*]*x-a-ni* [*x x x x x x*]
6′ [*x x x*]*x hu* [*x x x x x x*]
rest broken away

CT 53 387

1 [To the king, my lord]: your [serv]ant [Ṭab-šar-Aššur]. Good health t[o the king, my lord]!

4 As to what the king, my lord, wr[ote me]: "Why are the names of the gov[ernors] not fixed on [the *reliefs*]?" –

6 [the king, my lord], knows that our [*previous*] campaign which we directed to Mannea [... *is depicted*] o[n *the walls* of] the Ol[d] Palace. We [......]

(Break)

r.2 [the na]mes of the kings and the [...] officials

3 [di]adems in fr[ont of ...]

4 their [na]mes [......]

(Rest destroyed)

**282** Hand of Ṭab-šar-Aššur.

FIG. 40. *Sculpture caption naming a town (reign of Assurbanipal).*
BM 124802.

## 283. Arrival of a Royal Messenger

K 15394

beginning broken away
1′ [x x x x x] la [x x x x]
2′ [x x x x x]x x[x x x x]
3′ [ina] ŠÀ e-gír-te-[šú šá-ṭi-ir]
4′ ma-a ki-i an-na-[ka a-na-ku-ni]
5′ ma-a LÚ*.A—KIN ša KUR.[x x x x]
6′ [ina] UGU-[hi-i]a a-na URU.[x x x x]
7′ [i]t-tal-ka ma-a ina [x x x x]
8′ [l]a$^{?}$ ik-šu-da-ni [x x x x]
9′ [x x x]x ⸢É⸣ [x x x x x]
rest broken away
Rev. beginning broken away
1′ [x x x] e-ta[r-x x x x x]
2′ [x x x]x e x[x x x x x]
3′ [x x]-ik-tú [x x x x x]
4′ [x x]x ra tú [x x x x x]
5′ [e-gír]-tú an-ni-[tú ina UGU-hi-ia]
6′ [it-ta]l-ka [x x x x x]
rest broken away

CT 53 658

(Beginning destroyed)

3 [I]n [his] letter [it was written as follows]:

4 "While [I was] he[re], a messenger of [the king of ... c]ame [t]o [m]e in the city [...]; he had [no]t *reached* me in [...]

(Break)

r.5 thi[s lett]er [ca]me [to me ......]

(Rest destroyed)

## 284. Carnelian from Kumme

K 9212

Obv. totally broken away, except for (on the right edge):
1′ [x x x x x $^{m}$a-ri]-ia-e
rest broken away
Rev. beginning broken away
1′ [x x x] ⸢ta⸣ x[x x x x x]
2′ [x x x]x 1$^{!}$-e[n x x x]
3′ [x x re$^{?}$-h]a-ti la ⸢a-da⸣-n[a$^{!}$]
4′ [ina UG]U a-bi-te an-ni-te
5′ [x x x]-⸢i$^{!}$⸣ : i-sa-par
6′ [ma-a x x] ina UGU-hi-ia ina É.GAL
7′ [šá-áš-me] ina UGU-hi šú-u
8′ [a-na EN]-ia a-sa-par nu-uk la-áš-pur
9′ [ša ŠÀ]-bi-šú la-ah-ki-im
10′ [x x x] ša KUR.uk-ka-a-a šú-nu i-si-šú [x x]
11′ [x x $^{m}$a]-ri-ia-ṣa-a NA$_4$.GUG na-ṣa [0]
12′ [x x x] a-na $^{m}$si-lim—aš-šur
13′ [x x x r]ig$^{!}$ SIG$_5$-tú
14′ [x x x x] ⸢ši-ih-li⸣ [0]
rest broken away

ABL 1035

(Beginning destroyed)

1 [...... Ari]ye

(Break)

r.3 "I shall not giv[e the ...]...

4 [On acco]unt of this matter [NN] wrote: "[... *is*] against me; [make it known] in the Palace," and for that reason I wrote [to] my [lord]: "I shall write to find out [what] he has [in m]ind."

10 The [...] of the Ukkean are [...] with him.

11 [... A]riyaṣâ has brought carnelian

12 [...] to Silim-Aššur

13 [...] good

14 [...] second best

(Rest destroyed)

**283** Hand of Ṭab-šar-Aššur.
**284** r.5, 13 See coll.

## 285. Too Much Snow

K 15266

beginning broken away
1′ [*x x x x x x x x*]-⸢*ri*⸣
2′ [*x x x x x*] *ú-se-bi-la*
3′ [*i—su-ri* LUGAL] *be-lí i-qa-bi*
4′ [*ma-a a-ta-a a*]-*di a-kan-ni*
5′ [*la x x ku-pu-u a*]—*dan-niš da-an*
6′ [*x x x x x x*]*x* ITI.ŠE
7′ [*x x x x x* UG]U-*hi*-⸢*ia*⸣
rest broken away
Rev. beginning broken away
1′ [*x x x x x x x*] ⸢*x*⸣[*x*]
2′ [*x x x x x x x*]*x* ⸢*lum*⸣
3′ [*x x x x x x x x x*]*x*
4′ [*x x x x x* LÚ*].⸢*uk*⸣-[*ka-a*]-*a*
5′ [*x x x x x* L]UGAL *ú-x*[*x x*]-*ka*
6′ [*x x x x x x*]*x-ú-ni*
rest broken away

CT 53 629

(Beginning destroyed)
2 I am sending [......].
3 [Perhaps the king], my lord, will say:
4 "[Why *was it not* ...] until now?"
5 [The blanket of snow] is very thick,
6 [......] the month Adar (XII)
7 [......] to me
(Rest too broken for transalation)

## 286. A Journey to Dur-Šarruken

K 5493

beginning broken away
1′ [*x x x x x x*] *me i x*[*x x x x*]
2′ [*x x x x* L]Ú.*uk-ka-a*-⸢*a*⸣ [0]
3′ [URU.*x x x*]*x-na ú-ha-an-ni*-[*šú-ni*]
4′ [LÚ*.EN.NAM *ša*] *ina pu-tu-šú* TA* KUR.U[RI?]
5′ [*i-tal-k*]*a i-si a-ha-iš* [0?]
6′ [*ina* URU].*ir-mu-na bé-e-d*[*u* 0]
7′ [*an-nu-ri*]*g ki-lal-le-šú-nu x*[*x x*]
8′ [*x x x*]*x a-na* URU.BÀD—MAN—GI[N]
9′ [*x x x*] *i*-[*si*?]-*ia-m*[*a*]
10′ [*x x x x*] ⸢*x x ni*⸣ *har* [*x x*]
rest broken away
Rev. destroyed

CT 53 257

(Beginning destroyed)
2 [*After* ...] the Ukkean
3 had subjugat[ed ...],
4 [*the governor*] opposite him came from *Ur*[*arṭu*]
5 and they spen[t] the night together [in the town] Irmuna.
7 [No]w, both of them [...]
8 [...] to Dur-Šarruke[n ...]
9 [...] w[i]th me
(Rest destroyed)

## 287. Inspecting Bronze and Wooden Objects

K 15188

beginning broken away
1′ [*x x x x x x*] ⸢*an it*⸣
2′ [*x x x ma*]-*hi-ir nu-še-rib*
3′ [*x x i-b*]*a-ši* UTÚL.MEŠ URUDU
4′ [*x x x*] *sa-a-mu šar-pu šú-u*
5′ [*x x x n*]*é-em-mar ra-ʾi-ni*
Edge broken away

CT 53 628

(Beginning destroyed)
2 [... *has been rec*]*eived*, and we will enter (it);
3 [there] are vessels of bronze [...]
4 [...] it is burnt red.
5 We shall see [...]

**285** Hand of Ṭab-šar-Aššur. 5 Same form of *da* also in nos. 2, 3 and 16 (all from Liphur-Bel).
**286** 2f Or "[After NN] had subjugated the Ukkean (and) [...]."

Rev. lines 1-2 broken away
3 [*x x x*] *ša me* [[*x x*]] URUDU
4 [*x x x*]-*bi ni-ih-ti-*[*aṭ*]
5 [*x x* GI]Š.ÙR.MEŠ *x*[*x x x*]
rest broken away

(Break)
r.3 [...] of bronze
4 [...] we have weighed.
5 [...] beams [......]
(Rest destroyed)

## 288. Keeping Watch with Exempted Men

K 13060

destroyed
Rev. beginning broken away
1′ ⸢*ša*⸣ *ku-x*[*x x x x x x x x*]
2′ *ú-ma-a* LUG[AL *x x x x x x*]
3′ *le-pu-šá* ⸢*ù*⸣ [*x x x x x x*]
4′ LUGAL EN *li-ir-*[*ú*?*-ba*? *x x x*]
5′ *ana-ku* TA* *za-ku-*[*e x x x x*]
6′ EN.NUN *la-ṣur* [*x x x x x x*]
7′ *ina ku-tal ṣi-*[*x x x x x x*]
8′ *le-pu-šú* LÚ*.[*x x x x x x*]
9′ *ša* ᵐ*ú-a-x*[*x x x x x x x*]
10′ ⸢*ú*⸣*-da a-*[*x x x x x x x x*]
11′ [*x*] ⸢*ú*⸣ [*x x x x x x x x x*]
rest broken away
s.1 [*x x x x*]*x mar* MEŠ DÙ ᵈPA *x*[*x x x x x*]
2 [*x x x š*]*a a-*⸢*na*⸣ [*x x x x x x*]

CT 53 473

(Obverse destroyed)
r.1 of [......]
2 Now the ki[ng, my lord, ...]
3 *should exercise* [...]. And [......]
4 the king, my lord, should *rep*[*rimand* ......]
5 I shall keep watch [*in* ...] with the exempt[ed men ......]
7 behind [......]
8 let them do [......]
9 *of* Wa[......]
10 knows [......]
(Break; side untranslatable)

## 289. Distributing Corn

K 7333

beginning broken away
1′ [*x x x*]*-nu* URU.*mu-x*[*x x x x*]
2′ [*ú-še*]*-tu-qu ša* NINDA.ME[Š *x x x*]
3′ [*ša ṭu*]*p-pi-šú i-ba-šú-ni ù* ⸢ERIM⸣.[MEŠ-*šú*]
4′ [*i-b*]*a-ši* TA* ŠÀ-*bi* ŠE.*nu-sa-hi a-*[*laq-qi*]
5′ [*a-na*] EN.NUN-*šú a-na pa-na-tu-šú a-šak-*[*kan*]
6′ ⸢*ù*⸣ *ina* É *la-áš-šú-ni il-lak-u-ni*
7′ [*i*]*-qa-bu-ni a-na-ku a-da-an*
e.8′ ⸢*ù*⸣ ŠE.NUMUN-*šú-nu e-ru-šú*
9′ ⸢*ù*⸣ *šúm-mu la a-pa-qi-di*
r.1 [ŠE *pa*]*-ni-um-ma ša e-ṣi-du-ni*
2 ⸢*i*⸣*-na-ši-u e-ku-lu ù* ŠE.NUMUN *la e-ru-šú*
3 [*šá l*]*a* EN *ina* UGU-*hi-ia i-sa-hur-u-ni ma-a* NINDA.MEŠ
4 [*šak*?*-l*]*a*?*-na-ši* LUGAL *be-lí ú-da la x*[*x x*]

CT 53 323

(Beginning destroyed)
1 [*trans*]*ferring* [......] the town Mu[...].
2 For (any *cohort commander*) who has a bre[ad ration] entered on his tablet and who has men, I [take] from the corn tax and provide it to him in his garrison.
6 Even where there is no entry, they come and tell me, and I give it, so they can cultivate their fields.
9 If I did not allot it, they would take [the corn] they have harvested [prev]iously and eat it, and would not cultivate the fields but turn to me [with]out a superior, saying: "Bread [*is being with*]*held* from us!"
r.4 The king, my lord, knows that [...] no [...];

**288** Hand of Ṭab-šar-Aššur.
**289** Hand of Ṭab-šar-Aššur. r.4f Or: NINDA.MEŠ [*šá-ku-l*]*a-na-ši* "[give] us bread [to ea]t" (suggestion J. N. Postgate). There seems, however, to be too little room for the suggested restoration at the beginning of r.4; also, one would expect the verb to be *tadānu* rather than *šākulu*.

5 [*x x*] *a-na* LUGAL EN-*ia i-ta-n*[*u* 0]
6 [*x x*]*x* KUR.MEŠ-*šú-n*[*u x x x x x*]
rest broken away

5 they have give[n ...] to the king, my lord.
6 [...] thei[r] *countries* [......]
(Rest destroyed)

## 290. Ferrying Stone Thresholds Without Boats

K 1178

beginning broken away
1′ [*x x x x x x*]*x man x*[*x x*]
2′ [*x x x x x*]*x-ni ši-na*
3′ [*x x x x*]*x* ⌜KUR⌝-*e ša-ni-u*
4′ [*x x x x x*]*x-ha-ni i-sa-hu-ra*
5′ [*x x x x x*]*x dan-nu ina* URU.*ši-i-me*
6′ [*x x x x*]-*hi ša* GIŠ.MÁ.MEŠ KALAG.MEŠ
7′ [*x x x t*]*a*!-*ha-ni-šú-ni mar ša i-ba-*⌜*šu-ni*⌝
8′ [*x x x x*] GIŠ.MÁ.MEŠ *an-na-te pa-a-ṣa*
9′ [*x x x*]-*da-du i-sa-hu-r*[*a*]
10′ [*x x x x*]-*ha-ni-šú-nu i—s*[*u-ri*]
11′ [LUGAL *be-lí i*]-*qa-bi ma-a* [0]
12′ [*x* GIŠ.MÁ.MEŠ *an-n*]*a-te* [0]
rest broken away
Rev. beginning broken away
1′ [*x x x x x x x x x*] ⌜*i*⌝ [*x*]
2′ [*x x x x x x x x*] NA$_4$.I.[DIB.MEŠ]
3′ [*x x x x x x x na*]-*me-r*[*i*]
4′ [*x x x x x x x x*]-*ni*
5′ [NA$_4$.I.DIB.MEŠ] *ša* [*ina*] ⌜U⌝GU ÍD
6′ [*kar-ra-a-ni*] *ú-še-ba-ra*
7′ [*x x x x*] *dul$_6$-lu ša* GIŠ.MÁ.MEŠ
8′ [*e-pa-áš mi*]-⌜*i*⌝-*nu ša* LUGAL *be-lí*
9′ [*i-qa-bu-n*]*i*
rest uninscribed

CT 53 30

(Beginning destroyed)

2 [......] they
3 [......] another mountain [...]
4 [......] he returns [...]
5 [......] great [...] in Šimu
6 [......] *of* large boats
7 [......] ..., as many as there are,
8 [are ...]. These boats are absent.
9 [......]dadu will return, and
10 [......] their [...].
11 Perh[aps the king, my lord, wi]ll say:
12 "[... th]ese [boats]
(Break)
r.2 [......] the stone thres[holds]
3 [...... for the wa]tchtower
5 I shall bring across [*the thresholds*] which [have been deposited on] the river bank, [and ... do] the work on the boats. [Wh]at does the king, my lord, [say]?

**290** Hand of Ṭab-šar-Aššur.

# 14. Miscellaneous Letters

# 291. Giving Bricks to the Magnates

K 1246

beginning (about 5 lines) broken away

1′ [*x x x x x*] ⸢*x*⸣ [*x x x x x*]
2′ [*x x x*] ⸢56⸣ *tik-pi* SIG$_4$ ⸢KIN?.MEŠ⸣
3′ [*x x x x*]*-tú i-ta-sa-ha*
4′ [*i-sa-par ina*] UGU-*hi-šú ma-*⸢*a*⸣ [*a*]*-*⸢*ta-a*⸣
5′ [*x x x x*]*-tú ta-*⸢*su*⸣*-uh*
6′ [*ma-a re-eh*]*-ti dul*$_6$*-li-ia* ⸢*ša*⸣ *e-pa-šú-ni*
7′ [*x x x* SI]G$_4$.MEŠ *i-*⸢*ba-áš*⸣*-ši*
8′ [*x x x-d*]*i-šú ah—hu-*⸢*ur*⸣
9′ [*e-bir-tú*] ⸢*i*⸣*-šá-ha-aṭ*

10′ [*x x x x x*]*x-ni ša* S[IG$_4$].M[E *š*]*a* BÀD-*šú*
11′ [*ina* UGU LUGAL] EN-*ia ú-se-bi-la*

12′ [*i—su-ri* LUG]AL EN *i-qa-bi*
13′ [*ma-a a-na man*]*-ni* SIG$_4$.ME ⸢*x x*⸣
e.14′ [*ta*]*-a-din*
15′ [40?*-lim*] *a-na* URU.*ar-pad-d*[*a*]
16′ [40?*-lim a-n*]*a* URU.*sa-mi*[*r-na*]
r.1 [40?*-lim a-na*] URU.*ma-gi-d*[*u-u*]

2 [PAB 1?*-me*]—20*-lim* TA* IGI *li-bit*—MAN
3 [PAB 30*-lim* T]A IGI m*na-a'-di*—DINGIR
4 [PAB-*ma* 1?*-me*]-50*-lim* SIG$_4$.MEŠ *a-ti-din*
5 [*ù*?] SIG$_4$.MEŠ *ša* LÚ*.GAL—URU.⸢MEŠ MAN⸣
6 [*ša* LUG]AL EN *iš-pur-an-ni ur-ta-me*

7 [LUGAL E]N *ú-da* LÚ*.SAG.MEŠ NUMUN—LUGAL
8 [*ša*] SIG$_4$.ME TA* *pa-ni-šú-nu* ÍL*-u-ni*
9 [*a-na*] LÚ*.GAL.MEŠ *a-di-nu-ni*
10 [*a-na* L]UGAL EN-*ia i-ma-hu-ru*
11 [LUGAL E]N *ki-i ša* ZU*-u-ni le-pu-šú*
12 [LUGAL E]N *ú-da i—ti-ma-*⸢*li*⸣ [*i—šá-šu-m*]*e*
13 [SIG$_4$].ME *a-na li-bit*—M[AN *a-ti-din*]
14 [*x x du*]*l-lu ša* LUG[AL *x x x x*]
rest (about 3 lines) broken away

CT 53 38

(Beginning destroyed)

2 [...] 56 courses of bricks [...]

3 [...] he extracted [...].

4 [He wrote t]o him: "Why did you extract [...]?"

6 [He said: "The re]st of the work that I am doing [is ...; *I have receiv*]*ed from* him [x] bricks, but he is still glazing [the kiln-fired bricks]."

10 I am [herewith] sending [the ...]s of the br[ickwork o]f his wall (assignment) [to the king], my lord.

12 [Perhaps the ki]ng, my lord, will say: "[To who]m have [you] given bricks [...]?"

15 [*40*,000] to (the governor of) Arpad, [*40*,000 t]o Sama[ria, *40*,000 to] Megid[do], in all [*1*]20,000 (bricks taken) from the king's entourage.

r.2 [*In all* 30,000 f]rom Na'di-ilu.

4 [All told], I have given out [*1*]50,000 bricks; [*but*] I have *omitted* the bricks of the royal village managers [about which the ki]ng, my lord, wrote me.

7 [The ki]ng, my lord, knows that the eunuchs and the royal entourage, from [whom] I have been taking the bricks which I have given [to] the magnates, are going to petition the king. The king, my [lo]rd, may do as he deems best; [the ki]ng, my [lo]rd, knows that [I have] in the past [days given brick]s to the ki[ng's] entourage.

14 [...] the ki[ng's wo]rk [......]

(Rest destroyed)

## 292. Building the City Wall of Dur-Šarruken

ND 1108

1 [*a-n*]*a* LUG[AL] EN-*ia*
2 [ARAD-*k*]*a* $^{m}$⸢MAN$^{!}$⸣—IG[I].LAL-*an-ni*
3 [*lu* D]I-*mu a-na* ⸢LUGAL⸣ EN-*ia*
4 ⸢*ša* LUGAL⸣ EN *iš-pur-an-n*[*i*]
5 *ma-a ma-ʾa-ad* $^{m}$MAN—IGI.LAL-[*an-ni*]
6 *il-la-ka i-qa-*[*bi-a*]
7 *ma-a* BÀD *ša* URU.BÀ[D—MAN—GIN]
8 ⸢*ú*⸣-*x*[*x x x x x x x*]
rest broken away
Rev. beginning broken away
1′ ⸢*x*⸣ [*x x x x x x x x*]
2′ $^{md}$MES—*rém-*⸢*ni*⸣ *x*[*x x x x*]
3′ *ana-ku ina*$^{!}$ ŠÀ$^{!}$-*ma ana-ku ma*$^{!}$-*ṣ*[*ar*$^{!}$-*tu*]
4′ *ša* $^{m}$BA-*šá*—$^{d}$⸢MES *ù*⸣ [0]
5′ *ša is-si-šú a-*⸢*na-ṣar*$^{!}$⸣ *x*[*x x*]
6′ *a-du mì-ni ša* LUGAL *i-*⸢*šá*⸣-*p*[*a*$^{!}$-*ra-ni*]
7′ *a-*⸢*se*⸣-*me ma-a* $^{m}$MAN—IGI.LAL-⸢*an*⸣-*ni*
8′ [*it*]-*tal-ka ma-a ina* URU.⸢*x*⸣[*x*]
9e [*x x*]*x* ⸢*x*⸣ *ma-a du*[*l-lu*]
10e ⸢*i*⸣-*ba-ši e*$^{!}$-*pa-á*[*š* 0]

GPA 242

1 [T]o the ki[ng], my lord: [yo]ur [servant] Šarru-e[mu]ranni. [Good] health to the king, my lord!

4 As to what the king, my lord, wrote to m[e]: "Šarru-emur[anni] keeps coming and tel[ling me] that the city wall of Du[r-Šarruken ...]

(Break)

r.2 Marduk-remanni [...].

3 I shall be there too and keep wa[tch] over Iqiša-Marduk and his associates, until the king inst[ructs me] otherwise.

7 I have heard that Šarru-emuranni [has] come; [*he is*] in [...], and is indeed do[ing] the work.

## 293. Finishing the 'Winged Hoof'

K 1220

1 *a-na* LUGAL *be-lí-*[*iá*]
2 ARAD-*ka* $^{md}$PA—GÁL-*ši*
3 $^{m}$*ig-li-i*
4 *lu* DI-*mu a-na* LUGAL EN-*iá*
5 $^{d}$AG $^{d}$AMAR.UTU *a-na* LUGAL EN-*iá*
6 *lik-ru-bu*
7 *ina* UGU *ṣu-pur a-kap-pi*
8 *ša* LUGAL EN *iš-pur-an-ni*
9 *ma-a a-ta-a la ga-mì-ri*
10 *lu ina* IGI LÚ*.*aš-šur-a-a šu-u-tú*
r.1 *ni-iš-luh-šu-nu*
2 *ár-hi*[*š ni-i*]*g-mu-ru*
3 *x*[*x x x*] DUMU.MEŠ KÁ$^{!}$.DINGIR
4 ⸢*x*⸣[*x x-lu*]*h-u-ni*
5 *ud* [*x x x*]*x-ni*
6 *nin* [*x x x*] *pi* [*x*]
7 *la* [*x x x x x x*]
8 *a* [*x x x x x x x*]
s.1 *ina* UGU LUGAL *be-lí-iá ú-bal-ši*

ABL 271

1 To the king, [my] lord: your servant Nabû-ušabši, (and) Iglî. Good health to the king, my lord! May Nabû and Marduk bless the king, my lord!

7 As to the *winged hoof* about which the king, my lord, wrote me: "Why is it not finished?" —

10 had it been at the disposal of the Assyrians, we would have *retrieved it from* them and quick[ly fin]ished it!

r.3 [...] the Babylonians [... have been re]trieving it

(Break)

s.1 *I* shall bring it to the king, my lord.

**292** r.3, 5 See coll.
**293** 7 → ABL 180 (SAA I 51). The interpretation and precise translation of the object *ṣupur agappi* (lit. "nail/claw/hoof of/with a wing") remains uncertain. The amount of gold (250 g) needed for making it would fit the suggestion put forward in SAA I that an ornamented leg of a chair, possibly to replace a damaged one, is in question; for *agappi* "winged" cf. *ṣubāt agappi* "plumage," lit. "garment of wing/feather." s.1 Or: "*He* will bring it."

# 294. Request for Beams, Gold and Steel

K 942

beginning broken away

1′ [*ṭ*]*up-pu pi*-[*qid*?] LÚ*.⌈*ú*⌉-[*ra-si*?]

2′ [*ša*] ⌈Á⌉-*šú-nu ina* UGU *dul-li iš-k*[*un-u-ni*]

3′ [*a-n*]*a* 2-*i* UD-*me i-da-ab-bu-bu*

4′ [*ma*]-*a dul-lu an-ni-u ina* IGI $^{d+}$EN

5′ [*m*]*a-hi-ir a—dan-niš ma-a* UD.MEŠ *ša* LUGAL

6′ ⌈*i*⌉-*ri-ku ha-di-u a—dan-niš*

7′ *nu-uk qí-ba-a-ni mi-nu šu-u*

8′ *la im-ma-gu-ru la i-qab-bu-u-ni*

9′ 6 GIŠ.MES.MÁ.GAN.NA 6-*a-a* 1 KÙŠ

10′ GÍD.DA 1 KÙŠ *na-ku-pu* 1 GIŠ.HA.LU.ÚB

11′ 5 *ina* 1 KÙŠ GÍD.DA 1 KÙŠ *na-ku-pu*

12′ 10 GIŠ.MES.MÁ.GAN.NA *ša* 2 *qa-a-a*

13′ *kab-ba-ru-u-ni lu* 5 *lu-u* 6 *ina* 1 KÙŠ

14′ *li-ri-ku* 1 GIŠ.KU SIG$_5$ 2 *qa*

15′ *lu kab-ra* 6 *ina* 1 KÙŠ *li-ri-ik*

16′ 20 GIŠ.*šá-áš-šu-gi a-na tal-li*

17′ 10-*a-a ina* 1 KÙŠ *lu ár-ru-ku*

18′ LÚ*.SIMUG.KUG.GI *ma-a* KUG.GI

19′ *lu-rad-du-un-na-ši*

r.1 3 GÚ.UN AN.BAR *zag-ru ša a—dan-niš*

2 *am—mar a-na* LUGAL EN-*iá áš-pu-ra-an-ni*

3 *ár-hiš* LUGAL *be-lí lu-še-bi-la*

4 ŠE.PAD.MEŠ *a-na* LÚ*.UM.ME.A LUGAL

5 *liš-pu-ra lid-di-nu ri-ik-su*

6 *ša* LUGAL *be-lí* TA* É—DINGIR.MEŠ

7 *ir-ku-su-u-ni e-ṣa-šú-nu*

8 [*x*] LÚ*.ERIM.MEŠ *lu-u* LÚ*.*ša*—[*ziq*]-*ni*

9 [*lu*] LÚ*.ARAD—É.GAL LUGAL *lu-še-bi-la*

10 [*i-si*]-*ia a-na* EN.NUN *li-zi-zu*

11 [*x x*] ⌈*x*⌉ *lal*!-*li-ka pa-ni ša* LUGAL

12 [EN-*ia l*]*a-mur* TA* *bal-ṭu-ti*

13 [LUGAL? *la-ap-la*]-*ah ú-ma-a*

14 [*x x x x x x x x*]-*šá-ku*

rest broken away

ABL 566

(Beginning destroyed)

1 "*Cons*[*ult*] the tablet!" The *br*[*ick masons* who] star[ted] to work were gossiping the following day, saying: "This work is most acceptable to Bel! The king is going to live long!"

6 They were merry indeed, so I asked: "What is it? Tell me!" but they wouldn't tell me.

9 (I need) six *musukkannu* trees, each six cubits (3 m) long and one cubit (50 cm) in circumference;

10 one *haluppu* fir tree, five cubits long, one cubit in circumference;

12 ten *musukkannu* trees, each of which are two *qû* measures thick; they may be either five or six cubits long;

14 one good box tree; it should be two *qû* measures thick and six cubits long;

16 20 *šaššūgu* trees for the shafts; they should each be ten cubits (5 m) long.

18 The goldsmith says they need more gold.

r.1 The king, my lord, should quickly send the three talents of *steel* about which I wrote to the king, my lord.

4 The king should send grain rations to the artist and have them delivered; the contract that the king, my lord, made with the temple is too small for them.

8 The king should send [x] men, be it be[ard]ed courtiers [or] palace employees, to stand guard [with] me [...], so I can come and see the face of the king, [my lord], and [*fea*]*r* [*the king*] with those who are alive!

14 Now [...] I am [......]

(Rest destroyed)

**294** r.1 "Steel": lit., "extremely wrought iron."

# 295. Second-Rate Logs will not Do

Sm 456

1 [*a-na* LUGAL EN-*ia*]
2 [ARAD-*ka* $^{m}$*x x x*]
3 [*lu* DI-*mu a-na* LUGAL] EN-*ia*
4 [$^{d}$PA $^{d}$AMAR.UTU *a*]-*na* LUGAL EN-*ia lik-ru-bu*
5 [*x x x x x x x x*]*x-di-ru*
6 [*x x x x x x x x*]-*a-ni*
7 [*x x x x x x x x*]*x*.MEŠ
8 [*x x x x*]-⸢*ri*⸣ *a-na* LÚ*.GAL.MEŠ
9 [*x x x x*].MEŠ *ú-za-ʾi-zu-u-ni*
10 [*šúm-ma ina* IGI] LUGAL EN-*ia*
11 [*ma-hir x x x*] *ṭè*!-*e-mu*
12 [*a-na* LÚ*.*x x*.MEŠ] *liš-ku-nu*
13 [*x x x x x*] *lil-li-ku-u-ni*
14 [*x x x x la*]-*di*!-*na-áš-šú-nu*
15 [*x x x ú-šar*]-*ri-mu-u-ni*
16 [*x*] *an* [*x x x x*] *a—dan-niš*
17 ⸢*x*⸣-*šú-nu* [*x*] *x*[*x x x*]-ʾ*u-u*
18 *x*[*x x*]-⸢*šú-nu*?⸣ *ina*! *bat*!-*ta*!-*ta-a-a*
19 *a-sa*!-*ṭar*! *ina*! UGU! LUGAL EN-*ia*
20 *ú-se-bi-la ši*!-⸢*ih*!⸣-*li*
21 *ša*! *an*!-*na*!-*ka*! *nu*!-[*šar-ri*]-⸢*m*⸣*u*?-*u-ni*
22 *ma*!-*a*ʾ!-*da* [0] *a*!—*dan*!-*niš*
23 *ke-e-tú*! 1-*en* ⸢TA*!⸣ ŠÀ!-*bi-šú*!-*nu*!
24 *a*!-*na*! *dul*!-*li*! ⸢*la*!⸣ *il*!-*lak*!
25 [*x*] GIŠ.ŠÚ.A.MEŠ 1[2]-*a*!.*a* [*ina* KÙŠ GÍ]D
e.26 GÌR.PAD.DU DAGAL *pu*-⸢*su*!-*ku*!⸣ *mu*!-*bu-u*
27 *ša* GIŠ.*me-eh-ri ši-na*
28 *ra-qa-qa a—dan-niš*
r.1 *at-ti-ši an-na-ka ur-ta-am-me*
2 *lu ša* GIŠ.ERIN *ši-na*
3 *a-ka-an-ni ú-sa-ri-mì-ma*
4 *e-ti-mì-si-na-ma ú-ma-a*
5 *mi-i-nu ša* LUGAL *be-lí i-qab-bu-u-*(*ni*)
6 *šúm-ma* LUGAL *i-qab-bi ma-a li-in-ta-hu-ši-na*
7 *šúm-ma šal-ma-a-ti ni-mat-ta-ah*
8 *šúm-ma* 1-*et a-na* 2-*šú ni-ba-taq*
9 *mi-i-nu ša ši-ti-i-ni* LUGAL *be-lí*
10 *liš-pu-ra ba-si la-áš-me*
11 *ina* UGU *mi-ni-ti ša* LÚ*.*šá*—IGI—KUR
12 *la-ad-di-in-ši-na*
13 *dul-lum ug-da-mir ina* IGI LÚ*.ERIM.MEŠ
14 *ša* LÚ*.GAL.GAL.MEŠ *šu-u a-da-gal*
15 *a-du bé-et il-la-ku-ni-ni*
16 *a-šar-u-ni ad-da-na-áš-šú-nu-u-ni*
17 *ina* UGU GIŠ.*mu-us-ki* GIŠ.ÙR.MEŠ [[*x*]] *a*
18 *ša* LÚ*.GAL—*ka-a-ri* [[*x*]] 1 KUR.ʾ*a-ta-a-a*
19 *ša* $^{m}$*ig-li-i i-mat-ta-hu-u-ni*
20 *ki-i an-ni-i iq-ṭi-bi-u ma-a la-áš-šú*
21 *la nu-ša-an-ṣa ma-a* UD-10-KÁM *ša* ITI.NE
22 *la ni-il-la-ka ma-a ni-il-lak*

ABL 467

1 [To the king, my lord: your servant NN. Good health to the king], my lord! May [Nabû and Marduk] bless the king, my lord!

(Break)

8 [......] are distributing [...] to the magnates

10 [If it is acceptable to] the king, my lord, [the ...] should give orders [to ......]

13 [......] they should come

14 [I will] give them [...].

15 [The ... which *they have c*]*ut into shape*

16 [are] very [...];

17 their [...] are [...].

18 I have listed their [...] and sent (this information) to the king, my lord.

20 The second-rate (logs) we [*have been cut*]*ting into shape* here are quite plentiful but, frankly, none of them will do for the job.

25 There are [x] door-beams, each 1[2 cubits (6 m) long], a 'bone' (c. 32 cm) wide and a 'palm' (c. 8 cm) thick; they are of fir tree and much too thin. I have *tried them out* here but rejected them.

r.2 Had they been of cedar, I would already have cut them into shape and installed them.

5 Now, what are the king my lord's orders? If the king orders that they should be used, let the king, my lord, write specifically whether we should use them whole or whether we should cut them in two, and I will duly comply and give them over to the accounting of the palace superintendent.

13 I have finished the work, and will be waiting for the men of the *officers of the magnates*, until they come and I can check and give (*it*) to them.

17 As to the *musku* trees *and* the logs of the chief of trade that the 'Ateans of Iglî are lifting, they said as follows:

20 "There is no way we can come on the 10th of Ab (V). We shall go and get 30 wa-

**295** 26 W 172.

23 [*m*]*a* 30 GIŠ.*tal-lak*.MEŠ *ni-na-áš-ši*
24 [*ma-a*] *a-du bé-et* GIŠ.*in-gal-lu ina ši-ṭi-ri-šá*
25 [*x x*] ⌈*x x*⌉ *ma-a šúm-ma* UD-20-KÁM
26 [*ma-a šúm-ma* UD-*x*]-⌈KÁM⌉ *ša* ITI.KIN
rest broken away

gons, *and* until the *sickle* [...] in its ..., either on the 20th [or the ...]th of Elul (VI) [......]

(Rest destroyed)

## 296. Bricks for Dur-Šarruken

K 1544

Obv. destroyed
Rev. beginning broken away
1′ [*x x x* URU].⌈*a-di-a din x*⌉ [*x*]
2′ [*x* LÚ.B]UR.GUL.MEŠ *ina* UGU *ṣi-pi* [0]
3′ [*iq-ṭ*]*ar-bu* LÚ.*ṣa-pu-u*
blank
4′ *i-na* UGU *dul-li ša* URU.BÀD—MAN—GIN
5′ [U]RU.MEŠ-*ni ša* UN.MEŠ KUR
6′ *nu-se-ṣi* SIG$_4$ *ú-qar-ru-bu*
rest uninscribed

CT 53 188

(Beginning destroyed)

r.1 [...] Adia [...]

2 [*There are* x sto]ne cutters. The dyers have [beg]un to dye.

4 As to the the work of Dur-Šarruken, we have brought out the local population by villages; they will produce the bricks.

## 297. Transporting Stone Thresholds and Raising a Bull Colossus

K 932

beginning broken away
1′ *x*[*x x x x x x x*]
2′ *x*[*x x x*]-*an*-⌈*ni*?⌉
3′ *še* [*x x x x x*] ⌈*x x-ma*!⌉
4′ NA$_4$.I.D[IB.MEŠ *ú-se*]-⌈*bir*⌉
5′ 5 NA$_4$.[I.DIB.MEŠ *ina* Š]À-*bi*
6′ *re-e*-⌈*hu*?⌉ [LÚ*.GAL—*x x*].MEŠ
7′ *ina pa-ni* [*ap-ti-qi-di*]
8′ *muk* ⌈*še*!⌉-*b*[*ir-šú-nu x* LÚ*].⌈ERIM!⌉.MEŠ!—MAN!
9′ *ina qa-ti-*[*ia at*]-*ti-ši*
10′ UD-1-KÁM *ina* [URU.*tas*]-⌈*ti*!-*a*!⌉-*ti*
11′ *ina* UGU NA$_4$.$^{d}$ALAD.$^{d}$LAMA
12′ *ša-at-bu*-⌈*e*? *a-ta*!⌉-*lak*!
13′ *ba-ti-qi* ⌈*x*⌉ [*x x x*]*x*
r.1 [*an*]-*nu-rig ir-ti* 0!
2 [KA]R *ra-pa-ni a-ta-ra-aṣ*
3 [NA$_4$.$^{d}$A]LAD.$^{d}$LAMA *ú-ša-at-ba*
4 [*gab-b*]*u né-pa-áš*
5 [ŠÀ]-*bu ša* LUGAL EN-*ia lu* DÙG.GA
rest uninscribed

ABL 957

(Beginning destroyed)

4 [I have brought] stone thre[sholds acr]oss (the river), but five [of them] remain [the]re. [I have appoi]nted [the chief...] in charge of them, saying: "Bring [them] across!"

8 On the first day [I to]ok [x] king's men with [me] and went to [Tas]tiate to *raise* the bull colossus. It has been hewn and [...].

r.2 I am [n]ow spreading *poles* against [the qu]ay and *raising* the [bu]ll colossus. We will do it all right; the king, my lord, can be glad.

**297** 6, 8, 10, 12f, r.2 See coll.

# 298. Moving Bull Colossi Across the River

DT 289

beginning (probably one line only) broken away

1′ ⌜*x x*⌝[*x x x x x x x*]
2′ ⌜*x x*⌝[*x x x x x x x*]
3′ *x*[*x*] *a-na* [*x x x x x*]
4′ UGU LÚ.E[N—*pi-qit-ta-ti*]
5′ *ša* ŠÀ URU.*a-di-*[*a*]
6′ URU.*ta-as-*[*ti-a-te ša*]
7′ LUGAL *be-lí iš-*[*pur-an-ni*]
8′ *ma-a gab-bi-šú-nu* ⌜*a*!⌝-[*na* URU.BÀD—MAN—GIN]
9′ *lil-li-ku* $^{d}$A[LAD.$^{d}$LAMA.MEŠ]
10′ *ša* LÚ.GAL.MEŠ *ki-*⌜*i*⌝ [*a-ha*?-*iš*]
11′ *zaq-pu* LUGAL *be-lí* [*iq-ṭi-bi*]
12′ *ma-a* $^{d}$ALAD.$^{d}$LAMA.[MEŠ]
13′ *ar-hi-iš li-ik-ba*!-[*su-ni*]
14′ *a-du* A.MEŠ *ina* ÍD [*e-ṣu-ni*]
15′ ÍD! *lu*!-[*še-bi-ru*]
e.16′ LÚ.EN—*x*[*x x x x*]
17′ *man-nu pa-an* [$^{d}$ALAD.$^{d}$LAMA.MEŠ]
r.1 *i-za-za* ⌜*ú*⌝-[*ma-a*]
2 LÚ.GAL.MEŠ *ina pa-ni-*[*ia*]
3 *i-da-gul ina* ITI.SI[$G_4$ 0]
4 LUGAL *be-lí ina pa-ni-i*[*a*]
5 *lid-gul* $dul_6$!-*lu a-na* [LUGAL]
6 *lu-u-ša-ak-ši-di la-d*[*in*]
7 *šúm-ma* LUGAL *be-lí i-qab-*[*bi*]
8 *ma-a lil-li-ku* [0]
9 10 URU.ŠÀ—URU-*a-a* [0]
10 5 URU.*kal-ha-a-a* [0]
11 *ina pa-an* $^{d}$ALAD.$^{d}$LAMA.[MEŠ]
12 *lu-u šu-nu* ⌜*re*!⌝-[*hu-ti*]
13 *ina* URU.BÀD!—M[AN—GIN *lil-li-ku*]

rest (1-2 lines) broken away

ABL 1362

(Beginning destroyed)

4 As to the of[ficials] in Adi[a] and in Tas[tiate concerning whom] the king, my lord, wro[te me]: "All of them should go t[o Dur-Šarruken]!" —

9 the bu[ll colossi] of the magnates are set up to[gether] and the king, my lord, [(earlier) said]: "They should quickly ... the colossi and as long as the water in the river is [low, bring them across] the river!"

14 Who [...] would (then) stay (here) to look after the [bull colossi]?

r.1 N[ow], the magnates are waiting for [me]. May the king, my lord, wait for me (until) Siv[an] (III), and I will (then) get the work *done* and deliver it to [the king].

7 If the king, my lord, (nevertheless) ord[ers]: "They must go!" then let ten (officials) from the Inner City and five from Calah stay to look after the bull coloss[i]; the r[est may go] to Dur-Š[arruken].

# 299. Working and Loading Bull Colossi

K 1885

beginning broken away

1′ [*x ma*]-⌜*a*⌝-*te š*[*a x x x*]
2′ [*x x x*] ⌜m?⌝U—DÙ [*x x x x*]
3′ [*x x x*] *šá* [*x x x x*]
4′ [*x x x*] *i*[*š x x x x*]
5′ [*x x x*] *x*[*x x x x x*]
6′ [*x x x* L]UG[AL *x x x*]
7′ [*x x x*] *ku* [*x x x x*]

lines 8′-10′ destroyed

e.11′ [*x x x*] ⌜*ni*⌝ [*x x x x*]
12′ [*x*] ⌜*ub*? *te*⌝ *hi* [*x x x*]
r.1 [*dul*]-*lu ša in-né-*[*pa-šu-ni*]

CT 53 201

(Obverse too broken for translation)

**298** 1ff, 13, 15f, r.3ff, 12f See coll.

2 [*ša* LU]GAL EN *iš-pur-a*[*n-ni*]
3 [*ma*]-⌜*a*⌝ *pi-it-t*[*i*]
4 [*x*] ⌜NA$_4$⌝.$^{d}$ALAD.$^{d}$LAMA [*ša*]
5 [$^{m}$*du*$^{?}$-*i*]*a-nu-si te-pa-*[*áš*]
6 [*ina p*]*i-it-ti e-*[*pa-áš*]
7 [*du*]*l-lu pa-ni-šu d*[*a-an-qu*]
8 [*du*]*l-lu-šá in-né-*[*pa-áš*]
9 [ŠÀ-*b*]*u šá* LUGAL EN-[*ia*]
10 [*lu*] DÙG.GA NA$_4$.$^{d}$ALA[D.$^{d}$LAMA]
11 [*ša*] ⌜$^{m}$*du*$^{?}$⌝-*ia-nu-si* [*ga-mur*]
12 [*ina* Š]À GIŠ.MÁ *nu-*[*sar-kib-šú*]
13 [*mi-nu*] *šá* LUGAL EN [*i-qa-bu-ni*]
14 [*liš-p*]*a-*[*ru-u-ni*]
15 [*x x x x x*]*x* [*x x x*]
rest broken away

r.1 [As to the wo]rk to [be done about which the ki]ng, my lord, wrote [me]: "You shall exec[ute] it by the patte[rn] of the [...] bull colossus [of *Du*]yanusi" — I am do[ing acco]rdingly.

7 [The w]ork looks [*good*]; [i]t is being done. The king, [my] lord, [can] be glad.

10 The bull colo[ssus of] *Du*yanusi [is finished] and we have l[oaded] it [on] a boat. [Let them w]ri[te me wh]at the king my lord's [orders are].

(Rest destroyed)

# 300. Fragment Referring to a Bull Colossus

K 5523

beginning broken away
1′ [*x x x x x*]*x* ⌜*x*⌝[*x x*]
2′ [*x x x x*]*x e-pa-*[*áš*]
3′ [*ú-ga*]-*mar an-ni-*[*ú*]
4′ [NA$_4$.$^{d}$A]LAD.$^{d}$LAMA [0]
5′ [*ša*] LUGAL *be-*[*lí*]
6′ [*iš-pur*]-⌜*an-ni*⌝ [*x x*]
rest broken away
Rev. beginning broken away
1′ [*x x x x*] *sal* [*x x*]
2′ [*x x x*]*x ad* ⌜*an*⌝ [*x*]
3′ [*ina*] ⌜É!⌝ *kam-mu-s*[*u*]
4′ [*ša* LU]GAL EN *iš-pur-*[*an-ni*]
5′ [*x x x*]*x* ⌜*ni*⌝ *x*[*x x*]
rest broken away

CT 53 268

(Beginning destroyed)

1 I will d[o and fin]ish [......].

4 Thi[s bull] colossus [concerning which] the king, [my] lo[rd, wro]te me

(Break)

r.3 *they are* [*at h*]*ome.*

4 [As to what the ki]ng, my lord, wr[ote me]

(Rest destroyed)

**299** r.1 See coll.

# GLOSSARY AND INDICES

## Logograms and Their Readings

A.AN → *zunnu;* A.MEŠ → *mê;* A.ŠÀ, A.ŠÀ.GA → *eqlu;* Á, Á.2 → *ahu B;* AD → *abu;* AD.AD → *ab abi;* ALAM → *ṣalmu;* AN.BAR → *parzillu;* ANŠE → *imāru;* ANŠE.A.AB.BA → *gammalu;* ANŠE.BAD-HAL → *pēthallu;* ANŠE.GÌR.NUN.NA → *kūdunu;* ANŠE.KUR, ANŠE.KUR.RA → *sissû;* ANŠE.NUN.NA → *daddammu;* ANŠE.SAL.HÚB → *atānu;* ARAD → *urdu;*

BAD-HAL → *pēthallu;* BÀD → *dūru;* BANŠUR → *paššūru;* BE → *bēlu, šumma;* BE.LUM → *bēlu;* BURU$_{14}$ → *ebūru;*

$^{d}$AG → *Nabû;* $^{d}$ALAD.$^{d}$LAMA → *aladlammû;* $^{d}$AMAR.UTU → *Marduk;* $^{d}$EN → *Bēl;* $^{d+}$EN → *Bēl;* $^{d}$PA → *Nabû;* $^{d}$ŠÚ → *Marduk;* DAGAL → *rapāšu;* DI → *šulmu;* DINGIR → *ilu;* DU → *alāku;* DÙ → *kalu;* DÙG, DÙG.GA → *ṭiābu;* DUG$_{4}$.GA → *qabû;* DUMU → *marʾu;* DUMU—KÁ.DINGIR.RA.KI → *Bābili;* DUMU—LUGAL → *mār šarri;* DUMU—ŠEŠ → *mār ahi;* DUMU.MÍ → *marʾutu;*

É → *bētānu, bētu;* É—AD → *bēt abi;* É—BÀD → *bēt dūri;* É—DINGIR → *bēt ili;* É—EN → *bēt bēli;* É—ŠU.2 → *bēt qāti;* É.GAL → *ekallu;* É.KUR → *ekurru;* É.SIG$_{4}$ → *igāru;* EGIR → *urki;* EN → *bēlu;* EN—GIŠ.GIGIR → *bēl mugirri;* EN—URU → *bēl āli;* EN.NUN → *maṣṣartu;* ERIM → *ṣābu;* ERIM—LUGAL, ERIM—MAN → *ṣāb šarri;*

GABA → *irtu;* GAL → *rabû;* GAR → *šaknu;* GAZ → *dēktu, duāku;* GEŠTIN → *karānu;* GI.AMBAR → *appāru;* GI$_{6}$ → *mūšu;* GIBIL → *eššu;* GÍD.DA → *arāku;* GIM → *kî;* GÍR → *patru;* GÌR.2 → *šēpu;* GÌR.PAD.DU → *eṣintu;* GIŠ → *iṣu;* GIŠ.A.AM → *aṭāru;* GIŠ.APIN → *epinnu;* GIŠ.BAN → *qassu;* GIŠ.BÁN → *sūtu;* GIŠ.ERIN → *erēnu;* GIŠ.GAG.LIŠ.LAL → *saparru;* GIŠ.GEŠTIN → *karānu;* GIŠ.GIGIR → *mugirru;* GIŠ.GU.ZA → *kussiu;* GIŠ.HA.LU.ÚB → *haluppu;* GIŠ.KIN.GEŠTIN → *išhunnatu;* GIŠ.KU → *taskarinnu;* GIŠ.MÁ → *eleppu;* GIŠ.MES.MÁ.GAN.NA → *musukkannu;* GIŠ.MI → *ṣillu;* GIŠ.MURUB$_{4}$ → *qablu B;* GIŠ.PA → *haṭṭu;* GIŠ.SAR → *kiriu;* GIŠ.ŠÚ.A → *šibšutu;* GIŠ.UL → *ullu?;* GIŠ.ÙR → *gušūru;* GÚ → *libānu;* GÚ.UN → *biltu;* GUD, GUD.NITÁ → *alpu;* GUR → *tuāru;* GURUN.BURU$_{14}$ → *ebūru;*

HAL.ṢU → *bīrtu;*

I.DIB → *askupputu;* Ì → *šamnu;* ÍD → *nāru;* IGI → *pānu;* IGI.2 → *ēnu;* ÍL → *našû;* IM → *ṭuppu;* ITI → *urhu;* ITI.AB → *kanūnu;* ITI.APIN → *arahsamnu;* ITI.BARAG → *nisannu;* ITI.DUL → *tašrītu;* ITI.KIN → *elūlu;* ITI.NE → *ābu;* ITI.SIG$_{4}$ → *simānu;* ITI.ŠE → *addāru;* ITI.ŠU → *tamūzu;* ITI.ZÍZ → *šabāṭu;*

KA → *pû;* KÁ.DINGIR → *Bābili;* KAB → *šumēlu;* KALAG → *daʾānu, danānu;* KASKAL → *hūlu;* KASKAL.GÍD → *bēru;* KI.LAL → *šuqultu;* KI.TA → *šapal;* KIN → *šapāru;* KUG.GI → *hurāṣu;* KUG.UD → *ṣarpu;* KUR, KUR.KUR → *mātu;* KUR.RA → *sissû;* KUR.URI → *urarṭu;* KÚR → *nakru;* KUŠ → *mašku;* KÙŠ → *ammutu;*

LAL → *muṭê;* LÚ → *amēlu;* LÚ.03.U$_{5}$ → *tašlīšu;* LÚ.600—É.GAL → *nāgir ekalli;* LÚ.A → *mār;* LÚ.A—KIN → *mār šipri;* LÚ.A—SIG$_{5}$ → *mār damqi;* LÚ.A.BA → *ṭupšarru;* LÚ.ARAD → *urdu;* LÚ.ARAD—É.GAL → *urda ekalli;* LÚ.BAD-HAL → *ša-pēthalli;* LÚ.BUR.GUL → *parkullu;* LÚ.DAM.QAR → *tamkāru;* LÚ.DUMU → *marʾu;* LÚ.EME → *ša-lišāni;* LÚ.EN—GIŠ.GIGIR → *bēl mugirri;* LÚ.EN—NAM → *pāhutu;* LÚ.EN—URU → *bēl āli;* LÚ.ERIM → *ṣābu;* LÚ.ERIM—LUGAL, LÚ.ERIM.MAN → *ṣāb šarri;* LÚ.GAL → *rabiu, rab;* LÚ.GAL—É → *rab bēti;* LÚ.GAL—GAL → *rab rabê;* LÚ.GAL—HAL.ṢU → *rab bīrti;* LÚ.GAL—KAŠ.LUL → *rab šāqê;* LÚ.GAL—SAG → *rab ša-rēši;* LÚ.GAL—SUM.NINDA → *rab karkadinni;* LÚ.GAL—URU → *rab ālāni;* LÚ.GAL—URU.HAL.ṢU → *rab bīrti;* LÚ.GAR → *šaknu;* LÚ.GIŠ.GIGIR → *susānu;* LÚ.IGI.DUB → *masennu;* LÚ.KA.KÉŠ → *kāṣiru;* LÚ.KAB.SAR → *kapšarru;* LÚ.KAŠ.LUL → *šāqiu;* LÚ.KIN.A → *mār šipri;* LÚ.KUR → *māda;* LÚ.KÚR → *nakru;* LÚ.LUL → *parriṣu;* LÚ.MAH → *ṣīru;* LÚ.MU → *nuhatimmu;* LÚ.NAGAR → *naggār pāši;* LÚ.NAM → *pāhutu;* LÚ.NIGIR/NIGÍR—É.GAL → *nāgir ekalli;* LÚ.NINDA → *āpiu;* LÚ.SAG → *ša-rēši;* LÚ.SANGA → *sangû;* LÚ.SIMUG.KUG.GI → *ṣarrāpu;* LÚ.SIPA → *rāʾiu;* LÚ.SUKKAL → *sukkallu;* LÚ.ŠÁM → *ša-šīmi;* LÚ.ŠÚ.NIGÍR—É.GAL → *nāgir ekalli;* LÚ.TIN → *etinnu;* LÚ.TUR → *ṣehru;* LÚ.UM.ME.A → *ummânu;* LÚ.UN → *nīšī;* LÚ.UŠ → *rādiu;* LÚ.UŠ—ANŠE → *rādi imāri;* LÚ.ZI → *napšutu;* LUGAL → *šarru;*

MA.NA → *manû;* MAN → *šarru;* MÈ → *tāhāzu;* MI → *mūšu;* MÍ → *issu;* MÍ.ANŠE.KUR.RA → *urītu;* MÍ.HÚB → *urītu;* MÍ.NIN—ŠEŠ → *ahāt ahi;* MU → *šumu;* MU.AN.NA → *šattu;* MÚD → *dāmu;* MUN → *ṭābtu;* MURUB$_4$ → *qablu A;*

NÁ → *eršu;* NA$_4$.GUG → *sāmtu;* NA$_4$.I.DIB → *askupputu;* NA$_4$.KIŠIB → *kunukku;* NAM → *pāhutu;* NINDA → *kusāpu;* NUMUN → *zar'u;* NUMUN—LUGAL → *zēr šarri;*

PAB → *ahu, gimru;*

QÀL → *qalālu;*

SA$_5$ → *sāmu;* SAG → *rēšu;* SAG.DU → *kaqqudu;* SIG$_4$ → *libittu;* SIG$_5$ → *damāqu;* SU$_6$ → *ziqnu;* SUM → *tadānu;*

ŠÀ → *libbu;* ŠE → *še'u;* ŠE.IN.NU → *tibnu;* ŠE.NUMUN → *zar'u;* ŠE.PAD → *kurummutu;* ŠEŠ → *ahu;* ŠU, ŠU.2 → *qātu;*

TA → *issi/issu;* TÚG.GADA → *kitû;* TÙR → *tarbāṣu;*

Ú.ZAG.HI.LI.SAR → *sahlû;* UD → *ūmu;* UDU, UDU.HI.A → *immeru;* UDU.NITÁ → *iābilu;* UDU.SISKUR → *niqiu;* UGU → *muhhu;* UN.MEŠ → *nīšī;* URU → *ālu;* URU.BÀD—LUGAL—GI → *Dūr-Šarrukēn;* URU.BÀD—MAN—GIN → *Dūr-Šarrukēn;* URU.HAL.ṢU → *bīrtu;* URU.NINA → *Nīnua;* URU.ŠÀ—URU → *Libbi-āli;* URUDU → *siparru;* UŠ → *šiddu;* ÚŠ → *muātu;* UTÚL → *diqāru;* UZU → *šīru;*

ZAG → *imittu;* ZÁH → *halāqu;* ZI → *napšutu;* ZÍD → *eṣidītu;* ZU → *la'û, lē'u;*

# Glossary

**ab abi** "grandfather": AD—AD-*ia* 143 r. 7,

**abāku** "to haul, lead away": *a-ba-ak* 129 r. 6, *a-tab-ka* 117:14, *e-tab-ku-u-ni* 117:12,

**abarakku** see *masennu,*

**abati** (Šubrian word?): *a-ba-ti* 35:31,

**abātu** "(N) to flee": *in-[na-bit-u-ni]* 196:6,

**abiktu** "defeat": *a-bi-ik-tú* 92:10,

**abu** "father": AD-*ia* 143 r. 7, AD-*u-a* 31 r. 16,

**abutu** "word, matter": *a-bat* 108 e. 32, 260 r. 3, [*a-bat* 210 r. 1, [*a*]*-bat* 74:6, *a-bat-u-ni* 52 r. 19, *a-bi-te* 96 r. 2, 284 r. 4, *a-bu-tú* 104:14, *a-bu-t*[*ú*] 203 r. 22, [*a-bu-tú* 162 r. 4,

**ada** (Šubrian word?): *a-da* 35 r. 11,

**adanniš** "very": *a—dan-niš* 21:4, 10, 22:4, 23:4, 24:4, 25:4, 28:4, 31:3, 32:4, 34:3, 35 r. 8, 44:1, 45:1, 56 r. 8, 126 r. 13, 132:7, 152:9, 20, 199:9, 214 e. 4, 217:14, 242 r. 4, 249:7, 274:3, 281:7, 294:5, 6, r. 1, 295:16, 22, e. 28, *a—dan-niš*] 29:4, 33:3, 35:3, 37:3, 44:1, 218 r. 13, 276 e. 3, *a—dan-n*[*iš*] 249:10, *a—dan-*[*niš*] 27:4, 156 r. 2, *a—da*[*n-niš*] 30:4, *a—da*]*n-niš* 278:6, *a*]*—dan-niš* 34 r. 30, 285:5, *a—da-niš* 145 r. 8,

**adê** "treaty": *a-*[*de-e*] 78 r. 4,

**adi** "until, plus": *a-di* 3:13, e. 19, r. 19, 32 r. 17, 37:17, 46 r. 2, 64:16, 74:7, 10, r. 6, 91:11, 108:17, 114:10, 117:5, 12, 131:4, 147:6, 164 r. 1, 175:7, 210 r. 17, 215 r. 1, 2, 227:20, r. 1, 8, 229 r. 2, 5, 8, 257:11, 261:4, *a-di*] 33:10, *a-d*[*i* 165:8, 277:8, *a-*[*di*] 31 r. 25, *a-*[*d*]*i* 145 s. 2, *a*]*-di* 285:4, [*a*]*-di* 277:9, *a-du* 47:9, 48:14, 62:6, 92 r. 14, 98 r. 9, 99:1, 6, 103 r. 2, 152 e. 25, 205:4, 242:10, 244:7, 250 r. 20, 279:9, 292 r. 6, 295 r. 15, 24, 298:14, *a-d*]*u* 267:6, [*a*]*-du* 152 e. 26,

**adru** "threshing floor": *ad-r*[*a-te* 82:8, *ad-ra-te-šú-nu* 60:3,

**agappu** "wing": *a-kap-pi* 293:7,

**ahāiš** "each other": *a-ha-iš* 3 r. 16, 32:16, 33 s. 3, 286:5, *a-ha-*[*iš*] 249:11, [*a-ha-iš*] 298:10, *a-he-ii-ši* 227 r. 14, *a-he-iš* 118 r. 6, 123 r. 3, 202:10, *i-sa-he-iš* 150 r. 12,

**ahāt ahi** "brother's sister": MÍ.NIN—ŠEŠ-*ka* 108 r. 20,

**ahhūr** "still": *ah—hur* 280 r. 4, *a*]*h—hur* 54:10, *ah—hu-ru* 147:15, *ah—hu-ur* 291:8,

**ahītēšu** "secretly": *a-hi-te-šú* 90 r. 1, *a-hi-t*[*i-šú* 90:4,

**ahu A** "brother": PAB-*ia* 33 r. 19, PAB-*u-a* 81:2, 4, r. 5, PAB.MEŠ-*ku-nu* 257:11, ŠEŠ-*a-a* 81 r. 3, ŠEŠ-*šú* 32:14, 52:11, 91:14, 17, 108:27, 148:9, ŠEŠ-*u-a* 217 s. 1, ŠEŠ.MEŠ-*šú* 31:19, 53:7, ŠEŠ.MEŠ-*šú-nu* 42 r. 2,

**ahu B** "arm": *a-hi* 35:27, Á-*šú* 147 r. 6, Á-*šú-nu* 294:2, Á.2-*ka* 115:10, Á.2-*ni* 42 r. 6, Á.2-*š*[*ú* 176:10,

**aiābu** "enemy": *a-a-b*[*i-ka*] 146 r. 8,

**aiāka** "where": *a-a-ka* 54:3, 100 r. 10, 147:8, *ia-a-k*[*a*] 146:6, [*i*]*a-a-ka* 225:9,

**aiakamēni** "anywhere": *a-a-ka-me-ni* 95 e. 18, 108 r. 13, *a-a-ka-m*[*e-ni* 60:8,

**aiakku** "shrine": *a-a-k*[*i*] 121 r. 11,

**aiālu** "help": *a*]*-a-li* 131:5,

**aiāši** "me": *a-a-ši* 46 r. 2, 81:3, *a-*[*a-š*]*i* 46 r. 7, *ia-a-ši* 196 r. 10,

**aiēša** "whither?": *a-a-šá* 100 r. 11,

**aiu** "what, which?": *a-a-e* 194 r. 6, *a-a-ʾu* 262:4,

**akālu** "to eat": *e-ku-lu* 289 r. 2, *e-*[*ku*]*-lu* 37:23, *e-tak-la* 32:16, *e-tak-lu* 32:13, [*e*]*-tak-lu* 34:28, *e-ta-kal* 156 r. 4, *i-ku-ul* 225:12, *le*]*-kul* 106:21, *ša-ku-lu* 257:2, *šá-ki-il* 3 e. 19, *ta-kul* 243 r. 5, *ú-šá-ku-ul* 225:14,

**akanni** "now": *a-da-kan-ni* 245 r. 6, *a-kan-ni* 285:4, [*a-k*]*an-ni* 257 r. 10, *a-ka-an-ni* 246:9, 295 r. 3, *ka-a-ni* 146:8,

**akappu** see *agappu,*

**akê** "how?": *a-ke-e* 58:7, 147 r. 11, 182 r. 5, 212:3, *a-k*]*e-e* 212:1, *a*]*-ke-e* 86 r. 1,

**aki** "as": *a-ki* 35 e. 35, 69:9, 90 r. 6, 103 e. 10, 105 r. 1, 113 r. 1, 117:5, 121 r. 3, 143:10, 162:11, r. 6, 163 r. 7, 169 r. 6, 229:3, 248:5, *a-k*[*i* 208 r. 3, *a-*[*ki* 271:4, *a-ki-i* 92:8, 10, 218 r. 7,

**aladlammû** "bull colossus": $^{d}$ALAD.$^{d}$LAMA.[MEŠ] 298:12, r. 11, $^{d}$A[LAD.$^{d}$LAMA.MEŠ] 298:9, [$^{d}$ALAD.$^{d}$LAMA.MEŠ] 298 e. 17, NA$_4$.$^{d}$ALAD.$^{d}$]LAMA 17:12, NA$_4$.$^{d}$ALAD.$^{d}$LAMA 17 r. 2, 115 r. 5, 118:4, 297:11, 299 r. 4, NA$_4$.$^{d}$ALA[D.$^{d}$LAMA] 299 r. 10, NA$_4$.$^{d}$ALA]D.$^{d}$LAMA 57:4, [NA$_4$.$^{d}$A]LAD.$^{d}$LAMA 297 r. 3, 300:4, NA$_4$].$^{d}$ALAD.$^{d}$LAMA.MEŠ 58:11,

**alāku** "to go, come": *al-ka* 210 r. 11, *al-ka*]] 67:3, *al-k*[*a* 108 r. 5, *al-k*[*a*] 18 r. 2, *al-*[*k*]*a* 74 r. 10, *al*]*-ka-ni* 256 r. 2, *al-lak* 64:11, 172 r. 6, 199:13, 200:15, *al-la-ak* 146:11, *al-la-ka* 53 e. 26, 74 r. 11, 176:9, [*a*]*l-la-ka* 105 r. 10, *al-la-ku-u-ni* 31 r. 26, *al-*[*lik-an-ni*] 230:4, *al-*[*lik-u-ni*] 26 r. 3, *a*[*l-lik-u-ni* 63:13, *al-li-kan-ni* 176 s. 1, *al-l*[*i-x* 135 r. 2, *at-tal-ka* 4 r. 2, *at-tal-k*[*a* 37:24, [*a*]*t-ta-lak* 32 r. 9, *a-lik* 53:11, 18, e. 25, 200:8, 210 r. 11, *a-l*[*ik*] 126:10, *a-*[*lik* 117 r. 7, *a-lik-u-n*[*i* 125 r. 8, *a-li-k*[*u*]*-u-ni* 35 r. 1, *a-ta-al-ka* 146:12, *a-ta-lak* 297:12, *il-lak* 88 r. 7, 95:6, 218:8, 295:24, *il-la*[*k*] 122 r. 7, [*il-l*]*ak* 150:7, [*il*]*-lak* 38:9, *il-lak-a* 81:16, *il-lak-*[*an-n*]*i* 74:5, *il-l*[*ak-ma*] 38:9, *i*]*l-lak-ni* 279 r. 7, *il-lak-u-ni* 52:13, r. 10, 15, 249 r. 9, 289:6, *il-lak-u-ni-ni* 257 e. 12, *il-l*[*ak*]*-ú-n*[*i*] 74:12, *il-la-ka* 40 r. 3, 62:5, 172 r. 4, 292:6, *il-la-k*[*a*] 146:9, *il-la-*[*ka*] 51:5, *il-la-kan-ni* 210 r. 18, *il-la-ku-ni* 243 r. 15, *i*]*l-la-ku-*[*ni*] 180:4, [*il-l*]*a-ku-ni* 137 e. 9, *il-la-ku-ni-ni* 295 r. 15, *il-la-ku-u-ni* 40 e. 23,

113:13, 156 r. 7, 226:15, 246:7, *il-la-ku-u-[ni]* 137 r. 3, *il-la-ku-[u-ni]* 105:19, *il-lik-u-ni* 52:13, 92:9, *il-l]ik-u-ni* 106 e. 26, 178 r. 5, *i[l-lik-u-ni]* 55:7, 173:4, *il-lik-u-ni-ni* 52 r. 8, 14, *i]l-lik-u-ni-ni* 107 r. 1, *il-li-ka* 53:6, 54:11, 83 r. 6, 245 r. 7, *il-li-k[a* 146 r. 5, *il-li-k]a* 33 s. 1, *i[l-l]i-ka* 108:10, *i]l-li-ka* 196:8, *il-li-kan-a-ni* 53:6, *il-li-kan-ni* 21:8, 31 r. 18, 179 r. 2, *il-li-ku* 3 r. 12, 126:12, *il-li-ku-ni]* 46:7, *il-li-ku-ni-ni* 243:14, *il-l]i-ku-ni-ni* 220:6, *il-li-ku-u-ni* 105:18, *i]l-li-ku-u-[ni* 174:3, *[il-li-ku-u-ni* 54:10, *[il-l]i-ku-u-ni* 21 r. 21, *il-lu-ku* 92 r. 12, 100:10, 106:19, 113:13, 226 r. 18, *i[l-lu-ku]* 243 r. 14, *[i]l-lu-ku* 38:10, *it-tal-ka* 3:15, 33 s. 2, 34 r. 24, 53:12, 81:8, 155:5, 241:7, 281:13, *it-tal-[ka]* 34 r. 10, 145 e. 18, *i[t]-tal-ka* 2:9, *[it-tal-ka* 48:6, *[it-tal-ka]* 221:7, *[it-tal-k]a* 245:13, *[it-ta]l-ka* 38:6, 283 r. 6, *[it]-tal-ka* 292 r. 8, *[i]t-tal-ka* 283:7, *it-tal-ku* 40 e. 22, *it-tal-ku]* 13:7, 92 r. 6, 221:10, *it]-tal-ku* 34 e. 35, *it]-tal-ku-n[i]* 112 r. 6, *[i]t-tal-ku-ni* 106: 14, *it-tal-ku-nu* 245 r. 5, *it-tal-ku-u-ni* 52:6, 15, 53:10, r. 2, *it-tal-[k]u-u-ni* 52:10, *it-tal]-ku-u-ni* 279 r. 4, *it-t]al-ku-u-ni* 31:18, *[it-tal-k]u-u-ni* 186: 4, *it-tal-ku-ú-ni* 32:18, *it-ta-lak* 31 r. 24, 34 r. 19, 37 r. 1, 61 r. 11, 131:5, *it-ta-l[ak]* 204 r. 6, *it]-ta-lak* 177:2, *[it-ta-lak* 54:6, *it-(ta)-la-ka* 53:19, *[it-ta-la-ka* 54:8, *it-ta-tak-k[u]* 19 r. 7, *[it-t]a-ta-[ku* 130 r. 1, *i-lak* 89:12, 95:14, 97:13, 147:7, 14, 218 r. 6, *i-lak-ka* 126 r. 5, *i-lak-u-ni* 52 r. 4, 224 r. 9, *i-la-ka* 53:9, 81:6, 171:3, r. 6, 200:12, 226 r. 10, *i-la-k[a* 191:2, *[i-la-ka]* 200 r. 13, *i-la-ku-ni-ni* 69 r. 6, *i-la-ku-u-ni* 35 e. 35, 147 e. 16, 194 r. 5, 226 r. 21, 232 r. 9, *i-l[a-ku-u-ni]* 195:3, *i]-la-ku-u-ni* 35:13, *i-lik-an-ni* 147 r. 9, *i-lik-u-ni-ni* 202 r. 4, *i-li-ka* 1 r. 2, *i-li-kan-a-ni* 227:8, 21, *i-li-ki* 200 r. 6, *i-[li-ku-ni]* 121 r. 6, *[i-l]i-ku-ni-ni* 269:12, *i-lu-ku* 35 e. 34, *[i-l]u-ku-u-ni* 141 r. 3, *i-tal-ka* 83 r. 5, 91:17, 98:12, 133:8, 149 r. 1, 4, 162 r. 1, 164 r. 5, *i-tal-k[a* 138:10, *i-[tal-ka]* 148:10, *[i-tal-k]a* 286: 5, *i-tal-ku* 35 r. 7, 84 r. 2, 162:8, *i-tal-[ku* 74 r. 7, *i-tal-ku-ni* 87 r. 6, 104:6, 121 r. 13, 202 r. 17, *i-tal-k[u-ni* 208:5, *[i]-tal-ku-ni* 133 r. 12, *i-tal-ku-u-ni* 147:11, 164:8, 203 r. 10, 16, 223 r. 1, *i-tal-ku-ú-ni]* 149 r. 19, *i-tal-lak* 86:7, 9, 87 r. 2, 92 r. 11, 95:2, 162 r. 3, *i-tal-lu-ku* 126 r. 8, *i-ta[l-x* 216 r. 1, *i-t[al-x* 7:6, *i-ta-at-ku* 32:11, 217:9, *i-ta-at-k[u* 18:7, *i-ta-lak* 141 r. 6, 162:9, 216 r. 3, 223 r. 3, 227:13, *i-ta-la-ak* 184:2, *i-ta-la-k[a* 218:4, *i-ta-ta-ka* 163 r. 14, *i-ta-ta-ku* 36:4, *lal-lik-ka* 62:5, *lal-li-ka* 154 r. 5, 294 r. 11, *[la]l-li-[ka* 67 e. 14, *la-al-li[k* 99 e. 13, *la-al-lik-ka* 126:6, *la-al-li-ka* 47 r. 2, *la-li-ki* 78 r. 13, *la-li-[ki]* 133 s. 1, *lil-lik* 74:8, *lil-li-ka* 52 r. 17, 18, 257 r. 6, *lil]-li-ka* 194 r. 11, *li[l-li-ka* 108 r. 4, *[lil-l]i-ka* 98:13, *lil-li-ki* 199 r. 10, 11, 200 r. 11, *lil-li-ku* 104:11, 178 r. 8, 298:9, r. 8, *lil-li-ku]* 298 r. 13, *lil-li-ku-ni* 145 r. 3, *lil-(li)-ku-ni* 32 r. 15, *lil-li-ku-u-ni* 295:13, *li-li-i[k]* 231:3, *li-li-ka* 134:7, 217 r. 17, *ni-il-lak* 206 r. 7, 295 r. 22, *ni-il-la-ka* 295 r. 22, *ni-il-lik* 52 r. 9, *ni-il-lik-u-ni* 282:9, *ni-li-ka* 194 r. 6, *ni]-tal-ka* 98:9, *tal-lak-an-ni* 98 r. 10, *tal-l[a-ka]* 31 r. 28, *tal-li-kan-ni* 105:9, *ta-li-kan-ni* 263:4, *ta-li-ka-ni]* 117:3, *ta-li-ki* 233 r. 3, *ta-tal-ka]* 165:10, *t[a]-ta-al-[ka* 26:3, *ú-ša-la[k]* 97:7, DU-*ak* 133:5, DU-*a-ni* 217 r. 12, DU-*ka* 226 r. 7, DU-*u-ni* 42 r. 5, 169:4, 7, 8, 226 r. 17, DU-*u-ni-ni* 117:18,

**ali** "where?": *a-le-e* 46:12, 103:9, 129:2, 215 r. 4, *a-le-e]* 82:8, *a-li-i* 224:13,

**almattu** "widow": MÍ.*al-mat-te* 217 r. 8, MÍ.*a[l-mat-te* 218:2,

**alpu** "ox": GUD 37:17, 48:8, GUD.MEŠ 21:18, 37:20, 21, 22, 25, r. 14, 69 r. 7, 70:4, 122:7, 12, 238:4, 258:2, 4, 280 r. 1, GUD.M[EŠ 20:5, GUD].MEŠ 37:16, GU]D.MEŠ 133 r. 14, GUD.NITÁ.MEŠ 137:4, GUD.NITÁ.M[EŠ] 146:5, GUD.NITÁ.MEŠ-*šú* 133 r. 9,

**ālu** "city, town": URU 3:13, r. 14, 12 r. 3, 15:16, r. 8, 24:16, 54 r. 8, 78:4, 5, 80:8, 109:9, 206 r. 1, 213:5, 226:10, URU] 56 r. 5, 126 r. 7, UR[U] 4 r. 3, U[RU 13:7, U[RU] 67:6, [URU] 56:9, U]RU-*ka* 250 r. 5, URU.ME[Š 268:9, URU.MEŠ 37:23, r. 8, 13, 48:14, 232:12, URU.[MEŠ 232:4, URU.MEŠ-*ni* 12 r. 11, 46: 11, 78:10, 84:4, 152:16, 232 r. 8, URU].MEŠ-*ni* 232:8, [URU].MEŠ-*ni* 177:5, [UR]U.MEŠ-[*ni*] 232:9, [U]RU.MEŠ-*ni* 296 r. 5, URU.MEŠ-*ni-ia* 46:6, URU.MEŠ-*ni-ma* 232 r. 4, URU.MEŠ-*šú-nu* 250 r. 13,

**amāru** "to see, behold": *am-ra* 19 s. 1, *am-ra-š[u-nu-n]i* 149:5, *am-ru-te* 251:10, r. 4, *a-mar* 203 r. 6, *a-ma-ru-ni* 243:9, *a-mur* 108:6, *a-ta-mar* 37: 16, *a-ta-ma[r* 125 r. 9, *a-ta-[mar]* 34 r. 29, *[a-ta-m]ar-šú* 4:9, *e-mar-šú* 91 r. 5, *e-mar-u-ni* 154 r. 4, *e-mu-ru* 90 r. 5, *e-mu-ru-ni* 164:13, *e-tam-ru* 3:8, *e-ta[m-ru]* 267 s. 2, *e-tam-ru-šú-nu* 217:9, *e-ta-am-m[a]r-šú* 53:23, *i-ma-ru-ni* 260 r. 7, *la-mur* 47 r. 4, 126:7, *l]a-mur* 294 r. 12, *[l]a-mur* 47 r. 10, *n]é-em-mar* 287:5, *né-e-ta-[mar]* 156:16, *né-mur* 52 r. 10, *né-m[ur-u-ni]* 250 r. 24, *ú-mu-ru* 204:16,

**amēlu** "man": LÚ 53 r. 9, 54:18, 80:9, 125 r. 2, 3, 150 r. 4, 154 r. 6, 213 r. 5, 246 r. 4, L[Ú] 113:15, 250 r. 11, [LÚ] 204:16,

**ammāka** "there": *am-ma-kam-ma* 83 r. 7, *am-ma-kam-[m]a* 1:10, *am-ma-ka-ma* 105:20, *a-ma-k[a]* 224:15, *ma-ak-ka* 100 r. 4, *ma-ka* 92:11,

**ammar** see *mar,*

**ammiu** "that": *am-ma-ti* 206 r. 8, *am-mì-iu-u* 163 r. 12, *am-mì-ti]* 228:5, *am-mì-ú* 199:9, *am-mu-te* 54 r. 19, 92:14, 105:22, *am-mu-t[e* 92:13, *am-mu-[te]* 97:6, *am-[mu-te* 108:28, *[am-mu-te]* 97:5, *[am-mu]-te* 112 e. 7, *am-m[u-ti* 61 r. 7, *[am-mu-u-te]* 204:6, *a-mu-te* 202:6,

**ammutu** "cubit": KÙŠ 15 r. 7, 294:9, 10, 11, 13, 15, 17, 295:25,

**ana** "to": *ana* 15:3, 4, 5, 16:3, 169:11, 210 r. 12, *a-na* 1:1, 3, 4, 5, 2:3, 4, 3:1, 2, 3, 4, 13, 6:3, 10:5, 11:1, 4, 5, r. 2, 7, s. 3, 14:1, 5, 10, r. 4, 13, 16:1, 9, r. 3, 17:3, 4, 5, 18:3, 19:1, 3, s. 3, 20:11, 21:3, 5, 6, r. 14, 22:5, 23:1, 3, 5, 24:3, 5, 6, 25:1, 3, 5, 6, 27:3, 5, 6, 28:1, 3, 5, 6, 29:1, 4, 5, r. 7, 30:3, 5, 31:1, 3, 4, 5, r. 19, 32:1, 3, 5, 6, r. 15, 33:1, 3, 4, 5, 6, r. 1, 11, s. 3, 34:3, 4, 20, e. 37, r. 3, 6, 21, 28, 35:3, 4, 24, 27, 29, r. 3, 7, 36:4, 37:3, 4, 24, r. 5, 13, 38:3, 39:8, 40:3, 4, r. 1, 43:3, 5, 44 r. 5, 45:1, 46:7, 17, r. 3, 47:1, 3, 4, 6, 8, 13, 15, r. 1, 48:1, 49:1, 4, 52:1, 3, 15, 20, e. 23, r. 1, 8, 12, 53:1, 3, 5, 9, 11, 19, 54:5, 9, 10, r. 16, 55:3, 7, 56:1, 3, 5, 57:3, 9, 58:8, 59:3, 62:1, 3, 63:3, r. 13, 64:1, 3, 65:1, 4, 66:3, 68:1, 3, 69:1, 3, 10, r. 7, 70:1, 71:1, 3, 73:3, 74:1, 3, 75:1, 3, 78:1, 3, 79:1, 3, 80:1, 3, 4, 5, 81:2, 4, r. 2, 82:1, 3, r. 1, 83:1, 3, r. 2, 4, 84:1, 3, r. 3, 85:1, 2, 86:3, 6, 87:3, r. 5, 88:1, 3, 7, r. 4, 89:1, 90:4, r. 8, 91:1, 2, 4, 17, r. 9, 92:1, 2, 3, 4, 7, 94:3, 95:4, r. 3, 96:1, 3, 5, 6, 97:3, 98:1, 3, r. 4, 99:3, 8, e. 12, r. 8, 100:3, 15, r. 5, 11, 104:1, 3, 12, r. 1, 105:1, 18, r. 3, 108:1, r. 8, 15, 109:4, 110:1,

4, 113:1, 114:1, 115:7, 9, 116 r. 3, 117:1, 13, r. 6, 16, 118:1, 10, 119:1, 4, 8, 120:5, 7, r. 3, 121:1, 13, r. 5, 14, 122:1, 3, r. 2, 125:1, r. 9, 126:1, 3, 4, 9, r. 12, 15, 127:1, 3, 4, 5, 128:3, 4, 5, 7, 10, 129 r. 3, 4, s. 2, 130 r. 4, 132:1, 3, 4, 133:3, 134:3, 135:1, 136:1, 3, 140:1, 3, 141:1, 3, 142:5, 8, r. 6, 143 r. 3, 144:3, 5, 145:1, 146:3, 147:2, 3, 149:1, 2, r. 4, 150:12, 17, 152:1, 3, 8, 14, 15, r. 3, 5, 153:3, 154:1, 3, 6, r. 3, 155:1, 3, 156:5, e. 17, 157:4, 6, 7, 158:1, 159:3, 160:10, 161:1, 3, 162:3, 6, 163:1, 4, r. 13, 165:1, 3, 168:1, 4, r. 8, 169:1, r. 4, 6, 170:3, 171 r. 12, 172:1, 3, r. 5, 176:5, 6, r. 8, 181:3, 182:3, 192 r. 4, 194:3, 197 r. 4, 8, 199:1, 3, 8, 11, 12, 14, r. 4, 200:1, 3, 7, 11, 12, 16, r. 6, 201:3, 202:1, 3, 203:1, 3, 7, r. 6, 16, 204:3, 4, r. 6, 205:1, r. 2, 206:1, 3, r. 6, 207:3, 209:1, 210:1, 3, 4, 211:1, 3, 4, 213:3, r. 1, 2, 214 e. 3, 215:3, 216:1, 8, 217:1, 3, 218:10, 12, r. 7, 221:1, 3, 10, 223 r. 4, 224:1, 3, 226:1, 3, r. 11, 227:1, 3, 13, 20, r. 9, 229 e. 11, 12, 233:1, 3, 6, 234:3, r. 1, 237:1, 3, 238:3, 239:3, 241:1, 3, 242:1, 3, 243:1, 3, 17, r. 8, 244:1, 3, 4, r. 7, 245:1, 5, 6, 7, 246:1, 3, 10, 247:3, 250:1, 3, 251:3, 253:5, 256:6, 257:5, 264:5, 265:1, 3, 7, 266:1, 269:7, 271:3, 279:11, r. 10, 280:6, 8, r. 2, 8, 9, 281:3, 4, 5, 6, 10, 282:8, 283:6, 284 r. 12, 286:8, 288 s. 2, 289:5, r. 5, 291:13, e. 15, r. 13, 292:3, 293:1, 4, 5, 294:16, r. 2, 4, 10, 295:3, 8, 24, r. 8, 298:3, r. 5, *a-na*] 18:5, r. 3, 34:4, 36:7, 106:12, 108:5, 225:3, 240:3, 250 r. 22, 291 r. 1, *a-n*[*a* 14:4, 20:3, 34:24, 44:1, 48:3, 50:3, 55:6, 70:3, 72:3, 105:3, 108 s. 2, 122 e. 16, 130:5, 135:3, 144:4, 146 e. 22, 152:16, 176 r. 2, 197:2, r. 5, 205:3, 216:3, 251:1, 270:4, 281:1, 282:3, *a-n*[*a*] 35:18, *a-n*]*a* 8 r. 4, 17:9, 18:4, 22:3, 134:4, 150:3, 151:3, 196 r. 7, 291 e. 16, *a-*[*na* 2:2, 11:3, 14:7, 35:17, 89:3, 108:2, 126 r. 7, 143:3, 152:17, 158:4, 171:3, 192 r. 7, 208:2, 256:1, 267:3, 270:3, 298:8, *a-*[*na*] 173:9, *a-*[*n*]*a* 20:6, 76:3, 85:4, 89:7, 92:3, *a*]*-na* 6:4, 5, 34 r. 15, 232:3, 295:4, (*a-na*) 30:5, [*a-na* 2:1, 6:1, 14:3, 15:1, 17:1, 18:1, 20:1, 21:1, 22:1, 6, 29:6, 30:1, 34:1, 35:1, 5, 37:1, 38:1, 40:1, 5, 43:1, 45:7, 50:1, 55:1, 57:1, 59:1, 63:1, 72:1, 73:1, 76:1, 86:1, 87:1, 97:1, 100:1, 115:1, 120:1, 131:5, 134:1, 143:1, 144:1, 148:1, 3, 150:1, 151:1, 156:1, 170:1, 181:1, 182:1, 183 r. 3, 194:1, 204:1, 5, 215:1, 225:1, 232:1, 239:1, 240:1, 245:12, r. 2, 267:1, 268:1, 269:1, 3, 270:1, 271:1, 282:1, 284 r. 8, 291 r. 10, 295:1, 12, [*a-na*] 23:6, 24:1, 14, 27:1, 34:7, 66:1, 153:1, 159:1, 5, 164:1, 190 r. 7, 194 r. 6, 238:1, 289:5, 291 r. 9, [*a-n*]*a* 128:1, 162:1, 196 r. 9, 201:1, 247:1, 254:16, 292:1, 294:3, [*a*]*-na* 86:12, 94:1, 108:16, 109:8, 133:1, 146:1, 157:1, 189:1, 196 r. 10, 207:1, 218 r. 14, 280:7,

**anāku** "I": *ana-ku* 2 r. 1, 53:10, 13, 54 r. 3, 126:6, 18, 142 r. 9, 178 e. 10, 229 r. 3, 242:8, 270:18, 288 r. 5, 292 r. 3, [*ana*]*-ku* 67:12, [*ana-ku-m*]*a* 229 r. 9, *a-na-ku* 4 r. 6, 21 r. 12, 24:9, 31 r. 17, 32 r. 8, 37:10, 13, 25, 28, 48 r. 13, 62:5, 65:7, 105:5, 108:8, 19, 22, 117:13, 127:11, 143 r. 5, 148 r. 4, 152 e. 27, 162 r. 7, 199:16, 225:10, 227:8, 23, 243:5, 6, 249 r. 5, 257 r. 9, 260 r. 9, 261 r. 5, 289:7, *a-na-ku*] 106:10, *a-na-k*[*u*] 34 r. 26, *a-na-*[*ku* 14:9, *a-*[*na-ku*] 108:6, *a*]*-na-ku* 98:7, [*a-na-k*]*u* 162:11, [*a-n*]*a-ku* 152 e. 25, 162:10, [*a*]*-na-ku* 56 r. 6, 106:9, 154:8, *a-na-ku-ma* 129 r. 6, [*a-na-ku-ma*] 95:10, *a-na-ku-ni*] 283:4, *a-n*[*a-ku-ni*] 106:18, *a-na-ku-u* 118 r. 2, [*a-na-ku-u* 37 r. 11,

**anīnu** "we": *an-ni-nu* 53 r. 7, *a-ni-*[*ni*] 8:6, *a-ni-ni-*[*e*] 118 e. 13, *a-ni-nu* 2:12, 21:14, 105:12, 108 r. 28, 149 r. 21, 160:12, 182 r. 5, *a-ni-*[*nu* 21:20, *a*]*-ni-nu* 19 r. 6, [*a-ni*]*-nu* 36:5, [*a-n*]*i-nu* 113 r. 6, *a-ni-*[*nu-ma*] 106:15, *a-ni-nu-ni* 95:13,

**annāka** "here": *an-na-ka* 41:2, 106:18, 152:19, 295:21, r. 1, *an-na-*[*ka* 283:4, *an-na-*[*ka*] 37:13, *an-*[*na-k*]*a-a-ma* 156:11, *a-na-ka* 32 r. 12, 199 r. 12, *a-na-ka-*[*ni*] 215 r. 1, *ha-na-k*[*a* 268 r. 7, *na-ak* 233:5, *na-ka* 166:4, 5,

**annēša** "hither": *an-n*[*i-šá*] 60:6, *a-ni-šá* 36:5, *ni-šá* 100 r. 5,

**anniu** "this": *an-na-a-te* 280 r. 5, *an-na-te* 100 r. 10, 290:8, *an-n*]*a-te* 290:12, *an-ni-e* 21 r. 14, 45 r. 8, 48:10, 63:17, r. 11, 91:18, 98 r. 3, 103 e. 10, 104:9, 113 r. 1, 145 r. 16, 150 r. 15, 173:2, 188:9, 226 r. 8, 243 e. 18, *an-ni-*[*e* 95 r. 5, *an-ni-*[*e*] 8:5, *an-*[*ni-e*] 34:21, *an*]*-ni-e* 83:6, [*an-ni-e* 108:24, [*an-ni-e*] 95:11, 108 r. 19, *an-ni-i* 295 r. 20, *a*]*n-ni-i* 150:11, *an-ni-iu-ma* 98 r. 8, *an-ni-i-e* 3:8, *an-ni-i-u* 2 r. 8, *an-ni-i-ú* 3 r. 9, *an-ni-ma* 108 r. 17, *an-ni-te* 21:19, 96 r. 2, 6, 284 r. 4, *an-ni-tú* 44 r. 5, 52 r. 11, 152 r. 5, *an-ni-*[*tú* 283 r. 5, *an-n*]*i-tú* 250 r. 25, *an-ni-u* 54:18, 83 r. 3, 147 r. 11, 294:4, *an-ni-ú* 92:13, 95 r. 2, 145:5, 152 r. 12, 199:12, 217 r. 3, *an-ni-*[*ú*] 300:3, *an-n*[*i-ú* 106:4, *an-ni-*[*x* 176 r. 4, *an-nu-te* 24:7, 32 r. 17, 42 r. 5, 46 r. 3, 52:14, r. 7, 87:12, r. 7, 92:18, r. 7, 95 r. 1, 96 r. 8, 100:15, 16, r. 7, 14, 108:21, 118 r. 3, 232 r. 8, 257:3, *an-nu-*[*te*] 97 r. 8, *an-nu-ti* 100:9, 250:9, 256:13, *an-*[*nu*]*-ti* 149:19, [*an*]*-nu-ti* 56 r. 9, [*a*]*n-nu-ti* 176:15, *an-nu-tú* 150 r. 4, *an-nu-u-te* 35 r. 9, *an-nu-ú-te* 152:4, *a-ni-e* 162 r. 6, *a-ni-ú* 162 r. 5, *ha-an-ni-i* 204:10, *ha-*[*an-ni-im-ma*] 229:3, *ha-*[*an*]*-ni-ma* 25:10, *ha-ni-e* 121 r. 10, 199:13, *ha-ni-e*] 199:16, *ha-ni-u* 53:15, 154 r. 6, *ha-nu-te* 121 r. 19, *ha-*[*nu-t*]*e* 62 r. 2, *ha-nu-u-te* 121:8,

**annurig** "now": *an-nu-ra* 152:21, *an-nu-ri* 38:8, 172 r. 2, [*an-nu-r*]*i* 38:4, *an-nu-rig* 19 s. 2, 37:22, 40 r. 2, 52 r. 10, 62:4, 71:10, 78:13, 79:15, 107:2, 119:5, 122 r. 6, 126 r. 6, 134:8, 149 r. 6, 23, 162 r. 7, 169:3, 232 r. 6, 241:10, 243:16, 250:17, r. 6, 251 r. 8, 263:8, 279:7, *an-nu-rig*] 108:11, *an-nu-ri*[*g* 48:13, *an-nu-r*[*ig*] 28:10, 29 r. 3, *an-nu*]*-rig* 130 s. 1, 183 r. 2, [*an-nu-rig*] 35 r. 14, 156:14, [*an-nu-ri*]*g* 228 r. 6, 286:7, [*an-nu-r*]*ig* 196:10, [*an-nu*]*-rig* 277:2, [*an-n*]*u-rig* 42 r. 5, [*an*]*-nu-rig* 82 r. 9, 297 r. 1, *an-nu-*[*rí*]*g* 81:5, *a-nu-rig* 227 s. 3,

**apālu** "to answer": *ep-pa-lu-ka-a-n*[*i* 280 s. 1, *e-pal-ka-ni* 115 r. 3, *ú-sa-p*[*i-il* 108 r. 1, *ú-sa-pi-lu* 95:12,

**āpiu** "baker": LÚ.NINDA.MEŠ 215:17,

**appāru** "reed": GI.AMBAR 34 r. 5, GI.AMBAR.MEŠ 120:3, r. 2,

**arādu** see *urādu*,

**arāku** "to be long": *ár-ru-ku* 294:17, *i-ri-ku* 294:6, *li-ri-ik* 294:15, *li-ri-ku* 294:14, *lu-ri-ku-na-ši* 103 r. 2, GÍ]D 295:25, GÍD.DA 294:10, 11, GÍD.DA.MEŠ] 148:4, [GÍD].DA.MEŠ 49:5,

**arāšu** "to cultivate": [*a-ra-ši*] 82:6, *a-ru-uš* 225:8, [*e*]*-ra-áš* 225:11, *e-ru-šu* 14 r. 13, *e-ru-šú* 289 e. 8, r. 2, *i-ru-*[*šu*] 225:15, *le-ru-šú*] 14 r. 5, *le-ru-uš* 225:7, [*l*]*e-ru-uš* 225:6,

**arhiš** "quickly": *ar-hi-iš* 298:13, *ar-hi-i*[*š* 7 r. 5, *ár-hiš* 45:5, 115 r. 4, 226:13, 294 r. 3, *ár-hiš*] 67:2, *ár-hi[š* 293 r. 2, [*ár-hiš* 186 e. 9, [*á*]*r-hi*[*š*] 213 e. 10,

**ārišūtu** "cultivation": *a-ri-šu-*[*te* 16:9,

**arītu** "shield": GIŠ.*a-ri-te* 53 r. 1,

**arû** "millstone": $NA_4$.*a-ru-a-ti-šú-nu* 35 r. 6,

**askupputu** "threshold": I.DIB 15 r. 11, $NA_4$.I.DIB.MEŠ 118:3, $NA_4$.I.D[IB.MEŠ 297:4, $NA_4$.I.[DIB.MEŠ] 290 r. 2, $NA_4$.[I.DIB.MEŠ 297:5, N]$A_4$.I.DIB.MEŠ 17 r. 3, [$NA_4$.I.DIB.MEŠ] 290 r. 5,

**asunaka** (mng. uncert.): *a-su-na-ka* 31 r. 21,

**aṣappu** "pack-animal": *a-ṣap-pi* 250 r. 6, *a-ṣap*.MEŠ 119:8, *a-ṣa-pi*.ME[Š] 47:4, ANŠE.*a-ṣap-pi* 21:13, ANŠE.*a-ṣap-pu-šú* 88:9,

**aṣû** see *uṣû*,

**ašābu** see *ušābu*

**ašāru** "to check, to review": *a-šar-u-ni* 295 r. 16, *a-šá-ru-*[*u-ni*] 95 r. 8, *a-šur* 215:6, *a-ta-šar* 48:9, *a-ta-šar-šú-nu* 251:16, *a-ta-š*[*ar-šú-nu*] 251:8, see also *ušāru*,

**ašlu** "tow, string": *áš-la-ni* 117 r. 2,

**aššūrāiu** "Assyrian": *aš-šur-a-a* 16:8, KUR.*aš-šur-a-a* 215:21, KUR—*aš-šur*.K[I-*a-a*] 273:3, LÚ.*aš-šur-a-a* 293:10,

**atâ** "why?": *a-ta-a* 2:12, 14 r. 1, 3, 21 r. 19, 33 r. 18, 35:18, 21, 30, 37:19, 46 r. 4, 52:11, 63 r. 13, 95:7, 108 r. 19, 114 r. 6, 115 r. 1, 117:4, 126 r. 10, 149 r. 11, 152 r. 19, 179 r. 9, 199:5, 216 r. 4, 221:5, 227:6, 243 r. 4, 256:4, 260:5, 265:8, 277:5, 282:6, 285:4, 293:9, *a-ta-*[*a* 221 r. 5, [*a-t*]*a-a* 150:13, [*a*]*-ta-a* 109:9, 291:4,

**atānu** "mare": ANŠE.SAL.HÚB.MEŠ 122 r. 4, MÍ.HÚB.MEŠ 171:11, MÍ.AN[ŠE.KU]R.RA 47:9, MÍ.ANŠE.KUR.RA 47:15,

**atta** "you": *at-ta* 31 r. 14, 53:18, 54:13, 108:9, r. 22, 130:8, 150:13, 225:7, 227 r. 24, 279:5, r. 6, *at*]*-ta* 108:4, [*a*]*t-ta* 81 r. 1, *at-ta-a* 81 r. 3,

**attunu** "you": *at-tu-nu* 2:13, 14, 179 r. 10, 210 r. 7, 277:8, *at-t*]*u-nu* 210 r. 2, [*at-t*]*u-nu* 37:30, *at-tu-ú-ni* 81:13, *at-tú*]*-nu* 34 r. 4, *at-t*[*ú-nu*] 184:4, *a*]*t-tú-nu* 109:2, [*a*]*t-tú-nu* 184:6,

**aṭāru** "poplar": GIŠ.A.AM 34 r. 5,

**baʾʾû** "to seek": *ba-i-a* 2 r. 5, *ba-ʾu-ú* 125 r. 5, [*lu-ba-ʾi* 150:19, *ú-ba-ʾa-a* 37:26, *ú*]*-ba-ʾu-u-ni* 178 r. 3,

**balāṭu** "to live, recover": *bal-ṭu-ti* 294 r. 12, *ba-al-ṭa* 91 r. 3, [*ib-ta*]*l-ṭa* 127:7,

**bārtu** "rebellion": *bar-ti* 33 r. 15, *bar-tu* 33 r. 13,

**basi** "in order to, duly": *ba-si* 199:13, 295 r. 10,

**bašāʾu** (mng. unknown): *ba-ši-iʾ* 46:16,

**bašû** "to exist": *it-tab-ši* 34:24, *i-ba-áš-ši* 56 r. 3, 152 r. 6, 249:9, 291:7, *i-ba-á*[*š-ši-i*] 125:4, *i-*[*ba-áš-ši-i*] 103:2, *i-ba-áš-*[*šu*]*-u-ni* 221 r. 2, *i-ba-ši* 4 r. 7, 21 r. 17, 42 r. 3, 78 r. 12, 145 s. 1, 171 r. 9, 217:11, 243 r. 12, 292 r. 10, *i-ba-š*[*i*] 246 r. 4, *i-b*]*a-ši* 287:3, [*i-ba*]*-ši* 106:20, [*i-b*]*a-ši* 42 r. 4, 289:4, *i-ba-šu-ni* 290:7, *i-ba-šu-u-ni* 21 r. 8, 118 r. 4, 233:9, *i-ba-šú-ni* 25 r. 6, 120:4, 289:3, *i-ba-šú-u-ni* 82 r. 13,

**batāqu** "to hew, cut off, parcel out": *a-bat-taq* 176:11, *ab-t*[*a-taq* 259:2, *bat-qu-ni* 105 r. 2, *ba-ti-qi* 297:13, *ni-ba-taq* 295 r. 8,

**batiqtu** "information": *ba-te-*[*iq-tú*] 29 r. 6, *ba-ti-iq-*[*ti*] 29:9, *ba-ti-i*[*q-tú*] 173:7, *ba-ti-qí-tú* 164 r. 13, [*b*]*a-ti-qí-tú* 164 r. 11,

**batqu** "deficit": *bat-qi-ni* 182 r. 3, *bat-qu* 199 r. 14,

**battatāi** "one by one": *bat-ta-ta-a-a* 250 r. 7, 295:18,

**battibatti** "around": *bat*]*-ti—bat-ti* 126 r. 3, [*b*]*a-ta-ba-ti* 67:6, *ba-ta-ba-ti-ia* 79:7,

**battu** "side": *ba-te* 21:18, *ba-t*[*i* 228:5,

**bēl āli** "city lord": EN—URU 100:20, r. 7, 237:4, EN—URU.URU.MEŠ 117:11, LÚ.EN—URU 103:5, 243:4, [LÚ.EN—U]RU 245:11, LÚ.EN—URU-*a-ni* 203 r. 8, LÚ.EN—URU.MEŠ 217 s. 3,

**bēl ālūtu** "city-lordship": [EN—U]RU-*u-te-e* 277:7,

**bēl mugirri** "chariot owner/fighter": EN—GIŠ.GIGIR 141 r. 1, LÚ.EN—GIŠ.GIGIR.MEŠ 68:4, 251:13, r. 1, 3,

**bēl piqitti** "official": EN—*pi-qi-ti* 254:9, LÚ.E[N—*pi-qit-ta-ti*] 298:4, LÚ.EN—*pi-*[*qit-te* 248:8, LÚ.EN—*p*[*i-qit-ti-ia*] 122 r. 6, LÚ.EN—*pi-q*]*i-ta-ti* 37 r. 6,

**bēl pirri** "(cavalry) unit commander": LÚ.EN—*pir-ri* 87:13,

**bēltu** "lady, mistress": *be-lit* 146 r. 7,

**bēlu** "lord": *be-li* 16:4, r. 5, 104 r. 12, 152:24, 168:6, 243:7, r. 10, 244 r. 4, 7, *be-li*] 196 r. 8, [*be-li* 244:8, *be-l*[*i-ia* 196 r. 7, *be-lí* 2:10, 3 r. 15, 7 r. 3, 12 r. 7, 14:7, 8, 15:9, 14, 18 r. 4, 21 r. 2, 11, 27:8, 28:8, 31:7, r. 8, 32 r. 14, 18, 33:8, 34 r. 20, 35 r. 13, 37:6, 9, 18, 20, 27, 30, 46 r. 12, 52:11, r. 14, 17, 20, 54:1, 6, e. 21, 56:4, 62:4, 9, 10, 63:5, r. 1, 7, 66:4, 67:4, r. 1, 68:5, 69:4, 70:6, 71:8, 74:9, r. 1, 8, 75:5, 85:3, 86:14, 87 r. 3, 91:22, 92 r. 10, 93 r. 4, 96 r. 3, 97:5, 14, r. 3, 5, s. 1, 98:13, r. 2, 100 r. 6, 9, 105:4, 11, 24, r. 1, 4, 106:6, 108 s. 1, 114 r. 3, 119:10, 122 e. 17, 123 r. 5, 124:5, 126 r. 9, 128:6, 133 s. 1, 138:1, 142:8, r. 5, 7, 143:8, r. 6, 144:7, s. 2, 149:3, 12, r. 8, 24, 152:4, 8, 21, r. 5, 9, 19, 159:4, 160:17, 162:11, 163:7, 170:4, 6, 172:6, 9, 181:5, 198 r. 3, 202:4, r. 1, 203:5, 8, 11, 15, r. 9, 18, 22, 204:8, r. 2, 226:4, 7, r. 6, 13, 227:4, 14, 22, r. 4, 10, 16, 21, 228:7, 230:3, 233:4, 234 r. 2, 241:13, 242:6, 246:5, 247:5, 250:15, r. 3, 23, 251:13, 257 r. 5, 260 r. 6, 263:2, 7, 267 s. 3, 269:4, 282:4, 285:3, 289 r. 4, 290:11, r. 8, 294 r. 3, 6, 295 r. 5, 9, 298:7, 11, r. 4, 7, *be-lí*] 1:7, 14 r. 14, 34:5, 57:5, 58:6, 109:5, 110:5, 130 s. 2, 141:8, 182:5, 251:5, 282:6, *be-l*[*í* 265:4, *be-l*]*í* 101:3, 232 r. 10, *be-*[*lí* 160:21, 226:17, 279:12, *be-*[*lí*] 69:9, 105:20, 155:6, 161:4, 182 r. 6, 256:5, 258:6, 300:5, *be*]*-lí* 34 r. 34, 54:2, r. 13, 159:7, 160:7, 256 r. 8, *b*[*e-lí* 99 r. 9, 136 r. 8, 160:9, *b*[*e-lí*] 29:10, 82:4, 103 r. 5, *b*]*e-lí* 173:1, *b*]*e-*[*lí*] 127:8, [*be-lí* 15 r. 14, 54 r. 3, 62:8, 143 r. 9, [*be-lí*] 97 r. 9, 109:3, 132:9, 152:10, 252:10, 256:3, 263:11, *be-lí-i* 52:6, *be-lí-ia* 52:1, 3, r. 1, 53:1, 3, 56:1, 3, 62:1, 3, 63:1, 74:1, 75:1, 83:3, 86:1, 3, 92:1, 2, 98:15, 100:1, 3, 104:1, 3, 127:1, 3, 4, 130 s. 2, 132:3, 5, 152 e. 27, r. 18, 199:1, 202:1, 3, r. 6, 203:1, r. 6, 15, 206:1, 207:1, 226:14, 241:1, 4, 11, r. 3, 242:4, 260 r. 7, *be-lí-ia*] 38:3, 43:1, 73:1, 108:2, 122:1, 144:1, 182:1, 204:1, 250:1, 251:1, 265:1, 266:1, 269:1, 271:1, *be-lí-i*[*a* 130 r. 6, *be-lí-i*]*a* 250:3, *be-lí-*[*ia* 130:7, *be-lí-*[*ia*] 55:1, 3, 128:5, *be-lí*]*-ia* 132:1, *be-l*[*í-ia*] 72:1, *be-*[*lí-ia*] 159:1, *be*]*-lí-ia* 63:12, 73:3, 76:1, 83:1, *b*[*e-lí-ia*] 128:3, 205:1, *b*]*e-lí-*[*ia*] 38:1, [*be-lí-ia* 178 e. 12, [*be-lí-ia*] 128:1, 209:1, *be-lí-ia-a* 62:7, *be-lí-iá* 83 r. 2, 85:1, 2, 88:3, 91:1, 2, 4, 92:4, 94:1, 96:1,

3, r. 10, 100 r. 8, 206:3, 246:1, 250 r. 8, 22, 293 s. 1, *be-lí-iá* 97:1, *be-lí-*[*iá*] 268:2, 293:1, *be-*[*lí-iá*] 88:1, 94:3, [*be-lí-iá*] 97:3, 105:1, [*be-lí-i*]*á* 250:19, *be-lí-i-ni* 105:11, *be-lí-ni*] 157:1, *b*[*e-lí-ni*] 158:1, *b*]*e-lí-*[*ni*] 156:1, BE-*i* 146:4, BE-[*i* 146:18, BE-*ia* 146:3, BE-*iá* 168:2, 4, r. 8, BE-*ni* 105:15, BE.LUM 238:6, EN 45:4, 46:4, r. 3, 9, 59:6, 113:4, 114 r. 4, 121:4, e. 20, r. 15, 17, 122 r. 1, 9, 11, 124:2, 125:3, 137 r. 1, 148:4, 149:6, 150:15, 18, 163 r. 8, 187:9, 199:4, r. 7, 8, 200:4, 13, r. 9, 205:10, 210:16, 211 r. 1, 2, 215:4, r. 3, 217:17, 18, 218 r. 3, 10, 224:5, 225:4, 243 r. 6, 254:9, 269:14, 288 r. 4, 289 r. 3, 291:12, r. 6, 292:4, 293:8, 299 r. 2, 13, 300 r. 4, EN] 113 r. 7, E[N 221:4, r. 4, E[N] 210 r. 19, E]N 150 r. 14, 291 r. 7, 11, 12, EN-*a* 53 r. 3, 9, 59:3, 172:1, 3, EN-*a*] 59:1, EN-*i* 82 r. 11, EN-*ia* 1:1, 3, 6, 3:2, 5, 6:1, 3, 6, 14 r. 14, 15:3, 6, 17:6, r. 5, 21:1, 4, 24:1, 25:1, 4, 26 r. 3, 27:4, 28:4, 6, 30:4, 31:1, 3, 5, 13, 32:1, 4, 6, 33:1, 34:7, r. 28, 35:3, 6, 37:24, 40:3, r. 1, 3, 4, 43:3, 48:3, 15, 49:1, 4, 50:5, 52 r. 12, 57:3, 63:3, 64:3, 65:1, 4, 68:1, 3, 69:3, 16, 71:4, 74:3, 75:3, 76:3, 78:1, 79:1, 3, 80:1, 3, 6, 82:1, 3, 84:1, 98:1, 106:3, 8, 113:1, r. 13, 117:15, 118:1, 119:1, 121:1, 122 r. 8, 124:4, 125 r. 10, 126:1, 3, 4, 7, r. 12, 15, 133:1, 134:3, 4, 136:1, 140:1, 142:9, 145:2, 146:1, 149:1, 5, r. 7, 150:1, 3, r. 13, 152:1, 3, 20, r. 4, 154:1, 3, 4, r. 6, 161:1, 163:1, 4, 164:1, 165:3, 194:3, 199:3, r. 6, 13, 203:3, 204 r. 9, 207:3, 210:1, 4, 6, r. 14, 214 e. 3, 215:1, 3, 217:1, 3, 15, r. 5, 224:1, 3, 226:1, 227:1, 233:1, 3, 237:1, 3, 8, 238:1, 4, 239:1, 3, 240:1, 3, 242:1, 243:6, 10, 17, 244:1, 3, r. 3, 245:1, 8, 247:1, 3, 257 r. 11, 260 r. 1, 289 r. 5, 291:11, r. 10, 292:1, 3, 295:3, 4, 10, 19, 297 r. 5, EN-*ia*] 14:1, 3, 15:1, 17:1, 20:1, 3, 22:1, 29 r. 7, 30:1, 35:1, 5, 37:1, 50:1, 3, 57:1, 69:1, 70:3, 72:3, 87:1, 89:3, 114:1, 115:1, 122:3, 127:7, 135:1, 3, 138:5, 140:3, 143: 1, 3, 144:3, 148:1, 3, r. 5, 151:1, 162:3, 170:1, 3, 181:1, 204:3, 5, 205:3, 211:3, 216:1, 3, 221:1, 3, 225:1, 227 s. 2, 232:1, 3, 236:5, 251:3, 256:1, 267:1, 3, 269:3, 270:1, 3, 271:3, 276 r. 2, 281:1, 3, 282:1, 3, 295:1, EN-*i*[*a* 82 r. 7, 233 r. 2, EN-*i*[*a*] 155:1, 161:3, 201:1, 260:2, EN-*i*]*a* 19 s. 3, 98:3, EN-[*ia* 20:6, 99:2, 211:5, 244:5, 249:16, EN-[*ia*] 15 e. 18, 16:3, 23:1, 29:7, 34:1, 70:1, 71:1, 136:3, 151:3, 155:3, 167:4, 182:3, 200:1, 201:3, 232:5, 299 r. 9, EN]-*ia* 40:1, 105:3, 134:1, 284 r. 8, E[N-*ia* 14:6, 108:1, 143:11, 260 r. 12, 281:7, E[N-*ia*] 25:6, 27:6, 30:6, 33:5, 42 e. 9, 48:1, 87:3, 153:1, 162:1, 225:3, 243:1, E]N-*ia* 40:5, 120:1, 181:3, 194:1, E]N-[*ia*] 232 r. 9, [EN-*ia* 20:4, 33:3, 160:16, 186 e. 10, 294 r. 12, [EN-*ia*] 11:1, 16:1, 22:4, 27:1, 29:1, 66:1, 3, 89:1, 106:12, 116 r. 3, 117:1, 125:1, 149:2, 153:3, 159:3, 182 r. 8, 200:3, 211:1, 243:3, 12, [EN-*i*]*a* 152:19, [EN]-*ia* 23:6, 64:1, 165:1, [E]N-*ia* 23:4, 24:4, 6, 71:13E, 173:10, 205 r. 3, EN-*iá* 2:5, 3:1, 18:3, 4, 6, 21:6, 7, r. 14, 22:6, 28:1, 32 r. 12, 33:6, r. 1, 34:3, r. 21, 35 r. 1, 37:3, 24, r. 5, 38:10, 44:1, 45:1, 7, 47:1, 3, 5, 7, r. 3, 78:3, 8, r. 6, 84:3, 133:3, 138:7, 141:1, 169:1, 184:4, 199 r. 14, 211 r. 6, 213:3, 218:15, 226:3, 227:3, 234 r. 7, 245:5, 246:3, 10, 293:4, 5, 294 r. 2, EN-*iá*] 11:3, 4, 17:3, 18:1, 19:1, 3, 34:4, 37:4, 218 r. 12, EN-[*iá* 227 s. 4, EN]-*iá* 2:2, E]N-*iá* 46 r. 6, 141:3, E]N-[*iá* 2:1, [EN-*iá* 29:4, [EN-*iá*] 35 r. 16, EN-*lí* 78:6, EN-*ni* 150:10, 156 r. 8, 220:1, EN-*ni*] 110:1, 4, 156:5, 157:4, 158:4, EN-[*ni* 158:6, [EN-*ni*] 156:6, e. 17, EN-*šú* 34 r. 3, LÚ.EN-*ni* 169 r. 3,

**bēru** "double hour": KASKAL.GÍ[D 229:7,

**bēt abi** "father's house": É—AD-*šú* 15:8, r. 15, É—AD-*šú-u-ni* 190 r. 2,

**bēt bēli** "government": É—EN.MEŠ-[*ka*] 31 r. 26, É—EN.MEŠ-*ku-nu* 34:23, É—EN.MEŠ-[*šú-nu* 154 r. 3,

**bēt dūri** "fortified place": É—BÀD.MEŠ-*ni* 21:17,

**bēt ili** "temple": É—DINGIR 147:12, É—DINGIR.MEŠ 294 r. 6,

**bēt qāti** "storehouse": É—ŠU.2 206:9,

**bētānu** "interior, inside": É-*a-ni* 83:5,

**bētu** "house, where": *a—bé-e-ti* 146:5, *a—bé-e-t*[*i* 146 r. 4, *bé-et* 95:3, 98 r. 9, 114:6, 150:15, 173:4, 295 r. 15, 24, *b*[*é-e*]*t* 48:14, [*bé-et* 174:3, [*bé-et*]. 198 r. 3, *bé-te* 25 r. 5, 6, É 3 r. 13, 15:12, 26 r. 2, 33 r. 12, 35 r. 14, 41:5, 54:9, 63:12, 64:16, 91 e. 24, 100:11, 18, 103 r. 2, 104:10, 105:15, 108 r. 6, 113:7, 125 r. 4, 135 r. 9, 150:4, 159:5, 168 r. 7, 183:5, 196:5, 197 r. 6, 9, 205:4, 206:5, 6, 215:18, 218:2, r. 5, 221 r. 2, 226:4, 10, 227:22, r. 27, s. 3, 229 e. 10, 232:9, 244:8, r. 4, 256 r. 5, 259:1, 260 r. 5, 7, 10, 264:7, 283:9, 289:6, 300 r. 3, [É] 263:13, É-*su* 228:5, É-*šú* 261 r. 4, É-*šú*] 210 r. 3, É.MEŠ 52 r. 5, 94:4, 105:14, 260:11, É.[ME]Š 95:14, É.[MEŠ 149:18, É.MEŠ-*šú-nu* 80 r. 4,

**biādu** "to stay overnight": *bé-e-d*[*u* 286:6,

**biāru** "to examine": *ni-ib-ti-ar* 261:5,

**biltu** "talent, tax, tribute": *bi-*[*lat*] 29 r. 4, GÚ.UN 206:8, 294 r. 1, GÚ.U]N 206:11,

**birti** "between": *bir-te* 47:13, 92:6, 200:9, *bir-ti* 31:18, 47 r. 6, 149 r. 12, 169:13, *bir*]*-ti* 31:19, [*b*]*ir-ti* 54 r. 10,

**bīrtu** "fort": HAL.ṢU.MEŠ 1:5, 6:5, 15:5, URU]. *bir-te* 60:5, URU.*bir-te* 54 e. 22, 122 r. 10, 162:7, 199:14, URU.[*bi*]*r-te* 53:21, URU.*bir-ti-šú* 32 r. 10, URU.*b*]*ir-tú* 109:10, URU.*bi-rat* 21:5, 24:5, 25:5, 28:5, 29:6, 32:5, 34:4, 37:4, URU.*bi-*[*rat* 30:5, URU. *bi-*[*rat*] 27:5, URU.*b*[*i-rat* 14:5, 281:6, URU.[*bi-rat*] 23:5, U]RU.*bi-rat* 22:5, URU.*bi-ra-a-te* 80:4, URU. *bi-ra*]*-a-te* 152:17, [URU.*bi-ra*]*-a-te* 152:18, URU. *bi-ra-a-ti* 31:4, URU.*bi-ra-a-ti*] 35:4, URU.*bi-ra-a*]*-ti* 40:4, URU.*bi-ra-*[*a-ti*] 33:4, [URU.*b*]*i-ra-t*[*e* 173: 13, URU.*bi-ra-t*[*i*] 128:4, URU.*bi-*[*ra-ti*] 128:7, UR]U.*bi-ra-ti* 131:1, U]RU.*bi-ra-ti* 131:3, URU.HAL.[ṢU 10:4, URU.HAL.ṢU 15 r. 5, 45 r. 2, 80:7, 89:4, 92:3, 218 r. 14, ?245:6, URU.HAL.Ṣ[U 93 r. 8, URU. HAL].ṢU 199 r. 2, UR]U.HAL.ṢU 93 r. 6, URU.HAL.[ṢU].MEŠ 2:4, URU.HAL.ṢU.MEŠ 3:4, 4:8, 18:5, 92 r. 9, 115:7, 160:4, 199 r. 14, 210:5, r. 9, 244:4, 6, 273:4, URU.HAL.ṢU.MEŠ] 204:4, URU.HAL.ṢU.[MEŠ 244:7, URU.HAL.Ṣ[U.MEŠ] 211:4, URU.HAL.Ṣ]U.MEŠ 17:5, UR]U.HAL.ṢU.MEŠ 6 r. 4, UR]U.HAL.ṢU.M[EŠ 187:2, U[RU.HAL.ṢU.MEŠ] 144:5, U]RU.HAL.ṢU.MEŠ 124:3, [URU.HAL.ṢU.MEŠ] 11:5, URU.HAL.ṢU.MEŠ-*ku-nu* 2 r. 3, URU.HAL.ṢU.MEŠ-*ni* 2:14,

**bis** (mng. uncert.): *bi-is* 226 r. 3, *bi-i*[*s* 176:9,

**bītu** see *bētu*,

**buʾʾû** see *baʾʾû*,

**bubūtu** "hunger": *bu-bu-te* 126:13,

**būlu** "cattle": *bu-li* 47:14,

**burbānu** "foal(?)": *bur-ba-a-ni* 64 r. 6,

**daʾānu** "to be strong, harsh; (D) to strengthen": *da-an* 285:5, *da-ʾa-na* 200:10, *nu-ti-in* 227 r. 15, *ta-da-in* 227 r. 10, *ú-da-ʾa-na* 33 r. 14, KALAG-*an* 105 r. 6, KALAG-[*an*] 56 r. 8, see also *danānu*,

**dabābu** "to talk, plot": *ad-da-bu-ub* 95:11, *ad-du-bu-ub* 210:13, *a-da-bu-bu-ni* 243 r. 1, *a-du-ba-šú-nu* 226:9, *du-ub-ba*] 277:3, *du-ub-bu* 203:13, *d*]*u-ub-bu* 42:7, *id-bu-bu-ni* 108:22, *id-di-bu-ub* 95:10, *id-di-bu-ub-u-ni* 91:6, *id-du-ba-áš-šú* 2:11, [*id-du-ub-b*]*u* 43:9, *i-da-ab-bu-bu* 294:3, *i-da-bu-bu* 105:10, 107:5, 260 r. 11, *i-da-bu-ub* 147:13, 149 r. 3, 14, *i-da-bu-*[*ub*] 137 r. 5, *i-di-bu-u*[*b-u-ni*] 95 r. 2, *i-du-bu* 108 r. 19, *i-du-bu-bu* 34:22, 27, *i-du-bu-bu*]] 163 r. 6, *i-d*[*u-bu*]*-ub* 95 r. 6, *la-ad-bu-ub* 154 r. 7, *la-da-bu-ub* 78 r. 14, 133 s. 2, *li*]*d-bu-bu* 106:24, *lid-bu-ub* 98:14, *lid-di-bu-bu* 52 r. 19, [*ni*]*-du-ba-áš-šú-nu* 105:8, *ta-da-bu-bu* 108:24, 260:6,

**daddammu** "mule": ANŠE.NUN.NA 224 r. 11,

**dagālu** "to look": *a-da-gal* 19 s. 2, 199 r. 6, 202 r. 2, 246:8, 295 r. 14, *a-da-*[*gal* 200 r. 3, *a-da-ga-la* 146:9, [*du-g*]*ul* 108:6, *i-da-gal* 108:9, 200 r. 5, *i-da-gul* 298 r. 3, *lid-gul* 298 r. 5, *ta-ad-gul* 199:7,

**dāgil iṣṣūri** "augur": LÚ.*da-gíl*—MUŠEN.MEŠ 163:6, 12,

**daiālu** "scout, spy": LÚ].*da-a-a-li* 264:4, LÚ.*da-a-a-li* 3:7, 24:13, 54 r. 15, 87 r. 4, 246:6, LÚ.*da-a-a-l*[*i* 12 r. 10, LÚ.*da-a-a-*[*li* 13:6, LÚ.*da-*[*a-a-li*] 12 r. 1, L]Ú.*da-a-a-li* 12 r. 6, LÚ.*da-a-a-li-ia* 83:4, [LÚ.*da-a*]*-a-li-ia* 55:4, [LÚ.*d*]*a-a-a-li-ia* 55:8, LÚ.*da-a-a-li-ka* 85:3, LÚ.*da-a-a-*URU 11 r. 4, LÚ.*da-ia-a-li* 105:17,

**dakû** "to summon, mobilize": *d*[*a-ki-u*] 4 r. 5, *i-da-*[*ki-u*] 106:19,

**dâku** see *duāku,*

**dalāhu** "to disturb, perplex": *da-la-hu* 37:33, *da-li-ih* 79:14,

**dâlu** see *duālu,*

**damāqu** "to be good, nice": *dam-qu* 152 r. 7, *da-an-qu* 34 s. 1, 37 r. 17, *d*[*a-an-qu*] 299 r. 7, *da-mì-i*[*q*]*-qa* 34:26, SIG$_5$ 294:14, SIG$_5$-*a*[*t* 205 r. 6, [SIG$_5$-*iq* 278:6, SIG$_5$-*tú* 284 r. 13, SIG$_5$.MEŠ 152 r. 10, 200 r. 7, SIG$_5$.MEŠ] 200 r. 15,

**dāmu** "blood": MÚD.MEŠ 236:2,

**danānu** "to be strong": [*dan-nat*] 160:6, *dan-na-at* 21:9, 10, 210 r. 16, 217:13, [*dan-na-at* 160:16, *dan-na-te* 225:10, *dan-nu* 249:7, 290:5, *dan-nu-ti* 104:4, KALAG.ME[Š 184 r. 1, KALAG.MEŠ 179 r. 7, 290:6, KALAG.[MEŠ 281:8, see also *daʾānu,*

**dannutu** "stronghold": URU.*dan-ni-te* 169:10,

**dātu** "after": *a—da-at* 53 r. 7, *da-at* 180:3, *da-t*[*i* 63:9, *de-et* 86:11, 121 r. 10, *id—da-a-*[*te* 39:6, *i—da-at* 53 r. 2, 61 r. 7, *i*]*—da-a-te-šú-*[*nu*] 219:5, *i*]*—da-tuk-ka* 8:7, *i—da-tu-šu-nu* 87:16, *i—d*[*a-tu-šú-nu*] 56 r. 1, *i—da-tú-šú* 53:18, *i—d*[*a*]*-tú-u-a* 119:7, [*i*]*—da-tú-u-šu* 112:5,

**dēktu** "defeat": *de-ek-tu-šú-*[*nu* 173:5, *de-ek-tú* 46 r. 7, *de-ek-*[*tú*] 273:5, GAZ-*šú* 197 r. 7,

**dekû** see *dakû,*

**dēnu** "judgment, legal case": *de-e-ni* 213:4, *de-ni* 81:9, *de-ni-i*[*a*] 243 r. 6, *di-in-šú* 149 r. 10,

**dibbī** "words": *dib-bi* 204 r. 1, 210:12, *dib-*[*b*]*i* 204:17, [*dib*]*-bi* 46 r. 8, *di-bi* 241:7, *di-bi-šú* 108:21, *di-b*[*i-šú-ni*] 38:6, *di-bi-šú-u-ni* 241:14, *di-ib-bi* 46 r. 3, 87 r. 7, 95 r. 1, 96 r. 8, 108:28, r. 18, 121 r. 14, 152:4, 204:6, *di-ib-b*[*i* 106:23, [*d*]*i-ib-bi* 105:7, *di-ib-bi-šú-nu-ni* 40 r. 4,

**diqāru** "pot": UTÚL 77 r. 1, UTÚL.MEŠ 287:3,

**duāku** "to kill": *de-e-ku* 90:15E, 91:12, *de-e-k*[*u*] 90:5, *de-e-*[*ku* 174:4, [*d*]*e-e-ku* 173:7, *du-a-ki* 107:4, *du-a-ki-ia* 260 r. 10, *i-du-ak-*[*ši*] 108 r. 25, *i-d*]*u-ak-šú-nu* 149:23, *i-du-ka* 53:5, 260 r. 8, *i-du-ku* 53 r. 5, 173:6, *i-du-k*[*u* 175:3, 273:7, *i-*[*d*]*u-ku-ni* 143:10, *i-du-ku-šu* 93:5, *i-du-ku-šu-nu* 112 r. 1, *i-du-u*[*k-ku*] 273:6, *ta-du-ku-ni* 108 r. 23, *ta-du-uk* 108 r. 21, GAZ.ME[Š 184:3,

**duālu** "to run about, serve": *i*]*-du-al* 35:14, *i-du-lu* 119:7, *li-du-lu* 254:11,

**dullu** "work": *dul-la-a-ni* 152 r. 1, *dul-la-ku-nu* 210 r. 4, *dul-la-ni* 152:7, *dul-la-šú-nu* 210 r. 8, *dul-li* 3:16, 47 r. 8, 63 r. 14, 147 r. 6, 294:2, 295:24, 296 r. 4, *dul-l*[*i* 69:13, *dul-lu* 32 r. 21, 80:7, 85 r. 2, 108:16, 147:11, r. 2, 199 r. 12, 211 r. 5, 281 r. 8, 294:4, *dul-lu*] 33 r. 6, *du*[*l-lu*] 292 r. 9, *du*]*l-lu* 291 r. 14, *d*[*ul-lu*] 160:3, [*dul-l*]*u* 20:4, [*dul*]*-lu* 67 r. 3, 299 r. 1, [*du*]*l-lu* 299 r. 7, *dul-lum* 295 r. 13, [*du*]*l-lu-šá* 299 r. 8, *dul-lu-š*[*u* 113:17, [*dul$_6$*]*-la-šú-nu* 108:15, *dul$_6$-li* 16 r. 3, 52 r. 3, *dul$_6$-li-ia* 291:6, *dul$_6$-l*[*i-i*]*a* 118:10, *dul$_6$-lu* 3:17, 34 r. 25, 53:7, 56:9, 12, 15, 108 e. 31, 148 r. 4, 266:3, 4, 290 r. 7, 298 r. 5, *dul$_6$-l*[*u* 266 r. 2, 277:5, *dul$_6$-*[*lu* 56 r. 2, 266 r. 1, *dul$_6$-*[*lu*] 8:3, 34 r. 1, *d*[*ul$_6$-lu*] 56 r. 7, *d*]*ul$_6$-lu* 58:7, [*d*]*ul$_6$-lu* 106:4, 267:5, KIN-*i* 47 r. 4,

**dumāqu** "jewelry": *du-ma-qi* 31 r. 16,

**durāru** "debt remission": *du-ra-ru* 203 r. 17,

**dūru** "city wall": BÀD 56:10, 160:8, 292:7, BÀD-*šú* 291:10,

**ebāru** "to cross": *e-bi-ru-*[*u-ni* 26 r. 4, *e-tab-ru* 88:9, *lu-*[*še-bi-ru*] 298:15, *še-b*[*ir-šú-nu* 297:8, *ú-se*]*-bir* 297:4, *ú-še-bar-ru-šu-nu-u-ni* 100 r. 13, *ú-še-ba-ra* 290 r. 6, *ú-še-bir-šú-nu* 64:12,

**ebūru** "harvest": BURU$_{14}$ 127:6, GURUN.BURU$_{14}$ 97 r. 2,

**ēdānīu** "lone (horse)": *e-da-ni-e* 90 r. 2,

**edānu** "term, deadline": *e-da-nu* 202 r. 15, [*e-d*]*a-nu* 152:24,

**egirtu** "letter": *e-gir-a-te* 218:14, *e-gir-te* 218:12, *e-gir-ti* 44 r. 4, *e-gir-tú* 35 r. 10, *e-gír-te* 96 r. 5, *e-gír-te-*[*šú* 283:3, *e-gír-te*.MEŠ 52:21, *e-gír-ti* 210:6, 213:9, *e-gír-tú* 50:4, 52 r. 11, 63 r. 7, 79 r. 7, 107 e. 6, 113 r. 13, *e-gír-t*[*ú*] 263:3, [*e-gír*]*-tú* 283 r. 5,

**ehūla** (mng. obscure): *e-hu-la* 46 r. 4,

**ekal māšarti** "review palace": É.GAL—*ma-šar-ti* 206 r. 4, É.GAL—*m*]*a-šar-ti* 206 r. 2,

**ekallu** "palace": É.GAL 3 r. 10, 15 r. 8, 42 r. 8, 96 r. 6, 104:13, r. 3, 11, 108:29, s. 1, 151:5, 7, 8, 172 r. 6, 206:6, 210:9, 228:13, r. 4, 241:8, 243:15, e. 19, r. 5, 8, 277:4, 279:2, r. 3, 282:10, 284 r. 6, É.GAL] 13:3, 43:5, É.G]AL 245 r. 2, É].GAL 98:12, 142 e. 11, 183 r. 3, [É.GAL 268:5, [É.G]AL 25:9,

**ekurru** "temple": É.KUR 54 r. 6, 10, É.[KUR.MEŠ-*te*] 281:5,

**eleppu** "boat": GIŠ.MÁ 233:7, 299 r. 12, GIŠ.MÁ.MEŠ 290:6, 8, 12, r. 7,

**elû** "to go up; (D) to set aside, reserve, remove; (Š) to move up, raise": *e-l*[*i*] 133 r. 4, 200:15, [*e-l*]*u-ni* 194 r. 5, *e-lu-u-ni* 96:5, 150 r. 7, *e-te-li* 84:8, 90 r. 2, 133 r. 7, 199:15, *le-li-u* 106:22, *l*]*e-li-u* 17:10, *le-lu-ni* 97 r. 8, *le-lu-u-ni* 194 r. 8, *lu-še-li* 213 r. 7, [*lu-š*]*e-li-ú* 106:18, *tú-še-li* 150:14, *ú-li* 203:7, *ú-se-li* 97:6, 169:10, 227 s. 2, 274:6, *ú-se-l*[*i*] 131:3, *ú*]*-se-li* 37 e. 36, [*ú-se-li*] 150:18, [*ú-s*]*e-li* 117 r. 11, *ú-se-li-u* 32 r. 10, *ú-še-la* 117 r. 13, *ú-še-lu-u-ni* 34 s. 1, 115:8, *ú-ši-la* 150:12, *ú-ta-li* 203:9, *ú-tu-li-u* 87:17,

**emādu** "to impose, lean": *e-ti-mì-si-na-ma* 295 r. 4, [*lu-u*]*m-mi-*[*du* 182 r. 10, *ú-ta-me-di* 80 r. 7,

**emūqu** "(armed) forces, army": *e-mu-qe-šú* 114:4, *e-m*[*u-qe-šú-nu*] 114:10, *e-mu-qi* 44 r. 3, 67:11, 129 r. 4, 7, 145 r. 9, 200:14, 215:5, r. 6, 250:17, 278:4, *e-mu-q*[*i*] 215 r. 4, *e-mu-qi-ia* 67:5, 152 e. 26, *e-mu-q*]*i-ia* 279:8, *e-mu-qi-ka* 200:5, *e-mu-qi-k*[*a*] 145 r. 2, [*e-mu-qi-ka*] 67:1, *e-mu-qi-ku-nu*] 277:8, *e-mu-qi-šu* 164 r. 2, [*e-mu-qi-šú*] 131:4, *mu-qa-a-a* 37:11, *m*]*u-qa-a-a* 225:9, *mu-qa-ni* 95 e. 17, LÚ.*e-muq-qi* 86:10, LÚ.*e-muq-qi-šú* 147:6, LÚ.*e-mu-qe-e-*[*šú*] 220:5, LÚ.*e-mu-qi* 78 r. 7, 87:18, 217 s. 3, 223:4, LÚ.*e-*[*mu-qi* 158:5, LÚ.*e-*[*mu-qi*] 4 r. 9, LÚ.*e*]*-mu-qi* 66:5, LÚ.[*e-mu-qi* 216:4, [LÚ.*e-mu*]*-qi* 4 r. 5, LÚ.*e-*[*mu-qi*]*-ia* 240:4, LÚ.*e-mu-qi-ku-*(*nu*) 164 r. 8, LÚ.*e-mu-qi-šú* 2 r. 5, [LÚ.*e-mu-q*]*i-šú* 220:3,

**enāšu** "to become weak": *e-ta-*[*an-šú*] 156 r. 1,

**enû** "to change": *e-te-nu-na-š*[*i* 182 r. 2, *li-te-nu-ni* 17 r. 1,

**ēnu** "eye": IGI.2.MEŠ 92 r. 8, 126:7, 169: 13, IGI.2.MEŠ-*šú* 149 r. 12,

**epāšu** "to do": *ep-pa-á*[*š*] 210 r. 22, *ep*]*-pa-áš* 113:17, *ep-p*[*u-šu*] 89:6, *ep-pu-šú* 210 r. 8, *ep-šá* 34:24, 210 r. 4, [*e*]*p-šá* 34:26, *e-pa-áš* 84 r. 6, 148 r. 5, 211 r. 5, *e-pa-á*[*š* 292 r. 10, *e-pa-*[*áš*] 300:2, *e-*[*pa-áš*] 299 r. 6, [*e-pa-áš* 290 r. 8, *e-*[*p*]*a-áš-šú-u-ni* 56:12, *e-pa-ša* 165:9, *e-pa-šu-u-ni* 173:9, *e-*[*pa-šu-u-ni* 106:10, *e-pa-šú-ni* 291:6, *e-*[*pu-šu*] 85 r. 2, *e-pu-šú* 32 r. 21, 147:12, r. 2, *e-pu-šú*] 56:15, [*e-pu-šú*] 25:10, *e-pu-šú-ni* 147 r. 10, *e-pu-uš* 53:7, 56:9, 63 r. 6, 122 r. 12, *e-tap-šá* 147 r. 10, [*e-tap-šá*] 221:8, *e-tap-šu* 150:9, *e-tap-šú* 69:8, *e-ta-pa-áš* 106:7, *in-né-*[*pa-áš*] 299 r. 8, *in-né-*[*pa-šu-ni*] 299 r. 1, *le-pu-šá* 288 r. 3, *le-pu-šu* 199 r. 13, *le-pu-šú* 203 r. 13, 288 r. 8, 291 r. 11, *le-pu-*[*šú* 108:15, *le-pu-uš* 2 r. 1, 14:14, 16 r. 6, 56:7, 152 r. 5, *le-pu-uš*] 14 r. 15, *le-p*[*u-uš* 106:11, [*le-pu-uš*] 34 r. 3, [*le-p*]*u-uš* 46 r. 13, [*l*]*e-pu-uš* 6 r. 8, *né-ep-pa-áš* 206 r. 5, *né-pa-áš* 297 r. 4, *né-p*[*a-áš*] 250 r. 2, [*né-pu-uš*] 182 r. 5, *né-ta-pa-áš* 36:3, *te-pa-áš* 3:18, 58:7, *te-pa-*[*áš*] 299 r. 5, *te-pa-šá*] 108:16, *te-pu-š*[*ú-u-ni*] 108 r. 21, *te-pu-uš* 108 r. 20, *ú-pa-ša* 166 r. 4,

**epēšu** see *epāšu,*

**epinnu** "plough": GIŠ.APIN 263:13,

**epirtu** "fired brick": *e-b*[*ir-tú*] 211 r. 8, [*e-bir-tú*] 291:9,

**eqlu** "field": A.[Š]À 15 r. 3, A.ŠÀ 16:6, 8, 210 r. 12, 232:6, 259:1, 263:13, A.Š[À 15:16, A.Š]À 15 r. 14, A].ŠÀ 188:3, [A.ŠÀ 15 r. 15, A.ŠÀ-*šú* 109:7, 210 r. 3, A.ŠÀ.MEŠ 37 r. 12, 52 r. 5, 260:11, A.ŠÀ.MEŠ] 37 r. 9, A.ŠÀ.M[EŠ] 109:9, A.Š[À.MEŠ] 15:14, A.ŠÀ.MEŠ-*šú-nu* 60:2, A.ŠÀ.GA.MEŠ 15:7,

**erābu** "to enter": *e-rab* 63: 14, *e-rab-ba* 93 r. 3, *e-rab-u-ni* 257:7, *e-ra-b*[*a*] 33 s. 1, *e-ra-bu-u-ni* 52:20, *e-ru-bu* 100 r. 2, 170 r. 6, *e-r*[*u-bu*] 33 r. 9, *e-*[*ru-bu-ni*] 11 r. 7, *e-ru-bu-u-ni* 113:8, 217 r. 13, *e-tar-ba* 112:5, 135:5, 145:9, *e-tar-b*]*a* 35:25, [*e*]*-tar-ba* 112:4, *e-tar-bu* 53 r. 6, 87:15, 210 r. 15, *e-ta*[*r-bu*] 87:5, *e-ta*[*r*]*-bu* 53:22, [*e-tar-bu*] 12 r. 11, *e-*[*tar-bu-ni*] 173:12, *e-ta-rab* 31:22, 91:8, 133:13, *e-t*[*a-rab*] 5:2, *i-ru-bu* 126 r. 8, *le-ru-bu* 122 r. 8, *li-ir-*[*ú-ba* 288 r. 4, *né-er-r*[*ab* 144 r. 4, *né-rab* 176:13, *né-t*[*a-rab*] 160:5, *nu-se-rib* 242:11, *nu-še-rib* 287:2, *ú-se-r*[*ib*] 6 r. 4, [*ú-se-rib*] 89:10, *ú-se-ri-ba* 129:5, 218 e. 16, *ú-se-ri-bi* 5 e. 7, *ú-se-ri-bu* 4 r. 4, *ú-še-ra-ba* 166:6, *ú-še-r*[*i-bu-ni*] 5 r. 4,

**erāšu** "to request": *e-ri-*[*iš*] 258:2, *e-ri-ša-an-ni* 258:5, *e-r*[*i-ši*] 34 r. 13, [*e*]*-ta-ár-šú* 225:12, *e-*[*te-riš*] 188:3, *e-te-ri-iš* 21 r. 13, *le-r*[*iš* 7 r. 2, see also *arāšu,*

**erēbu** see *erābu,*

**erēnu** "cedar": GIŠ.ERIN 295 r. 2,

**esāpu** "to gather, collect": *e-si-ip-ka* 46 e. 19,

**eṣādu** "to reap, harvest": *e-ṣa-du* 3 r. 19, 199 r. 5, *e-ṣi-di* 199 r. 5, *e-ṣi-du-ni* 289 r. 1, *e-t*[*a-ṣi-di*] 97 r. 2,

**eṣānu** "to smell": *né-*[*ṣi-in* 113:16,

**eṣāru** "to draw": *e-te-ṣir* 15 r. 10,

**eṣemtu** see *eṣintu,*

**eṣidītu** "travel provisions": ZÍD.*e-ṣi-di-a-te* 115:6,

**eṣintu** "bone": GÌR.PAD.DU 295 e. 26,

**ēṣu** "to be scarce, insignificant": *e-ṣa-šú-nu* 294 r. 7, *e-ṣi-i* 37 e. 34, [*e-ṣu-ni*] 13:5, 117 e. 22, 298:14,

**ešāru** "to be, go straight": *i-ta-áš-ru* 202:10,

**ešer** "ten": 10-*a-a* 294:17,

**eššu** "new": *eš-šu-u-te* 152 r. 7, GIBIL 105 r. 7, GIB[IL 191:5,

**etāku** "to be alert": *et-ka-ka* 200:6, *et-ku* 53 r. 4, *e-ta-ka* 179 r. 3, *e-te-ka* 200 r. 12,

**etāqu** "to pass, move on": *e-ta-*[*qi* 69:10, *e-te-te-q*[*i* 82:7, [*e*]*-te-ti-iq* 96:8, *e-ti-iq* 250:17, *e-ti-q*[*u*] 226 r. 4, *lu-u-še-ti-qu-u-ni-šú* 218 r. 8, *nu-še-taq* 74 r. 3, *ú-se-te-qa* 3 r. 4, *ú-s*[*e-ti-q*]*u* 74 r. 8, *ú-še-taq-u-ni* 4 r. 9, [*ú-še*]*-tu-qu* 289:2,

**etēqu** see *etāqu,*

**etinnu** "master builder": LÚ.TIN.MEŠ 56:4, 11, r. 3, LÚ.TIN.[MEŠ 56 r. 4, LÚ.TIN.MEŠ-*ni* 56 r. 9, LÚ.TIN.MEŠ-*ni-ia* 56:7,

**ezābu** "(Š) to escape": *ú-se-zi-bu* 32 r. 4, *ú-š*[*e-zib-u-ni*] 90 r. 6, [*ú-še*]*-zib-u-ni* 12 r. 11,

**ezēbu** see *ezābu,*

**gabbu** "all": *gab-bi* 99:7, 105:11, *ga*]*b-bi* 149:18, *g*]*ab-bi* 98:17, *gab-bi-šá* 108:26, [*gab-bi-šu* 107:3, *gab-bi-šú* 106:14, 109:9, 145 r. 6, *gab-bi-šú-nu* 79:10, 257 r. 3, 298:8, *gab-bi-*[*šú-nu*] 224 r. 6, *gab-bi-*[*x*] 60:1, *gab-bu* 21:16, r. 5, 25 r. 4, 34 r. 2, 37 r. 10, 53:16, 63 r. 3, 10, 78 r. 4, 79:12, 84 r. 7, 86:11, 119:3, 152 r. 14, 226:9, 249:8, r. 3, 250:11, 267:5, 268:10, 281 r. 3, *gab-bu*] 281:6, *gab-b*[*u* 30:8, 130:2, *gab-b*[*u*] 67:5, *ga*[*b-bu*] 146 r. 12, *ga*]*b-bu* 174:4, [*gab-b*]*u* 297 r. 4,

**galādu** "to frighten": *ig-la-du-u-ni* 202 r. 12, *ig-ta-al-du* 202 r. 8,

**galītu** "deportation": *ga-li-te* 203 s. 1,

**gallubu** "to shave": *gal-l*[*u-bu* 108:26,

**galû** "(Š) to exile, deport": *šá*]*-ga-lu-u-ni* 54:4, *ú-šá-gal-u-šú-nu* 112 r. 2, *ú-šá-ga-lu-šú-nu* 105:23,

**gamāru** "to finish": [*g*]*am-mu-ra* 74 e. 15, *ga-am-mu-ru* 152 r. 8, *ga-a*]*m-ri* 160:13, *ga-ma-ri-šú* 58:8, *ga-me-ri* 293:9, [*ga-mur*] 299 r. 11, *i-ga-mar* 149 r. 12, *ni-i*]*g-mu-ru* 293 r. 2, *ug-da-dam-*[*mar* 176:7, *ug-da-me-er* 16 r. 4, *u*[*g-d*]*a-me-*[*r*]*a* 74:9, *ug-da-mir* 33 r. 7, 295 r. 13, *ú-gam-*[*x* 34:19, [*ú-ga*]*-mar* 300:3, *ú-ga-m*[*ar-u-n*]*i* 79 r. 10,

**gammalu** "camel": ANŠ]E.A.AB.BA 48:7,

**gammuzu** "to press hard(?)": *ga-mu-zu* 64 r. 4,

**garāru** "to become scared": *ig-da-na-ru-*[*ru* 95: 7, *ig-du-ru* 103:9, *li-gi-ru-ru* 203 s. 1, *ta-ag-da-na-ra-*[*ra* 95:8,
**garû** "to contest": *i-gi-ru-ú-ni* 37:28,
**giltu** (mng. unknown): *gi-il-te* 254 r. 8,
**gimru** "total": PAB 14 r. 7, 10, 69 r. 3, 90:14, 100:6, 111 e. 6, r. 1, 117:11, 171 r. 2, 177:4, 215:12, 14, 18, 21, 228 r. 1, 250 r. 10, 12, 251 r. 3, P[AB] 56:11, 100:8, [PAB 250 r. 15, 17, 19, 291 r. 2, 3, [PAB] 138:5, PAB-*ma* 215 e. 23, [PAB-*ma* 291 r. 4,
**girūtu** "hostility": *gír-ru-tú* 113:18,
**gišru** "bridge": *giš-ri* 61 r. 10,
**gubbu** "well": *gu-ub-bu* 15:12,
**gušūru** "log, roof-beam": GIŠ.ÙR.MEŠ 34 r. 21, GI]Š.ÙR.MEŠ 287 r. 5, GIŠ].ÙR.MEŠ 8 r. 3, 39:5, 254 r. 13, GIŠ.ÙR.ME[Š 33 r. 2, GIŠ.ÙR.ME[Š] 8 r. 1, GIŠ.ÙR.MEŠ 3 r. 1, 25 r. 6, 32 r. 17, 33 r. 10, 34 r. 13, 14, 111:1, 117:17, r. 11, 129:1, 4, s. 1, 253:5, 7, 295 r. 17, GIŠ.ÙR.M[EŠ 127:8, GIŠ.ÙR.[MEŠ 117 r. 1, GIŠ.ÙR.[MEŠ] 4 r. 6, 111 r. 4, GIŠ.ÙR].MEŠ 34 r. 27, GIŠ.Ù[R.MEŠ 7:2, 117 r. 3, 254 r. 4, GIŠ.Ù[R.MEŠ] 6:8, GIŠ.Ù]R.MEŠ 178:5, GIŠ.[ÙR.MEŠ] 117:19, [GIŠ.ÙR.MEŠ 117:4, [GIŠ.ÙR.MEŠ] 4 r. 8, [GIŠ.Ù]R.MEŠ 254 r. 6,
**habālu** "to borrow, be indebted": *hab-bu-ul* 149: 14, *ih-b*[*il-u-ka-ni*] 260 r. 2,
**habātu** "to plunder": [*i*]*h-ta-bat* 145 r. 19, *i-ha-bat* 260 r. 8,
**hadû** "to be glad": *ha-di-u* 294:6,
**hahhu** "peach": GIŠ.*ha-ah-hi* 27:12,
**hakāmu** "to understand": *ha-ki-*[*im*] 56:17, *la-ah-ki-im* 284 r. 9, *li-ih-hi-*[*kim*] 243 e. 19,
**halāqu** "to disappear": *hal-qu* 54 e. 23, 79:11, 100 r. 17, *hal-qu-te* 79:5, r. 11, [*hal-q*]*u-te* 35:21, *hal-qu-u-te* 100 r. 15, *ha-la-qu-ni-ni* 35:19, *ih-hal-li-qu-u-ni* 52 r. 4, *ih-li-qa-an-ni* 218 r. 6, *i*[*h-li-qu-ni*] 36:7, *ih-li-qu-u-ni* 11 r. 6, 52:19, *ih-l*]*i-qu-u-ni* 54:9, *ih-tal-qa* 245:11, *ih-tal-qu* 35 r. 3, 48:12, r. 4, *ih-tal-qu-u-ni* 121 r. 12, *ih-ti*]*-liq* 54:5, *ni-ih-ti-liq* 34:21, LÚ.*ha-al-qu-*[*t*]*e* 35:18, ZÁH.MEŠ 32:9,
**haluppu** "oak": GIŠ.HA.LU.ÚB 294:10,
**hanāšu** "to submit": *ha-an-šu-ni* 78:12, *ha-an-šú-ti* 78 r. 12, *i*]*h-ta-an-šu* 149:7, *ih-ta-an-šú* 78:9, 184:6, *t*]*a-ha-ni-šú-ni* 290:7, *ú-ha-an-ni-*[*šú-ni*] 286:3,
**hanniu** see *anniu,*
**hanumešu** (mng. unknown): *ha-nu-me-šú* 108 r. 7,
**hapû** "to break, destroy": *ha-pe-e* 95:9, [*i*]*-ha-pi-u* 56 r. 11, *u*]*h-ta-pi-ú* 149:8,
**hapūtu** "destruction": *ha-pu-su-*[*nu* 149:8,
**harādu** "to watch, attend, prompt; (D) to warn": [*l*]*a-ah-ri-di* 213 r. 8, *uh-t*[*ar-rid*] 4:8, *ú-hu-ta-ri-du-šú-nu* 217:12,
**harammāma** "later": *ha-ram-ma-*[*ma* 280 r. 3, *ha-ram-me-ma* 160:3, [*ha-ra*]*-me-ma* 126:18,
**harāpu** "to be early, first": *ah-tú-ru-pu* 199:14, [*ah-tú-r*]*u-up* 200 r. 2, *har-pu-ti* 253 r. 3, *ha-ri-ip* 150:6, *ih-tú-ur-pa-ni* 200 r. 4, [*l*]*a-ah-ru-ub* 6 r. 5, *ta-ha-ru-pu* 199:5,
**harāṣu** "to clear up, to dig": *ah-ru-ṣa* 173:8, *ah-ru-uṣ*] 144 r. 7, *har-ṣu* 40 e. 23, 85:5, *har-ṣu*] 34:6, *har-ṣ*[*u* 144:8, *hur-ṣa* 144 r. 11, [*hu*]*-ur-ṣu* 128:9, *ih-tar-ṣa* 217 r. 3, *i-ha-ra-aṣ* 25:9,
**harbu** (a kind of plough): *har-bi* 21 r. 7,
**hardūtu** "prompting, attendance": *ha-ar-du-ut-te* 152:7,
**harimtu** "prostitute": MÍ.*ha-ri-ma-te* 24:11,
**harrānu** "road, journey": *har-ra-nu* 176:8, see also *hūlu,*
**harru** "canal, moat": *i—ha-ri* 166:2,
**hasā'u** "to mistreat, molest": *ih-t*[*i-si*] 260:4,
**haṭṭu** "sceptre": GIŠ.P[A-*ka*] 146 r. 11,
**haṭû** "to make a mistake, sin": *ah-ti-ṭí* 2 r. 4, *ah-ṭi* 176 s. 3,
**hazannu** "mayor, inspector": LÚ.*ha-za-ni* 53:5,
**hepû** see *hapû,*
**hiāṭu** "to weigh": *ni-ih-ti-*[*aṭ*] 287 r. 4, *n*]*i-ih-*[*ti-a*]*ṭ* 206:12, [*n*]*i-ih-ti-aṭ* 206:9,
**hibiltu** "debt": *hi-bi-la-te-ia* 260 r. 4, *hi-bi-la-te-ka* 260 r. 2,
**hiṭṭu** "fault, crime": *hi-i-ṭu* 210:16,
**hubtu** "booty, captives": *hu-ub-ti* 145 r. 15, *hu-ub-tú* 120:8, 145 r. 18, 226 r. 7, LÚ.*hu-ub-te* 242:5, LÚ.*hu-ub-*[*te*] 156:10, LÚ.*hu-ub-*[*tú* 156:15, LÚ.*hu-*[*ub-tú*] 166:3,
**hūlu** "road, way": *hu-li-ni* 282:7, *i—*KASKAL-*šú-nu* 221 r. 13, KASKAL 19 r. 2, 31 r. 25, 53:6, r. 3, 79:14, 90 r. 8, 173:4, 194 r. 6, 199:9, 12, 200:7, r. 6, 226 r. 19, 230:8, [KASKAL 34 r. 15, KASKAL-*šu* 92:17, KASKAL-*šú* 152 r. 20, KASKAL.MEŠ 146:7, 260 r. 8, see also *harrānu,*
**hurāṣu** "gold": KUG.GI 234:5, 294:18,
**hušê** "(metal) scraps": *hu-še-e* 206:5, 8,
**iābilu** "ram": UDU.NIT]A.MEŠ 133 r. 15, UDU.NITÁ.MEŠ 146:6, 263:6, UDU.[NITÁ.MEŠ 136 r. 3,
**iābu** see *aiābu*
**iāmuttu** "each": *ia-a-mut-tu* 210 r. 2, 12, *ia-mut-*[*tu*] 109:6, *ia-mu-tú* 34 r. 24, *i*]*a-mu-tú* 48:13, *i*]*a-mu-ut-tum* 113:16,
**iāši** see *aiāši*
**igāru** "wall": É.$SIG_4$.MEŠ] 282:9,
**ijû** "mine": *ia-u* 56 r. 7, *ia-ú* 34 r. 11, 146:15,
**ilku** "(labour) duty": *il-ka-šú-ni* 78 e. 17, *il-ki* 52:18, 149:6, [*i*]*l-ku* 232 r. 7, *il-ku-šu* 78 r. 1,
**ilu** "god": *i-lu-u* 33 s. 1, DINGIR 105 r. 7, 149:4, DINGIR.ME-*ni* 117:15, DINGIR.MEŠ 35:23, 32, 106: 10, 236:5, DINGIR.MEŠ-*ku-nu* 95:5, DINGIR.MEŠ-*ni* 69:8, 203 r. 13, DING]IR.MEŠ-*ni* 178 e. 11, [DI]NGIR.MEŠ-*ni* 106:3, DINGIR.MEŠ-*ni-šu* 256:6, DINGIR.MEŠ-*šu* 37 r. 2,
**imāru** "donkey": AN[ŠE 48:7, 250 r. 12, ANŠE 34 e. 38, 60:4, 98 r. 5, 203:6, 250 r. 9, 10, 11, 12, 15, 16, 19, 259:1, 274:5, ANŠE] 250 r. 17, A[NŠ]E 74:8, A]NŠE 250 r. 18, ANŠE.MEŠ 52 r. 13,
**imēru** see *imāru,*
**imittu** "right side": ZAG 46 r. 5, 63:15, 93:7, Z[AG] 229 e. 11, ZAG-*ka* 46:2,
**immeru** "sheep": UDU.MEŠ 21:18, 37:12, 16, r. 14, 122:7, 256:2, 4, 12, r. 6, 257:3, UDU.M[EŠ] 258:4, [U]DU.MEŠ 256:6, 11, UDU.MEŠ-*ia* 256 r. 5, UDU.MEŠ-*šú* 133 r. 9, UDU.HI.A.MEŠ 98 r. 6,
**ina** "in": *ina* 2:6, 7, r. 2, 3, 4, 7, 3:6, 11, 16, r. 1, 4, 6, 7, 10, 15, 18, 4 r. 2, 4, 7, 10, 5:3, e. 5, r. 3, 6 r. 2, 5, 8:8, 12 r. 3, 13:5, 7, 14:11, r. 5, 15:16, e. 18, r. 4, 5, 10, 12, 19 r. 5, 6, 8, 9, s. 2, 20:5, 21:11, 12, 13, 15, 17, 18, e. 21, r. 3, 16, 24:15, 16, 25:8, 9, r. 4, 5, 26 r. 1, 27:7, 28:7, 29:8, 31:6, 9, 11, 19, 20, r. 6, 11, 13, 23, 24, 32:8, 9, 13, 15, e. 20, r. 7, 8, 10, s. 1, 33 r. 2, 5, 10, 12, s. 1, 34:23, r. 5, 8, 9, 10, 11, 14, 15, 24, 25, 27, 32, s. 1, 35:19, e. 34, r.

1, 5, 8, 10, 12, 14, 15, 37:12, 14, 21, 23, 24, r. 21, 38:7, 39:1, 3, 40:13, r. 3, 42:3, r. 6, 44 r. 3, 4, 45:3, r. 4, 6, 46:2, 9, 14, e. 18, r. 1, 6, 48:15, r. 1, 5, 7, 51 r. 1, 52:5, 12, 17, 19, 21, r. 4, 6, 7, 53:9, 14, 17, 21, r. 3, 4, 6, 10, 54:12, 15, 19, r. 1, 2, 55:4, 56:4, 6, 8, 9, 10, 16, r. 1, 5, 8, 10, 60:5, 62:7, 63:9, 12, r. 4, 8, 14, 64:7, 9, 11, 14, 65:6, 9, 67:7, r. 3, 68:4, 69:4, 6, 12, 13, r. 8, 70:4, 5, 71:5, 11, 74:8, r. 10, 75:4, 77 r. 2, 78:6, 8, 15, r. 8, 13, 79:5, 11, r. 2, 5, 6, 8, 80:8, r. 6, 81:7, 8, 11, 82:4, 85 r. 1, 86:8, 87:5, 14, r. 1, 88:11, r. 6, 89:10, 11, 90 r. 1, 2, 91:3, 6, 8, 15, 16, 21, r. 4, 92:9, 10, 17, r. 5, 6, 8, 13, 15, 93 r. 2, 95:3, 6, 9, 15, e. 16, r. 4, 5, 10, 96:7, 8, r. 6, 97:4, 12, 13, r. 11, s. 1, 98:5, 6, 9, r. 10, 100:10, 17, r. 2, 3, 6, 8, 102 r. 3, 103:1, 3, e. 11, r. 3, 7, 104:6, 7, 13, r. 3, 5, 6, 7, 11, 105:4, 9, 13, 24, r. 3, 4, 8, 106:12, 13, 20, 107:4, r. 1, 108:7, 8, 20, 21, 28, 29, r. 18, 24, 25, s. 1, 110:6, 111:2, r. 3, 112:2, 3, 6, 113:3, 5, 7, 10, 11, 12, r. 11, 13, 114:4, 115:11, 116:5, 117:16, 17, 20, e. 22, 118:5, 119:4, 121:5, 8, 11, 17, r. 2, 19, 122 r. 3, 5, 8, 10, 124:8, 125:5, 126:5, 13, r. 11, 129:5, r. 5, 130 s. 2, 131:2, 3, 6, 132:8, 133:7, r. 5, 6, 8, 135:7, r. 11, 136:5, 6, 7, 8, 9, 137:4, 5, 139:1, 5, 9, 140:4, 141 r. 5, 143 r. 1, 144:6, r. 5, 6, 145:8, r. 1, 4, 5, 14, 15, 146:10, r. 10, 147:12, 14, r. 1, 6, 148:6, r. 3, 149:10, r. 2, 19, 21, 23, 150:6, 7, 9, 18, r. 5, 151:6, 152:5, 7, 18, e. 26, 27, r. 9, 17, 154:4, r. 5, 155:4, 9, 156:6, 13, 157:8, 158:5, 160:5, 161:4, 162:10, 163:5, 9, r. 10, 164:3, 7, 11, 15, r. 7, 165:4, 7, 166:6, r. 4, 168:7, r. 4, 5, 6, 169:6, 8, 10, 170:8, 172:4, r. 6, 176:12, 14, 177:1, 2, 179 r. 4, 180:3, 182:10, 11, r. 8, 183:1, 184:3, 185:2, 186:6, 187:3, 5, 6, 190 r. 1, 191:3, 6, 194 r. 10, 196:15, r. 10, 197 r. 3, 199:6, 11, 15, r. 3, 5, 200:17, r. 3, 5, 12, 202:7, 10, r. 2, 3, 15, s. 1, 203:4, 10, 12, r. 8, 11, 12, 15, 204:7, 9, 11, 14, r. 3, 205:7, 8, r. 2, 5, 7, 206:6, 7, 9, r. 5, 207:6, 210:9, r. 3, 15, 211 r. 9, 10, 213:7, r. 9, 217:5, 6, 7, 8, 10, 11, r. 1, 5, 6, 10, 11, 13, 14, s. 2, 4, 218:1, 6, 8, 12, 15, r. 12, 220:3, 6, 9, 221:7, 10, r. 6, 14, 223:1, 5, 224:4, 8, 10, r. 15, 226:4, 5, 10, 12, 13, 16, r. 3, 5, 12, 14, 16, 19, 227:4, 8, 10, 11, 12, 15, 16, 19, 23, 24, r. 6, 13, 15, 17, 18, s. 1, 2, 4, 228:5, r. 4, 229:2, 230:1, 6, 232:4, 5, 11, r. 3, 5, 9, 233:10, 234:6, 235:4, 236:4, 5, 238:4, r. 3, 241:6, 8, 11, r. 3, 242 r. 1, 243:7, 10, 12, 13, 15, e. 18, 19, r. 5, 7, 8, 9, 11, 13, 14, 245 r. 3, 246:4, 8, 248:1, 2, r. 3, 249:1, 3, 5, 6, 11, 12, 14, r. 2, 7, 250:4, 10, 16, 18, r. 3, 7, 8, 14, 21, 253 r. 3, 254:5, 8, 12, r. 10, 13, 15, 255:2, 256:7, 9, r. 8, 9, 257:7, 9, r. 4, 8, 9, 259:5, r. 1, 3, 260:11, 261 r. 4, 262:8, 263:3, 6, 8, 10, 266 r. 3, 267:4, 268:4, r. 2, 269:6, 9, 270 s. 2, 3, 271:6, 272 r. 1, 3, 4, 273:1, 275:1, 276:2, 277:4, 6, 281:12, 14, r. 4, 282:5, r. 3, 283:7, r. 5, 284 r. 6, 7, 286:4, 288 r. 7, 289:6, r. 3, 290:5, 292 r. 3, 8, 293:7, 10, s. 1, 294:2, 4, 11, 13, 15, 17, 295:18, 19, r. 11, 13, 17, 24, 296 r. 2, 297:5, 7, 9, 10, 11, 298:14, r. 2, 3, 4, 11, 13, *ina*] 31 r. 13, 42 r. 8, 54 r. 15, 107:3, 151:5, 176 s. 3, 186 e. 9, 187:4, 257:2, 279 r. 11, 291:4, *in*[*a* 15:7, 46:9, 47 r. 9, 154:7, 249:4, 251:12, 282:9, *in*[*a*] 32 r. 20, *i*[*na* 203 r. 5, *i*[*na*] 200 r. 4, *i*]*na* 15 r. 7, 63:6, 232 r. 8, 279 r. 9, [*ina* 4 r. 1, 6 r. 4, 11 r. 8, 12 r. 6, 12, 21 r. 20, 22:7, 25 r. 2, 31 r. 3, 34:5, 35 e. 35, 37:25, 27, 43:4, 57:4, 63:4, 12, 14, 72:4, 86:4, 89:4, 90 r. 8, 92:12, 94:4, 95:5, 98:12, 104:16, 106:11, 107 e. 6, 112:3, r. 6, 126 r. 3, 134:7, 135:4, 138:7, 142 e. 11, 143:5, 145:10, 12, 148:10, 150:5, 14, r. 13, 17, 151:4, 162 e. 18, r. 3, 173:12, 174:2, 181:4, 182:4, 186:8, 188:8, 189:2, 194 r. 7, 196:11, 199 r. 2, 203:17, r. 3, 210 r. 3, 225:4, 232:7, 237:5, 239:4, 245 r. 1, 247:4, 251:4, 254 r. 3, 5, 256:2, r. 5, 257 r. 11, 262:2, 269:9, 273:6, 277:1, 284 r. 4, 286:6, 291:11, r. 5, 295:25, 299 r. 6, 12, [*ina*] 5 e. 6, 6:9, 31:18, 40 r. 4, 44 r. 2, 46 r. 14, 50:7, 63:16, 71:12, 81:15, 92 r. 16, 93:1, 95:13, 109:7, 117 r. 10, 146:14, 149:15, 164 r. 12, 165:11, 173:4, 179 r. 8, 204 r. 9, 253:2, 259 r. 2, 283:3, 6, 290 r. 5, 300 r. 3, [*in*]*a* 228:13, [*i*]*na* 142:2, 168:5, [[*ina* 67:3, 163 r. 6, *i-na* 84:4, r. 1, 5, 121 r. 13, 133:12, r. 1, 3, 143 r. 2, 149:4, r. 7, 11, 168 r. 3, 175:5, 260:8, 9, 296 r. 4, *i-n*[*a* 135 r. 5, [*i-na*] 133 r. 11, [*i-n*]*a* 143:7,

**ingallu** "sickle": GIŠ.*in-gal-lu* 295 r. 24,

**īnu** see *ēnu*,

**irginu** (a breed of horse): *ir-gi-ni* 171:7,

**irtu** "breast": *in*$_6$*–ni-ir-ti-ia* 224 r. 16, *in*$_6$*–ni-ir-ti-iá* 224:9, *in*$_6$*–ni-i*[*r-ti-iá*] 224 r. 3, *in*$_6$*–ni-ir-ti-i-k*[*a*] 224 r. 8, *in*$_6$*–ni-ri-te* 164 r. 9, *ir-ti* 297 r. 1, *ir-ti-ia* 126:9, *i–ni-ir-ti-šú-nu* 223 r. 2, GABA 53:14, 62:7, GABA] 194 r. 7, [GA]BA-*ia* 133:7, GABA-*ni* 194 r. 10,

**ishunnatu** see *išhunnutu*

**isītu** "(depot) tower": *i-si-te* 120:9, *i-si-*[*te*] 60:5, É*–i-si-te-ia* 120 r. 3, [URU].*i-si-tú* 5 e. 5,

**ispillurtu** "cross, crossroads": *is-pi-lu-ur-te* 227 r. 6,

**issēniš** "also, in addition": *is-se-niš* 152 r. 11, 176:11, [*is-s*]*e-niš* 24:12, *i-se-niš* 37 r. 3, 64 r. 3, 228:8, [*i-se*]*-niš* 36:6, 126:17,

**issēnīu** "single, individual": *i-se-nu-te* 87 r. 6, *i-se-nu-te-ma* 87 r. 8,

**issi/u** "with/from": *is-s*]*i-ia* 17 e. 13, [*is-s*]*i-ia* 152 r. 3, *is-si-*[*ni* 157:9, *is-si-šú* 246 r. 5, 292 r. 5, *is-si-šú*] 108:23, *is-si-šú-nu* 78 r. 14, [*is-si-šú-nu* 106:24, *i-si* 286:5, *i-si-ia* 3 r. 18, 21 r. 18, 32 r. 15, 121 r. 4, 122:6, 200 r. 6, 8, 10, 13, 15, 270:14, [*i-si*]*-ia* 294 r. 10, [*i-s*]*i-ia* 195:3, *i-*[*si*]*-ia-m*[*a*] 286:9, *i-si-ka* 199 r. 9, 254:11, [*i*]*-si-k*[*a* 270:16, *i-si-ku-nu* 260:7, *i-si-ni* 226 r. 20, *i-s*]*i-ni* 250:9, *i-si-šu* 3 r. 6, 38:9, 91:5, 171:5, 179 r. 4, *i-si-š*[*u* 35:25, [*i-si-šu*] 38:5, *i-si-šu-nu* 162:9, *i-si-šú* 2 r. 6, 3:11, 52:10, 53:24, 98:13, 108 r. 19, 122 r. 7, 164 r. 5, 166 r. 2, 245 r. 5, 249 r. 8, 284 r. 10, *i*]*-si-šú* 133 r. 17, 141 r. 2, [*i-s*]*i-šú* 133 s. 2, [*i*]*-si-šú* 203:13, *i-si-šú-nu* 32:8, 11, 43:8, 52 r. 16, 18, 68:10, 91:10, 169:7, 171 r. 5, 210:12, 228 r. 3, 5, *i-si-šú-n*[*u*] 137 r. 4, *i-*[*s*]*i-šú-nu* 34:22, *i*]*-si-šú-nu* 95:2, [*i-si-šú-nu*] 34:27, [*i-s*]*i-šú-nu* 137 r. 7, [*i*]*-si-šú-nu* 34:27, 137:3, *i-si-šú-nu-ma* 32:15, TA 1 r. 1, 3 r. 3, 11, 12, 13, 14, 5 r. 1, 11 r. 1, 12 r. 2, 13:3, 15 r. 1, 13, 18 r. 5, 21:13, 26 r. 2, 31 r. 23, 32 r. 2, 33 r. 15, 34 r. 30, 35:16, 22, 32, r. 4, 37 r. 8, 46:10, 15, 52:12, 18, r. 3, 13, 53:6, 7, 8, 15, 20, e. 27, 54:4, 7, 9, 59:4, 72:5, 79:7, r. 5, 86:5, 87:13, 19, 89:5, 92:11, 16, 95 r. 7, 96:7, 99:11, 100:13, 14, r. 2, 4, 10, 12, 16, 103:6, 105:17, r. 2, 107:1, e. 7, 108:27, e. 30, r. 21, 111 r. 2, 113:7, r. 4, 117 r. 4, 121:18, r. 11, 122:10, 126:9, r. 4, 7, 133:4, 6, 138:2, 4, 141:12, 144 r. 8, 145:6, 149 r. 9, 13, 151:5, 154 r. 6, 156:10, 160:2, 19, 162:5, 163:6, 12, r. 4, 166:4, 5, 169 r. 3, 172:9, 173:11, 182 r. 3, 195:4, 196:13, r. 8, 199:10, r. 10, 203 r. 19, s. 1,

206:4, 208:4, 210:7, r. 9, 211:7, 213 r. 6, 216 r. 8, 217 s. 1, 218 r. 1, 5, 9, 221:12, r. 3, 224 r. 4, 225:12, 14, 16, 17, 227:7, 18, r. 8, 229 r. 1, 4, 7, 233:5, r. 2, 241 r. 1, 242:5, 9, 243:11, 13, r. 1, 244:6, 251:15, 253 r. 1, 256:4, 257:4, r. 3, 260 r. 1, 5, 10, 261:3, 264:4, 268:5, 273:4, 277:3, 280 r. 1, 286:4, 288 r. 5, 289:4, 291 r. 2, 8, 294 r. 6, 12, 295:23, T[A 11 r. 5, 146:12, T[A] 149:21, T]A 18:8, 37 r. 11, 46 r. 15, 95:3, 196 r. 6, 230:4, 278:5, 291 r. 3, [TA 34 r. 2, 7, 55:6, 174:5, 176 s. 2, 198 r. 2, [TA] 138:6, 190 r. 3, 197:7, 225:13, 238 r. 2, 254:4, [T]A 34:9, 67:13, 83:5, 130:10, 197 r. 12, 262:5, [[TA 163 r. 3,

**issu** "woman, wife": MÍ 108 r. 23, 197 r. 10, MÍ.M[EŠ 265:6,

**issurri** "perhaps": *is]–su-ri* 220:7, *is–su-ur-ri* 52:6, *is]–su-ur-ri* 58:5, *i–su-ri* 33 r. 13, 37:18, 47 r. 5, 54 r. 18, 86:13, 145 r. 10, 152 r. 18, *i–su-ri]* 62:9, *i–su-r[i]* 101:2, *i–su-r]i* 54:6, *i–su-[ri* 1:7, *i–s[u-ri]* 105:21, 290:10, *i–[su-r]i* 143 r. 9, *[i–su-ri* 34 r. 34, 285:3, 291:12, *[i–s]u-ri* 93 r. 4, 215 r. 3, *[i]–su-ri* 194 r. 3, 195:1, *i–su-ur-ri* 40 r. 5, 52:10,

**iṣu** "tree, wood": GIŠ 280 r. 7, GIŠ.MEŠ 255:2,

**išātu** "fire": *i-šá-tu* 12 r. 12,

**išhunnutu** "bunch of grapes": GIŠ.KIN.GEŠTI[N 281 r. 5, GIŠ.KIN.GE[ŠTIN.MEŠ] 41:3,

**iškāru** "assigned quota, tax": *iš-ka-šú* 197 r. 1,

**išpatu** "quiver": *iš-pat* 101 r. 4,

**kabāru** "to be thick": *kab-ba-ru-u-ni* 294:13, *kab-ra* 294:15,

**kabāsu** "to tread upon": *li-ik-ba-[su-ni]* 298:13,

**kaiamānu** "constantly": *ka-a-a-ma-nu* 243 r. 13, *k]a-a-a-m[a-nu]* 108:3,

**kal amāri** "early morning": *ka-la-ma-ri* 243 r. 14,

**kalakku** "kelek": KUŠ.*ka-la-ki* 200:12,

**kallāp šipirti** "dispatch rider": LÚ.*kal-lap–ši-pir-[te* 197 e. 11, LÚ.*kal-lap–ši-pir-t[ú* 197 r. 2,

**kallāpu** "outrider(?)": LÚ.*kal-ba-te* 215:20, LÚ.*kal-[la-bu]* 46:13, LÚ.*kal-[la-pu* 277:11,

**kalliu** "mule express": *kal-li-ú* 74:4, *ka-li-e* 122 r. 2, 227:20, *ka-li-ie* 227:4, *ka-li-iu-u* 227:6, 19, *ka]]-li-iu-ú* 227 r. 12,

**kallumu** "to show": *[u]k-tal-li-[x* 197:9, *ú-kal-lam* 37:25,

**kalu** "all": *kal* 48 r. 6, 211 r. 7, 9, DÙ 288 s. 1,

**kalû** "to hold back": *ak-la-šú-nu* 64:15, *ak-tal-šú-u* 147 r. 9, *ak-ta-la* 163 r. 11, *a-kal-la* 256:8, *ik-la-[šú-nu-u]* 12 r. 8, *ik-lu-u-ni* 3 r. 2, *ik-ta-la* 200 r. 7, *ik-ta-[la* 143 r. 4, *ik-[ta-la]* 256:6, *ik-ta-la-šú* 31 r. 25, *ik-ta-na-la-a-na-ši* 234:7, *i-kal-li-ú* 106:25, *i-kal-lu-u* 87:18, *i-ka-al-la* 200 r. 16, *ka-la-ʾu* 106:23, *ki-la-šú-nu* 37 r. 7, *lak-la-šú* 147 r. 12, *la-ak-la* 37 r. 6, *la-ak-l[a* 248:7, *lik-la-šú* 150:4, *lik-li-u* 226 r. 15, *[šak-l]a-na-ši* 289 r. 4, *ša-a[k]-lu* 119:5, *[t]a-ka-la-šú* 256:5,

**kammusu** "to sit, live, stay": *kam-ma-su-u-ni* 53 r. 10, *kam-mu-sa-ka* 31 r. 15, *kam-mu-sa-ni]* 157:8, *kam-mu-su* 52 r. 7, 54:15, *kam-mu-s[u]* 300 r. 3, *kam-mu-[su]* 109:7, *[kam]-mu-su* 126 r. 4, 228:6, *ka-mu-sa-[ka-ni* 95:4,

**kanāku** "to seal": *ni-kan-na-ak* 206 r. 8,

**kannušu** "to gather": *nu-ka-na-šú-ú-ni* 3 r. 20,

**kapšarru** "engraver": [LÚ.K]AB.SAR 205:12,

**kaqqudu** "head": SAG.DU 105 r. 7, 191:5, S]AG.DU 86:4, SAG.DU.MEŠ-*šú-nu* 108:20,

**kaqquru** "earth, ground": *kaq-qu-ru* 200:9,

**karābu** "to bless": *lik-ru-bu* 126:5, 127:5, 293:6, 295:4,

**karāku** "to gather": *i[k-ti-rik]* 89:9, *kar-ka-te-e* 147:7, *kar-ka-ti* 279:8, *kar-ku* 200:10,

**karāmu** "to hinder": *kar-ma-šu* 199:9, *ka-ri-im* 79:15,

**karānu** "wine": GEŠTIN.MEŠ 98 r. 5, 203:4, 6, GIŠ.GEŠTIN 122:9,

**karāru** "to lay, throw": *ak-t[ar-ra]* 4 r. 7, *ak-ta-ra-ar* 15 r. 6, *[a-kar-ra-ár* 25 r. 3, *a-ka-ra-ár* 117 r. 12, *ik-ta-ra-ra* 33 r. 6, *i-ka-ru-[ru]* 33 r. 10, *kar-[ra* 95:15, *[kar-ra-a-ni]* 290 r. 6, *kar-ru* 244 r. 5, 254 r. 14, *[kar-ru* 34 r. 16, *[k]a-ár-ri* 118:6, *ka-ra-ri* 200:11, *ka-ri-ru-u-ni* 227 r. 7, *kur-ru* 216 s. 2,

**karkadinnu** "confectioner": LÚ.*kar-ka-di-ni* 215:17,

**karṣī** "slander, calumny": *kar-ṣi-ia* 243 r. 4,

**kāru** "quay, harbour, trade colony": [KA]R 297 r. 2, *ka-a-ri* 150:12, URU.*ka-a-ri* 150:17,

**kaspu** "money": *kas-pi* 149 r. 21, *kas-pu* 169:9, *kas-pu-šú* 150:7,

**kaṣāru** "to bind, organize": *a]k-ṣur* 31 s. 3, *ak-ṣur-u-ni* 121:7, *ik-ṣur-u-ni* 121 r. 18, 182 r. 7, *ka-ṣa-ra* 164 r. 8, *ku-ṣ[u-ru]* 200:5, *lik-ṣu-ru* 199 r. 15,

**kāṣiru** "tailor": LÚ.KA.KÉŠ 215:16,

**kāša** "you": *ka-[šá]* 147:3, *ka-[[šá* 227 r. 12,

**kašādu** "to reach, conquer; (D) to persecute; (Š) to deliver": *ik-šu-da-ni* 283:8, *i-kaš-šad* 46:11, *i-[k]aš-šad* 46 r. 7, *i-[kaš-šu-du* 46:6, *ka-ši-du* 146:17, *li-ik-šu-du* 146 r. 9, *lu-u-ša-ak-ši-di* 298 r. 6, *uk-ta-ši-di* 256:11, *ú-k[aš-ša-da]* 46:11,

**kāšunu** "you": *ka-a-šu-nu* 34:20,

**katāru** "to wait": *ni-ik-te-ti-[ir]* 249:5,

**kettu** "truth": *ke-et-tu* 176 s. 2, *ke-e-tu* 52 r. 11, *ke-e-tú* 295:23, *[k]e-e-tú* 121:18,

**kî** "as": *ki* 3 r. 16, 8:5, 92 r. 4, 104:9, 199 r. 8, 202 r. 3, 205:10, 213 e. 10, *ki-i* 2:10, 3:8, 13:3, 14:7, r. 15, 16 r. 4, 21 r. 13, 25:10, 27:9, 34:21, 45:6, r. 8, 46 r. 5, 12, 63 r. 11, 79 r. 9, 11, 92:15, 95:11, 12, 98 r. 3, 106:9, 21, 108:24, r. 10, 16, 19, 109:3, 118 r. 6, 129 r. 7, 138:11, 147 r. 8, 149:3, 160:9, 182 r. 9, 202 r. 11, 203 r. 17, 204:10, 12, r. 1, 226 r. 8, 227:7, 21, r. 5, 24, 243 e. 20, 256 r. 9, 277 r. 7, 279:5, r. 6, 283:4, 291 r. 11, 295 r. 20, 298:10, *ki-[i* 108 s. 1, *ki-[i]* 173:8, *ki-[[i]]* 108 r. 22, *k[i]-i* 48:10, *k]i-i* 11 r. 6, 60:7, 123 r. 3, *[ki-i* 83:6, 142:7, 150:11, 188:9, 203:15, 230:4, *[ki-i]* 108 r. 17, 150 r. 6, 15, 152:23, 159:4, *[ki]-i* 108 r. 11, 173:2, 179 r. 10, 196:6, *[k]i-i* 6 r. 7, 63:17, 106:10, 114 r. 5, 170:9, GIM 204 r. 7,

**kibru** "shore, bank": *ki-b[ir* 117:20,

**kibsu** "track, trail": *kib-sa-ti* 32 r. 8,

**kilallī** "both": *ki-lal-le-šú-nu* 286:7, *ki-la-li* 32 r. 4,

**kīma** "when, after, if": *ki-ma* 7:5, 37:23, 52 r. 15, 97:11, 145 r. 11, 150 r. 10, 156:8, 277:2, 280 e. 14, *ki-[ma* 33 r. 6, *[ki-ma* 19 s. 3, *[ki-ma]* 6 r. 3, *ki-ma-a* 186:7,

**kipputu** "circle, disc": *kip-pu-tú* 15 r. 7,

**kiriu** "orchard, garden": GIŠ.SAR 42 e. 8, 213 r. 7, 281:15, GIŠ.SAR-*šú* 109:7, GIŠ.SAR.MEŠ 37 r. 9, 12, 52 r. 5,

**kissutu** "fodder": ŠE.*ki-su-tú* 233:5, 8, 250 r. 6, 9, 11, 19, ŠE.[*ki-su-tú* 250 r. 15,

**kiṣru** "cohort, corps": *ki-iṣ-ri-ia* 69:4, *ki-iṣ-r*[*u* 182 r. 6, *ki-ṣar-ka* 69:5, *ki-ṣir* 121:6, 250:13,

**kitru** "aid": [*kit-ri*] 145 r. 1,

**kitû** "linen, tunic": TÚG.GADA 152 r. 10, TÚG. GADA.MEŠ 206 r. 7,

**kuānu** "to be firm, true; (D) to confirm, decree": *ku-un-nu-te* 96 r. 9, *k*]*u-un-tú* 162 r. 4, *lu-uk-ta-ti-ni* 163:10, [*uk-tin-nu* 31:20, *ú-ki-nu-šu-u-*[*ni*] 31:10,

**kudimmu** (a kind of salt): ŠE.*ku-dim-me* 242 r. 2,

**kūdunu** "mule": AN[ŠE.*ku-din*] 227:15, ANŠE. *ku-din* 227:9, 11, 16, 19, 24, ANŠE.*ku-di*[*n*] 5:3, ANŠE].*ku-din-*[*ni*] 9:6, ANŠE.*ku-din*.MEŠ 48:6, ANŠE.*ku-di-ni* 215:8, ANŠE.*ku-du-nu* 52 r. 13, ANŠE. GÌR.NUN.NA 35:25, ANŠE.GÌR.NUN.NA.MEŠ 35:26, ANŠE.GÌR.NUN.NA.MEŠ-*šú* 171 r. 1,

**kuintu** (reading and mng. obscure): *ku-in-ti* 44 r. 5,

**kullu** "to hold": *ú-k*[*al-la*] 74:11, *ú-kal-lu-u-ni* 105:14, *ú-ka-lu-ni* 32 r. 13,

**kūmu** "instead": *ku-mu* 268 r. 9, *ku-um* 126 r. 2, 244 r. 9, 259:7,

**kunukku** "seal": $NA_4$.KIŠIB 32:8, 53 e. 25,

**kuppû** "snow, ice": *ku-*[*pe-e*] 126 r. 4, *ku-pu* 92 r. 4, *ku-pu-u* 142:6, 145 r. 11, 285:5, *ku-pu-ú* 146: 7, *ku-up-pu* 105 r. 5, *ku-up-p*[*u*] 26 e. 10,

**kurummutu** "barley (ration)": (ŠE.)PAD.MEŠ 82 r. 12, [ŠE.PAD.MEŠ] 242:12, ŠE.PAD.ME[Š] 98 r. 5, ŠE.PAD.MEŠ 16:7, 234:8, 250 r. 16, 18, 259:6, 269: 5, 294 r. 4, ŠE.PAD.M[EŠ] 185:5, ŠE.PAD.[MEŠ 278:9, ŠE.PA[D].MEŠ 217:10, ŠE.P[AD.MEŠ] 269:8,

**kusāpu** "bread": NINDA.ME[Š 289:2, NINDA.MEŠ 32:13, 34:27, 37:28, 216 r. 5, 289 r. 3, [NINDA.ME]Š 32:15, [NINDA.MEŠ 106:21, [NINDA.MEŠ] 126:15, NINDA.[MEŠ-*šú*]-*nu* 68:7,

**kussiu** "throne, seat": GIŠ.GU.ZA 95:3, GIŠ.[GU. ZA] 108 r. 25,

**kuṣṣu** "cold, winter": *ku-ṣi* 151:10,

**kutallu** "rear, reserves": *ku-tal* 288 r. 7, *ku-tal-l*[*i* 278:7, *ku-tu-li-šu-nu* 249:4,

**la** "not": *la* 1 r. 2, 4, 3:18, r. 12, 11 r. 4, 12 r. 13, 14 r. 13, 16:11, 31 r. 12, 21, 34:20, r. 4, 35:22, 32, 37:11, r. 18, 40:12, 46:1, 13, 16, r. 9, 11, 52:13, r. 11, 53:6, 7, r. 5, 8, 54:11, 16, r. 7, 56:15, 17, r. 4, 61 r. 8, 63:11, 13, r. 15, 74:11, 13, r. 12, 78:12, r. 12, 83 r. 6, 87 r. 9, 88 r. 8, 91 e. 23, r. 2, 5, 7, 93 r. 7, 95:10, 11, e. 17, 18, 97:7, 10, 103:4, 104 r. 4, 10, 105:19, 106:4, 15, 19, 22, 108:10, 16, 23, 24, r. 7, 26, 113:16, r. 5, 9, 114 r. 4, 7, 115:11, 117 e. 22, 118:9, 11, r. 1, 7, 121 r. 20, 122 r. 11, 12, 126:12, r. 5, 130:1, 133 r. 4, 135 r. 1, 137 r. 5, 142:7, r. 4, 143 r. 5, 146:9, 11, 147 r. 4, 7, 149 r. 14, 150:12, r. 5, 152 r. 7, 8, 157:9, 163 r. 5, 169 r. 4, 176 s. 3, 184:5, 187:10, 188:4, 199:7, r. 2, 200:8, 11, 12, 14, r. 6, 13, 203:14, 208 r. 2, 210 r. 1, 212:1, 217 s. 2, 218 r. 6, 221:6, r. 7, 8, 226 r. 2, 3, 10, 18, 227:14, r. 21, 23, 232 r. 4, 243:11, 245 r. 7, 246:7, 251:14, 254:6, 7, 14, 16, 256:7, 260:9, 10, r. 10, 268:13, e. 15, r. 4, 270:19, 272 r. 3, 277 r. 2, 279 r. 5, 280 r. 6, 282:6, 283:1, 284 r. 3, 289 e. 9, r. 2, 4, 293:9, r. 7, 294:8, 295:24, r. 21, 22, *la*] 40:10, 124:5, 150:10, 220:9, *l*[*a* 46 r. 13, 126 r. 5, 225:9, 277 r. 5, *l*[*a*] 37:7, *l*]*a* 86 r. 3, 106:25, 174:5, 289 r. 3, [*la* 12 r. 8, 33 s. 1, 54:11, 18, 63:10, 108:9, 144 r. 7, 250:13, 285:5, [*la*] 31 r. 29, 56 r. 10, 63 r. 18, 90 r. 6, 93 r. 3, 98:11, [*l*]*a* 114:6, 121:12, 142 r. 3, 254:15, 262:6, 277 r. 5, 283:8, *la-a* 13:4, 14 r. 12, 26 e. 9, 10, 31 r. 20, 34 r. 22, 37:9, 26, 40 r. 11, 48 r. 16, 74 r. 11, 13, 81 r. 3, 82 r. 5, 90 r. 5, 91:19, 104 r. 11, 112 e. 7, 116:5, 117:20, 121:15, 122:9, 144 s. 1, 149 r. 5, 173:10, 202 r. 4, 211 r. 5, 216 r. 5, 220:10, 243:4, r. 6, 246 r. 3, 260 r. 4, 270:12, *la-*[*a*] 211 r. 2, *l*]*a-a* 55:13, [*la-a* 37:6, 104:18, 196:8, [*la-a*] 149:19, [*la*]-*a* 150:16, [*l*]*a-a* 104 r. 2, 173:8, 260 r. 5,

**la'û** "to be able": *i-la-u-ni* 6 r. 7, 14 r. 15, 204:17, *i-la-u-ni*] 46 r. 12, *i-la-*[*u-ni*] 16 r. 5, *i-la-'u-ú* 200:14, ZU-*u-ni* 291 r. 11,

**labīru** "old": *la-bir-*[*te* 282:10, *la-bir-tú* 233:7, *la-bi-*[*ru* 16 r. 2, *la-bi-ru-ú-te* 53 r. 10,

**labû** "to surround, go around": [*a-l*]*a-bi-a* 200: 17, *a-la-bi-ia* 199:13, [*i*]*l-ti-bi-ú-šu* 93:4,

**lānu** "body, figure": *la*[*m-šú-nu*] 156 r. 3,

**laqû** "to buy": *a-*[*laq-qi*] 289:4, *a-si-qi* 15 r. 3, *a-*[*si-qi*] 37:22, [*a-s*]*i-qi* 224 r. 1, *i-laq-qi-u* 100: 14, *i-la-*[*qi*] 149:18, *i-si-qi-u* 21 r. 7, *li-qi-a* 238 r. 3, *ni-la-qi* 238 r. 4, *ni-si-qi* 224 r. 7,

**laššu** "is not": *la-áš-šu* 120 r. 4, 200:8, r. 13, [*l*]*a-áš-šu* 121:17, *la-áš-šú* 53 r. 4, 63:10, 83 r. 5, 91 r. 5, 95:5, r. 9, 119:9, 295 r. 20, *la-áš-*[*šú* 268:12, *la-áš*]-*šú* 243 r. 7, *la-*[*áš-šú*] 26 r. 1, [*l*]*a-*[*áš-šú*] 68:8, [[*la-áš-šú*]] 121 r. 21, *la-áš-šú-ma* 108 r. 6, *la-áš-šú-m*[*a* 108:14, *la-áš-šú-ni* 289:6, *la-a-*[*šu* 259:5, *la-a-šú* 69:15, 113:18, *la-a-šú*] 21 r. 3, *la-šu* 31 r. 29, 126 r. 11, *la-šu-u-ni* 118 r. 5, *la-šú* 118 r. 7, 227:6, r. 20,

**le'û** see *la'û,*

**lē'u** "writing-board": GIŠ.*le-'i* 121:5, 11, 16, GIŠ. *le-'i*]] 121 r. 20, GIŠ.*le-'*[*i*] 121 e. 19, [GIŠ.*l*]*e-*[']*u-ú* 152 r. 1,

**leqû** see *laqû,*

**libānu** "neck": G[Ú 170 r. 2,

**libbu** "heart": *il—li-bi-ni* 105:7, *lib-ba-šú-nu* 54 r. 4, 5, *lib-bi* 46 r. 7, 126:9, r. 11, 132:6, *lib-bu* 148 r. 5, [ŠÀ 6:6, 17:6, 35:6, ŠÀ 1:6, 3:5, r. 4, 6, 14, 4 r. 5, 5:3, e. 6, r. 3, 21 r. 3, 35:24, r. 4, 37:21, 23, 42 r. 6, 46 e. 18, 52 r. 6, 55:4, 67:13, 79 r. 5, 6, 84:4, 85 r. 1, 86:8, 87:5, 19, r. 1, 88 r. 6, 89:10, 90 r. 2, 91:15, r. 4, 92:10, 16, r. 8, 95 r. 5, 96:7, r. 5, 100:10, 17, 105 r. 2, 107 e. 6, 108 r. 18, 109:7, 111 r. 3, 112:3, 113 r. 4, 117:16, 122:10, r. 3, 135 r. 8, 142 r. 8, 144 r. 6, 145:13, 150 r. 5, 162:5, 10, 173:11, 176 s. 2, 3, 187:3, 191:3, 198 r. 2, 210 r. 3, 9, 217 r. 11, 227 r. 6, s. 1, 238 r. 3, 241 r. 1, 254:4, r. 13, 256 r. 4, 263:12, 273:4, 281:14, 283:3, 298:5, Š[À 15:6, 92 r. 5, 93 r. 1, 135 r. 11, 211 r. 10, 220:6, 256:4, Š]À 80:8, 95:5, 173:12, 299 r. 12, ŠÀ-*ba-ku-nu* 210 r. 5, [ŠÀ-*bi*] 225:14, [ŠÀ]-*bi* 42 e. 9, ŠÀ-*bi* 1 r. 1, 4 r. 10, 5 e. 5, r. 1, 15 r. 5, 10, 12, 32:13, 15, 35 r. 3, 7, 37 r. 11, 52:19, 21, r. 4, 7, 53 r. 10, 56:6, 60:5, 67:7, 69:16, 79:11, 87:14, 100 r. 2, 3, 103:3, e. 11, 105:4, 121:18, 133:6, r. 3, 145:6, 8, 150:7, 164:7, 165:7, 166:6, 168:7, r. 5, 6, 174:5, 182 r. 3, 197:7, 199:11, 204:14, 205 r. 5, 210:14, r. 15, 213 r. 6, 217:8, 10, 11, 218:12, 220:3, 225: 12, 13, 229:2, r. 1, 8, 233:10, 236:5, 243 e. 18, 249:3, 5, 11, r. 2, 259:5, 262:8, 263:3, 264:4, 278:5, 281 r. 4, 289:4, ŠÀ-*b*[*i* 146:15, 265:7, 266 r. 3, ŠÀ]-*bi* 150:9, Š[À-*bi* 14 r. 5, 166 r. 4, Š[À]-*bi* 4 r.

4, Š]À-*bi* 297:5, ŠÀ]-*bi-i-ni* 222:4, ŠÀ-*bi-ku-*[*nu*] 107:1, ŠÀ-*bi-ma* 64:9, ŠÀ-*bi-šá* 205 r. 7, ŠÀ-*bi-š*[*u* 168 r. 4, ŠÀ-*bi-šú* 213 r. 9, ŠÀ]-*bi-šú* 284 r. 9, ŠÀ-*bi-šú-nu* 34 r. 30, 53 r. 4, 79 r. 5, 179 r. 8, 184:3, 253 r. 1, 257:9, 295:23, ŠÀ-*bi-šú-*[*nu*] 56:16, ŠÀ-*bi-šú*]-*nu* 273:6, [ŠÀ-*bu* 18:6, [ŠÀ-*bu*] 249:16, [ŠÀ-*b*]*u* 237:6, 299 r. 9, [ŠÀ]-*bu* 297 r. 5, ŠÀ-*bu* 2:5, 14:6, 38:10, 78 r. 6, 127:7, 217:14, 276 r. 2, 281:7, ŠÀ-*b*[*u* 152:20, ŠÀ]-*bu* 160:16, ŠÀ-*ma* 292 r. 3, ŠÀ-*šú-nu* 3 r. 7, 115:11,

**libittu** "brick": SIG$_{4}$ 291:2, 296 r. 6, SIG$_{4}$-*ma* 56 r. 11, SIG$_{4}$.ME 291:13, r. 8, S[IG$_{4}$].M[E 291:10, [SIG$_{4}$]. ME 291 r. 13, SIG$_{4}$.MEŠ 80 r. 6, 291 r. 4, 5, SI]G$_{4}$.MEŠ 291:7,

**libītu** "entourage": *li-bit*—LUGAL 250:11, *li-bit*—MAN 291 r. 2, *li-bit*—M[AN 291 r. 13,

**līdiš** "the day after toworrow": *li-di-iš* 104 r. 6,

**līmu** "thousand": *lim* 34 r. 14, *li-mi* 263:6,

**lišānu** "tongue": *li-šá-ni* 217:18, 246:4,

**lu** "let, may, be it": *lu* 1:3, 2:2, 5, 6:6, 14:6, 15:6, 16:3, 5, 17:6, 21:9, 25:3, 28:3, 30:3, 31:3, 32:3, 33:3, 35:6, 37:6, 9, 31, 38:10, 46 r. 9, 52:3, 53 e. 26, 62:3, 74 r. 1, 75:3, 82:3, 83:3, 85:2, 88:3, 89:3, 91:2, 92:2, 4, 96:3, r. 3, 98:3, r. 2, 104:3, 106:3, 19, 20, 23, 25, 108:2, 109:7, 121:8, 122:3, 124:5, 127:8, 132:3, 135:3, 139:10, 144:3, 147:3, r. 7, 148:3, r. 6, 149:2, r. 14, 152:3, 20, 154:3, 155:3, 156:5, r. 8, 158:4, 160:16, 162:3, 165:3, 168:3, 172:3, 199:3, 200:3, 6, 202:3, 203:3, 205:3, 213:3, 214 e. 3, 217:3, 15, 226 r. 2, 227:3, r. 23, 232:3, r. 6, 235:6, 238:3, 241:3, 242:3, 245:5, 246:3, 249: 16, 251:3, 267:3, 271:3, 277 r. 3, 281:3, 7, 282:3, r. 1, 293:4, 10, 294:13, 15, 17, 295 r. 2, 297 r. 5, *l*[*u* 19:3, 78 r. 6, 278 r. 4, [*lu* 6:3, 17:3, 18:6, 20:3, 22:3, 34:3, 35:3, 37:3, 38:3, 40:3, 42 r. 1, 43:3, 57:3, 63:3, 66:3, 72:3, 73:3, 76:3, 86:3, 87:3, 97:3, 110:3, 143:3, 150:3, 151:3, 153:3, 159:3, 181:3, 182:3, 194:3, 201:3, 204:3, 207:3, 215:3, 225:3, 239:3, 240:3, 247:3, 269:3, 270:3, 292:3, 295:3, [*lu*] 94:3, 100:3, 137 r. 5, 237:3, 294 r. 9, 299 r. 10, [*l*]*u* 21:3, 23:3, 24:3, 27:3, 50:3, 128:3, 157:4, *lu-u* 1:6, 3:2, 5, 11:3, 14:3, 29:3, 45:2, 47:3, 48:3, 49:3, 59:3, 64:3, 65:3, 68:3, 69:3, 7, 16, 70:3, 71:3, 74:3, 78:3, 79:3, 80:3, 81:4, 84:3, 105:3, 114 r. 3, 4, 122 r. 11, 126:3, 127:3, 133:3, 136:3, 140:3, 141:3, 146:3, 150:12, 161:3, 163:3, 206:3, 210:3, r. 5, 211:3, r. 1, 2, 216:3, 221:3, 224:3, 226:3, 233:3, r. 3, 243:3, 244:3, 250:3, 294:13, r. 8, 298 r. 12, *lu-*[*u* 44:2, 276 r. 3, [*lu-u* 18:3, 55:3, 134:3, 170:3, 256: 1, [*lu*]-*u* 15:3, [*l*]*u-u* 21 r. 19, 67:2, *lu-ú* 53:3, 56:3,

**ma** "thus": *ma* 2:12, 31 r. 29, 37:19, 46 e. 18, 104:12, 14, 108:9, 130:3, 4, 5, 6, 8, r. 8, 152:11, 212:3, 227:6, r. 3, 236:6, 254:10, 268 r. 5, *m*[*a* 121 r. 9, 270 r. 10, [*ma* 104:17, [*ma*] 63 r. 13, 104 r. 1, 141 r. 5, 262:4, [*m*]*a* 115 r. 1, 295 r. 23, *ma-a* 2:15, r. 2, 3:9, 13, 15, 16, 17, 18, 7 r. 4, 8:6, 11 r. 4, 5, 12 r. 5, 14 r. 2, 3, 5, 15:12, 16:5, 19 r. 4, 8, 20:7, 21:9, 28:9, 31:8, 11, r. 15, 25, 27, 32 r. 6, 33:9, s. 1, 34:23, 24, r. 1, 7, 13, 35:22, r. 8, 11, 37:15, 20, 31, r. 7, 40:11, 13, 19, 42 r. 7, 43:9, 45:4, r. 3, 46:1, 3, 48:11, 51:2, 52:7, 11, 14, r. 9, 15, 16, 53 e. 25, 54 r. 3, 56:5, 6, 61:5, 6, 7, 63 r. 2, 4, 5, 68:6, 9, 69:5, 74:6, 7, 77 r. 2, 79:14, 81:12, 85:3, 5, 87 r. 4, 88 r. 5, 93 r. 5, 95:5, 6, 7, 12, 14, 15, e. 17, r. 6, 8, 9, 97 r. 10, 98 r. 1, 4, 103:9, e. 11, r. 1, 104:10, r. 5, 8, 10, 105:12, 13, 106:14, 15, 16, 17, 20, 23, 108:4, 6, 7, 8, 16, 25, 26, e. 31, r. 3, 5, 12, 14, 19, 21, 22, 24, 27, 113 r. 3, 114 r. 5, 6, 115:5, 117:4, r. 8, 118 e. 12, 121:5, 6, 8, 9, 122 r. 12, 123 r. 2, 125:4, r. 2, 3, 4, 126:10, 12, r. 10, 128:7, 8, 129:4, r. 4, 130 r. 7, 133:11, r. 3, 134:6, 135 r. 3, 137 r. 2, 141:11, r. 1, 142 r. 8, 144:8, 145 r. 2, 10, 13, 18, s. 1, 2, 146:19, 147:5, 8, 13, 15, r. 4, 149:17, r. 1, 5, 22, 150:11, 151:6, 152 r. 19, 154:5, 156:8, 161:6, 163:9, 11, 164:10, r. 9, 165:11, 169:11, r. 3, 171 r. 8, 11, 13, 172:7, r. 5, 173:6, 177:1, 179 r. 9, 184:4, 5, 188:9, 192 r. 3, 197 r. 7, 9, 199:5, 6, r. 9, 200:5, 6, 202:5, 8, 203:6, r. 10, 11, 204:10, 210:9, 211:9, r. 3, 4, 212:2, 4, 5, 6, 213 r. 5, 215:5, 216 r. 7, 11, s. 1, 217 r. 16, 18, s. 1, 218:1, 3, 7, 9, 220:4, 5, 6, 221 r. 5, 223:4, r. 2, 224:14, r. 1, 6, 7, 225:6, 7, 226 r. 7, 10, 11, 14, 15, 18, 20, 227 r. 17, 22, 23, 229:9, e. 11, 232 r. 2, 4, 234:8, 241:7, 8, 243 r. 4, 250:16, 256:10, r. 10, 257:8, r. 6, 260:5, 7, 8, 10, r. 2, 263:12, 265:5, 6, 268 r. 1, 3, 270 s. 3, 279 r. 4, 283:4, 5, 7, 289 r. 3, 290:11, 291:4, 292:5, 7, r. 7, 8, 9, 293:9, 294:5, 18, 295 r. 6, 20, 21, 22, 25, 298:8, 12, r. 8, *ma-a*] 34 r. 29, 34, 82:7, 141:9, 221:4, 256 r. 11, 282:4, *ma-*[*a* 40:21, 59:7, 72:7, 108:5, 109:1, 144:10, 152 r. 2, 155:10, *ma-*[*a*] 34:30, 52:13, 133:8, 156:9, *ma*]-*a* 1:8, 12 r. 4, 18 r. 2, 31 r. 14, 95:8, 178 r. 6, 256 r. 9, 279:12, *m*[*a-a* 34:22, 75:6, 135 r. 10, 149 r. 20, 182:6, *m*[*a-a*] 74 r. 10, *m*]*a-a* 12 r. 10, 31 s. 3, 40:12, 95:7, [*ma-a* 11 r. 9, 12 r. 3, 19 r. 6, 34 r. 4, 14, 42 r. 8, 45 r. 5, 54:3, 4, 7, 9, 55:11, 58:7, 63:6, 66:5, 82:5, 86 r. 1, 101:4, 123 r. 3, 124:6, 129 r. 9, 178 r. 8, 225:5, 250 r. 4, 254 r. 13, 256 r. 2, 284 r. 6, 285:4, 291:6, 13, 295 r. 26, [*ma-a*] 12 r. 7, 34:6, 148:11, 150 r. 16, 256:4, 295 r. 24, [*ma*]-*a* 13:8, 14 r. 1, 31 r. 19, 33 r. 18, 42 r. 6, 63 r. 17, 82 r. 1, 103:1, 105:11, 121:13, 162 r. 2, 173:3, 192 r. 1, 203:12, 215 r. 4, 216 r. 4, 224:15, 232:6, 256:12, 269:5, 7, 277:5, 6, 294:4, 299 r. 3, [*m*]*a-a* 34:25, 62:11, 67:1, 104 r. 3, 108: 17, 170:7, 173:5, 196 r. 2, 262:8, 277 r. 7,

**maʾādu** "to be much": *in-ta-aʾ-da* 260:12, *ma-aʾ-da* 36:2, 79:10, 169 r. 1, 229 e. 11, 295:22, *ma-aʾ-da*] 173:5, [*ma-aʾ-da*] 273:2, 275:4, [*ma-a*]ʾ-*da* 149:12, [*m*]*a-aʾ-d*[*a* 276 e. 3, [*m*]*a-aʾ-d*[*a*] 274:2, *ma-a-aʾ-du* 203 r. 20, *ma-a-d*[*u-u-t*]*e* 46 r. 8, *ma-ʾa-ad* 292:5, *ma-ʾa-a*[*d* 196 r. 4,

**madādu** "to measure": *lu-ma-di-du* 149 r. 13, *lu-u-ma-di-du* 169:15,

**madāktu** "military camp": *ma-dak-te* 160:8, *m*[*a-dak-te*] 160:15, *ma-da*[*k-ti* 12 r. 4, [*ma-dak-tú*] 144 r. 6, *ma-dàk-t*[*i*] 90 r. 4, *ma-dàk-tú* 217 r. 7, 9,

**madbaru** see *mudaburu*,

**maddattu** "tribute": *ma-da-at-tú* 92:7,

**magāru** "to agree": *im-ma-gúr* 104 r. 10, 118:9, *im-ma-gu-ru* 294:8, *i-ma-*[*gur* 268:13, *i-*[*ma-gur* 16:11, *i-ma-gúr* 254:6, [*i-ma-gúr*] 254:14, *i-ma-gu-ru* 226 r. 18, *i-ma-*[*gu-ru*] 14 r. 12, *ma-gu-ri* 11 r. 2, [*n*]*i-ma-ag-gu-ru* 144 r. 4,

**mahāru** "to accept, receive": *at-tah-*[*ra* 46 r. 10, *at-ta-har* 48:10, *at-ta-har-šú-ma* 257 r. 10, *a-hu-ru-u-ni* 43:5, 260 r. 6, *a-ta-har* 117 r. 9, [*i*]*h-hu-ru-ni* 106:13, *it-ta-ha-*[*ar* 281 r. 6, *i-ma-har-u-ni* 100 r. 12, *i-ma-hu-ru* 291 r. 10, *i-ta-ah-ru-šu* 35: 26, *i-ta-har-šu* 149:16, *li-hur-šú-nu* 226 r. 8, *m*]*ah-ru* 144 r. 3, *ma*]-*hi-ir* 287:2, [*m*]*a-hi-ir* 294:5, *ni-mah-har* 257 r. 4, *ta-ma-har* 31 r. 21,

**mahāṣu** "to strike, fight": *it-tah-ṣ[u* 269:13, *ma-hu-ṣu* 3 r. 7, *ut-ta-hi-ṣu* 3 r. 8, *ú-[ta]-hi-iṣ-ṣi* 53:17, *ú-ta-hi-iṣ-ṣu* 53 r. 5,
**mahirtu** "past": *ma-hi-ir-te* 203 r. 16,
**māhiṣu** "archer": [L]Ú.*ma-hi-ṣi* 263:11,
**mala** "once": *ma-la* 152 r. 21, *nam—ma-la* 88:10,
**malāku** "to advise, counsel": *tu-um-ta-l[ik-x* 197 r. 6,
**malû** "to be full": *ma-lu-ú* 108:18,
**mannu** "who?": *man-ni* 37:25, 46:9, *man-n[i* 117:5, *man]-ni* 291:13, *man-ni-ma* 98 r. 4, *man-nu* 46:3, 52:7, 100 r. 12, 13, 176:10, 265:6, 270 s. 3, 277:6, 298 e. 17, *ma-ni-ma* 81 r. 2,
**manû** "mina": M]A.NA 149:14, M]A.N[A 271 r. 1, M]A.NA-*a-a* 150:14,
**maqātu** "to fall": *im-qu-ut* 54:16, *in-qut-u-ni* 227 s. 4, *in-q[u-tu]* 103:4, *i-ma-qa-tu-ni-ni* 103 r. 4, *i-ma-qu-ut* 200 r. 12, *i-tuq-tu-u-ni* 202:7, *i-tú-uq-tu* 227 r. 19, LÚ.*ma-aq-tu-tú* 245:13, [LÚ].*ma-aq-tú* 245 r. 3,
**mar** "as much/many as": *am—mar* 21 r. 8, 37 r. 8, 105:7, 13, 217 r. 6, 226:7, 278:6, 294 r. 2, *am—mar]* 12 r. 10, *am—m[ar]* 33 r. 8, *[am—mar* 124:8, *a—mar* 92:11, 121 r. 17, 203:8, *mar* 53:6, 54:4, 69 r. 5, 120:4, 172:9, 223:2, 260 r. 2, 288 s. 1, 290:7,
**mār ahi** "nephew": DUMU—ŠE[Š-*ka*] 108 r. 20,
**mār damqi** "chariot fighter, nobleman": LÚ.A—[SIG] 186:2, LÚ.A.SIG$_5$ 215:10,
**mār šarri** "crown prince": DUMU—LUGAL 109:8, 150:10, 171:2, r. 2, 228:11, D]UMU—LUGAL 277 r. 4,
**mār šipri** "messenger": LÚ].A—*šip-ri* 130 r. 9, LÚ.A—*šip-ri* 33 r. 18, 121 r. 3, [LÚ.A—*šip-ri* 112 r. 5, [LÚ.A—*š]ip-ri* 112 r. 3, [LÚ.A]—*šip-ri* 143:4, LÚ].A—*šip-ri-ia* 35:8, LÚ].A—*šip-ri-i[a]* 252:8, LÚ.A—*šip-ri-ia* 53:14, LÚ.A—*šip-ri-i[a]* 35:15, LÚ.A]—*šip-ri-ia* 35:9, LÚ.A—*šip-ri-šú* 262:3, LÚ.A—*šip-ri*.MEŠ 221:11, [LÚ].A—*šip-ri*.MEŠ 245 r. 4, LÚ.A—KIN 3:15, e. 19, 81:14, 91 r. 4, 95 r. 2, 6, 96:4, 107 e. 7, 108 r. 8, 9, 11, 129 s. 2, 199 r. 5, 204 r. 3, 283:5, LÚ.A—KI[N 280:8, LÚ.A—K[IN] 51:3, [LÚ.A—KIN 194 r. 10, LÚ.A—KIN-*ia* 2:7, 71:11, 81:6, 108:3, 6, 130 s. 1, 133:5, LÚ.A—KIN-*i[a* 188:7, LÚ.A—KIN-*[ia]* 134:6, [LÚ.A—KIN-*i]a* 186:6, [L]Ú.A—KIN-*ia* 108 r. 10, LÚ.A—KIN-*iá* 46:15, 17, 97:12, LÚ.A—KIN-*ka* 104:12, 108:10, 128:7, 210:9, LÚ.A—[KIN-*ka*] 108:8, LÚ].A—KIN-*šú* 8:6, 178:6, LÚ.A—KIN.MEŠ 92 r. 12, LÚ.A—KIN.MEŠ-*šú* 243 r. 12, LÚ].DUMU—*šip-ra-a-ni* 31:15, LÚ.DUMU—*šip-ra-ni* 169:5, LÚ.DUMU—*šip-ra-ni-ia* 113:9, LÚ.DUMU—*šip-ri* 31 r. 22, 145:14, [LÚ].DUMU—*šip-ri* 31 r. 18, [LÚ.DUMU—*šip-ri* 31 r. 13, [LÚ.DU]MU—*šip-ri* 162 e. 16, LÚ.DUMU—*šip-ri-ia* 34 r. 12, 149 r. 23, 260:3, 4, 263:9, LÚ.DUMU—*šip-[ri-š]u* 34 r. 8, LÚ.DUMU—*šip-ri-šú* 31 r. 23, LÚ.KIN.A 164:5, 6, LÚ.KIN.A.MEŠ 164:12,
**marāqu** "to crush": *[i]m-tar-qu-šú-nu* 156 r. 5,
**marāṣu** "to be ill, painfull": *[in-ta-ra-ṣa]-áš-šú* 45 r. 4, *mar-ṣa-ak* 217 r. 16, *mar-ṣa-te* 117 e. 23, *ma-ri-ṣi* 35 r. 8, 52:14, r. 9, 200:9, *ma-ri-ṣi-ma* 217 r. 18,
**marʾu** "son": A-[*šú*] 190 r. 7, DUMU 98:6, 122 r. 4, 141:7, 199 r. 9, 200 r. 5, 204:11, 210:11, 217 r. 8, 222:5, 243:4, 249 r. 6, [DUMU] 237:4, DUMU-*ia* 197 r. 8, DUMU-*ka* 217 r. 17, DUMU-*šu* 196:6, DUMU.MEŠ 293 r. 3, DUMU.MEŠ-*šú-nu* 56:13, LÚ.A-*šú* 114:8, LÚ.DUMU 210:15, see also *mār,*
**marʾutu** "daughter": DUMU.MÍ 259 r. 3,
**mardītu** "stage, stretch": *mar-di-a-[te]* 117:11, *mar-di-tú* 117:14, 227 r. 7, *mar-[di-tú]* 67:12, *ma-di-tú* 164 r. 4,
**maršu** "leather strap": KUŠ.*mar-šá-n[i* 142 r. 8,
**mārtu** see *marʾutu,*
**māru** see *marʾu,*
**masennu** "treasurer": LÚ].I[GI.DUB 97:1, LÚ.IGI.DUB 96:1, 108:3, 5, 7, 9, LÚ.IGI.D[UB 110:4, 5, LÚ.[IGI.DUB 108 r. 8, L[Ú.IGI.DUB 110:1,
**masû** "to wash": *i-ma-su-ni* 257 r. 7,
**maṣi** "enough; as though, as if": *ma-ṣi* 15 r. 13, 108 r. 21, 22, *ma-ṣ[i* 196 r. 8, *ma-ṣi-en* 199 r. 8, *ma-ṣi-in* 202 r. 3,
**maṣṣartu** "watch, guard": *ma-ṣar-ta-šú-nu* 217:13, *ma-ṣar-te* 24:14, 84 r. 3, 203:7, *[m]a-ṣar-te* 80:5, *ma-ṣar-ti* 32 r. 16, 113:5, *ma-ṣ[ar-tu]* 292 r. 3, *ma-ṣar-tú* 78 r. 9, 113 r. 6, *ma-ṣar-tú-šú* 54 r. 9, 172:8, 11, EN.NUN 2 r. 7, 3:12, r. 17, 8 r. 4, 17:9, 21:10, 15, 33 r. 14, 99:10, 127:11, 12, 160:6, 162:12, 210 r. 16, 249 r. 8, 288 r. 6, 294 r. 10, E]N.NUN 160:15, [EN.NUN 80 r. 2, EN.NUN-*ka* 21:9, EN.NUN-[*šu*] 162 r. 8, EN.NUN-*šú* 163 r. 13, 246 r. 8, 289:5, EN.NUN-*šú-nu* 63:9, 264:5, EN.NUN-*šú-n[u]* 33 r. 11, EN.NUN]-*šú-nu* 40:21, EN.NUN.MEŠ 152:6, 14,
**maṣû** "(Š) to be able to": *nu-ša-an-ṣa* 295 r. 21, *ú-šam-ṣa* 226 r. 10,
**mašālu** "(Š) to make match": *ú-sa-an-[šil]* 6 r. 3,
**māšartu** "review, inspection": *ma-šar-te* 234:3, *ma-šar-ti* 52:12, 230:4,
**mašennu** see *masennu,*
**mašku** "skin": *maš-ki* 160:10, KUŠ.MEŠ 101 r. 3,
**maškunu** "tent": TÚG.*maš-kan*.MEŠ 249:8,
**maškuru** "wineskin": KUŠ.*maš-ki-ri* 200:11,
**māt nakiri** "enemy land": KUR.*na-ki-ri* 146:14,
**matāhu** "to lift, pick up, use": *[a]t-ta-at-ha* 253:8, *i-mat-ta-hu-u-ni* 295 r. 19, *i-ma-tú-hu* 105 r. 9, *i]-ma-tú-hu* 254 r. 11, *le-ma-tú-hu* 105 r. 7, *li-in-ta-hu-ši-na* 295 r. 6, *li-in-tú-hu* 43:6, *ni-mat-ta-ah* 295 r. 7, *[ni]-mat-ta-ah* 123 r. 4,
**mati** see *immati,*
**mātu** "land, country": *ma-a-te* 127:5, *ma]-a-te* 299:1, *ma-a-t[i]* 149 r. 11, *m]a-a-ti-ni* 143:5, *ma-a-tu* 179 r. 2, *ma-te-ni* 120:5, *ma-ti-i]a* 12 r. 12, KUR 1:4, 3:3, 6:4, 11:4, 14:4, 15:4, 17:4, 18:4, 21:6, 22:6, 23:6, 24:6, 25:6, 27:6, 28:6, 31:5, 32:6, 33:5, 34 r. 24, 35:5, 37:4, 40:5, 52:9, 16, 54:10, 79:5, r. 11, 87:17, 92:3, 96:7, 104:15, 106:19, 108:11, 26, r. 18, 118:7, 128:5, 129 s. 3, 130:2, 132:4, 6, 144:4, 171:9, 10, 11, 179 r. 7, 204:5, 210:10, 264:8, 296 r. 5, KUR] 29:6, 30:5, 7, [KUR 34:4, [KUR] 2:3, KUR-*ia* 21 r. 16, 32 r. 7, 46 r. 2, 119:4, 173:12, 243 r. 16, 17, [KUR-*ku-nu*] 95:9, KUR-*šú* 34:29, 52 r. 6, 218 r. 8, KUR-*šú-nu* 4 r. 5, 36:4, KUR.MEŠ 79:11, 114 r. 1, 136 r. 2, 171:7, 8, r. 2, KUR.MEŠ-*šú-n[u* 289 r. 6, KUR.KUR.MEŠ 105:13, 146 r. 12, KUR.KUR.[MEŠ 143 r. 2, KUR.*ma-ti-ia* 260:8,
**maṭû** "to be defective, lacking": *i-ma-ṭi* 226 r. 2, *ma-ṭi-a-ku-ú-ni* 152 r. 13,
**mazzassu** "stand, post": *ma-za-si* 69 r. 7,
**mê** "water": A.MEŠ 7 r. 6, 21 r. 4, 26 r. 1, 106:21, 117 e. 22, 200:10, 13, 249:3, 274:5, 298:14, A.[M]EŠ 13:5,

**mehru** (a fir tree): GIŠ.*me-eh-ri* 295 e. 27, GIŠ. *mi-ih-r[i* 253:3,

**mehû** "storm": *mi-[hu-u]* 249:8,

**memmēni** "anybody, anything": *me-me-ni* 31 r. 12, 91:18, e. 23, r. 1, 6, 113:18, 147 r. 5, 150:11, 157:9, 163 r. 3, 243:11, 250:12, *me-me-ni]* 259:4, *me-me-n[i]* 33 r. 13, *me-me-(ni)* 227 r. 20, *m[e]-me-ni* 113:15, *[me-m]e-ni* 137 r. 4, *me-me-ni-šú* 243 r. 7, 11, *mi-me-ni* 1:12, *mi-mi-e-ni* 118:8, *mi-mi-ni* 53 r. 4, *mi-mi-n[i* 61 r. 3, *mi-mi-[ni* 56:15, *[mi-mi-ni]* 56 r. 3,

**mihru** "equal, colleague": *me-eh-ri-iá* 47 r. 6,

**milhu** (a precious stone): NA$_4$.*mil-hu* 205:5,

**milku** "advice, counsel": *mì-li[k-ka* 46:12,

**minītu** "number": *mi-ni-ti* 295 r. 11,

**mīnu** "what?": *ana—mi-ni* 108 r. 15, *mi-i-ni* 122 r. 3, *mi-i-nu* 31:8, 34 r. 20, 36:1, 37 r. 9, 52 r. 19, 62:8, 96 r. 4, 104 r. 12, 122 r. 9, 123 r. 5, 243:8, 280 r. 4, 295 r. 5, 9, *mi-[i-nu]* 55:9, *mi]-i-nu* 290 r. 8, *m[i-i-nu]* 171 r. 13, *m[i-i]-nu* 1:8, *m]i-i-nu* 101: 4, *[mi]-i-nu* 45:5, *mi-i-nu]-u[m-ma]* 182:6, *mi-ni* 121 r. 14, *mi-nu* 38:6, 40 r. 4, 46 r. 6, 63 r. 5, 78 r. 15, 81 r. 4, 105:12, 108 s. 1, 109:5, 115 r. 3, 119:10, 136 r. 7, 137 r. 8, 149 r. 8, 194 r. 9, 294:7, *mi-nu]* 19 s. 1, *[mi-nu* 267 s. 3, *[mi-nu]* 112 e. 8, 299 r. 13, *mì-i-nu* 43:10, 143 r. 6, 163:11, 232 r. 10, 233:9, *mì-i-n[u* 221:5, *mì-i-[nu]* 115:4, 228:6, *m[ì]-i-nu* 118 r. 3, *[mì-i-nu* 160:7, *[mì-i-nu]* 144 s. 1, *mì-ni* 129 r. 4, 210 r. 19, 292 r. 6, *mì-nu* 2 r. 1, 130 r. 5, 199 r. 7, 204 r. 7, 234 r. 2, 241:14,

**mišlu** "half": *meš-la-a-ti* 272 r. 4, *meš-li* 31 r. 24, 95 r. 7, 1/2 242 r. 1,

**muātu** "to die": *[a-mu-at]* 146:14, *a-mu-tu-ni* 244 r. 9, *i-mut-tú* 126:13, 226 r. 19, *in-tu-a-[ta* 106:2, *mé-e-te* 91 r. 3, ÚŠ 3 r. 7, ÚŠ.ME[Š 149:17, ÚŠ.MEŠ 31 s. 2,

**mūbû** "thickness": *mu-bu-u* 295 e. 26,

**mudaburu** "desert, steppe, plain": *mad-bar* 139:6, *mad-bar-ma* 139:9, KUR.*m]u-da-bar* 256 r. 5,

**mugirru** "chariot": GIŠ.GIGIR 74 r. 11, GIŠ. GIG[IR] 74 r. 3, GIŠ.GI[GIR 277:9, GIŠ.GIGIR.MEŠ 152:22, 215:6, 12, see also *narkabtu*,

**muhhu** "top, on": UGU 2:6, 7, 3:6, 16, r. 11, 15, 6:9, r. 5, 12 r. 6, 14:11, 20:5, 22:7, 27:7, 29:8, 31:6, 11, 20, r. 23, 32:9, 34:5, r. 15, 35 r. 8, 12, 37:14, 43:4, 44 r. 2, 3, 45:3, 46:9, 48:15, 50:7, 51 r. 1, 54:12, r. 2, 15, 56:4, r. 5, 57:4, 59:4, 63 r. 8, 14, 68:4, 69:4, 12, 13, 70:4, 71:5, 75:4, 78:8, r. 13, 79:5, 80 r. 6, 82:4, 84 r. 1, 91:3, 6, 21, 92:9, r. 6, 95:9, 96 r. 10, 97:4, 98:6, 100 r. 6, 8, 105 r. 4, 107:3, 4, 108:7, 28, r. 24, 111:2, 112:6, 113:3, 5, 10, 11, 12, r. 13, 115:3, 13, 116 r. 3, 117:3, 121:3, 130:7, r. 6, 132:8, 139:1, 140:4, 141:4, 143:7, 144:6, r. 9, 145 e. 17, r. 1, 4, 5, 15, 146 r. 12, 148:8, 149 r. 2, 150 r. 8, 151:4, 152:5, 6, 7, 18, r. 9, 17, 154:4, 156:6, 158:5, 161:4, 162:14, 163:5, 164:3, r. 12, 165:4, 168:5, 169:6, 8, r. 3, 172:4, 181:4, 182:4, 186 e. 9, 187:4, 188:8, 194 r. 3, 196:15, 200 r. 12, 202:10, s. 1, 203:4, 10, r. 8, 15, 204:11, r. 9, 205:8, 206:7, 208:1, 210 r. 12, 217:7, r. 5, 10, 218:8, r. 1, 9, 221 r. 3, 14, 223:5, 224:4, r. 4, 226:5, 10, 13, r. 5, 12, 227:4, r. 15, 17, 232 r. 8, 9, 235:4, 238:4, 239:4, 243:12, 246:4, 249:14, 250:16, r. 3, 8, 21, 251:4, 253:2, 254:8, 12, 256 r. 8, 257 r. 4, 260:5, 11, r. 10, 263:6, 10, 265:3, 268:4, 277:6, 279 r. 11, 290 r. 5, 291:11, 293:7, s. 1, 294:2, 295:19, r. 11, 17, 296 r. 2, 4, 297:11, 298:4, UGU] 15:7, 63:4, 72:4, 131:2, 225:4, 251:12, 291 r. 5, UG[U 67 r. 3, 89:11, 176:14, 177:2, 248 r. 3, 270 s. 2, 273:1, UG[U] 183:1, UG]U 37:27, 94:4, 126:19, 162 r. 3, 247:4, 254 r. 5, 256:2, 262:2, 284 r. 4, U[GU 110:6, 149:4, 155:9, 176:12, 218 r. 12, 275:1, 277:4, U[GU] 45 r. 6, 226:16, 249:12, U]GU 4 r. 1, 72:5, 130 s. 2, 138:7, 162 e. 18, 188:5, 190 r. 1, 254 r. 3, (UGU) 242:5, [UGU] 232:4, [U]GU 115 r. 6, 143 r. 2, UGU-*hi* 15 r. 4, 44 r. 4, 81:7, 8, 11, 15, 95 e. 16, 144 r. 5, 185:2, 187:6, 248:2, 254 r. 15, 256:7, 257:2, 284 r. 7, UGU-*h[i* 102 r. 3, UGU-*hi-ia* 34 r. 10, 35 r. 10, 56 r. 8, 78:15, 95:6, 97:13, 98 r. 10, 107 r. 1, 112 r. 6, 117:12, 17, 118:5, 121 r. 13, 129 r. 5, 151:5, 202 r. 15, 203 r. 12, 241:6, 243 r. 9, 284 r. 6, 289 r. 3, UGU-*hi-ia]* 283 r. 5, UGU-*hi-i[a]* 202 r. 3, UGU-*hi-[ia* 149 r. 19, UGU-*[hi-i]a* 98:5, 283:6, UG[U-*hi-ia]* 106:13, 218:6, UG]U-*hi-ia* 237: 5, 285:7, UGU-*hi-iá* 226 r. 16, UGU-*hi-ni* 95:15, 164:11, 204:9, 234:6, UGU-*[hi-ni]* 95:13, UGU-*hi-šu* 31:9, 35 e. 34, 145 r. 14, UGU-*hi-šú* 31 r. 13, 34 r. 11, 53:17, 79 r. 8, 163 r. 6, 221:10, 272 r. 1, 3, 291:4, UGU-*hi-[šú]* 186:6, UGU-*hi-šú-nu* 78:6, 92 r. 13, 15, 105:9, 243:15, 257:7, UG]U-*ia* 186:8, UGU-*iá* 46 r. 14, U]GU-*ka* 95 r. 10, UGU-*šú* 217 r. 14,

**muk** "thus": *muk* 46:12, 210 r. 6, 11, 217 r. 15, 297:8, *[muk* 210 r. 2, *[mu]muk* 217 r. 16, 224:12, *mu-ku* 53:11, 15, 16, 18, 55:9, 56 r. 2, *mu-uk* 103:8, *[mu-uk* 150:10, *[mu-u]k* 277 r. 2, *[mu]-uk* 196 r. 8,

**mukīl appāti** "chariot driver": LÚ.*mu-kil*—KUŠ. PA.MEŠ 215:9, LÚ.*mu-kil*—KUŠ.PA.MEŠ-*ia* 74 r. 13, LÚ.*mu-[kil*—KUŠ.P]A.M[EŠ-*ia]* 74 r. 4, [LÚ.DIB]—*a-pa*.MEŠ 230:6,

**murṣu** "disease": *mur-ṣi* 200 r. 12,

**mūru** "foal": *mu-ru* 35:31,

**musku** (a tree): GIŠ.*mu-us-ki* 295 r. 17,

**musukkannu** (a tree): GIŠ.MES.MÁ.GAN.NA 294: 9, 12,

**mušarkisu** "recruitment officer": LÚ.*mu-šar-[kis* 82 r. 3, LÚ.*mu]-šár-kis* 251 r. 5, LÚ.*mu-šár-kis*.MEŠ-*ni* 119:6,

**mūšu** "night": MI 168 r. 3, 211 r. 7, 249:6,

**mutīr ṭēmi** "information officer": LÚ.*mu-tir—ṭè-me* 215:20,

**muṭê** "deficit": LAL-*e]* 251:10, [LA]L-*e* 251 r. 4,

**nabalkutu** "to cross over, rebel, back off": *[i]t-ta-bal-kàt-u-ni* 137:6, *i-bal-ka-ta* 200 r. 11, *ú-šá-bal-ku-tú* 169 r. 2,

**naggār pāši** "axe maker": LÚ.[NA]GAR—*pa-a-ši* 71:6,

**nāgir ekalli** "palace herald": LÚ.NIGIR—É.GAL 44 r. 2, LÚ.NIGIR—É.[GAL] 147:2, LÚ.NIGÍR—É.GAL 145: 1, LÚ.NIGÍR—É.[GAL 130 r. 8, LÚ].600—É.GAL 160: 12, LÚ.[600—É.GAL 149 r. 9, LÚ.600—É.GAL 56:8, r. 6, 160:11, 216 r. 6, LÚ.600—É.GA[L] 159:5, LÚ.600—É.[G]AL 149:15, LÚ.600]—É.GAL 149:24, L]Ú.600—É.GAL 150 r. 9, LÚ.600—KUR 149:20, LÚ.ŠÚ.NIGÍR—É.GAL 227 r. 27,

**nagiu** "district": *i—na-gi-e* 84:6, *na-gi-e* 131:6, 145 s. 1, *na-gi-[e]* 34 r. 5, 27, *na-g]i-e* 31 r. 5, *na-gi-ia-a* 260:9, *na-[gi-u* 44:3, KUR.*na-gi-ú* 92:5,

**nāgurtu** "hire": *na-gúr-te* 46:7, 105 r. 3, *na-gúr-tú* 105:18,

**nakāru** "to be hostile": *i-ti-ki-ri* 166 r. 2, *na-ka-ra-ka* 260:7,

**nakāsu** "to cut": *a-na-kis* 47:12, *i-na-ki-si* 34 r. 19, *i-na-ki-su* 25 r. 7, *i-ti-ki-si* 33 r. 5, [*t*]*a-ki-sa-ni* 34 r. 6,

**nakkamtu** "treasure": *na-kam-ti* 206:5,

**nakru** "enemy": KÚR.MEŠ-*ka* 146 r. 8, LÚ.KÚR-*š*[*u* 92:16, [LÚ.KÚR.MEŠ 107:1,

**nakuppu** "circumference": *na-ku-pu* 294:10, 11,

**namarkû** "to be late": *a-ma-ra-kù* 47 r. 7, *li-mar-ku* 199 r. 12, *n*]*a-mar-ku* 215 r. 5, [*na*]*-mar-ku* 277 r. 3, *na-mar-ku-u*] 117:4,

**nammušu** "to set out": *nam-mu-ši* 234:2, *na-me-šá* 217 r. 15, *nu-ta-me-ši* 194:5, *tu-na-me-še* 199:6, *ut-t*[*a-mi-iš*] 40:11, [[*ut-ta-mì-ši*]] 62:4, *ú-nam-maš* 88 r. 8, *ú-n*[*am-ma-šá*] 33 r. 7, *ú-na*[*m-mi-iš*] 40:12, *ú-na-maš-ú-ni* 97:10, 11, *ú-na-ma-áš* 199: 10, *ú-na-me-šá-a-ni-ni* 217 r. 12, *ú-na-me-šá-ni* 129 r. 7, *ú-na-miš-u-ni* 14:8, *ú-na-mu-šú* 64:10, *ú-tam-me-šá* 172 r. 3, *ú-ta-me-šá* 240:4, *ú-ta-me-š*[*i* 165:6, *ú-ta-me-š*[*i*] 198 r. 5, *ú-ta-me-šu* 88:8, *ú-ta-mi-šu* 162:6, *ú-ta-mi-šu-ma* 88 r. 3, *ú-ta-mi-šu-šu* 162 r. 2, *ú-ta-mì-ši* 164:14,

**namaddu** "measure": *na-me-di* 202:6,

**nāmurtu** "audience gift": *na-mur-tú* 171 r. 8, *na-mur-*[*tú* 212:5, *na-mu*[*r-tú* 136 r. 6,

**nāmuru** "watchtower": *na*]*-me-r*[*i*] 290 r. 3,

**napāhu** "to light up": *ta-na-pa-ha* 11 s. 1,

**napšutu** "life; person": *nu-up-šá-te* 11 s. 3, LÚ.ZI.ME 94:6, L[Ú.ZI.MEŠ] 261:2, ZI 145 s. 2, ZI.MEŠ 79 r. 4, ZI.M]EŠ 149:17,

**narkabtu** "chariot": GI]Š.*nar-kab-tu* 252 r. 4, see also *mugirru*,

**nāru** "river": ÍD 4 r. 7, 6:9, 13:5, 21:19, 26 r. 1, 33 r. 10, 34 r. 15, 39:3, 61 r. 5, 111:2, 115 r. 6, 117 e. 22, 187:4, 200:10, 254 r. 5, 290 r. 5, 298:14, 15, ÍD] 33 r. 5, 117:20, Í[D 6 r. 2, Í[D] 6 r. 5, Í]D 25 r. 2, [ÍD 117 e. 23, ÍD-*ma* 255:3,

**nasāhu** "to pull out, uproot": *a-ta-s*[*a*]*h* 27:14, [*is-s*]*u-hu-u-ni* 82 r. 11, *i-ta-as-hu* 35 r. 6, *i-ta-sa-ha* 291:3, *ta-su-uh* 291:5, *ú-ta-s*[*i-hi*] 249:9,

**nasāqu** "to choose": *i*[*s-si-qu-u-ni*] 33 r. 4, *i-ta-*[*as-qu* 33 r. 3,

**nasīku** "sheikh": LÚ.*na-sik*.MEŠ 3 r. 15,

**naṣāru** "to watch, guard": *a-na-ṣar* 127:12, 14, 162 r. 8, 292 r. 5, [*a-na-ṣa*]*r* 162:14, *it-ta-aṣ-ru* 172 e. 13, *i-na-ṣa-ar* 2 r. 8, *i-na-ṣur* 3:12, 227 s. 2, *i-na-ṣu-ru* 40:21, *i-na-ṣ*]*u-ru* 80 r. 2, *i-na-ṣu-ru-šu* 35:17, *i-na-ṣ*[*u-ru-šú*] 182 r. 4, *i-ṣu-ru* 21 r. 19, *i-ta-ṣar* 78 r. 5, *la-ṣur* 288 r. 6, *li-ṣur* 246 r. 8, *l*]*i-ṣur* 63:9, *li-ṣu-ru* 3 r. 19, 172:8, *li-ṣu-ur* 78 r. 10, *ni-na-ṣar* 21:16, e. 22, *ni-na-*[*ṣar*] 113 r. 9,

**našû** "to lift, carry, take": *at-ta-ṣ*[*a* 280:9, *at-ti-ši* 295 r. 1, *at*]*-ti-ši* 297:9, *a-na-ši* 232 r. 4, [*a*]*-na-ši* 108:13, *a-na-ši-a* 203 r. 7, *a-ta-ṣa* 202 s. 2, *a-ti-ši* 37 r. 11, [*i*]*ṣ-ṣa* 53 e. 26, *iš-šú-u-ni* 208:6, *iš*]*-šú-ú-*[*ni*] 149 r. 9, [*it-ta*]*-ṣu* 90 r. 7, *it-ta-ṣu-šú-nu* 176 s. 2, *i-na-ši* 141 r. 4, *i-na-ši-u* 289 r. 2, *i-na-ši-ú* 106:15, 109:10, [*i*]*-na-ši-ú* 232 r. 6, *i-na-šu-ni* 100 r. 11, *i-ṣa* 202:8, 203 r. 11, *i-ṣal-ka* 14:13, *i-ši* 163 r. 5, 216 s. 1, *i-ši*] 141:10, *i-šu-u-ni* 139:4, 163:13, *i-ta-ṣu* 32 r. 2, *i-ti-ši* 84:8, 91:19, 179 r. 5, *i-ti-ši-*[*a* 259:8, *na-aṣ* 234:6, *na-aṣ-ṣa* 79 r. 4, 228:13, *na-ṣa* 78:15, 284 r. 11, *na-ṣa-an-ni* 48:5, *na-ṣa-ni* 98:5, 106:16, 215 r. 2, *na-ṣ*[*u-ni-šu*] 142 r. 6, *na-ṣu-u-ni* 52 r. 1, *na-ṣu-*[*u-ni*] 28 r. 3, *na-ṣ*]*u-u-ni* 202 s. 1, *na-ṣu-ú-ni* 103:7, *na-ši* 24:10, 104:12, *ni-na-áš-ši* 250:15, 295 r. 23, [*ni-n*]*a-ši* 106:16, [*ni-ti-ši*] 182 r. 3, *ta-at-ta-ṣa* 280 r. 2, [*t*]*a-ti-*[*š*]*i* 37:21, ÍL-*u-ni* 291 r. 8,

**natanaia** (mng. obscure): [*n*]*a-ta-na-a-a* 117 e. 21,

**naṭû** "to beat, whip": *li-ṭu-šú* 142 r. 9,

**nazāru** "to curse": *i-na-zi-ra-a-ni* 46 r. 2, *i-na-*[*zi*]*-ru-šú* 46 r. 8,

**nērubu** "pass": *né-e-r*[*i-bi*] 5:1, *né-rab-a-ni* 53: 16, *né-ri-bi* 117 r. 10, 206:6, *né-ri-b*[*i*] 24:14, *né*]*-ri-bi* 176 s. 2, [*né-r*]*i-b*[*i*] 34 r. 9, *né-ru-bu* 150 r. 10, KUR.*né-ru-bu* 129 s. 1,

**niqiu** "offering, sacrifice": UDU.*ni-qi* 165:8, [UD]U.SISKUR.MEŠ 36:3, UDU.SISKUR.MEŠ-*šú* 84 r. 6, 221:8,

**nirtu** see *irtu*,

**nīšī** "people": LÚ.UN.MEŠ 52:16, LÚ.UN.M[EŠ 212:2, [L]Ú.UN.MEŠ-*šú* 89:9, UN.ME[Š 68:9, UN.MEŠ 21:16, 24:7, 37:12, 27, 52:9, 79:5, r. 11, 108 r. 18, 118:7, 121:3, 5, 9, r. 16, 132:8, 149:18, 19, 156 r. 1, 202 r. 9, 203 r. 19, 210:10, 215:18, 243 r. 16, 17, 249:10, 296 r. 5, UN.M[EŠ 108:11, UN.[MEŠ 248:4, U]N.MEŠ 264:6, [UN.ME]Š 121 e. 19, [[UN.MEŠ 121 r. 20, UN.MEŠ-*ia* 149 r. 1, UN.MEŠ-*ma* 121:15, UN.MEŠ-*ni* 104:10, UN.MEŠ-*šú* 149:19, UN.MEŠ-*šú-nu* 35 r. 5, 36:6,

**nuāhu** "to rest": [*i*]*t-tu-ú-ah* 249:15, *né-e-hu* 210 r. 7, *né-ha-ku* 26 r. 5,

**nuhatimmu** "cook": LÚ.MU 215:18,

**nuk** "thus": *nu-ku* 21 r. 15, 32 r. 5, 33:7, r. 2, 37:29, [*nu-ku* 37 r. 6, [*nu-ku*] 21 r. 22, *nu-uk* 12 r. 13, 14:12, 16:10, 19 s. 1, 35:21, 54:13, 14, 83 r. 3, 91:5, 108:23, 109:2, 115:4, 10, 12, r. 2, 117 r. 7, 126:6, 129:1, 134:5, 142:4, 144 r. 10, 178:1, 226 e. 18, r. 3, 229:5, 280 e. 14, r. 3, 284 r. 8, 294:7, *nu-uk*] 130 r. 4, *nu-u*[*k* 142:10, r. 3, 229:8, *nu-u*[*k*] 254:3, *nu-u*]*k* 35:30, 54 r. 11, *nu-*[*uk* 142 r. 10, [*nu-uk* 43:6, [*nu*]*-uk* 35:18, 205 r. 4,

**nūru** "light": *nu-ru* 146 r. 3,

**nusāhu** "corn tax": ŠE.*nu-sa-hi* 82 r. 10, 289:4,

**pa'āṣu** "to remove": *pa-a-ṣa* 290:8, *ú-pa-ṣu-ni* 149 r. 5,

**pahāru** "to assemble": *ip-tu-uh-*[*ru*] 167:2, *i-pa-hu-ru* 67:8, *lu-pa-hi-ra* 63 r. 10, *pa-hi-ir* 63 r. 3, *pu-uh-ra* 200:15, [*pu*]*-uh-ra* 277:12, *pu-uh-ru* 2 r. 6, 21:14, *pu-*[*uh-ru* 67:2, [*pu*]*-uh-ru* 4 r. 6, *up-tah-hir*] 184:2, *up-tah-hi-ir* 114:5, *up-ta-at-hu-ru* 227 s. 1, *up-ta-hi-i*[*r*] 78:14, *ú-pa-har* 33 r. 8, *ú-p*[*a-har*] 67:11, *ú-pa-har-an-ni* 79 r. 12, *ú-pa-har-šú-nu* 108:18, *ú-*[*pa-har-šú-n*]*u* 63:11, *ú-pa-hu-ru* 145 r. 9,

**pāhutu** "governor; province": LÚ.EN.NAM 2:8, 3:9, 10, 11 r. 6, 34:25, 81:9, 83 r. 3, 84:9, 11, 87:6, 88:6, 13, 89:6, 90:9, 10, 11, 13, 100 r. 1, 104 r. 8, 114:9, 145:15, 147:9, 10, 179 r. 3, 199:6, 8, 210:7, r. 17, 258:3, LÚ.EN.NA[M 211:7, LÚ.EN.N[AM] 41:1, LÚ.EN.[NAM] 156:8, LÚ.E[N.NAM] 228:3, L[Ú.EN.NAM] 53 e. 25, 254:13, [LÚ].EN.NAM 34 r. 13, 90:8, 190 r. 5, [LÚ.EN.NAM 286:4, [LÚ.EN.N]AM 90:6, 201:4, [LÚ.EN].NAM 90:7, [LÚ.EN].NA[M 258:1, [LÚ.E]N.NAM 33 r. 16, LÚ.EN.NAM.MEŠ 21:11, 84 r. 7, 87:4, 90:12, 148:7, LÚ.EN.NAM.[MEŠ 250:7, LÚ.EN.NA[M.MEŠ] 180:2, LÚ.EN.N[AM.MEŠ 282:5, LÚ.EN.NAM.MEŠ-*šú* 90:14, LÚ.EN].NAM.MEŠ-*šú* 90:5, LÚ.NAM.MEŠ 21:12, 85 r. 1, 92 r. 7, 147:15, LÚ.NAM.MEŠ] 92 r. 4, LÚ.NA]M.MEŠ 44:7, L]Ú.NAM.M[EŠ

23:7, NAM 250 r. 14,

**palāhu** "to fear": *ap-t]a-làh* 37 e. 35, *ip-la-[hu-ni]* 90:3, *ip-tal-hu* 249:10, *ip-ta-al-hu* 202 r. 13, *ip-ta-làh* 53:8, 145 r. 7, *i-pal-l]àh-u-ni* 154 r. 3, *la-ap-la]-ah* 294 r. 13, *lip-lu-hu* 109:8, *pal-ha-[k]a* 35:32, *pal-ha-ku* 33 r. 15, 35:23, *pal-ha-ku-u* 34 r. 8, *up-ta-lìh-an-ni* 15:11,

**pānāt** "fore": *i—pa-na-tú-šú* 133 r. 10, *i—pa-na-tú-šú-nu* 227:9, *pa-na-at-(u)-šú-[nu]* 97:12, *pa-na-tu-šú* 289:5, *pa-na-tu-šú-nu* 256 r. 7, *pa-na-tu-uš-šú* 250:21, *[pa-n]a-tu-u-a* 106:19, *pa]-na-tu-u-[šu]* 112:2, *pa-na-tú-šú-nu* 69 r. 8, *pa-na-tú-š[ú-nu]* 32 e. 20, *pa-na-tú-u-[a]* 4 r. 2, 205:7, *pa-n]a-tú-u-a* 150:6, IGI-*at* 152 e. 26,

**pāniu** "previous, former": *pa-ni-iu-te* 64:5, *pa-ni-ti* 106:12, *pa-ni-tú* 108 r. 16, 263:4, *pa-ni-u* 250:14, *pa-ni-um-[ma* 7:3, *pa]-ni-um-ma* 289 r. 1, *pa-ni-(u)-te* 52 r. 2, *pa-n]i-u-te* 264:5, *pa-ni-u-ti* 5 r. 2, *[pa-ni-ú]* 282:7, *pa-ni-ú-te* 152 r. 6, 215 r. 1,

**pānu** "face, presence": *i—pa-an* 167:4, *i—pa-ni-šú* 84 r. 8, 170:7, *pa-an* 52:18, r. 3, 53:8, 56:8, 71:12, 89:5, 92:17, 95:13, r. 4, 104:7, r. 7, 8, 9, 122 r. 8, 142:4, 9, r. 9, 154:4, r. 5, 160:19, 182 r. 8, 203 r. 2, 218:15, r. 2, 5, 238 r. 2, 241:11, r. 3, 243:10, 250:18, 256 r. 9, 260 r. 1, 12, 298 e. 17, r. 11, *pa-a[n* 95 r. 4, *pa-a[n]* 226 r. 3, *pa-a]n* 104:16, *p[a-an* 149 r. 7, *p]a-an* 61 r. 5, *[pa-a]n* 24:11, *pa-an-šú-nu* 246:8, *pa]-né-e-a* 38:11, *pa-ni* 120:7, 160:2, 213:7, 279 r. 9, 294 r. 11, 297:7, *p]a-ni* 148:12, *pa-ni-ia* 56 r. 10, 67:3, 104:6, 121:17, r. 19, 122 r. 5, 149 r. 4, 200 r. 4, 256:9, *pa-ni-ia]* 108:21, 196:11, 281:12, *pa-ni-i[a* 130:10, 221 r. 6, *pa-ni-i[a]* 298 r. 4, *pa-ni-[ia* 243 r. 7, *pa-ni-[ia]* 243 r. 11, 298 r. 2, *pa-n]i-ia* 203 r. 3, *[pa-ni-ia]* 269:9, *pa-ni-i]a-a-ni* 124:8, *pa-ni-ka* 121:8, 203 r. 11, *pa-ni-[ka]* 269:6, *pa-ni-ni* 19 r. 9, *pa-ni-šu* 88:11, 299 r. 7, *pa-ni-šú* 12 r. 2, 121 r. 2, 149 r. 9, 165:11, 200 r. 3, 257 r. 8, *pa-ni-šú]* 11 r. 8, *pa-ni-šú]]* 163 r. 3, *pa-ni-šú-ni* 168 r. 7, *pa-[ni]-šú-ni* 114:6, *pa-ni-šú-nu* 163 r. 4, 182:10, 203 r. 19, 226 r. 14, 291 r. 8, *pa-ni-šú]-nu* 19 s. 2, *pa-n[i-šú-nu]* 202 r. 2, *pa-ni-[x* 170:8, IGI 15 r. 1, 20:8, 31 r. 11, 33 r. 15, 35:32, r. 1, 15, 37:12, 24, 40 r. 3, 4, 46:10, r. 6, 52:18, 63:12, r. 4, 79 r. 2, 97 s. 1, 103 r. 7, 108:6, 8, 126 r. 4, 146:10, 150 r. 13, 163:12, 199:6, r. 5, 203 s. 1, 210:7, 227 s. 4, 232:5, 11, r. 5, 243:11, 257 r. 3, 291 r. 2, 3, 293:10, 294:4, 295 r. 13, IGI] 12 r. 3, 34 r. 7, 257 r. 11, IG[I 227 s. 2, IG[I] 35:22, IG]I 148:10, I[GI 282 r. 3, [IGI 26 r. 2, 108:3, IGI-*ia* 8:8, 32 s. 1, 37 r. 21, 46:14, 63:16, 65:9, 78 r. 8, 217 s. 2, 4, 254:5, IGI-*ia]* 155:4, IGI-*i[a]* 70:5, IGI-*i]a* 63:14, (IGI)-*ia* 74:8, IGI-*iá* 3 r. 10, IGI-*ka* 54:15, 106:20, 163:9, IGI-*k]a* 134:7, IGI-*šu* 33 s. 1, IGI-*šú* 18 r. 5, 46 r. 1, IGI-*šú-nu* 163 r. 10, IGI-[*x*] 255:2, IGI.MEŠ 47 r. 3,

**paqādu** "to appoint, entrust": *ap-ta-aq-da-šú* 237:7, *ap-ti-[qid* 248:9, *ap-ti-qi-di* 67:9, *[ap-ti-qi-di]* 297:7, *ap-ti-qi-su* 122 r. 12, *a-pa-qi-di* 289 e. 9, *ip-qi-[da]-ni-ni* 69:9, *ip-q[i-du]-ni* 46:14, *ip-taq-da-ni* 243:8, *ip-taq-du* 257:8, *ip-t[aq-du]* 95 r. 7, *i]p-ti-qi-su* 31 r. 10, *i-pa-qí-d[u]* 8:2, *nu-up-ta-qid* 242:11, *paq-da-šú-nu* 9:1, *pa-qi-du-ú-ni* 79 r. 3, *pi-iq-da* 257:9, *pi-[qid]* 294:1, *up-t[a-qid]* 137 r. 7, *ú-pa-qa-da-šú-nu* 152:17,

**paqānu** (mng. obscure): *pa-qi-ni* 120:7,

**parāsu** "to decide": *lip-ru-us]* 136 r. 8, *li-ip-ru-s[u]* 149 r. 10,

**parkullu** "stonecutter, sculptor": LÚ.B]UR.GUL.MEŠ 296 r. 2,

**parriṣu** "criminal, traitor": LÚ.*par-ri]-ṣu* 124:6, [L]Ú.*par-ri-ṣu* 210:17, LÚ.*pa-ri-ṣu-u-te* 227 r. 25, LÚ.LUL.MEŠ 176 s. 1, 227 r. 15, 22, 228:9, r. 5, 231:2, LÚ.LUL.MEŠ-*te* 227 s. 3,

**parzillu** "iron": AN.BAR 35:28, 202 r. 9, 294 r. 1, AN.BAR] 108 r. 8,

**passuku** "to clear away, remove": *pa-su-k[u* 230:2, *ú-pa-sa-ak* 229 r. 3, 9, *ú-pa-su-ku* 229 r. 6,

**pašāhu** "to relent, relax": *lip-šu-hu* 64 r. 5,

**paššūru** "table": BANŠU[R 219:2,

**patru** "sword": GÍR 91:18, 202 r. 9,

**patû** "to open, be distant; (D) to dismiss": *ip-ti* 142 r. 3, *ni-ip-te-te* 206:7, *ni-ip-t[i* 130:1, *pa-a-tu* 179 r. 5, *pa-te* 203:14, *p]a-ti-ú-te* 186:5, *pa-tu-ú* 179 r. 7, *ta-[ap-te-e* 108:23,

**paṭāru** "to release": *i-ba-ṭar-[šú* 254:15, *li-ip-ṭu-ur-u-ni* 97 r. 9, *pa-ṭi-ir* 126:11, *pu-ṭu-ur-šú* 254:10,

**paṭīru** "reed altar": *pa-ṭi-ra-a-te* 97 r. 4,

**pazzuru** "to conceal": *up-ta-zi-ir* 37 r. 12, *ú-ba-zar* 243:11, *ú-pa-za-ar* 37:8,

**pēthallu** "cavalry": ANŠE.BAD.HAL-*lu* 95:13, 215:9, BAD.HAL 226 r. 14, BAD.HAL-*li* 217:5, BAD.HAL-*lum* 152:22,

**petû** see *patû*,

**pilku** "work assignment": *pil-ki* 56:10, r. 5, *p[i]l-ku-šú-nu* 56:6,

**piqittu** "charge; office": *pi-qi-tú* 70:5, LÚ.*pi-qí-ti* 31:11,

**pisannu** "gutter": GIŠ.*pi-s[a-nu]* 275:6, [G]IŠ.*pi-sa-nu* 274:4,

**pitti** "according to": *pi-it-t[i]* 299 r. 3, *pi-[it-ti]* 33:9, *p]i-it-ti* 299 r. 6, *pi-i-te* 202:6, *pi-ti* 247:6, *p]i-ti* 106:11,

**pitūtu** "diadem": *[p]i-tu-a-te* 282 r. 3,

**pû** "mouth, utterance": *pe-e* 78:8, r. 13, *pi* 293 r. 6, *pi-i* 34 r. 9, 54 r. 1, 147 r. 4, 202 r. 9, 203:12, 17, 204 r. 3, *[pi]-i-ia-a-ma* 203:14, *pi-i-ka* 108:23, KA 169:8, KA-*ia* 241:8, K]A-*ia* 189:2, KA-*šú-nu* 169 r. 2,

**puāgu** "to take away": *ip-tu-gu* 53 r. 9, *pu-a-gi* 149 r. 2,

**pu'u** "hay, chaff": Ú.*pu-e* 47:11,

**puhhu** "to modify(?)": *ú]-pa-ha-šú-nu* 57:10,

**pusku** "palm (a measure)": *pu-su-ku* 295 e. 26,

**pūtu** "front, opposite": *i—pu-tú-u-a-a* 217 r. 9, *pu-tu* 87:7, *pu-tu-ni* 21:13, *p[u-t]u-ni* 87:6, *pu-tu-šu-nu* 21:15, *pu-tu-šú* 286:4, *[p]u-tu-uš-šu-nu* 196 r. 5, *pu-tu-uš-š[ú* 187:5, *pu-tu-u-a* 88:7, *pu-tú-ni* 90:7, *pu-tú-un-ni* 3:10, *pu-tú-u-a* 254 r. 10, *pu-tú-u-[a]* 22:8, *pu-[tú-u-a]* 34 r. 23, *pu]-tú-u-a* 41:2, *p]u-tú-u-a* 33 r. 17, *pu-ut* 3:12, 88 r. 1, 90:6, 8, 9, 12, 133 r. 11, 175:6, 225:9, *pu-u[t* 199:16, *pu-u-tú* 12 r. 3, *pu-u-tú-u-a* 2:8,

**pūtuhu** "responsibility": *pu-tu-hu* 106:16, 108 r. 14,

**qabassu** "middle": *qab-si* 149:15, *qa-ab-si* 218 r. 8,

**qablītu** (a tool): GIŠ.*qab-li-tú* 257 r. 8,

**qablu A** "middle (parts)": MURUB$_4$ 56:9, 80:8, [MURUB$_4$ 56 r. 5, 146 r. 7,

**qablu B** "grove": GIŠ.MURUB$_4$-*šú-nu-ma* 34 r. 32, GIŠ.MURUB$_4$.MEŠ 25 r. 5,

**qabsu** see *qabassu,*

**qabû** "to say, tell": *aq-bu-u-ni*] 196 r. 7, *aq-b[u-u-ni*] 205 r. 3, [*aq-ṭi-ba-á*]*š-šú* 254:3, *aq-ṭi-ba-šú-nu* 226 r. 17, *aq-ṭí-bi* 142 r. 10, *a-qab-bi* 243:10, *a-qa-ba-kan-ni* 213:6, [*a-q*]*a-ba-šú-ni* 108 r. 12, *a-qa-bu-u-ni* 31 r. 27, 232 r. 5, *a-qa-b*[*u*]*-u-*[*ni*] 126 r. 12, *iq-bu-ni* 145 r. 17, 257 r. 5, [*iq-bu-ni* 256 r. 9, *iq-bu-u-ni* 52:13, 154:5, 163 r. 8, 226 r. 6, 13, *iq-bu-*[*u-ni*] 170:6, *iq-bu-*[*u-n*]*i* 127:9, [*iq-bu-u*]*-ni* 162:12, [*i*]*q-*[*b*]*u-u-ni* 232:6, *iq-bu-ú-ni* 104:11, *iq-ṭi-ba-a-na-a-ši* 217 r. 4, *iq-*[*ṭi-ba-šú*] 34 r. 12, *iq-ṭi-ba-*[*šú-nu* 256 r. 11, *iq-ṭi-*[*ba-šú-nu*] 256 r. 1, *iq-ṭi-bi* 34:30, 264:1, [*iq-ṭi-bi*] 298:11, *iq-ṭi-bi-a* 28:8, 48:11, 63 r. 16, 129:3, [*iq-ṭi-b*]*i-a* 129 r. 8, *iq-ṭi-bi-u* 295 r. 20, *iq-ṭi-bu-ni* 226 r. 9, [*iq-ṭi-bu-ni*] 173:2, *iq-ṭi-bu-u-ni* 103 e. 10, *iq-ṭí-ba-a*[*n-na-ši*] 155:8, *iq-ṭí-ba-*[*ni* 108:4, *iq-ṭí-bi* 9:2, 106:17, 108:25, 162 r. 1, 257 r. 2, *iq-ṭí-b*[*i*] 129 r. 3, 142 r. 7, *iq-*[*ṭí-bi* 108:16, *iq-ṭí-bi-a* 52 r. 14, 106:20, *iq-ṭí-bi-*[*a*] 16:4, 159:7, *i*]*q-ṭí-bi-a* 188:9, *iq-ṭí-bi-ú-ni* 3:9, *iq-ṭí-bu-ni* 87 r. 7, [*iq-ṭí-bu-n*]*i* 141 r. 1, *iq-ṭí-bu-*[*ni-šú*] 108 r. 26, *iq-ṭí-bu-u-ni* 53:10, 54:3, 83:6, *i*]*q-ṭí-bu-u-ni* 40:11, *iq-ṭí-bu-ú-n*[*i*] 104:9, *i-iq-ṭí-bi* 164 r. 7, *i-qab-ba-áš-šú* 91 r. 7, *i-qab-ba-na-ši-ni* 204 r. 8, *i-qab-bi* 52:7, 11, r. 17, 54:6, r. 13, 58:6, 86:14, 101:3, 114 r. 5, 122 r. 11, 124:5, 211 r. 3, 250:15, 254 r. 12, 295 r. 6, *i-qab-bi*] 143 r. 9, *i-qab-b*[*i* 1:8, *i-qab-*[*bi*] 298 r. 7, *i-qab*]*-bi* 152 r. 19, *i-q*[*ab-bi* 92 r. 10, *i-*[*qab-bi*] 62:10, *i-*[*qab-b*]*i* 250 r. 23, [*i-qab*]*-bi* 93 r. 5, *i-qab-bi-a* 91 r. 2, *i-qab-bi-u* 145 s. 1, *i-qab-bi-ú* 46 r. 6, *i-qab-bu-ni*] 62:8, *i-qab-bu-niš-šú* 44:3, *i-qab-bu-u-ni* 40 r. 1, 78 r. 16, 294:8, *i-qab-bu-u-*(*ni*) 295 r. 5, *i-qab-bu-u-*[*ni*] 123 r. 5, *i-*[*qab-bu-u-ni*] 143 r. 6, *i-*[*q*]*ab-bu-u-ni* 234 r. 3, *i-qab-*[*x* 160:14, *i-qa-ba-kan-ni* 63 r. 6, *i-qa-ba-na-*[*ši-ni* 130:9, *i-qa-bi* 103 r. 5, 133 s. 1, 175:4, 215 r. 3, 285:3, 291:12, *i-qa-*[*bi* 34 r. 34, 258:7, *i*]*-qa-bi* 290:11, [*i-qa-bi*] 232 r. 2, [*i*]*-qa-bi* 37:19, *i-qa-*[*bi-a*] 292:6, *i-qa-bu-ni* 104 r. 13, 144 s. 2, 199 r. 7, [*i-qa-bu-ni*] 299 r. 13, [*i-qa-bu-n*]*i* 290 r. 9, [*i*]*-qa-bu-ni* 109:6, 289:7, *i-qa-bu-u-ni* 34 r. 20, 119:11, 244 r. 5, 267 s. 3, *i-q*[*a*]*-bu-u-ni* 228:8, [*i-q*]*a-bu-u-ni* 232 r. 11, *i-qi-bu-ni* 199 r. 8, *i-qi-ṭí-bu-ni-šú* 164:9, *liq-ba-šú* 108 r. 5, *liq-bi* 78 r. 17, *l*[*i-i*]*q-ba-š*[*u*] 98 r. 3, [*l*]*i-qi-ba-áš-šú-nu* 63 r. 12, *l*]*i-qi-bu-ni-šú-nu* 203 s. 1, *ni-iq-ṭí-bi* 104 r. 10, *n*]*i-qa-ba-ka* 104:18, *ni-qa-bi* 104:16, r. 2, 7, 105:12, *qi-bi* 213:8, *qi-*[*bi*] 108:5, [*qi-bi-a* 19 s. 2, [*qi*]*-bi-a* 108:14, *qí-ba-a-ni* 294:7, *ta-qa-bi* 31 r. 20, DUG$_4$.GA 54 r. 8,

**qalālu** "to be small": *qàl-li* 33 r. 19, *qa-lu-te* 200 r. 8, *q*[*a-lu-te*] 200 r. 14, QÀL.MEŠ 56:5, 13,

**qannu** "outside": *qa-an-ni* 32:16, 44 r. 4, 85:4, 94:5, 227 s. 4, *qa-an-n*[*i* 259 r. 2, *qa-ni* 52:8, 105:22, 147:10, 232 r. 2, *qa*]*-ni* 232:7, *q*]*a-ni* 93:2,

**qaqqadu** see *kaqqudu,*

**qaqqaru** see *kaqquru,*

**qarābu** "to approach, arrive": *aq-ṭí-rib* 113 r. 11, *iq-rib-an-ni* 204:13, *iq*]*-ri-ba* 250:13, *iq-ri-bu-u-ni* 250:10, *iq-ṭar-ba* 156:9, 14, [*iq-ṭ*]*ar-bu* 296 r. 3, *iq-ṭar-bu-u-ni* 249 r. 10, *iq-ṭa-ra-bu-u-ni* 64:8, *iq-ṭa-*[*ra-bu-u-ni*] 192 r. 5, *iq-ṭí-ri-ib* 14:9, *i-qar-bu-u-ni-ni* 64 r. 2, *i-qar-rib-an-ni* 250:14, *i-qa-rib-u-ni* 217 s. 2, [*l*]*u-qa-rib* 6 r. 6, *ni-i*]*q-ṭi-rib* 250:4, *ni-qar-ri-ib* 123 r. 3, *qur-bu* 91:19, 111:2, *qur-*[*bu* 268:8, *qur-bu-ni* 150 r. 5, [*uq*]*-ṭar-rib* 280 r. 11, *uq-ṭ*[*ar-ri-ba*] 211:8, *u*[*q-ṭa-rib*] 6:9, *uq-ṭa-r*[*i-bi* 205:9, *uq-ṭ*]*a-ri-bu* 255:4, *uq-ṭa-ri-ib* 115 r. 6, *ú-qar-rab* 17 r. 6, *ú-qar-ru-bu* 296 r. 6, *ú-qa-ra-*[*bu-ni* 7:4, *ú-qa-ru-b*[*u* 211 r. 11,

**qarābu** "battle": *qa-ra-bi* 3 r. 4, *qa-r*]*a-bu* 166 r. 4,

**qarāhu** "to freeze": *iq-ru-hu* 272 r. 3,

**qarbāti** "personally(?)": *qar-ba-te-šú* 27:11,

**qarhu** "ice": *qar-hu* 105 r. 6, 272 r. 2,

**qassu** "bow": GIŠ.BAN 3 r. 6, GIŠ.BAN-*šu* 16:6,

**qātu** "hand": *qa-at* 242 r. 1, *qa-a-ti-šú* 53:9, *qa-ta-a-a* 32 r. 8, *qa-ti* 172:7, 12, *qa-ti-*[*ia* 297:9, *qa-ti-ni* 103 r. 3, *qa-ti-*[*šú*] 150:18, ŠU 48 r. 1, 116:2, 4, ŠU.2 38:7, 54:19, 71:11, 100:6, 8, 19, 149 r. 23, 150 r. 1, 3, 186:3, 196 r. 6, 204:7, 218 r. 11, 224 r. 14, 227:5, 232:10, 251:11, r. 5, 263:8, ŠU].2 37:25, ŠU.2-*a-a* 213:5, ŠU.2-*ia* 2 r. 4, 199 r. 3, ŠU.2-[*ia*] 149 r. 13, ŠU.2-*ka* 202:7, ŠU.2-*šú* 224:10, 245 r. 3, [ŠU.2-*šú-nu*] 103:3, ŠU.2-*šú-nu* 32:8, 35 r. 5, 100 r. 12, 137:4, 226:12, ŠU.2-*ti-ku-n*[*u-u*] 171 r. 10,

**qēpu** "(royal) delegate": LÚ.*qe-e-pu* 38:5, 106:24, [L]Ú.*qe-e-pu* 106:15, LÚ.*qe-pi*] 107:5, LÚ.*qe-pu* 38:9, 261 r. 3,

**qerēbu** see *qarābu,*

**qiāpu** "to entrust": *ta-qí-pu-*[*ni* 248:6,

**qinnu** "family": *qi-i-ni* 93:7,

**qirsu** "cart": GIŠ.*qir-si* 152 r. 10, GIŠ.*qir-si-ia* 152 r. 6,

**qû** "litre": *qa* 242 r. 1, 262:9, 269:9, 294:14, [*qa* 261 r. 5, *qa-a-a* 126:15, 294:12, *q*]*a-a-a* 126:16,

**quālu** "to be silent": *qa-la-*[*ka*] 149 r. 5,

**qubbāti** "ague(?)": *qu-ba-te-šú-nu* 156 r. 6,

**qurbu** "relative": LÚ.*qur-b*[*u*] 98 r. 7, see also *qarābu,*

**qurbūtu** see *ša-qurbūti,*

**ra'ābu** "to rage": *ir-tu-'u-b*[*u*] 179 r. 8,

**rā'iu** "shepherd": *ra-'i-ni* 287:5, LÚ.SIPA 96:7, 176:14, 264:3,

**ra'û** "to shepherd": [*i-ra*]*-'u-u-ni* 256 r. 6, *li-ir-'u-ú-šú-nu* 257:10, *li-ri-'u* 256 r. 7, *ra-'i-*[*a* 256 r. 2, *re-'i-šu-nu-u* 256:8,

**rab ālāni** "village manager": LÚ.GAL—URU 3 r. 3, LÚ.GAL—URU.MEŠ 21 r. 5, 152:15, 291 r. 5, LÚ.GAL—URU.MEŠ-[*ma*] 179 r. 6, LÚ.GAL—URU.MEŠ-*šú* 52:8, LÚ.GAL—URU.MEŠ-*šú-nu* 3 r. 5,

**rab bēti** "major-domo": LÚ.GAL—É 115:9, 152:10, L]Ú.GAL—É 34 r. 36, LÚ.GAL—É-*i*[*a* 215 r. 5, LÚ.GAL—É-*i*[*a*] 67:10, LÚ.GAL—É-*k*[*a*] 126 r. 10,

**rab bīrti** "fort commander": LÚ.GAL—*bir-te* 204:18, r. 4, LÚ.GA]L—HAL.ṢU 12 r. 8, LÚ.GAL—URU.HAL.ṢU 245:3,

**rab daiāli** "chief scout": LÚ.GAL—*da-a-a-li* 31 r. 7, LÚ.GAL—*d*[*a-a-a-li*] 35:23,

**rab danibāti** "chief victualler": LÚ.GAL—*da-ni-bat* 143 r. 8, LÚ.GAL—*da*]*-ni-bat* 48 r. 12,

**rab eširti** "commander-of-ten": LÚ.GAL—10.MEŠ-*te* 257:5,

**rab hanšê** "commander-of-fifty": LÚ.GAL—50 53:15, 20, r. 5, 7, LÚ.GAL—50-*ia* 53:4, e. 27, LÚ.GAL—50.MEŠ-[*k*]*u-nu* 43:12,

**rab kallāpi** "commander of riders(?)": LÚ.GAL—*kal-lab*.MEŠ 88:5,

**rab kāri** "chief of trade": LÚ.GAL—*ka-a-ri* 295 r. 18,

**rab karkadinni** "chief confectioner": LÚ.GAL—

SUM.NINDA 227 r. 18,
**rab kāṣiri** "chief tailor": LÚ.GAL—*ka-ṣir* 91:3,
**rab kiṣri** "cohort commander": LÚ.GAL—*ki-ṣir* 234:4, [LÚ].GAL—*ki-ṣir-ia* 250:18, LÚ.GAL—*ki-ṣir*.MEŠ 32:10, 217:4, LÚ.GAL—*ki-ṣir*.MEŠ-*ia* 32 r. 3,
**rab rabie** "officer of a magnate": LÚ.GAL—GAL.MEŠ 295 r. 14,
**rab šāqê** "chief cupbearer": LÚ.GAL—KAŠ.LUL 63 r. 4, 100:11, LÚ.GAL—KAŠ.LU[L] 90:6, LÚ.GA]L—KAŠ.LUL 250:5,
**rab ša-rēši** "chief eunuch": LÚ.GAL—SAG 81:7, LÚ.GAL—[SAG] 81:15, 232:10, L]Ú.GAL—SAG 279:10,
**rab urāti** "team commander": LÚ.GAL—*ú-r[a-te* 211:6,
**rabiu** "magnate": LÚ.GAL.MEŠ 56:5, 69 r. 5, 226:5, r. 9, 12, 250:9, 12, r. 20, 257 r. 7, 291 r. 9, 295:8, 298:10, r. 2, LÚ.GA]L.MEŠ 45:9, [L]Ú.GAL.MEŠ 162:5, LÚ.GAL.MEŠ-*šú* 164 r. 7, LÚ.GAL.MEŠ-*šú*] 165:8, LÚ.GA[L.MEŠ-*šú* 173:6, LÚ.[GAL.MEŠ-*šú*] 173:3, [L]Ú.GAL.MEŠ-*šú* 93:3,
**rabû** "to be great, grow": GAL 96:7,
**rabušeni** "three years ago": *ra-bu-še-ni* 52:17,
**radāpu** "to pursue": *ir-ti-di-bi* 53:19, *ra-da-bi* 47:13, *ri-di-pi* 53:18,
**rādi imāri** "donkey driver": LÚ.UŠ—ANŠE.MEŠ 215:19,
**rādiu** "guide": LÚ.UŠ-*x*[*x* 282 r. 1, LÚ.UŠ—IGI.DUB 257 r. 4, [*ra*]-*di-a-te-šú-nu* 137:7,
**radû** "to lead, rule; (D) to add to": *a-ra-di* 211 r. 8, [*i*]-*ra-di-a* 86:13, *li-ir-di-ia* 231:1, *lu-rad-du-un-na-ši* 294:19, *ur-ta-di* 15 r. 4, *ú-ra-da* 256:7,
**rakābu** "to ride, mount; (Š) to service mares, to load": *nu-*[*sar-kib-šú*] 299 r. 12, [*ú-sa*]*r-kib* 5 e. 4, *ú-šar-kab* 47:10,
**rakāsu** "to bind, attach": *ar-ta-kas* 227:10, e. 25, *ir-ku-su-u-ni* 294 r. 7, *ir-ta-kas* 227:12,
**raksu** "recruit(?)": [LÚ].*rak-su*.MEŠ 137 r. 6,
**rammû** "to leave, abandon, release": *lu-ra-*[*mi-š*]*ú-nu* 78 r. 8, [*lu*]-*ra-mu-ni* 120 r. 1, [*lu-ra*]-*mu-u-ni* 21 r. 23, *nu-ra-ma* 272 r. 5, *ra-am-me* 32 r. 6, *r*]*a-am-me* 15:13, *ra-me-a* 108:17, *ur-ta-am-me* 295 r. 1, *ur-ta-me* 24:12, 291 r. 6, *u*[*r-t*]*a-me* 129:6, *ur-ta-mi-ú-šú-nu* 91:20, [*ur*]-*ta-mu-*[*u*]-*ni* 48:12, *ú-ra-ma* 199 r. 2, *ú-ra-ma-ka* 260:10, *ú-*[*r*]*a-mu-ka* 31 r. 28, *ú-ra-mu-ni* 54 r. 14, *ú-ra-mu-u-ni* 33:11, 122 r. 10,
**rapāšu** "to be wide, extensive": DAGAL 295 e. 26,
**rappu** "bridle, pole": *ra-pa-ni* 297 r. 2,
**raqāqu** "to be thin": *ra-qa-qa* 295 e. 28,
**raqû** "to hide": *ra-qi-ú* 14 r. 11,
**rāqūtu** "emptiness": [*r*]*a-qu-te-ia* 146:10,
**raṣāpu** "to build": *á*[*r*]-*ṣip-u-ni* 15 e. 17, *ár-te-ṣip* 15 r. 9, *i-ra-ṣip-u-ni* 56:11, *i-ra-ṣi-pu* 80 r. 4, *li-ir-ṣip* 210 r. 13,
**reʾû** see *raʾû*,
**rēʾû** see *rāʾiu*,
**redû** see *radû*,
**rēhtu** "rest, remainder": *re-eh-te* 215 r. 5, 226 r. 15, *re-*[*e*]*h-te* 215 r. 4, *re-eh-ti* 12 r. 4, 206 r. 5, 217 s. 3, 224:12, *re-eh*]-*ti* 291:6, *re-e*[*h-ti*] 42 r. 1, *re-eh-tu* 37:17,
**rēšu** "head, top, beginning": *re-eš* 13:7, 69:6, *re-s*[*u* 141:10, *re-šu* 250:14, *re-šu-šu-n*[*u*] 24:15, SAG] 245 r. 1, SAG-*su-nu* 139:3,
**riāhu** "to be left": *re-e-hu* 79 r. 7, 297:6, *re-ha-ti* 216 r. 10, *re-h*]*a-ti* 284 r. 3, *re-he* 223:3, *re-hu-te* 91:9, [*re-hu*]-*te* 117 r. 12, *re-hu-ti* 33 r. 11, 260:10, *re-*[*hu-ti*] 298 r. 12, *re-hu-u-ni* 34 r. 31,
**riāqu** "to be empty, free": *re-*[*qa-ka*] 53 e. 26,
**ridpu** "pursuit": *ri-id-pu* 53 r. 7,
**riksu** "agreement": *ri-ik-su* 31 r. 20, 294 r. 5,
**sadāru** "to array": *a-sa-di-ri* 164 r. 10, [*ni-is-dir* 250 r. 24, *sa-ad-ra* 3:14, *sa-di-ri* 164 r. 12, *si-id-ra* 250:16,
**sadirtu** "battle array": *sa-dir-te* 250 r. 21, *sa-*[*d*]*ir-tú* 250:16,
**sagullu** "herd": *sa-kul-la-te* 264:3,
**sahāru** "to return": *a-su-uh-ru* 146:13, *a-su*[*h-ra*] 4:9, *is-hu-r*[*a* 174:5, *is-hu-r*]*a* 54:11, [*is-hu-r*]*u-u-ni* 72:6, *is-suh-ra* 204 r. 7, *is-suh-ru-ni* 19 s. 3, *is-su-hur* 53 r. 6, [*is*]-*su-uh-ru-ni* 106:13, *i-sa-hur-u-ni* 289 r. 3, *i-sa-hur-ú-ni* 74:13, *i-sa-hu-ra* 290:4, *i-sa-hu-r*[*a*] 290:9, [*i-sa-hu-ra*] 97:13, *i-suh-ra* 186:8, *i-s*]*uh-ra* 54:7, *i-suh-ru-ni* 3 r. 11, *i-s*[*uh-ru-ni*] 12 r. 2, *i-su-hur* 129:3, *i-su-hu-ra* 164 r. 6, *i-su-hu-ru* 221: 9, *i-su-hu-*[*ru* 148:11, [*i-su-u*]*h-ru-*[*ni* 36 e. 8, *li-is-hu-ra* 108 r. 4, *l*]*i-is-hu-ru* 9:3, *lu-sa-hi-ir-šú-nu* 105:25, [*l*]*u-u-sa-hi-ri* 163 e. 14, *sa-*[*hi*]-*ra* 31 r. 17, *ta-sa-hur* 31 r. 29, *ú-sa-hi-ir* 31 r. 9, 53:13, 178 r. 5, *ú-sa-hi-ra-a-ni* 126:10, *ú-sa-hi-ru* 35:29, *ú-s*]*a-hi-ru* 8:3,
**sahlû** "cress": Ú.ZAG.HI.LI.[SAR 126:16,
**sakāru** "to refine": *zag-ru* 294 r. 1,
**salāmu** "to make peace": *sa-al-ma-ni* 2:13, *tu-sa-lim* 99:5, *ú-sa-li-im-šú-nu* 78:16,
**sāmtu A** "carnelian": $NA_4$.GUG 284 r. 11,
**sāmtu B** "red light, dawn": *sa-an-ti* 206:4,
**sâmu** see *siāmu*,
**sanāqu** "(D) to question": *ú-sa-ni-iq-šú-nu* 91:9, *ú-sa-ni-qu-šú-nu* 228 r. 4,
**sangû** "(high) priest": LÚ.SANGA 31:6, 20, 232:9,
**saparru** "cart": G[I]Š.GAG.LIŠ.LAL.MEŠ 48:8,
**sartinnu** (a high official): LÚ.*sar-tin-ni* 162 e. 18, LÚ.[*sar-tin-ni*] 227 s. 3, L]Ú.*sar-tin-ni* 216 s. 1,
**sarru** "thief": *sa-ra-nu* 176 s. 1,
**sasû** "to read": *i-si-si-i-u* 218 r. 1,
**siāmu** "to be red": *sa-a-mu* 287:4, $SA_5$.MEŠ 171:6,
**simunu** "time": *si-mìn*] 82:5, *si-*[*mìn*] 106:21,
**sinnutu** "brandmark": *si-*[*ni-t*]*i* 37:21,
**siparru** "bronze": *si-bar-*[*ri*] 46 e. 18, *si-par-ri* 108 r. 8, *si-pa-ri* 35:28, URUDU 101 r. 4, 206:8, 11, 287:3, r. 3, URUDU.MEŠ 101 r. 1, 2, 257 r. 6,
**sissû** "horse": ANŠE.KUR.MEŠ 133 r. 8, 234 r. 4, 249:11, ANŠE.KUR.[MEŠ] 137:3, A]NŠE.KUR.MEŠ 133 r. 13, ANŠE.KUR.RA 64:5, 95 r. 7, 8, ANŠE.KUR.[RA 208:8, ANŠE.KUR.RA-*ka* 3:18, ANŠE.KUR.RA.ME 64 r. 3, ANŠE.KUR.RA.MEŠ 82 r. 6, 169:12, 171:6, 202:5, 215:7, 226 e. 18, ANŠE.KUR.RA.[MEŠ 62:11, ANŠE.KUR.R[A.MEŠ 14 r. 2, ANŠE.KU[R.RA.MEŠ] 251 r. 6, ANŠ]E.KUR.RA.M[EŠ 199 r. 1, [AN]ŠE.KUR.RA.MEŠ 250:20, ANŠE.KUR.RA.MEŠ-*šú-nu* 226 r. 16, KUR.RA.MEŠ 218:9, 10, 224:10, r. 10, KUR.RA.[MEŠ] 224:14, [KUR.RA.MEŠ] 224 r. 4, KUR.RA.MEŠ-*ka* 224:13, KUR.RA.MEŠ-[*šú-nu*] 225:13,
**sukkallu** "vizier": LÚ.SUKKAL 3:12, r. 12, 168:1, 4, r. 8,
**sulummû** "peace": *su-lum-me-e*] 157:6,
**surrāti** "lies": *sur-rat* 45:6,
**sūsānu** "horse trainer, chariot-man": LÚ.GIŠ.

GIGIR.MEŠ 215:11, 13, 15,

**sūtu** "seah": GI]Š.BÁN 269:9,

**ṣāb šarri** "king's men": ERIM.MEŠ–L]UGAL 250 r. 20, ERIM.MEŠ–MAN 215 e. 23, ERIM.MEŠ–MAN-*ia* 152 e. 25, LÚ.ERIM.MEŠ–LUGAL 52:16, [LÚ].ERIM.MEŠ–LUGAL-*ia* 152:22, LÚ].ERIM.MEŠ–MAN 297:8, LÚ.ERIM.MEŠ–MAN 78 r. 3, LÚ.ERIM.MEŠ–MAN-*šu*-[*ni*] 78 r. 2, LÚ.ERIM–LU[GAL.MEŠ 14:11, LÚ.ERIM–MAN 3 r. 16, LÚ.ERIM–MAN-*šú-nu* 251 r. 2,

**ṣāb šarrūtu** "military service": ERIM.MEŠ–MAN-*te* 52:18,

**ṣabātu** "to seize; (Š) to provide": *a-ṣa-bat* 33:12, 46 e. 18, *a-*[*ṣa-bat*] 199 r. 3, *a-ṣa-ba-su* 150:9, *a-ṣa-b*[*a-ta*] 16 r. 3, *iṣ-ṣab-*[*tu-ni-šú*] 55:8, *iṣ-ṣa-bat*] 89:8, *i-ṣab-bat* 53:9, *i*]*-ṣab-bat* 54 r. 7, *i-ṣab-ta-ni* 151:9, *i-ṣab-tú* 35 r. 5, *i-ṣa-ab-*[*tu* 220:2, *i-ṣa-ab-t*[*u-šú-nu*] 116 r. 2, *i-ṣa-bat* 90 r. 3, 92:14, 227:11, *i-ṣa-bat-s*[*u*] 190 r. 5, *i-ṣa-ba-s*[*u-nu*] 116: 6, *i-ṣa-ba-ta* 166:3, (*i*)*-ṣi-bu-tú* 53 r. 8, *lu-ṣa-bi-it* 100 r. 8, [*lu*]*-šá-aṣ-bi-t*[*u*] 252 r. 2, *n*]*u-ṣa-bat* 187:3, *ṣa-ab-bu-tú* 91:7, *ṣa-bit* 4 r. 3, *ṣa-*[*bit* 33:10, *ṣa-bi-ti* 91:15, *ṣa-bu-tú* 169:7, *tu-ṣa-bat* 35:20, *tu-ṣa-ba-ta* 2:15, *tu-ṣa-bit* 227 r. 23, *tu-ṣa-bi-ta* 115 r. 2, *ú-sa-aṣ-bit* 243:17, *ú-ṣab-bi-tú* 115:8, *ú-ṣab-bu-tú* 46:8, *ú-ṣa-bit* 33:8, *ú-ṣa-bit-u-ni* 227 s. 2, *ú-ṣa-bi-it* 146:8, *ú-ṣa-bi-ti* 228:12, [*ú*]*-ṣa-bi-tu* 225:17, *ú-ṣ*]*a-bi-tú* 25:11, *ú-ša-aṣ-bat-su-nu* 52 r. 6,

**ṣābu** "men, troops": ERIM.ME[Š 95 r. 9, 215:12, ERIM.MEŠ 52 r. 12, 60:6, 91:9, 12, 97:4, r. 8, 106: 17, 111 e. 6, r. 1, 112:6, 200:13, r. 7, 250 r. 10, 12, 17, 257:8, 277:9, [ERIM.MEŠ 200 r. 15, ERIM.MEŠ-*ia* 217 s. 1, ERIM.ME[Š-*ka*] 118 e. 12, ERIM.MEŠ-*ku*-[*nu*] 35 r. 11, ERIM.MEŠ-*ni* 199 r. 10, ERIM.[MEŠ-*šú*] 289:3, [ERIM.MEŠ-*šú* 131:3, LÚ.ERIM.MEŠ 3 r. 6, 5 e. 4, r. 1, 6 r. 3, 14 r. 10, 21 r. 22, 32:7, 12, r. 2, 5, 9, 33 r. 8, 9, 35 r. 2, 4, 9, 41:4, 52 r. 2, 63 r. 17, 79:7, 88:4, 92:11, 103:8, 9, e. 11, r. 3, 104:4, 111:3, 130:6, 139:1, 294 r. 8, 295 r. 13, LÚ.ERIM.M[EŠ 10:3, 129 s. 3, LÚ.ERIM.[MEŠ 14:12, 126:19, LÚ.ERIM.[MEŠ] 25 r. 4, LÚ.[ERIM].MEŠ 21 r. 16, L[Ú.ERIM.MEŠ 92 r. 3, 184:2, L[Ú.ERIM.MEŠ] 53 e. 27, L]Ú.ERIM.MEŠ 5 r. 3, 24:10, 13, 37 r. 16, [LÚ.ERIM.MEŠ 106:25, [L]Ú.ERIM.MEŠ 103:2, LÚ.ERIM.MEŠ-*e* 21 r. 12, LÚ.ERIM.MEŠ-*ia* 32 r. 19, [LÚ.ERIM.MEŠ-*ia*] 33:7, LÚ.ERIM.MEŠ-*ka* 33:10, 126:11, 226 r. 1, LÚ.ERIM.[MEŠ-*ka*] 126:12, LÚ.ERIM.MEŠ-*ni* 115 r. 1, LÚ.ERIM.[MEŠ-*ni*] 115:5, LÚ.ERIM.MEŠ *ni-šú-nu* 3 r. 8, LÚ.ERIM.MEŠ-*šu* 88 r. 2, LÚ.ERIM.MEŠ-*šú* 33:9, 53:15, 20,

**ṣahittu** "wish, desire; luxury item": *ṣa-hi-ta-a-te* 100:12, r. 4, 10, [*ṣa-hi-ta*]*-a-te* 101:5, *ṣa-hi-ti* 34 r. 33, 37:20,

**ṣalālu** "to sleep": N[Á] 261 r. 4,

**ṣalāmu** "to be black": $GI_6$.MEŠ 171:8,

**ṣalmu** "image, likeness": ALAM 15 r. 9,

**ṣāpiu** "dyer": *ṣa-p*[*i-ú-ti*] 205:8, LÚ.*ṣa-pu-u* 296 r. 3,

**ṣarbutu** "poplar": GIŠ.*ṣar-bu-tú* 253:6,

**ṣarpu** "silver": KUG.UD 149:14, 238 r. 3,

**ṣarrāpu** "goldsmith": LÚ.SIMUG.KUG.GI 294:18,

**ṣehru** "child": LÚ.TUR.MEŠ 200 r. 7, LÚ.TUR.MEŠ-*ni* 227 r. 17, LÚ.TUR.MEŠ-*ni-ma* 200 r. 14,

**ṣēru** "back": *ṣe-er* 160:10,

**ṣillu** "shadow": GIŠ.MI 15 e. 18,

**ṣīpu** "dyeing": *ṣi-pi* 296 r. 2,

**ṣīru** "emissary": LÚ.*ṣi-ra-a-ni* 35 e. 33, LÚ.MAH 40 r. 2, 169 r. 4, 171 r. 4, LÚ.M[AH] 171:4, [LÚ.MA]H 75:4, LÚ.MAH.MEŠ 52:4, r. 13, 169:3, 14, r. 1, 194 r. 7, LÚ.MAH.MEŠ-*ni* 52 r. 7, 15,

**ṣuʾubtu** (a designation of sheep): *ṣu-ʾu-bat* 256:12,

**ṣupru** "nail, claw, hoof": *ṣu-pur* 293:7,

**ša** "that; what; of": *ša* 1:6, 9, 2:3, 6, 10, 3:3, 5, 6, 10, 16, r. 5, 10, 6:5, 11 r. 5, 7, 13:2, 14:5, 6, r. 10, 15:4, 8, 9, r. 2, 8, 16:8, 9, r. 5, 17:4, 6, 18:4, 19 s. 1, 20:4, 5, 21:6, 7, 8, r. 2, 7, 10, 16, 22:7, 8, 23:6, 24:6, 8, 14, 15, 25:6, 27:6, 8, 12, 28:6, 29:7, 10, 30:6, 7, 31:5, 6, 7, 9, 11, 16, 17, r. 3, 16, 18, 32:6, 9, 14, r. 12, 33:5, 6, r. 1, 3, 4, 16, 19, 34:4, 5, r. 2, 4, 8, 10, 15, 20, 23, 27, 31, 35:5, 6, 19, 31, e. 33, r. 13, 37:4, 5, 20, 21, 23, 27, 29, r. 13, 14, 38:6, 40:5, 10, r. 4, 44 r. 3, 45:3, 5, r. 2, 46:7, 14, r. 5, 47:5, 7, 14, r. 1, 3, 50:4, 6, 51:4, 52:4, 8, 9, 12, 17, r. 3, 8, 13, 19, 53:4, 5, 22, e. 25, r. 1, 3, 7, 9, 10, 54:2, r. 2, 11, 55:4, 10, 56:4, 10, 12, r. 5, 6, 10, 57:4, 59:6, 62:8, 63:6, r. 6, 64:6, 65:8, 9, 66:5, 67:6, 68:5, 10, 69:4, 6, 8, 14, r. 5, 70:5, 6, 71:8, 74:4, 5, 8, 12, 75:5, 78:6, 8, 10, 11, e. 17, r. 2, 8, 15, 79:5, r. 2, 9, 11, 80:6, 7, r. 5, 81:9, 10, 82:4, r. 7, 10, 83 r. 2, 84:5, 6, 10, 12, r. 2, 85:3, 86:4, 10, 87:4, 6, 7, 9, 10, 11, r. 3, 88:6, 7, 10, 12, r. 1, 89:8, 90:6, 7, 8, 9, 10, 11, 12, 13, r. 4, 91:4, 6, 10, 14, 22, r. 4, 92:3, r. 2, 5, 93:7, 94:4, 5, 95:9, 13, r. 2, 96:4, 5, r. 4, 5, 97:4, 5, r. 6, 7, 9, 98:5, 7, 15, 100:6, 8, 11, 13, 19, r. 1, 104:5, 17, r. 12, 105:4, 17, r. 4, 8, 106:3, 8, 18, 107:1, 108:3, 29, r. 8, 11, 14, 16, 18, s. 1, 109:3, 5, 11, 110:5, 111:3, 4, 5, e. 6, 112 e. 8, r. 3, 113:4, 6, 15, r. 7, 12, 114:9, 115:3, 6, r. 3, 116:2, 4, 117:15, 17, e. 23, r. 5, 10, 118 r. 4, 5, 119:10, 121:3, 4, 5, 7, 15, e. 19, r. 4, 17, 20, 122:11, r. 5, 123 r. 5, 124:7, 125:3, 126:7, 14, r. 3, 9, 12, 127:6, 8, 13, 128:5, 6, 129:2, 6, r. 4, s. 2, 130:2, 4, 9, s. 1, 131:1, 4, 6, 132:5, 9, 135:4, 5, 138:5, 139:3, 6, 141:6, 8, 143:10, r. 1, 6, 144:4, 7, r. 2, 10, 145 r. 17, 146:18, r. 2, 147:10, r. 4, 5, 148:8, 9, r. 2, 4, 5, 149:4, 15, 18, 20, 24, r. 8, 13, 150 r. 2, 3, 152:4, 7, 10, 19, 20, 23, 24, r. 1, 10, 11, 13, 18, 20, 154:4, 155:6, 156:6, 157:5, 160:7, 15, 16, 20, 161:4, 6, 162:4, 7, 163:6, 7, 12, r. 7, 164:4, 5, 6, 12, 165:5, 166:4, 168:6, 169:5, 6, 9, 14, r. 3, 171 r. 2, 172:6, 174:1, 175:6, 176:8, 10, 14, r. 3, 7, s. 1, 178 e. 11, 179 r. 7, 181:4, 182:8, 10, 184:4, 5, 186:3, 187:9, 193:2, 194 r. 9, 196:5, 197 e. 10, 199:4, 7, 8, r. 6, 7, 13, 14, 200:4, 7, 201:4, 202:4, 6, r. 6, s. 2, 203:4, 8, 11, 15, r. 9, 13, 204:5, 7, 18, r. 1, 4, 8, 206:5, 6, 7, r. 4, 208:7, 210:5, 11, r. 6, 14, 19, 211:5, r. 6, 213:5, 6, 215:5, 7, 8, r. 1, 2, 216:4, 5, r. 11, 217:5, 7, 8, 10, 11, 14, r. 6, 7, 11, s. 3, 218:11, 14, r. 2, 3, 10, 219:1, 221:4, 6, 13, r. 4, 9, 223:5, r. 5, 224:5, r. 12, 14, 226:16, r. 6, 11, 13, 227:4, 15, 16, r. 16, 18, 26, 27, s. 3, 4, 228:3, 7, 11, r. 5, 232:5, 6, 8, 9, r. 5, 7, 233:8, 9, 234:2, r. 2, 235:5, 236:2, 3, 241:14, 242:6, 12, r. 1, 243:4, 6, 9, 12, 13, 15, r. 16, 244:5, 245:4, 8, r. 1, 5, 246:4, r. 3, 247:5, 248:1, 4, 5, r. 1, 5, 249:3, 4, 6, 7, 16, r. 6, 250:7, 14, 18, r. 3, 5, 6, 7, 10, 12, 13, 15, 16, 17, 18, 20, 24, 251:11, r. 5, 253:5, 254:9, 13, 256:2, r. 12, 257:3, 4, 6, r. 5, 7, 258:1, 3, 260:2, 6, r. 7, 261 r. 3, 263:3, 7, 11, 264:2, 7, 265:4, 7, 266:5, 267:4, s. 3, 268:5, 269:5, 9, 272 r. 4, 276 r. 2, 277:9, 278:4, 279:4, r. 2, 3, 281:6, 7, 9, 11, 15, r. 8, 282:4, 5, 8, 283:5, 284 r. 10, 287 r. 3, 288 r. 1, 9, 289:2, r. 1,

290:6, 7, r. 5, 7, 8, 291:6, 10, r. 5, 11, 14, 292:4, 7, r. 4, 5, 6, 293:8, 294:5, 12, r. 1, 6, 11, 295:21, e. 27, r. 2, 5, 9, 11, 14, 18, 19, 21, 26, 296 r. 4, 5, 297 r. 5, 298:5, 10, 299 r. 1, *ša*] 6:6, 18:6, 22:6, 55:5, 56 r. 2, 92 r. 15, 112 r. 5, 128:8, 150 r. 1, 165:9, 232:4, 269:11, 286:4, 298:6, *š*[*a* 34 s. 1, 37 r. 20, 46 r. 12, 106:12, 127:7, 137 r. 8, 144:6, 149:5, 10, 221:11, 244:6, 250:9, 256:2, 266:3, 267:5, 299:1, *š*[*a*] 105:11, *š*]*a* 8:4, r. 1, 9:5, 15:6, r. 15, 31 r. 9, 34 r. 28, 39:1, 7, 74 r. 7, 93 r. 8, 94:7, 95:4, r. 5, 107 e. 6, 113 r. 10, 143:11, 152:16, 160:4, 170 r. 5, 177:4, 178 r. 10, 182 r. 6, 219:2, 232:10, 288 s. 2, 291:10, [*ša* 11:4, 12 r. 2, 7, 31 r. 5, 8, 33 r. 17, 36:7, 37:28, 38:7, 10, 41:2, 43:5, 57:5, 66:4, 72:5, 80:8, 93:2, 107:5, e. 7, r. 1, 108:21, 109:10, 117:3, 121 e. 20, 131:2, 134:4, 136 r. 7, 137 r. 1, 141 r. 2, 143:4, 144 s. 2, 150:6, 151:5, 162:13, 15, e. 17, 170:4, 173:1, 181:5, 182:5, 190 r. 1, 8, 196 r. 7, 205 r. 2, 206:10, 220:6, 230:3, 236:5, 250 r. 5, 20, 22, 251:5, 256 r. 8, 284 r. 9, 289:3, 291 r. 6, 299 r. 2, 300 r. 4, [*ša*] 2:8, 15:16, 63:5, 92 r. 8, 95 r. 8, 104:15, 105:9, 138:1, 152 r. 2, 170:6, 190 r. 2, 195:2, 238:6, 269:4, 282:10, 291 r. 8, 294:2, 299 r. 4, 11, 300:5, [*š*]*a* 2:7, 21:19, 31 r. 17, 34 r. 5, 35:19, 24, 37:32, 45:4, 48:5, 50:5, 54 r. 12, 74 r. 2, 93:7, 121:11, 143:8, 147:4, 158:6, 173:9, 204:17, 215:4, 225:4, 245:10, 254:14, 260:13, 263:2, 269:6, 280 s. 1, *šá* 1:4, 5, 2:5, 3:15, r. 1, 10, 4 r. 8, 6:4, r. 7, 14:4, 61 r. 2, 81 r. 4, 145:15, s. 1, 2, 147:9, r. 3, 10, 171 r. 14, 232 r. 10, 255:2, 299:3, r. 9, 13, [*šá* 14 r. 15, 289 r. 3,

**šaʾālu** "to ask": *a*[*s-sa-ʾa-al-šú*] 108:22, *a-sa-al* 227 r. 19, *a-*[*sa-a*]*l* 35:17, *a-sa-al-šu* 35 r. 9, *a-sa-al-šú* 171 r. 7, *a-sa-al-š*[*ú*] 188:8, [*a-s*]*a-al-šú* 55:9, *a-sa-aʾ-la* 163 r. 1, *a-sa-na-al* 91 r. 1, *a-sa-ʾa-a*]*l* 54:8, *a-sa-ʾa-al-šú* 224:11, *a-sa-ʾa-*[*al-šú*] 224 r. 5, *a-sa-ʾa-al-šú-nu* 103:8, 149 r. 20, *a-šá-ʾa-al* 32 r. 6, *iš-ʾa-al-*[*x* 182:8, [*iš*]*-ʾa-lu-ni* 37:18, *i-sa-al-šú-nu* 91:18, *i*]*-sa-*(*a*)*ʾ-lu* 37:15, *i-sa-na-al* 91 r. 6, *i-ša-ú-lu* 91 r. 8, *i-šá-ʾu-u-l*[*u*] 40 e. 22, *liš-al* 46 r. 4, 105:21, 169 r. 5, *liš-a*[*l* 227:14, *liš-al-šu* 241:13, [*liš*]*-al-šu* 82 r. 12, [*liš-al-šú* 149 r. 8, [*liš*]*-al-šú* 130 s. 3, *liš-al-šú-nu* 100 r. 9, 122 r. 9, *liš-ul* 31:12, *liš-ul-lu* 85:5, *liš-ʾa-al* 197 r. 3, *liš-ʾa-a*[*l* 243 r. 10, *li*[*š-ʾa-a*]*l* 74 r. 9, *liš-ʾa-al-šú-nu* 150 r. 14, *liš-*[*ʾa*]*-al-šú-nu* 149 r. 25, *ni-sa-a*[*l* 136 r. 4, *šá-a-la* 265:5, *šá-ʾa-al* 34:6, 68:6,

**šabāṭu** (Shebat, name of the 11th month): ITI.ZÍZ 272 r. 4, ITI.ZÍ[Z] 9:5,

**šadādu** "to drag, haul, extend": *a-sa-da-*[*ad* 127:10, *i-sa-du-ú-ni* 91:10, *i-šá-du-*[*du*] 8 r. 3, *liš*]*-du-du* 17 e. 14,

**šaddaqdiš** "last year": *iš–šad-*[*dag-diš*] 170:4, *šad-daq-diš* 52:17, *šad-dàq-diš* 200 r. 5, *šad-dàq-diš-ma* 199:15, [*šá-da*]*q-di-iš* 150:15, *šá-dàq-di-iš* 28:7,

**šadû** "mountain; east": KUR-*e* 25 r. 4, 83 r. 4, 116:5, 191:4, 290:3, K]UR-*e* 180:1, 196:13, KUR-*i* 55:7, K[UR-*i*] 55:4, KUR-*ú* 53:16, 78 r. 4, 90 r. 3, KUR.MEŠ-*ni* 200:9, KUR.MEŠ-[*ni*] 156 r. 4,

**šahāṭu** "to glaze": *i-šá-ha-aṭ* 291:9, *i-šá-hu-ṭu* 211 r. 10,

**šahšūru** "apple": [GI]Š.*šá-ah-šu-ru* 27:13,

**šakānu** "to place, set": *áš-kun-ka-a-ni* 3:17, *a-sa-kan* 169:11, *a-sa-*[*kan* 281 r. 7, *a-s*[*a-kan-šu*] 280 e. 13, *a-sa-kan-šú* 237:6, *a-sa-kan-šú*] 229:4, *a-sa-kan-šú-nu* 202 r. 16, *a-šak-*[*kan*] 289:5, *a-šak-kan-šú* 108 r. 9, [*is-sak*]*-nu-uš* 90 r. 9, *iš-k*[*un* 142 r. 4, [*iš-kun*] 46:16, *iš-kun-an-ni* 152:24, *iš-k*[*un-an-ni*] 128:6, [*iš-kun-an-ni*] 70:7, *iš-kun-an-ni-ni* 224:6, 226:8, 17, *iš-kun-a-ni-*[*ni*] 29 r. 2, *iš-kun-na-na-ši* 98:11, *iš-kun-u-ni* 169 r. 7, 203 r. 18, *iš-k*[*un-u-ni*] 294:2, *iš-ku-na-*[*an-ni*] 251:7, *iš-*[*k*]*u-na-an-ni* 251:14, *iš-ku-na-ni* 109:4, *iš-ku-na-ni-ni* 113:4, 215:4, *iš-*[*ku-na*]*-ni-ni* 113 r. 8, *iš-ku-nu-šu-u-*[*ni*] 210 r. 21, *iš-ku-nu-šú-*[*u-ni*] 155:7, *iš-ku-*[*x* 130 r. 2, *i*]*-sak-nu-uš* 187:7, *i-sa-a*[*k-na*] 53:24, *i-sa-ak-nu* 52 e. 24, 107:3, 202 r. 10, *i-sa-ak-nu-šu* 35:28, *i-sa-kan* 144 r. 7, *i-sa*]*-kan* 168 r. 4, *i-šak-kan* 46:13, 92:15, *i-šak-ka-nu-ni* 108 s. 2, *liš-kun* 227 r. 11, [*l*]*iš-kun* 67 r. 2, *liš-ku-nu* 146 r. 11, 295:12, [*liš-ku-nu*]*-šu-nu* 256 r. 4, *ni-is-sa-k*[*an*] 206:10, *ni-iš-ku-*(*nu*)*-u-ni* 53 r. 8, *ni-sa-kan* 204 r. 4, *ni-šak-kan* 95 e. 18, [*šak-na* 86 r. 2, *šak-na-ni* 160:6, *šak-nu-u-ni* 121:6, *š*[*a*]*k-nu-u-ni* 226:10, *šá-ak-na-ku-u-ni* 27:10, 217 r. 8, [*šá-áš-kin-šú*] 263:12, *šá-ki-in* 217 r. 10, *šá-ki-ni* 69:7, 145:13, 168 r. 7, *ta-áš-šá-ki-nu-ni* 92:11, *ta-sa-kan-an-ni* 108:5, *ú-sa-áš-kin-šú-nu* 210:14,

**šaklulu** "ungelded bull": [*šak-l*]*a-lu-tu* 238:5,

**šaknu** "prefect": GAR-*nu-u-ti* 57:9, LÚ.*šak-ni* 251:12, LÚ.*šak-nu* 213 r. 3, LÚ.GAR-*nu* 268 r. 6, 10, LÚ.GAR-*nu-te* 88:5, LÚ.GAR-*nu*.MEŠ 34 r. 23, LÚ.GAR-*nu*.MEŠ-*šú-nu* 32 r. 13,

**šalāhu** "to retrieve": *ni-iš-luh-šu-nu* 293 r. 1,

**šalāmu** "to be sound, whole, safe": *la-áš-la-mu-te* 121 r. 15, *šal-ma-a-ti* 295 r. 7, *šal-mu* 218:5, *tu-šal-lum-ni* 227 r. 24,

**šalimtu** "safety": *šá*]*-li-in-ti* 160:5,

**šallūru** "apricot": GIŠ.KIB 281:14,

**šalšu** "third": *šal-ši-u-te* 129:4, *šá-al-še* 199:11,

**šalšūmi** "the day before yesterday": [*i–šá-šu-m*]*e* 291 r. 12,

**šaluššeni** "two years ago": *šal-še-ni* 52:17,

**šamāru** "to be fierce": *ša-mu-ru* 126 r. 13,

**šamnu** "oil": Ì.MEŠ 108:20, r. 24, 126:15,

**šamû** "to hear, listen to": *áš-me* 54:18, 86 r. 3, 112 e. 7, 114:6, *áš-mu-u-ni* 45:6, *a-se-e-me* 35 r. 7, *a-se-me* 45 r. 8, 88 r. 5, 95:6, 150 r. 15, 292 r. 7, *a-se*]*-me* 177:1, [*a-se*]*-me* 162 r. 7, *a-šam-mu-ni* 243:9, *a-šá-me* 144 s. 1, *iš-me* 33 s. 4, 108 r. 7, 260 r. 4, *i-sa-na-me* 121 r. 16, *i-šam-u-ni* 118 r. 7, *i-šam-*[*u-ni*] 118 r. 1, *i-ša-ma-a-ni* 142:7, *i-šá-am-me* 210 r. 1, *i-šá-man*]*-ni* 63:10, [*i-š*]*á-mu-na-ši* 194 r. 4, *i-šá-mu-u-ni* 63 r. 18, *la-áš-me* 295 r. 10, *ni-iš-me* 169 r. 4, 227 r. 21, *ni-sa-*[*n*]*am-me* 113 r. 2, *ni-šam-me* 1 r. 4, [*nu*]*-sa-šá-me-šú-nu* 105:10, [*šá-áš-me*] 284 r. 7, *taš-*[*me* 221:6, *taš-mu-u-ni* 45:5, *taš-m*[*u*]*-u-ni* 114 r. 6, *ta-šá-me-a* 63 r. 15, *ú-ša-áš-ma* 152 r. 4, *ú-šá-áš-mu-u-ni* 52 r. 2, 12,

**šangû** see *sangû*,

**šaniu A** "deputy": LÚ.2-*e* 152:5, 226 r. 11, 264:2, LÚ.2-[*e* 154:6, 208:4, LÚ.2-*i-šú* 46 r. 1, 52:12, LÚ.2-*u* 21 r. 4, 179 r. 6, [LÚ.2-*u* 150 r. 9, LÚ.2-*ú* 3 r. 5, 192 r. 7, 242:9, LÚ.2-*ú*] 149 r. 8, L[Ú].2-*ú* 149:14, [LÚ.2-*ú* 149:24, [LÚ.2]-*ú* 149:20,

**šaniu B** "second, other, different": *š*[*a*]*-ni-e* 95 r. 3, *ša-ni-u* 290:3, *šá-ni-ti* 104:15, *šá-ni-ú-te* 152 r. 7,

**šanû** "(D) to repeat": *lu-šá-an-ni* 34:8,

**šapal** "under": *šap-la* 146 r. 10, 172:12, *šap-li* 172:7, *ša-pal* 108 r. 2, *šá-pal* 4 r. 8, 218 r. 11, KI.TA

54:19, 152 r. 11, 227:10, 12, KI.TA-*šú* 227:19, KI.T[A-*šú*] 227:24,

**šapāru** "to send": [*as-sap-ra*] 125 r. 10, *áš-par* 217 s. 1, *áš-pur-an-ni* 91:4, 181:7, *áš-pur-[an-ni* 108:29, *áš-pu[r-an-ni*] 33:6, [*áš-pur-an-ni* 34 r. 29, [*áš-pur-an-ni*] 33 r. 1, *áš-pur-a-ni* 83 r. 2, [*áš-pur*]-*a-ni* 134:5, *áš-pur-u*]-*ni* 12 r. 2, *áš-pur-ú-ni* 2:9, *áš-p[u-ra*] 173:10, *áš-pu-ra-an-ni* 250:19, r. 22, 294 r. 2, *áš-pu-ra-ni* 243:16, *a-sap-ár-šu* 217 r. 2, *a-sap-ra* 96 r. 11, 113 r. 14, 150 r. 9, 168 r. 9, s. 2, 178 r. 4, 217 r. 15, s. 2, 246:6, *a-sap-r[a* 248:3, *a-sap-(ra)* 168 s. 1, *a-sap-[r]a* 217:8, *a-[sap-ra*] 144 r. 9, *a-sa-ap-ra* 3 r. 3, 254:12, *a-sa-ap-ra*] 14:11, [*a-sa-ap-ra* 14 r. 14, [*a-s*]*a-ap-ra* 254 r. 16, [*a*]-*sa-a[p-ra* 192 r. 8, *a-s[a-ap-rak-ku-nu* 277:2, *a-sa-ap-ra-šú-nu* 3 r. 13, *a-sa-bar* 21 r. 15, 34:7, 37:29, r. 5, [*a-sa-bar*] 46:15, *a-sa-bar-áš-šú* 32 r. 5, *a-sa-bar-šú-nu* 32:10, *a-sa-na-par-šú* 63:15, *a-sa-par* 3:7, 40 e. 22, 44 r. 5, 45:7, 87 r. 5, 103:7, 108 s. 1, 115:4, 9, 172:11, 202 r. 5, 245 r. 2, 263:5, 270 s. 2, 284 r. 8, *a-sa-par*] 13:6, *a-sa-[par* 61:3, 203 r. 4, 257:2, [*a-sa-par* 130 r. 4, [*a-sa-par*] 186:7, *a-sa-par-a-[šu* 35:30, *a-sa-par-ra* 126 r. 15, *a-sa-par-šú* 130 s. 2, *a-sa-pa-ar* 34 r. 12, [*a*]-*sa-pa-*[[]]*ar-šú* 190 r. 4, *a-sa-pa-ra* 53:11, 14, 244 r. 4, *a-sa-pa-[ra*] 260:3, *a-šab-bar* 46:12, *a-šap-par* 91 r. 8, 10, 108:7, *a-šap-par-kan-ni* 3 e. 20, *a-šap-par-u-ni* 91 r. 5, *a-šap-pa-ra* 40 r. 2, *a-šap-pa-ra*] 38:7, *a-šap-pa-r[a*] 218 r. 11, *a-ša*]*p-pa-ra* 186 e. 10, *a-š[ap*]-*pa-ra* 19 s. 3, [*a*]-*šap-pa-r[a*] 204 r. 10, *a-šá-par-a-ka* 35 r. 12, [*is-s*]*ap-ra* 134:6, *iš-pur-an-na-ši-ni*] 158:6, *iš-pur-an-na-ši-[ni*] 156:7, *i[š-pur-an-na-ši-ni*] 157:5, *iš-pur-an-ni* 2:10, 12 r. 7, 15:9, 31:8, 10, 45:4, 54:2, 56:5, 57:5, 59:6, 63:5, 68:6, 69:5, 71:9, 78:7, 85:3, 87 r. 3, 91:22, 97:5, r. 10, 126 r. 9, 152:8, 23, r. 2, 163:8, 172:6, 10, 199:4, 202:4, 203:5, 9, 11, r. 9, 204 r. 2, 218 r. 4, 10, 221:4, 227:5, r. 16, 242:7, 254:10, 263:7, 291 r. 6, 293:8, *iš-pur-an-ni*] 20:6, 146:18, 221 r. 4, 265:4, *iš-pur-an-n[i*] 292:4, *iš-pur-an-n*]*i* 54 r. 3, *iš-pur-an-[ni*] 182:5, 230:3, *iš-pur-a[n-ni*] 204:9, 299 r. 2, *iš-pur-[an-ni*] 263:2, 300 r. 4, *iš-pur-[an*]-*ni* 37:27, *iš-pu[r-an-ni* 141:9, *iš-pu[r-an-ni*] 200:4, *iš-p[ur-an-ni*] 225:4, *iš-p[ur*]-*an-ni* 21 r. 11, *iš-p*]*ur-an-ni* 75:5, *iš-[pur-an-ni* 282:4, *iš-[pur-an-ni*] 27:8, 66:4, 298:7, *iš-[pur*]-*an-ni* 161:5, *iš*]-*pur-an-ni* 181:5, *i[š-pur-an-ni* 69:14, *i[š-pur-an-ni*] 138:1, 143:8, 144:7, [*iš-pur-an-ni*] 21 r. 2, 125:3, 269:4, [*iš-pur-an-n*]*i* 168:7, [*iš-pur-an*]-*ni* 34:6, [*iš-pur-a*]*n-ni* 238:7, 247:6, [*iš-pur*]-*an-ni* 300:6, [*iš-pu*]*r-an-ni* 203:16, [*iš-p*]*ur-an-ni* 137 r. 2, [*i*]*š-pur-an-ni* 263:12, *iš-pur-an-ni-ni* 226:6, *iš-pur-an-ni-ni*] 196 r. 9, *iš-pur-a-ni* 35 r. 13, 82:5, 121:4, *iš-pur-a-[ni*] 256:3, [*i*]*š-pur-ni* 110:6, [*iš-p*]*ur-ni-ni* 170:5, [*i*]*š-pur-ra-ni-ni* 198 r. 4, *iš-pur-šu-u-ni* 227:22, *iš-pur-[u-ni-ni* 268:6, [*iš-pur-u-ni-ni*] 151:6, *iš-pu-ra-an-ni* 246:5, 250 r. 4, *iš-pu-ra-ni* 105 r. 5, [*iš-pu*]-*ra-ni-ni* 159:6, *i-sap-ra* 178 r. 7, 218:7, 227 r. 22, [*i-sap-ra*] 33:8, *i-sa-ap-ra* 152:21, *i-sa-a[p-ra*] 142 r. 5, 192 r. 2, *i-s[a-ap-ra-šú*] 11 r. 3, *i-sa-bar* 31 r. 24, 33 r. 17, 37:20, [*i-sa-bar* 31 r. 14, *i-sa-par* 270:15, 284 r. 5, *i-sa-[pa*]*r* 35 r. 10, [*i-sa-par* 291:4, *i-sa-pa-[ra-šu*] 188:6, *i-sa-pa-ru-u-ni* 202 r. 14, *i-sa-ta-pa[r* 26:2, *i-šap-pa-[ra-an-ni*] 160:7, *i-ša[p-pa-ru-ni-ni*] 13:4, *i-šap-pu-r[u*] 229 e. 12, *i-šá-p[a-ra-ni*] 292 r. 6, *la-áš-pur* 96 r. 7, 284 r. 8, [*la-áš-pu-ra*] 34:8, *liš*]-*pa-ru-[ni*] 267 s. 3, [*liš-p*]*a-[ru-u-ni*] 299 r. 14, *liš-pur* 97 r. 5, 100 r. 7, 268 r. 11, *liš-pur-áš-šu* 63 r. 1, *liš-pur-ú-ni* 79 r. 8, *liš-pu-ra* 3 r. 16, 32 r. 14, 52 r. 20, 63 r. 9, 74 r. 9, 200 r. 10, 294 r. 5, 295 r. 10, *liš-pu-r*]*a* 108 s. 2, *liš-p[u-ra* 62:9, [*liš-pu-ra* 194 r. 11, [*li*]*š-pu-[ra*] 136 r. 9, *liš-pu-ru* 213:9, r. 4, *liš-pu-[r*]*u* 62 r. 3, *l*]*i-iš-pa-ru-u-ni* 144 s. 2, *li-iš-pur* 81 r. 5, *li-iš-pur-ra* 244 r. 8, *l[i-iš-pur*]-*ú-[ni*] 152 r. 12, *li-iš-pu-ra* 152 r. 9, *ni-iš-pu-u-ru* 139:7, *ni-sap-ra* 217 r. 5, *ni-sa-ap-[ra*] 156 e. 18, *š*]*ap-ra-a-ni* 279 r. 5, *šup-ra* 68:9, 81 r. 2, 115 r. 4, 204:12, 215:6, *šup-ra*] 144:8, *šup-[ra* 128:9, [*šup-ra*] 45:6, [*šu*]*p-ru* 128:8, *šu-pur* 87 r. 4, *šu-pur-šu* 278:3, *šu-pu-ur* 85:4, *šu-up-ru* 115:12, *taš-pur*] 108:9, *taš-pur-an-ni* 147:4, r. 3, *taš-pur-ni* 95:5, *taš-pu-ra* 114 r. 7, *taš-pu-ra*] 221:6, *ta-šap-pa-r[a* 11 r. 10, KIN.MEŠ 291:2,

**šāqiu** "cupbearer": LÚ.KAŠ.LUL 215:16, L]Ú.KAŠ.LUL 206:10,

**šarāmu** "to cut into shape": *nu-[šar-ri*]-*mu-u-ni* 295:21, *ú-sa-ri-mì-ma* 295 r. 3, *ú-šar*]-*ri-mu-u-ni* 295:15,

**šarāpu** "to burn": *šar-pu* 287:4,

**šarāṣu** (mng. uncert.): [*i*]-*sa-ra-aṣ* 152:9,

**šarbu** "cold weather": *šá-ár-bu* 156 r. 3,

**šarru** "king": LUGAL 1:1, 3, 4, 5, 6, 7, 2:2, 5, 10, 3:1, 2, 3, 5, r. 15, 6:3, 4, 6, 10, r. 7, 7 r. 3, 11:1, 3, 4, 14:3, 6, 7, r. 14, 15:1, 4, 9, 14, e. 17, r. 8, 9, 11, 13, 16:1, 3, 4, r. 5, 17:1, 3, 6, 18:1, 3, 4, 6, r. 4, 19:3, s. 3, 20:1, 3, 4, 6, 10, 21:3, 6, 7, r. 2, 10, 14, 22:1, 3, 6, 23:1, 6, 24:1, 3, 6, 25:1, 6, 27:1, 6, 8, 28:1, 3, 6, 8, 29:1, 4, 7, 10, 30:1, 6, 31:1, 3, 5, 7, 9, 13, r. 8, 32:1, 3, 6, r. 12, 14, 18, 33:1, 3, 5, 6, 8, r. 1, 34:3, 4, 5, 7, e. 37, r. 2, 3, 4, 20, 21, 28, 34, 35:1, 3, 5, 6, r. 1, 13, 16, 37:1, 3, 4, 6, 9, 18, 24, 27, 29, 30, 32, 38:1, 10, 40:1, 5, 8, r. 1, 3, 4, 42 e. 9, 43:1, 44:1, 45:1, 4, 46:4, 14, r. 3, 9, 12, 47:1, 3, 5, 7, r. 3, 48:1, 15, 49:1, 4, 50:1, 3, 5, 52:1, 3, 6, 11, r. 1, 3, 12, 14, 17, 20, 53:1, 3, r. 3, 9, 54:2, 6, e. 21, r. 2, 11, 12, 13, 14, 55:3, 56:1, 3, 4, 57:1, 5, 59:1, 3, 6, 62:1, 3, 4, 7, 8, 9, 10, 63:3, 5, 12, r. 7, 64:1, 3, 65:1, 4, 8, 66:1, 3, 68:3, 5, 69:3, 9, 14, 70:1, 3, 6, 71:1, 3, 12, 72:3, 73:1, 3, 74:1, 9, r. 1, 8, 75:1, 3, 76:1, 3, 78:1, 3, 6, 8, r. 5, 6, 13, 15, 79:1, 3, 80:1, 3, 6, r. 1, 82:1, 3, 4, r. 7, 11, 83:3, r. 2, 84:1, 3, 85:1, 2, 3, 86:3, 11, 14, 87:1, 3, 19, r. 3, 88:1, 3, r. 5, 89:3, 91:1, 2, 4, 6, 7, 22, r. 9, 92:1, 2, 3, 4, r. 6, 10, 15, 93 r. 4, 94:1, 3, 98:1, 13, 15, r. 2, 99:2, r. 9, 100:3, r. 6, 8, 9, 103 r. 5, 104:1, 3, 10, 16, r. 7, 12, 105:1, 3, 4, 11, 15, 20, 24, r. 1, 4, 106:12, 108:1, 2, e. 32, r. 27, s. 1, 109:3, 112:4, 113:1, 4, r. 13, 114 r. 3, 4, 115:1, 116 r. 3, 117:1, 15, 118:1, 119:1, 10, 120:1, 121:1, 4, r. 4, 15, 17, 122:3, r. 1, 8, 9, 11, 123 r. 5, 124:7, 125:1, 3, 126:1, 127:1, 3, 4, 6, 7, 8, 128:1, 3, 5, 6, 129:2, r. 4, 130:7, r. 6, s. 2, 132:3, 5, 9, 133:1, 3, s. 1, 134:1, 3, 4, 135:3, 136:1, 3, r. 8, 138:1, 7, 139:3, 140:1, 141:1, 3, 142:9, r. 5, 7, 143:1, 3, 8, 11, r. 6, 9, 144:1, 3, 7, s. 2, 146:1, 3, 4, 18, e. 23, 147:5, 13, r. 5, 8, 148:1, 3, 149:1, 2, 3, 12, r. 7, 8, 24, 150:3, 15, 18, 151:1, 3, 152:1, 3, 4, 8, 10, 19, 21, 23, 24, r. 2, 5, 9, 153:1, 3, 154:1, 3, 4, r. 5, 155:1, 3, 6, 156:1, 6, e. 17, 157:4, 5, 158:1, 4, 6, 159:1, 3, 4, 160:7, 9, 16, 17, 21, 161:1, 3, 4, 162:1, 11, 163:1, 4, 7, r. 7, 164:1, 10, r. 9, 165:1, 3, 167:4, 169:1, r. 5, 170:1,

6, 172:1, 3, 6, 9, 176:12, 178 r. 6, 181:1, 3, 5, 182:1, 5, r. 6, 8, 183:5, 184:4, 186:4, e. 9, 194:1, 196 r. 6, 7, 8, 198 r. 3, 199:1, 3, 4, r. 6, 7, 8, 13, 14, 200:1, 3, 4, 13, r. 9, 201:1, 3, 202:1, 3, 4, r. 6, s. 1, 2, 203:1, 3, 4, 8, 11, r. 6, 9, 13, 15, 18, 22, 204:1, 3, 5, 8, r. 9, 205:1, 3, 206:1, 3, 207:1, 3, 209:1, 210:1, 3, 5, r. 6, 14, 19, 211:1, 5, r. 1, 2, 6, 215:3, 4, 216:3, 217:1, 3, 7, 14, 17, r. 5, 218:15, r. 3, 10, 12, 221:3, 4, r. 4, 224:1, 3, 5, 225:1, 3, 4, 226:1, 3, 4, 7, 14, 16, r. 4, 6, 13, 227:1, 3, 4, 14, 22, r. 4, 10, 16, 21, s. 2, 4, 228:7, 232:1, 5, r. 5, 233:1, 3, 4, r. 2, 234 r. 2, 236:5, 237:1, 3, 238:1, 3, 6, 240:3, 241:1, 3, 11, 13, r. 3, 242:1, 3, 6, 243:1, 3, 6, 7, 10, 11, 12, 17, r. 1, 10, 244:1, 3, 5, 8, r. 3, 4, 7, 245:1, 5, 8, 246:1, 3, 4, 247:1, 3, 5, 6, 249:16, 250:3, 11, 15, 18, r. 8, 22, 251:1, 3, 5, 252:10, 254:9, 256:1, 5, r. 8, 257 r. 2, 5, 11, 258:6, 260:2, 6, 13, r. 1, 3, 5, 7, 12, 261 r. 1, 263:2, 7, 11, 265:4, 267:1, 3, s. 3, 269:1, 3, 4, 270:1, 3, 271:1, 3, 279:12, 281:1, 6, 7, 282:1, 3, 4, 6, 288 r. 4, 289 r. 4, 5, 290 r. 8, 292:3, 4, r. 6, 293:1, 4, 5, 8, s. 1, 294:5, r. 2, 3, 4, 6, 9, 11, 295:1, 4, 10, 19, r. 5, 6, 9, 297 r. 5, 298:7, 11, r. 4, 7, 299 r. 9, 13, 300:5, LUGAL] 12 r. 7, 14:4, 5, r. 13, 17:4, r. 5, 21:1, 26 r. 2, 30:3, 37 r. 5, 40:3, 43:3, 48:3, 57:3, 63:1, 66:4, 125 r. 9, 137 r. 8, 142:7, 144:4, 149:5, 150:1, 152:20, r. 18, 182:3, 194 r. 10, 205 r. 2, 210 r. 1, 230:3, 240:1, 250 r. 23, 256:2, 268:1, 285:3, 291: 11, 295:3, LUGA[L 98:3, 114:1, 130 s. 2, 216:1, 270:11, LUGA[L] 178 e. 11, LUGA]L 45:7, 239:1, LUG[AL 7 r. 1, 38:3, 44 r. 1, 46 r. 6, 69:1, 92 r. 8, 109:2, 5, 117 r. 6, 138:5, 162:3, 266:1, 288 r. 2, 291 r. 14, LUG[AL] 23:3, 292:1, LUG]AL 55:1, 72:1, 124:4, 170:4, 203:15, 215:1, 269:14, 291:12, r. 6, LU[GAL 14:8, 20:8, 29 r. 7, 69:15, 16, 83:1, 143 r. 3, 232 r. 10, 246:10, 276 r. 2, LU[GAL] 27:3, 146: 10, 204 r. 1, 251:13, LU]GAL 6:1, 34:1, 54:1, 86:1, 100:1, 124:2, 137 r. 1, 150 r. 13, 194:3, 237:8, 250 r. 3, 299 r. 2, 300 r. 4, LU]GA[L 2:1, L[UGAL 106:8, 113 r. 7, 130:4, 132:1, 141:8, 148 r. 5, 156:5, 170:3, 235:5, 250:1, 265:1, 281:3, 291 r. 10, L]UGAL 37:24, 121 e. 20, 239:3, 250 r. 2, 285 r. 5, L]UG[AL 299:6, [LUGAL 14:1, 19:1, 58:6, 75:5, 92: 15, 101:3, 106:3, 112 r. 4, 122:1, 124:5, 135:1, 140:3, 150 r. 14, 152 r. 19, 157:1, 159:7, 211:3, 221:1, 232:3, r. 9, 290:11, 291 r. 7, 11, 12, 294 r. 13, [LUGAL] 6:5, 25:3, 68:1, 71:8, 89:7, 152 r. 3, 180:3, 205:10, 298 r. 5, [LUGA]L 46 r. 10, [LUG]AL 2:3, 69:8, 86:5, 89:1, [LU]GAL 15 e. 18, 63 r. 1, 15, 67:4, 152 e. 27, 215 r. 3, [L]UGAL 37:20, 67 r. 1, 106:6, 156 r. 8, LUGAL-*šú-nu* 90 r. 1, 173:3, [LU]GAL-*šú-nu* 90 r. 5, LUGAL.MEŠ 282 r. 2, LUGAL.MEŠ-*ni* 260 r. 8, MAN 15:3, 6, 74:3, 6, 126:3, 4, 7, r. 9, 12, 15, 189:3, 256 r. 4, 291 r. 5,

**šarrû** "to begin": *ú-s[ar-ri]* 249:13, *ú-sa-[ri-ia]* 275:3,

**šarrūtu** "kingship": LUGAL-*u-t[e* 90 r. 8, [LUGAL]-*ú-tú* 90 r. 10, *šar]-ru-tú* 219:1,

**šartinnu** see *sartinnu,*

**šāru** "wind": *šá-a-r[u]* 249:6, *šá]-a-ru* 108 r. 26,

**šasû** see *sasû,*

**šasumu** (mng. uncert.): *šá-su-ma-[te]* 27:11,

**šāši** "her": *ša-ši-ma* 108:16,

**šaššūgu** (a tree): GIŠ.*šá-áš-šu-gi* 294:16,

**šāšu** "him": *ša-šú* 254:16, *šá-šú* 54 r. 16, *šá-a-šu* 35:27, *šá-a-šú* 91:17,

**šattu** "year": MU.AN.NA 15:15, 218 r. 4, MU.A[N.NA] 122 r. 4,

**šatû** "to drink": *li-is-si-u* 106:21,

**šaṭāru** "to write": *áš-ṭa-ru-u-ni* 121:12, *a-sa-ṭar* 232 r. 9, 295:19, [*a-s*]*a-ṭar* 48:15, *i-sa-ṭar* 218:13, 250 r. 25, *i-sa-ṭa-ru* 52 e. 22, *ni-sa-ṭar* 250 r. 8, *šá-ṭi-ir*] 283:3,

**ša-bēti-šanie** "lackey": LÚ.*šá*—É—2-*e* 215:15,

**ša-bēt-kūdini** "mule stable attendant": LÚ.*ša*—É—*ku-din* 79:4, 13, r. 1, LÚ.*šá*—É—*ku-din* 200 r. 9, L]Ú.*šá*—É—*ku-din* 48:4,

**ša-bīrti** "garrison troops": LÚ.*ša*—HAL.ṢU.[MEŠ] 4 r. 3,

**ša-lišāni** "informer": LÚ.EME 55:5,

**ša-maṣṣarti** "guard": LÚ.*šá*—EN.NUN 163:5, r. 9,

**ša-muhhi-āli** "city overseer": LÚ.*šá*—UGU—URU 213 r. 1,

**ša-muhhi-bēti** "overseer of the household": LÚ.*šá*—UGU—É 245:9, [L]Ú.*šá*—UGU—É 254:13,

**ša-pān-ekalli** "palace superintendent": LÚ.*šá*—IGI—KUR 295 r. 11,

**ša-pēthalli** "cavalryman": *ša*—BAD.HAL-*a-[te* 35 r. 2, *ša*—LÚ.BAD.HAL 246 r. 7, LÚ.*ša*—BAD.HAL.MEŠ] 251:4, LÚ.*š[a*—BAD.HAL.MEŠ] 251:9, LÚ.*ša*—BAD.[HAL.ME]Š-*ma* 251:15, [LÚ.*šá*]—*pet-hal* 44 r. 1, LÚ.*šá*—*pet-hal-[a-t]e* 215:13, LÚ.*šá*—*pet-hal-la-ti* 32 s. 1, LÚ.*šá*—BAD.HAL-*l[i]* 34 r. 18,

**ša-qurbūti** "royal bodyguard": LÚ.*qur-bu-te* 59: 5, 78:14, 120:6, 126:8, 207:4, 215 r. 2, 227:7, LÚ.*qur-bu-[te* 208:3, LÚ.*qur]-bu-te* 109:11, [LÚ.*qur]-bu-te* 82 r. 8, [LÚ.*q]ur-bu-te* 82 r. 10, LÚ.*qur-bu-ti* 31:21, 37:19, 104:7, r. 9, 279 r. 2, LÚ.*qur-b[u-ti]* 279 r. 8, LÚ.*q[ur-b]u-ti* 98:4, LÚ.*q[u]r-[b]u-ti* 74:5, L[Ú.*qur-bu-t*]*i* 98:8, L]Ú.*qur-bu-ti* 31:14, [LÚ.*q]ur-bu-ti* 74 r. 5, LÚ.*qur-bu-ti-ma* 104 r. 1, LÚ.*qur-bu-tú* 43:7, 105:6, LÚ.*qur-bu-[tú]* 204:8, 262:7, LÚ.*qur-bu-u-ti* 15:10,

**ša-rēši** "eunuch": LÚ.SAG 95 r. 4, 182:9, 218 r. 2, 245:9, LÚ.SA[G] 48 r. 2, 170:5, LÚ.S[AG 34:10, 137:2, L]Ú.SAG 183:3, L]Ú.S[A]G 181:6, LÚ.SAG.MEŠ 91:5, 11, 291 r. 7, LÚ.SAG.MEŠ-*ia* 32:7, r. 1,

**ša-šīmi** "bought slave": LÚ.ŠÁ[M] 35 r. 12, [LÚ.Š]ÁM 150:17, LÚ.ŠÁM.MEŠ 150:13, [LÚ.ŠÁM].MEŠ 150:12,

**ša-ziqni** "bearded (courtier)": LÚ.*ša*—[*ziq*]-*ni* 294 r. 8, LÚ.*ša*—$SU_6$.MEŠ 91:11,

**še'u** "corn": [ŠE 289 r. 1,

**šemû** see *šamû,*

**šēpu** "foot": GÌR.[2 108 r. 2, GÌR.2 24:16, 50:7, 104:17, GÌR.2-*šú* 108 r. 13, GÌR.2.ME-*ia* 74 r. 10, GÌR.2.MEŠ 35:27, 88:4, 130:4, [G]ÌR.2.[MEŠ-*ka*] 146 r. 10, GÌR.2.MEŠ-*ni* 95 e. 17,

**šî** "she, it": *ši-i* 104:14, 164 r. 11, 13, 233:7, 246 r. 4,

**šiāhu** "earnest talk(?)": *ši-a-hu* 126 r. 14, 243 e. 20,

**šiāru** "tomorrow": *ši-a-ri* 104 r. 5,

**šiāṣu** "to diminish": *i-si-ṣu* 21 r. 4,

**šiāṭu** "to be negligent": *i*]-*si-a-aṭ* 273:3, *ni-si-[aṭ* 106:5, *ni-ši-aṭ* 113 r. 9, *še-e-ṭu* 211 r. 4,

**šibšutu** "log, door-beam": GIŠ.ŠÚ.A 34 r. 5, GIŠ.[ŠÚ.A.MEŠ] 6:7, GIŠ.ŠÚ.A.MEŠ 25:14, r. 5, 43:9, 295: 25, GIŠ.ŠÚ.A].MEŠ 43:6, GIŠ.Š[Ú.A.MEŠ 26 r. 6, [GIŠ.ŠÚ.A.MEŠ 25 r. 2, 34 r. 27,

**šību** "witness": [LÚ.IGI].MEŠ-*ia* 150 r. 5,

**šiddu** "long side; along": *šid-di* 34 r. 14, 84:6,

226 r. 19, *ši*[*d-di* 33 r. 5, *ši-du* 103 r. 1, U]Š 90 r. 8,

**šihlu** "second-best": *ši-ih-li* 284 r. 14, 295:20,

**šikin ṭēmi** "commandant": [LÚ].*ši-kin*—[*ṭè-mi*] 244:9,

**šina** "they": *ši-i-na* 101:4, *ši-na* 290:2, 295 e. 27, r. 2,

**šipirtu** "message": *ši-bir-te* 117:3, *ši*-[*pir-tu* 165:9,

**šīr šumê** "roasted meat; scent, whiff": *ši-ir*—*šu-me-e* 113:14,

**šīru** "flesh": UZU.MEŠ-*ni* 218:12,

**šīti** "she, it": *ši-i-te* 52 r. 11, *ši-i-ti* 74:6, 162 r. 4, *ši-ti-i-ni* 295 r. 9, *ši-ti-ni* 19 s. 1, 96 r. 4, 112 e. 8, *ši-ti-ni*] 221:5,

**šiṭru** (mng. uncert.): *ši-ṭi-ri-šá* 295 r. 24,

**šû** "he": *šu-u* 1:11, 12 r. 3, 39:2, 83 r. 7, 84 r. 5, 148:6, 150 r. 8, 152 r. 12, 196:10, r. 2, 199:11, r. 10, 218:5, 226 r. 7, 241:6, 294:7, 295 r. 14, *šu*-[*u* 220:7, [*š*]*u-u* 196 r. 3, 277:8, *šu-ú* 41:3, 88:11, 92:7, r. 16, 126 r. 14, 129:3, 150:5, 197 r. 10, 199:14, 16, 200:10, 210:16, 17, 217 r. 2, 228:4, 243 r. 6, 245 r. 6, 278:1, *šu*-[*ú* 55:5, *š*]*u-ú* 278:3, [*šu*]-*ú* 102:5, 105:12, *šú-u* 53:4, 58:2, 61 r. 9, 217:18, 284 r. 7, 287:4, *šú-ú* 124:6, 211 r. 4,

**šubtu** "seat, ambush": *šu-ub-te-šú-nu* 33 r. 12, *šu-ub-tú* 32 e. 20,

**šuh** "concerning, as to": *šu-uh* 21 r. 1, 9,

**šuharruru** "to lay waste": *ú-sa-ha-ri-ri* 260 r. 9,

**šulmu** "health, well-being": *šul-me* 143 r. 3, 172 r. 5, *šul-mu* 31 r. 19, 48:3, 49:3, 50:3, 52:3, 53:3, 56:3, 62:3, 84:3, 144:4, 5, 150:3, 151:3, 158:4, 206:3, 210:3, 4, 241:3, 281:3, 4, 5, 6, *šul-mu*] 63:3, *šul-m*[*u* 250:3, *šul*-[*mu* 157:4, *šul*-[*m*]*u* 156:5, *šul*]-*mu* 72:3, *šu*[*l-mu*] 29:3, *š*]*ul-mu* 55:3, [*šul-mu* 122:3, 144:3, [*šu*]*l-mu* 143:6, DI 216:3, DI-*me* 18 r. 3, DI-[*me* 221:10, DI-*me-ia* 95:4, DI-*mu* 1:3, 4, 5, 2:2, 3, 4, 3:2, 3, 4, 11:3, 14:3, 4, 5, 15:4, 16:3, 17:3, 19:3, 21:3, 5, 22:3, 23:3, 24:3, 25:3, 5, 27:3, 5, 28:3, 5, 29:5, 30:5, 31:3, 4, 32:3, 5, 33:3, 4, 35:3, 37:3, 40:3, 43:3, 44:2, 45:2, 47:3, 4, 6, 57:3, 59:3, 64:3, 65:3, 10, 68:3, 69:3, 70:3, 71:3, 73:3, 74:3, 75:3, 78:3, 79:3, 80:3, 6, 81:3, 4, 82:3, 83:3, 85:2, 88:3, 89:3, 91:2, 92:2, 3, 4, 94:3, 96:3, 98:3, 100:3, 104:3, 105:3, 108:2, 4, 126:3, 127:3, 5, 128:3, 5, 132:3, 4, 133:3, 135:3, 136:3, 140:3, 146:3, 147:3, 148:3, 149:2, 152:3, 154:3, 155:3, 161:3, 162:3, 163:3, 165:3, 168:3, 172:3, 181:3, 182:3, 194:3, 199:3, 200:3, 202:3, 203:3, 204:3, 205:3, 211:3, 4, 213:3, 214 e. 3, 217:3, 221:13, 224:3, 225:3, 226: 3, 227:3, 233:3, 237:3, 238:3, 239:3, 240:3, 242:3, r. 3, 243:3, 244:3, 4, 8, 245:5, 6, 7, 246:3, 267:3, 282:3, 293:4, 295:3, DI-*mu*] 18:3, 34:3, 76:3, 110: 3, 207:3, 270:3, DI-*m*[*u* 30:3, 221:3, DI-*m*[*u*] 47:8, DI-*m*]*u* 38:3, 143:3, DI-[*mu* 218 r. 13, DI-[*mu*] 11:4, 15:3, DI]-*mu* 6:3, 66:3, 134:3, 153:3, 159:3, 170:3, 201:3, 256:1, D[I-*mu* 141:3, 232:3, D[I-*m*]*u* 15:5, D]I-*mu* 20:3, 86:3, 87:3, 97:3, 215:3, 247:3, 269:3, 292:3, [DI-*mu* 6:4, 5, 17:4, 5, 18:4, 5, 22:5, 34:4, 35:4, 37:4, 40:4, 204:4, 251:3, 271:3, [DI-*mu*] 11:5, 270:4, [DI]-*mu* 23:5, [D]I-*mu* 24:5, 128:4,

**šumēlu** "left, south": KAB 63:15, K[AB 46 r. 5, 150 229 e. 12,

**šumma** "if": *šum-ma* 52 r. 17, 203 r. 10, 243 r. 11, [*šum-ma* 178 r. 1, *š*]*um-mu* 54 r. 4, [*š*]*um-mu* 182 r. 8, *šúm-ma* 45 r. 3, 68:7, 103 r. 5, 117:16, 20, 123 r. 2, 130 r. 8, 133 r. 3, 154 r. 2, 197 r. 3, 202:5, r. 17, 205 r. 6, 227 r. 22, s. 2, 295 r. 6, 7, 8, 25, 26, 298 r. 7, *šúm-m*[*a* 233 r. 1, *šú*]*m-ma* 227:14, *š*[*úm-ma*] 258:6, [*šúm-m*]*a* 105:11, 133 s. 1, 137 r. 3, [*šú*]*m-ma* 256 r. 4, [*š*]*úm-ma* 256:7, *šúm-mu* 31 r. 14, 37:10, 82 r. 12, 91 r. 2, 3, 97 r. 3, 106:22, 200:6, 213 r. 2, 250:15, 272 r. 2, 289 e. 9, *šúm-mu*] 106:3, *šúm-m*[*u*] 37 r. 17, *šú*[*m-mu*] 31 r. 27, 126:11, *šú*]*m-mu* 45 r. 5, [*šúm-mu*] 112 r. 2, [*šúm-m*]*u* 112 r. 1, [*šú*]*m-mu* 32 r. 7, 106:5, BE-*ma* 2 r. 2, 11 r. 9,

**šumu** "name": *šúm* 8 r. 3, MU-*ku-nu* 34:26, MU.MEŠ 282:5, [M]U.MEŠ 282 r. 2, MU.MEŠ-*šú* 48:13, MU.MEŠ-*šú-nu* 87:12, [M]U.MEŠ-*šú-nu* 282 r. 4,

**šunu** "they": *šu-nu* 19 r. 7, 21:17, 19, r. 18, 32 r. 7, s. 1, 34 r. 29, 37 r. 10, 21, 67:7, 79:12, 84 r. 8, 91:12, 94:6, 95:11, 96 r. 10, 100 r. 15, 103 r. 1, 139:6, 10, 149:5, 6, 7, 20, 22, r. 1, 150 r. 4, 17, 160:18, 225:11, 270 s. 4, 298 r. 12, *šu-nu*] 56:14, *š*[*u-nu*] 106:20, *š*]*u-nu* 35 r. 2, [*šu-nu*] 106:17, 186:5, [*šu-n*]*u* 36:4, 78 r. 7, *šu-nu-ni* 44 r. 4, 187:8, [*šu-n*]*u-u-ni* 55:5, *šú-na-šú-nu* 52:20, *šú-nu* 52:7, 64:9, 104:4, 105:20, 108:21, 126 r. 2, 5, 217 s. 4, 228:9, 232 r. 6, 250:9, 257:5, 284 r. 10, *šú-n*[*u* 11 r. 6, *šú-nu-ni* 48:14, 105 r. 3,

**šuqultu** "weight": [K]I.LAL-*šu* 271 r. 2,

**šurmēnu** "cypress": GIŠ.ŠUR.M[AN 281 r. 2,

**šūtu** "he": *šu-tu-ma*] 200 r. 3, *šu-tú* 46:9, 54 r. 6, 164 r. 1, 182:9, *šu-t*]*ú* 63:13, *š*]*u-tú* 54:3, [*šu*]-*tú* 63 r. 16, 277:4, *šu-tú-ni*] 142:8, *šu-u-tu* 98 r. 8, *šu-u*-[*tu*] 182 r. 7, *šu-u-tú* 25:12, 37:17, 154:7, 169 r. 5, 293:10, *šu-ú-tu-u-ni* 91 e. 24, *šú-u-tú* 52:9, r. 8, 58:1,

**tabāku** "to pour, shed": [*a-tab-ba-ak*] 108:20, *it-bu-uk* 255:6, *it-ta-ad-bu-ku* 249:12, *i-du-ba-ka-nu-ni* 43:11, *i-ta-bu-ku* 108:19, *t*[*a-t*]*a-ba-ak* 108 r. 24,

**tabku** "stored grain": ŠE.*tab-k*[*i* 248 r. 2, Š[E.*tab-ki* 250 r. 3, [ŠE.*ta*]*b-ku* 250 r. 10, ŠE].*tab-ku* 250 r. 4, ŠE.*tab-ku* 126:14, 250 r. 7, 17, 19, ŠE.*tab*-[*ku* 82 r. 5, ŠE.*tab*]-*ku* 250 r. 12,

**tabrību** "red wool": SÍG.*tab-ri-bu* 28:9,

**tabû** "to rise, get up; (Š) to raise": *i-tab-ba* 98:12, *ni-tab-ba* 98:8, *ša-at-bu-e* 297:12, *ú-sat-bi-šu* 35:15, *ú-š*]*at-ba-šú-nu-u-ni* 57:6, *ú-ša-at-ba* 297 r. 3, *ú-šá-da-ba* 58:9,

**tadānu** "to give, sell; (Š) to collect": *ad-da-na-áš-šú-nu-u-ni* 295 r. 16, *ad-din* 124:4, *at-ti-din* 242 r. 3, *at-ti-di*-[*ni*] 77 r. 3, *a-dan-na* 56 r. 4, *a-da-an* 25 r. 3, 32 r. 7, 289:7, *a-da-n*[*a*] 284 r. 3, *a-di-a-kan-ni* 31 r. 17, *a-di-na-kan-ni* 121:7, *a-di-nu-ni* 108 r. 17, 291 r. 9, *a-tan-na* 252 r. 7, *a-tan-na-šú-nu* 126:17, *a-t*[*an-na-šú-nu*] 126:14, *a-ta-na-áš*-[*ši-na* 259:3, *a-ta-n*[*a-x* 259 r. 4, *a-ti-din* 56 r. 7, 243 e. 18, 291 r. 4, *a-ti-din*] 291 r. 13, *din* 296 r. 1, *di-i-ni* 56:6, *di-ni* 121:14, *di-ni*] 280 r. 2, [*di*]-*ni* 269:8, *id-da-na-šú-nu* 52 r. 5, *it-tan-na* 122:8, *it-tan-nu-ni* 57:8, *i-dan-u-ni* 15 r. 14, *i-da-an* 92:8, *i-da-na* 270 s. 3, *i-da-nu-ni* 100 r. 11, *i-da-nu-ni-šú-nu* 257 r. 1, *i-di-in* 97 r. 1, *i-di-i-ni* 145 r. 12, *i-di-na* 260 r. 5, [*i-d*]*i-na-an-ni* 121 r. 1, *i-d*]*i-na-áš-šu* 188:4, *i-di-na-ni* 121 r. 18, *i-di-na-šú-u-ni* 218:11, *i-di-nu* 53 r. 8, *i-du-nu* 53 r. 11, 100:16, *i-ta-an-na* 79:8, *i-ta-an-nu* 21 r. 9, *i-ta-n*]*a-áš-šu* 188:6, *i-ta-n*[*u* 289 r. 5, *i-ta-nu-šu* 35:30, *i-ti-din* 218:10, *i-ti*-[*din*] 78 r. 1, 3, *la-ad-di-in-ši-na* 295 r. 12, *la-d*[*in*] 298 r. 6, *la*]-*di-na-áš-šú-nu* 295:14, [*l*]*id-din* 163 e. 15, *lid-di-nu* 246 r. 2, 294 r. 5, *lid-di-nu-niš-šú* 246 r. 6, *li-din* 31 s. 4, 34 r. 3, 22, [*l*]*i-di-na-ka* 260 r. 3, *li-di-nu-ni* 253 r. 2, *li-di-n*[*u-nik-ka* 148:5, *li-di-nu-u-ni* 232:7, *ni-da-an* 226 r. 12, *ni-*[*d*]*a-nu-ni* 74:4, *ta-ad*]*-nu-ni* 37 r. 14, [*ta*]*-a-din* 291 e. 14, *ta-da-an-ni* 149 r. 21, *ta-da-na-na-a-ši* 35:22, *ta-din* 98 r. 6, *ú-šá-da-an* 150:8, SUM-*an* 54 r. 7, SUM-[*an*] 34 r. 22, SUM-*ka* 169:12, SUM-*ka-nu-ni* 264:6,

**tāhāzu** "battle": MÈ] 146 r. 7,

**tahūmu** "border": *t*]*a-hu-ma-*[*ni*] 252:9, *ta-hu-ma-t*[*e* 30:7, *ta-hu-me* 52:8, 129:5, 217 r. 6, 223:6, *ta-hu-me*] 33 r. 2, *ta-hu-m*[*e*] 84 r. 1, *ta-hu-me-ku-nu* 2 r. 2, *ta-hu-me-šu* 217 r. 10, *ta-hu-mi-šú* 131:2, *ta-hu-mì-i-ni* 221:7, *ta-hu-u-me* 190 r. 1, *ta-hu*]*-ú-me* 31 r. 3,

**takālu** "to trust": *tak-lu* 204:16,

**tallaktu** "wagon": GIŠ.*tal-*[*lak-a-te*] 280 r. 1, GIŠ.*tal-lak*.MEŠ 48:9, 295 r. 23,

**tallu** "crossbar": *tal-li* 294:16,

**talmīdu** "apprentice": LÚ.*tal-mi-da-*[*ni* 56:14,

**tamītu** "oath": [*t*]*a-mit-tú* 53:24,

**tamkāru** "merchant": LÚ.DAM.QAR 150:4, r. 6, 218 r. 9, LÚ.DAM.QAR-*ni-ni* 149 r. 22, LÚ.DAM.QAR.MEŠ 143:9, 202:9, 224:4, L[Ú.DAM.QAR.MEŠ] 143: 7, LÚ.DAM.QAR.MEŠ-*ia* 143 r. 4, LÚ.DAM.QAR.MEŠ-*šu* 143 r. 5,

**tamlû** "terrace": *tam-le-e* 206:7,

**tāmtu** "sea": *ti-amat* 84:7,

**tarāṣu A** "to be proper, all right": *i-ta-at-ra-ṣa-áš-šú* 45 r. 5, *tar-ṣa-at* 97:9, *ta-ri-iṣ*] 233 r. 1, [*ta-ri-iṣ*] 200:6, [*t*]*a-ri-iṣ* 182 r. 9, *ta-ri-ṣi* 200:8,

**tarāṣu B** "to stretch out": *a-ta-ra-aṣ* 297 r. 2,

**tarbāṣu** "courtyard, pen": T]ÙR 151:8,

**targumānu** "interpreter": LÚ.*tar-gu-ma-nu* 203 r. 5, LÚ.*tar-*[*gu-ma-nu*] 212:4, LÚ.*tur-gu-ma-*[*ni* 108 e. 30,

**taskarinnu** "boxwood": GIŠ.KU 294:14,

**tašlīšu** "third man (reading uncert.)": LÚ.3.U$_5$ 14:15, 21:7, 217 s. 1, LÚ.3.[U$_5$ 141:5, LÚ.3.U$_5$-*ia* 33 r. 4, 217 r. 14, LÚ.3.[U$_5$-*ia*] 230:5, LÚ.3.U$_5$.MEŠ 215: 10,

**tebal** (Šubrian word?): *te-bal* 35 r. 11,

**tebû** see *tabû*,

**tēgirtu** "bargain(?)": *te-gír-te* 52:15, r. 8, *te-gír-te-šú-nu* 52 e. 23,

**tēlītu** "yield": *te-lit* 82:8,

**tibnu** "straw": *ti-ib-nu* 233:8, ŠE.IN.NU 16 r. 2, 21 r. 6, ŠE.IN.N[U] 16:6, ŠE.IN.[NU] 21 r. 1, ŠE.IN.NU.MEŠ 119:3, 8, ŠE.IN.[NU.MEŠ] 62 r. 2,

**tikpu** "brick course": *tik-pi* 291:2,

**tillī** "equipment, arms": *til-li* 208:2, 217:10,

**timāli** "yesterday": *i—ti-ma-li* 291 r. 12, *i—ti-ma-l*[*i* 110:7,

**tuānu** (a breed of horses): *tu-a-nu* 171:10,

**tuāru** "(D) to turn": *ú-ta-ra* 105 r. 10, *ú-ta-ra*] 246:10, *ú-te-re* 142:10, *ú-ti-*[*ra*] 46:17,

**tukku** "oppression": *tuk-ka-ni* 149 r. 11,

**tunimmu** (a kind of leather): KUŠ.*tu-nim-me* 152 r. 11,

**tūra** "again": *tu-ra* 53 r. 9, *tu-*[*u-r*]*a* 149:16,

**turtānu** "commander-in-chief": LÚ.*tur-tan* 169 r. 6, LÚ.*tur-ta-nu* 91:13, 93:6, 250:5, [LÚ.*tur-t*]*a-nu* 131:4, LÚ.*tur-ta-nu-šu* 86:8, 166 r. 3,

**ṭābtu** "salt": MUN 242 r. 2,

**ṭēmu** "order, report, mind": *a—ṭè-mu* 227 r. 11, [*ṭ*]*e-e-mu* 70:7, *ṭé-mu* 224:5, *ṭè-en-šú-nu* 1 r. 3, 2 r. 9, 3 r. 9, 115:5, *ṭè-*[*en-šú*]*-nu* 182:7, [*ṭè*]*-en-šú-nu* 158:7, *ṭ*]*è-en-šú-u-ni* 38:7, *ṭè-e-me* 3:6, 31:6, 45:3, 113:3, 144:6, 148:8, 210 r. 20, *ṭè-e-*[*me* 140:4, 279 r. 11, *ṭè*]*-e-me* 34:5, *ṭè-e-mu* 40 e. 23, 42 r. 8, 85:5, 108 s. 1, 113 r. 7, 128:6, 144 r. 7, 169 r. 7, 215:4, 226:8, 246:9, 251:14, 280 e. 13, 281 r. 7, 295:11, *ṭè-e-m*[*u* 128:8, *ṭè-e-m*[*u*] 27:9, *ṭè-e-*[*mu* 144 r. 10, 229:4, *ṭè-e-*[*mu*] 108:4, 155:5, 256 r. 3, *ṭè-*[*e-mu* 92 r. 15, *ṭ*[*è-e-mu* 61:4, *ṭ*]*è-e-mu* 226:17, [*ṭè-e-mu* 34: 6, 86 r. 3, [*ṭè-e-mu*] 25:7, 67 r. 1, 251:6, [*ṭè-e-m*]*u* 109:4, [*ṭè-e*]*-mu* 55:10, *ṭè-e-mu-ma* 98:11, *ṭ*]*è-e-mu-ma* 54:17, *ṭè-e-mu-ni* 194 r. 9, *ṭè-ma-a-ni* 152: 6, *ṭè-ma-ni* 99:9, *ṭè-me* 2:6, 29 r. 1, 105 r. 10, 115:3, 162:14, 164:3, 165:4, 168:5, 181:4, *ṭè-me*] 22:7, *ṭè-mu* 1:9, 3:16, 130 r. 5, 144:8, 217 r. 3, 268 r. 8, [*ṭè-mu*] 142:9, [*ṭè*]*-mu* 162 r. 5, [*ṭ*]*è-mu* 13:2, 142 r. 4, *ṭè-mu-ma* 46:13, 16, *ṭè-mu-ni*] 136 r. 7, *ṭè-mu-u-ni* 81 r. 4,

**ṭiābu** "to be good": *lu-ṭa-i-*[*bu*] 146 r. 13, *ṭa-a-ba* 132:7, *ṭa-bu-u-ni* 105:15, DÙG 2:5, 3:5, 15:6, DÙG] 14:6, 17:6, 18:6, 249:16, [DÙG] 6:6, [DÙ]G 1:6, DÙG.GA 54 r. 1, 148 r. 6, 152:20, 203:12, 217:15, 276 r. 3, 297 r. 5, 299 r. 10, DÙG.GA] 38:10, 42 r. 1, 69:16, 78 r. 6, 160:16, 281:7, DÙG].GA 35:6, D[ÙG.GA] 127:8, DÙG.GA-*ku-nu* 210 r. 5, DÙG.G]A-*ma* 203:17, DÙG.GA.MEŠ 210:12, DÙG.GA.MEŠ] 106: 23,

**ṭūbu** "goodness": *ṭu-bi* 157:6,

**ṭuppu** "tablet": *ṭu*]*p-pi-šú* 289:3, *ṭup-pi-šú-nu* 217:11, [*ṭ*]*up-pu* 294:1, IM 81:1, 213:1, 214:1, [I]M 147:1,

**ṭupšarru** "scribe": LÚ.A.BA 122 r. 7, L]Ú.A.BA 250 r. 24, LÚ.A.BA.MEŠ 269:11,

**u** "and": *u* 31 s. 2, 63:15, 81 r. 1, 126:4, 127:4, 146 r. 7, 196 r. 5, 222:1, [*u* 157:6, *ú* 8 r. 6, 102:3, 147 r. 11, 288 r. 11, *ù* 42 r. 1, 46 r. 5, 52 r. 2, 53:16, 56:13, r. 7, 60:4, 6, 69 r. 5, 90 r. 1, 95:6, 98:8, 105:16, 106:8, 108 r. 15, 18, 23, 113 r. 6, 121:9, 146:6, 164 r. 3, 166 r. 1, 196 r. 11, 211 r. 7, 227 r. 21, 232 r. 3, 250:7, 11, r. 3, 7, 21, 280 r. 7, 288 r. 3, 289:3, 6, e. 8, 9, r. 2, 292 r. 4, [*ù* 108 r. 26, [*ù*] 228:4, 269:11,

**ubālu** "to bring; (Š) to send": *at-tu-bíl* 242:8, *bi-la*] 152 r. 2, *b*[*i-la* 14:13, [*it-tu-bi-l*]*a-an-ni* 207: 7, *lu-bíl* 210:10, *lu-bi-la* 246 r. 6, *lu-bi-la-na-ši* 104:13, *lu-bi-li* 105:16, *lu-b*[*i-lu-ni*] 246 r. 2, *lu-bi-lu-ni-šu-nu-u* 139:8, *lu-bi-lu-u-ni* 241:9, *lu-še-bi-la* 100 r. 9, 294 r. 3, 9, [*ni-t*]*u-bíl* 42 r. 7, *nu-se-bi-la* 250 r. 8, *nu-še-ba-lu-u-ni* 233:10, *še-bi-la* 203 r. 12, 254:5, [*še*]*-bi-la* 28:10, *še-bi-la-áš-šú-nu* 202:8, *še-bi-la-a-ni* 250 r. 5, *tu-bal* 115:11, *tú-ba-la* 129 r. 5, *tú-bi-la-na-a-ši* 104 r. 4, *ub*]*-bal-u-ni-šú* 58:3, *u*[*b-ba-la*] 224 r. 1, [*u*]*s-s*[*e-bi-la*] 132 r. 1, *ú-bal* 130:3, 150 r. 13, 277 r. 5, *ú-bal-an-ni* 79 r. 13, *ú-bal-ši* 293 s. 1, *ú-bal-u-ni-šú* 218 r. 12, *ú-bal-u-ni-šú-nu* 227 s. 3, *ú-bal-*[*x* 34:31, *ú-ba-al-u-ni* 100 r. 5, *ú-ba-la* 147 r. 7, 152 r. 3, 215 r. 6, *ú*]*-ba-la-ni* 73:6, *ú-ba-lu-na-ši* 104 r. 11, *ú-ba-lu-ni-šú* 263:5, *ú-bu-lu* 100 r. 3, 105 r. 9, *ú-se-bíl* 228:2, *ú-se-bi-la* 35 r. 16, 149 r. 24, 218:13, 263:9, 285:2, 291:11, 295:20, *ú-se-bi-la*] 149 r. 7, 227 s. 4, *ú-se-*[*bi-la*] 29 r. 8, *ú-s*[*e-bi-l*]*a* 228 r. 6, [*ú-se-bi-la*] 138:7, [*ú-s*]*e-bi-la* 277:3, [*ú*]*-se-bi-la* 48:16, 232 r. 10, *ú-se-bi-la-šu* 241:12, r. 4, *ú-se-bi-la-šú* 71 r. 1, 257 r. 11, *ú-se-bi-la-*[*šú-nu*] 116 r. 4, [*ú-se-bi-l*]*a-šú-nu* 183 r. 4, *ú-še-bal* 203 r. 7, *ú-še-*

*bal-a-ni* 105:5, *ú-še-bal-a-šú* 218 r. 13, *ú-še-bal-šú-nu* 202 s. 1, *ú-še-ba-la* 254:7,

**udê** "utensils": *ú-de-e* 206:11,

**udīna** "yet": *ú-di-na* 87 r. 8, 88 r. 7, 97:7, *ú-d*]*i-na* 86 r. 2, *ú-*[*di-na*] 97:9, [*ú-d*]*i-na* 112:6, [*ú*]*-di-na* 93 r. 2, *ú-di-ni* 37 r. 15, 105:19, r. 6, 217 s. 2, 246:7, *ú-di-*[*ni* 13:3, *ú-*[*di*]*-ni* 1:11,

**udī-** "alone": *ú-di-ia* 117:13, *ú-di-*[*šú* 34:25,

**udû** "to know": *lu-u-di-ú* 117:16, *l*]*u-u-du-u* 178 e. 12, *nu-ú-da* 40:10, 108 r. 22, 149 r. 22, *tu-da* 227 r. 23, *tu*]*-ú-da* 279:5, r. 6, *ú-da* 15:15, 31 r. 8, 32 r. 19, 67:4, 74:10, r. 1, 91 e. 23, 96 r. 3, 97:14, 105 r. 1, 114 r. 3, 124:2, 149:3, 156 r. 8, 160:9, 200:13, 217:17, 227 r. 4, 233:4, 282:7, 288 r. 10, 289 r. 4, 291 r. 7, 12, *ú-d*[*a* 235:3, *ú-d*[*a*] 146:4, *ú-*[*da*] 186:4, *ú-*[*di*] 211 r. 1, *ú-du-u* 37 r. 10, 90 r. 6, 106:3, *ú-d*[*u-u* 93 r. 7, ZU 169 r. 6,

**uhur** (mng. uncert.): *ú-hur* 121 r. 11,

**ukkušu** "to be delayed": *ú-ki-iš* 37:19,

**ulâ** "or, if not": *ú-la-a* 69:11, 78 r. 9, 15, 104 r. 3, 109:6, 130:5, 133 r. 6, 139:9, 194 r. 8, 200 r. 11, 206 r. 3, 246 r. 3, *ú-*[*la-a*] 146:11, [*ú*]*-la-a* 182 r. 11,

**ullūtu** "levy(?)": *ul-lu-a-te* 3:14, 87:17, *ul-lu-tú* 31 r. 4,

**ullu** (a tree; reading uncert.): GIŠ.UL.MEŠ 35:16,

**ūmâ** "now": *ú-ma-a* 10:6, 12 r. 5, 24:8, 31 r. 10, 35:15, 42 r. 5, 45:7, 46:4, 52 r. 3, 53 r. 7, 54:14, 78:13, 81:5, 14, 82 r. 2, 87:15, 91:7, r. 8, 98 r. 7, 106:22, 108 r. 3, 17, 119:9, 123 r. 4, 125 r. 6, 126 r. 6, 149:16, 152:21, 163 r. 7, 169:13, 172 r. 1, 173:11, 182 r. 4, 194 r. 7, 196 r. 4, 200 r. 9, 203 r. 4, 227:21, 232 r. 1, 241:10, 243:16, r. 2, 8, 257 r. 2, 258:6, 260 r. 11, 288 r. 2, 294 r. 13, 295 r. 4, *ú-ma-a*] 33 r. 3, *ú-ma-*[*a* 108:11, 227 s. 1, *ú-ma-*[*a*] 69:7, *ú-m*]*a-a* 34:8, *ú-*[*ma-a*] 51:2, 298 r. 1, *ú-*[*ma*]*-a* 15 r. 13, *ú*]*-ma-a* 107:2, [*ú-ma-a* 130 s. 1, [*ú-ma*]*-a* 134:8, 137 r. 8, [*ú-m*]*a-a* 46 r. 9, [*ú*]*-ma-a* 38:8, 46 r. 11, 189:3, 190 r. 6,

**umāmu** "animal": *ú-ma-me* 227 r. 9,

**umma** "thus": [*um-ma* 250 r. 23,

**ummânu** "scholar, artist": LÚ.*um-ma-ni* 215:19, 257:3, LÚ.UM.ME.A 294 r. 4,

**umnīnu** "chest": *ú-ni-na-a-te* 56 r. 1, *ú*]*-ni-na-a-ti* 57:7,

**ūmu** "day": UD 243 r. 15, U[D 165:5, 276:1, UD-*me* 35:12, 67:12, 95 r. 3, 107 e. 6, 178:4, 250 r. 10, 13, 17, 294:3, UD-*me*] 250 r. 15, UD-*m*[*e*] 117:16, UD-[*me* 108:17, U[D-*me* 108 r. 18, UD-*me-ni* 206 r. 6, UD-*mi* 263:3, UD-*mì-*[*im*]*-ma* 204:14, UD-*mu* 108:7, 133 r. 10, 150:5, 164:12, 211 r. 9, 216:4, 217 r. 11, UD-[*mu* 211 r. 7, UD-*mu*.MEŠ 217 r. 6, UD-*x*]-KÁM 73:7, 295 r. 26, UD.MEŠ 17 r. 1, 19 r. 8, 78:10, 97:14, 106:18, 148:4, 157:8, 242:12, 250 r. 7, 275:4, 294:5, [UD.MEŠ] 67:7, UD.MEŠ-*te* 250 r. 5, UD.1.KÁM 123 r. 2, 297:10, UD.1.[KÁM 135:5, UD.2.KAM 250:4, UD.2.KÁM 130:10, UD.3.KÁM 111:2, UD.4.KAM 249:6, r. 7, UD.4.KÁM 204 r. 5, UD.5.KAM 281:9, UD.5.KÁM 155:4, UD.6.KÁM 156:12, UD.7.KAM 281:11, UD.10.KÁM 136:4, 295 r. 21, UD.11.KAM 267:4, UD.[11.KÁM] 136:6, UD.11.KÁM 65:5, [UD.1]2.KÁM 137:5, [UD.12.KÁM] 136:7, [UD.13.KÁM 136:8, UD.14.KÁM 192 r. 6, [UD.14.KÁM 136:9, UD.16.[KAM 113 r. 10, UD.17.KAM 115 r. 5, UD.20.KAM 113 r. 12, UD.20.[KAM 267:6, 275:2, UD.20.KÁM 80 r. 5, 162:4, 295 r. 25, UD.22.KAM 126:5, UD.23.KÁM 52:4, UD.24.KÁM 133:11, UD.25.KÁM 117 r. 9, UD.26.KÁM 117 r. 11, 133 r. 5, UD.27.KAM 206:4, UD.27.KÁM 64:4, 133 r. 7, UD.28.KAM 241 r. 1, UD.28.KÁM 64:9, UD.29.KAM 206 r. 4, UD.29.KÁM 64:10, UD.30.KÁM 64:13, 135:4,

**unqu** "signet ring, sealed order": *un-qi* 105:4, 247:6, *un-qu* 98:5, r. 9, 105:8, 234:5,

**unūtu** "utensils, equipment": *a-nu-su-nu* 97:9, *a-*[*nu*]*-su-nu* 31 r. 5, *a-nu-t*[*e* 117 r. 8,

**unzarhu** "domestic slave": LÚ.*un-za-ar-h*[*u*] 243:5,

**urādu** "to descend; (Š) to bring down": [*it*]*-tu-ur-du-u-ni* 34:28, *i-tu-rid* 177:5, *i-tu-ri-di* 96:6, *i-tu-ur-*[*d*]*a* 237:5, *i-tu-ur-du* 21 r. 6, *še-ri-da* 53:12, 142:6, *še-ru-di* 218 r. 7, *tú-ra-da* 260:9, *ú-ra-*[*da*] 199 r. 4, *ú-ra-du-ni* 85 r. 2, *ú-se-ri-da-a* 53:13, *ú-se-ri-du-ni* 32:12, [*ú*]*-še-ra-da-šú-nu* 109:5, *ú-še-ra-ni-ni* 117:19,

**urāsu** "brick mason": LÚ.*ú-*[*ra-si*] 294:1,

**urda ekalli** "palace servant": LÚ.ARAD—É.GAL 294 r. 9,

**urdu** "servant, subject": ARAD 106:8, 150 r. 2, [ARAD 152 r. 18, ARAD-*ka* 1:2, 2:1, 3:1, 11:2, 14:2, 16:2, 23:2, 25:2, 28:2, 29:2, 31:2, 32:2, 33:2, 44:2, 45:2, 47:2, 48:2, 49:2, 52:2, 53:2, 56:2, 59:2, 62:2, 64:2, 65:2, 68:2, 69:2, 70:2, 71:2, 74:2, 75:2, 78:2, 79:2, 80:2, 82:2, 83:2, 84:2, 85:1, 88:2, 89:2, 91:1, 92:1, 94:2, 96:2, 98:2, 104:2, 105:2, 108:1, 110:2, 113:2, 114:2, 117:2, 118:2, 119:2, 121:2, 125:2, 126:2, 127:2, 132:2, 133:2, 135:2, 136:2, 140:2, 141:2, 145:3, 146:2, 149:1, 152:2, 154:2, 155:2, 161:2, 163:2, 164:2, 165:2, 168:2, 169:2, 172:2, 199:2, 200:2, 202:2, 203:2, 205:2, 206:2, 209:2, 210:2, 211:2, 213:2, 214:2, 217:2, 221:2, 224:2, 226:2, 227:2, 233:2, 237:2, 241:2, 242:2, 243:2, 244:2, 245:2, 246:2, 250:2, 265:2, 266:2, 268:3, 281:2, 293:2, ARAD-*k*[*a* 267:2, ARAD-[*ka* 19:2, 122:2, 251:2, 271:2, ARAD-[*ka*] 115:2, [ARAD-*ka* 15:2, 17:2, 18:2, 20:2, 21:2, 22:2, 30:2, 35:2, 37:2, 38:2, 40:2, 43:2, 57:2, 63:2, 73:2, 76:2, 87:2, 97:2, 134:2, 143:2, 144:2, 148:2, 150:2, 151:2, 181:2, 182:2, 194:2, 204:2, 225:2, 232:2, 239:2, 240:2, 270:2, 295:2, [ARAD-*ka*] 34:2, 55:2, 66:2, 72:2, 86:2, 153:2, 159:2, 215:2, [ARAD-*k*]*a* 100:2, 170:2, 269:2, 292:2, [ARAD]-*ka* 6:2, 128:2, 201:2, 207:2, 238:2, 247:2, [ARA]D-*ka* 120:2, 282:2, [AR]AD-*ka* 24:2, 162:2, [A]RAD-*ka* 27:2, 50:2, ARAD-*šú* 108 s. 2, 152:8, r. 5, 228:3, 244 r. 7, [ARA]D-*šú* 228:11, ARAD.MEŠ 54 r. 11, 12, 95:12, 257 r. 7, ARAD.MEŠ-*ia* 220:8, ARAD.MEŠ-*ka* 158:2, ARAD.MEŠ-*ni* 65:8, 138:5, 152:18, [ARA]D.MEŠ-*ni* 50:6, ARAD.MEŠ-*ni-iá* 46:11, ARAD.MEŠ-*ni-iá*] 46:6, [ARAD.MEŠ-*n*]*i-k*[*a*] 156:2, [ARAD].MEŠ-*n*[*i-ka* 157:2, ARAD.[MEŠ-*x*] 256 r. 9, LÚ.ARAD 15 r. 11, 211 r. 3, 236:3, 243:6, LÚ.AR[AD] 100:20, L]Ú.ARAD 160:20, LÚ.ARAD-*ka* 216:2, LÚ.ARAD-*šú* 35 r. 14, LÚ.ARAD.MEŠ 37:29, 32, r. 20, 47:6, 210 r. 6, 14, 211 r. 6, 217:7, 245:7, LÚ.ARAD.M[EŠ] 48 r. 15, LÚ.ARAD].MEŠ 34 r. 2, L]Ú.ARAD.MEŠ 124:7, [LÚ.A]RAD.[MEŠ] 15 r. 1, LÚ.ARAD.MEŠ-*e* 34 r. 4, LÚ].ARAD.M[EŠ]-*ia* 48 r. 11. LÚ.ARAD.MEŠ-*ia* 48:11, 81:12, LÚ.ARAD.MEŠ-*ka* 254:4, LÚ.ARAD.MEŠ-*ni* 53 r. 3, 9, 184:4, 5, 202 r 5, 243:12, 260:5, r. 6, LÚ.ARAD.MEŠ-*ni-ka* 53:12, LÚ.ARAD.MEŠ-*ni-šú* 53:13,

**urhu** "month": ITI 86:4, 242:12, 245 r. 1, 250 r. 5, 16, 18, 20, ITI.MEŠ 126:14,

**urki** "after": EGIR.MEŠ 64 r. 1,

**urkītu** "rearguard": *ur-ke-te* 184:2,

**urkīu** "later, junior": *ur-ki-iu-u* 163 r. 9, *ur-ki-ti* 6 r. 6, *ur-k[i-tú]* 108 r. 23, *ur-ki-ú-te* 24:8,

**urû** "team": *ú-rat* 189:4, *ú-rat*.MEŠ 74 r. 2, *ú-ra-a-a* 74 r. 4, 12, *ú-ru-u* 74:11, 227:15, 16, ANŠE.*ú-[rat* 280:7, ANŠE.*ú-ra-te* 215:8, [ANŠ]E.*ú-ra-te* 215:11, ANŠE.*ú-ra-te-ia* 74 e. 14,

**ussuku** "to assign": *ú-sa-ak* 152:23, *ú-tu-si-i[k* 251 r. 7,

**uṣṣuṣu** "to investigate": *lu-ṣi-ṣi* 105:21, *ú-ṣi-ṣi* 68:7, [*ú-ṣi-ṣi*] 265:5, *ú-ṣu-uṣ* 91 r. 9, *ú-ta-ṣi-ṣi* 54:8, 163 r. 2, 227 r. 20,

**uṣû** "to emerge": *at-[tu-ṣi]* 126:18, *it-tu-ṣi* 86:6, 145:6, *it-[tu-ṣi]* 278:5, *it-tu-ṣu-u-ni* 3 r. 14, 83:5, *it-tu-ṣu-ú-ni* 32:17, *it-tu-uṣ-ṣi* 204 r. 5, *i-tu-ṣi* 87:20, *i-tu-ṣ[i]* 133 r. 2, [*i-tu*]*-ṣu-u-ni* 273:5, *i-tú-ṣi* 223 r. 3, 227:18, *l*]*u-ṣu-u-ni* 17:11, *lu-še-ṣi-šú* 200 r. 10, *lu-še-ṣu-ú-ni* 3 r. 17, *nu-se-ṣi* 296 r. 6, *še-ṣi-[a* 280 r. 5, [*še-ṣi-a* 107:2, *ú-se-ṣi* 4:7, 200 r. 8, [*ú-s*]*e-ṣi* 5 r. 2, *ú-se-ṣi-a* 79:8, 203 r. 21, *ú-se-ṣi-ia-a* 210:8, *ú-se-ṣi-šú-nu* 210 r. 10, *ú-ṣa* 55:13, 260 r. 10, *ú-[ṣe-e* 189:1, *ú-ṣi* 220:9, *ú-ṣi-a* 113 r. 5, *ú-ṣu-ni* 87 r. 9, *ú-ṣu-ni-ni* 257:5, *ú-ṣu-u* 56 r. 10, *ú-[ṣu-u-ni*] 118:11, *ú-še-ṣa* 37:14, 200 r. 15, *ú*]*-še-ṣa-a* 34 r. 35, *ú-še-ṣa-an-ni* 79:6, r. 10, *ú-še-ṣ[u-ni*] 42 r. 2, *ú-še-ṣu-u-ni* 24:9, 32 r. 18, 53 r. 11,

**ušābu** "to sit, dwell": *lu-ši-ib* 210 r. 13, *tu-šab* 108 r. 26, *ú-se-ši-bu* 32 e. 21, *ú-se-ši-ib* 15 r. 12, *ú-šab* 147:8, 14, *ú-še-šá-[ab*] 33 r. 12, *ú-še*]*-šib-ú-n[i*] 8 r. 5, *ú-ši-bu-u-ni* 150:16, *ú-šu-bu* 100:11,

**ušāru** "to be humble, pious": *ú-še-er* 146:16,

**uššuru** "to let go": *ú-še-ra-ni-ni* 117:19,

**utāru** "to exceed": *ut-ru* 246 r. 4, *ut-ru-te* 21 r. 17, *ut*]*-ru-te* 25 r. 2, *ut-ru-u-ti* 121:10,

**uttartu** "large-wheeled chariot": GIŠ.*ut-tar-a-te* 215:7,

**uzuzzu** "to stand, to be present": *it-t[i]-it-su* 11 r. 9, *it-zi* 63 r. 5, *iz-za-az* 136:5, *iz-za-a[z*] 45 r. 4, *i*]*z-za-zu* 35:11, *i-te-et-zi* 149 r. 4, *i-ti-it-zi* 256:10, [*i-t*]*i-ti-is-s[u* 196:12, *i-ti-ti-su* 104:8, *i-za-az* 63:16, *i-za-za* 46 r. 1, 246 r. 5, 298 r. 1, *i-za-zu* 31 r. 6, 32 r. 2, *i-za-z[u-ni*] 254:2, *li-zi-zi* 246 r. 7, 254:6, *li-zi-zu* 32 r. 16, 294 r. 10, *lu-šá-zi-zu* 227 r. 14, *ni-it-te-et-[zi*] 8 r. 2, *ni*]*-za-az* 21:20, *ú-sa-zi-[zu* 50:8, *ú-šá-za-zu* 69 r. 9, *ú-šá-zi-zu-ú-ni* 227:17,

**za''û** (mng. obscure): *ú-za-'u-u-na-ši* 42 r. 7,

**zabālu** "to carry, transport": *a-z*]*a-bíl* 25 r. 3, *i-za-bil-(u)-ni* 4:6, *i-za-bi-lu* 56 r. 2, 111 r. 4, *ni-za-bi-lu-ni* 233:6, *ta-za-bi-la-ni* 34 r. 7, *za-ab-lu* 102:3, *zi-ib-la* 234:9,

**zagru** see *sakāru,*

**zakû** "to be clean, exempt": *ú-za-ka* 33 r. 9, *za-ki-ti* 31:20, *za-ku-a-[ni* 268 r. 5, *za-ku-[e* 288 r. 5, *za-k[u-ti* 268 r. 9, *za-ku-u* 16:7, *z[a-ku-u*] 16:5, LÚ.*za-ku-ú* 199 r. 3,

**zanānu** "to rain": *i-za-nun* 272 r. 2, *i-zi-nu-nu-[ni*] 26 e. 11, *i-z[u-nun*] 274:3, *i-zu-nu-u[n* 273:2, *i-zu-[nu-un*] 275:5, 276 r. 1,

**zaqāpu** "to plant, erect; to attack": *a-za-qa-ap* 148 r. 3, *iz-zu-qu-pu* 45 r. 7, *i-za-qu-pu* 114 r. 2, 227 s. 1, *i-zu-ku-pu* 53 r. 3, *i-zu-qu-pu* 84:7, *i-zu-q[u-pu*] 131:2, [*i-zu-q*]*u-pu* 12 r. 5, *ni-za-qu-pu* 145 r. 13, *zaq-pu* 298:11, *za-qu-[pa* 282:6,

**zar'u** "seed, offspring": NUMUN.MEŠ-*šú-n[u* 14 r. 13, [ŠE].NUMUN 225:15, ŠE.NUMUN 225:4, 11, 289 r. 2, ŠE.NU[MUN] 225:5, ŠE.NUMUN-*šú-nu* 289 e. 8, ŠE.NUMUN.MEŠ 14 r. 5, 82:6, ŠE.NUM[UN.MEŠ] 60:4, ŠE.NU[MUN.MEŠ 15:13, ŠE.NUMUN.MEŠ-*ši-n[a* 259:4, ŠE.NUMUN.MEŠ-[*ši-na*] 259:7, ŠE.NUMUN.MEŠ-*šú-nu* 68:8,

**zēr šarri** "royal line": NUMUN—LUGAL 37 r. 13, 291 r. 7, NU]MUN—LUGAL 37 r. 8,

**ziāqu** "to blow, waft": *i-z[i-qa*] 249:7,

**zēru** see *zar'u,*

**zibbutu** "tail": *zi-ba-te* 90 r. 4, *zi-bu-[tú* 92 r. 14,

**zīnu** "rain": *zi-i-nu*] 275:2, *zi-i-[nu*] 26 e. 9, *z*]*i-i-nu* 273:1, [*zi*]*-i-[nu*] 274:1, see also *zunnu,*

**ziqnu** "beard": SU$_6$.MEŠ 108:25,

**ziqpu** "sapling": *zi-iq-p[i*] 27:7, GIŠ.*ziq-pi* 105 r. 4, GIŠ.*ziq-[pi* 268 e. 16, GIŠ.*zi[q-pi* 268:7,

**zuāzu** "to divide": *ú-za-'i-zu-u-ni* 295:9,

**zūku** "infantry(?)": [LÚ].*zu-ku* 277:11,

**zunnu** "rain": A.[AN 21 r. 3, [A.AN.M]EŠ 272 r. 1, see also *zīnu,*

**zunzurahhu** (a class of soldiers): LÚ.*zu-un-zu-ra-hi* 215:14,

# Index of Names

## *Personal Names*


**Abaliuqunu** (Urarṭian governor): ᵐ*ab-li-uq-nu* 91:14, 16, ᵐ*a-ba-*[*l*]*i-ú-qu-nu* 114:8, ᵐ*a-ba-lu-qu-nu* 84:9,

**Abat-šarri-uṣur** (Mannean emissary): ᵐ*a-bat*—LUGAL—PAB 171 r. 4, ᵐ*a-bat*—MAN—PAB 172:2,

**Abilê:** ᵐ*a-bi-le-e* 115:13,

**Abī-iaqâ** (a Šubrian): ᵐ*a-bi—ia-qa-a* 52:9,

**Abī-rāme** (an Arzuhinaean): ᵐAD—*ra-me* 228: 14,

**Abī-ul-īde** (Chaldean bodyguard): ᵐAD—*ul—i-di* 59:4,

**Adâ** (king of Šurda?): ᵐ*a-da-a* 129 s. 2, 168:3, 190 r. 6, [ᵐ*a-d*]*a-a* 138:2,

**Adad-aplu-iddina** (royal bodyguard): ᵐᵈIM—A—AŠ 98:4,

**Adad-ibni:** ᵐᵈIM—DÙ 241:2, ᵐᵈIM—*ib-ni* 152 r. 9, ᵐU—DÙ 299:2,

**Adad-issīja** (governor of Mazamua): ᵐᵈIM—KI-*ia* 215:2, 217:2, 224:2, ᵐ[ᵈIM—KI-*ia*] 216:2, 221:2, ᵐᵈIM—KI—*ia*] 225:2,

**Adad-rēmanni** (fort of): ᵐ10—*rém-a-ni* 162:7,

**Ahutun:** ᵐ*a-hu-tu-un* 14 r. 9,

**Am-ra'i:** ᵐ*am—ra-i* 138:9,

**Arbailāiu:** ᵐURU.*arba-ìl-a-a* 227:5, 12,

**Argista** (Argišti II, king of Urarṭu): ᵐ*ar-gi-is-ta* 3:15,

**Arije** (ruler of Kumme): ᵐ]*a-ri-e* 102 r. 4, ᵐ*a-ri-e* 95 r. 3, 97:8, 98:10, 100:8, 107:3, 111:4, ᵐ*a-r*[*i-e* 89:12, ᵐ*a-*[*ri-e*] 110:2, 116:2, [ᵐ]*a-ri-*[*e* 236:1, [ᵐ*a-r*]*i-e* 55:7, ᵐ*a-ri*]*-ia-e* 284:1,

**Ariṣâ** (son of Arije?): ᵐ*a-ri-a-ṣa-a* 100:6, ᵐ*a-ri-a-ṣa-*[*a*] 116:4, ᵐ*a*]*-ri-ia-ṣa-a* 284 r. 11, ᵐ*a-ri-ṣa-a* 89:11, 97:8, 110:3, ᵐ*a*]*-ri-ṣa-a* 95 r. 4, ᵐ*ú-ri-ṣa-a* 111:5, 112 r. 5,

**Arzāiu:** ᵐ*ar-za-a-a* 121:3, ᵐ*ar-za-a-*[*a*] 121:13,

**Ašipâ** (governor of Tidu?): ᵐ]*a-ši-pa-a* 21:2, ᵐ*a-ši-pa-a* 24:2, 25:2, 28:2, 46:10, ᵐ*a-ši-pa-a*] 22:2, 30:2, ᵐ*a-ši-pa-*[*a*] 23:2, 27:2, ᵐ[*a*]*-ši-pa-a* 15 r. 2, [ᵐ*a-ši-pa-a*] 29:2,

**Aššūr-ālik-pāni** (Assyrian governor?): ᵐ*aš-šur—a-lik—pa-an* 154:2, ᵐ*aš-šur—a-lik—pa-ni* 152: 2, 161:2, ᵐ*aš-šur—a-lik—pa-ni*] 157:2, ᵐ*aš-šur—a-lik—pa-n*[*i*] 155:2, ᵐ*aš-šur—a-lik—*[*pa-ni*] 153:2, 159:2, ᵐ[*aš-šur—a-lik—pa-ni*] 158:2, [ᵐ*aš-šur—a*]*-lik—pa-ni* 156:3,

**Aššūr-balti-nīši** (palace superintendent): ᵐ*aš-šur*—TÉŠ—UN.MEŠ 242:2,

**Aššūr-bēlu-da'an** (Assyrian governor?): ᵐ*aš-šur*—EN—KALAG-*an* 113:11, 126:2, 127:2,

**Aššūr-bēlu-da''in** (governor of Halziatbar?): ᵐ*aš-šur*—EN—KALAG-*in* 78:2, 79:2, 80:2,

**Aššūr-bēlu-[...]:** ᵐ*aš-šur*—EN-*x*[*x* 155:4,

**Aššūr-bēssunu:** ᵐ*aš-šur—bi-su-nu* 52 r. 16,

**Aššūr-dūr-pānīja** (governor of Šabirešu?): ᵐ*aš-šur*—BÀD—*pa-ni-*[*ia*] 59:2, ᵐ*aš-šur*—BÀD—IGI-*ia* 52:2, 53:2, 55:2, 56:2, ᵐ*aš-šur*—BÀD—IGI]-*ia* 57:2,

**Aššūr-lē'i** (king of Karalla): ᵐ*aš-šur*—ZU 218:10, r. 2, ᵐ*aš-šur*—Z[U 218:3, 7, 219:4,

**Aššūr-pātinu:** ᵐ*aš-šur—pa-ti-nu* 49:2, ᵐ*aš-šur—pa-*[*ti-nu*] 48:2, 51:4, ᵐ*aš-šur—*[*pa-ti-nu*] 50:2,

**Aššūr-rēmanni:** ᵐ*aš-šur—rém-a-ni* 15:8, 127: 13, ᵐ[ᵈ*aš-šur*]*—rém-an-ni* 132:2,

**Aššūr-rēṣūwa** (royal delegate in Kumme?): ᵐ]*aš-šur—r*[*e-ṣu-u-a*] 97:2, ᵐ*aš-šur—re-ṣu-u-a* 84: 2, 85:1, 86:2, 88:2, 91:1, 92:1, 94:2, 96:2, 100:2, 111 r. 2, 113:12, ᵐ*aš-šur—re-ṣu-u-a*] 87:2, ᵐ*aš-šur—re-ṣu-u-*[*a* 117:6, ᵐ*aš-šur—re-ṣu-*[*u-a*] 60:7, ᵐ*aš-šur—re-ṣ*]*u-u-a* 107 e. 7, ᵐ[*aš-šur*]*—re-*[*ṣu-u-a*] 98:2, [ᵐ*aš-šur—re-ṣu-u-a*] 89:2, [ᵐ*aš-šur*]*—re-ṣu-u-a* 106:17,

**Aššūr-šarrāni:** ᵐ*aš-šur*—MAN-*a-ni* 190 r. 3,

**Aššūr-šarru-uṣur:** ᵐ*aš-šur*—MAN—PAB 213:7,

**Aššūr-šarru-[...]:** ᵐ*aš-šur*—MAN—[*x* 219:3,

**Aššūr-zēru-ibni** (of Ehiman): ᵐ*aš-šur*—NUMUN—DÙ 81:1,

**Ātanha-Šamaš:** ᵐ*a-ta*]*n-ha—*ᵈ[UTU] 151:2, ᵐ*a-t*]*an-ha—*ᵈUTU 150:2,

**Atār-hām** (merchant): ᵐ*a-tar—ha-am* 150 r. 6, [ᵐ*a-tar—ha-a*]*m* 150:4,

**Attâ-idrī** (a Hubuškian?): [ᵐ*a-t*]*a-a—id-ri* 196: 11,

**Azâ** (king of Mannea): ᵐ*a-za-a* 216:6,

**Babisu** (a Kummean): ᵐ*ba-bi-su-*[*x*] 116:3,

**Babû** (city lord): ᵐ*ba-bu-*[*u*] 264:7, ᵐ*ba-bu-ú* 237:4,

**Bazia** (Ukkean prince): ᵐ*ba-zi-ia* 190 r. 7,

**Bēl-ahhē** (merchant): ᵐEN—PAB.MEŠ 218 r. 9,

**Bēl-ēmuranni:** ᵐEN—IGI.LAL-*ni* 246:2,

**Bēl-iddina** (king of Allabria): ᵐᵈ⁺EN—SUM-*na* 210:11, 15, ᵐEN—AŠ 164:2, ᵐE[N]—AŠ 165:2, ᵐEN—SUM-*na* 154:4, 199 r. 9, 200 r. 5, ᵐE[N—SUM-*na* 249 r. 6,

**Bēl-qātū'a:** ᵐEN.ŠU-*u-a* 196 r. 3,

**Biriaun** (Kummean smuggler): ᵐ*bi-ri-a-un* 100:7,

**Burê** (Kummean smuggler): ᵐ*bu-ri-e* 100:4,

**Dādâ** (ruler of Arzizu): ᵐ*da-da-a* 243 r. 2, 5,

**Dalâ-il** (an Arzuhinaean): ᵐ*da-la*—DINGIR 228 r. 1,

**Dinānu:** ᵐ*di-*[*na-nu*] 170:2,

**Duianusi:** ᵐ*du-ia-nu-si* 299 r. 11, [ᵐ*du-i*]*a-nu-si*

299 r. 5,
**Dūrī-Adad:** $^{m}$BÀD—$^{d}$IM 38:8, $^{m}$BÀD—$^{d}$I[M 38:4,
**Ēa-šarru-ibni:** $^{md}$É.A—MAN—DÙ 162:8,
**Ehije** (Kummean smuggler): $^{m}$*e-hi-ie-e* 100:5,
**Ezije** (Kummean smuggler): $^{m}$*e-zi-ie-e* 100:4,
**Gabbu-āmur:** $^{m}$*gab-bu]—a-mur* 279:4,
**Gabbu-ana-Aššūr** (palace herald): $^{m}$*gab-bu—ana—aš-šur* 113:2, 118:2, 119:2, 121:2, 261:6, $^{m}$*gab-[bu—ana—aš-šur]* 114:2, $^{m}$*g[ab-bu—ana—aš-šur]* 125:2, $^{m}$*[gab-bu—ana—aš-šur]* 115:2, 117:2, $^{m}$*gab-bu—a-na—aš-šur* 120:2,
**Gamalu** (Kummean smuggler): $^{m}$*ga-ma-lu* 100:5,
**Habsu** (merchant): $^{m}$*hab-si* 150 r. 16, [$^{m}$*hab]-si* 150 r. 8,
**Haldi-abu-uṣur:** $^{m}$*hal-di*—AD—PAB 14 r. 7,
**Humamatu:** $^{m}$*hu-ma-ma-ti* 14 r. 6,
**Hu-Tešub** (king of Šubria): $^{m}$*hu—te-šub* 31 r. 19, 45:2, 52:14, r. 9, $^{m}$*hu]—te-šub* 44:2, $^{m}$*hu—te-šu-bu* 31 r. 11, 22, $^{m}$*hu—t]e-šu-ub* 31 r. 8,
**Iala[...]** (crown prince of Andia): $^{m}$*ia-la-[x* 171:1,
**Ianzû** (king of Hubuškia): $^{m}$*ia-an-zu-ú* 133:9,
**Iataʾ** (Šubrian official in charge of towns near the Urarṭian border): $^{m}$*ia-ta-aʾ* 52:7,
**Iaū-[...]:** $^{m}$*ia-ú—ʾ[a-x* 196:9,
**Iglî:** $^{m}$*ig-li-i* 293:3, 295 r. 19,
**Ilu-illika** (mule stable attendant): $^{m}$DINGIR—DU-*k[a* 48:4,
**Il-dalâ:** $^{m}$DINGIR—*da-la-a* 53:10, 14, 23, r. 2,
**Inṣabru** (Mannean city lord?): $^{m}$*in-ṣab-ri* 204:11,
**Iqīša-Marduk:** $^{m}$BA-*šá*—$^{d}$MES 292 r. 4,
**Issār-dūrī** (royal bodyguard): $^{m}$15—BÀD 105:6, see also *Sardūri,*
**Issār-šumu-iqīša** (vassal king?): $^{md}$15—MU—BA-*šá* 169:2,
**Iṣije:** $^{m}$*i-ṣi-ie-e* 91:21, $^{m}$*i-ṣi-[ie-e* 108:27,
**Išmanni-Aššūr** (official in Laqê?): $^{m}$HAL-*n]i—aš-šur* 250:6,
**Išme-ilu** (cohort commander): $^{m}$*iš-me*—DINGIR 234:4, [$^{m}$]*iš-me*—DINGIR 170:8,
**Kakkullānu** (royal bodyguard): $^{m}$*ka-ku-la-a-ni* 126 r. 7, $^{m}$*ka-ku-la-nu* 126:8,
**Kanūnāiu:** $^{m}$*ka-nun-a-a* 14 r. 8,
**Kaqqadānu** (Urarṭian commander-in-chief): $^{m}$*kaq-qa-da-a-ni* 103:6, $^{m}$*kaq-q[a-da-ni]* 89:5, $^{m}$*kaq-qa-da-nu* 87:7, $^{m}$*kaq]-qa-[da-nu]* 112:1, $^{m}$SAG.DU-*a-ni* 100:18, $^{m}$SAG.DU-*a-nu* 86:7,
**Kiṣir-Aššūr** (governor of Dur-Šarruken): $^{m}$*ki-ṣir—[aš-šur]* 232 r. 1, $^{m}$*ki-ṣir—[aš-š]ur* 232:5, $^{m}$*ki-ṣi[r—aš-šur]* 269:7, $^{m}$*ki-ṣ[ir—aš-šur* 69:12, $^{m}$*k[i-ṣir—aš-šur]* 232:11,
**Kubāba-ilāʾi** (interpreter): $^{md}$*kù*-KÁ—DINGIR-*a-a* 217:16,
**Kubāba-satar** (Median chieftain): $^{m}$*kù*-KÁ—*sa-tar* 203:10,
**Kuiakâ** (a Hargean): $^{m}$*ku-ia-ka-a* 149:21,
**Kummāiu** (Kummean smuggler): $^{m}$*ku-ma-a-a* 100:7, 9, 15, 16, r. 7, 14,
**Kuškāiu:** $^{m}$*ku-uš-ka-a-a* 213:2, 214:2,
**Liphur-Bēl** (governor of Amidi, eponym 705): $^{m}$]NIGIN—E[N] 18:2, $^{m}$NIGIN—EN 1:2, 3:1, 6:2, 20:7, $^{m}$NIGIN—EN] 17:2, 19:2, 20:2, $^{m}$NIGIN—[EN] 16:2, $^{m}$NIGIN]—EN 2:1, $^{m}$NIG]IN—E[N] 15:2, $^{m}$[NIGIN—EN] 11:2, [$^{m}$NIGIN—EN] 14:2,
**Lullupāiu:** $^{m}$*lu-ul-lu-pa-[a-a* 138:6,
**Lūqu** (merchant): $^{m}$*lu-qu* 150 r. 11,
**Mahdê** (governor of Nineveh, eponym 725): $^{m}$*mah-de-e* 74:2, 75:2, $^{m}$*ma]h-de-e* 76:2,
**Mannu-kī-Adad** (governor): $^{m}$*man-nu—ki*—$^{d}$IM 225:6, 237:2, $^{m}$*man-n]u—ki*—$^{d}$IM 240:2, $^{m}$*ma]n-nu—ki*—$^{d}$IM 239:2, $^{m}$*man-nu—ki*—10 238:2, [$^{m}$*m]a-nu—ki-i*—$^{d}$[IM 277 r. 6,
**Mannu-kī-ahhē** (royal bodyguard): $^{m}$*man-nu*—GIM—PAB.ME[Š] 82 r. 9,
**Mannu-kī-Arbail:** [$^{m}$*man]-nu—ki—arba-ìl* 269:10, $^{m}$*man-nu—k]i*—URU.*arba-ìl* 194:2,
**Marduk-rēmanni** (1. merchant, 2. governor of Calah): $^{md}$AMAR.UTU—*rém-ni* 150 r. 16, $^{md}$MES—*rém-ni* 292 r. 2,
**Mār-Issār** (royal bodyguard): $^{m}$DUMU—$^{d}$15 104:7,
**Melarṭua** (crown prince of Urarṭu): $^{m}$*me-la-ar-ṭu-a* 114:7, $^{m}$*me-la-ar-[ṭu-a]* 90 r. 7, $^{m}$*me-la-a[r-ṭu-a]* 90 r. 9,
**Meṣate-ibni:** $^{m}$*me-ṣa-te—[i]b-ni* 247:4,
**Mitunu** (governor of Isana, eponym 700): [$^{m}$]*me-tu-[nu* 28:11,
**Musani:** $^{m}$*mu-sa-ni* 261 r. 2,
**Mušallim-Adad:** $^{m}$*mu-šal-lim*—$^{d}$IM 244:2,
**Nabûa** (1. mule stable attendant, 2. royal bodyguard): $^{md}$PA-*ú-a* 79:16, $^{md}$PA-*u-a* 74 r. 5,
**Nabû-ahu-uṣur** (royal bodyguard): $^{md}$PA—PAB—PAB 204:12, 226:2, [$^{md}$PA—PAB—PAB] 204:7,
**Nabû-ēreš** (a Chaldean noble): $^{md}$PA—KAM-*eš* 172:4,
**Nabû-erība** (merchant): $^{md}$PA—SU 224 r. 12,
**Nabû-hamātūʾa** (deputy governor of Mazamua): $^{md}$PA—*ha-am-mat-u-a* 213:1, 214:1, $^{md}$PA—*ha-mat-u-a* 199 r. 11, 218:6, 11, 14, r. 3, 5, 226 r. 5, $^{md}$PA—*ha-mat-u-[a]* 210:2, $^{md}$P[A—*ha-mat-u-a]* 211:2,
**Nabû-lēʾi** (governor of Birate): $^{md}$PA—ZU 113:10, $^{md}$P[A—ZU] 128:2,
**Nabû-rēmanni** (governor of Nikkur?): $^{md}$PA—*rém-a-ni* 64:6,
**Nabû-šarru-uṣur:** $^{md}$PA—MAN—PAB 83:2,
**Nabû-uṣalla** (governor): $^{md}$PA—*ú-ṣal-l[a]* 104:2,
**Nabû-ušabši:** $^{md}$PA—GÁL-*ši* 293:2,
**Nabû-zēru-iddina:** $^{md}$PA—NUMUN—AŠ 256:9, r. 8,
**Nanû** (eunuch): $^{m}$*na-nu-u* 247:2, [$^{m}$*na]-nu-u* 137:2,
**Naragê** (chief tailor of Urarṭu): $^{m}$*na-ra-ge-e* 91:3,
**Naṣīb-il** (of Bit-Amukani): $^{m}$*na-ṣib*—DINGIR 63:4, [$^{m}$*n]a-ṣib*—DINGIR 63 r. 14,
**Naʾdi-ilu** (chief cupbearer): $^{m}$*na-aʾ-di*—DINGIR 291 r. 3, $^{m}$]I—DINGIR 63:2, $^{m}$I—DINGIR 62:2, 64:2, 65:2, 66:2, 69:2, 71:2, 261:7, $^{m}$I—[DINGIR] 70:2, 72:2, $^{m}$[I]—DINGIR 68:2,
**Nergal-bēlu-uṣur** (Andian emissary): $^{md}$MAŠ.MAŠ—EN—PAB 171:4, 217 r. 11,
**Nergal-ēṭir:** $^{m}$U.GUR—KAR-*ir* 81:2, $^{m}$U.[GUR—K]AR-*ir* 250:13,
**Nergal-šarrāni** (adjunct of Aššur-alik-pani): $^{md}$U.GUR—M[AN-*a-ni]* 158:3, [$^{md}$U.GU]R—MAN-*a-ni* 156:4, [$^{m}$]$^{d}$U.GUR—M[AN—*a-ni]* 157:3,
**Nimarkāiu** (servant of the crown prince): [$^{m}$]*ni-mar-ka-a-a* 228:10,
**Pihame** (deputy governor): $^{m}$*pi-ha-me* 152:5,
**Qurdi-Issār** (archer): $^{m}$*qur-di*—$^{d}$I[5] 263:10,

**Rusâ** (Rusa I, king of Urarṭu): $^{m}$*ru-sa-a* 31 r. 9, $^{m}$*ur-sa-a* 162 r. 3, $^{m}$*ur-sa-a-ma* 95:8, $^{m}$*ur-sa*]*-a-ma* 187:6,
**Sakuatâ** (Urarṭian governor): $^{m}$*sa-ku-a-ta-a* 87:8,
**Sanî** (merchant): $^{m}$*sa-ni-i* 224 r. 14,
**Sanije** (city lord): $^{m}$*sa-ni-ie* 103:5, r. 6, 130 r. 4, $^{m}$*sa-ni-ie-e* 100:19, $^{m}$[*sa-ni*]*-ie-e* 100 r. 6,
**Sardūri** (1. Urarṭian commander, 2. king of Urarṭu): $^{md}$15—BÀD 145:11, [$^{m}$]$^{d}$[15]—BÀD 93:8,
**Sētinu** (Urarṭian governor): $^{m}$*se-e-ti-ni* 88:6, 10, $^{m}$*se-ti-nu* 87:6,
**Sē'-gabbāri** (priest of Nerab?): $^{m}$*se-e*]*—gab-bar* 17 r. 4,
**Silim-Aššūr** $^{m}$*si-lim—aš-šur* 284 r. 12,
**Sīn-ahhē-rība** (Sennacherib, crown prince of Assyria): $^{m}$30—[PAB.MEŠ—SU] 281:2,
**Siplia** (Urarṭian governor): $^{m}$*si-ip-li-a* 87:9,
**Suitkâ** (city lord): $^{m}$*su-it-ka-a* 245:10,
**Ṣunâ** (Urarṭian governor): $^{m}$*ṣu-na-a* 88:12,
**Šamaš-bēlu-uṣur** (governor of Arzuhina, eponym 710): $^{md}$UTU—EN—PAB 227:2, 233:2, $^{md}$UTU—EN—PAB] 232:2,
**Šamaš-ilā'ī** (eponym 818): $^{md}$UTU—DINGIR*-a-a* 78:11,
**Šamaš-išmanni:** $^{md}$UTU—HAL*-ni* 102 r. 2,
**Šamaš-ukīn:** [$^{md}$]UTU—GIN-[*i*]*n* 204:15,
**Šarî** (horse trader from Kannu'): $^{m}$*šá-ri-i* 224:7,
**Šarru-ēmuranni** (1. governor of Mazamua, 2. of Bit-Zamani, 3. city lord of Qumbuna): $^{m}$LUGAL—*e-mur-an-ni* 199:2, 206:2, $^{m}$LUGAL—*e-mur-*[*an-ni*] 201:2, $^{m}$LUGAL—IGI.LAL-[*an-ni*] 200:2, 243:2, $^{m}$LUGAL—IGI.LAL*-a-ni* 47:2, $^{m}$LUGAL—IGI.LAL*-ni* 202:2, 203:2, 207:2, $^{m}$LUGAL—IGI.LAL*-ni*] 204:2, $^{m}$MAN—IGI*-ni* 226:16, $^{m}$MAN—IGI.LAL*-an-ni* 292 r. 7, $^{m}$MAN—IGI.LAL-[*an-ni*] 292:5, $^{m}$MAN—IG[I].LAL*-an-ni* 292:2, $^{m}$MAN—IGI.LAL*-ni* 63 r. 8, $^{m}$MAN—IGI.[LAL*-ni*] 205:2, $^{m}$MAN—[IGI.LAL*-ni*] 209:2,
**Ša-Aššūr-dubbu** (governor of Tušhan, eponym 707): $^{m}$*šá—aš-šur—du-bu* 32:2, 34:2, $^{m}$*šá—aš-šur—du-bu*] 37:2, $^{m}$*šá—aš-šur—du-b*[*u*] 4 r. 1, $^{m}$*ša—aš-šur—du-bu* 33:2, 90:8, $^{m}$*ša—aš-šur—du-bu*] 35:2, $^{m}$*š*]*a—aš-šur—d*[*u-bu*] 38:2, $^{m}$*ša—aš-šur—du-ub-bu* 31:2,
**Ṣa-ili-dubbu:** $^{m}$*ṣa*—DINGIR—*du-bu* 256:10,
**Šimkaia** (axe maker from Damascus): $^{m}$*ši-im-ka-ia* 71:5,
**Šulmu-bēli** (deputy of the palace herald): $^{m}$]DI-*mu*—EN 193:3, $^{m}$DI-*mu*—EN 133:2, 136:2, 148:10, 150 r. 8, $^{m}$DI-*mu*—EN] 143:2, $^{m}$DI-*mu*—[EN] 140:2, $^{m}$DI-*m*[*u*—EN 221 r. 12, $^{m}$D[I-*mu*—E]N 141:2, $^{m}$D]I-*mu*—EN 134:2, [$^{m}$DI-*mu*—EN] 135:2,
**Šulmu-bēli-lašme:** $^{m}$DI-*mu*—EN—*la-áš-me* 82:2, $^{m}$DI—EN—*la-áš-me* 97 s. 1,
**Taklāk-ana-Bēl** (governor of Naṣibina, eponym 716): $^{m}$*tak-lak—a-na*—E[N 250:6,
**Tarditu-Aššūr:** $^{m}$*tar-d*[*i*]*-tú—aš-šur* 152 r. 17,
**Tutî** (recruitment officer): $^{m}$*tu-t*[*i-i* 251 r. 5,
**Tu'āiu:** $^{m}$*tu-'a-ia* 125:6, $^{m}$*tu-ú-a-a* 281:12,
**Ṭāb-šār-Aššūr** (treasurer, eponym 717): $^{m}$[DÙG—IM—*aš-šur*] 282:2,
**Ṭuki** (Urarṭian governor): $^{m}$*ṭu-ki* 87:10,
**Ṭunbaun** (Urarṭian governor): $^{m}$*ṭu-un-ba-un* 84:11,
**Ubru-Harrān** (royal bodyguard): $^{m}$SUHUŠ—KASKAL 227:7, 10,
**Ubru-Pālil:** $^{m}$SUHUŠ—$^{d}$IGI.D[U] 46 r. 3,
**Ullusūnu** (king of Mannea): $^{m}$*ul-su-un-n*[*u*] 220:4, $^{m}$*ú-li-su-ni* 218:8, $^{m}$*ú-li-su-nu* 218:9,
**Upāq-Šamaš:** $^{m}$*ú-paq—*$^{d}$*šá-maš* 163:2, $^{m}$*ú-pa-*[*qa—*$^{d}$UTU] 162:2,
**Urda-Sīn:** $^{m}$ARAD—$^{d}$30 145:3,
**Uriṣâ** see *Ariṣâ*
**Urmakinnu:** $^{m}$*u*]*r-ma-ak-in-n*[*u* 196:7,
**Ursâ** see *Rusa,*
**Urṣenê** (deputy commander-in-chief of Urarṭu, brother of Abliuqnu): $^{m}$*ur-ṣe-né-e* 91:13,
**Urzana** (king of Muṣaṣir): $^{m}$*ur-za-a-ni* 89:7, $^{m}$*ur-za-na* 136:4, 144 r. 9, $^{m}$*ur-za-na-a* 112 r. 3, 146:2, $^{m}$*ur-za-na-*[*a*] 147:1, $^{m}$*ur-za-n*[*a-a*] 148:9, $^{m}$*ur-za-ni* 130 r. 7, $^{m}$*ur-*[*za*]*-ni* 145 e. 17, $^{m}$*ur*]*-za-ni* 187:1,
**Zābāiu** (fort commander): $^{m}$*za-ba-a-a* 245:2,
**Zāba-iqīša** (vassal king): $^{m}$Í]D.*za-ba*—BA-*šá* 162:13, 15,
**broken:** $^{m}$*aš-šur—x*[*x* 211:10, $^{m}$*a-r*[*a-x* 144 r. 2, $^{m}$*da-a-*[*x* 138:8, $^{m}$*da-*[*x* 138:4, $^{md}$[*x* 221 r. 3, 251:11, $^{md}$*x*[*x* 49:6, [$^{md}$*x—bal*]*-liṭ* 43:7, $^{md}$*x—x*]*x*—GIN-*in* 40:2, [$^{md}$*x—x*.M]EŠ—AŠ 254 r. 15, [$^{md}$*x*—API]N-*eš* 186:2, [$^{md}$*x*]—PAB-*ir* 207:4, $^{md}$]AG—*x* 225:5, $^{md}$AMAR.UTU—*x*[*x* 197:6, $^{md}$MAŠ—*ku-x*[*x* 197:8, $^{md}$PA—*x*[*x* 262:2, $^{m}$*e-*[*x* 116:1, $^{m}$*har-mi-*[*x*] 150 r. 3, $^{m}$*qa-*[*x* 61 r. 6, $^{m}$*sal-*[*x* 135 r. 4, $^{m}$*sa-*[*x*]*x-x-*[*x* 280 e. 12, $^{m}$*tu-ú-x*[*x* 196:5, $^{m}$*ú-a-x*[*x* 288 r. 9, $^{m}$*za-m*[*i-x* 150 r. 1, $^{m}$*x* 20:5, 43:2, 61 r. 8, 73:2, 108:1, 122:2, 144:2, 148:2, 181:2, 182:2, 239:4, 251:2, 267:2, 270:2, 271:2, 295:2, $^{m}$[*x* 14 r. 6, 141:4, 149:1, 156:12, 192 r. 6, 265:2, 280 r. 2, [$^{m}$*x* 43:8, 105:2, 141:6, 186:3, 228:2, 250:2, 261:6, 7, 266:2, 268:3, 269:2, 277:3, $^{m}$*x*[*x* 150 r. 2, 265:3, 277 r. 4, [$^{m}$*x-x*]*x-a* 150 r. 11, [$^{m}$*x-x*]*x-na-a* 247:5, [$^{m}$*x-x*]*x-tú-šú* 38:5, [$^{m}$*x-x*]*-am* 150 r. 12, [$^{m}$*x-x*]*-ra-a* 31 r. 7, $^{m}$*x-*[*x*]*-ur-da-a* 98:6, [$^{m}$*x-x-x*]*x-a'* 150 r. 2, [$^{m}$*x-x-x*]*-am* 150 r. 3, $^{m}$ARAD—[*x* 38:7, $^{m}$EN—[*x* 261:5,

## *Place Names*

**Abâ** (a town in Kurdistan): [URU.*a-ba*]*-a* 24:15, URU.*a-ba-a-a* 24:7,
**Adia** (town in central Assyria, mod. Sheikh Adi?): URU].*a-di-a* 296 r. 1, URU.*a-di-*[*a*] 298:5, URU.*a-d*[*i*]*-a* 57:4, UR]U.*a-di-a* 58:10,
**Adian** (or Adi-il, town in central Assyria): URU.EN-*an* 133:7,
**Aira** (town near Kumme): URU.*a-i-ra* 100:17,
**Alamu** (town near Muṣaṣir): URU.*a-la-mu* 136:5,
**Alzi** (Urarṭian province): KUR.*al-zi* 87:10,
**Alzunu** (Urarṭian province): KUR.*al-zu-nu* 31:17,

**Ampihābi** (town in the province of Arzuhina): KUR.*am-pi-ha-a-bi* 233:6,
**Andia** (contry SE of Lake Urmia): KUR.*an-d[i-a* 176:5, KUR.*an-di-a-a* 164:5, 171 r. 3, 177:3, KUR. *an-d[i-a-a]* 171:2,
**Anīsu** (city in Habhu, near Muşaşir): URU.*a-ni-su* 133:6, r. 11,
**Appina:** URU.*ap-pi-na* 245:4, U]RU.*ap-pi-na* 245:12,
**Araza** (city in Urarṭu): URU.*a-ra-za-a-[a]* 278:2,
**Arbail** (Arbela, mod. Erbil): URU.*arba-ìl* 141 r. 5, 149:15, 151:6, 152 e. 27, URU.*arb]a-ìl* 136:9, UR]U.*arba-ìl* 150 r. 17,
**Argistiani** (city in Urarṭu): URU.*i]r-gi-is-ti-a-ni* 55:6,
**Arhi** (city in Urarṭu): URU.*ar-hi* 145 s. 2,
**Armiraliu** (Urarṭian province): KUR.*ár-mir-a-li-u* 87:11,
**Arpadda** (city N of Aleppo): URU.*ar-pad-d[a]* 291 e. 15,
**Arrakdi** (city in Mazamua, near mod. Suleimaniya): URU.*a-ra-ak-di* 227:20, r. 9,
**Arrapha** (city in Assyria, now Kerkuk): URU. *arrap-ha* 199:7, 8, 227:11, r. 26, UR]U.*arrap-ha* 252 r. 1, URU.*arrap-ha-a-a* 228 r. 3, 229 r. 6, URU.*arrap-ha-a-[a* 253:4,
**Arzizu** (city in Mazamua): LÚ.*ar-zi-za-a-a* 243 r. 3, URU.*ar-[zi-zi]* 243:13,
**Arzūhina** (city on the lower Zab, mod. Gok Tepe?): URU.*ár-z[u-hi-na]* 201:4, URU.*ar-zu-hi-na* 227 r. 5, URU].*ur-z[u-hi-na* 277:1, URU.*ur-zu-hi-na* 64:7, 224:8, r. 15, 227:8, 18, 23, r. 8, s. 4, 232 r. 2, URU.*ur-zu-hi-na-a-a* 228 r. 2,
**Aššūrāiu** "Assyrian": *aš-šur-a-a* 16:8, KUR.*aš-šur-a-a* 215:21, KUR—*aš-šur*.K[I-*a-a*] 273:3, LÚ.*aš-šur-a-a* 293:10, see also *māt Aššūr*,
**Azari** (city in Mazamua): URU.*a-za-ri* 229 r. 8,
**ʾAtā** (region in Syria): KUR.*ʾa-ta-a-a* 295 r. 18,
**Bābili** (Babylon): DUMU—KÁ.DINGIR.RA.KI 203 r. 14, 241:5, KÁ.DINGIR 293 r. 3,
**Babiti** (mountain in Mazamua, mod. Bazian): KUR.*ba-bi-ti* 227 r. 18,
**Babutta** (city state near Ukku and Kumme): KUR.*ba-bu-ta-[a-a* 117:8,
**Baqarru** (town near Arzuhina): URU.*ba-qar* 142:5,
**Barzaništa** (town in Bit-Zamani): URU.*bar-za-ni-iš-[ta]* 97 r. 7,
**Bīrāti** (town in Habhu): KUR.*bi[r-a-te]* 170 r. 5,
**Bīt-Abdadāni** (Median city-state): KUR.É—*a[b-da-da-a-ni]* 157:7,
**Bīt-Amukāni** (Chaldean tribe): É—$^{m}$*ú-kan-a-a* 63 r. 2, 9,
**Bīt-Hamban** (Assyrian province in the Diyala valley): KUR.*ha-ban* 226 r. 11, KUR.É—*ha-ban* 200: 17,
**Bīt-Zamāni** (Assyrian province around mod. Diyarbakir): KUR.É—*za-ma-na* 48 r. 5, KUR.É]—*za-ma-na* 17:8, KUR.É—*za-ma-ni* 47:8, 79 r. 6, KUR.É—*za-ma-n[i* 14:10,
**Būrtu** (town in Kurdistan, near Harrania): URU. PÚ-*te* 133 r. 5, 8,
**Bususu** (town near Kumme): URU.*bu-s]u-sa-a-a* 170 r. 4, URU.*bu-su-sa-a-a* 100:12, URU.*bu-su-si* 100:10,
**Danibanu** (town in Urarṭu): URU.*da-ni-ba-ni* 21: 12,
**Denia** (reading uncert., perhaps rather Šulmubelija): URU.DI.EN-*ia* 117 r. 10,
**Dimašqa** (Damascus): URU.*di-maš-qa-a-a* 71:7,
**Dūr-atānāti** (town in Mazamua): URU.BÀD—*a-ta-na-t[e]* 229 r. 2, 4, URU.BÀD—MÍ.ANŠE.MEŠ-*te* 227 r. 13,
**Dūr-Iakīni** (Chaldean city, capital of Bit-Yakin): URU.BÀD—*ia-ki-na-a-a* 257:6, URU.BÀD—*ia-ki-ni* 257:4,
**Dūr-Šamaš** (Assyrian garrison city): URU]. BÀD—$^{d}$U[TU] 198 r. 2, URU.BÀD—$^{d}$UTU 97 r. 6,
**Dūr-Šarrukēn** (city in Assyria, now Khorsabad): UR]U.BÀD—LUGAL—*i-ku* 47 r. 9, URU.BÀD—LUGAL—GI 133:4, URU.BÀD—MAN—GIN 206 r. 6, 296 r. 4, URU.BÀD—MAN—GIN] 298:8, URU.BÀD—MAN—GI[N] 286:8, URU.BÀD—M[AN—GIN 298 r. 13, URU. BÀ[D—MAN—GIN] 292:7, URU.BÀD—$^{m}$LUGAL—GIN 34 r. 6, URU.[B]ÀD—$^{m}$[LUGAL—GIN] 34 e. 36, URU. BÀD—$^{m}$LUGAL—GI.NA 105 r. 8, URU.BÀD—$^{m}$MAN—GIN 32 r. 20, URU.BÀD—$^{m}$MAN—GIN.NA 119:4,
**Dūr-tālitti** (city in the Arzuhina province, near the Babite pass): URU.BÀD—*ta-li-ti* 227:15, r. 1, 229 r. 5, 7, 232 r. 3,
**Ehiman** (town in the vicinity of Mardin): URU.*e-hi-man-a-a* 81:11,
**Elizzadu** (city in Urarṭu): URU.*el-iz-za-da* 86:6, URU.*el-iz-za-du* 86:12,
**Eziat** (city on the Tigris, near Amedi/Diyarbakir): URU.*e-zi-at* 3 r. 1, 4 r. 8, 5 e. 6,
**Gargamis** (Carchemish, mod. Kargamis/Jarablus): URU.*gar-ga-mis* 243:13,
**Gimir** (Bibl. Gomer, Cimmeria): KUR.*ga-mir-ra* 92:6, 9, KUR.*gi-mir]* 174:2, KUR.*gi-mir-a-a* 144 r. 5, KUR.*g[i]-mir-[a-a* 144:9, [LÚ].*ga-me-ra-a-a* 145:4,
**Guriania** (land between Urarṭu and Cimmeria): KUR.*gu-ri-a-ni-a* 92:5, KUR.*g]u-ri-a-ni-a* 92:12,
**Gurru** (Aramean tribe): LÚ.*gur-ra-a-a* 53:4, 8, LÚ.*gur-ru* 215:22, [LÚ].*gur-ru* 277:10,
**Gūzāna** (Bibl. Gozan, class. Gizania, now Tell Halaf): U]RU.*gu-za-a-ni* 21 r. 20, URU.*gu-za-na* 48 r. 7, URU.*gu-za-n[a* 250:8,
**Habhu** (district N of Assyria): KUR.*hab-hi* 108 r. 23,
**Habrūri** (or *Kirrūri*, mod. Herir plain NE of Erbil): KUR.*hab-r]u-ri* 150:5,
**Hadattu** (city between Carchemish and Harran, mod. Arslan Tash): URU.*ha-da-at-ti* 65:6,
**Halzi-atbāri** (district N of Halahhu): KUR.*hal-zi*—AD.BAR 81:10, KUR.*hal-z[i*—AD.BAR 98:7, KUR. *hal-zi*—AD.BAR-*a-a* 79:9,
**Hamban** see *Bīt-Hamban*,
**Harda** (city in Urarṭu, N of Diyarbakir): URU. *har-da* 2 r. 7, URU.*ha-ar-da* 3:11,
**Hargu** (territory in eastern Kurdistan): KUR.*har-ga-a-a* 149 r. 3, KUR.*har-ga-a]-a* 149:4, [KUR.*h]ar-ga-a-a* 149 r. 6, KUR.*har-gi* 149 r. 2, KUR.*har-gu* 149:13, URU.*ha[r-g]a-a-a* 197 r. 5, URU.*har-gi* 150:6,
**Harmasu** (city near Hargu, mod. Harmashe 6 km E of Atrush?): URU.*har-ma-s[a-a-a* 197 r. 4,
**Harrānia** (town near Hubuškia, SW of Lake Urmia): URU.*har-ra-ni-a* 133 r. 4, 6, URU.*har-ra-[ni-a]* 133 r. 1,
**Haršu** (territory in Media?): *har-šá-a-a* 171:9,

**Hāu** (district in the province of Arzuhina): KUR.*ha-a-ú* 232:4, r. 7,
**Hiptūnu** (mod. Tell Haftun in the region of Dasht-i-Harir): URU.*hi-ip-tú-ni* 136:6, 137:5,
**Hirītu** (town in the Diyala valley): URU.*hi-ri-te* 200:7,
**Hubuškia** (country N of Muṣaṣir): KUR.*hu-buš-a-a* 133:10, KUR].*hu-buš-ka-a-a* 12 r. 9, KUR.*hu-buš-ka-a-a* 11 r. 3, 135:6, KUR.*hu-bu*[*š-ka-a-a*] 134:5, KUR.*hu-bu*]*š-ka-a-a* 12 r. 1, KUR.*hu-*[*buš-ka-a-a*] 192 r. 3, KUR.*h*[*u*]*-buš-ka-a-a* 11 r. 8, [KUR. *hu-buš-k*]*a-a-a* 160:19, KUR.*hu-buš-ki-a* 135:7, KU]R.*hu-buš-ki-a* 194:4, KUR.*hu-bu-uš-*[*ki-a* 196: 14, r. 9, KUR.*hu-b*[*u-uš-ki-a*] 196:13, K]UR.*hu-b*[*u*]*-uš-*[*ki-a* 196 r. 12, KUR.*hu-ub-buš-a-*[*a* 144 r. 8, KUR.*hu-ub-ka-a-a* 164 r. 3, KUR.*hu-ub-ka-a-*[*a* 165:10, KUR.*hu-ub-uš-ki-a* 44 r. 3, U]RU.*hu-bu-us-ka-a-a* 162 e. 17, URU.*hu-bu-u*[*š-ki-a*] 195:2,
**Huʾdidae** (town in Urarṭu): UR]U.*hu-uʾ-di-a-da-e* 145:10,
**Iasūmu** (mod. Karaca Dagh, a mountain 50 km E of Diyarbakir): KUR.*ia-su-me* 79 r. 5,
**Ieri** (town in Habhu): URU.*ie-e-ri* 162:5, 10,
**Irmuna:** URU].*ir-mu-na* 286:6,
**Iršumu** (town in Media): URU.*ir-šu-mu* 226:11,
**Isana** (city in the upper Habur Area): URU.*i-sa*]*-na* 250:8, [URU.*i-sa*]*-na* 254 r. 14, URU].*i-sa-na-a-a* 254 r. 9,
**Issēte** (town in NE Assyria, reading uncert.): U]RU.1-*te* 136:8,
**Ituʾu** (Aram. tribe): KUR.*i-tú* 215:22, LÚ.*i-tú-a-a* 3 r. 2, 10, LÚ.*i-tú-u* 21 r. 15, LÚ.*i-tú-ʾa-a-*[*a*] 238 r. 2, LÚ.*i-tú-ʾu* 178 r. 1, LÚ.*i-tú-ʾu-u* 32 r. 11, LÚ.*i-tu-ʾa-a-a* 16:5, LÚ.*i-tu-*[*ʾa-a-a*] 97 r. 5, 10, LÚ.*i-tu*]*-ʾa-a-a* 36 r. 6, LÚ.*i-t*]*u-ʾa-a-a* 264:2, LÚ.*i-*[*tu-ʾa-a-a*] 72:4, LÚ.*i-tu-ʾe-e* 21 r. 10, LÚ.*i-tu-*[*ʾu* 277:10, LÚ.*i-t*[*u-ʾu-u* 270:13,
**Izirtu** (capital of Mannea): URU.*i-zir-te* 204 r. 6,
**Kaldu** (Chaldea): KUR.*kal-dà-a-a* 59:5, KUR.*kal-da-a-*[*a* 14 r. 4, KUR.*kal-da-*[*a-a*] 79 r. 9, LÚ.*kal-da-a-a* 79 r. 2, 80 r. 3, 172:5,
**Kalhu** (Calah, mod. Nimrud): URU.*kal-ha* 74 r. 2, 254:14, U]RU.*kal-*[*ha* 205 r. 2, URU.*kal-ha-a-a* 224 r. 13, 298 r. 10, URU.*kal-hi* 100:13, r. 1, 142 r. 6, URU.*k*[*al-hi* 142:8,
**Kannuʾ** (city in Mesopotamia, Bibl. Kanneh): URU.*kan-nu-uʾ-a-a* 224:7,
**Kār-Aššūr** (city E of the Tigris, on the border of Elam): URU.*kar—ᵈaš-šur* 250:10, U[RU.*kar—ᵈaš-šur* 250:4,
**Kār-Nērigal** (city in Babylonia, near Cutha): URU.*kar*—ᵈMAŠ.MAŠ 207:6,
**Kār-siparri** (Urarṭian province): [KUR].*kar*-UD. KA.BAR 90:12, URU.*kar-si-par-*[*ri*] 84:12, URU.*kar*-URUDU.MEŠ 166 r. 1,
**Kār-Šamaš** (town on the Tigris S of Samarra): URU.*kar*—ᵈUTU 242:10,
**Kibatki:** URU.*ki-ba-at-ki* 202 r. 7, 11,
**Kipšūna** (city in Kurdistan, mod. Gefše 15 km NE of Zakho): URU.*kip-šú-na* 108:8,
**Kirmesi** (mountain): KUR.*ki-ir-me-si* 83 r. 4,
**Kulimmeri** (city in Šubria, Byzantine Khlomaron): URU.*ku-li-im-me-*[*ri*] 25:8,
**Kumisu:** KUR.*ku-me-sa-a-a* 202:9,
**Kumme** (city in Kurdistan, mod. Komane on the Upper Zab 9 km SE of Imadiya?): KUR.*ku-ma-a-a* 117:7, [L]Ú.*ku-ma-a-a* 106:12, LÚ.*ku-ma-a-a-e* 105:13, 16, LÚ.*ku-um-ma-a-a* 104:5, URU.*ku-ma-a-a* 111 e. 6, URU.*ku-me* 105:17, 24, URU.*ku-mu* 102: 4, URU.*ku-um-me* 95:14, r. 5, 100 r. 16, URU.*ku-u*[*m-me* 98:9, URU.*ku-*[*um-me*] 94:5, URU.*k*]*u-um-m*[*e*] 101:1, UR[U.*ku-um-me*] 97:4, UR]U.*ku-um-me* 107:1, URU.*ku-um-mu* 106:14, URU.*ku-um-m*[*u*] 107:2,
**Kurbail** (city in Assyria): URU.*kur-ba-ìl* 113:7, r. 11, URU.*kur-ba-*[*ìl*] 121 r. 5,
**Labdūdu** (Aram. tribe): LÚ.*lab-*[*d*]*u-da-*[*a-a*] 194 r. 4,
**Labir:** URU.*la-bir-a-a* 42 r. 3,
**Lahīru** (city E of the Tigris, probably in the Diyala valley): URU.*la-h*[*i-ri* 250 r. 14,
**Laruba** (town in Bit-Zamani): URU.*la-ru-ba* 3 r. 18,
**Libbi-āli** ("Inner City," an appellative of Assur): URU.ŠÀ—URU-*a-a* 298 r. 9, [URU.Š]À—URU-*a-a* 102:2,
**Māda** (Bibl. Madai, Media): KUR.*ma-d*[*a-a-a*] 225:16, LÚ.KUR.*ma-da-a-a* 210:8,
**Magidû** (Megiddo): URU.*ma-gi-d*[*u-u*] 291 r. 1,
**Manna** (Bibl. Minni, kingdom S of lake Urmia): KUR.*man-a-a* 84:4, r. 2, KUR.*man-na-a-a* 45 r. 4, 171 r. 5, 217 r. 7, 13, 221:6, 236:4, KUR.*man-na-a-*[*a* 282:8, KUR.*man*]*-na-a-a* 222:2, KUR.*ma-na-a-a* 145:7,
**Marhuha** (town in Šubria): URU.*mar-hu-ha* 53: 21, r. 6, URU.*mar-hu-ha-a-a* 53 r. 1,
**māt Aššūr** (Assyria): KUR—*aš-šur* 37:23, 105 r. 3, 164:10, r. 9, KUR—*aš-šu*[*r* 99:8, KUR—*aš-šu*[*r*] 34 r. 4, KUR—*aš-š*[*ur* 99 e. 12, 176:3, KUR—*a*[*š-šur* 10:5, KUR—*aš-šur*.KI 42 r. 6, 96:6, 7, 100:13, 147 r. 8, 176:12, KUR—*aš-šur*.K[I 176:6, KUR—*aš-šur*. [KI] 35:19, [KUR—*aš-šur*.KI] 95:12, 281:4, see also *Aššūrāiu,*
**Māzamua** (province of Assyria, mod. Sulaimaniya): KUR—*za-mu-u* 234 r. 1, KUR—*za-mu-u-a* 199 r. 4, 215:5, KUR.*ma-za-mu* 227:13,
**Mēṣi** (city-state in Kurdistan): KUR.*me-ṣa-*[*a-a*] 117:10, KUR.*me-*[*ṣa-a-a* 99:3, [KUR].*me-ṣa-a-a* 138:4,
**Mēturna** (city on the Diyala river, mod. Tell Haddad): URU.*mu-dur-na* 53:5, URU.*mu-dur-na-a-a* 53:4,
**Mumu** (town in Kurdistan, on the slopes of Judi Dagh): URU.*mu-ma-a-a* 78 r. 11,
**Muṣaṣir** (city in Kurdistan, now Mudjesir): KUR. *mu-ṣa-ṣir* 11 s. 2, KUR.*mu-ṣa-ṣi*[*r* 89:8, K[UR].*mu-ṣa-ṣir* 11 r. 7, KUR.*mu-ṣa-ṣir-a-a* 139:2, KUR.*mu-ṣa-*[*ṣi-ri* 191:6, KUR.*mu*]*-ṣa-ṣi-ri* 112 r. 4, KUR.*mu-uṣ-*[*ṣa-ṣir* 148:6, URU.*mu-ṣa-ṣir* 88:7, r. 4, 96:8, 147 r. 1, URU.*mu-ṣa-ṣi-ri* 84:10, 90:9,
**Muši** (town in Kurdistan, near Hiptuna): URU. *mu-ši* 136:7,
**nāru ṣalmu** ("Black River," probably Gadar Chai SW of Lake Urmia): ÍD.MI 88:8,
**Nīnua** (Nineveh): URU.*ni-nu-a* 100:14, 257 r. 9, URU.NINA 125:5, 218:15,
**Nuru** (town in Kurdistan): URU.*nu-ra-a-a* 11 r. 5,
**Paiê:** URU.*pa-ie-e* 129 s. 3,
**Parsua** (Assyrian province in Media, SE of Mazamua): KUR.*par-su-a* 199:12,
**Paššate** (town in Mannea): KUR.*pa-áš-šá-te* 169: 11,

**Penzâ** (city in Šubria): URU.*pe-en-za-a* 31:7, 32: 9, 34 r. 11,
**Pulua** (city in Urarṭu): URU.*pu-li-a-a* 145 r. 4, URU.*pu-lu-a* 21:11, URU.*pu-lu-u-a* 31:16, 33 r. 16,
**Purattu** (Euphrates): ÍD.*pu-rat-te* 3 r. 11, Í[D.*pu-rat-ti*] 72:5,
**Qaniun** (Urarṭian province): KUR.*qa-ni-un* 87:9,
**Quda** (city in Kurdistan, on the slopes of Judi Dagh): URU.LÚ.*qu-da-a-a* 78:5,
**Que** (country in Asia Minor, Bibl. Coa): KUR.*qu-ú-a-a* 68:5,
**Qumbuna** (city in Mazamua): URU.*qu-un-bu-na* 243:7,
**Quruba** (city in Kurdistan): KUR.*qu-ru-ba* 129: 6, KUR.*qu-ru-b*[*a* 117 r. 5,
**Raṣappa** (Bibl. Rezeph, class. Risafe, mod. Riṣafa?): KUR.*ra-ṣa-pa-a-a* 254:8,
**Sakkuanu:** URU.*sak-ku-a-na-a-a* 42 r. 4,
**Sāmirīna** (Samaria): URU.*sa-mi*[*r-na*] 291 e. 16,
**Sanha** (town in Mannea): URU.*sa-an-ha* 217:5,
**Sarduriani** (city in Urarṭu): URU.15—BÀD-*a-ni* 97 r. 11,
**Sarê** (city in NE Assyria, mod. Altun Kupri?): URU.*sa-re-e* 64:11, 229 r. 1, URU.*sa-re-e-ma* 64:14,
**Sazanâ** (town in the province of Ṣupat): URU.*sa-za-n*[*a-a*] 261:4,
**Sihana** (town in the vicinity of Muṣaṣir?): URU.*si-ha-na* 139:5,
**Sirura** (region in the province of Arzuhina): KUR.*si-ru-ra* 232:8,
**Si'immê** (Ass. provincial capital in the upper Habur area): KUR.*si-*[*'i-me-e*] 258:3, URU.*si-'i-me*]*-e* 250:7,
**Sua** (mountain in Mazamua): KUR.*su-a* 176:13,
**Sumbu** (district in Mazamua): KUR.*su-um-bi* 200:16,
**Suriana** (city in Urarṭu): URU.*su-ri-a-na-a-a* 145 r. 5,
**Šabirēšu** (Assyrian city, mod. Basorin?): URU.*šá-bi-ri-šú* 52:5, 62:6, 74:7, 10, URU.*šá-bi-r*[*i-š*]*ú* 73:8, U[RU.*šá*]*-bi-ri-šú* 74 r. 6, U[R]U.*š*[*á*]*-bi-ri-šú* 74 r. 7,
**Šarru-iqbi** (Assyrian fortress on the Mannean border): URU.MAN—*iq-bi* 249:2,
**Šattera** (Urarṭian province): KUR.*šá-at-te-ra* 90: 13,
**Šīmu** (town in central Assyria): URU.*ši-i-me* 290:5,
**Šubria** (country SW of Lake Van): KUR.*šub-ri-a* 54:5, 7, 9, KUR.*šub-ri-*[*a*] 54 e. 20, KUR.*šub-ri-a-a* 32:14, e. 19, 34 r. 22, s. 2, 40 r. 3, 75:4, KUR.*šub-ri-a-*[*a*] 34 r. 7, KUR.*šub-ri-a*]*-a* 35:17, KUR.*šub-r*[*i-a-a*] 77 r. 2, [KUR.*šub-ri*]*-a-a* 34:9, KUR.*šu-bur-a* 53:11, 19, KUR.*šu-bur-a-a* 52:5, 53:22, KUR.*šu-u*[*b-ri-a*] 31 r. 3, KUR.*šu-ub-ri-a-a* 25:7, KUR.*šu-u*[*b*]*-ri-a-a* 33:7,
**Šūru** (city in Ṭur Abdin, mod. Savur): URU.*šu-u-r*[*i* 281:10,
**Tabālu** (Bibl. Tubal, Cappadocia): KUR].*ta-ba-li* 255:5,
**Tagalāgi** (town in the Zagros, near the Bazian pass): URU.*ta-ga-la-gi* 227:16,
**Tahālu** (town near Kar-Šamaš): URU.*tah*-URU 242:9,
**Tāsi** (city in western Kurdistan, Urart. Taše): URU.*ta-si* 34 r. 15, URU.*ta-*[*si*] 48 r. 8, URU.[*ta-s*]*i* 31:11, URU.[*t*]*a-si* 34 r. 10,
**Tastiāti** (town on the Tigris, near Nineveh): [URU.*tas*]*-ti-a-ti* 297:10, URU.*ta-as-*[*ti-a-te* 298:6,
**Taziru** (Aram. tribe): LÚ.*ta-zi-ru* 32 r. 11, LÚ.*ta-zi-r*[*u* 37:7, LÚ.*ta-*[*zi-ru*] 37:16,
**Tīdu** (Assyrian garrison city, mod. Kurh?): URU].*ti-di* 31 r. 2,
**Tikriš** (city in Mannea): URU.*ti-ik-ri-iš* 217 r. 1,
**Tillê** (city in the Habur triangle): URU.*til-e* 250:8,
**Ṭurušpâ** (capital of Urarṭu, mod. Van): URU.*ṭu-ru-uš-pa-a* 3:13, 84 r. 5, URU.*ṭ*]*u-ru-uš-pa-a* 178 r. 2, UR]U.*ṭu-ru-*[*u*]*š-pa-a* 145:12, URU.*ṭu-ru-uš-pi-a* 113 r. 4, URU.*ṭu-ur-uš-pa-a* 85:4, 91:8, 15, 16, 92 r. 16, URU.*ṭu-ur-uš-pa-*[*a*] 86:5, URU.*ṭu-ur-uš-*[*pa-a*] 179 r. 4, URU.*ṭu-ur-uš-*[*pa*]*-a* 87:19, URU.*ṭu-u*[*r-uš-p*]*a-a* 93 r. 2, URU.*ṭ*[*u-ur-uš-pa-a*] 94:7, URU.[*ṭu-ur-uš-pa-a*] 85 r. 1,
**Ukku** (city at the foot of Judi Dagh, N of Kumme): KUR.*uk-ka-a-a* 284 r. 10, K]UR.*uk-ka-*[*a-a*] 190 r. 8, KUR.*ú-ka-a-a* 87:8, 88 r. 1, 96:4, 111:3, 117:9, 129 r. 3, 8, [KUR].*ú-ka-*[*a-a* 102:6, KUR.*ú-ki* 91 r. 4, KUR.*u-ka-a-a* 147:10, LÚ].*uk-*[*ka-a*]*-a* 285 r. 4, L]Ú.*uk-ka-a-a* 286:2,
**Ulua** (city state in Kurdistan): KUR.*ú-li-a-a* 117: 10, [UR]U.*ul-ú-a-a* 138:3,
**Uluaza:** KUR.*ú-lu-a-za* 168 r. 6,
**Ulušia** (town in Mannea): URU.*ú-lu-ši-a* 217:6,
**Upūmu** (capital of Šubria, Byzant. Aphumon, mod. Fum): URU.*pu-u-me* 31 r. 6, 13,
**Ura** (city in Kurdistan, near Ukku and Kumme): URU.*ú-ra* 111 r. 3,
**Urarṭu** (Bibl. Ararat, Armenia): KUR.*u*[*r-ar-ṭa-a-a*] 184:5, KUR.*ú-ra-ar-ṭa-a-a* 113:6, r. 3, KUR.*ú-ra-ar-ṭa-a-*[*a*] 114:3, KUR.URI 36:7, 86:10, 92:6, 96:5, 100 r. 3, 105 r. 2, 145:8, r. 6, 176 s. 3, 183:4, 223:5, KUR.U[RI] 286:4, KUR.URI-*a* 53:9, KUR].URI-*a-a* 167:1, KUR.URI-*a-a* 2:6, 3:6, 31:9, r. 23, 33 r. 3, 34 r. 23, 35:19, 24, 45:3, 52:9, 84:5, r. 4, 86:5, 91:7, 92:7, 8, 10, r. 5, 131:4, 147:5, 164:4, 165:5, 169:5, 177:4, 178 r. 6, 216 r. 7, KUR.URI-*a-a*] 92: 15, 144:6, KUR.URI-*a-*[*a* 178 r. 9, 216:5, KUR.URI-*a-*[*a*] 22:7, KUR.URI-[*a-a* 92 r. 6, KUR.URI-[*a-a*] 35: 31, 87:4, 148:8, KUR.URI]-*a-a* 182:4, 188:8, KUR.UR[I-*a-a*] 131:1, KUR.UR[I]-*a-*[*a*] 222:6, KUR.U[RI-*a-a* 34:5, KUR.U[RI-*a-a*] 12 r. 6, 55:10, 115:3, KUR.U]RI-*a-a* 90:2, 185:3, 222:3, KUR.[URI-*a-a*] 108 r. 24, 128:8, KUR.[U]RI-*a-a* 35 e. 33, KU]R.[U]RI-*a-a* 181:4, K]UR.URI-*a-a* 174:2, [KUR].URI-[*a*]*-a* 1:9, [KUR.URI]-*a-a* 35:29, 168:6, KUR.URI-*a-a-e* 34 r. 21, MÍ.KUR.URI-*tú* 108 r. 25,
**Uṣunali:** KUR.*ú-ṣu-na-li* 144 r. 6,
**Ušhu** (town at the foot of Mt. Nipur/Judi Dagh, mod. Ṣah?): URU.LÚ.*uš-ha-a-a* 78:4,
**Ušti:** URU.*uš-ti* 185:4,
**Waisi** (Urarṭian city SW of Lake Urmia, mod. Ušnaviyeh?): *ú-e-si* 89:10, K[UR].*ú-a-si* 11 r. 7, URU].*ú-a-si* 167:3, URU.*ú-a-si* 164:7, URU.*ú-a-*[*si*] 133:12, U]RU.*ú-a-s*[*i* 167:5, URU.*ú-e-si* 86:9, 87:5, 14, 88 r. 6, URU.*ú-e-s*[*i*] 145 e. 16, URU.*ú-e-*[*si*] 93:2, 112:3, URU.*ú-*[*e-si* 93 r. 9, URU.*u-a-si* 147:9, 14,
**Wazaun** (Urarṭian province): KUR.*ú-a-za-e* 90:10, KUR.*ú-a-za-na* 114:4, URU.*ha-za-un* 87 r. 1,
**Zabban** (town on the Diyala, possibly between Kifri and Qara Tepe): URU.*za-ban* 199:10, URU.*za-*

*ba*[*n* 259 r. 1,
**Zaddi** (town on the border of Babylonia, near Zabban): URU.*za-ad-di* 241 r. 2,
**Zikirtu** (kingdom on the E side of Lake Urmia): KUR.*zi-g*[*ír-te*] 188:5, KUR.*zi-kir-ta-a-a* 45 r. 6, KUR.*z*[*i-kir-te* 189:3, KUR.*zi-ki-ra-a-a* 164:6, KUR.*zi-ki-ti-a* 164:15, LÚ.*zi-gír-ta-a-a* 169:4, 9, LÚ.[*zi*]-*gír-ta-a-a* 169:6,
**broken:** KUR.*i*[*l-x-a-a*] 117:9, KUR.*ni-x*[*x* 117 r. 4, KUR.*ni*-[*x-x-a-a*] 138:2, KUR.*ši-ib*-[(*x*)-*x*]*x* 90:11, KUR.*ú*-[*x* 129:7, KUR.*x* 14:7, 117:6, 8, 258:1, KUR.[*x* 18:8, 93 r. 5, 128:10, 191:3, 283:5, K[UR.*x* 117:7, [KUR.*x* 114:9, 173:11, KUR.*x*]*x-ti-na-a-a* 55:11, URU.*a*-[*x* 165:7, U]RU.*a-x*[*x* 45 r. 1, URU.*il*-[*x* 34 r. 9, URU.*mu-x*[*x* 289:1, URU.*ša-x* 222:5, URU.*šu*-[*x* 156:13, URU.*š*[*u*-(*x* 166:2, URU.*tú-ur*-[*x* 125 r. 7, URU.*x* 89:4, 135:4, URU.[*x* 19 r. 8, 35:20, 66:6, 67:13, 93:1, 99 r. 8, 103:1, 200:16, 220:3, 283:6, UR[U.*x* 39:1, 126 r. 3, 129 s. 4, 130 r. 7, 142:2, 187:3, 262:8, 276:2, U[RU.*x* 243:4, [URU.*x* 35:24, 286:3, URU.*x*[*x* 19 r. 5, 94:4, 138:3, 148 r. 3, 192 r. 4, 243 r. 13, 261 r. 3, URU.*x*[*x*] 292 r. 8, UR[U.*x*]*x-ri* 35 r. 4, URU.[*x*]-*li-te* 126:9, [URU.*x*]-*ši-ma-a-a* 207:5, URU.[*x-x-a-a*] 192 r. 1, URU.DU$_6$—*da*-[*x* 261:3, URU.MAŠ-*d*[*a-x* 221:12,

## *God and Star Names*

**Aššūr** (national god of Assyria): *aš-šur* 95:5, 148:4, *aš*]-*šur* 48:5, [d]*aš-šur* 146 r. 6,
**Bēl** ("lord," an appellative of Marduk): [d]E[N 146 r. 6, [[d]]EN 232:10, [d+]EN 294:4,
**Issār** (Ištar, Assyrian war goddess): [d]*iš-tar* 146 r. 7,
**Kipputu** ("Circle," Assyrian name of Corona): MUL.*kip-pi-te* 249:13,
**Marduk** (supreme god of Babylon): [d]AMAR.UTU 126:4, 293:5, 295:4, [d]ŠÚ 127:4,
**Nabû** (Nebo, son of Marduk): [d]AG 126:4, 293:5, [d]PA 127:4, 288 s. 1, [d]PA] 146 r. 6, [d][PA 148:4, [[d]PA 295:4,
**Taškâti** ("Triplet," α Herculis): MUL.*taš-ka*-[*a-ti*] 249:14,

# Subject Index


able 37 204
absent 290
accept 31
acceptable 294
accomplices 228
accountable 37
accounting 295
achieve 122
acquire 203
act 25 46 202 243
action 69 106
Adar 52 105 135 285
add 15 256
advanced 223
aegis 15
affair 146
afraid 33 34 35 37 53 90 202
agree 11 104
agreed 14 16 254
agreement 31 53
ague-stricken 156
aid 145
alarm 179
alert 200
alerted 4
alive 91 294
allegations 121
allocation 56
allot 289
alone 34 117
altars 97
alternate 17
alternatively 109 206
amassed 260
ambush 32 33
animals 21 47 88 119 227
another 21 104 227 290
appealed 43 46 106 260
apple 27
appoint 8 152 170 257
appointed 31 46 67 69 79 108 122 137 142 237 242 243 248 297
apprentices 56
appropriated 37
arable 14 15
Arbela 136 141 149 150 151 152
arbitrated 31
archer 263
area 53 78
Argisti 3
arms 35
army 69 86 87 114 152 200 216 220 250 277 278
Arpad 291
array 3 164 250
arrest 53 100
arrested 31 91 116 150 190 243
artist 294
assemble 33 63 67 79 277
assembled 2 4 67 78 114 147 167 184 200 279
assembling 63 145
assign 152
assigned 24 251
assignment 56 291
associates 292
Assyria 10 34 35 37 95 96 99 105 147 164 176 281
Assyrian 42 100 164
Assyrians 16 215 273 293
attack 114 145
attacked 12 32 45 53 84 131
attendant 48 79 200 257
attention 121
audience 104 136 149 171 196 212 256
augurs 163
authority 95
axe 71
axes 35
α Herculis 249
Babylon 203
Babylonian 241
Babylonians 293
bakers 215
bank 6 34 111 115 117 290
bargain 52
barley 16 82 98 185 217 234 259 269 278
base 33
battle 3 146 166 250
beams 4 7 32 33 34 39 43 111 117 178 253 254 287
bearded 91 294
beards 108
believe 37
Bel 146 148 232 294
beneficial 146
black 171
bless 126 127 293 295
blocked 146
blood 236
blowing 249
boat 233 299
boats 290
bodyguard 15 31 37 43 59 74 78 82 98 104 105 109 120 126 183 204 207 208 215 227 262 279
bone 295
booty 120 145 226

border 31 44 52 84 100 129 131 190 217 221 223
borders 30 252
bought 15 35 150 224
bow 3 16
box 294
boys 200
branded 37
bread 37 126 216 289
brick 56 294
bricking 56
bricks 80 211 291 296
brickwork 291
bronze 101 206 287
brother 14 32 33 52 81 91 108 148 217
brothers 31 42 257
build 15 210
builders 56
building 80 89
bull colossi 57 58 118 298
bull colossus 17 115 297 299 300
burden 56
burnt 287
buy 100 238
buying 149 238
Calah 74 100 142 205 224 254 298
calendar 250
calf 35
camels 48
camp 12 90 144 160
campaign 282
captives 92 156 166 169 242
capture 2 33 116 187
captured 32 33 55 115 166
Carchemish 243
careless 273
carnelian 284
carts 48 152
case 149 213 250
catch 227
cavalry 34 44 95 152 217 251
cavalryman 246
cavalrymen 32 35 215 251
cedar 295
centre 56 80
chains 46
Chaldean 59 172
Chaldeans 14 79 80
charge 52 70 71 79 297
chariot 68 74 141 215 230 251 252 277
chariotry 152
chariots 215
check 295
checked 48
chests 56 57
chief 46 91 143 250 295 297
chief confectioner 227
chief cupbearer 63 90 100 250
chief eunuch 34 81 232 279
chief of 295
chief scout 31
chief tailor 91
chief victualler 48 143
Cimmeria 92
Cimmerians 92 144 145 174
Circle Star 249
circumference 294
cities 37 84 177 250
citizens 203
city 3 4 12 13 19 35 39 56 67 99 103 106 107 112 126 129 142 148 165 166 187 206 213 222 243 245 250 262 276 277 279 281 283 292
city lord 100 103 237 243
city lords 117 138 203 217
claims 149 232
clay 52 218
clean 31
cohort 32 121 182 217 234 250 289
colleagues 47
collected 3
collecting 150
colony 150
colour 218
commandant 244
commander 12 35 204 211 234 245 250 289
commanders 32 87 88 217
commander-in-chief 86 91 93 131 166 169 250
commander-of-fifty 43 53
commanders-of-ten 257
complain 163
comply 295
conceal 37 243
confectioners 215
conquer 46
conspire 91
constricted 200
consumption 250
contingent 250
contract 294
contrast 225
cooks 215
copper 257
corn 60 143 225 259 289
corn-tax 82
Corona 249
counsel 197
countries 79 105 143 146 289
country 4 12 14 18 21 30 32 34 36 46 52 54 79 87 95 104 106 108 118 119 120 128 130 143 146 149 173 179 191 218 232 243 260 264
countrymen 210
courses 291
court 54 63 260
courtiers 91 294
courtyard 151
cover 67
cress 126
criminals 176 210 227 228 231
crossroads 227
crown prince 109 150 171 228 277
cubit 15 294 295
culmination 249
cultivate 14 82 225 289
cup 242
cupbearer 206
cupbearers 215
curse 46
cut 34 47 176 295
cutters 296
cypresses 281
Damascus 71
daughter 259

dawn 206
dead 31 91
deadline 152 202
debt 260
debt-remission 203
decide 136 149
decree 31
deed 53
defeat 92 273
defeated 173
delayed 37 215 277
delegate 38 106 107
deliver 25 298
delivered 294
depart 126 162 217
departed 88 97 126 129 145 162 194 227 278
depicted 282
deportation 203
deported 54 105 112
deposited 169 290
depot 120
deputy 3 21 46 52 91 149 150 152 154 179 192 208 226 242 264
deserted 34 35
deserter 245
deserters 32 35 245
desire 34
desperate 79
destroying 95 149
detain 37 106
detained 106 143
detour 200
devoted 154
diadems 282
die 3 106 126 146 226 244
difficult 117 200
dined 32
dinner 32 34
disagreed 226
disappear 106 121
discharge 179
disclose 130
discuss 104
disobey 118
dispatch riders 215
dispense 246
distance 117
distributing 295
district 31 34 44 84 92 131 145 260
disturb 37
domain 35 100
domestics 215
donkey 215
donkeys 48 52
door-beams 6 7 25 26 34 43 295
downstream 4
drag 17
dragged 91
draw 250
drawn 15 91
drink 106
drive 211 256
driver 74 230
drivers 215
duty 52 149 232
dye 296
dyers 205 296
dying 149
earnest 126
earnestly 243
eat 37 156 225 289
elapse 82
Elul 80 295
emerge 220
emissaries 35 52 169 194 195
emissary 40 75 169 171
employees 294
employment 46
empty-handed 146
encamped 160 168 217 226
encouraged 210 237
enemies 107 146
enemy 92 146
engraver 205
enquire 68
enquired 227
enthroned 150
entourage 250 291
entrance 206
entrusted 9 70 257
entry 289
environs 85 94 126 232
equal 6 33
equipment 31 97 117 208 217
erect 15
errands 63 229
escape 32 52 90 92
eunuch 95 137 170 181 182 183 218 245
eunuchs 32 91 291
Euphrates 3 72
exempt 16 268 277 288
exercise 288
expedition 53 152 173 200 221
explanation 46
express 74 227
express-station 227
extend 103
extract 82 232 291
fall 103 200 202
fallen 54 103 227
false 45
family 93 228
father 31 143 190
favour 152
fear 35 109 294
fed 257
feed 3 225
feet 35 50 95 130 146
felled 33
felling 25
fellow 91
fellows 53
field 15 16 109 188 210 232 259 263
fields 14 15 32 37 52 60 82 109 260 289
fierce 126
fight 146
fighters 215
fighting 3
fir 294 295
fire 12
first 19 64 86 87 150 199 200 250 297
firstly 24

fled 36 54 196 218 245
fleeing 35
float 4
floors 60
foals 64
fodder 233 250
foes 146
food 68 106
force 115
foreman 95
fort 4 10 12 15 32 45 53 54 60 80 89 92 93 109 122 162 199 204 218 245
fortified 21
forts 1 2 3 4 6 11 14 15 17 18 21 22 23 24 25 27 28 29 30 31 32 33 34 35 37 40 80 92 115 124 128 131 144 152 160 173 187 199 204 210 211 244 270 273 281
free 33 53 106 199
frightened 145
garden 42 109
gardens 37 52
garrison 80 163 203 264 289
garrisons 33 152
gather 108
gathered 21 89
gift 136 171 212
glazing 211 291
goats 256
god 33 149
gods 35 37 69 95 106 117 178 203 236 256
gold 294
golden 234
goldsmith 294
gossiping 294
government 31 154
governor 2 3 11 31 33 34 41 53 81 83 84 87 88 89 90 100 104 114 145 147 152 156 179 190 199 201 210 211 226 228 242 254 258 286 291
governors 21 23 44 84 85 87 90 92 147 148 174 178 180 250 282
grain 82 126 248 250 294
grandfather 143
grapes 41 281
graze 256 257
grazed 256
Great Shepherd 176
greet 18 31 95 143 172 221
greeted 108
greetings 221
grinding 35
grooms 215
groves 25 34
guard 21 24 32 33 53 54 84 160 163 210 217 246 294
guarding 182
harnessed 227
harsh 225
harvest 3 97 127 199
harvested 289
haul 58 117
hay 47
head 13 69
heads 108
heap 249
heart 46 96 146 222
hectares 15 232 259
help 56 131 145 236
herds 47
herdsman 264
hewn 29 297
hiding 14
hire 105
hired 46 254
hit 269
homers 60 98 203 225 250 259 269 274 275
hoof 293
hoplites 53
horse 90 171
horses 3 14 62 64 82 95 133 136 169 171 189 199 202 208 215 218 224 225 226 234 249 250 251 279
horse-drawn 215
hostility 113
house 34 100 125 159 183 196 197 206 210 218 227 232 260 261 263 264
household 190 245 254
houses 3 52 80 94 95 105 149 260
house-born 243
humble 146
hunger 126
hurt 53
ice 105 142 272
ill 35 52
impasse 79
implanted 204
import 100
incapable 56
inciting 106
indebted 149
infantry 277
inflicted 273
information 48 173 215 250 295
informed 3 55 103 150 173 188 203
informer 55
informers 164
inhabitant 52
inhabitants 100
Inner City 102 298
inquire 32 34 40 91 105
inquired 37 173
inquiring 91
inside 4 15 21 218
insists 106
inspect 47
inspected 34 156
inspector 3
inspectors 152
installed 295
installment 129
instructions 119 123 143
instructs 292
insulted 260
insurrection 33
interpreter 108 203 212
inventory 206
investigate 68 74 91 105 227 243 265
investigated 54
investigation 163
iron 35 46
irons 108
itemized 218 250
items 100

jewelry 31
journey 31
junior 56
jurisdiction 149 232
keleks 200
kill 108 197 260
killed 53 90 91 93 108 112 143 173 174 175 184 273
killing 107 149 260
kiln-fired 211 291
kings 282
kingship 90
labour 52 78 149 232
lackeys 215
lagging 47
lake 84
language 217
large-wheeled 215
late 117
lawsuit 243
leather 101 142 152 160
legate 261
letter 35 44 50 63 79 96 107 113 210 211 213 214 250 263 283
letters 218
levied 3
levies 87
light 11 146
linen 152
litigate 243
litre 126
litres 242 261 269 274
little 13 33 37
loaded 299
local 52 296
logs 3 8 127 129 254 295
low 117 298
luxury 100
magnates 45 56 69 93 162 164 165 173 226 250 257 291 295 298
major-domo 34 67 115 126 152 215
maker 71
manager 179
managers 21 291
march 86 92
Marchesvan 45 245
Marduk 126 127 293 295
mares 47 122 171
masons 294
master 56
mayor 53
measured 269
measures 294
Mede 210
Medes 225
medlars 281
Megiddo 291
men 3 14 21 24 25 32 33 35 37 41 52 53 63 78 79 80 91 100 103 104 106 111 112 115 118 126 129 139 150 152 184 199 200 215 226 250 251 257 268 288 289 294 295 297
menservants 227
merchandise 100
merchant 150 218
merchants 143 149 150 202 224
merry 294
message 117 165
messenger 2 3 31 33 34 35 46 51 53 71 81 91 95 96 97 104 107 108 112 121 128 129 130 133 134 143 145 149 162 164 178 186 188 194 197 199 204 210 252 260 262 263 280 283
messengers 8 31 92 113 164 169 221 243 245
metal 206
mid-Shebat 272
mighty 179
military 52
mina 150
minas 149 271
moat 166
mobilized 4
modify 57
moment 53 172 260
money 150 169
month 191 242 250 285
months 126
moon 105
morning 243
Mount 83
mountain 34 53 55 78 116 137 180 196 237 290
mountains 21 25 84 90 156 191 200
mounting 5
mouth 34 108 189 203 204
move 69 117
moved 3 37 87 97 115 117 227
moving 115
mule 48 52 74 79 200
mules 5 9 35 48 171 224 227
mule-drawn 215
mule-express 227
name 34 95
names 48 87 121 282
negligent 106 113 211
negotiate 78
new 105 152
news 1 2 3 13 22 31 34 45 55 81 92 99 115 140 144 148 158 162 164 165 168 181 182 221 279
night 168 211 249 286
Nineveh 100 125 218 257
Nisan 281
number 6 33 79
obey 63 142 194 210 260 268
objects 206
occupy 131
officer 82 215 251
officers 119 295
official 31 48 117 122 248 254 269
officials 37 98 282 298
offspring 37
oil 108 126
Old Palace 282
one-year-old 122
opposite 2 3 12 21 22 33 34 41 87 88 90 133 175 187 196 217 254 286
oppression 149
orchard 37 213 281
order 11 27 32 74 97 98 105 128 130 155 169 215 229 243 247 260 268
orders 29 34 52 62 67 70 78 97 98 103 104 108 109 113 130 133 136 137 142 144 160 194 199 210 224 226 227 228 232 244 250 251 256 258 267 280 281 295 298 299

organize 164 200
organized 53 121
outskirts 93
overseer 179 213 245 254
owner 141
owners 251
oxen 20 21 37 69 70 122 133 136 146 238 258 280
pack-animal 250
paid 260
palace 15 96 142 148 151 206 268 279 282 294
Palace 3 13 25 42 43 98 104 108 150 172 183 206 210 228 241 243 245 277 284
palace herald 44 56 130 145 147 149 150 159 160 216 227
palace superintendent 295
'palm' 295
panicked 249
pass 5 24 34 100 117 129 176 220 226
passes 53
patrimony 15
pay 92 121 227
peace 2 78 157
peaceful 210
people 21 24 35 36 37 42 46 52 68 79 89 91 104 108 118 121 132 145 149 156 202 203 212 243 248 249 261 264
perimeter 15
permission 147
persecute 46
persons 79 94 149
petition 291
pick 105 254
pile 117
piled 33 34 249 254 255
plain 139
planted 225
plentiful 295
plot 91 149 259 260
plough 263
plum 27
poplar 34 253
population 296
position 69
positioned 3 86
positions 33
possession 74 203 243
posthaste 122
pots 77
pour 108
powerful 104
prefect 16 213 251 268
prefects 32 34 57 88
present 53 213
presented 221
pressed 64
priest 31 232
prince 277
proclaimed 184
produce 296
progress 152
promise 169
promoted 277
property 15 37
prostitutes 24
protect 35
provide 74 78 289
provided 78 106 205 252
province 250
provisions 115 242
punish 31
purchase 21 100
pursuing 53
pursuit 53
quarreled 37
quay 297
question 149 150 199
questioned 37 91 228
quivers 101
quota 197
raging 179
raids 227
rain 21 275
rained 26 274 275 276
raining 272 273
raise 57 58 297
raised 31 87 274 275
rams 146 263
rations 185 217 234 250 289 294
read 52 152 218
reap 97 199
reason 46 199 284
receive 100 226 257
received 48 98 117 144 149 217 257 281 287 291
reconnoiter 3
recruitment 82 119 251
recruits 137
red 28 171 287
reeds 34 97 120
refined 257
refuse 118 268
rejected 295
relations 157
relative 98
release 21 31 32 33 78 126 203 254 260
reliefs 282
relieve 97
remove 213 229
removed 34 106 230
repair 199
repay 260
replacement 182
report 3 19 25 34 38 40 42 54 85 86 105 128 142 144 217 246
reported 53 83 115 162
reporting 12 13
reports 152
reprimand 288
request 7 188
reserve 119 163
respect 154
responsibility 106 108
retrieved 293
review 52 95 215 230 234
Review Palace 206
reviewed 202 251
revolted 166
riding 215 226
rites 281
river 4 6 7 13 21 25 26 33 34 39 64 72 111 115 117 187 228 254 255 290 297 298
road 34 53 90 176 199 200

roads 146 260
robbing 260
roof-beams 6 7 25 33 34
ropes 117
round-trip 199
royal 15 31 32 37 38 43 74 78 82 98 104 105 106 107 109 120 126 183 204 207 208 215 227 250 262 279 291
rule 146 150
ruled 100
ruler 149 192
rumor 108 162
rumour 246
runaway 79
runaways 100
Rusa 31 95 162 187
sacrifices 36 84 165 221
safe 218
safely 160
sale 150
salt 242
Samaria 291
saplings 27 105 268
Sarduri 93 145
scarce 21
scared 95 103 203
scattered 79
scholars 215 257
scout 35 54
scouts 12 13 24 40 55 83 87 105 246 264
scraps 206
scribe 122 250
scribes 269
seah 242 269
seahs 250 261
seal 53 206 234
sealed 32 98 105 247
search 79
searched 125
second 34 169 284
second-rate 295
secretly 54 90 108 172 218
seed 60 68 225 259
seize 35 46 54
seized 25 89 115 151 220 225 228
selected 33 250 261
selection 33
sell 100 169
serious 56
servants 37 48 50 53 81 152 156 157 158 202 211 220 245 256 257 260
serve 254
service 46 52 85 121 124 147 163 170 227
serviced 47
serving 35
settle 35
settled 8 15
settles 52
shackles 35
shafts 294
shape 295
Shebat 9
sheep 21 37 48 98 122 133 136 256 257 258
sheikhs 3
shepherd 96
shepherds 256
shipping 233
shocked 15
shore 84
sick 217
sickle 295
signals 12
silent 149
silver 149 238
Sennacherib 281
sister 108
Sivan 298
slabs 15 35
slain 46
slander 46
slandered 243
slave 35 243
slow 199
snow 92 105 126 145 146 285
snowed 26
sold 21 149
soldiers 3 5 32 35 53 88 92 115 130 250
son 98 108 114 141 190 196 197 199 200 204 210 217 237 243 249
sons 56
spies 3 11 12 85 91
stable 48 79 200
stage 117 164 227
stamp seal 234
star 249
started 80 249 275 294
starve 126
state 179
station 227
steel 294
steppe 256
stock 202
stone 15 17 29 118 205 290 296
stored 82 126 248 250
storehouse 206
storm 249
strain 227
straps 142
straw 16 21 62 119 233
strengthen 33 227
stretch 67
stronghold 169
subject 100
subjects 15 34 37 46 47 53 54 65 95 124 138 184 210 217 243 254 260
subjugated 286
submissive 78
submitted 78 149 184
submitting 246
subordinate 116 150 186 224
suffered 92
summon 139 141
superior 95 289
surplus 21
surround 93
swear 106 117
swim 200
sword 91 202
sworn 53
table 219
tablet 52 81 147 217 218 289 294
tablets 52

tailors 215
talents 29 206 294
Tammuz 21 47 113 162
tax 16 289
team 74 189 211 227
teams 74 215 280
temple 54 85 121 147 294
temples 281
tenancy 16
tents 249
terrace 206
terrain 200
territory 2 33 42 176 217
terror 202
terrorize 202
thick 285 294 295
thieves 176
thin 295
'third man' 14 21 33 141 215 217 230
threshing floor 60 82
thresholds 17 118 290 297
throne 31 95 108
timber 34
Tishri 112
tow 127
tower 5 120
town 3 15 24 34 35 45 54 80 94 100 109 126 129 130 166 185 213 226 286 289
towns 12 37 46 48 52 78 152 232 268
trade 150 295
trail 32
traitor 124 210
transport 25 102 233 268
transporting 34 111
treasurer 96 97 108 110 257
treasury 206
treaty 78
tree 253 281 294 295
trees 25 27 34 255 281 294 295
trespass 2 176
tribute 92
trip 92
Triplet Star 249
troops 2 3 4 6 10 21 32 33 44 53 60 66 67 68 78 88 92 95 97 114 126 129 131 145 147 158 164 174 178 199 200 215 217 220 223 227 240 277 279
trunks 25
trust 248
trustworthy 204
truth 52
tunics 206
unanimously 118
understanding 56
understood 243
ungelded 238
unit 69 87
unsubmissive 78
unsubstantiated 108
urging 47
valuables 100 101
value 37
vanguard 5
vanquish 146
vessels 287
vigil 213
village 3 21 152 179 291
villages 296
vizier 3 168
wagons 48 280 295
wall 56 160 291 292
walls 282
war 260
warn 217
waste 260
watch 2 3 8 17 21 63 78 80 99 113 127 162 227 249 288 292
watching 172
watchtowers 290
water 7 13 21 26 117 249 274 275 298
waters 200
water trough 274 275
weak 156
weather 156
weigh 206 287
weight 271
whiff 113
whipped 142
widow 217 218
wind 249
wine 98 122 203
wineskins 200
winged 293
withhold 256 289
woman 108
women 265
wool 28
work 3 8 16 20 34 47 52 53 56 58 63 67 69 80 106 108 113 118 160 197 199 210 211 250 266 267 277 290 291 292 294 295 296 298 299
working 32 56 80 148
works 152
wounded 3 53
wrap 46
write 3 19 38 40 45 52 62 63 68 81 91 96 100 108 114 115 121 126 130 136 144 152 173 186 204 215 267 284 295 299
writing 46 96 156 277
writing-board 121 152
written 33 37 48 52 96 134 144 152 168 178 192 232 254 257 277 283
year 28 52 150 170 199 200 218
years 15 52
yield 82
young 200

# List of Text Headings


1. No News is Good News
2. Attacks on Forts
3. Urarṭu gets Ready for War
4. Floating Logs down the River
5. Bringing Soldiers into Eziat
6. Transporting Logs
7. *Log Driving
8. *Fragment Referring to Messengers and Timber
9. ———
10. ———
11. An Urarṭian Governor in Muṣaṣir
12. Fragment Referring to Military Operations and Spies
13. ———
14. Chaldeans in Bit-Zamani
15. Building a Town, a Fort and a Palace
16. Exempt Land Provides no Straw
17. *Work on a Bull Colossus and Stone Thresholds
18. ———
19. *Rendezvous
20. ———
21. Tension on the Urarṭian Border
22. *News from the Urarṭian Border
23. ———
24. People from a Mountain Town
25. Felling Trees in Šubria
26. No Water in the River
27. Pulling up Fruit Tree Saplings
28. *Red Wool for the King
29. Forwarding Hewn Stone Objects
30. ———
31. Argisti Puts Pressure on Ḫu-Tešub of Šubria
32. Soldiers Captured by the Šubrians
33. Cutting Timber in Urarṭian Territory
34. Problems with Cutting Timber in Šubria
35. The King of Šubria Refuses to Extradite Deserters
36. *Joint Sacrifices
37. Defense Against Accusations
38. A Visit by Duri-Adad and a Royal Delegate
39. *Fragment Concerning Tree Trunks
40. A Šubrian Emissary on His Way to the King
41. ———
42. ———
43. Fetching Beams
44. *Troops in Hubuškia
45. Urarṭian Offensive against Mannea and Zikirtu
46. A Wronged Vassal
47. Having Mares Serviced
48. Receiving a Shipment of Animals and Wagons
49. ———
50. ———
51. *Fragment Referring to a Messenger
52. Šubrian Emissaries on their Way to the King
53. A Murderer Flees to Šubria
54. A Sanctuary for Fugitives
55. A Captured Informer
56. Master Builders and Apprentices
57. Raising Bull Colossi in Adia
58. *Raising Bull Colossi in Adia
59. *A Chaldean Bodyguard
60. *Providing for Troops
61. ———
62. Meeting the King on the Way
63. Subjugating Bit-Amukani
64. Horses from the East
65. An Arrival Report
66. *Fragment of a Military Report
67. Assembling Troops
68. Chariot Troops from Que
69. On an Army Unit
70. *Fragment Referring to Oxen
71. An Axe Maker from Damascus
72. *Returning from the River
73. ———
74. Mule Express not Available
75. *News from Šubria
76. ———
77. ———
78. Imposing the King's Treaty
79. Capturing Runaways
80. Building a Fort and Houses for Deportees
81. A Case Against the Governor
82. Paying the Corn Tax
83. Fragment of a Military Report
84. The Mannean King Raids Urarṭian Cities
85. Spying on the Urarṭian Capital
86. The Army of Urarṭu on the March
87. The Urarṭian Troops Concentrate in Waisi
88. The Urarṭian Troops Set out to Muṣaṣir
89. The King of Muṣaṣir Taken to Urarṭu
90. The Urarṭian King Flees and his Son is Made King
91. Revolt against the King of Urarṭu
92. The Urarṭian King Gathers his Troops after Defeat
93. A Coup d'État in Urarṭu
94. Houses in the Environs of Kumme
95. Argisti's Message to the Kummeans
96. An Ukkean Messenger and his Dispatch
97. Troop Movements in Kumme
98. Where Did All That Wine Go?
99. ———

100. Smugglers on the Assyrian Border
101. Fragment of a List of Valuables
102. ———
103. Manhunt
104. For his Royal Ears Only
105. The Kummean Leaders Comply with the King
106. The Kummeans versus the Royal Delegate
107. Kill the Assyrian Delegate!
108. An Urarṭian Woman on the Throne of Habhu
109. Allocating Fields for Garrison Troops
110. *A Letter to the Treasurer
111. Report on Timber Transport
112. Urarṭian Movements in Waisi
113. All Quiet on the Northern Front
114. The King of Urarṭu Gathers his Army
115. Retrieving Captured Soldiers
116. Arrests in Kumme
117. Delays in Timber Delivery
118. Complaint on Disobedience
119. Complaint on Lack of Straw
120. Leave me Some Booty, Please
121. Protest against False Accusations
122. Anticipating Criticism
123. ———
124. *A Matter of Loyalty
125. ———
126. Feeding the Troops
127. Log Towing
128. Fragment of a Report on Urarṭu
129. Where are the King's Logs?
130. Urzana has Left the Town
131. An Attack on Urarṭian Border Forts
132. Letter of Accompaniment
133. King of Hubuškia Arrives with Tribute
134. A Message from Hubuškia
135. Information about the King of Hubuškia
136. Urzana on his Way to Assyria
137. Arrival of Tributaries
138. Forwarding Local Rulers to the King
139. Troops from Muṣaṣir Summoned by the King
140. *Fragment of a Military Report
141. Summoning a Chariot-Man
142. Having an Official Whipped
143. Merchants Killed and Detained
144. Cimmerians and the Urarṭian King
145. Cimmerian Invasion of Urarṭu
146. A Letter of Excuse
147. Urarṭian Governors in Muṣaṣir
148. A Visit by Urzana's Brother
149. The Foul Dealings of the Deputy
150. Curbing a Slave Trader
151. ———
152. Request for New Carts
153. ———
154. *Fragment on Allegations
155. *Fragment Concerning a Royal Order
156. Inspecting Deportees
157. ———
158. *Fragment of a Military Report
159. *Fragment Concerning a Royal Utterance
160. Guarding the Camp
161. ———
162. Zaba-iqiša Joins the Camp of Rusa
163. Settling a Complaint by the Augurs
164. King of Urarṭu Facing Battle with Sargon
165. King of Urarṭu Sacrificing on a Campaign
166. Revolt in Urarṭu
167. *Military Movements in Urarṭu
168. Report on the Urarṭian Camp
169. King of Zikirtu as Horse Trader
170. Appointing an Attendant to a Eunuch
171. Arrival of Foreign Princes with Horse Tribute
172. Nabû-ereš under Surveillance
173. Report on an Urarṭian Defeat
174. The Defeat of the King of Urarṭu
175. ———
176. Military Movements in the Northeast
177. *Military Movements in the Urarṭian Camp
178. *Fragment of a Report on Urarṭu
179. Purge in an Urarṭian Province
180. *Troubles in Urarṭu
181. News of Urarṭu
182. Fragment of a Military Report
183. *Sending People to Palace
184. Urarṭian Subjects Submit to Assyria
185. *Fragment of a Report on Urarṭu
186. Exchanging Messengers
187. *Military Operations in Muṣaṣir
188. *Fragment referring to Zikirtu
189. ———
190. Arrested by the Governor
191. ———
192. *The Hubuškian has Arrived
193. *Fragment Mentionning Šulmu-beli
194. Emissaries from Labdudu
195. *Messenger from Hubuškia
196. *A Letter from Hubuškia
197. ———
198. *On the Road Again
199. Time to Set Out for a Campaign
200. Sending Boys to War
201. ———
202. Horses for the King
203. When the King Established the Debt Remission
204. Sending a Message to Mannea
205. *Precious Stones
206. Opening the Treasury
207. ———
208. ———
209. ———
210. Taking over the Forts of Allabria
211. Building Forts
212. *Fragment Mentioning an Interpreter
213. A Case Concerning a Town
214. Envelope of the Previous Letter
215. The Troops of Mazamua
216. *Fragment Mentioning Azâ, King of Mannea
217. Preparing for War in Mannea
218. Ullusunu Bribes Aššur-le'i of Karalla
219. *Fragment of a Report on Mannea
220. *Military Operations in Mannea
221. News from Mannea
222. *Military Movements in Mannea
223. *Preparing for Battle with Urarṭian Troops
224. Buying Horses in the East
225. Not All Reap What They Sow
226. Orders to Magnates
227. Post Stations and Criminals
228. Criminals Again
229. *Clearing up the Royal Road to Mazamua

230. *A Military Review
231. *Fragment Concerning Criminals
232. The Governor of Dur-Šarruken Wants More Fields
233. The King Gets an Old Boat
234. Barley to Mazamua
235. ———
236. ———
237. *Appointing a City Lord
238. *Buying Ungelded Bulls
239. ———
240. ———
241. A Babylonian Asks for Audience
242. Resettling Captives
243. Portrait of a Vassal
244. The Forts are Fine
245. Flooded by Refugees
246. Waiting for Scouts to Come back
247. A Sealed Royal Order
248. ———
249. Stormy Night
250. Assembling Troops for War and Counting Rations
251. Reviewing Cavalry and Chariot Troops
252. ———
253. *Beams from the Zagros
254. Logdriving in Isana
255. *Transport of Beams
256. Problems with Sheep
257. Sheep from Dur-Yakin
258. *Supplying Oxen and Sheep
259. *Distributing Provisions
260. Insults and Accusations
261. *Dividing the Booty
262. ———
263. Arrival of Rams
264. ———
265. *Cherchez la Femme
266. *Fragment Referring to Public Works
267. *Fragment Concerning Public Works
268. Refusal to Transport Saplings
269. Delivery of Barley
270. ———
271. ———
272. Rain and Travel Problems
273. *An (Urarṭian?) Defeat
274. Heavy Rain
275. Steady Rain
276. *Fragment Reporting on Rainfall
277. Assembling Troops
278. ———
279. *Military Matters
280. *Oxen and Wagons
281. *Trees for the Royal Orchards
282. Palace Reliefs
283. *Arrival of a Royal Messenger
284. *Carnelian from Kumme
285. Too Much Snow
286. A Journey to Dur-Šarruken
287. *Inspecting Bronze and Wooden Objects
288. *Keeping Watch with Exempted Men
289. Distributing Corn
290. Ferrying Stone Thresholds Without Boats
291. Giving Bricks to the Magnates
292. Building the City Wall of Dur-Šarruken
293. Finishing the 'Winged Hoof'
294. Request for Beams, Gold and Steel
295. Second-Rate Logs will not Do
296. Bricks for Dur-Šarruken
297. Transporting Stone Thresholds and Raising a Bull Colossus
298. Moving Bull Colossi Across the River
299. Working and Loading Bull Colossi
300. *Fragment Referring to a Bull Colossus

# Index of Texts

## *By Publication Number*


ABL 112 145
ABL 121+ 121
ABL 122 119
ABL 123 113
ABL 124 120
ABL 125 118
ABL 138 32
ABL 139+ 31
ABL 144 91
ABL 145 96
ABL 146+ 92
ABL 147 97
ABL 148 85
ABL 192 64
ABL 193 71
ABL 194 63
ABL 195 66
ABL 200 1
ABL 201 16
ABL 205 169
ABL 206 104
ABL 207 242
ABL 208 210
ABL 215 45
ABL 243 126
ABL 244+ 127
ABL 245 79
ABL 246 78
ABL 247 80
ABL 251 53
ABL 252 52
ABL 253+ 56
ABL 271 293
ABL 309 246
ABL 310 202
ABL 311 199
ABL 312 200
ABL 317 243
ABL 319+ 206
ABL 321 201
ABL 342 217
ABL 343 245
ABL 380 88
ABL 381 84
ABL 387 203
ABL 408 227
ABL 409 147
ABL 410 163
ABL 411 172
ABL 424 3
ABL 431 28
ABL 441 162
ABL 444 87
ABL 448 139
ABL 463 260
ABL 466 171
ABL 467 295
ABL 490 111
ABL 491 94
ABL 492 86
ABL 506 21
ABL 507 25
ABL 508 23
ABL 509 24
ABL 510 27
ABL 515 164
ABL 522 241
ABL 529 224
ABL 544 105
ABL 548 2
ABL 566 294
ABL 567+ 251
ABL 579 115
ABL 582 234
ABL 590 103
ABL 596 223
ABL 599 228
ABL 619+ 117
ABL 624+ 68
ABL 635 229
ABL 646 90
ABL 703 38
ABL 705 33
ABL 729 62
ABL 732 6
ABL 741 55
ABL 742 59
ABL 757 47
ABL 758 205
ABL 761 207
ABL 768 146
ABL 769 83
ABL 783 161
ABL 784 152
ABL 785 159
ABL 786 153
ABL 787 154
ABL 788 155
ABL 802 233
ABL 867 257
ABL 884 226
ABL 890 133
ABL 891 136
ABL 902 237
ABL 903 238
ABL 904 239
ABL 905 240
ABL 921+ 48
ABL 922 49
ABL 931 134
ABL 936 194
ABL 946 244
ABL 952 29
ABL 957 297
ABL 978 132
ABL 987 75
ABL 988+ 156
ABL 1012 82
ABL 1018 70
ABL 1035 284
ABL 1043 12
ABL 1048 148
ABL 1058 218
ABL 1068 211
ABL 1081 168
ABL 1083 11
ABL 1176 54
ABL 1192 232
ABL 1193 14
ABL 1196 89
ABL 1206 263
ABL 1265 274
ABL 1273 149
ABL 1288 256
ABL 1290+ 250
ABL 1295 179
ABL 1298+ 165
ABL 1305 272
ABL 1325 166
ABL 1359 158
ABL 1362 298
ABL 1407 213
ABL 1407A 214
ABL 1414 125
ABL 1416 221
ABL 1419 58
ABL 1466 135
CT 53 4 40
CT 53 7 114
CT 53 30 290
CT 53 33 56
CT 53 35 117
CT 53 36 281
CT 53 37+ 108
CT 53 38 291
CT 53 40 68
CT 53 42 98
CT 53 47+ 250
CT 53 54 44
CT 53 56 204
CT 53 57+ 31
CT 53 58 48
CT 53 59 150
CT 53 63 127
CT 53 65 15
CT 53 79 225
CT 53 85 67
CT 53 95 34
CT 53 98 107
CT 53 99 173
CT 53 101 37
CT 53 114 112
CT 53 122 177
CT 53 124 178
CT 53 125 69
CT 53 126 254
CT 53 127 110
CT 53 131 141
CT 53 132 46
CT 53 133 176
CT 53 135 236
CT 53 137 122
CT 53 138 106
CT 53 160 35
CT 53 163 36
CT 53 164+ 121
CT 53 170 116
CT 53 172+ 95
CT 53 188 296
CT 53 192 138
CT 53 194 190
CT 53 197 249
CT 53 200 271
CT 53 201 299
CT 53 204 170
CT 53 210 4

| | |
|---|---|
| CT 53 213 | 26 |
| CT 53 215 | 128 |
| CT 53 225+ | 206 |
| CT 53 240 | 230 |
| CT 53 250 | 220 |
| CT 53 257 | 286 |
| CT 53 261 | 193 |
| CT 53 264 | 20 |
| CT 53 268 | 300 |
| CT 53 271 | 219 |
| CT 53 272 | 188 |
| CT 53 280 | 7 |
| CT 53 283 | 43 |
| CT 53 296 | 61 |
| CT 53 305 | 277 |
| CT 53 323 | 289 |
| CT 53 324 | 269 |
| CT 53 328 | 30 |
| CT 53 335 | 18 |
| CT 53 343 | 253 |
| CT 53 346 | 57 |
| CT 53 365+ | 93 |
| CT 53 370+ | 108 |
| CT 53 386+ | 17 |
| CT 53 387 | 282 |
| CT 53 389 | 60 |
| CT 53 394 | 109 |
| CT 53 398 | 261 |
| CT 53 403 | 279 |
| CT 53 407 | 186 |
| CT 53 409 | 196 |
| CT 53 414 | 137 |
| CT 53 415 | 192 |
| CT 53 420 | 252 |
| CT 53 424 | 42 |
| CT 53 427 | 187 |
| CT 53 432 | 212 |
| CT 53 440 | 124 |
| CT 53 442 | 280 |
| CT 53 445 | 184 |
| CT 53 454 | 131 |
| CT 53 462+ | 93 |
| CT 53 470 | 157 |
| CT 53 473 | 288 |
| CT 53 478 | 5 |
| CT 53 480 | 259 |
| CT 53 485 | 197 |
| CT 53 492 | 102 |
| CT 53 509 | 140 |
| CT 53 513+ | 247 |
| CT 53 517+ | 258 |
| CT 53 519 | 183 |
| CT 53 522+ | 156 |
| CT 53 527 | 208 |
| CT 53 533 | 198 |
| CT 53 553 | 231 |
| CT 53 558 | 276 |
| CT 53 560+ | 247 |
| CT 53 569 | 255 |
| CT 53 573 | 50 |
| CT 53 578 | 76 |
| CT 53 579+ | 17 |
| CT 53 581 | 195 |
| CT 53 583 | 174 |
| CT 53 584 | 22 |
| CT 53 585 | 222 |
| CT 53 586 | 181 |
| CT 53 615 | 167 |
| CT 53 616 | 9 |
| CT 53 617 | 267 |
| CT 53 621 | 175 |
| CT 53 625 | 19 |
| CT 53 628 | 287 |
| CT 53 629 | 285 |
| CT 53 631 | 8 |
| CT 53 637 | 151 |
| CT 53 641 | 51 |
| CT 53 651 | 266 |
| CT 53 656 | 99 |
| CT 53 658 | 283 |
| CT 53 676 | 262 |
| CT 53 677 | 278 |
| CT 53 679+ | 108 |
| CT 53 695 | 275 |
| CT 53 697 | 41 |
| CT 53 708 | 10 |
| CT 53 726 | 39 |
| CT 53 729 | 73 |
| CT 53 730 | 248 |
| CT 53 766+ | 258 |
| CT 53 777 | 235 |
| CT 53 779 | 209 |
| CT 53 789 | 185 |
| CT 53 793+ | 165 |
| CT 53 795 | 273 |
| CT 53 797+ | 251 |
| CT 53 799 | 180 |
| CT 53 808+ | 156 |
| CT 53 827 | 270 |
| CT 53 836 | 268 |
| CT 53 840 | 142 |
| CT 53 847 | 77 |
| CT 53 852 | 72 |
| CT 53 856 | 264 |
| CT 53 858+ | 95 |
| CT 53 859 | 123 |
| CT 53 872 | 129 |
| CT 53 874 | 143 |
| CT 53 882 | 265 |
| CT 53 885 | 216 |
| CT 53 891 | 182 |
| CT 53 912 | 189 |
| CT 53 914 | 160 |
| CT 53 918 | 130 |
| GPA 242 | 292 |
| GPA 243 | 144 |
| GPA 244 | 191 |
| Iraq 7 99 | 65 |
| K 17736 | 101 |
| K 19621 | 13 |
| NL 62 | 74 |
| NL 89 | 215 |
| RCAE III 65+ | 92 |
| TCL 9 67 | 100 |
| TCL 9 68 | 81 |


## *By Museum Number*


| | |
|---|---|
| K 146 | 64 |
| K 194 | 91 |
| K 463 | 149 |
| K 464 | 105 |
| K 468+ | 121 |
| K 469 | 32 |
| K 485 | 145 |
| K 488 | 1 |
| K 491 | 119 |
| K 498 | 241 |
| K 503 | 118 |
| K 506 | 53 |
| K 510 | 226 |
| K 513 | 79 |
| K 525 | 52 |
| K 534 | 162 |
| K 536 | 40 |
| K 537 | 169 |
| K 539 | 104 |
| K 541 | 242 |
| K 542 | 71 |
| K 567 | 126 |
| K 574 | 113 |
| K 593 | 2 |
| K 610 | 202 |
| K 617 | 210 |
| K 621 | 164 |
| K 630 | 199 |
| K 635 | 114 |
| K 645 | 87 |
| K 665 | 63 |
| K 669 | 78 |
| K 676 | 133 |
| K 678 | 21 |
| K 689 | 200 |
| K 690 | 16 |
| K 746 | 111 |
| K 826 | 139 |
| K 847 | 29 |
| K 903 | 120 |
| K 910 | 96 |
| K 932 | 297 |
| K 942 | 294 |
| K 946+ | 251 |
| K 951 | 35 |
| K 1021 | 246 |
| K 1027 | 80 |
| K 1028 | 132 |
| K 1029 | 161 |
| K 1031+ | 152 |
| K 1037 | 45 |
| K 1042 | 83 |
| K 1043 | 115 |
| K 1046 | 237 |
| K 1067+ | 31 |
| K 1071 | 238 |
| K 1077 | 25 |
| K 1079 | 136 |
| K 1080+ | 92 |
| K 1093 | 234 |
| K 1111 | 103 |
| K 1120 | 223 |
| K 1124 | 228 |
| K 1137 | 36 |
| (K 1154+) | 121 |
| K 1170 | 97 |
| K 1175+ | 56 |
| K 1178 | 290 |
| (K 1179+) | 56 |
| K 1182+ | 117 |
| K 1183 | 281 |
| K 1186+ | 108 |
| (K 1207+) | 56 |
| K 1211 | 75 |
| K 1213+ | 68 |
| K 1220 | 293 |
| K 1224 | 116 |
| K 1231+ | 156 |
| K 1246 | 291 |
| (K 1251+) | 152 |
| K 1252A | 224 |
| K 1258+ | 95 |
| K 1424+ | 250 |
| K 1426+ | 258 |
| K 1438 | 260 |
| K 1501+ | 98 |
| K 1516 | 229 |
| (K 1543+) | 117 |
| K 1544 | 296 |
| K 1613 | 138 |
| K 1862 | 190 |
| K 1871 | 44 |
| K 1875 | 204 |
| K 1876 | 249 |
| K 1884 | 271 |
| K 1885 | 299 |
| (K 1886+) | 31 |
| K 1889+ | 48 |
| K 1892 | 170 |
| K 1897 | 150 |
| K 1907 | 85 |
| (K 1917+) | 117 |
| K 1924 | 4 |
| K 1931 | 26 |

K 1932+ 127
K 1940 128
K 1966+ 15
K 1987+ 206
K 4277 256
(K 4282+) 250
K 4306 82
K 4677 179
K 4695+ 165
K 4701 70
K 4756 272
K 5291 243
K 5392 230
K 5435B+ 225
K 5462 166
K 5481 220
K 5493 286
K 5503+ 67
K 5507 20
K 5518 193
K 5523 300
K 5528 219
K 5533 188
K 5555 7
K 5568 43
(K 5572+) 48
K 5609 61
K 7301 277
(K 7303+) 108
(K 7304+) 225
(K 7327+) 48
K 7333 289
K 7334 269
K 7336+ 34
K 7352 30
(K 7360+) 225
K 7367 18
K 7370 134
(K 7384+) 206
K 7389 253
(K 7391+) 34
(K 7393+) 98
K 7398 57
K 7402 107
K 7420 173
K 7458 37
K 7466+ 93
(K 7477+) 108
K 7493 66
K 7509+ 17
K 7517 282
K 7528 60
K 7551 109
K 7797 261
K 8989 38
K 9212 284
K 9526 279
(K 9783+) 98
K 9971 186
K 10363 196
K 10875 137
K 10895 192
K 10913 252
K 11315 42
K 11801 187
K 12010 212
(K 12957+) 127
K 12959 124
K 12964 280
K 12970 184
(K 12992+) 92
K 13004 131
K 13006 194
(K 13008+) 34
(K 13024+) 93
K 13027 239
(K 13037+) 108
K 13048 157
K 13060 288
(K 13082+) 98
K 13085 259
K 13088 5
K 13096 197
K 13120 240
K 13140 102
K 13142 159
K 13147 112
K 14093 201
K 14096 140
K 14109 153
K 14113+ 247
K 14291 183
K 14571 135
(K 14575+) 156
K 14578 208
K 14588 198
(K 14622+) 68
K 14635 231
K 14641 276
(K 14643+) 247
K 14655 255
(K 14663+) 67
K 14665 50
K 14672 76
(K 14673+) 17
K 14675 195
K 14683 174
K 14684 22
K 14685 222
K 14686 177
K 14687 181
K 15015 178
K 15081 167
K 15085 9
K 15090 267
K 15114 175
K 15154 19
K 15188 287
K 15266 285
K 15268 8
K 15291 151
K 15321 51
K 15380 266
(K 15383+) 48
K 15389 99
K 15394 283
K 15606 262
(K 15607+) 15
K 15608 278
K 15610+ 108
K 15638 275
(K 15639+) 251
K 15640 41
K 15661 10
K 16047 39
K 16050 73
K 16055+ 248
(K 16074+) 248
(K 16478+) 258
K 16496 235
K 16500 209
K 16522 185
(K 16529+) 165
K 16534 273
K 16551 180
(K 16578+) 156
K 17736 101
K 19621 13
Sm 51 171
Sm 96 12
Sm 163 274
Sm 333 69
Sm 339 254
Sm 358 148
Sm 456 295
Sm 521 62
Sm 548+ 47
Sm 677 94
Sm 754 205
Sm 760 3
Sm 770 270
Sm 807 55
(Sm 887+) 47
Sm 935 218
Sm 984 28
Sm 1045 203
Sm 1056 146
Sm 1162 110
Sm 1189 141
Sm 1231 268
Sm 1293 142
Sm 1675 77
Sm 1742 189
Sm 1809 46
Sm 1821 72
Sm 1872 264
Sm 1933 211
(Sm 1934+) 95
Sm 1961 176
Sm 2071 123
DT 68 236
DT 218 158
DT 264 23
DT 289 298
Rm 55 154
Rm 68 54
Rm 557 168
Rm 978 11
Rm 993 232
Rm 998 14
Rm 2,1 227
Rm 2,2 147
Rm 2,3 88
Rm 2,4 163
Rm 2,5 172
Rm 2,410 6
Rm 2,460 129
Rm 2,462 59
Rm 2,474 207
Rm 2,539 143
79-7-8,52 125
79-7-8,154 122
79-7-8,160 221
79-7-8,234 217
79-7-8,260+ 316 106
79-7-8,262 265
79-7-8,264 216
79-7-8,267 182
79-7-8,273 58
79-7-8,292 90
80-7-19,30 89
81-2-4,55 84
81-2-4,60 86
81-2-4,94 257
81-2-4,100 263
81-2-4,123 24
81-2-4,438 160
81-7-27,35 27
81-7-27,39 233
81-7-27,46 130
82-5-22,109 33
82-5-22,140 49
83-1-18,18 245
83-1-18,103 244
Bu 89-4-26,1 155
Th 1905-4-9, 281 213
Th 1905-4-9, 281A 214
Th 1932-12-10, 302+ 65
BM 123359+ 65
AO 4506 81
ND 1107 144
ND 1108 292
ND 1112 191
ND 2367 74
ND 2631 215
N. III 3158 100

# List of Joins


| Join | No. |
|---|---|
| K 468 (ABL 121) + K 1154 (CT 53 164) | 121 |
| K 946 (ABL 567) + K 15639 (CT 53 797) | 251 |
| K 1067 (ABL 139) + K 1886 (CT 53 57) | 31 |
| K 1186 (CT 53 37) + K 7303 + K 7477 (CT 53 370) + K 13037 + K 15610 (CT 53 679) | 108 |
| K 1231 (ABL 988) + K 14575 (CT 53 522) + K 16578 (CT 53 808) | 156 |
| K 1258 (CT 53 172) + Sm 1934 (CT 53 858) | 95 |
| K 1424 (CT 53 047) + K 4282 (ABL 1290) | 250 |
| K 1426 (CT 53 517) + K 16478 (CT 53 766) | 258 |
| K 1987 (CT 53 225) + K 7384 (ABL 319) | 206 |
| K 4695 (ABL 1298) + K 16529 (CT 53 793) | 165 |
| K 7466 (CT 53 365) + K 13024 (CT 53 462) | 93 |
| K 7509 (CT 53 386) + K 14673 (CT 53 579) | 17 |
| K 14113 (CT 53 513) + K 14643 (CT 53 560) | 247 |


# List of Illustrations


| | |
|---|---|
| AO 19909 | 28 |
| AO 19913 | 34 |
| BM 118800 | 3 |
| BM 118905 | 27 |
| BM 124557 | 14 |
| BM 124558 | 30 |
| BM 124652 | 10 |
| BM 124652 | 18 |
| BM 124652 | 23 |
| BM 124789 | 7 |
| BM 124793 | 21 |
| BM 124802 | 19 |
| BM 124802 | 40 |
| BM 124822 | 2 |
| BM 124945 | 16 |
| BM 134386 | 25 |
| BM 135198 | 6 |
| Botta and Flandin II, 141 | Frontispiece |
| Botta and Flandin II, 145 | 9 |
| Iraq Museum, Baghdad | 4 |
| Menant, *Catalogue* Pl. VII | 24 |
| Mosul Museum | 1 |
| Or. Dr. I, 32 | 11 |
| Or. Dr. I, 70 | 5 |
| Or. Dr. I, 70 | 36 |
| Or. Dr. II, 65 | 13 |
| Or. Dr. IV, 20 | 31 |
| Or. Dr. IV, 77 | 32 |
| Or. Dr. IV, 78 | 29 |
| Or. Dr. V, 26 | 26 |
| Or. Dr. V, 31 | 8 |
| Or. Dr. V, 31 | 35 |
| Or. Dr. V, 31 | 39 |
| Or. Dr. VI, 5 | 22 |
| Or. Dr. VI, 5 | 37 |
| Or. Dr. VI, 7 | 38 |
| Or. Dr. VI, 13 | 17 |
| Or. Dr. VI, 15 | 33 |
| Or. Dr. VI, 20 | 20 |
| Or. Dr. VI, 33 | 12 |
| Or. Dr. VI, 34 | 15 |

# COPIES AND COLLATIONS

K 14113+ (+) K 16055+, Obv.
(Nos. 247 and 248)

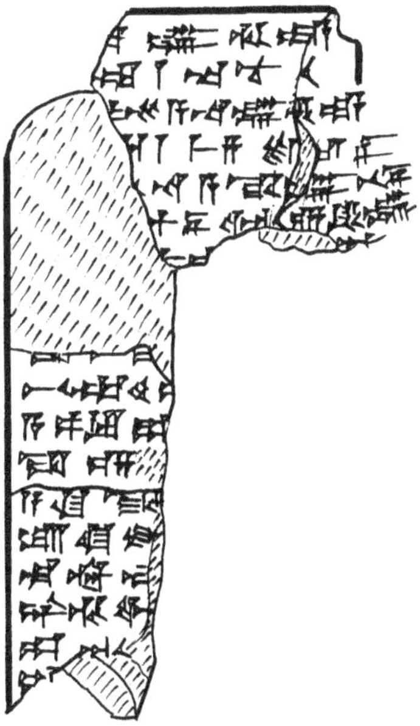

K 19621 (No. 13)

79-7-8,273 (No. 58)

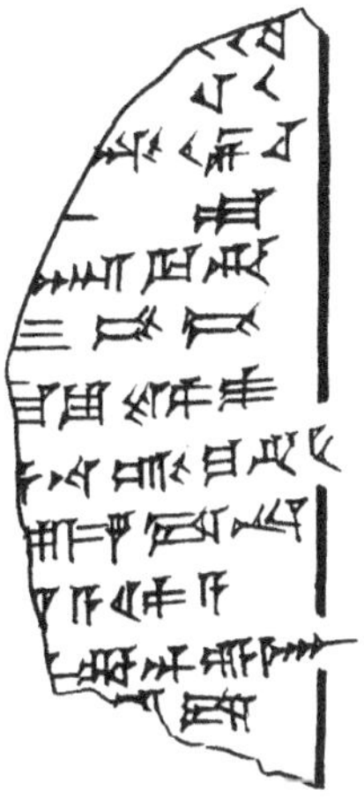

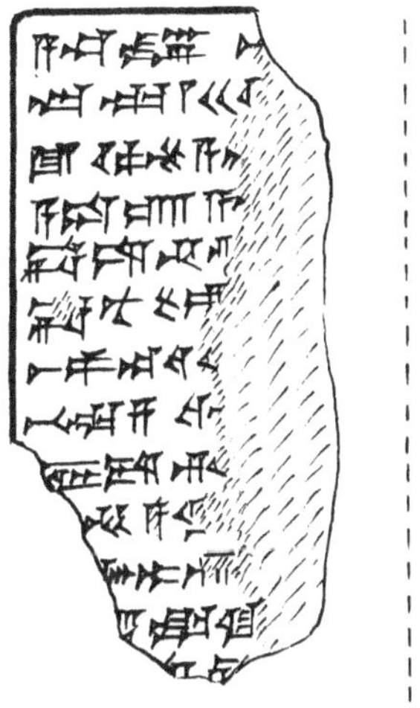

K 17736 (No. 101)

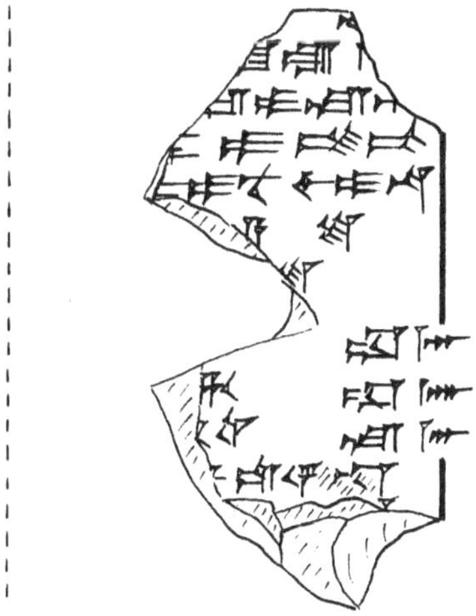

Sm 754 (No. 205)

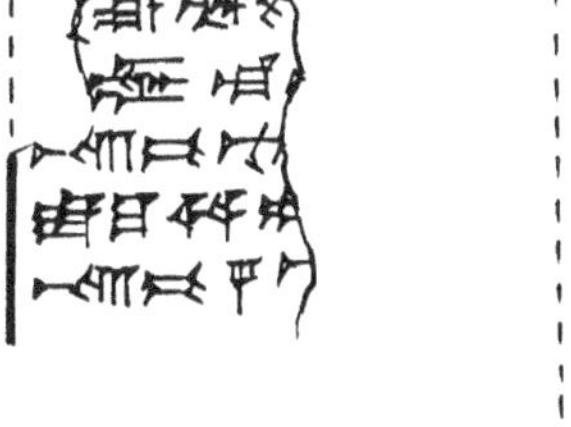

**1**: 1, 3 *na* written

6 *ša* written ; end

10

11

12

r.2 *la* written

**2**: 3 (end)

3f, r.8 *na* written

5 *bu* written

6 URI written

13 *tu* written

r.7 *da* written

**3**: 7 *da-a-a-*

10, 12, r.11 *pu* written

16 *ina* UGU

r.18 URU -*ru-ba*

**6**: 4f *na* written

8 (end) GIŠ

r.1 (end)

2

4 *ú* written

**7** r.2

**8** r.6 *ú* written

**9**: 6

**11** r.1

3 (end) *i-* .

**12** r.1 [*x* KUR.*hu-* -*a-a* LÚ*.

2 (end)

4 *ma-*

8 (end) *ik-*

13 *uk* written

**14**: 4f *mu* written

5, 8, r.4 *na* written

6, 14 *bu* written

9 *iq* written

15 [

**15**: 17 LUGAL

**16**: 6 (end) ŠE

7

8

9 *na* written

11

r.2 IN.NU -*bi-*[*ru*]

3

**21**: 11, 13f, 16 *pu* written

13 *tu* perfectly normal

19 *an-ni-te*

21

r.16 *ša ina* KUR-

**24**: 10 (end)

11

15 *ina re-šu-*

16 URU

**25**: 11 *ú-ṣ*]*a-bi-tú*

r.1

2

3

4

**27**: 11

12

13 (end)

**28**: 9

11 (end)

**29** r.2

**31**: 4 *ti* written

11

12 (end)

r.3

4

8

12

21 *a-su-* -*ka*

23 URI written

24 (end)

27

29

s.3

4 *li-*

**32**: 5 *na* written

20 *ina pa-na-*

r.14 *pu* written

16 *li-zi-*

**33**: 11

12

r.4 (end)

8 *ú-pa-*

9 (end)

s.1

**34**: 8

**36**: 2

8

9

**38**: 3 *na* written

5

8 (end)

11

**40**: 2

**44** r.1

2

3

4 *ina* UGU-

5

**45**: 1, r.4 *na* written

3 URI written , *ša* written

6 *ki-*
7 [*a-na*
r.1
2
5
**46** r.3 (end)
7 *a-*[*a-š*]*i*
**47**: 1, 3, 6 *na* written
4 *a-ṣa-pi*
7, 14 *ša* written
9 *a-du*
11, 14 *bu* written
12 *kis* written
r.4 *la-* KIN-*i*
9 (end)
**49**: 2 *aš-šur-pa-*
5
7
**52**: 4, 8f, r.8 *ša* written
6, 10, r.6 *su* written
6 (end)
12
r.8 *il* written
13 ANŠE written
**53**: 2ff *ša* written
3ff *ú* written throughout
6 *il* written
13 *ú-se-ri-da*
17 (end)
21 *te* written
24 *-mit-tú*
25 (end)
r.5 (end)
**54**: 3 *-tú*
7 *-ra*
12 (end)
13 *uk* written
15, r.18 *su* written
17 *t*]*è-e-*
18 LÚ
21 LUGAL
22 URU
r.6 normal KUR ( )
10
**55**: 5 (end)
11
12
**56**: 4, 13 MEŠ written
11 *ra* written
16 *ina*
r.1 *-na-a-te*
6 LÚ.600-É.

11
**59**: 7
8
**62**: 4 (end)
5 *il* written
7 LUGAL *be-lí-*
8 *ša* written
12
r.1
2
3
**63**: 4
9
15 *na* written
r.6 *ša* written
12 [*l*]*i-*
14 [ *-ṣib-*DINGIR
**64**: 6 *ša* written
7 *zu* written
8 *bu* written
13
r.4 *ga-mu-*
6 *-a-ni*
**65**: 6 URU.*ha-*
8f *ša* written
**66**: 5
6
**68**: 7 (end)
**69**: 5 *ma-a* *-ka*
6 *ina re-eš*
7 (end)
9 LUGAL
12
16
**70**: 3 *mu* written
5 *qi* written , *ša* written
**71**: 6
**75**: 4
: 5 *ša* written
**78**: 6 *ni* written
10f, 17 *ša* written
r.10
**79**: 4, 7, 13 LÚ* written
15 *im* written
8, 12 *hi, har* written
**80**: 3 *mu* written
6f, r.5 *ša* written
8
r.4 *pu* written
**82**: 4 *ša* written
6 ŠE.NUMUN.MEŠ
7 *e-te-te-*

r.4 *e-ta-*
9 [*an-n*]*u-* ᵐ*man-nu*-GIM-
10 *ša* written , *hi* written
11 (end)
23 *šúm* written
**83**: 6, r.2 *ni* written
r.2 *na* written
7
**84**: 5f, 10ff *ša* written
9 ᵐ*a-* *-lu-qu-nu*
11 ᵐ*ṭu-un-* *-un*
**85** r.2 (end)
**86**: 1, 3, 14 *ni* written
3 *mu* written
4, 10 *ša* written
7 *-tal-lak*
12 *el* written
r.4
**87**: 3, r.5 *na* written
4, 6f, r.3 *ša* written
4, 13 LÚ* written
6 (end)
10 ᵐ*ṭu-*
13
14f *ú* written
r.1 *ina* ŠÀ
**88**: 3 *mu* written
6f, 10ff *ša* written
**89**: 5 TA* *pa-an*
6 EN.NAM
7 ᵐ*ur-za-a-ni*
8 KUR.*mu-ṣa-*
9 UN.MEŠ
12
**90**: 6ff *ša* written
10 KUR.*ú-a-za-*
11 KUR.*ši-ib-*
13 KUR.*šá-* *-te-ra*
r.8 [
**91**: 3 (end)
4, 7, 10f *ša* written
7 *bu* written , URI written
12 (end) *-•-ku*
18 *me-me-ni*
r.4 A-KIN
7 *la* written
8 *ú* written
**92**: 2ff *mu* written
3
6 *te* written , URI written
12
13
14 (end)
r.1
2
4
7 LÚ*.NAM.MEŠ
10
12 LÚ*.A-KIN.MEŠ
13 (end)
**94**: 4f *ša* written
**95**: 5 *ma-a*
**96**: 3 *mu* written
4f, r.5 *ša* written
5 URI written
7 (end)
r.2, 5 *te* written
7 *pur* written
**97**: 4, r.6, 9 *ša* written
11 *ú* written
12 *ina pa-*
r.3 (end)
5 *i* written
11
12
**103**: 1
2
3
4
5
8 *uk* written
r.5 *šúm-ma*
6
7
**104**: 5 *ša* written
8 *su* written
9 *ki an-ni-e*
17
r.3 *ú* written
4
8 LÚ* written
11 *ba* written
**105**: 9, 17 *li* written
10 *-šá-me-šú-nu i-* *-bu-bu*
11
12
13
18, r.3, 8 *na* written
r.2 TA* ŠÀ KUR. *-qu-ni*
4 *ša* written
8 ITI written
10 *-la-ka*
**109**: 8 [*x x* LÚ*.*qur*]-
**111**: 3f *ša* written

**113**: 4, 6 *ša* written
6, r.3 *ú* written
9, r.3, 14 *ra* written
14
15
r.12 KAM written
**114**: 2
8 (clear)
9 (end)
**115**: 3, 6, r.3 *ša* written
7, 9 *na* written
r.4 *ra* written
5 KAM written
**117**: 21
r.2
5
14
**118**: 1, 10 *na* written
r.1
2
4f *ša* written
**119**: 1, 4, 8 *na* written
5
10 *ša*
**120**: 7
8
9
**121** r.10 (end)
11 (end)
12 (end)
20
21
**126**: 1, 9 *na* written
7, 14, r.9 *ša* written
8 (end)
9 URU -*li-te*
11 (end)
14 (end) *a*-
15 -*a-a*
20 [
21 [
r.1 [
4 [*kam*]-*mu*-
10 (end)
11 (end)
14
**127**: 6
7
9
14
**129** r.6
**132**: 2
5 *ša* written
8 MEŠ written
r.1
**133**: 1, 3 *na* written
6 URU.*a-ni*-
7 (end)
9
10
12
13 *e-ta*-
r.2
14 [
17
s.1 (end) *la*-
**134**: 3 *na* written
5 *nu*- KUR
**135**: 1 *na* written
5 normal *tar* ( )
r.2
4
7
10
11
**136**: 1, 2 *na* written
6 *hi* written
r.2
**141** r.5 URU
**145**: 5
6
7
8
9
10
11
12
13
16 URU.*ú*-
r.11 *pu* written
s.1
2
**146**: 3 (end)
6 (end)
15 *ia-ú* :
r.13 *da* written
**147**: 2, 9f LÚ* written
5 URI written
7 *kar* written
10, 15 NAM written
10, r.4f *ša* written
**148**: 8 (end)
10 [*ina*
12 [*x x*

r.1
2 É
3 (end)
4 (end)
**149**: 4
5
7 -*ta-an-šu*
8
11
12
13
14
15
18 UN
20 (end)
21
22
23
r.4 *i-te-et-*
5
10 -*šú*
13 (end)
14
18
20 *a-sa-ʾa-al-*
21 (end)
24
25
**150**: 4 (end)
14 [
18 (end)
r.5
**151**: 10 (end) *ku-*
**152**: 4, 7, 24 *ša* written
9
11
r.4 *ša* written
8
11 *ša* KI.TA
20
21
**153** r.1
2
**154**: 6
r.4
**155**: 3 *mu* written
4 (end)
6 LUGAL
7 (end)
8
**156**: 10
11

r.3
4
5
**159**: 5
6
7
**161**: 4 *ina* UGU
r.1
**162**: 17 [TA* U]RU.*hu-*
18 *sar* written
**163**: 5ff LÚ* written
6f, 12 *ša* written, MEŠ written
10 *uk* written
r.3
5
8 *bu* written
**164**: 4 URI written
5f *ša* written
7 *ú* written
r.3 KUR.*hu-* -*ka-a-a*
5
6, r.8 *ra* written
**165**: 5
8 (end)
10 KUR.*hu-* -*ka-a-[a*
12
**166**: 1
2
3
4
5
**168**: 1, 4, r.8 *na* written
6 (end)
r.2 (end)
3
4 *ina* ŠÀ-*bi*
5 *ina* ŠÀ-*bi*
6 *ina* ŠÀ-*bi*
**169**: 5, 12 *ra* written
5f *ša* written, URI written
r.3 (end)
6 : *a-ki*
**171**: 3
4
10 *tu* written
r.1, 5 *na* written
2 *ša* written
11
12
**173**: 13 [*i-*
**176** s.1 LÚ*.LUL.MEŠ -*ra-nu*
**179** r.1

3 *ta* written
5 (end)
7
8
9
**182**: 8
**194**: 4 [
r.2 [
3 [
4 [
5 [
6 [
8 [
10
**196** r.5
**199**: 3 *mu* written
5, r.8 *pu*/*bu* written
8, r.3 LÚ* written
15 -*te-li*
16 *a-na-ku šu*-
17
r.2
8 *qi* written
**200**: 3 *mu* written
5 *e-mu*- -*ka ku*-
7 (end) *ša*
15, r.10 *pu* written
17
r.13 (end)
**201**: 4
5
**202**: 1, 3 *na* written
5 ANŠE written
10
r.1
3 (end)
s.2 [ -*ki*
**203**: 1, r.6 *na* written
10
14
15
16
17
r.3 [*ina pa*]-
11 (end)
13
17 *ki-i* -*ra-ru*
s.1 TA written
2 [ *li-gi-ru-ru*
**207**: 6
7
8

**210**: 9, 15 LÚ* written
13, r.15 *bu* written , NAM written
r.6
**211**: 3 *mu* written
4 (end)
r.9 *ina kal* UD-*mu*
10
11
**213**: 10
r.2
**217**: 2 MEŠ written
3f LÚ* written, *ša* written
10 (end)
16
r.15 *a-sap-ra*
**218**: 2
r.13 (end)
14
**221**: 4, 6 *ša* written
8 UDU.SISKUR.MEŠ-
11 A-*šip-ri*
12 TA*
13 *mu* written
r.12
**223**: 3
5
r.5
**224**: 5 *ša* written, *mu* written
14 (end)
15
r.1
2
7 *ni-si*- *ma-a*
**225**: 6 (end)
**226**: 1 EN-
11
r.3
8 -*šú-nu*
11
12 *da* written, MEŠ written
19
**227**: 7, r.15ff, 27 LÚ* written
14 LUGAL *be-lí*
r.2
3 sup. ras.
11
12
13, 17 MEŠ written
**228**: 3 (end)
5
6 (end)
8

13
14
**229** r.4 TA* written, BÀD written
7 *li* written
9 *ú-pa-sa-ak*
**232**: 4 *ina* [UGU]
11 (end)
r.6 *šú-nu*
9 *-ku-u-ni*
11 *bu* written
**234**: 1
2
3 *a-na ma-* *-te*
7 *la* written
r.7 (end)
8
**237**: 6 [ *-sa-kan-šú*
**238**: 4 MEŠ written
5 [ *-lu-tu*
r.4 *la* written
**239**: 5 [
**242**: 8
9 LÚ*.2-*ú*
11
12
r.1
2
**243**: 11 (end)
19
20
r.9 *ina* UGU-*hi-ia*
13 (end) URU
14 (end)
15 (end)
**244**: 6 URU.HAL.ṢU
9
r.4
6
8 *ra* written
**245**: 10 *su-it-ka-a*
r.1 [
2 [*a-na* É.
**246**: 6f *ra* written
11
r.3 (end)
**250**: 4 (end) *ni-* *-ṭi-rib*
5 (end)
6 (end)
9 (end)
13
14
16 *si-id-ra*
r.2 (end)
3 *ù ina* UGU
9 *-me*-70 ANŠE ŠE.*ki-su-tú* 5-*me*
10 [ŠE.*ta*]*b-ku ša*
13 *ša* 1/
14 *ina* URU
20 [
21 [*x x x x*]-
22 (end) *áš-pu-*
23 (end) *i-*[*qab-*
25 [
**254** r.16 [
**256**: 2
5 [*t*]*a-ka-la-*
7 (end) *ú-ra-*
10
r.1 [ *-a'*
2 [ ]*-ka-ni* *-'i-*[*a*
4 (end)
5 [*ina* KUR.
**260**: 2 LUGAL
r.1
9
**261**: 2 URU
r.2
**263**: 1 [
**267**: 6 [
**284** r.5 [
13 [
**292** r.3
5 *a-na-*
**297**: 6 *re-e-*
8 (end)
10 (end) URU.*tas-*
12
13
r.2 (end)
**298**: 1
2
3
13 *ar-hi-iš li-*
15
16 LÚ
r.3 *i-da-gul*
4 (end) *ina pa-*
5 *lid-gul* *-lu*
6 (end)
12
13
**299** r.7 *pa-ni-*

# PLATES

PLATE I. N. III 3158 (= No. 100), Obverse

PLATE II. N. III 3158 (= No. 100), Reverse

# State Archives of Assyria

VOLUME I
THE CORRESPONDENCE OF SARGON II, PART I
*Letters from Assyria and the West*
Edited by Simo Parpola
1987

VOLUME II
NEO-ASSYRIAN TREATIES AND LOYALTY OATHS
Edited by Simo Parpola and Kazuko Watanabe
1988

VOLUME III
COURT POETRY AND LITERARY MISCELLANEA
Edited by Alasdair Livingstone
1989

VOLUME IV
QUERIES TO THE SUNGOD
*Divination and Politics in Sargonid Assyria*
Edited by Ivan Starr
1990

VOLUME V
THE CORRESPONDENCE OF SARGON II, PART II
*Letters from the Northern and Northeastern Provinces*
Edited by Giovanni B. Lanfranchi and Simo Parpola
1990

www.ingramcontent.com/pod-product-compliance
Lightning Source LLC
Chambersburg PA
CBHW081439070526
44586CB00019B/2178
* 9 7 8 1 5 7 5 0 6 3 2 6 3 *